Integrating Multi-User Virtual Environments in Modern Classrooms

Yufeng Qian
Northeastern University, USA

A volume in the Advances in Educational Technologies and Instructional Design (AETID) Book Series

Published in the United States of America by
IGI Global
Information Science Reference (an imprint of IGI Global)
701 E. Chocolate Avenue
Hershey PA, USA 17033
Tel: 717-533-8845
Fax: 717-533-8661
E-mail: cust@igi-global.com
Web site: http://www.igi-global.com

Library of Congress Cataloging-in-Publication Data

Names: Qian, Yufeng, 1967- editor.
Title: Integrating multi-user virtual environments in modern classrooms / Yufeng Qian, Editor.
Description: Hershey, PA : Information Science Reference (an imprint of IGI Global), [2018] | Includes bibliographical references.
Identifiers: LCCN 2017021154| ISBN 9781522537199 (hardcover) | ISBN 9781522537205 (ebook)
Subjects: LCSH: Virtual reality in education. | Shared virtual environments.
Classification: LCC LB1044.87 .I5473 2018 | DDC 371.33/468--dc23 LC record available at https://lccn.loc.gov/2017021154

This book is published in the IGI Global book series Advances in Educational Technologies and Instructional Design (AETID) (ISSN: 2326-8905; eISSN: 2326-8913)

British Cataloguing in Publication Data
A Cataloguing in Publication record for this book is available from the British Library.

Advances in Educational Technologies and Instructional Design (AETID) Book Series

Lawrence A. Tomei
Robert Morris University, USA

ISSN:2326-8905
EISSN:2326-8913

Mission

Education has undergone, and continues to undergo, immense changes in the way it is enacted and distributed to both child and adult learners. From distance education, Massive-Open-Online-Courses (MOOCs), and electronic tablets in the classroom, technology is now an integral part of the educational experience and is also affecting the way educators communicate information to students.

The **Advances in Educational Technologies & Instructional Design (AETID) Book Series** is a resource where researchers, students, administrators, and educators alike can find the most updated research and theories regarding technology's integration within education and its effect on teaching as a practice.

Coverage

- Adaptive Learning
- Digital Divide in Education
- Web 2.0 and Education
- Hybrid Learning
- Game-Based Learning
- Social Media Effects on Education
- Educational Telecommunications
- Curriculum Development
- Instructional Design
- Instructional Design Models

IGI Global is currently accepting manuscripts for publication within this series. To submit a proposal for a volume in this series, please contact our Acquisition Editors at Acquisitions@igi-global.com or visit: http://www.igi-global.com/publish/.

The Advances in Educational Technologies and Instructional Design (AETID) Book Series (ISSN 2326-8905) is published by IGI Global, 701 E. Chocolate Avenue, Hershey, PA 17033-1240, USA, www.igi-global.com. This series is composed of titles available for purchase individually; each title is edited to be contextually exclusive from any other title within the series. For pricing and ordering information please visit http://www.igi-global.com/book-series/advances-educational-technologies-instructional-design/73678. Postmaster: Send all address changes to above address.

Titles in this Series

For a list of additional titles in this series, please visit: www.igi-global.com/book-series

Deviant Communication in Teacher-Student Interactions Emerging Research and Opportunities
Eletra Gilchrist-Petty (The University of Alabama in Huntsville, USA)
Information Science Reference • copyright 2018 • 133pp • H/C (ISBN: 9781522527794) • US $125.00 (our price)

Culturally Engaging Service-Learning With Diverse Communities
Omobolade O. Delano-Oriaran (St. Norbert College, USA) Marguerite W. Penick-Parks (University of Wisconsin – Oshkosh, USA) and Suzanne Fondrie (University of Wisconsin – Oshkosh, USA)
Information Science Reference • copyright 2018 • 359pp • H/C (ISBN: 9781522529002) • US $225.00 (our price)

Enhancing Education and Training Initiatives Through Serious Games
John Denholm (The University of Manchester, UK & University of Warwick, UK) and Linda Lee-Davies (The University of Manchester, UK & Wroxton College of Fairleigh Dickinson University, USA)
Information Science Reference • copyright 2018 • 311pp • H/C (ISBN: 9781522536895) • US $185.00 (our price)

A Simplex Approach to Learning, Cognition, and Spatial Navigation Emerging Research and Opportunities
Pio Alfredo Di Tore (University of Salerno, Italy)
Information Science Reference • copyright 2018 • 116pp • H/C (ISBN: 9781522524557) • US $125.00 (our price)

Digital Transformation and Innovation in Chinese Education
Hiller A. Spires (North Carolina State University, USA)
Information Science Reference • copyright 2018 • 362pp • H/C (ISBN: 9781522529248) • US $195.00 (our price)

Applications of CALL Theory in ESL and EFL Environments
James Perren (Alliant International University, USA) Ken Kelch (Alliant International University, USA) Jin-suk Byun (Alliant International University, USA) Seth Cervantes (Alliant International University, USA) and Setareh Safavi (Alliant International University, USA)
Information Science Reference • copyright 2018 • 360pp • H/C (ISBN: 9781522529330) • US $195.00 (our price)

Visual Imagery, Metadata, and Multimodal Literacies Across the Curriculum
Anita August (Sacred Heart University, USA)
Information Science Reference • copyright 2018 • 295pp • H/C (ISBN: 9781522528081) • US $210.00 (our price)

Cases on Audio-Visual Media in Language Education
Catherine Hua Xiang (London School of Economics and Political Science, UK)
Information Science Reference • copyright 2018 • 419pp • H/C (ISBN: 9781522527244) • US $195.00 (our price)

IGI Global
DISSEMINATOR OF KNOWLEDGE

701 East Chocolate Avenue, Hershey, PA 17033, USA
Tel: 717-533-8845 x100 • Fax: 717-533-8661
E-Mail: cust@igi-global.com • www.igi-global.com

Table of Contents

Detailed Table of Contents

This chapter investigates whether a problem-solving task with an environment exploration component mediates learner autonomy in a 3D virtual world (VW). Two groups of English as a foreign language (EFL) learners were to collect information by exploring the 3D VW and eliciting information from player avatars to complete the task. An analysis of student interaction reveals that only one of the groups acted as autonomous learners by generating new topics based on their observations in the environment; eliciting information and controlling the topics when interacting with the player avatars; and initiating repair leading to input modification, negotiation of meaning, and modification of output. Results suggest that learner autonomy could be promoted in 3D VWs by improving the clarity of task instructions and by designing learning tasks in such a way that students would be able to complete the tasks only if they share their observations with peers and player avatars.

The latest street view technology enables language learners to look around and navigate interactively from remote worldwide locations via the internet. In addition to the enhanced feeling of immersion, the realistic scenes in a street view panorama help to represent the real world and make language learning more engaging and meaningful. This chapter explores the potential for extending a virtual English as a foreign language classroom with online street view panoramas. The program aims to create an immersive environment within which students complete a task-based learning activity; the task design is based on Schank's (1996) goal-based scenarios. The results reveal that street view technologies hold great potential to enhance language learners' communicative competence. Future research is needed to look into learners' experience in this new learning environment and to examine the use of street view panoramas in other disciplines.

The purpose of this chapter is to examine participants' perceived affordances of three-dimensional virtual learning environments (3D VLEs) in developing interpersonal emotional connections with their partners during the initial stage of the virtual exchange. To fulfill the purpose, two Japanese and two American students were paired and participated in sessions within two differently designed virtual environments using the same 3D virtual application. The results indicate that the participants tend to find avatars useful as a cue that helps in recalling previous conversations and in avoiding long silences. Additionally, the affordances of the 3D VLEs heightened the experience of co-presence. However, for non-native speakers, this experience also created increased anxiety. Finally, the results show the affordances affected the participants much more strongly during the first several sessions but were mitigated by other factors as the sessions continued.

Section 2
MUVE and Twenty-First Century Learning

The multi-user virtual environment (MUVE) described in this chapter is aimed to promote learner agency and motivation by engaging students in authentic and challenging learning experiences aligned with educational goals to foster twenty-first century competencies. Principles of assessment for learning (AfL) and gamification will be integrated to design a MUVE governed by students. The students will engage in learning, assessment, and instruction-related activities. They will also initiate, manage, and monitor the activities. The relationship between The Learners' Isle virtual environment and the physical classroom environment will be complementary and reciprocal. The teacher (a digital immigrant) and the students (the digital natives) will be partners in the teaching-learning process. The design principles of The Learners' Isle, a scenario to illustrate blended learning, and its conceptualization through an activity theory framework will be presented. In addition, this chapter will discuss the educational context characteristics conducive to successful implementation of the MUVE.

This chapter maps the types of interactions that relate to the use of virtual worlds in hybrid virtual learning scenarios. Students were asked to state their opinions regarding their experiences and were also observed along the way. The results highlight that the learning activities and students' attitudes and experiences greatly affect learner engagement. It is vital, though, that instructional designers plan the learning activities thoughtfully and provide learners with enough time and support. Offering content with examples of the expectations of the teaching team can be invaluably helpful. Furthermore, a game-like content can be considered a great source of motivation. Moreover, the vividness of the virtual world makes the learning process more stimulating and less tedious. Additionally, avatars enable users to interact with the content and increase the opportunities for interactions with others. Nevertheless, learners' simultaneous co-presence in the physical classroom is a more immediate and preferred option, since it offers increased opportunities for collaboration.

The aim of this chapter is to argue how create-and-learn pedagogy can be used to direct and drive the development of virtual reality applications in academic settings. The chapter discusses the development of a synthetic learning environment that provides a context for new learning and twenty-first century education. A case study of an interdisciplinary project by university undergraduates in Japan designing,

Foreword

As we approach (arguably) the fifth decade of the application of Multi-User Virtual Environments to learning, the publication of a book that charts the application of such environments in school and university classrooms is timely. From the early use of text based Multi-user Dungeons (MUDs) in the 1970s and 1980s and their Object-oriented extensions (MOOs) in the 1990s, the potential for learners to become deeply engaged and psychologically immersed while undertaking exploratory learning activities alongside their peers within virtual environments has been very clear. As the hardware and software platforms required for 3D virtual environments became more readily available in the 2000s MUVEs providing a much greater degree of sensory immersion emerged, most prominently Active Worlds and Second Life. However, despite regular predictions of their potential to revolutionise education, the mainstream application of such environments within classroom curriculums has been only modest. This book addresses the need for documented examples of successful applications of MUVEs achieving curriculum outcomes across a range of disciplines.

While there have been numerous articles over many years highlighting the learning potential of virtual environments in general and MUVEs in particular, studies providing strong evidence for their educational effectiveness are harder to find (Mikropoulos & Natsis, 2011). Nevertheless, meta-analyses such as that conducted by Merchant, Goetz, Cifuentes, et al. (2014) show that their educational value can be and has been empirically demonstrated. Despite this, integration into the curriculum within contemporary classrooms has been found challenging even by some of the most passionate early adopters (Dalgarno, Lee, Carlson, et al., 2011; Dickey, 2011). Common challenges reported include technical and usability barriers as well as policy and attitudinal constraints imposed by other teachers and administrators. Examples such as those reported within the chapters of this book will encourage educators considering applying MUVEs in their own contexts to persevere despite some of these potential barriers.

In some ways there is a more natural application of MUVEs in informal learning settings or in university settings where much of the learning occurs outside of formal class time. In school settings, the need to connect students to their peers through a virtual environment can on the surface appear less compelling given that the students are collocated in the physical environment when the learning occurs. A number of the chapters in this book, however, help to show the benefits of immersive virtual environments for achieving curriculum outcomes in a school setting, and most importantly the benefits of cooperative and collaborative activities with peers inside these environments.

One of the things that makes the educational applications of MUVEs so exciting is the way in which they draw on the representational, interactive and communicative capabilities of contemporary connected technologies. This combination of capabilities can afford identity construction, sense of presence and co-presence, and enable a wide range of learning tasks with benefits including spatial knowledge representation, experiential learning, high engagement, contextual learning and collaborative learning (Dalgarno & Lee, 2010).

However, despite the clear potential of MUVEs, when considering their use as a platform on which to base learning activities designed to achieve particular learning outcomes, it is important to be clear on the needs of the learning activity. Because of the potential usability and technical challenges in using MUVEs an analysis of their fit for purpose is important. Firstly, for activities that first and foremost require the immersive, experiential capabilities of a virtual environment, there is the question of whether the communicative, cooperative or collaborative capabilities of a MUVE are required or whether a single user environment may be sufficient. On the other hand, for activities which are primarily social or collaborative, there is the question of whether the immersive capabilities of a virtual environment are required or whether a simpler non-immersive environment such as a video conferencing or web conferencing platform might be adequate. The unique potential for MUVEs to enable immersive learning in a social context is illustrated by a number of the chapters within this book.

In recent years substantial changes in teaching approaches have begun to emerge, building on a deeper understanding of cognitive and social learning processes from a solid evidence base of empirical educational research, drawing on the affordances and ubiquitous availability of contemporary connected learning technologies, and responding to important developments in the socio-political contexts in which education occurs (Steffens et al., 2015). These changes include a greater emphasis on learners constructing their own knowledge representation in the context of well-designed purposeful learning activities, in a cooperative environment with peers providing support, feedback and collaborative generation of ideas. These changes in accepted teaching approaches and learning contexts will potentially open up new opportunities for the use of MUVEs which have the potential to afford exactly the kinds of learning activities demanded by these developments. It is also likely that some of the barriers to mainstream adoption of MUVEs will gradually diminish as base technology platforms and minimum internet bandwidths improve and as experience in playing 3D video games becomes a commonplace expectation within adult and youth learning cohorts. In this context books like this will become increasingly important in highlighting the strengths, limitations and unique benefits of MUVEs in contemporary digitally enabled classrooms.

Barney Dalgarno
Charles Sturt University, Australia

Barney Dalgarno *is Director of Learning Online at Charles Sturt University, leading strategic innovation for Australia's largest online learning provider. Professor Dalgarno's research contributions have been in three broad areas: the relationship between learning technology and learning theory; learning in polysynchronous learning environments, including 3D virtual environments; and university teacher and student use of learning technologies. He has had international influence over many years through journal editorship, conference program committee leadership, and assessing of teaching awards and research grants for international bodies. He has obtained numerous grants and consultancies for higher education research and innovation and has authored over 75 refereed publications. Professor Dalgarno has received recognition for his innovative teaching and research including Australian Learning and Teaching Council Citations in 2007 and 2011 and the 2013 ASCILITE Fellow Award.*

REFERENCES

Dalgarno, B., & Lee, M. J. W. (2010). What are the learning affordances of 3D virtual environments? *British Journal of Educational Technology*, *41*(1), 10–32. doi:10.1111/j.1467-8535.2009.01038.x

Dalgarno, B., Lee, M. J. W., Carlson, L., Gregory, S., & Tynan, B. (2011). An Australian and New Zealand scoping study on the use of 3D immersive virtual worlds in higher education. *Australasian Journal of Educational Technology*, *27*(1), 1–15. doi:10.14742/ajet.978

Dickey, M. D. (2011). The pragmatics of virtual worlds for K-12 educators: Investigating the affordances and constraints of ActiveWorlds and SecondLife with K-12 in-service teachers. *Educational Technology Research and Development*, *59*(1), 1–20. doi:10.1007/s11423-010-9163-4

Merchant, Z., Goetz, E. T., Cifuentes, L., Keeney-Kennicutt, W., & Davis, T. J. (2014). Effectiveness of virtual reality-based instruction on students' learning outcomes in K-12 and higher education: A meta-analysis. *Computers & Education*, *70*, 29–40. doi:10.1016/j.compedu.2013.07.033

Mikropoulos, T. A., & Natsis, A. (2011). Educational virtual environments: A ten-year review of empirical research (1999–2009). *Computers & Education*, *56*(3), 769–780. doi:10.1016/j.compedu.2010.10.020

Steffens, K., Bannan, B., Dalgarno, B., Bartolomé, A. R., Esteve-González, V., & Cela-Ranilla, J. M. (2015). Recent developments in technology- enhanced learning: A critical assessment. *RUSC. Universities and Knowledge Society Journal*, *12*(2), 1–14.

Preface

INTRODUCTION

Since its inception in 1975 as an adventure game and dubbed as MUD (multi-user dungeon), multi-user virtual environment (MUVE) has emerged as one of the most exciting instructional platforms in education. Starting in the early 2000s, a variety of MUVE-based learning environments have been developed, including the popular platform of MUVE in higher education, Second Life, ActiveWorlds, Open Wonderland, OpenSimulator and Minecraft, with the latter being used primarily in K-12 setting. Over the past few years, enabled by mobile devices and 3D applications and recent advances in immersive technologies, such as virtual reality and augmented reality, MUVE-based learning is further enhanced and the use of MUVE in the classroom is continuously growing. MUVE is believed to be a promising and powerful approach for twenty-first century education.

MUVE is a unique instructional platform with a set of distinct technological affordances, such as multi-user interaction, realism, concretization of abstraction, free of spatial, temporal, and corporeal barriers, which enable a number of significant instructional benefits, including immersion, engagement, immediacy, authenticity, co-presence, and learning community. If designed and implemented appropriately, MUVE has great potential to provide a viable learning environment for promoting higher levels of learning, thinking and doing, such as critical thinking, problem solving, creativity, inquiry spirit and skills, collaboration and teamwork skills, autonomous learning, and lifelong learning. As both an instructional technology and strategy, MUVE holds great potential to enhance and transform education by engaging and challenging learners in a socially situated and distributed learning environment that simulates real-life tasks and situations. Such a learning environment is consistent with current thinking on how people learn as well as with the highly dynamic twenty-first century work and life environment characterized by ubiquitous technology, instant networking, and increasingly diversified challenges.

To harness the power of MUVE in education and explore its full potential in preparing this generation of learners for the new demands and challenges of the twenty-first century, this book brings together distinguished education scholars and practitioners from around the world who offer their most current scholarship and practices in using MUVE in modern classrooms. The purposes of this collection are threefold: (1) to examine the theoretical underpinnings and pedagogical frameworks that guide the design, development, and implementation of MUVE in education, (2) to highlight current leading-edge research efforts and exemplary uses of MUVE in different educational settings, and (3) to identify challenges and future trends in integrating MUVE into the classroom.

ORGANIZATION AND OVERVIEW

This book is organized around three themes: (1) MUVE in science education and language learning, (2) MUVE and twenty-first century learning, and (3) the future of MUVE in education. What follows is a brief overview of the three sections, each representing a theme.

The first section, "MUVE in Science Education and Language Learning," includes current research efforts in science education and language learning, both of which have been at the forefront of integrating MUVE into the curriculum and classroom. This section updates the field by highlighting new developments and exemplary uses of MUVE to enhance science education and language learning. In the opening chapter, Shari J. Metcalf, Amy M. Kamarainen, Eric Torres, Tina A. Grotzer, and Chris Dede discuss the design of *EcoMUVE*, a MUVE-based middle school science curriculum for ecosystem science education and explicate how the affordances of MUVE can support pedagogical strategies that are powerful for science learning, which include (1) immersive virtual interface for situated learning, (2) team-based, student-centered virtual exploration for constructivist learning, (3) investigating mysteries for inquiry-based learning, (4) visualizing complex scientific phenomena for simulation-based learning, (5) taking scientific roles and using avatars for identity exploration, and (6) shared online presence for social network knowledge construction. As a pioneering and leading project in MUVE-based science education, *EcoMUVE* has attracted significant attention and has been used in the U.S. and worldwide since 2012, and various studies have been conducted to explore a range of research topics. In this chapter, the authors highlight the curriculum's feasibility in practicality, integration, and acceptance, as well as its power in engaging, motivating students in collaborative, inquiry-based science learning, and its effectiveness in supporting students' acquisition of core concepts in ecosystem and scientific inquiry skills. The authors also identify several important aspects that are critical to the successful implementation of MUVE-based curricula in science classroom, including teacher professional development, school technological infrastructure and support, school culture, and teachers' comfort level with being "guide on the side." Although the focus of this chapter is on science education, Metcalf, Kamarainen, Torres, Grotzer, and Dede illustrate the connection between contemporary pedagogical concepts and MUVE features, which serves as a roadmap for readers to explore and understand MUVE-based learning further discussed in later chapters.

Similarly, MIT Education Arcade has been exploring the use of MUVE to support K-12 students' STEM learning and scientific inquiry since early 2000s. In the second chapter, Louisa Rosenheck looks into MIT Education Arcade's current research effort on The Radix Endeavor, an online game that capitalizes on the unique features of both games and MUVEs. Rosenheck describes in detail the design process of Radix, which combines the principles of game design, social and collaborative learning, and deep learning. Emphasizing the value of collaborative inquiry-based play, the author contends that an intentionally designed content-rich game for STEM learning, set in an open-ended MUVE environment, can engage students in a more authentic scientific inquiry process, thus provide them deeper learning experiences. Based on the data collected during the Radix pilot phase, Rosenheck identifies three areas that teachers need to plan and design in advance for a successful MUVE implementation in the classroom: making wise implementation decisions regarding classroom challenges, embracing the mindset and role of "guide on the side," and using formative assessment strategies to assess and scaffold students' learning, thought processes, and collaborative inquiry process. Rosenheck's explication on connecting play and deep learning sheds light on future research in optimizing MUVE-based learning environments to make learning both fun and deep.

Learner autonomy is important in teaching and learning and this topic has been researched for decades in second language acquisition. In Chapter 3, "Task-Based Language Learning and Learner Autonomy in 3D Virtual Worlds," Iryna Kozlova examines the effect of a problem-solving task with an environment exploration component in a 3D virtual world on learner autonomy in second language learning. The study reveals that 3D virtual worlds that simulate real-life situations (locations and experiences) are a promising medium to facilitate autonomous learning when learners are involved in a problem-solving task that requires environment exploration. Kozlova identifies two design elements that are critical to the successful implementation of this instructional strategy in the classroom: clarity of task instructions and team-based tasks that require sharing and collaboration. While this study is focused on second language learning, Kozlova formulates a promising instructional strategy to promote autonomous learning in 3D virtual worlds, which could be applicable to other subject areas. Moreover, this instructional strategy may benefit the acquisition of teamwork skills and contribute to the long-term educational goal of preparing students to be independent learners.

Contextualized learning can be an effective pedagogical approach to facilitating active and meaningful learning if designed and implemented appropriately. In Chapter 4, "Contextualizing Language Learning With Street View Panoramas," Ya-Chun Shih uses Google street view panoramas technology to immerse English as foreign language learners in real-life contexts, exploring real street-view scenes, imagery of popular places, and real objects, interacting with other avatars, and completing goal-based tasks, such as role play of virtual tour guides, and hometown instructions. Shih considers teachers' willingness and readiness to incorporate this innovative instructional tool into their classrooms as critical to the successful implementation of contextualized learning enabled by street view panoramas technology. The focus of this chapter is on communicative competence of language learners; however, the instructional techniques for contextualized learning using virtual reality technology (such as street view panoramas) found in this study may serve as a catalyst for future research on facilitating communicative competence in other disciplines.

The first section concludes with "The Affordances of 3D Virtual Learning Environments: Designing for Learner's Interpersonal and Emotional Connections," authored by Hisae Matsui and Terence C. Ahern. This chapter examines native and non-native Japanese speakers' perceived affordances of 3D virtual learning environments in developing interpersonal emotional connections with their partners during their virtual interaction. The results indicate that the experience of co-presence is enabled in 3D virtual learning environments via avatars, which, however, creates increased social anxiety for non-native speakers. The authors argue that regardless of non-native speakers' intimidation in social interaction caused by anxiety, 3D virtual learning environments with avatar embodiment provide an optimal learning platform for non-native speakers to practice real-world interactions and acquire real-life communicative skills. Co-presence, the sense of being together physically and psychologically, has been recognized as critical to building a learning community in virtual learning environment. Matsui and Ahern's study contributes to the extant literature on co-presence by looking deeper into its impact on learners who differ in competency levels on a subject.

The second section of the book, "MUVE and Twenty-First Century Learning," explores the features, affordances and instructional benefits of MUVE and how this learning environment can be used to optimize higher levels of learning for 21st century competencies. In Chapter 6, "Integrating Virtual Spaces: Connecting Affordances of 3D Virtual Learning Environments to Design for Twenty-First Century Learning," Peggy Hartwick and Nuket Savaskan Nowlan explore the connections between contemporary learning theories and affordances of 3D virtual learning environments, based on which they explicate a pedagogical design process for learning environments, learning processes and learning outcomes. The authors emphasize the importance of making great use of MUVE's unique technological affordances (e.g., high fidelity simulation, multi-user environment, synchronicity in space and time) in space and task design, to promote the sense of authenticity, learning community, knowledge sharing and co-construction, and real-life learning. Hartwick and Nowlan advocate drawing on multiple learning theories to guide the design of a MUVE space to help promote higher levels of learning for twenty-first century skills.

In Chapter 7, "Creating Contexts for Collaborative Learning in a 3D Virtual World for Distance Education," Anders I. Mørch, Valentina Caruso, Melissa D. Hartley, and Barbara L. Ludlow identify two types of contexts that are instrumental in promoting collaborative learning in virtual learning environments: social context (social interaction) and pedagogical context (instructor's scaffolding). The authors find that the sense of anonymity represented by avatars in the 3D environment helps engage learners more freely and effectively in social interactions and in practicing collaboration skills. At the same time, instructor's scaffolding throughout the learning process is critical to the success of collaborative learning. Scaffolding comes in four forms: technology support, course structure planning, procedure implementation, and activity transition facilitation. The authors also identify a third context, emotional context (unsupported in this study), as necessary in supporting collaborative learning in virtual learning environments. Learner emotion, an integral part of any learning experience, is one of the less studied topics in online learning. This chapter is a reminder that future research studies are needed to probe into learner's emotion and how to make use of the unique features and affordances of MUVE to support learner's emotional presence.

Like collaborative learning, team-based learning is important in multi-user virtual learning environments. In Chapter 8, "Team-Based Learning and Team-Based Playing: How World of Warcraft and Similar Games Can Make Better Learners," Abi Johnson explores the use of World of Warcraft, a popular massively multiplayer online role-playing game to prepare college students for team-based learning and practice teamwork skills. Johnson includes a flowchart for the general phases of the World of Warcraft assignment and identifies four tenets that are connected to successful team functions: (1) permanent, small, and correctly formed learning groups, (2) accountable group members for individual and group participation, (3) group activities that promote both learning and group development, and (4) frequent and immediate feedback on performance to group members. Team-based learning has been a potentially powerful instructional strategy to facilitate students' acquisition of real-life work competencies; teamwork skills are of paramount importance in twenty-first century learning. Johnson's study on the use of World of Warcraft (or a similar MUVE program) as an assignment in the early phase of a semester long class provides a novel and promising approach to accelerating early team development and promoting the learning of teamwork skills.

Section two ends with Chapter 9, "Factors Affecting Primary School Students' Learning Experience When Using MUVEs: Development and Validation of a Scale," in which Emmanuel Fokides and Pinelopi Atsikpasi report the development and validation of a survey instrument that measures the key factors that affect students' learning experience in MUVE programs. The validated instrument consists of 24 survey items grouped into seven factors: (1) perceived learning effectiveness, (2) perceived ease of use, (3) presence, (4) enjoyment, (5) motivation, (6) collaboration, and (7) realism. Many extant empirical studies on MUVE have touched upon learner's affective domain (such as engagement, motivation, enjoyment, and satisfaction) when primarily examining the effect of MUVEs on learning outcomes; very few studies, however, have identified the major factors and investigated how they have interacted to affect students' learning experience in MUVE programs. Fokides and Atsikpasi's study fills this gap in the field by developing and validating such a scale, which can be used to evaluate user experience and thus further improve the design of a MUVE program.

To maximize the potential of MUVE and optimize the use of its emerging tools, unique affordances, and educational benefits, the third and final section of the book, "MUVE: Exploring the Future," collects current innovative pedagogical uses of MUVE in the classroom. In Chapter 10, "Multi-User Mixed Reality Environments for Distance Learning," Anasol Peña-Rios, Victor Callaghan, and Michael Gardner pinoint the lack of support for collaborative hands-on experience as a serious shortcoming in their distance education courses in science and engineering, which is also a common challenge in other disciplines when using virtual learning environments, including MUVE. The authors explore how the multi-user mixed reality approach has offered a solution to this problem, through their case study of the Blended Reality Lab (BReal Lab), which involves students from eight universities in six countries. This mixed-reality learning environment provides a set of unique affordances to promote collaboration across geographically dispersed learners, including simulated physical objects, mixed physical and virtual mirrored objects (digital twins), and physical-virtual mashups. While the study is focused on science and engineering, the distributed mixed reality framework proposed by the authors points to a promising future direction in the innovative use of MUVE to improve distance education.

Similarly, Chapter 11, "The Learner's Isle: A Multi-User Virtual Environment to Foster Learner Agency and Motivation," by Menucha Birenbaum and Elhanan Gazit, describes a blended learning environment in which a multi-user virtual learning program, The Leaners' Isle, is integrated into a physical classroom environment. The activities in the two systems are coordinated so as to maximize the affordances of both learning environments. Based on the design principles of Assessment for Learning (AfL) and gamification, The Learner's Isle is designed to promote learner agency and motivation, both of which play important roles in facilitating effective and active learning. AfL is believed to be a potentially powerful instructional strategy to improve teaching and learning; Birenbaum and Gazit's study explores AfL's role in fostering learner agency through active-reflective learning activities in the learning process, including formulating objectives, developing rubrics, and performing self- and peer assessments. This chapter serves as a reminder of a significant area in learning—learner agency, and the use of AfL to facilitate autonomous learning points to a promising direction for future research on how to promote self-regulated learners in MUVE.

Chapter 12, "The Added Value of the Hybrid Virtual Learning Approach: Using Virtual Environments in the Real Classroom," by Athanasios Christopoulos, Marc Conrad, and Mitul Shukla, examines college students' interaction and engagement in a hybrid virtual learning environment, in which both the teaching team and students are present simultaneously in a Second Life-based virtual environment as well as in the physical classroom. The study identifies immediate interactions with peers and instructors in the physical classroom as a more preferred option; the in-world interactions with learning materials, however, are more attractive than studying in the traditional sense for practical sessions. Christopoulos, Conrad, and Shukla reiterate the importance of designing and implementing varied types of interactions in a hybrid learning environment, so as to maximize the benefits of both virtual and physical environments.

The book ends with a study on a synthetic learning environment—a mixed-reality learning environment aiming to promote new learning and twenty-first century education. In this chapter, "Create-and-Learn: Education 'in' a Synthetic Learning Environment," Michael Vallance discusses the development of a multi-user mixed reality learning environment, in which university undergraduates in Japan develop an interdisciplinary project on virtual nuclear power plant through a "create-and-learn" approach. Vallance argues that there needs to be a shift in education from learning "from" or "with" technology to education "in" a synthetic learning environment characterized by immersive technologies (e.g., virtual reality, augmented reality, mixed reality), real-life tasks, and create-and-learn pedagogy. Experiential learning ("learning through reflection on doing") aims to prepare students for real-world work, life, and learning; it holds great potential for education for the twenty-first century. Vallance's study sheds light on future research on twenty-first century education and how emerging immersive technologies can be used to help promote experiential learning.

CONCLUSION

This book showcases leading-edge research efforts in using MUVE in education worldwide. Twenty-eight contributors from nine countries share insights on connecting theories and practices in MUVE design, as well as recommendations for successful classroom implementations of MUVE through authentic case studies and other empirical research methods. The 13 chapters together cover a range of topics from MUVE integration in science education and language learning, to MUVE design for twenty-first century competencies, and to innovative use and forward-thinking on MUVE for education.

As shown across the chapters, current research in MUVE has primarily focused on affective, cognitive, and social aspects of learning; the metacognitive aspect has scarcely been touched upon. Metacognitive strategies are especially important in open-ended learning environments, such as MUVE, in which learners are given more control of their own learning. For future development and research of MUVE in education, attention should be paid to the design of metacognitive support and how it, in return, can help enhance student learning outcomes in affective, cognitive, and social aspects. Moreover, as evidenced in the recommendations made across the chapters, teachers' willingness and readiness for MUVE-based learning and "guide on the side" mindset are critical to the success of MUVE implementation and the cultivation of inquiry spirit among learners; it is therefore imperative to establish a pedagogically and pragmatically sound professional development framework of MUVE implementation for teachers, with the goal to make the best use of this powerful pedagogy to enhance and transform teaching and learning.

The goal of the editor and contributors of this book is to advance scholarly inquiry in MUVE's features, affordances, educational benefits, and theoretical underpinnings by considering advances in MUVE and other immersive technologies and the advent of new areas in educational research; they seek to share research-informed, evidence-based best practices and implementation recommendations in the use of MUVE in the classroom for twenty-first century education. It is hoped that this book will help researchers, practitioners, and policy makers in education gain a deeper understanding of the roles, benefits, potential, and challenges of integrating MUVE in the classroom so as to enhance and transform teaching and learning and to better prepare students for the real world.

Yufeng Qian
Northeastern University, USA

Acknowledgment

I would like to acknowledge the many individuals who made this book possible. First, my sincere thanks go to the authors who generously contributed their time and expertise. Their research and thought-provoking insights made this project a timely contribution to the research and practice in 3D multi-user virtual learning environments.

Further, I would like to express my deep indebtedness to members of the editorial advisory board and all the reviewers of individual chapters for their rigorous critiques offered during the double-blind review process. This book would not have been such a strong product had it not been for their constructive feedback.

I also want to acknowledge the staff at IGI Global for their highly professional and prompt assistance throughout the whole process. My special thanks go to Mariah Gilbert, Acquisitions Editor, who provided the opportunity for this project. Extra special thanks must be extended to Jordan Tepper, Assistant Development Editor, who was always prompt and cordial in providing guidance and assistance during my work on the book.

Finally, I want to thank my husband and best friend, Dr. Guiyou Huang who, while running the busy operations of a university, provided unwavering support of my professional endeavors, with patience and humor. This book would not have come to light without his continuous support. To my parents and my children George and Claire – Thank you for being an endless source of inspiration, motivation, and strength in my life.

Yufeng Qian
Northeastern University, USA

Section 1

MUVE in Science Education and Language Learning

Chapter 1
EcoMUVE:
A Case Study on the Affordances of MUVEs in Ecosystem Science Education

Shari J. Metcalf
Harvard University, USA

Amy M. Kamarainen
Harvard University, USA

Eric Torres
Harvard University, USA

Tina A. Grotzer
Harvard University, USA

Chris Dede
Harvard University, USA

ABSTRACT

This chapter considers classroom strategies that have been shown to support student science learning and discusses the affordances of multi-user virtual environments (MUVEs) as a platform to implement those strategies. EcoMUVE, a middle school curriculum for ecosystem science education, is presented as a case study to demonstrate the design of a MUVE-based curriculum that enhances science learning and engagement. The chapter concludes with a summary of research findings on student learning and engagement, and suggestions for consideration in implementing MUVE-based curricula in classrooms.

DOI: 10.4018/978-1-5225-3719-9.ch001

INTRODUCTION

The National Research Council *Framework for K-12 Science Education* outlines a vision for science education:

In which students, over multiple years of school, actively engage in science and engineering practices and apply crosscutting concepts to deepen their understanding of the core ideas in these fields. The learning experiences provided for students should engage them with fundamental questions about the world and with how scientists have investigated and found answers to those questions. Throughout the K-12 grades, students should have the opportunity to carry out scientific investigations and engineering design projects related to the disciplinary core ideas. (National Research Council, 2012, pp. 8-9)

This vision has grown out of work in areas such as constructivism and situated learning theory, which recognize science and science learning as social processes of knowledge construction and argue for leveraging student-centered approaches as well as inquiry- and project-based pedagogies (National Research Council, 2005). The integration of knowledge and practice suggested by the NRC Framework and Next Generation Science Standards (NGSS) is heralded as a powerful approach to science learning (National Research Council, 2012; NGSS Lead States, 2013), but there are currently few curricula that can deliver on this promise.

The book *Learning Science Through Computer Games and Simulations*, published by the National Research Council (2011) presents a framework of five learning goals for quality science education. These learning goals have to do with cultivating the motivation to learn about natural phenomena, the conceptual understanding of how science represents the world, the ability to understand and apply scientific methods, the awareness of and participation in scientific discourse, and the development of a scientific identity (National Research Council, 2011). The authors present research suggesting that computer games and simulations have the ability to advance each of these learning goals. The Next Generation Science Standards (NGSS Lead States 2013), likewise, call for student learning experiences that involve engaging in investigation, data analysis, developing and using models, and constructing explanations. Computer-based models and simulations offer rich opportunities for supporting students in these activities.

Multi-user virtual environments (MUVEs) offer opportunities to provide rich learning experiences like those described by NGSS and the National Research Council. MUVEs are 3-D graphical worlds used to construct simulated immersive experiences. In a MUVE, each user has a virtual representation, an avatar, which they can move through a 3-D virtual world. These simulated contexts provide rich, *immersive* environments in which participants can interact with digital objects and tools, with each other and with computer-based agents, providing a sense of presence in a virtual place (Dede, 2009a; Fishman, Dede, & Means, 2015; Slater, 2009). MUVEs are a promising platform for educational applications, in part because MUVEs can simulate environments and experiences otherwise impossible in school settings (e.g., Barab et al., 2005; Kafai, 2010; Schaller et al., 2009). Research with MUVEs for science education has shown that these platforms can be effective in engaging middle and high school students in various science topics (Clarke et al, 2006; Lim et al., 2006; Nelson & Ketelhut, 2007; Trindade et al., 2002).

This chapter describes the ways in which curricula based on MUVEs can be designed to provide a situated context for enacting these powerful science pedagogies. It reviews classroom strategies that have been shown to support student science learning, and discusses the affordances of MUVEs as a platform to implement those strategies. EcoMUVE, a middle school curriculum for ecosystem science education, is presented as a case study to demonstrate the design of a MUVE-based curriculum that enhances science learning and engagement.

POWERFUL APPROACHES FOR SCIENCE LEARNING

Influential science education frameworks argue that students should be given opportunities to practice skills in the context of larger investigations within a rich problem space that is compelling to the students and within which they can pursue their own questions and lines of inquiry (Duschl, Schweingruber, & Shouse, 2007). This argument arises out of constructivist and situated learning theories, which suggest that students construct new knowledge through meaningful interaction with social, physical and cognitive resources embedded in a particular context. Building on these learning theories, the pedagogical approaches of inquiry and project-based learning are powerful tools to help support teachers in achieving these goals. Finally, research suggests that inquiry and project-based pedagogies can be used most fruitfully when they are framed through a lens of student-centered instruction, and with opportunities for identity exploration as well as social knowledge construction. Below we review some of the primary literature that supports the value of these approaches for science learning, and then elaborate on how these approaches can be powerfully integrated through immersing students in problem-based simulations using multi-user virtual environments.

Situated Learning

Situated learning theory contends that learning is properly understood as contextualized – a process that occurs within a given social and cultural paradigm with associated activities and practices. Per situated learning theory, authentic learning of a given skill or capacity cannot be effectively abstracted from the context in which the skill is situated (Brown, Collins, & Duguid, 1989; Chaiklin & Lave, 1993). Thus in the context of science learning, situated learning theory would suggest that learning the content and process of science could be best supported by engaging students in activities in which the knowledge and practices of science are leveraged to address authentic problems. This also includes supporting students in adopting scientific habits of mind and strategies toward investigation that support developing ways to parse complex systems and phenomena, ways to evaluate and construct evidence-based arguments through discourse and communication, and ways to leverage tools and representations specific to science.

MUVEs, as immersive 3D environments, are well suited to supporting authentic science learning as described by situated learning theory. An immersive virtual environment can mimic scientific phenomena, and simulate important features of the scientific context in which the targeted skills and practices are embedded (Dalgarno & Lee, 2010). The ability to virtually move around a graphically rich, dynamic setting or simulation provides up front a highly engaging setting in which to learn, e.g., visiting a virtual pond or forest to learn about ecosystem science.

Additionally, virtual environments can support science learning by scaffolding and structuring complex science tasks and reducing cognitive load associated with typical science activities, for example, by using a single click to collect new data, by making the problem-relevant features more visually prominent, and by providing linked tables and graphs for data representation. Such scaffolds support novice science learners as they develop content knowledge and skills that ultimately contribute to success in use of authentic scientific practices (Kamarainen et al., 2015). With careful scaffolding, the multi-user portion of the virtual environment also provides affordances that can be leveraged to support socially-mediated construction of evidence-based arguments, for example, a team of students might explore different parts of an ecosystem, or use different tools to collect data, and compare and discuss their findings using embedded discourse tools.

Constructivist Learning

Constructivist theory posits that knowledge is constructed rather than transmitted and that learners' active constructions of reality are therefore central to the learning process (Duffy & Cunningham, 1996; Jonassen, 1999; Johnson & Johnson, 1996). Rather than tightly curating a course of experiences and specific interpretive outcomes, constructivist pedagogy allows students to take a more exploratory approach, generating their own interpretations and understandings as they proceed. Students have more autonomy to learn and construct their own understanding through open-ended exploration. While purely discovery-based learning may not be optimal, research suggests that constructivist learning frameworks can be paired with appropriate and flexible scaffolds to support productive inquiry learning experiences (Hmelo-Silver, Duncan & Chinn, 2007; Quintana et al. 2004).

MUVEs for science education can create opportunities for students to learn-by-doing in the virtual world (Dickey, 2005). Virtual worlds permit exploration well beyond what can typically be accommodated in the physical classroom environment. The ability for students to engage in undirected play and exploration in simulations has been linked to improved science content learning (Podolefsky, Rehn, & Perkins, 2013). Rather than be provided with a set of comprehensive instructions for resolving the issues they encounter, students using MUVEs can work together and use in-world tools to collect data, gather information, manipulate the environment, and analyze their experiences in order to make meaning of the phenomena they encounter. The congruence between the visual features of a MUVE and real-world objects, environments and phenomena may support students' construction of knowledge by activating student's prior knowledge about similar objects or environments. As students build on this prior knowledge, the MUVE can provide multiple modes of accessing problem relevant information and, therefore, result in multiple sources from which students can build new knowledge. These features of MUVEs may make new science ideas more accessible, relevant and compelling than if students learned about the same ideas by reading about them.

Inquiry-Based and Project-Based Learning

Student-centered active learning pedagogies for science education, including inquiry-based and project-based strategies, pique student curiosity and generate engagement by framing learning with respect to a motivating question or mystery in need of resolution. In an inquiry-based or project-based model, the skills students develop and apply and the information that they gather are combined to solve a compelling problem (Blumenfeld et al., 1991; Crawford, 2000; Savery, 1995).

MUVEs can support inquiry-based learning through the inclusion of designed frustration points (Warren et al., 2009) and intentional structures to promote student engagement in authentic scientific behaviors (Dede, 2009a). MUVEs that incorporate emergent obstacles, problems, and narratives that students may discover in the course of their interaction can be effective in eliciting student curiosity and structuring scaffolded inquiry behavior without explicit didacticism on the part of either the teacher or an instructional relay in the game world.

The design of a MUVE-based curriculum can provide wide berth for independent approaches to inquiry in the game world, and enable active learning through inquiry, collaboration, and self-directed problem-solving (Ketelhut et al. 2010; Metcalf et al., 2014).

Simulation-Based Learning

Simulation-based learning refers to learning that takes advantage of the power of technology to simulate scientific phenomena. The phenomena and its context are authentic models of the real world, simplified so as to focus attention on particular aspects, and to allow the development of skills or practices in scaffolded, uncluttered, or safer settings than authentic practice would allow. Simulated environments can also provide a range of illustrative visualizations, and can facilitate transfer of learning for future application by presenting interactive simulations of greater complexity and context than is possible in traditional classroom teaching (Bransford & Schwartz, 1999; Rutten, van Joolingen, & van der Veen, 2012).

MUVEs can situate learners in a virtual world in which they can experience and interact with simulated phenomena in rich detail. Simulated, virtual tools can mimic the authentic tools that scientists actually use, but also allow learners to travel through time and alter spatial and temporal scales to see phenomena at different sizes, over time, or over large distances, and to change variables or rules in the world and observe what happens. Students can see and interact with objects and processes in new ways, and the virtual world can enhance understanding through visualizations of hard to understand processes. For science education, MUVEs provide an effective means by which to simulate environments and scenarios otherwise implausible or impossible in school settings (e.g., Barab et al, 2005; Kafai, 2010; Schaller et al, 2009).

Through the affordances of a MUVE, we can create scenarios with real-world verisimilitude that are safe, cost effective, and directly target learning goals. Like other computer-based simulations, MUVEs can also allow students to explore in ways that would not be possible in the real world, through manipulating time and space, or doing experiments that would be dangerous or impossible in real life. With MUVEs, the opportunities to explore virtual environments are limitless – students can shrink to the size of an atom or molecule, travel through the solar system, or explore the human digestive system. In doing so, they can "take apart" or "go inside" structures or phenomena that could not otherwise be subject to observation, and activating these kinds of "inside" views of phenomena by clicking on a macroscopic visual representation of a realistic object that is situated in a realistic virtual context can help students solidify the connections between concrete objects and microscopic phenomena or abstract ideas associated with those objects. MUVEs provide a unique opportunity for linking representations across scales in ways that can be particularly powerful for science learning.

These capacities to strategically distort space and time enable students to interrogate and interact with game-world entities in a manner that is reflective of their real-world analogues, but without many of the limitations that would inhibit having salient experiences and making robust connections between phenomena. While it might be argued that in-game capacities which distort space, time, or other logistical realities are unrealistic, the advantages that these simulated experiences offer for enabling perspective on ecological phenomena are nonetheless powerful.

Identity Exploration

Learning experiences that provide opportunities for identity exploration permit students to reflect on their own identity and to explore alternative possible selves. Identity exploration has been recognized as an important aspect of engagement and persistence in science-based career paths, and most critically, is an important factor for groups who tend to be under-represented in science and STEM fields (Stake & Nickens 2005; Winn, 2003).

Simulated embodiment in virtual environments can allow students to explore features of their identity by enabling them to construct and inhabit a virtual identity. This affordance of virtual spaces, including games, has been explored and elaborated by a number of researchers, who have outlined ways in which virtual and online spaces can support identity development (Foster, 2008; King et al., 2014). The ability to modify avatars or in-game characters enables students to participate in the virtual world as agents with different aesthetic characteristics or imagined histories than the students' own (see Laurel, 1993; Murray, 1998).

More profoundly, students have the opportunity to inhabit the role ascribed to the avatar in the game world. The implication for science education is that, by moving through a virtual environment and performing the tasks of a scientist, students are offered the opportunity to develop first-person identification with the actions of professional scientists through the proxy of the in-game avatars that they control.

Social Network Knowledge Construction

Social Network Knowledge Construction (SNKC) is a pedagogy that uses the communications and networking tools of digital environments to support knowledge construction (Dawley, 2009). MUVEs provide a platform for applying an SNKC model – MUVE can include tools for sharing files or data, messaging and interacting with other students in the environment, creating or joining groups, distributing tasks, and taking collective action. These communications and networking tools may also generate increased engagement thanks to students developing a stronger sense of community or affiliation (Warburton, 2009).

MUVEs can be designed so as to include tools and features that encourage student collaboration (Metcalf et al., 2013). Shared presence is supported by the multi-user aspects of the technology; the software can support virtual interactions through avatars, as well as online chat and other opportunities for sharing data and experience. Student can learn collaboratively by sharing artifacts and data collected in the virtual world. Distributing roles or access to information across individuals or teams can provide further means of in-game collaboration.

In summary, MUVEs offer a valuable platform to implement many powerful pedagogical strategies for science education, both through affordances of the technology itself and through ways in which the technology can be embedded in classroom contexts. Here we describe EcoMUVE as a case study on the affordances of MUVEs for science education, through demonstrating how the design of the software and curriculum are informed by the science learning theories outlined above.

Case Study: EcoMUVE

EcoMUVE is a MUVE-based ecosystem science curriculum for middle-school students to learn about complex causality in ecosystems. There are two EcoMUVE modules, Pond and Forest, each representing an ecological scenario for students to investigate. The two modules are designed to be complementary, covering different aspects of ecosystem science with a similar immersive, virtual interface and the same inquiry-based approach. Table 1 shows an overview of the structure and learning goals for each module.

EcoMUVE Pond

The Pond module provides a 3D virtual representation of pond that is typical of those in the northeastern United States (Figure 1). Students can explore the pond and its surroundings over two months. On one day they discover that all of the large fish in the pond have died. Students may assume there is an isolated cause (such as poisoning), but in fact it is the result of a complex series of events and changes.

Runoff from nearby housing developments carries excess fertilizer to the pond. The phosphorus and nitrogen in the fertilizer support algae growth, leading to an algal bloom. When levels of phosphate become too low to support further growth of the algae population, dead algae accumulate on the bottom of the pond. Bacteria, the dominant decomposers in aquatic ecosystems, consume the dead algae and the bacteria population increases. During decomposition, the bacteria use up a lot of the oxygen in the pond. Eventually, there is not enough oxygen produced during photosynthesis during one virtual day to support the amount of oxygen used during respiration that night. Cloudy days with little wind further deplete the oxygen in the pond. Dissolved oxygen concentrations in the pond became very low overnight, leading to the death of the large fish in the pond from inadequate oxygen.

EcoMUVE Forest

The Forest module simulates two islands, Dover and Willis, which are part of a forested state park (Figure 2). Initially, the ecological communities are quite similar on the two islands; however, Willis Island has populations of wolves and deer, while on Dover Island the deer have no natural predators. Students visit the forested islands over fifty years, to observe, collect data, and investigate how and why the patterns of change are different between the two islands, and to hypothesize why fewer visitors are coming to the park.

On Dover, the deer population increases to its carrying capacity over time, and the flowers, shrubs, and saplings that deer like to eat disappear from the island. The bird species that use the shrubs as habitats likewise decrease, through birds who nest in trees still thrive. Meanwhile, on Willis Island, students

Table 1. EcoMUVE modules:setting, virtual time scale, content areas and learning goals

	Pond	Forest
Setting	Pond and watershed, Northeast US	Two forested islands Great Lakes region
Virtual Time Scale	8 visits 2 months	10 visits 45 years
Content areas, learning goals	Photosynthesis Respiration Decomposition Abiotic/biotic factors Food webs and energy transfer Microbes Oxygen cycle, Carbon cycle Conservation of matter	Food webs and energy transfer Producers, consumers, and decomposers Populations, communities, ecosystems Habitat Carrying capacity Predator-prey relationships Decomposition

Figure 1. EcoMUVE Pond virtual world

Figure 2. EcoMUVE Forest virtual world

observe predator-prey cycles of the deer and wolf populations, as well as an impact of predation on small mammals. Students also learn about the life cycle of deer ticks and monitor Lyme disease risk, learning that the ticks that cause Lyme disease are more closely related to the small mammal populations than to the deer (Kamarainen et al., 2015).

Here we describe the design of the EcoMUVE curriculum using the framework of affordances of MUVEs for science education.

Situated Learning via Immersive Virtual Interface

Immersion in the virtual environment can add significantly to the learning experience by superimposing perceptual overlaps on phenomena to support student understanding. In EcoMUVE, as students explore the virtual world, they experience a sense of presence. In the Pond module, they can walk around the pond, and even under the water to see the different kinds of fish and aquatic plants that live there. They can hear the sounds of the pond – the chirps, buzzes and quacks of insects and ducks. When it rains, they see the splashing and hear the sound of rain. It is an uphill walk to the housing development, and students can walk down along a drainage ditch and through the pipe where runoff flows into the pond. There are also tacit sensory clues to help students understand changes in the ecosystem variables. The pond becomes significantly greenish when the algae population grows in the water (Figure 3). Students can measure pond turbidity, but also experience it directly as the clarity or cloudiness of the water when they go into the pond on different days.

In the Forest module, students visit the two forested islands over time, and walk through the dense hardwood forests, dominated by hemlock, maple, and beech trees, including both saplings and mature trees, and also shrubs, ferns, and trillium flowers. As they explore the forest, students view both tree-dwelling and ground birds, small mammals such as mice, chipmunks, and rabbits, deer, and on Willis Island, wolves as well. A hawk circles overhead. Students can see differences between the two islands over time by observing changes in the numbers and diversity of flora and fauna on each island – e.g., flowers and shrubs disappear on Dover due to overgrazing by deer as their population grows unchecked (Figure 4).

Constructivist Learning Through Student-Centered Exploration

During the EcoMUVE curriculum, students are grouped into teams of four, but each student works individually on computers to explore the 3D immersive environment. They can also chat and collaborate with their teammates. Teachers introduce activities, and provide guidance and support to students, but the primary orientation of the classroom is student-centered exploration. Students observe, collect and interpret data, and develop hypotheses about relationships in the ecosystem through their activities in the virtual world.

To begin, on their first day in the virtual world, students are encouraged to use a camera tool to take photos of the species they find (Figure 5). The photos are linked to a virtual Field Guide, which provides background information about each species, including where it lives, its food sources and predators. At first this activity can be an engaging orientation to familiarize students with the virtual world, but they often revisit the Field Guide later in the unit during their investigations, as important evidence for the causal connections they are making between organisms and factors in the environment.

Figure 3. Examples of immersion in Pond: changes in pond water over time

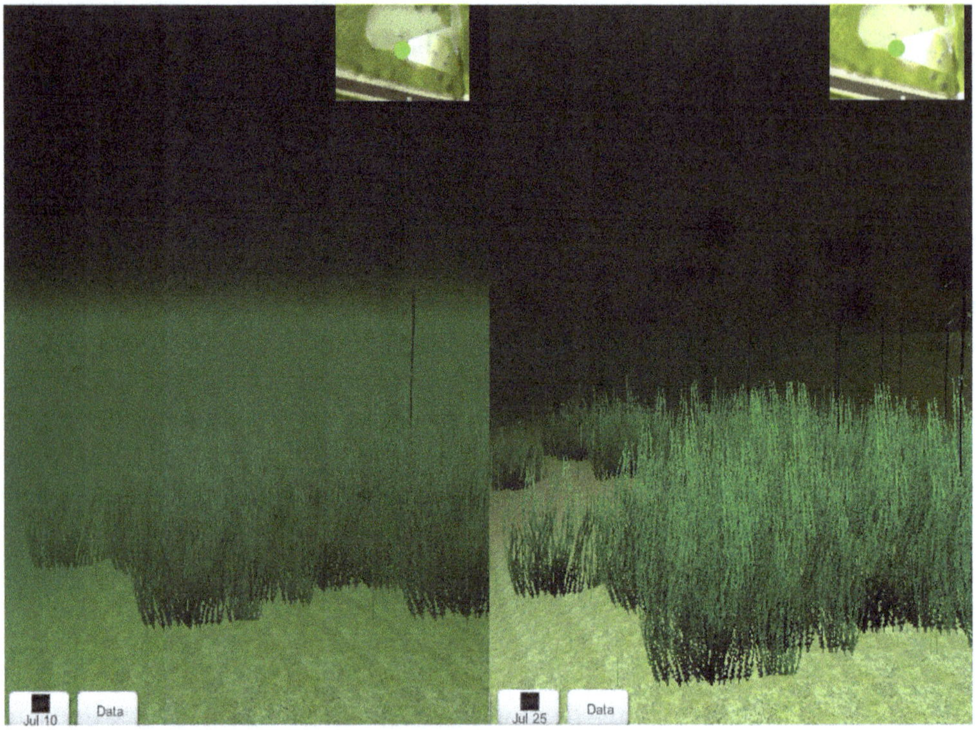

Figure 4. Examples of immersion in Forest: changes in forest composition over time

Figure 5. Exploration in EcoMUVE begins with camera and field guide tools

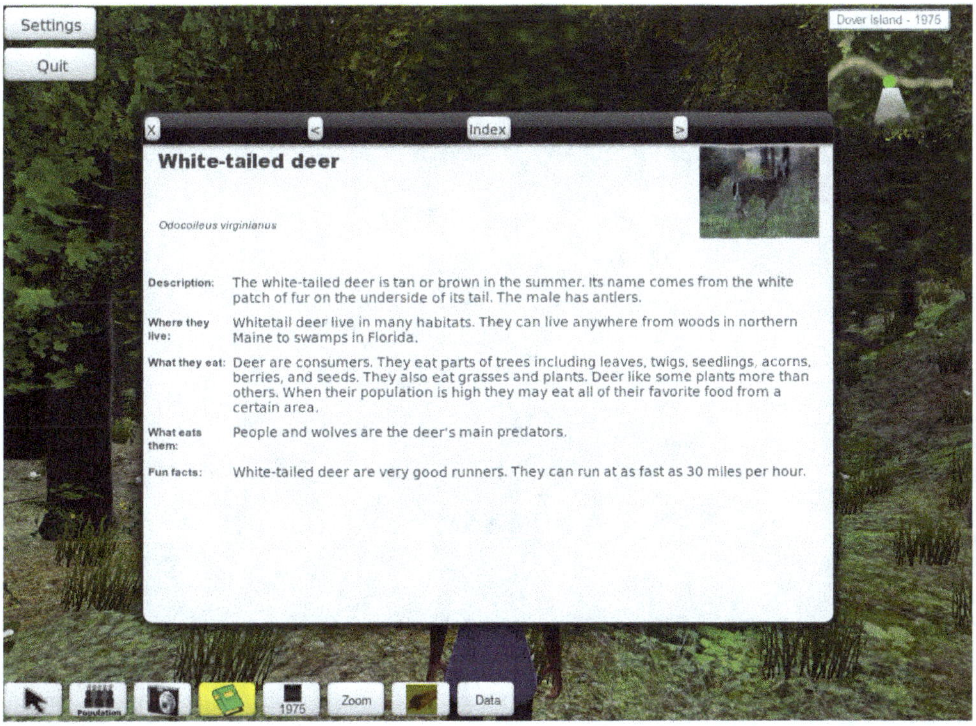

Inquiry-Based Learning by Investigating a Mystery

Student investigation in EcoMUVE begins with open-ended exploration and observation in the immersive virtual world, but is soon framed by a problem for students to investigate – an ecological scenario involving complex causality. In Pond, students investigate "what killed the fish?" (Figure 6) and in Forest, a virtual Park Ranger introduces the problem by informing students that park visitor numbers to the island are down by 40% over the last 10 years, and the state is considering slashing the funding for the park. Students are asked to investigate why fewer visitors are coming to the park.

To investigate these questions, students use the MUVE to explore, make observations, and talk to virtual characters in the world (Figure 7). Measurement tools allow students to collect data on a number of abiotic and biotic factors over time. For Pond, these include water measurements such as dissolved oxygen, nitrates, phosphates, and turbidity, weather measurements like air temperature, cloud cover, and wind speed, and populations of macro- and microscopic organisms. Students click on the measurement tools to collect data, and travel in time to collect measurements on different days. Tables and multi-line graphs support visualizations of the factors and relationships between these factors over time (Figure 8).

The Forest module supports students collecting population data for fifteen species of flora and fauna every five years. The animal species include deer, wolves, several types of birds, small mammals, and deer ticks; the plants include four types of trees, trillium, wood fern, and shrubs. Students collect these populations on each of the two islands; two graphs allow students to look at changes both across time and between the two islands. At first the islands may appear quite similar, except that Dover Island has no wolves, but Willis Island does. Over time, the deer population begins to grow on Dover, but it fluc-

Figure 6. Pond mystery: what killed the fish?

Figure 7. Talking to virtual characters in the world

Figure 8. Collecting and viewing data over time

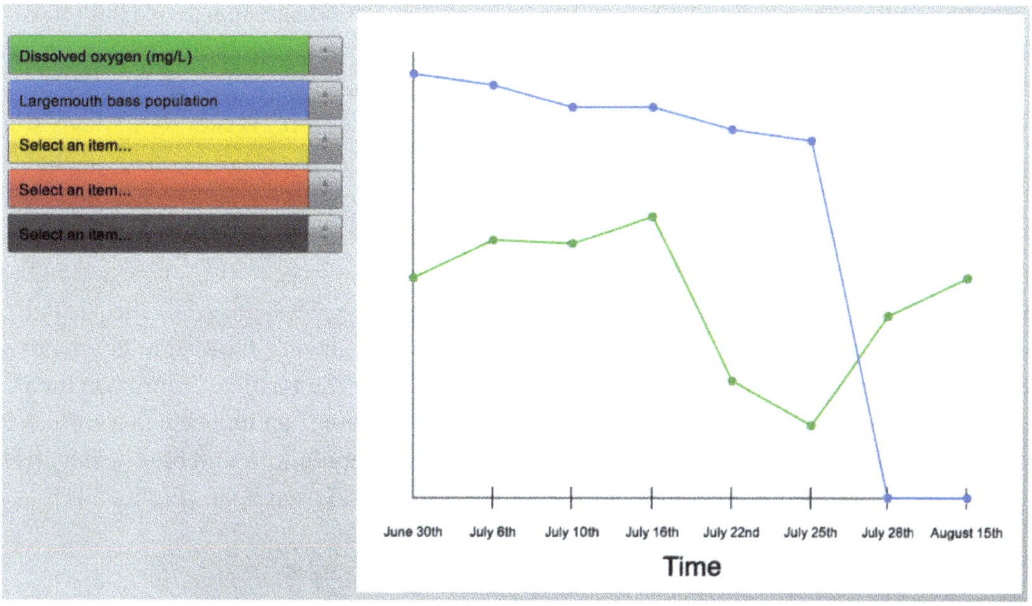

tuates on Willis in a predator-prey cycle. Students also discover that population dynamics are different for different species, because different species grow at different speeds and have different life spans.

In providing students with an open-ended virtual setting with interesting questions to solve, EcoMUVE allows students to engage in science inquiry at a level rarely seen in classroom practice, particularly in middle school. Students conduct their own investigations – choosing which tools to use, what data to collect, and which variables to compare on graphs over time, in order to gather evidence, look for patterns and understand the ecosystem relationships.

Simulation-Based Learning to Visualize Complex Scientific Phenomena

EcoMUVE provides richly detailed ecosystem simulations, with specialized tools that help students visualize phenomena at different scales, across space and over time. Because the world is virtual, there need not be any physical boundaries. Students can explore a large area – a particularly important feature for ecosystem education – in order to understand effects over distance. The Pond module includes not only the pond itself but also the surrounding watershed area, including a nearby golf course and a housing development, from which fertilizer runoff is the distant cause of the algae bloom at the pond. The Forest module supports students moving around and between two large, forested islands. Each island has its own populations of plants and animals, and students travel from one island to the other by using a virtual boat.

Virtual simulations can also help students view and understand that organisms too small to see can play a critical role in the ecosystem. The Pond ecosystem includes organisms ranging in size and phyla from the great blue heron down to microscopic plankton and bacteria suspended in the water and sediment. A virtual submarine tool allows students to explore the microscopic organisms in the pond, with three levels of magnification – at 10x, students see tadpoles, snails, and insect larvae, while at 500x students can see the algae and bacteria (Figure 9). The Forest module provides a "zoom" tool to find smaller animals in the forest that are hard to find, such as field mice and sparrows (Figure 10). And a virtual "rotting log" can be examined at different magnifications to view organisms from earthworms to paramecia.

The Pond even supports visualizations at the atomic scale. An Atom Tracker tool allows students to track three specific simulated atoms over time – oxygen, carbon, and phosphorus, to learn about ecosystem processes like photosynthesis and respiration from an atom's perspective. For example, an oxygen atom starts out as part of a water (H_2O) molecule in the ground near the roots of a tree; later it is taken up into a leaf where, through photosynthesis, it becomes part of an oxygen (O_2) molecule in the air.

Virtual worlds also facilitate exploration of changes over time. Students visit the virtual pond on eight days over a virtual summer, collecting data over time and viewing multi-line graphs to see how changes in one factor might affect another, for example, how after the fertilizer runoff on the rainy day, the phosphate levels in the pond increase, and shortly after that there is an increase in the algae biomass of the pond. For the Forest module, students observe changes in populations and biodiversity over larger time scales – visiting the two islands in 5-year increments over a 45-year span (Figure 11).

Identity Exploration Using Avatars and Scientific Roles

In EcoMUVE, students begin by selecting their avatar, and can choose its appearance from a range of options. A student can explore the world in 1st person point of view, through the eyes of an avatar, or in 3rd person, controlling an avatar as if looking over the character's shoulder (Figure 12). With either

Figure 9. Virtual submarine to see microscopic life in the pond

Figure 10. Zoom tool to find smaller animals in the forest

Figure 11. Viewing forest populations on two islands over 45 years: deer and trillium flowers

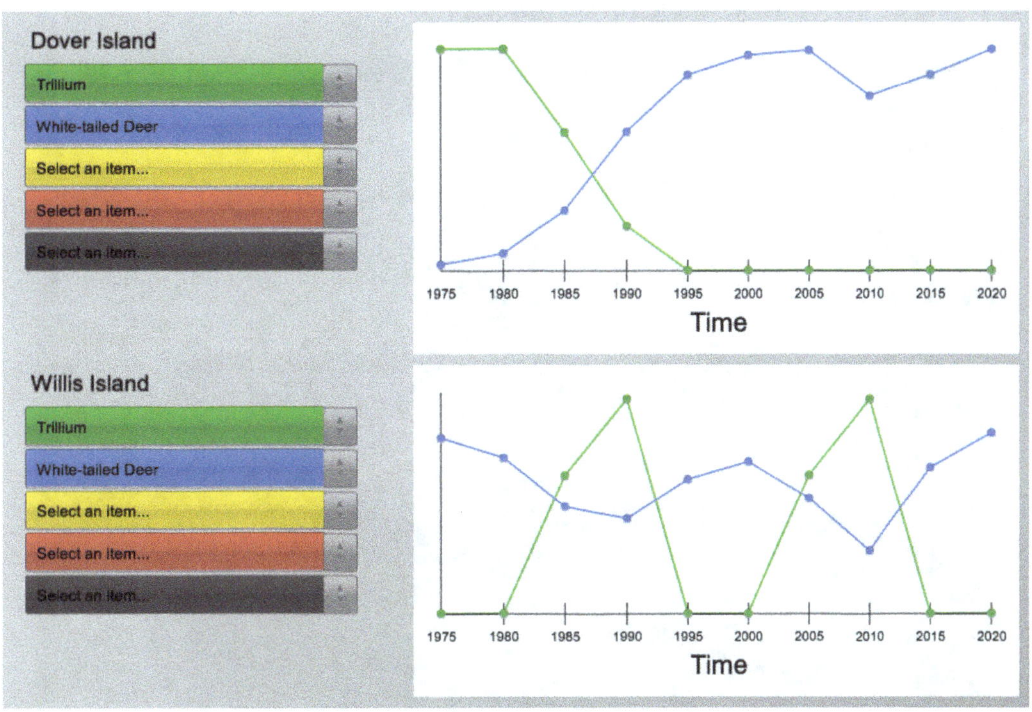

viewpoint, this situated embodiment provides a personal connection and sense of 'being there' – walking through the trees, around the pond, and even under the water.

Students experience identity exploration by taking on the role of a scientist. Throughout the EcoMUVE curriculum, students work in teams of four, each with a different role. For Pond, the roles are Water Chemist, Microscopic Specialist, Naturalist and Private Investigator, and for Forest, they are Bird Watcher, Public Health Worker, Population Specialist, and Botanist. Learning Quests provide important background information related to each role, and Role Worksheets guide students to collect and analyze the data related to their role, and also scaffold students in their roles by prompting them to look for patterns in that data over time and reflect on possible explanations. For example, in Forest, the Bird Watcher worksheet asks students to look at how the populations of birds on the islands change over time. It also asks students what factors might cause changes in bird populations, suggests they consider what kind of habitat each bird species needs, and reminds them to use the Field Guide as a resource.

Social Network Knowledge Construction Through Teams and Shared Online Presence

The curriculum uses a jigsaw approach, in which each of the four students in a team is assigned a specific role (e.g., botanist, bird watcher); students work independently on the data related to their role, and share their findings with the team. Together, the group must synthesize and make sense of the collective findings. In this manner, not only do students still gain exposure to all aspects of the activity through their classmates, but they also gain a much deeper understanding of their area of expertise than they would have by reviewing all of the material quickly.

Figure 12. 1st and 3rd person views of the virtual world

EcoMUVE supports student collaborative learning in a model that blends face-to-face dialogue with interaction in immersive virtual environments. During the curriculum, students work individually on computers to explore the 3D immersive environment, but can see each other's avatars in the world, use in-world chat and share data with their teammates (Figure 13). The role worksheets encourage collaboration – for example, the forest population specialist collects data on deer over time, but is also prompted "What happens to the plants that deer like to eat? Work with the Botanist on your team to answer this question." The unit culminates in each team creating and presenting to the class an evidence-based concept map that represents their hypotheses of the ecosystem relationships (Figure 14). Students work collaboratively as a team to identify connections between data across roles – e.g., the population specialist might find that without wolves the deer population increased, and work with the botanist to identify the overpopulation of deer as the reason there are fewer shrubs. The birdwatcher might then realize that the lack of shrubs explains the decline in population for birds that use the shrubs as habitat (Metcalf et al., 2013a).

Findings

Research with EcoMUVE has been conducted over five years, during 2009-2014, to explore a range of research questions. In this section, some highlights of this research are presented, with a focus on the findings that relate to the effectiveness of aspects of the design of the software and curriculum.

Figure 13. In-world chat in multi-user virtual environment

Figure 14. Concept map example of students' evidence-based hypotheses of ecosystem relationships

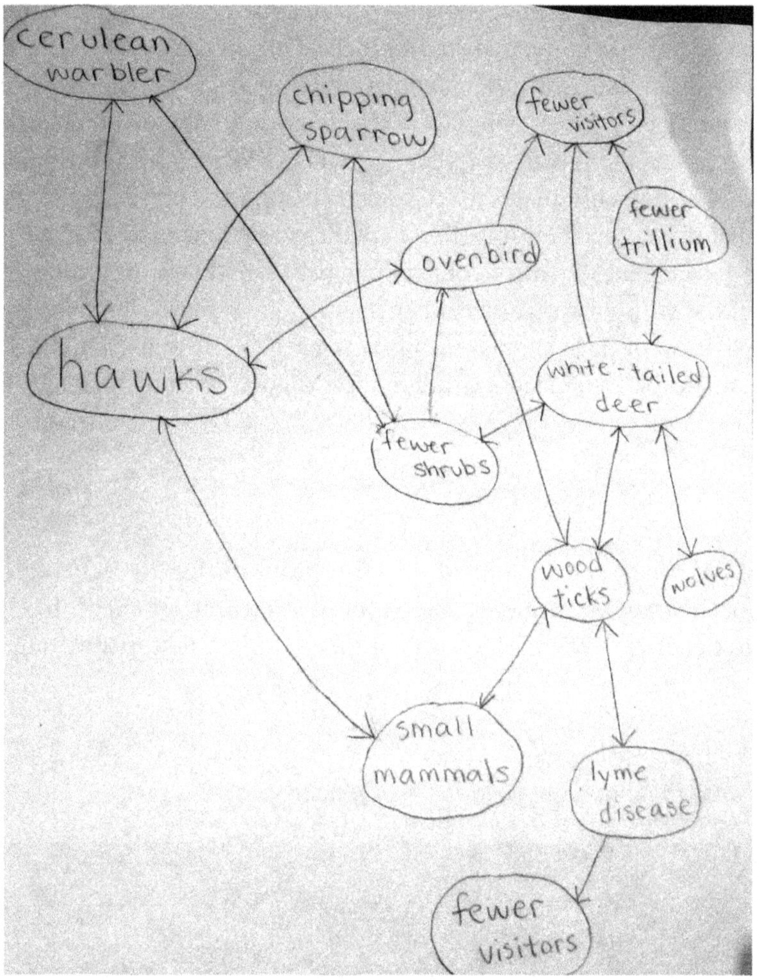

A feasibility study was conducted on the practicality, integration, and acceptance of the MUVE-based curriculum for student engagement and learning (Metcalf et al., 2016). The study included 18 science teachers and approximately 1330 students in grades 5 through 9. Teachers participated in the project on a voluntary basis, primarily by invitation through their principal or district science coordinator. Findings indicated that EcoMUVE was very well received. Teachers felt the curriculum was effective, aligned well with standards, and compared favorably with a non-MUVE alternative. Technical issues, primarily simply access to technology, were considered to be manageable.

Teachers found that students were highly engaged in the immersive virtual environment, and described the ease with which students could collect and compare data using graphs as particularly valuable for understanding how variables change over time. Teachers also valued the inquiry, role-based pedagogy, and specifically mentioned active, hands-on exploration, students' investment in the activity, and the value of students taking on specific roles and working with a team.

In general, teachers most often cited as advantages of EcoMUVE that students were more active in learning and that the information was more visual. As one teacher described it, "They visually saw something was up in the world and physically were able to collect data."

Another teacher described the student-centered, inquiry-based learning as follows:

The freedom to walk and click wherever they want allowed students to stumble upon questions. Most of the virtual world was familiar to students, but many question marks existed within the virtual world. As soon as one person found something perplexing, the whole class wanted to investigate it too. Everyone was participating together, at their own pace (Metcalf et al., 2016, p.33).

Pre-post assessments of student learning were collected over several research studies that include the following findings:

- Significant learning of ecosystems content (Metcalf, et al. 2013b).
- More complex causal reasoning about non-obvious causes; distant drivers of ecosystems dynamics and the system parameters; and processes, steady states and change over time (Grotzer, et al., 2013).
- Gains in self-efficacy and attitudes towards science (Kamarainen, et al., 2012; Metcalf et al., 2013b).
- Students reporting greater self-efficacy in scientific inquiry and more sophisticated views about the role of authorities in justifying scientific claims on the post-test (Chen et al., 2014).

A study of student motivation and perspectives on the EcoMUVE pond module found that from the beginning, students were very interested and engaged in EcoMUVE, and that interest and engagement remained high during the two-week curriculum. Responses to open-ended questions about what students liked about the MUVE shifted from a focus on the 3D virtual environment itself, towards more frequent mention of the self-directed, collaborative, and inquiry-based design elements (Metcalf et al., 2014).

The opportunity for students to take on scientific roles in EcoMUVE supported identify exploration, and particularly, self-efficacy – believing in their ability to succeed in investigating problems in science. Affective survey findings showed significant increases to measures of self-efficacy, and this was reinforced by student comments about EcoMUVE, such as "It made me actually think that I could solve problems like actual scientists do," and "I like to use EcoMUVE because I love to play different roles with my friends to find a solution to a problem" (Metcalf et al., 2014).

In looking at collaborative learning in EcoMUVE, one study of 91 seventh graders using the Forest module found that 91% of students reported having learned from their teammates and 95% of students liked the roles they played on their team. These results were paired with significant gains in student learning based on pre-post measures over the course of the implementation (Metcalf et al., 2013a).

Fundamentally, EcoMUVE supports students in engaging in collaborative sense making through the use of evidence to support claims. While immersed in the virtual world, students are able to collect data, make inferences, and collaboratively reason about claims. Students considered both numerical data and perceptual clues from the virtual environment to guide data interpretation, for example, noting both turbidity readings and the "murkiness" of the pond. The tools provided for easy transitions among representations – quick access to multiple sources of evidence for comparison and pattern seeking. Research findings demonstrate that the concept mapping activity motivated students to bolster the scope and validity of their evidence, while the immersive world provided ready access to resources that supported evidence collection (Kamarainen et al., 2015).

CONCLUSION

The EcoMUVE ecosystems science curriculum engages students in collaborative, inquiry-based experiences in which they adopt the role of scientists to study two immersive, simulated ecosystems. The two virtual ecosystems, Pond and Forest, illustrate core concepts in ecosystem science and complex causality. Findings included that the curriculum is feasible to use in typical classroom settings, well-aligned with standards, and supports student engagement and learning of science content, complex causality, and inquiry. Students made significant gains in ecosystem science understanding, and also in attitudinal measures. EcoMUVE helped students to shift their thinking about causal dynamics within ecosystems.

In considering classroom implementation of MUVE-based curricula, we wish to emphasize the importance of considering both the design of the tool and the design of the instructional context in which it is to be used. Dede (2009b) identifies salient features of the conventional science classroom that bear upon the success of MUVEs as a curricular device. In particular, it is important to consider the following points:

- Supporting successful teacher use of a MUVE-based curriculum requires effective professional development.
- Schools provide access to and support for the technology that enables students to use MUVEs, but effective implementation requires both the technological infrastructure and support services be of adequate quality.
- Grading requirements and their resultant pressures may either increase or reduce student engagement and focus within the context of the MUVE.
- Teachers may meet high levels of resistance when trying to use MUVEs in a school culture dominated by high-stakes testing.
- While schools offer an opportunity to uniformly deliver educational MUVEs to an entire population, implementing at scale remains difficult.

Since 2012, EcoMUVE has been available for download through a free license from Harvard University. By registering their contact information, interested parties are given access to a webpage that provides a downloadable version of the software, the full curriculum and teacher's guide. EcoMUVE has received significant attention around the country and the world; the project continues to receive inquiries from educators, and several school districts around the country have adopted it as part of their regular curriculum. The EcoMUVE project team is continuing to conduct research around immersive technologies for science education – including research blending MUVEs and mobile augmented technologies (EcoMOBILE), and supporting experiment-based inquiry in MUVEs (EcoXPT). For more information visit the project website at http://ecolearn.gse.harvard.edu.

The process of adopting EcoMUVE in the classroom has demonstrated some of the critical hurdles that must be overcome and the support that teachers need in order to use the EcoMUVE curriculum in its full richness. MUVEs offer support for student-directed learning, yet we find this learning process is most fruitful when teachers are willing to adopt student-centered strategies. Guiding without directing the inquiry process is a difficult challenge for many teachers (Furtak, 2006; Tabak & Reiser, 1997; Williams et al., 2004), and doing so in a MUVE environment can sometimes magnify a feeling of "loss of control" for some teachers. We have found it important to help teachers see how student-directed learning can lead to deeper student engagement and understanding.

This chapter articulates the types of learning affordances that MUVEs can provide for implementing the classroom strategies and pedagogies that are powerful for science learning. MUVEs are part of the future of education. Rather than learning by listening to lectures or reading textbooks, students are increasingly able to access new ways of learning that include simulations in virtual worlds, that support science learning by exploring and solving problems in realistic environments. Inquiry-based learning can be made accessible to all students, through the experiences and tools that are possible in virtual worlds.

EcoMUVE demonstrates the technical feasibility of actualizing these affordances in a modern, MUVE-based curriculum, and serves as a proof of concept that immersive virtual worlds can offer powerful and practical learning experiences that integrate cutting edge approaches to science teaching and learning, particularly in teaching difficult-to-teach concepts like ecosystem science and complex causality. This suggests the importance of pursuing the development and use of these environments in classroom settings, to invest in research and development of virtual worlds for learning across the curriculum, and to promote and support this learning medium.

ACKNOWLEDGMENT

This research was supported by the Institute of Education Sciences [grant no. R305A080514]. All opinions, findings, conclusions, or recommendations expressed here are those of the authors and do not necessarily reflect the views of the Institute of Education Sciences.

REFERENCES

Barab, S. A., Thomas, M., Dodge, T., Carteaux, R., & Tuzun, H. (2005). Making learning fun: Quest Atlantis, a game without guns. *Educational Technology Research and Development*, *5*(1), 86–108. doi:10.1007/BF02504859

Blumenfeld, P. C., Soloway, E., Marx, R. W., Krajcik, J. S., Guzdial, M., & Palincsar, A. (1991). Motivating project-based learning: Sustaining the doing, supporting the learning. *Educational Psychologist*, *26*(3-4), 369–398. doi:10.1080/00461520.1991.9653139

Bransford, J. D., & Schwartz, D. L. (1999). Rethinking transfer: A simple proposal with multiple implications. *Review of Research in Education*, *24*(1), 61–100. doi:10.3102/0091732X024001061

Brown, J. S., Collins, A., & Duguid, P. (1989). Situated cognition and the culture of learning. *Educational Researcher*, *18*(1), 32–42. doi:10.3102/0013189X018001032

Chaiklin, S., & Lave, J. (Eds.). (1993). *Understanding practice: Perspectives on activity and context*. Cambridge, UK: Cambridge University Press. doi:10.1017/CBO9780511625510

Chen, J. A., Metcalf, S. J., & Tutwiler, M. S. (2014). Motivation and beliefs about the nature of scientific knowledge within an immersive virtual ecosystems environment. *Journal of Contemporary Educational Psychology*, *39*(2), 112–123. doi:10.1016/j.cedpsych.2014.02.004

Clarke, J., Dede, C., Ketelhut, D. J., & Nelson, B. (2006). A Design-based research strategy to promote scalability for educational innovations. *Educational Technology*, *46*(3), 27–36.

Crawford, B. (2000). Embracing the essence of inquiry: New roles for science teachers. *Journal of Research in Science Teaching*, *37*(9), 916–937. doi:10.1002/1098-2736(200011)37:9<916::AID-TEA4>3.0.CO;2-2

Dalgarno, B., & Lee, M. J. (2010). What are the learning affordances of 3-D virtual environments? *British Journal of Educational Technology*, *41*(1), 10–32. doi:10.1111/j.1467-8535.2009.01038.x

Dawley, L. (2009). Social network knowledge construction: Emerging virtual world pedagogy. *On the Horizon*, *17*(2), 109–121. doi:10.1108/10748120910965494

de Freitas, S., & Neumann, T. (2009). The use of 'exploratory learning' for supporting immersive learning in virtual environments. *Computers & Education*, *52*(2), 343–352. doi:10.1016/j.compedu.2008.09.010

Dede, C. (2009a). Immersive interfaces for engagement and learning. *Science*, *323*(5910), 66–69. doi:10.1126/science.1167311 PMID:19119219

Dede, C. (2009b). Learning context: Gaming, simulations, and science learning in the classroom. In *National Research Council Workshop on Gaming and Simulations*. Retrieved from http://www7.nationalacademies. org/bose/Gaming_Sims_Commissioned_Papers.html

Dickey, M. D. (2005). Engaging by design: How engagement strategies in popular computer and video games can inform instructional design. *Educational Technology Research and Development*, *53*(2), 67–83. doi:10.1007/BF02504866

Duffy, T. M., & Cunningham, D. J. (1996). Constructivism: Implications for the design and delivery of instruction. In D. H. Jonassen (Ed.), *Handbook of research for educational communications and technology* (pp. 170–198). New York, NY: Macmillan.

Duschl, R. A., Schweingruber, H. A., & Shouse, A. W. (2007). *Taking science to school. Learning and teaching science in grades K-8*. Washington, DC: National Academies Press.

Fishman, B., Dede, C., & Means, B. (2015). Teaching and technology: New tools for new times. In D. Gitomer & C. Bell (Eds.), *Handbook of research on teaching* (5th ed.). Washington, DC: American Educational Research Association.

Foster, A. (2008). Games and motivation to learn science: Personal identity, applicability, relevance and meaningfulness. *Journal of Interactive Learning Research*, *19*(4), 597–614.

Furtak, E. M. (2006). The problem with answers: An exploration of guided scientific inquiry teaching. *Science Education*, *90*(3), 453–467. doi:10.1002/sce.20130

Grotzer, T. A., Kamarainen, A., Tutwiler, M. S., Metcalf, S., & Dede, C. (2013). Learning to reason about ecosystems dynamics over time: The challenges of an event-based causal focus. *Bioscience*, *63*(4), 288–296. doi:10.1525/bio.2013.63.4.9

Hmelo-Silver, C. E., Duncan, R. G., & Chinn, C. A. (2007). Scaffolding and achievement in problem-based and inquiry learning: A response to Kirschner, Sweller, and Clark (2006). *Educational Psychologist*, *42*(2), 99–107. doi:10.1080/00461520701263368

Johnson, D. W., & Johnson, R. T. (1996). Cooperation and the use of technology. In D. Jonassen (Ed.), *Handbook of research for educational communications and technology*. New York, NY: Macmillan.

Jonassen, D. (1999). Designing constructivist learning environments. In C. M. Reigeluth (Ed.), Instructional-design theories and models: A new paradigm of instructional theory pp. 215-239. Hillsdale, NJ: Lawrence Erlbaum Associates.

Kafai, Y. B. (2010). The world of Whyville: An introduction to Tween Virtual Life. *Games and Culture*, *5*(1), 3–22. doi:10.1177/1555412009351264

Kamarainen, A., Metcalf, S., Grotzer, T., & Dede, C. J. (2015). Exploring ecosystems from the inside: How immersion in a multi-user virtual environment supports epistemologically grounded practices in ecosystem science instruction. *Journal of Science Education and Technology*, *24*(2), 148–167. doi:10.1007/s10956-014-9531-7

Kamarainen, A. M., Metcalf, S., Grotzer, T., & Dede, C. (2012). *EcoMUVE: Shifts in affective beliefs and values about science through learning experiences in immersive virtual environments*. Paper presented at American Educational Research Association (AERA) Conference, Vancouver, Canada.

Ketelhut, D. J., Nelson, B. C., Clarke, J., & Dede, C. (2010). A multi-user virtual environment for building and assessing higher order inquiry skills in science. *British Journal of Educational Technology*, *41*(1), 56–68. doi:10.1111/j.1467-8535.2009.01036.x

King, A., Marietta, G., & Gehlbach, H. (2014). The role of role-taking: Social perspective taking and interpersonal relationships in virtual simulations. In D. B. Zandvliet (Ed.), *Interpersonal relationships in education: From theory to practice* (pp. 95–110). Rotterdam, The Netherlands: Sense Publishers. doi:10.1007/978-94-6209-701-8_7

Laurel, B. (1993). *Computers as theatre*. New York, NY: Addison-Wesley.

Metcalf, S. J., Chen, J. A., Kamarainen, A. M., Frumin, K. M., Vickrey, T. L., Grotzer, T. A., & Dede, C. (2014). Shifts in student motivation during usage of a multi-user virtual environment for ecosystem science. *International Journal of Virtual and Personal Learning Environments*, *5*(4), 1–15. doi:10.4018/IJVPLE.2014100101

Metcalf, S. J., Kamarainen, A., Grotzer, T. A., & Dede, C. (2013a). *Collaborative learning in virtual environments: Role-based exploration of causality in ecosystems over time and scale*. Paper presented at Conference on Computer Supported Collaborative Learning (CSCL), Madison, WI.

Metcalf, S. J., Kamarainen, A. M., Cooke, C. B., Turkay, S., Grotzer, T., & Dede, C. (2016). Teacher perceptions of the practicality and effectiveness of immersive ecological simulations. In K. Terry & A. Cheney (Eds.), *Utilizing virtual and personal learning environments for optimal learning* (pp. 22–45). Hershey, PA: Information Science Reference. doi:10.4018/978-1-4666-8847-6.ch002

Metcalf, S. J., Tutwiler, M. S., Kamarainen, A. M., Grotzer, T. A., & Dede, C. (2013b). *Multi-user virtual environments to promote middle school ecosystem science learning and attitudes about science*. Paper presented at American Educational Research Association (AERA) Conference, San Francisco, CA.

Murray, J. H. (1998). *Hamlet on the holodeck: The future of narrative in cyberspace*. Cambridge, MA: MIT Press.

National Research Council. (2005). *How students learn: History, mathematics, and science in the classroom*. Washington, DC: The National Academies Press. doi:10.17226/10126

National Research Council. (2011). *Learning science through computer games and simulations*. Washington, DC: The National Academies Press. doi:10.17226/13078

National Research Council. (2012). *A framework for K-12 science education: Practices, crosscutting concepts, and core ideas*. Washington, DC: The National Academies Press. doi:10.17226/13165

Nelson, B., & Ketelhut, D. J. (2007). Scientific inquiry in educational multi-user virtual environments. *Educational Psychology Review*, *19*(3), 265–283. doi:10.1007/s10648-007-9048-1

NGSS Lead States. (2013). *Next generation science standards: For states, by states*. Washington, DC: The National Academies Press.

Podolefsky, N. S., Rehn, D., & Perkins, K. K. (2013). Affordances of play for student agency and student-centered pedagogy. In AIP Conference Proceedings: Vol. 1513. *No. 1* (pp. 306–309). AIP. doi:10.1063/1.4789713

Quintana, C., Reiser, B. J., Davis, E. A., Krajcik, J., Fretz, E., Duncan, R. G., & Soloway, E. et al. (2004). A scaffolding design framework for software to support science inquiry. *Journal of the Learning Sciences*, *13*(3), 337–386. doi:10.1207/s15327809jls1303_4

Roseman, J. E., & Koppal, M. (2008). Using national standards to improve K-8 science curriculum materials. *The Elementary School Journal*, *109*(2), 104–122. doi:10.1086/590521

Rutten, N., Van Joolingen, W. R., & Van der Veen, J. T. (2012). The learning effects of computer simulations in science education. *Computers & Education*, *58*(1), 136–153. doi:10.1016/j.compedu.2011.07.017

Savery, J. R., & Duffy, T. M. (1995). Problem based learning: An instructional model and its constructivist framework. *Educational Technology*, *35*(5), 31–38.

Schaller, D. T., Goldman, K. H., Spickelmier, G., Allison-Bunnell, S., & Koepfler, J. (2009). *Learning in the wild: What Wolfquest taught developers and game players*. Retrieved from http://www.archimuse.com/mw2009/papers/schaller/schaller.html

Slater, M. (2009). Place illusion and plausibility can lead to realistic behaviour in immersive virtual environments. *Philosophical Transactions of the Royal Society of London. Series B, Biological Sciences*, *364*(1535), 3549–3557. doi:10.1098/rstb.2009.0138 PMID:19884149

Stake, J. E., & Nickens, S. D. (2005). Adolescent girls' and boys' science peer relationships and perceptions of the possible self as scientist. *Sex Roles*, *52*(1), 1–11. doi:10.1007/s11199-005-1189-4

Tabak, I., & Reiser, B. J. (1997). *Complementary roles of software-based scaffolding and teacher-student interactions in inquiry learning*. Paper presented at The 2nd International Conference on Computer Support for Collaborative Learning, Toronto, Canada. doi:10.3115/1599773.1599809

Trindade, J., Fiolhais, C., & Almeida, L. (2002). Science learning in virtual environments: A descriptive study. *British Journal of Educational Technology*, *33*(4), 471–488. doi:10.1111/1467-8535.00283

Warburton, S. (2009). Second Life in higher education: Assessing the potential for and the barriers to deploying virtual worlds in learning and teaching. *British Journal of Educational Technology*, *40*(3), 414–426. doi:10.1111/j.1467-8535.2009.00952.x

Warren, S. J., Stein, R. A., Dondlinger, M. A., & Barab, S. A. (2009). A look inside a MUVE design process: Blending instructional design and game principles to target writing skills. *Journal of Educational Computing Research*, *40*(3), 295–321. doi:10.2190/EC.40.3.c

Williams, M., Linn, M. C., Ammon, P., & Gearhart, M. (2004). Learning to teach inquiry science in a technology-based environment: A case study. *Journal of Science Education and Technology*, *13*(2), 189–206. doi:10.1023/B:JOST.0000031258.17257.48

Winn, W. (2003). Learning in artificial environments: Embodiment, embeddedness and dynamic adaptation. *Technology, Instruction. Cognition and Learning*, *1*(1), 87–114.

KEY TERMS AND DEFINITIONS

Constructivism: A learning theory that states that people construct their own understanding of the world through their own experiences and reflections.

Ecosystem: A community that includes all the living and nonliving things found in a certain area.

Identity Exploration: The opportunity to reflect on one's own identity and to explore alternative possible selves.

Immersive: Feeling as if one is really taking part in the experience.

Inquiry-Based Learning: Active learning that is based on posing questions, problems, or scenarios to investigate.

Project-Based Learning: Active learning in which students learn through engaging with an authentic, and complex project or problem.

Role: The part or function played by a person in a particular situation.

Simulation-Based Learning: Learning through experiences with artificial representations of real-world processes or phenomena.

Situated Learning: Learning while participating in authentic settings and situations in which one would normally engage with the knowledge being learned.

Chapter 2
Designing for Collaborative Play:
Why Games Need MUVEs and MUVEs Need Games

Louisa Rosenheck
Massachusetts Institute of Technology, USA

ABSTRACT

Games and MUVEs each have distinct features that make them rich environments for learning. The MIT Education Arcade has worked to capitalize on the affordances present in both genres by designing The Radix Endeavor, a multiplayer online game for STEM learning set in a rich virtual world. This chapter presents the game as an example of how collaborative learning theory can be applied to game design within a MUVE. It will discuss the process of intentionally designing game features and content with the goal of bringing about social experiences, as well as the concrete game features that resulted. Then it will describe the importance of implementation design and the ways that teachers can leverage a multiplayer educational game based on the Radix pilot project. More broadly, it will explore how this type of social game can lead to authentic scientific inquiry and deep STEM learning.

INTRODUCTION

Games can be rich environments for learning, given their playful qualities and opportunity for scaffolded experimentation. MUVEs can also be rich environments for learning, due to their immersive nature and support for collaboration. While the design of games often focuses on a set of rules and mechanics, MUVEs tend to be more open-ended and invite exploration of the virtual world. When it comes to designing for learning, many games could benefit from the exploratory affordances of a MUVE. Similarly, many MUVEs could benefit from the framing and scaffolding of a game. When we combine these characteristics into one digital experience, we get something like an educational MMO. An MMO, or massively multiplayer online game, is a game genre in which hundreds or thousands of players simultaneously interact with the game and with each other. They typically take place in a large, persistent, open

DOI: 10.4018/978-1-5225-3719-9.ch002

world in which players are given quests, or loosely guided tasks, to complete as they progress through the game. By incorporating key design elements of both games and MUVEs, the resulting MMO has the potential to provide a deep and authentic learning experience for its players.

To capitalize on the affordances present in both genres, and build on the commonalities between MMOs, science inquiry, and collaborative learning, the MIT Education Arcade set out to design a multi-user virtual environment that deeply integrates science and math practices as core game mechanics and allows players to learn by doing, in authentic contexts and in social ways. In this chapter, we will present this game, called *The Radix Endeavor*, as an example of how collaborative learning theory can be applied to game design within a MUVE. We will discuss the process of intentionally designing game features and content with the goal of bringing about social experiences, as well as the concrete game features that resulted from that design process. Then we will describe the importance of implementation design and the ways that teachers can leverage an educational MMO based on the *Radix* pilot project. Through this journey, we will explore how this type of social game can lead to authentic scientific inquiry and deep STEM learning.

Radix Background

The Radix Endeavor game is set in a virtual multiplayer world with embedded biological and mathematical systems that involve the world's flora, fauna, and fictional civilizations. Players take on quests that guide them to probe the game's systems and develop a firsthand understanding of math and biology concepts in a variety of topic areas. The game is exploratory, leaving a lot of experimenting and problem-solving up to the players, much of which they can do either individually or by working together. It incorporates a wide variety of content as well as STEM practices, such as problem-solving, and even soft skills, such as perseverance. Rather than teaching players directly, it builds a conceptual understanding, leaving students open to make connections between experiences in the game and experiences in their classroom and even their lives outside of school. It is a long-form game, meant to be played over the course of a semester and revisited during each relevant curricular unit. In addition, it presents opportunities for players to collaborate both in and outside of the game, leading to a unique deep learning experience.

The central *Radix* gameplay is designed around systems that players can interact with and manipulate, many of which are built upon the world's biomes. Figure 1 shows players in the forest region, one of the five distinct biomes with unique fauna, flora, structures, and characters. In each of these biomes, players can engage in activities such as collecting data on the heights of plants in different regions, and using statistical tools to compare the means and medians. They can also experiment with simulations to see how a species in a biome has evolved over time and manipulate variables to test out changes in the environment, as seen in Figure 2. Engaging in these activities gives players a foundation to compare their findings and discuss their discoveries with each other, be it in the game or in person. To further engage players in the authentic practices of biologists and mathematicians, they have a set of tools available to them in the game. Some of the tools are open-ended and creative, allowing players to draw geometric objects on scale maps, build fences with appropriate areas and perimeters, or create and share food web diagrams. The gameplay is centered on quests that target specific content areas in biology and math. These quests are designed to encourage players to explore the different systems and biomes as well as to engage in inquiry, problem-solving, and collaborative learning in order to complete the task and provide evidence needed to support their solution.

Figure 1. The forest biome

Figure 2. The Evo Globe, an evolution simulation tool

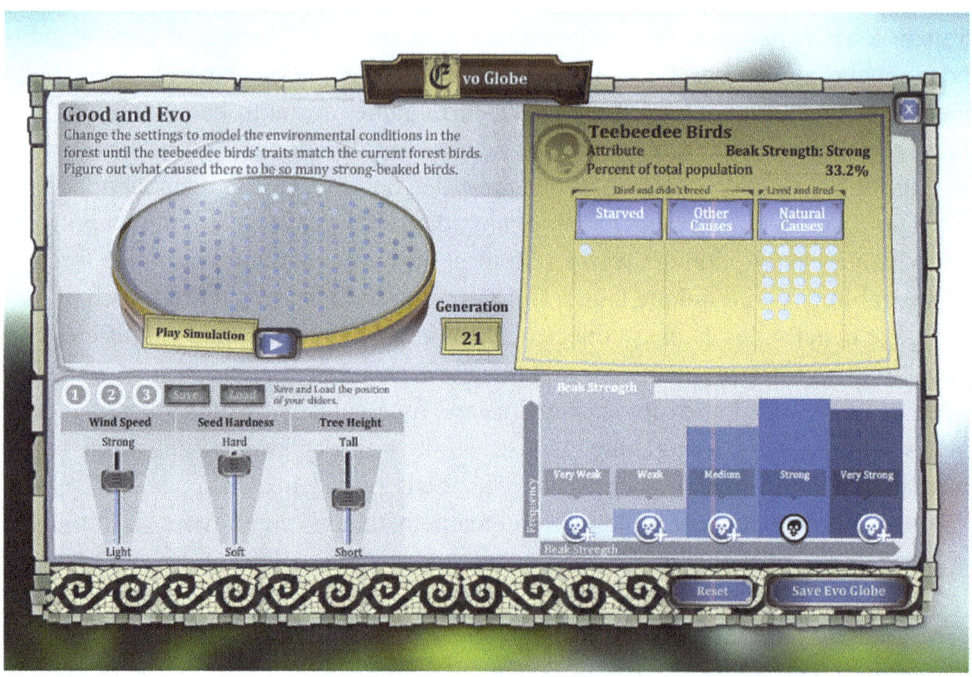

When a new player enters the *Radix* game, she finds herself in a grassland biome on the island of Ysola, an earth-like world full of fictional but realistic plants and animals such as lumabells and blackburns. She is likely to see the avatars of other players moving around the world working on tasks in the same area. There is a character nearby with an exclamation point over her head, so she talks to her to take on her first challenge, which starts the series of introductory quests. Once she has completed those quests she will be familiar with navigating the world, talking with in-game characters, and using the basic tools for collecting objects, examining them, and analyzing data about them. From there, a wide array of other quest lines is unlocked. The player can explore any topic area she is interested in, or the specific ones that her teacher has asked her to work on.

Each quest line starts with one of the island's residents explaining some problem or question that is causing the people trouble. This way, the game's challenges are situated in a contextual narrative that gives the player a reason to care, and a motivation to solve problems that will save the island or its people. The player will then use her tools to explore the environment, ostensibly "messing around" but in reality experimenting and making discoveries. Through collecting and analyzing data, and discussing those data with her peers, the player gains an understanding of the mathematical and biological systems embedded within the game world, such as Mendelian genetics or evolution. Once she understands each system, she can adjust the inputs to that system in order to get the outputs necessary to solve the problem. She then returns to the character in need of help to turn in an artifact or explain a solution, which requires not only an answer but also data that explains how she knows her solution will work. Quests take place across the *Radix* world, with different tools becoming useful in different domains.

The virtual *Radix* world provides an environment where students can gain both content knowledge and the skills and practices critical to STEM fields. They do this both by working through quests on their own, and by talking with other players to make meaning from their discoveries. The game covers topics in biology (genetics, evolution, ecology, human body systems) and math (algebra, geometry, statistics) which were carefully selected to complement what students can already do in a hands-on lab or classroom setting. The particular content for each of the topic areas is aligned with standards from the Next Generation Science Standards and Common Core State Standards, including an emphasis on science and math practices. These include things like model building, investigation, interpreting data, and evaluating information, which are incorporated into game tasks. In addition, the game creates a space for students to practice inquiry, meaning that when players encounter a problem in the game, they must think through how to solve the problem and determine their own course of action. For example in the evolution quest lines, players collect data about the traits of animals in different regions of the world in order to learn about adaptation. They have a known question to investigate, looking at the various traits in the menji species (a fictional but realistic type of primate), but they must figure out for themselves, or together with others, what process to use to do that. As the players examine menjis in different regions, they study patterns, interpret data, and construct explanations. In this and all of the quest lines in the game, players must use 21st century skills such as collaboration and critical thinking in order to solve problems. This emphasis on skills and practices is critical to students as they learn concepts from science and math, and *Radix* provides an innovative place for students to engage with these skills.

GAMES, LEARNING, AND COLLABORATION

The design process of *The Radix Endeavor* was a highly interdisciplinary process. This was essential for a project that aimed to combine principles of deep learning, game design, and social and collaborative learning. In this section we will start by looking at the research on what students can learn from games, and the research on benefits and types of cooperative learning. Then we will discuss the intersection of these two areas, examining the role that cooperative player interactions can have in learning games. Finally, in order to bring about these digital interactions, we must consider the importance of intentional design for both games and educational experiences.

Games for Learning

As the field of educational games has grown, designers and researchers have clearly shown how games as a medium naturally employ many good pedagogies. In video games, players engage in active and critical thinking, they take on different identities, and they have opportunities to practice skills and find intrinsic rewards as they work on increasingly difficult challenges on their path to mastery (Gee, 2003). Video games are engaging, exemplify good pedagogical principles, provide opportunities for ongoing assessment, and can be scaled up (Steinkuehler & Squire, 2014). They can incorporate theory from learning and psychology to support cognitive, behavioral, affective, and sociocultural engagement with the subject matter (Plass et al., 2015). When designed purposely for learning, and when combined with a thoughtful game-based curriculum, games can also be successfully implemented in classrooms (Squire, 2011). These are some of the characteristics of games that give them their pedagogical value. As open-ended worlds, MUVEs don't always incorporate elements that add structure and scaffolding, but they certainly can if the designer chooses to build them in. This is one reason why game mechanics and playful features can add value to an educational MUVE.

In addition to these strong connections between games and good learning, empirical research has shown that games can indeed enhance student learning. Clark et al. (2013) conducted a metastudy and found that compared to other non game-based instruction, digital games had a moderate to strong effect in terms of cognitive competencies. They also found that certain enhanced game designs were associated with significant benefits for learning, showing that it matters how the games are designed to support learning. A literature review done by Boyle et al. (2016) found that the current research on games for learning reports outcomes in knowledge acquisition, as well as affect, behaviour change, perception and cognition. More specifically, a number of studies on specific games have shown how they can support learning in domains such as science (Li, 2013; NRC, 2011) and math (Divjak, 2011; Starkey, 2013).

What's even more interesting about the power of games for learning is that they can support conceptual understanding and problem solving (Gee, 2009) as well as domain-specific skills and practices (Bressler & Bodzin, 2016; Zimmerman, 2011) that go beyond the basic content knowledge more commonly taught in the classroom. Gee (2003) writes about how learning in games is social and distributed - within players' own minds, across others they can call on for help, and across tools that they learn how to use with the help of affinity groups. Steinkuehler and Duncan (2008) have found players in virtual worlds frequently engaging in social knowledge construction, systems based reasoning, and other scientific habits of mind. This body of work shows that games in general, and social gaming experiences more specifically, have a lot of potential for contributing to a deep learning environment.

Cooperative Learning

As we look more deeply at how these social experiences can support learning, we find that the field of cooperative learning has a lot to tell us about designing multi-user environments. While this body of research is not focused on technology or game experiences, we can take theories developed in this area and apply them to educational game design. Self-determination theory suggests a framework in which autonomy, competence, and relatedness all need to be present in order for a learner to feel intrinsic motivation (Ryan & Deci, 2000). Relatedness here describes the need to feel belongingness and connectedness with others. In an educational setting, this could be one's peers, teachers, or a larger community of learners.

One way to foster and strengthen this sense of relatedness in a classroom of individual learners is through the use of cooperative learning techniques. According to Johnson and Johnson (1996) cooperative learning occurs when students work together to accomplish shared learning goals. This idea is based on a view of learning as an active process, that is dependent on a rich context, that benefits from diverse learners, and that is inherently social (Smith & MacGregor, 1992). It is a very well-researched area, with over 900 studies showing its effectiveness as one type of teaching method (Johnson & Johnson, 2000). Cooperative learning includes an array of techniques including group investigation, constructive controversy, jigsaw procedures, and many more. Individual implementations of these have been studied in detail such as small group discourse in science classrooms (Howe, 2014), the relationship between help-seekers and help-givers (Webb, 2002), and creative problem solving in small groups (Cardellini, 2006). As an overarching method, it has been shown to have a positive effect on areas such as cognitive development, learner control, social competency, and attitudes toward learning (Johnson & Johnson, 1996).

How cooperation brings about the construction of knowledge is a topic that has been studied as well. Roschelle (1992) describes a process called convergent conceptual change, in which learners with naturally divergent ideas work together to construct a shared meaning. They go through an iterative cycle of displaying, confirming, and repairing their ideas, while using progressively deeper pieces of evidence to come to agreement on the concept at hand. In order to make this happen in any particular learning environment, educational activities must be purposefully designed to enable productive cooperation around conceptual change. Positive interdependence is a key way to ensure that the necessary elements are present. This idea is based on social interdependence theory, whose premise is that the way that an activity's goals are structured determines how individuals interact, and those interactions lead to learning outcomes. Positive interdependence then, is when the actions of individuals promote the achievement of joint goals. Cooperative interactions increase the likelihood of each other's success, and in order for the group to succeed, each individual must contribute and succeed as well. Interactions that can come into play include mutual help and assistance, exchange of needed resources, trust, management of conflict, and more (Johnson & Johnson, 2005).

To produce activities that have positive interdependence, teachers or learning designers must thoughtfully design both the goal structure and these key interactions among group members. When these mechanisms are in place and working smoothly, the stage is set for learners to cooperate in building knowledge and skills together. This can happen in activities that don't use technology at all, or it can happen through computer-supported cooperative learning. Within this category, learners may either interact around computers, with the software facilitating some face-to-face discussions or activities, or through computers, with the software making the direct connection between learners that wouldn't otherwise interact (Johnson & Johnson, 1996). As we will see later in this chapter, both types of computer-supported cooperative learning can be valuable in an educational MUVE.

Player Interactions in Digital Games

At the intersection of game mechanics and collaboration sit the mechanisms by which players interact with each other and with the virtual world. It is through these interactions—among players, tools, game objects, rule systems, and the community—that students collaborate and learn (Paraskeva, 2010). Therefore when embedding cooperative learning into a game, this is one of the most important elements to examine. In fact, there is an increasing amount of work being done to try and guide these interactions within games because they have such a great impact on players' experiences and even on their lives.

Virtual worlds can act as third spaces - informal places outside of home and school where young people gather (Steinkuehler & Williams, 2006). MUVEs which require collaboration for successful play can become these social environments where players not only work together to complete game tasks but also simply chat and hang out. For many players, this is an important way to feel connected to others and build social capital. Video games can also spark unique player interactions and shape interpersonal relationships outside of the technology, when players are together in real life. Stevens et al. (2008) observed kids playing video games in their homes and identified a number of different learning arrangements created by the kids themselves. They organized themselves to teach and learn together, based on the types of interactions that would best support their own social context and game goals. Both types of interactions - those that happen through technology and those that happen around technology - are valuable to learning because they present an opportunity for distributed intelligence and cross-functional teams (Gee, 2008). Knowing where to find information and how to use the tools available, and being able to create and work in teams of people with varied expertise, are important skills in today's workplaces. Cooperative learning in a game environment is a powerful way for learners to build these skills.

One well-known example of a MUVE experience with embedded cooperative learning is River City. Teams of students explore the virtual city, designing and conducting in-world experiments to try and understand why residents are becoming sick. They interpret the results and form hypotheses together, thereby engaging in convergent conceptual change. They take on different roles within the team, becoming experts in various areas of investigation. These cross-functional teams support cooperative learning both through and around the technology. These player interactions bring a pedagogical value supported by the research on games for learning and cooperative learning. In addition, this style of learning works especially well for students who are already comfortable using technology and the internet for creating, sharing, communicating, and problem solving, which includes an increasing majority of today's youth (Dieterle, 2009).

A number of other MUVEs have also taken advantage of meaningful player interactions to support learning. In Quest Atlantis, players explore a virtual world and narrative designed to inspire them to work for social change. They participate in both online communities as well as offline group learning at QA centers (Barab et al., 2007). Minecraft is a well-known virtual world game where players can easily work together to build and create. There are many instances of Minecraft in education, including assigning collaborative projects to students to build community and form cross-functional teams, which can result in a creation more brilliant than any one student could have come up with on their own (Kiang, 2014). Another complex simulation-based virtual world game, ECO, requires players to collectively make decisions to build a civilization while keeping the world's ecosystems balanced ("ECO," 2017). These examples all demonstrate innovative ways of incorporating cooperative mechanics into virtual worlds, with varying levels of game mechanics framing the experience. They show that this combination of educational elements can deepen the learning of domain-specific concepts as well as build important STEM skills and practices.

The Power of Design

Another key area for successful cooperative learning in games is the field of design. It may seem obvious but the power of intentional design is often overlooked. When we talk about intentional design here, we are referring to the way we set up a game's environment and rule systems purposely to enable or elicit certain player behaviors. We can't expect cooperative learning or any kind of deep learning to just emerge organically from a MUVE. Rather we must thoughtfully design the activities and mechanics that encourage the desired interactions. But this too is easier said than done. As discussed previously, we know that well-designed games can be good for learning. But there is much less research and reporting on *how* to design a good educational game - that is, the process of how design elements have evolved throughout the development process, and what has influenced them along the way (Gaydos, 2015). There is no clear-cut set of steps that will produce a good learning game. However, there are exemplars that accomplish related goals, whose design approaches we can draw on.

As an example of a game intentionally designed with a certain cooperative learning outcome in mind, *I Love Bees* was an alternate reality game meant to give players firsthand experience with collective intelligence. To do this, the designers crafted three stages of gameplay to form a community, identify the skill sets distributed throughout that community, and work through a challenge that required cooperation and coordination among the community. The narrative scenarios and multiuser applications crafted for this experience purposely got players to connect and work together in meaningful ways (McGonigal, 2008). This type of intentional design can easily be seen in any commercial MMO, where the designers have strategies to get users to exhibit (or not exhibit) certain behaviors. For instance adding opportunities for proximity, similarity, reciprocity, and disclosure will increase the likelihood that players will be able to make meaningful friendships in a game (Cook et al., 2017). Of course, adding those elements into a game doesn't mean that players will definitely make friends. While Barab (2003) discusses the educational potential of learning communities and the need to define what we mean by a community, he also makes the point that we can't directly design a community, or force any type of social interaction to occur. Rather, we can only design *for* it - putting the elements in place that will enable and even encourage those interactions to emerge from the participants themselves. The same is true for collaborative learning in general—we cannot design the actual interactions among people, but we can design situations where the desired type of learning is more likely to occur (Dillenbourg, 1999). This relationship between the design of an activity and the actual experience of it demonstrates the power of design to bring about learning in a game or MUVE.

Here we have presented an array of work showing the value of educational games, the value of cooperative learning, ways to build player interactions into games, and the importance of intentional design. Techniques and principles from each field came together to form an interdisciplinary foundation for designing *The Radix Endeavor.* Based on this body of research, our aim was to understand the mechanics that could motivate player interaction, embed those into a virtual world rich in math and science systems, and provide challenges that encourage players to draw on both socially-relevant and content-specific resources. In the next section, we will look closely at the application of these ideas from the literature to show how *Radix* designers created tools and systems in the game world with the intention of eliciting collaborative STEM learning.

MULTIPLAYER ELEMENTS

To bring about deep collaborative learning, we want a multi-user virtual environment to be more than simply an environment where multiple users exist together. Beyond sharing the virtual space, we want users to have meaningful interactions that help them learn together. For this to happen, the multiplayer elements of a game or other learning experience must be thoughtfully designed to target this goal, with the research literature in mind. *Radix* has a number of elements and tools built into the game world that were designed to do this by enabling players to find each other, to have some meaningful interactions, and to engage with each other around the curriculum content. The live feel of the game and ability to connect with other players lay the groundwork for small groups and a larger community. Chat and mail provide for basic interactions that keep players connected. Partying and multiplayer quests and tools take this a step further by enabling and encouraging players to collaborate on domain-specific tasks, in ways they couldn't do individually. Finally, the overarching approach to game systems provides enough uncertainty and variation to support meaningful discussions. To be effective, these elements rely on both the rich virtual world and the game mechanics, demonstrating what is possible when features of games and MUVEs are combined into one experience. In this section we will first describe the design of the smaller, supportive multiplayer elements that must be present in an MMO. We will then move on to the more complex elements that support the core pedagogy of the game, to show how they foster meaningful collaborative learning within *Radix*.

Live Feel

One of the foundations of a MUVE, which is not to be underestimated, is creating a "live" feel to the world. This means the users know that other users are there at the same time, and the world feels like a place that is bustling and active, as is the case in Figure 3. This is a prerequisite in a way for building community and presenting an exciting world that users want to explore. It establishes the feeling of relatedness that is a key element of self-determination theory as discussed previously. People have a natural curiosity about things that other people are doing, and they are social creatures, so a world that is clearly full of other users is appealing to many learners. MMOs are particularly good at creating this live feel, and in *Radix* we drew on the designs from this genre. The *Radix* world is split up into zones, different locations of the world that connect together to form the world players explore. When players walk around the world, they control their own avatar, and they can see other players' avatars walking around as well. They can see if a player is leaving the zone to go somewhere else, walking around the zone to collect animals or plants, or standing still talking to an NPC or using a tool station. The ability to see other players and have some general idea of what they're doing means that even upon their first entrance into the world, a player will understand that this is a place where players are active and like to explore - exactly the tone we want to set for inquiry learning. In addition, when a whole class enters the world at the same time, they can see their classmates and friends and immediately understand that they are engaging in a shared experience, which sets the stage for some powerful learning opportunities.

Figure 3. Players can see each other exploring the world

Connecting with Others

The next step beyond knowing that other players are exploring the world around you, is of course being able to find and connect with those players. Avatars in *Radix* have their usernames displayed above their heads to help players recognize people they may already know, such as classmates, and to recognize people they run into frequently in the game and could potentially get to know. When players are in the same zone, they can add each other to their buddy list to facilitate communication. This means that for example if a player is working on an evolution quest where they go back and forth between the forest and plains biomes to investigate bird traits, and they see another player visiting those same zones, they might guess that player is working on the same quest. When they are in the same zone, they can friend each other, which enables them to then use other features such as in-game chat to ask questions and share quest strategies. The ability to connect with others, in combination with actual conversation channels such as chat and mail, lets players take advantage of the distributed cognition afforded by the game, its tools, and all of its players.

In-Game Chat

In-game chat is one of the ways in which *Radix* players can collaborate, and it allows this to happen within different groups. We felt that being able to use open-ended chat was very important to let players get to know each other and use their own words to describe phenomena they observed in the game. For this reason, the chat system was designed to let players type directly but with a blacklist of words that would be filtered out. Using this feature, players can chat with other individuals on their buddy list about game-related topics, or just use it as a social space. In the zone chat, they can say things "out loud" which will be seen by all other players in the same zone (Figure 4). This may be especially useful if new players are looking for something for a quest, say a rare type of lumabell, and want to ask if it can be found in this area. The ability to do this helps players check their hypotheses about quest tasks, and sets up a community of collaborative inquiry. In party chat, players can communicate with other players that they have temporarily grouped with (parties will be discussed in more detail later). These players may be a group of friends from school, or a group that is partnering on the same quest but working in different zones. In either case, party chat creates a common channel to coordinate efforts or ask for tips. Similarly, class chat (which was designed but not implemented in the first version of *Radix*) is a group chat that automatically includes everyone in the same real-life biology or math class. This way no students are left out, and when they are playing outside of school they can easily see who else from their class is currently in the game. This variety of chat enables players to form and maintain relationships. While it certainly doesn't force players to chat about game strategies or STEM content, it provides the opportunity to engage in those conversations should players choose to, an element that must be present before we start using other game design techniques to encourage that collaboration.

In-Game Mail

While in-game chat enables players to communicate synchronously, mail lets them send messages asynchronously, useful if the other player is not online at the time. This way players can share their latest discoveries or tips for the recipient to read whenever they log in. Beyond the straightforward email functionality however, is the ability for players to send game objects to each other, as shown in figure 5. If a player has bred a particularly rare flower, or collected a reptile that can only be found in the farthest reaches of the world, they can send one to a friend who might not have made those discoveries yet. In

Figure 4. Players can talk "out loud" so others see what they say

Figure 5. A player sending objects through the mail

addition, if a player has found a particularly interesting solution to a quest by drawing a clever map or doing a certain genetic cross, those maps and Punnett square objects can be shared with others as well. By using in-game mail, players can make informal trades, show each other their work, or simply share cool stuff. The ability to do this increases opportunities for community-building and collaboration during quests and exploration of the world.

Partying

In addition to these more basic multiplayer elements, *Radix* also offers a partying feature. Though common to most games in the MMO genre, partying is not often found in educational games as it requires both real-time gameplay and a rich world environment. In general, partying means that a group of players form a party to work on some in-game task that is beneficial to do collaboratively. It could be a task where all party members are present in the same zone and take on different roles, or a task where party members are spread out to carry out the work in different zones of the world. Being in a party enables the party members to communicate easily with their group via party chat. It may mean that the work any party members do contributes to the shared team goal, and it may mean that those members all share in the reward given for completing a quest. In *Radix*, the benefits of partying center around shared data collection. As described previously, *Radix* players use in-game tools to collect data about objects they encounter in the world, from plant traits to animal genotypes to measurements of structures. This data is aggregated in their data library so they can then analyze it to understand world systems and complete quests. If players collect this kind of data while they are in a party, the data is saved to the data libraries of all party members. This means that if one player is collecting data about crocodiles in the swamp and her friend is collecting data about mushrooms in the forest, they both end up with access to both the crocodile and mushroom data. This interaction can prove useful in two main ways, both of which enable cooperative learning experiences.

First, it becomes possible to collect much larger data samples. Sampling is one of the science practices that is addressed in *Radix*, where players have to consider an appropriate sample size when they make claims in the game. If someone is trying to find the average blackburn height but has only sampled five birds, the quest giver will ask them to think about how they might get a more accurate sample. By partying, players can easily complete quests that require much larger samples because each member only needs to collect a fraction of the data points. So a group of three players can agree to all measure blackburns, pooling their data to easily obtain a sample of fifteen or much more. Then they can each do their analysis on the whole data set, and perhaps even observe differences in the average height between the whole sample and the smaller sample collected individually.

Second, it becomes possible to split up the data collection work for a given quest, for example one that calls for examining teebeedee birds in a number of different zones. Players can each travel to different parts of the world to collect an agreed-upon number of data points, and easily access the information on teebeedee birds without taking the time to do it all themselves. They can then compare notes on their qualitative observations from different areas, for example very long beaks, or different diets, and confirm these with quantitative analysis using the data explorer tool.

Setting up the partying functionality in this way has multiple affordances for learning. For one, it mimics the realistic way that science is a collaborative domain. In real-world experiments, scientists often work with other researchers to collect data or build on previous data sets, and in *Radix* players can have a first-hand experience showing them the value of this collaboration. In addition, working with other players to collect data and complete tasks necessitates communication. Whether players are partying remotely and using the chat channel, or playing in class sitting next to each other and talking out loud, they must articulate what the task is, make a plan for how to split up the work, and coordinate the execution of that plan. They have an opportunity to practice working in cross-functional teams, one of the key skills we have seen built by games. With this in place, players are invested and may even progress to discussing their results, thereby learning from each other in the context of authentic science inquiry.

Multiplayer Quests and Tools

The elements discussed so far are structural elements that can be built into any MUVE. They create a foundation for a multiplayer world so that more content-specific collaboration can be built on top. In *Radix*, we took this collaboration further by intentionally designing quests and tools that required different kinds of interactions with other players. Although these designs were not implemented in the first version of *Radix*, they were an integral part of the game's design goals from the outset. Some of them have been prototyped and tested with users, and as such they provide exciting prospects for future work on the game. We describe some of these designs here to illustrate the kinds of tasks and interactions that game mechanics built into MUVEs can foster.

There are five related yet distinct quest formats that we identified as a good fit for *Radix* multiplayer tasks, each of these inspired by the designs of other games as well as techniques for cooperative learning in the classroom. In each type, we aimed to bring about collaboration by structuring the problem space in such a way that it would not be feasible for one player to complete the entire task on their own. Choosing problems that are large or require varied tools or expertise can ensure that each player has a role to play on the quest. However, those tasks cannot be entirely separable either. Rather they must have some element in common that necessitates players' communication, planning, and interaction. Following are the main ways we went about solving this design problem.

1. **Large-Scale Problems:** Situations where large amounts of data need to be collected, or many objects need to be created, such that it would not be feasible (or enjoyable) for one player to do on their own. In this case players in a party would be doing essentially the same task, with variations, and they would have to agree on how to split up the problem before tackling it individually.
2. **Unique Roles:** Problems that require multiple steps, different tools, or various areas of expertise, and can be done by splitting up the project according to roles. Players may do similar tasks in series, preparing an artifact to be used by the next player, or they may take on the job of researching a specific aspect of the problem to inform the group's solution.
3. **Asynchronous:** Tasks that, once split up among team members, do not need to be done at the same time, enabling players to log in and complete their part of the task at a time convenient for them. This may be in the form of a large-scale problem that is split up, or a number of different tasks requiring unique roles that must happen sequentially. At least some asynchronous tasks are essential in a long-form game as it is not always possible for students to be online at the same time.
4. **Unique Resources:** Challenges where each player starts with different resources, either tools or objects, and must collaborate to determine how best to combine or trade those resources.
5. **Unique Goals:** Narratives that provide a context where each player has a different goal, possibly creating different artifacts or artifacts with different properties. Team members cannot tell each other directly how to complete the task but they can share resources and strategies that their goals and solutions may have in common.

Similarly, tools can be designed such that they allow or even require input from multiple players in order to accomplish tasks in the game. Here we aimed to apply the theory of positive interdependence, designing for interactions in which the whole group succeeds only when each individual also succeeds. These are the designs used in *Radix* tools to bring players together in service of a quest goal.

1. **Collaborative Work:** Tools that enable players to not only create artifacts but simultaneously work on a shared game artifact, much like real world shared documents. This means that players in a group can see what each other are working on, discuss what they contribute to the artifact, and how to integrate their work.
2. **Multiplayer Input:** Using this type of tool, players invite other players into some kind of interaction. This could be for the purpose of exchanging items or information, or contributing objects or data necessary to conduct an experiment.

3. **Limited Access:** While not really one tool per se, this functions as more of a structured system for tools. Limiting access to tools, objects, or data for different players in a group means that each player brings a unique contribution to the group, and must rely on other players for what they don't have.

Given this variety of quest formats and multiplayer tools that can be used in the quests, the key to designing meaningful interactions is choosing the right combination that will support the content and skills being targeted.

One example is a task designed into the geometry quest line in which we want players to discover for themselves why scale factor is so important. In this task, players have to infiltrate the enemy leader's compound to find out what his evil plans are. To do this, team members split up a large area to map out different sections of the compound. They then come together and use a collaborative map-drawing tool (figure 6) to draft and position all the surveyed buildings on one comprehensive map to be turned in and used for the next part of the challenge. As they begin mapping their buildings onto the same plans and they see what others are adding, they will likely discover that each has selected their own scale factor, which means that while each building may be proportional to the world, they are not to scale with respect to each other. Once they realize this, players discuss the need to use one consistent scale factor, agree on the most appropriate factor to use, and work together to complete the collaborative map. This task utilizes a large-scale problem and a collaborative work tool to provide opportunities to check each other's work and communicate about the integration of discrete pieces - important real-world skills that are not often practiced in schools.

Figure 6. A mockup of the collaborative cartogram tool

Another example is a point in the ecology quest line where we wanted players to experience the collaborative process of doing science and the interdisciplinary nature of inquiry. Players find out that local residents have noticed a significant increase in the rodent population which is causing health problems in many villages. They are asked to help uncover the connection between the rodents and the disease outbreak, as well as help devise a solution. Players have access to a wide array of tools but they are limited to bringing only one with them when they journey to this region. To be successful, they must coordinate within their group and ensure that each tool is represented, meaning that each player will choose a specialty and develop their expertise in that area during the quest. The health worker uses the Doctor's Bag tool to diagnose residents' ailments and confirm that there is a rodent-borne disease. The zoologist uses the Food Webs toolset to estimate population sizes and determine predator-prey relationships, discovering that the rodent boom has coincided with a sudden decrease in the snake population. The ecologist uses the Eco Globe to simulate population changes over time based on the snake and rodent data to test hypotheses about what would happen if a new group of snakes were introduced into the area. And finally, the geneticist uses the Breeding toolset to breed the agreed upon quantity of snakes with resistant traits. This whole process takes careful coordination - players must discuss the problem and possible solutions, then make sure each member of the team understands what needs to be done and when to play their part. This task utilizes unique roles and an asynchronous quest design, facilitated by limited access tools. It provides players with a feeling of individual expertise, alongside the shared team victory, both empowering learning experiences for budding scientists.

Identifying the learning objectives and designing tools and quests that elicit the desired player interactions to build certain skills, as we attempt to do in these quest designs, is no small feat. It requires a long iterative process of prototyping and user testing, and during the *Radix* project we by no means perfected this type of collaborative learning. We did however experience enough of the process to witness how these social interactions built into the context of a world can produce some unique and powerful learning moments. These are moments brought about by the unique affordances of game mechanics embedded into multi-user virtual environments.

Approach to Game Systems

In addition to the concrete game mechanics and tools that enable or require players to interact with each other, the general approach to designing the game's systems and challenges can be equally important. We wanted a world where different players would have experiences that were similar enough that they could talk about their shared experiences easily, but just different enough that they had to explain exactly what they had found and could compare it to their friends. The goal was to design a world that was open-ended enough that different players could come up with qualitatively different hypotheses about how the world's systems worked, setting the stage for their interactions and discussions to lead to convergent conceptual change. This goal was infused into the design of the world, quests, and tools built into the first version of *Radix*, and would continue to support any tools added in future versions.

As an example of variation in the game, two players might run the same ecosystems simulation (Figure 7) but set it to start with different numbers of each species. These players can easily converse about the mudweaver and caracal relationships, but they have to take the time to explain what inputs and outputs they got in their own run of the simulator. This means the players have to explain their process using relevant terminology, and they have the opportunity to learn from what others have tried and work

Figure 7. Players use the Eco Globe to run simulations with varying inputs

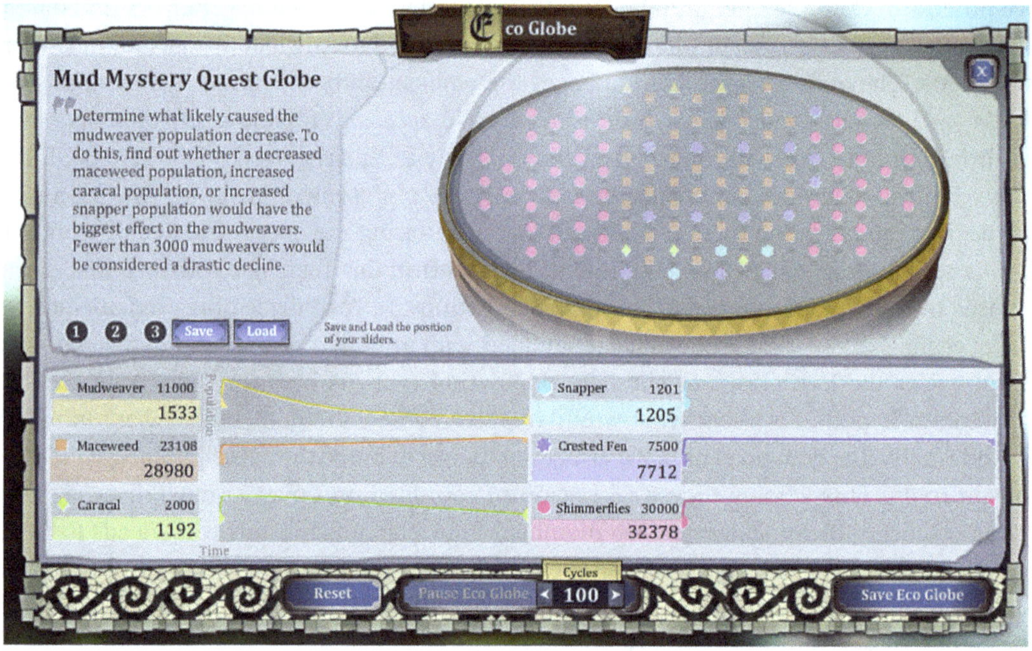

toward a shared understanding of the ecosystem's relationships. Another example of variation is that the game world is set up so that certain species have different population sizes and even distributions of traits, depending on which biome or area a player is exploring. In addition, the individual organisms are spawned randomly according to specified probabilities. This means that players can strategize about their method of collecting population or genetic data, but when they carry out their experiments they won't get the exact same results. Rather, they will have some motivation to share their findings, knowing that others may not have made the same discoveries. This sets the stage for interesting in-person discussions where players work together to make meaning out of their gameplay.

Another game design strategy that supports inquiry learning as well as a community of practice is to provide only enough guidance in the game to get players started, but not so much that they know exactly what to do. *Radix* quests attempt to find a balance between directing players so much that they are simply following directions, and leaving quests so open-ended that no one knows what to do. When this is done well, we find that players are more likely to take advantage of the community's collective intelligence, checking in with each other throughout the quest, even if the actual in-game tasks are done individually. Players ask each other what the quest task means, where to find certain characters or animals, how to use the breeding tool, how they figured out which trait was dominant, what step they are on, and much more. In a game with specific procedural instructions, players would have less reason to turn to their neighbors because discussing the game wouldn't provide them with any tangible benefits. On the other hand, setting the quests up in such a way that players are curious what others are doing and how they are doing it promotes social interactions and a sense of community. Intentionally designing for this is tricky because player interactions can depend heavily on play styles and existing player culture, but it is also a powerful tool in the design of social learning experiences.

IMPLEMENTATION DESIGN

We have looked at some of the educational benefits of learning games and cooperative learning, as well as how these ideas have been combined and applied in the design of *The Radix Endeavor.* The next step in understanding *Radix* and its potential for collaborative learning is to examine how the design of a game influences the needs of its implementation. While we can design for collaborative learning, we know that doesn't mean that meaningful player interactions and high quality discussions will necessarily occur. When a learning game is used in conjunction with a school or other formal educational setting, teachers can act as another catalyst, making implementation choices that complement the elements embedded in the game, and promoting the desired interactions. Since the focus of this chapter is on designing game elements that support multiplayer interactions, we won't go into great detail on designing classroom implementations. However, we present here a sampling of some complementary teaching strategies to demonstrate the power that teachers' actions have to leverage the game and its embedded elements for learning.

To find out how *Radix* fit into existing classrooms and which teaching strategies best supported the game's approach, we observed students and teachers and collected feedback in a number of ways. As part of the Radix project, our game and curriculum designers conducted an array of user testing involving paper prototypes and digital prototypes of individual tools and quests. Radix researchers also conducted a large-scale pilot that spanned three semesters and involved teachers at varying levels of involvement, including 2,125 teachers who created accounts, 324 teachers with at least one student who played the game, and 37 teachers who participated in a survey or interview. We observed students in small focus groups and whole class computer labs, and teachers as they taught classes and described their implementations in interviews. During the Radix pilot, teachers had a great deal of freedom in how they designed their implementations and how they integrated the game into their curriculum. This meant that the Radix researchers were able to witness a wide variety of teaching styles, school environments, and student populations and try to understand what was a good fit, what worked, and for what purposes. The factors presented here that can help or hinder the success of a multiplayer educational game are based on observations, interviews, surveys, and game data collected during the pilot period.

Classroom Challenges

When teachers integrate a new tool or initiative into their classroom, they have many decisions to make about how to do it. These implementation decisions shape the student experience and therefore the learning as well. For example there are tradeoffs between having students play together in class, or on their own time outside of school. Teachers must decide whether to assign specific quests to students based on the curricular unit, or to give them more autonomy by letting them explore freely. And they need to be cognizant of their own role and the level of guidance they want to provide–whether they want to be a central resource for gameplay and content, or to step back and let students take the lead. While there are no right or wrong ways to design an implementation, it must be based on the particular school and group of students, and teachers may need time to experiment and revise their implementation choices.

Aside from these aspects that are generally under teachers' control, there are often a number of barriers to using an MMO or other type of MUVE in schools. Students need access to technology, and time to play and explore, which can be a big challenge in schools with short class periods and limited availability of computers. Students need a teacher who is comfortable putting them in control, to let collaborative learning and discoveries happen. Similarly, students need a classroom culture of inquiry in order for an inquiry-based game to feel like something they can freely explore. These challenges, both practical and pedagogical, may take time and persistence to change. For this reason it is essential to take them into account when designing the game, as well as its classroom implementation.

Teaching Strategies

The challenges mentioned above which are pedagogical in nature are perhaps the most difficult to change but are likely also the ones that can have the biggest impact. A culture of inquiry and a supportive environment for collaboration are essential for the multiplayer interactions in a MUVE to really be used. Without this, students are likely to treat the MUVE more like other classroom activities they are used to - problems to be worked on individually until they obtain the "right" answer. In a well-designed game, especially one targeted at inquiry learning, we believe players will get more out of the game by working with others, both directly through the features of the software, as well as through discussions about the experience of using the software. In addition, while there may be a clear moment of completion, there may also be multiple pathways and lines of reasoning to arrive at the solution. For students to feel comfortable working in these ways, teachers must create an environment conducive to these pedagogies. There are a number of strategies they can use to establish that culture and to take advantage of it once it is in place.

One way to approach this goal is for teachers to embrace the role of a "guide on the side," by limiting direct instruction and giving students more autonomy. Pilot teachers who had the most success with *Radix* in their classrooms were the ones who saw their role as providing encouragement through frustration, and suggesting resources, but rarely telling students what they should be doing. Those teachers found that there was an adjustment period for everyone in the class but then students really began to take ownership of their learning, rely on each other, and figure things out for themselves—gaining unique experience in collaborative problem-solving. Another important role of the teacher as a guide is to facilitate discussion based on students' shared experience. Just because they have figured out the pattern among bird beak characteristics in different regions doesn't mean they will immediately recognize the more abstract concept of natural selection. So teachers can ask questions about different strategies and discoveries, soliciting students' hypotheses and leading them to converge on key ideas in evolution. With quality group discussions, students can ultimately build their own understanding of evolution, a much deeper way to learn than traditional instruction. Building on these discussions, and knowing what kinds of experiences the class as a whole has had, teachers can also make important connections between game content, other related classroom activities, and even examples from students' own lives. Identifying these types of connections, where students can apply their growing skills and knowledge to new situations, is invaluable to an inquiry classroom and a great fit for the rich experiences provided by an MMO.

Teachers can also play an important role in encouraging students to utilize some of the specific multiplayer elements of a game that they may have overlooked. During the Radix pilot, not many players used features like partying and mail of their own accord, because they weren't explicitly required to complete quests. Some students found these features and explored them on their own, but these interactions were not widespread. Teachers can encourage these cooperative learning experiences by layering additional tasks onto the game environment, even when they are not built into the digital experience. For instance they could select a rare species and ask groups of students to join a party and spread out around the world to collect data on this species. This would foster conversations about the findings both within parties and across parties, and the particular research question could be tailored to the class or even smaller groups. This brings in an element of personalization and takes advantage of the rich world of a MUVE to generate new inquiry experiences.

Formative Assessment

Formative assessment strategies are another area that can be tailored to take advantage of the multiplayer interactions and cooperative learning formats of a virtual world game. We saw *Radix* teachers developing a variety of methods that fit with the game and met their goals. Once students are used to working on their own and not looking to the teacher for information, teachers are freed up to circulate more or less unnoticed, listening in to students' conversations as they play. They may hear students checking in about how much they have accomplished, asking each other how to read the map or create a Punnett square, or even discussing why red myzle flowers are so much more prevalent in the forest. Teachers can treat all of this information as formative assessment data. It provides insight into students' thought processes, what they find engaging, and where they are struggling, all without interrupting the flow of their game experience. This picture of individual students and the class as a whole, combined with back-end data available to teachers, can then be used to tailor the feedback and class discussions that teachers have throughout their *Radix* implementation. As part of this strategy, teachers can ask about specific experiences from the game, either in whole class discussions or in thoughtfully designed small group tasks. They can provide prompts that get students to describe in detail their understanding of systems embedded in the game - for example why breeding two red myzle flowers might result in yellow offspring. By eliciting explanations of how the simulated breeding system works, teachers are able to see whether students still have misconceptions about Mendelian genetics more generally, and address them right away.

Throughout this section we have seen how Radix teachers adjusted their teaching to scaffold students' inquiry experiences, and how the multiplayer elements of the game can also support that pedagogical approach. It is worth noting as well that teachers committed to creating a culture of inquiry and a student-driven classroom should not shy away from being explicit about these efforts. Some of the teachers in the Radix pilot worked hard to highlight the scientific inquiry practices they saw students doing in the game. They led students to identify the steps they were taking to complete a quest - things like identifying a question, designing experiments, using models, collecting data, analyzing findings, and reporting results. This made it easy to connect their in-game actions to the scientific method, something that was taught throughout the year, and help students see that by playing the game together they were doing real science. Similarly, these teachers also pointed out the ways they saw students working together to solve problems - whether it was discussing together, asking someone who had already completed the quest, or recommending outside resources. This helped their students recognize the value of collaboration and feel that everyone had something to contribute in the class. The teachers we observed implementing this approach were also the teachers that were most enthusiastic about the value of *Radix* for their teaching, which underscores the importance of a good fit between an MMO and its classroom implementation.

CONCLUSION

We have seen the value of games in education and the value of cooperative learning, and this chapter has examined how *The Radix Endeavor* went about combining those pedagogies through specific multiplayer elements in a virtual world game, and how they were leveraged in classrooms. As just a MUVE, *Radix* players would lack direction and motivation for interacting with each other, which game mechanics provide. As just a game, *Radix* would feel flat and predictable, but the systems-based world that draws on MUVE characteristics makes it rich and interactive. By intentionally designing a game set in a multi-user virtual environment, we can immerse players in a content-rich MMO for STEM learning that balances directed and open-ended experiences.

Beyond providing learners with a deeper way to learn STEM concepts and practices, this approach addresses a broader need in STEM learning. Real scientists see doing science as a collaborative process of exploration, rather than simply carrying out predictable experiments in an isolated lab. However, this doesn't always come across in science classrooms where it can be hard to provide authentic experiences within the constraints of school walls and class periods. MUVEs with embedded game mechanics, such as MMOs, are one interesting way to provide a relevant and engaging context, along with meaningful experiences working with others. Designing realistic systems or simulations in conjunction with social interactions within a community can produce an engaging way to participate in the science inquiry process. This type of experience can help get students interested in science and begin to see themselves as scientists.

While MUVEs are a natural fit for rich content and social experiences, in order to be effective the multiplayer interactions must be carefully designed and tightly integrated with the content and STEM skills. While open-ended communication channels like chat and mail should be present, intentional multiplayer designs need to go further, including more explicit ways that players collaborate on problems directly involving STEM concepts. In addition, teachers must employ their own thoughtful design process to ensure that their implementation of the game is a good fit for its pedagogies and objectives. *Radix* has only begun the process of designing deeply integrated multiplayer interactions, but from the piloting conducted so far we have seen the potential for great impact. Based on this, we hope to continue building deeper multiplayer interaction into the next version of *Radix*, as well as apply this combination of learning theory and game design to future educational games. We also hope that other learning games designers will take inspiration from the methods, design elements, and implementation ideas presented here to create their own games that incorporate deep collaborative learning. We believe that if the learning games field works together to intentionally design multiplayer game elements into MUVEs and thoughtfully implement their tools in classrooms, we can bring students more authentic scientific inquiry and deeper STEM learning experiences.

REFERENCES

Barab, S., Dodge, T., Tuzun, H., Job-Sluder, K., Jackson, R. C., & Gilbertson, J. (2007). The Quest Atlantis Project: A socially-responsive play space for learning. In B. E. Shelton & D. A. Wiley (Eds.), *The educational design of computer games* (pp. 159–186). Rotterdam, The Netherlands: Sense Publishers.

Barab, S. A. (2003). An introduction to the special issue: Designing for virtual communities in the service of learning. *The Information Society*, *19*(3), 197–201. doi:10.1080/01972240309467

Boyle, E. A., Hainey, T., Connolly, T. M., Gray, G., Earp, J., Ott, M., & Pereira, J. et al. (2016). An update to the systematic literature review of empirical evidence of the impacts and outcomes of computer games and serious games. *Computers & Education*, *94*, 178–192. doi:10.1016/j.compedu.2015.11.003

Bressler, D. M., & Bodzin, A. M. (2016). Investigating flow experience and scientific practices during a mobile serious educational game. *Journal of Science Education and Technology*, *25*(5), 795–805. doi:10.1007/s10956-016-9639-z

Cardellini, L. (2006). Fostering creative problem solving in chemistry through group work. *Chemistry Education Research and Practice*, *7*(2), 131–140. doi:10.1039/B5RP90019K

Clark, D., Tanner-Smith, E., Killingworth, S., & Bellamy, S. (2013). *Digital games for learning: A systematic review and meta-analysis*. Menlo Park, CA: SRI International.

Cook, D., Bialoskursky, Y., Fulton, B., Fitch, M., & Gonzales, J. (2017, January 27). *Game design patterns for building friendships*. Retrieved from http://www.lostgarden.com/2017/01/game-design-patterns-for-building.html

Dieterle, E. (2009). Neomillennial learning styles and River City. *Children, Youth and Environments*, *19*(1), 245–278.

Dillenbourg, P. (1999). What do you mean by collaborative learning? In P. Dillenbourg (Ed.), *Collaborative-learning: Cognitive and computational approaches* (pp. 1–19). Oxford, UK: Elsevier.

Divjak, B., & Tomić, D. (2011). The impact of Game-based learning on the achievement of learning goals and motivation for learning mathematics-literature review. *Journal of Information and Organizational Sciences*, *35*(1), 15–30.

ECO. (n.d.). *Build a civilization in a simulated ecosystem*. Retrieved May 4, 2017, from https://www.strangeloopgames.com/eco/

Gaydos, M. (2015). Seriously considering design in educational games. *Educational Researcher*, *44*(9), 478–483. doi:10.3102/0013189X15621307

Gee, J. P. (2003). What video games have to teach us about learning and literacy. *Computers in Entertainment*, *1*(1), 20–20. doi:10.1145/950566.950595

Gee, J. P. (2008). Learning and games. *The Ecology of Games: Connecting Youth, Games, and Learning, 3*, 21-40.

Gee, J. P. (2009). Deep learning properties of good digital games. In U. Ritterfeld, M. Cody, & P. Vorderer (Eds.), *Serious games: Mechanisms and effects* (pp. 67–82). Abingdon, UK: Routledge.

Howe, C. (2014). Optimizing small group discourse in classrooms: Effective practices and theoretical constraints. *International Journal of Educational Research, 63*, 107–115. doi:10.1016/j.ijer.2013.03.011

Johnson, D. W., & Johnson, R. T. (1996). *Cooperation and the use of technology. In Handbook of research for educational communications and technology* (pp. 1017–1044). Abingdon, UK: Routledge.

Johnson, D. W., & Johnson, R. T. (2005). New developments in social interdependence theory. *Genetic, Social, and General Psychology Monographs, 131*(4), 285–358. doi:10.3200/MONO.131.4.285-358 PMID:17191373

Johnson, D. W., Johnson, R. T., & Stanne, M. B. (2000). *Cooperative learning methods: A meta-analysis. University of Minnesota*. Minneapolis, MN: Cooperative Learning Center.

Kiang, D. (2014). *Minecraft 101: The underwater dome project.* Retrieved from https://www.iste.org/explore/articleDetail?articleid=155

Li, M. C., & Tsai, C. C. (2013). Game-based learning in science education: A review of relevant research. *Journal of Science Education and Technology, 22*(6), 877–898. doi:10.1007/s10956-013-9436-x

McGonigal, J. (2008). Why I love bees: A case study in collective intelligence gaming. In K. Salen (Ed.), *The ecology of games: Connecting youth, games, and learning* (pp. 199–227). Cambridge, MA: MIT Press.

National Research Council. (2011). *Learning science through computer games and simulations*. Washington, DC: National Academies Press.

Paraskeva, F., Mysirlaki, S., & Papagianni, A. (2010). Multiplayer online games as educational tools: Facing new challenges in learning. *Computers & Education, 54*(2), 498–505. doi:10.1016/j.compedu.2009.09.001

Plass, J. L., Homer, B. D., & Kinzer, C. K. (2015). Foundations of game-based learning. *Educational Psychologist, 50*(4), 258–283. doi:10.1080/00461520.2015.1122533

Roschelle, J. (1992). Learning by collaborating: Convergent conceptual change. *Journal of the Learning Sciences, 2*(3), 235–276. doi:10.1207/s15327809jls0203_1

Ryan, R. M., & Deci, E. L. (2000). Self-determination theory and the facilitation of intrinsic motivation, social development, and well-being. *The American Psychologist, 55*(1), 68–78. doi:10.1037/0003-066X.55.1.68 PMID:11392867

Smith, B., & MacGregor, J. (1992). What is collaborative learning? In A. Goodsell, M. Mahler, V. Tinto, B. L. Smith, & J. MacGreger (Eds.), *Collaborative learning: A sourcebook for higher education* (pp. 9–22). University Park, PA: National Center on Postsecondary Teaching, Learning and Assessment.

Squire, K. (2011). *Video games and learning: Teaching and participatory culture in the digital age*. New York, NY: Teachers College Press.

Starkey, P. L. (2013). *The effects of digital games on middle school students' mathematical achievement* (Doctoral dissertation). Lehigh University, Bethlehem, PA.

Steinkuehler, C., & Duncan, S. (2008). Scientific habits of mind in virtual worlds. *Journal of Science Education and Technology*, *17*(6), 530–543. doi:10.1007/s10956-008-9120-8

Steinkuehler, C., & Squire, K. (2014). Videogames and learning. In R. K. Sawyer (Ed.), *The Cambridge handbook of the learning sciences* (pp. 377–396). Cambridge, UK: Cambridge University Press. doi:10.1017/CBO9781139519526.023

Steinkuehler, C. A., & Williams, D. (2006). Where everybody knows your (screen) name: Online games as "third places". *Journal of Computer-Mediated Communication*, *11*(4), 885–909. doi:10.1111/j.1083-6101.2006.00300.x

Stevens, R., Satwicz, T., & McCarthy, L. (2008). In-game, in-room, in-world: Reconnecting video game play to the rest of kids' lives. *The Ecology of Games: Connecting Youth, Games, and Learning, 9*, 41-66.

Webb, N. M., Farivar, S. H., & Mastergeorge, A. M. (2002). Productive helping in cooperative groups. *Theory into Practice*, *41*(1), 13–20. doi:10.1207/s15430421tip4101_3

Zimmerman, C. (2011). Developing scientific thinking in the context of video games: Where to next? In F. C. Blumberg (Ed.), *Learning by playing: Video gaming in education* (pp. 54–68). Oxford, UK: Oxford University Press.

KEY TERMS AND DEFINITIONS

Collaborative Learning: A process of learning in which learners work together and interact to build their shared understanding.

Cooperative Learning: Used interchangeably with collaborative learning in this chapter.

Formative Assessment: Assessment strategies used by teachers during the learning process to inform and modify teaching practices.

Inquiry Learning: A process of learning in which learners pose their own questions and find their own ways to solve problems rather than following proscribed processes.

MMO or MMOG: Massively Multiplayer Online Game – a genre of game in which many players explore a persistent, shared world at the same time.

Quest: A specific task players must complete within an MMO.

Quest Line: A sequence of related quests within an MMO.

Chapter 3
Task-Based Language Learning and Learner Autonomy in 3D Virtual Worlds

Iryna Kozlova
University of Pennsylvania, USA

ABSTRACT

This chapter investigates whether a problem-solving task with an environment exploration component mediates learner autonomy in a 3D virtual world (VW). Two groups of English as a foreign language (EFL) learners were to collect information by exploring the 3D VW and eliciting information from player avatars to complete the task. An analysis of student interaction reveals that only one of the groups acted as autonomous learners by generating new topics based on their observations in the environment; eliciting information and controlling the topics when interacting with the player avatars; and initiating repair leading to input modification, negotiation of meaning, and modification of output. Results suggest that learner autonomy could be promoted in 3D VWs by improving the clarity of task instructions and by designing learning tasks in such a way that students would be able to complete the tasks only if they share their observations with peers and player avatars.

INTRODUCTION

Autonomy has been one of the central topics in Second Language Acquisition (SLA) research for more than three decades, as evidenced by Benson's (2016) bibliography on autonomy in language learning, which includes 2,500 references. The concept of autonomy has been broadly explored; though many scholars acknowledge that this concept is "hard to grasp" (Schwienhorst, 2003), they tend to agree that autonomy refers to learners' ability or capacity to be in charge or to take control of their learning (Cotterall, 1995; Little, 2007). Autonomous learners are viewed as active agents whose learning depends on their ability and willingness "to make and carry out the choices which govern [their] actions" (Littlewood, 1996, p. 428). Learner autonomy is important for second language pedagogy because it concurs with "our view that language learning requires the active involvement of learners; our attempts to introduce

DOI: 10.4018/978-1-5225-3719-9.ch003

"learner-centred" methods; and our goal of helping learners to become independent from their teachers in their learning and use of language" (Littlewood, 1996, p. 427).

The concept of learner autonomy is of particular interest in Computer Assisted Language Learning (CALL) research (see Darasawang & Reinders, 2016; Kozlova, 2013; Schwienhorst, 2003; Smith & Craig, 2013; Vanijdee, 2003) because technology offers plentiful opportunities for learners to interact through audio-, text-, and video-based communication channels. As language-learning contexts expand to 3D virtual worlds (e.g., Second Life), scholars have begun to explore whether these immersive environments that resemble real-life geographical locations (Peterson, 2011) and offer real-life experiences (Schroeder, 2002) support autonomous learning. Although scholars argue that 3D VWs foster autonomous learning (Dalton, 2016; Deutschmann, Panichi, & Molka-Danielsen, 2009; Lan, Kan, Sung, & Chang, 2016; Schwienhorst, 1998), only one study to date, Collentine (2011), examines the relationship between learner autonomy and language learning, specifically, how learners' choices to interact with non-player characters and objects in the environment (e.g., notes and letters) influence accuracy and complexity of their language production. Collentine's (2011) study suggests that 3D tasks can facilitate learner autonomy, but the frequency and length of learner interaction with non-player avatars and objects in the environment do not guarantee the accuracy and linguistic complexity of the language they produce. Considering the findings of Collentine's (2011) research, the present study takes a sociocultural perspective to investigate whether a problem-solving task with an environment exploration component encourages autonomous learning in 3D VWs.

BACKGROUND

Sociocultural theory considers learners to be active agents. Within this framework, autonomy is defined as the "human ability to act through mediation, with awareness of one's actions, and to understand their significance and relevance" (Lantolf, 2013, p. 19). Mediation is defined as a learner's interaction with others and with their experiences with culturally constructed objects, or artifacts, which help carry out various tasks (Lantolf, 2000). While language is viewed as a culturally constructed artifact, it is also a learning object; therefore, autonomous language learners are those who make the conscious choice of using a language in order to learn it. Likewise, learning tasks and computer technology are artifacts that mediate language learning (Lantolf, 2000) and seem to have the potential to also mediate learner autonomy.

Artifact Mediation: Task as a Mediation Means

Ellis (2003) defines a task as a workplan that requires learners to process language pragmatically in order to achieve an outcome, convey appropriately propositional content, communicate meaning using their own language resources, and use language that resembles language used in real life. Since participation in language tasks requires learners to produce language, learners make both linguistic choices and the choice to interact (or not). When working on a task, learners must take initiative in making input more comprehensible through the modification and negotiation of meaning, and in modifying their output in order to make "themselves understood whenever their own message is unclear" (Pica, Kanagy, & Falodun, 1993, p. 12). Therefore, communicative tasks have the capacity to mediate learner autonomy as they compel learners to control their own learning.

While all types of tasks have the capacity to mediate learner autonomy, problem-solving, decision-making, and opinion-exchange tasks seem to require a more autonomous approach to task completion. In these tasks, students' participation is expected, but by design, they do not force students to interact (Pica et al., 1993). Instead, students need to take the initiative to contribute to task completion. In contrast, jigsaw and information-gap tasks require all of the students to hold pieces of information without which task completion is impossible. In other words, participation in jigsaw and information-gap tasks is obligatory.

Pica et al. (1993) emphasize that two task features, goal and activity, are instrumental for autonomous learning. Since tasks are goal oriented, in order to carry out a communicative task and reach its outcome, learners are expected to interact and "take an active role" in an interactional activity which they are to carry out on their own. The interactional activity is also referred to as task-in-process (Breen, 1989). Task-in-process is constructed by students and may differ from the task-as-workplan because learners' interpretation of the task may differ from the instructor's pedagogical intention (Breen, 1989; Seedhouse, 2004). Moreover, learners or groups of learners may interpret the same task in different ways and engage in different types of activities than intended (e.g., Coughlan & Duff, 1994; Foster, 1998; Roebuck, 2000). In Mori's (2002) study, for example, learners of Japanese were instructed to participate in a discussion meeting with native speakers where both learners and native speakers were to share their experiences and express opinions on a suggested topic; instead, learners asked native speakers a series of questions, thus constructing an interview-type interaction.

Artifact Mediation: 3D Virtual Worlds as a Mediation Means

According to Lantolf (2000), learning can be mediated by technology through text- and voice-based communication tools. While these communication channels also mediate interaction in 3D VWs, the 3D environment has even more to offer. 3D VWs immerse learners in environments resembling real-life locations (Peterson, 2011), simulate real-life experiences (Gerhard, Moore, & Hobbs, 2004), and create "learning spaces conceptually different from the face-to-face classroom" (Kozlova & Priven, 2015, p. 83). As learners control their avatars and navigate through the environment, they have opportunities for "experiential problem solving and spatially distributed forms of collaboration" (Cornille, Thorn, & Desmet, 2012, p. 245). Some of the features that differentiate 3D VWs from other virtual environments are the possibilities for visual and auditory information (e.g., landscape, landmarks, sounds of waves in the ocean, twittering of birds in the trees) that can minimize learners' reliance on imagination, provide learners with a "culturally authentic experience" (Collentine, 2011, p. 63), and prompt learners to interact based on their experiences in the 3D environments. Because learners can choose which of the landmarks in the environment to explore and which experiences to incorporate in their activity, virtual worlds also seem to have the capacity to mediate autonomous learning.

Task-Based Learning in 3D Virtual Worlds

Both tasks and technology have the potential to mediate learner autonomy; tasks enable learners to process and produce language, while technology provides a means for interaction and collaboration, as well as visual and auditory information that may prompt learner interaction. Despite growing research on task-based learning in 3D VWs, few studies focus on the tasks that incorporate an environment exploration component in their design (see Collentine, 2011; Lan et al., 2016). Lan et al. (2016) report that not all task types encourage learners to make and discuss observations, request additional information about what has been observed, and incorporate this information in their language production. Information-gap tasks, for example, limit students' oral interaction to question-answer sequences and do not encourage learners to talk about their observations. Reasoning-gap tasks, on the other hand, compel learners to share and integrate information collected when, for example, exploring the environment, which results in the production of modified input and better performance.

Collentine (2011) examines the relationship between learner autonomy and the accuracy and complexity of learner output. In her study, she includes environment exploration segments in the learning task, which was for learners to explore 3D worlds in order to collect information from non-player characters and objects to solve a murder mystery. After collecting the information—presented as text-based messages and interactive question-answer sequences—learners worked in pairs to solve the murder mystery using text-based chat. Collentine reports that learner autonomy, or learners' choices to interact with the input, does not necessarily lead to error-free and lexically dense output. She concludes that while 3D VWs encourage learner autonomy, the accuracy and complexity of learner output depends on the type of input the learner chooses to interact with.

Peterson (2006) investigates whether task design affects learner interaction in 3D VWs. He shows that there were twice as many instances of negotiation of meaning in decision-making tasks than in jigsaw tasks, and three times more than in opinion-exchange tasks. Peterson's (2006) study supports the findings of Lan et al. (2016) in that although jigsaw tasks require information exchange, participants view the completion of jigsaw tasks as a more important goal than the negotiation of meaning of new lexical items. The results of Lan et al. (2016) and Peterson's (2006) studies suggest that reasoning-gap and decision-making tasks are more facilitative of autonomous learning, as they encourage learners to initiate negotiation of meaning and produce modified output. Likewise, Lan et al. (2016) and Collentine's (2011) research advocates for integration of an environment exploration component, which also mediates autonomy.

Research Question

Drawing on the theoretical underpinnings of autonomous and task-based language learning, the present study embeds a problem-solving task with an environment exploration component in the context of a 3D VW. By comparing two groups of learners working towards completion of a given task with the pedagogical focus on meaning and fluency, this study seeks to answer the following question: Does a problem-solving task with an environment exploration component promote learner autonomy in a 3D VW?

METHODS

The data for this study comes from a larger project on teaching and learning in 3D VWs administered jointly by the Language Institute of a Canadian college and the English Language School of a university in Turkey. One of the goals of the project was to explore whether task-based instruction in 3D VWs provides language learners with opportunities to improve speaking skills. Six tasks were developed for the project; this chapter reports on one of the tasks.

Participants

Six Canadian teachers enrolled in Teaching English as a Second/Foreign Language (TES/FL) certification program and eight EFL students from Turkey volunteered to participate in this study. At the time of the study, the EFL students were preparing to enter a Turkish university and were enrolled in upper-intermediate courses at the university's English Language School. The university's language of instruction is English, and so students are required to demonstrate at least an intermediate-high English proficiency level based on the American Council on Teaching of Foreign Languages (ACTFL) guidelines at the time of admission.

Both the teachers and the students participating in the study used pseudonyms (used throughout this chapter) to log in to the 3D environment. Five female teachers, Diane, Gerri, Joan, and Simone were English native speakers whereas the one male teacher, Jack, was a native speaker of Korean and a near-native speaker of English. Six EFL learners were female—Anna, Aylin, Dilara, Maria, Miss Jane, Princess—and two were male, Daniel and Onur.

At the beginning of the project, all of the participants had a one-hour session with a 3D technology consultant who showed them how to navigate their avatars, introduced the collaboration tools, and provided a tour of the 3D VWs used in the project. In addition, a navigation manual provided to the participants assisted in their further exploration of the VWs.

3D Virtual Worlds

Developed on a cloud-based platform, AvayaLive™ Engage, Tipontia Island is an immersive 3D environment with real-time collaboration and web-conferencing tools. Surrounded by the ocean, the island has a large territory with mountains, two smaller islands, a lake, and a river with waterfalls. The island has ample vegetation and wildlife. Birds and mosquitoes signal their presence with their associated sounds, and crabs are visible as they scuttle across the shoreline. Some of the island's landmarks include a lighthouse, tree houses, waterfalls, a campfire, and two teleporting pads.

When logging in to the 3D VW, participants embody personalized avatars that are able to walk, run, jump, and perform gestures (e.g., clapping, raising a hand, waving hello and good-bye). The VWs are multimodal environments where users can interact via audio- and text-based chat and share web-cam video. Text-based chat messages can be sent to a single user or to a group in close proximity or globally. Screens that can be used as presentation or collaboration boards or as computers are available in the environment to browse the Internet.

Rationale for the Task Design

The task for this study was developed based on the findings of previous research on task-based instruction in 3D VWs (e.g., Collentine, 2011; Deutschmann et al., 2009; Peterson, 2006) and literature on task-based learning (Ellis, 2003; Pica et al., 1993). The pedagogical focus of the task was on meaning and fluency, and the task was designed to promote learner autonomy. In focusing on meaning rather than on form, learners develop fluency by focusing less on the production of error-free utterances and more on the meaning they want to express (Seedhouse, 2004). Although expressing personal meanings is the primary focus of interaction in the meaning-and-fluency context, learners still need to make linguistic choices in order to be understood by interlocutors. When expressing personal meanings, learners also need to take the initiative to develop topics and manage their interaction (Seedhouse, 2004). Thus, the meaning-and-fluency context mediates learner autonomy in that it requires learners to make decisions on both linguistic and interactional levels. Since interaction focuses on conveying meaning, 3D worlds seem to be suitable for tasks with a meaning-and-fluency pedagogical focus. Resembling real-life locations and having visual and auditory information readily available (e.g., crabs on the beach or sounds of twittering birds), 3D VWs can reduce learners' reliance on imagination and promote interaction.

The nature of 3D VWs provides ample material that may prompt interaction; so, a problem-solving task used in this study incorporates an environment exploration component in order to provide learners with opportunities to make observations and integrate these observations into their oral language production. The environment exploration component also provides learners with "culturally authentic experience" (Collentine, 2011, p. 63) because 3D VWs take learners out of the traditional classroom by immersing them in a real-life-like context and providing them with real-life experiences. Like in the real world, learners can move around within the environment, explore it, and talk about their experiences and observations with others in the environment. Because 3D VWs can prompt topics for discussion, they can also mediate learner autonomy in that learners need to make decisions on which experiences to include in their interaction.

The task scenario matches the environment because "the design of the physical (digital) space may influence the learning event, just as the choice of arrangements of desks in a classroom, for example, may do" (Panichi & Deutschmann, 2012, p. 205). The task scenario used in the present project was as follows:

There has been a nuclear accident at the power reactor on the mainland. People are being evacuated to our island for safety. Boats full of people from the city will be arriving in two hours. Our team was sent to the island to find out what resources the island has and how these resources can be used to help survivors.

This task was developed by Joan, an instructor for this task. Four of the other teachers -- Diane, Gerri, Jack, and Simone -- played the roles of park workers, and one teacher, Lynn, provided assistance when needed.

At the task onset, both groups received the same instructions that were posted on a collaboration board and provided orally. The task consisted of five stages:

1. *Brainstorming* what resources are needed to help survivors;
2. *Going on an island tour* with the team leader (instructor Joan) to locate key landmarks;
3. *Exploring the island and collecting information from park workers* about the island resources;
4. *Putting together a plan* for how island resources could be used to help survivors;
5. *Presenting the plan* to the evacuation committee.

Although the task incorporated five stages, this chapter focuses only on the third, the island exploration stage. Students were instructed to explore the island and ask park workers questions about how the island's resources could be used. Students did not receive a grade for participation, but they were informed that the successful completion of the task involved incorporation of the collected information into their presentation of the survival plan. The task was designed to allow students to interact with each other and park workers via an audio communication channel.

The eight EFL learners were randomly assigned to two groups, Group 1 and Group 2. Since two learners were unable to log in due to technical problems, only six learners ended up participating in the task, three in each group. The two groups completed the same task on different days during a class session of an hour and a half. Joan was supposed to teach both sessions, but during the second session Joan's computer crashed after the brainstorming stage, and so Lynn, who knew the task very well, took over the class.

Data Collection

The screen-capturing software Camtasia Relay was used to record live class sessions. Since 3D VWs resemble a real-life context in that only those who are in close proximity to the participant avatars can hear their talk, the researcher and one of the teachers followed the groups of learners to record their interaction. On several occasions, learners started interaction before the recorders had approached them, and so some recordings start shortly after the beginning of a conversation. Approximately three hours of recordings were transcribed using transcription conventions from Jefferson (1984).

Data Analysis

To explore whether a problem-solving task with an environment exploration component facilitates autonomous learning in 3D VWs, learner interaction was analyzed using conversation analysis (CA) techniques. According to CA, humans organize their interaction "as an emergent collectively organized event" (ten Have, 1999, p. 9), and they manifest their actions, or what they intend to accomplish in the event, through their contributions to the talk (Seedhouse, 2004, p. 13). Heritage (1984) argues that participants' contributions to the talk are shaped by the interactional context, as they are designed and can be understood by reference to the previous utterances. Thus, current utterances shape next contributions, or renew the interactional context, as the next action is performed in reference to the current one. Since human actions are sequentially organized, the sequential analysis of human talk explains how participants act in a certain way (ten Have, 1999, p. 9). In this study, CA techniques are applied to explain how learners organize their talk to achieve learner autonomy.

Conversationalists contribute to talk in turns, and how they organize their conversational turns reflects participants' orientation towards the activities in which they are engaged (Sacks, Schegloff, & Jefferson, 1974). Turn-taking organization of an ordinary conversation, for example, reflects conversationalists' orientation towards equal participation rights through their freedom for self-nomination to be the next speaker. In addition, if there is any kind of interactional trouble - e.g., comprehension or hearing problems - theoretically, any participant can initiate repair, or substitute a problematic item with the "correct" one (Schegloff, Jefferson, & Sacks, 1977). Because each participant can self-select to be the next speaker, there is no pre-allocation of turns. Pauses between turns are minimal, and turns often overlap.

Classroom talk, however, may constrain students' rights for self-selection to be the next speaker because *"[o]nly teachers can direct speakership in any creative way"* (McHoul, 1978, p. 188, italics in original). McHoul (1978) shows that in the teacher-centered classroom, conversational turns are pre-allocated and organized in teacher-initiated three-part sequences consisting of question-answer-comment turns. Since only the teacher is in a position to nominate the next speaker, classroom talk is characterized by longer pauses between turns, minimal possibility for turn overlap, and little possibility to change the turn-taking pattern.

Seedhouse (2004) argues that the second language classroom fosters more than one speech exchange system and that a particular exchange system and the pedagogical focus of an activity are related. A pedagogical focus on form and accuracy, which requires learners to produce error-free structures, is reflected in turn-taking organization of talk where the teacher controls "who says what and when" (Seedhouse, 2004, pp. 104-105). In a meaning-and-fluency context, learners "express personal meanings and develop topics" (Seedhouse, 2004, p. 111); the turn-taking organization of the talk thus becomes more flexible and resembles the turn-taking organization of an ordinary conversation in that learners can take control by self-selecting for speakership, initiating new topics, and initiating repair on problematic items they hear or try to produce. In sum, the meaning-and-fluency context promotes learner autonomy as learners are put in situations where they need to manage interaction on their own.

Since this study focuses on a meaning-and-fluency task, the way that learners accomplish learner autonomy in 3D VWs can be observed through learner-initiated turns in which they (1) generate the topics prompted by their observations in the environment, (2) ask park workers questions on specific topics and control the topics, and (3) initiate repair on incomprehensible input and on their own output.

Topical Organization of the Talk

Learners' initiation and control over the topics are some of the properties of meaning-and-fluency tasks (Seedhouse, 2004). Topical coherence can be observed through participants' organization of the talk rather than through relatedness of the subjects of the talk (Schegloff, 1990). In other words, participants can talk about different subjects connected by the same line of talk, but their relatedness can be observed through topical continuity, or organization of talk in such a way that different topics seem to be somehow related (Garcia, 2013).

There are several basic techniques that participants employ to control the topic and to create topical continuity, including asking questions and changing topics (Garcia, 2013). Topics can be controlled by producing interrogative series (Zimmerman, 1987), or a chain of question/answer adjacency pairs used "as a device to maintain control over the topic" (Garcia, 2013, p. 79). Adjacency pairs are "paired utterances such that on production of the first part of the pair (e.g., question) the second part of the pair (e.g., answer) becomes *conditionally relevant*" (Seedhouse, 2004, p. 14, italics in original).

Producing a topicalizer - an utterance that shows participants' interest in the possible topic and invites further talk on that topic (Button & Casey, 1984) - is a technique employed to maintain the topic. For example, a topicalizer for the utterance "I have a question about mosquitos" could be a response "Yeah?", which encourages talk on the suggested topic.

Topic change occurs at a point in conversation "where the prior topic has been 'bounded' or closed down" (Garcia, 2013, p. 122). One of the common techniques to close a topic is providing an assessment, or an utterance that evaluates the prior topic or event (Pomerantz, 1984), for example, "It's ridiculous!" An initial assessment can be followed by a subsequent assessment of the same referent. The second assessment does not add any new information to the talk; rather, it either displays the current speaker's agreement or disagreement with the previous speaker's evaluation of the topic. Since assessments do not add new information, they either lead to a closure of the conversation or a transition to another topic (Garcia, 2013).

Learner-Initiated Repair

In the second language classroom, repair may lead to interactional modifications, or making input or output more comprehensible. In this way, repair is claimed to facilitate language learning (Seedhouse, 2004). Repair is classified based on who initiates the repair and who performs the repair. Repair on the speaker's utterance can be initiated by someone other than the speaker, but performed by the speaker or by another participant. For example, self-initiated self-repair is initiated and performed by the current speaker. Self-initiated other-repair is initiated by the speaker, but performed by any other participant. These two classifications of learner-initiated repair result in input modification, negotiation of meaning, and modification of learner output. This type of repair is of interest in this study because learners who "take initiative in seeking help with whatever they do not understand and in making themselves understood whenever their own message is unclear" (Lantolf, 2013, p. 12) can be characterized as autonomous learners. Although this study employed CA techniques to explain how learners achieve autonomy, the presentation of findings in the sections that follow may not be conventional from the perspective of traditional CA.

STUDY RESULTS

The analysis of the sequential organization of students' interactions with each other and with park workers shows that although the same artifacts, i.e., the task and 3D VWs, mediated students' actions, they mediated learner autonomy only in Group 1. Students from Group 1 (1) generated new topics based on their observations in the environment, (2) asked park workers questions about specific topics and controlled the topics when interacting with the park workers, and (3) initiated repair leading to input modification, negotiation of meaning, and modification of learners' output. Group 2 students failed to do so. Results suggest that these differences are due to learners' interpretation of the task, specifically, their interpretation of the learning context and their learner roles.

Generation of New Topics

Example 1 illustrates how visual and auditory information available in 3D VWs mediate learner autonomy by prompting learners to generate new topics. When approaching the lake, Onur, Princess, and Maria, all students from Group 1, hear the sound of mosquitoes and talk about this observation (transcription conventions are included in Appendix).

(1) 16 Onur: there some mosquito sounds
17 [really >>annoying<<
18 Princess: [oh yes yes yes ((moves towards Onur))
19 it's very annoying I can- there are um
20 [on the island
21 Onur: [it is ridiculous, but bugs in the lake
22 Princess: [not like that everywhere

Onur: [all the water-
all the water are clean? But if it's clean, why there
are bugs, in the lake, it's [just ridiculous
Princess: [I don't know
((Maria and Onur run in the lake and return))

As shown in this example, students generate new topics, but they design their turns in such a way that allows them to prepare for the smooth transition from one topic to another, thus creating a series of new topics. The introduction of one topic is immediately followed by the topic's assessment, or a new topic is pre-empted by an assessment; so, students employ assessments as a resource to change or terminate topics. In line 16, Onur offers a new topic, "mosquito sounds", and immediately makes an initial assessment of the sound as "really annoying" (line 17). Princess agrees with Onur's assessment by producing an agreement series (Pomerantz, 1984, p. 66). First, she agrees with Onur by providing the same evaluation "yes, yes, yes" (line 18), and then upgrades her assessment of mosquitoes from really to very annoying (line 19). In line 21, Onur introduces another topic, "bugs in the lake", with its pre-assessment, "it is ridiculous". Princess' turn, "not like that everywhere" (line 22), supports Onur's observation that the bugs are concentrated in the lake and overlaps with an introduction of another topic. In lines 23-25, Onur relates students' previous observation of the bugs in the water to the information received from Joan that the island has fresh water, which challenges Joan's information. His assessment of the situation, "it's ridiculous" (line 26), overlaps with Princess' negative response of "I don't know" (line 26) to Onur's question, "why there are bugs, in the lake" (lines 24, 25). Onur's assessment and Princess's negative response terminate the conversation, and Onur and Maria run to check the water in the lake (line 27).

After having made these observations about the lake, students then walk towards the bridge and make additional observations about an airplane in the air and dancing rocks in the river. Altogether, Group 1 generated five topics: (1) annoying mosquitoes, (2) bugs in the water, (3) unclean water, (4) an airplane, and (5) dancing rocks. Although these topics do not seem to be related at first, they constitute a line of talk related to students' experiences in the environment.

Eliciting Information and Controlling the Topics

One of the goals of the task exploration stage was to elicit information about the island's resources from the park workers. Although the park workers provided both groups of students with the same information, the two groups obtained the information in different ways. Group 1 elicited information by asking questions on specific topics related to their observations and was able to control these topics. Group 2, on the other hand, opened conversation with a general question, which did not focus on any specific topics, and then passed the initiative to offer and control topics to the park workers.

Examples 2, 3, 4, and 5, below, illustrate how Group 1 elicits information from the park workers. Students ask Jack whether he sees a ship with the survivors (ex. 2, lines 16-17) and Gerri about the purpose of the bridge near the waterfalls that could be observed in the background (ex. 3, lines 15, 16). They also start an interaction with Diane by requesting information about the tree houses (ex. 4, line 7) and with Simone by asking about the mosquitoes near the lake (ex. 5, line 59).

(2) 15 Jack so, how can I help you?
16 Onur: (we have a question) Can you see the ship that the
17 survivor people coming? =
(3) 15 Onur: I think I wann- just want to ask you question why
16 there's why did they built bridges to rocks to rocks?
17 Gerri: [Um
18 Onur: [it's m- makes more sense. It's I think they are not used.
19 why they are there? It's my question.
(4) 5 Onur: I have a question
6 Diane: yeah?
7 Onur: it's facing the lake, people are there
8 Diane: well ((clearing the throat)), people use the tree houses
(5) 57 Princess: We got a question emm- [about
58 Simone: [oh, okay
59 Princess: [mosque-[mosquits?

Group 2 learners, alternatively, ask park workers general questions, which do not incorporate their observations (ex. 6, line 1), or simply tell park workers that they can start sharing information with them (ex. 7, line 13).

(6) 1 Daniel: how can we use the lighthouse?
2 Jack: umm (2) we use the lighthouse as a communication area
(7) 13 Daniel: we can start
14 Simone: okay, okay, did you have any questions?
15-18 ((Simone notices that one student is missing and asks
where that student is))
19 Okay, well, let me tell you about the lake then.

Different ways of eliciting information lead to different interactional patterns between the park workers and the students from the two groups as demonstrated in examples 8 and 9, below. The interaction between Gerri and Group 1 (ex. 8) consists of question-answer adjacency pairs where students initiate questions and Gerri provides responses.

(8) 15 Onur: I think I wann- just want to ask you question why
16 there's why did they built bridges to rocks to rocks?
17 Gerri: [Um
18 Onur: [it's m- makes more sense. It's I think they are not used.
19 why they are there? It's my question.
20 Gerri: So that they can reach the waterfall.
21 Onur: Ah, there is waterfall in there!
22 Gerri: uh-huh there are many- many sources of fresh drinking
23 water on this island. There's lakes that you've seen,

rivers, and the waterfall. And the water from the
waterfall comes from the mountains and it's very fresh
and very clean. A:nd- yeah and the waterfall is also a
source of power for the island
Princess: uh-huh
Gerri: uh-huh and don't drink the water from the ocean
as the [salt water will make you sick
Onur: [xxx
Gerri: yes yeah [it will make you sick
Princess: [a:nd
u:m what did- what do you think about animals? Is
they live in there- what kind of animals in- live um in
this place?
Gerri: hm, I've seen birds and crabs [and there probably=
Princess: [yes
Onur: =I saw them too
Princess: ha-hah-ha=
Gerri: =hah-hah-hah
Gerri: just probably fish in the lake and the ocean
Princess: Yes, it's imaginish, [um yes
Gerri: [hu huh
yes. And the waterfall keeps um the fr- the fish alive
because its very fresh and clean water
Princess: yes [yes
Gerri: [hu huh

In lines 15, 16, 18, and 19, Onur asks about the bridges that connect the rocks, and Gerri responds to his question (line 20). Onur's acknowledgement of new information about the waterfalls (line 21) functions as a topicalizer that expresses his interest in the topic (Button & Casey, 1984). This prompts Gerri to provide more information (lines 22-27). Princess produces another topicalizer (line 28), which invites more information from Gerri (lines 29, 30). Gerri's turn in line 32 repeats her previous turn and does not introduce any new information, and so Princess uses this opportunity to initiate another question about the animals on the island (lines 34-36), to which Gerri responds (lines 37, 42, 45, 46). Although Gerri supplies the information to the students, the interaction develops in such a way that students control the interaction by producing interrogative series and maintain the topic by producing topicalizers. In addition, the sequential organization of the students-Gerri interaction resembles ordinary talk in that students and Gerri self-select for speakership, their turns often overlap (lines 17 and 8, 30 and 31, 32 and 33, 37 and 38, 43 and 44, 47 and 48) and latch (lines 37, 39, 40, 41), and are not separated by any observable pauses. Their interaction also incorporates humor when Onur responds to Gerri's turn (line 37) with an ironic comment. Simone had told the students that the island has wildlife, but most animals except for the crabs and some birds are imaginary. In the interaction, students ask Gerri about the animals, as she saw the same animals as the students did. Onur then makes an ironic comment, "I saw them too" (line 39), that evokes Princess and Gerri's laughter.

While the sequential organization of the talk between Gerri and the students from Group 1 incorporates student-initiated question-answer sequences and resembles ordinary talk, the interaction between Gerri and the students from Group 2 follows the turn-taking pattern of a teacher-centered classroom, i.e., the three-part teacher-initiated question-answer-comment sequences (McHoul, 1978). As shown in example 9, Gerri scaffolds the students' responses by asking a series of questions on specific topics and modifying her input (lines 5, 6, 7, 10, 13, 15, 18, 19). Students then answer her questions (lines 11, 16, 21, 23) and Gerri comments on their responses (17, 22). There is no turn overlap and the turns are separated by long pauses (lines 7, 12, 14, 20). While students manage some of the pauses (lines 7, 20) by asking a clarification question (line 8) or answering Gerri's question (line 21), Gerri manages most other pauses (lines 12, 14). She interprets the pause after Daniel's negative response (lines 11, 12) as a topic closure and initiates a new topic in line 13, and she treats the pause in line 14 as students not comprehending the word "power" and modifies her input (line 15).

(9) 5 Gerri: But have you ever seen waterfalls provide other sources
6 of resources?
7 (6)
8 Anna: on this island?
9 Gerri: have you ever seen a place (.) where water fall actually
10 provides a resource more than just drinking?
11 Daniel: no
12 (2)
13 Gerri: how about power?
14 (4)
15 Making electricity?
16 Miss Jane: [yes, we can use this for making electricity
17 Gerri: [yes, (of course)
18 Yes, now it's important that you don't drink the water
19 from the ocean. Why?
20 (4)
21 Daniel: because it contain a lot of salt
22 Gerri: yes
23 Daniel: it's not drinkable=

The sequential organization of the students-Gerri interaction provides evidence that the groups orient to different learning contexts. Group 1 orients towards the student-centered meaning-and-fluency context reflected in the turn-taking organization that resembles an ordinary talk. Group 2, meanwhile, orients towards the teacher-centered context reflected in teacher-initiated question-answer-comment sequences.

Student-Initiated Repair

3D worlds mediate learner autonomy not only by prompting the topics for interaction, but also by encouraging students to use words that they either did not know or were not sure how to pronounce. This leads students to initiate repair on those vocabulary items. The students from Group 1 initiated repair on four vocabulary items that referred to objects in the environment: mosquitoes, seagulls, tree houses, and stairs. They also initiated repair on the word "skunk", introduced by Simone (ex. 10, line 124).

When Onur initiates repair on the word "skunk" (line 126), Princess, Maria, and Onur negotiate the meaning of this word in Turkish (lines 129-131, 133, 134, 136-139). Simone, who does not know Turkish, asks students to describe the animal (140-141) to make sure they understand the word. After the students demonstrate that they correctly interpreted the word meaning (line 142), she explicitly states what this animal is called in English (line 146).

(10) 122 Simone: (I just say) they are, there is a lot of wildlife on the
123 island, there are the fish and crabs, and birds, but we
124 also have a problem with skunks
125 (2)
126 Onur: A problem I- sorry, I could not hear you
127 Simone: A problem with skunks
128 Onur: hm
129 Princess: skunks?
130 Maria: *Kokaraca?*
131 Princess: *Kokaraca?*
132 Simone: is maybe how you say it in Turkish?
133 Princess: *kokara- Ahh kokarca*!
134 Maria: Umm! Ha hah hah
135 Simone: umm!! ((laughing)) [xx
136 Princess: [((in Turkish))!
137 Maria: ha.
138 Onur: ha hah. *kokarca*
139 Princess: *kokar ha. ca* ha hah
140 Simone: can you describe this animal to me? Do you know
141 anything about it?
142 Onur: it smells really bad [I don't know
143 Simone: [I see
144 Princess: [yeahh
145 Onur: [uh-huh
146 Simone: [In English, we call it a skunk

The following excerpt (ex. 11) exhibits how Princess initiates repair on the word "mosquitoes" (line 59). Princess and Onur collaborate on explaining the meaning of the problematic word to Simone (lines 62-64), who eventually conducts repair on this item (line 65).

(11) 57 Princess: We got a question emm- [about
58 Simone: [oh, okay
59 Princess: [mosque-[mosquits?
60 Maria: [okay
61 Simone: [mosquits?
62 Princess: mosquits

63 Onur: bugs
64 Princess: they are- it's very annoying
65 Simone: oh, you mean the mosquitoes?

Unlike Group 1, Group 2 did not initiate any repair leading to input/output modification or negotiation of meaning. To make sure students understood the vocabulary, park workers themselves initiated repair (see ex. 9, lines 13, 15) and scaffolded students' production of the new words. In example 11, Simone asks Group 2 which landmark students are going to explore next. Although the word "lighthouse" was introduced earlier in the task, students do not seem to remember the word (lines 43-47) and do not initiate repair on this item until Simone scaffolds their production of the word (lines 48, 51, 53, 56).

(11) 43 Miss Jane: where is Jack?=
44 Anna: light- light[x
45 Miss Jane [tree- tree [house?
46 Daniel: [the white great building
47 Anna: yeah, [(that building)
48 Simone: [the white great building, do you remember what it's
49 called?
50 Miss Jane: um
51 Simone: like a house, but a special kind of a house
52 Daniel: yeah
53 Simone: [do you know the word?
54 Anna: [xxxx
55 (1)
56 Simone: it starts with an L
57 Daniel: lighthouse [or xxxx
58 Simone: [that's right the lighthouse

The examples provided in this section demonstrate that the 3D VWs encouraged Group 1 to incorporate new words in their language production and to initiate repair on them, but Group 2 was not responsive to the environment mediation, so park workers initiated negotiation of meaning themselves.

Learner Autonomy and Task-Based Learning in 3D Virtual Worlds

The focus of this study is whether a problem-solving task with an environment exploration component facilitates learner autonomy in a 3D VW. Results show that although the 3D task mediated learner autonomy in Group 1, Group 2 was not responsive to this type of mediation. From a CA perspective, the sequential organization of the talk reflects participants' actions, or what they intend to accomplish through the talk (Seedhouse, 2004). The turn-taking organization of student-student and students-park worker interaction demonstrates that while both groups worked towards achieving the same goal of collecting information about the island's resources, they were engaged in different interactional activities. This suggests that the two groups interpreted the learning context and their learner roles differently. The students from Group 1 oriented towards a student-centered meaning-and-fluency context reflected in the turn-taking organization of their interaction, which took the shape of ordinary talk. Because in the meaning-and-fluency context learners control their interaction at both linguistic and interactional levels, this context fosters learner autonomy. Group 1 achieved learner autonomy by generating new topics, asking park workers questions about specific topics based on their observations in the environment, controlling the topics, and by initiating repair leading to negotiation of meaning and modification of input and learner output. Group 2, on the other hand, oriented towards a teacher-centered learning context as reflected in the teacher-initiated three-part question-answer-comment sequences. Since the teacher directs interaction in the teacher-centered context (McHoul, 1978), students' autonomous actions were restricted, and so learner autonomy was not achieved in Group 2.

The groups' interpretation of the learning context and their learner roles is also reflected in the turn-taking organization of the closing sequences of the students-park worker encounters. When Onur, a student from Group 1, finishes exploring the lighthouse, he asks Princess and Maria if they asked any questions (ex. 12, line 69). He states that he could not come up with any ideas (line 73), and Princess says that she could not either (line 74). Similarly, in example 13, Onur takes responsibility for not being able to think about another question to ask Gerri (line 51).

(12) 69 Onur: Did you ask some questions to Jack [except that
70 Maria: [no
71 Onur: Ah, okay, xxx
72 Princess: hey, I don't have any questions. I don't- I don't-
73 Onur: yeah, me too I could not come up with an idea
74 Princess: me too
(13) 51 Onur: Yes, I think that's all I can't think of another question
52 Gerri: [okay
53 Princess: [yes, me too

Group 2, on the other hand, puts the responsibility for providing information on the park workers. Jack's turn, "Any questions?" (ex. 14, lines 13), does not elicit any questions from students and is followed by Daniel's response "okay, thanks" (line 14). In line 15, Jack repeats his question (line 15). After a six-second pause (line 16), he again tries to elicit students' questions (line 17), but Anna responds negatively (line 18). Daniel also provides a negative response (line 19), followed by his counter question, "Is it all?" Daniel's question passes the responsibility for adding information to Jack. After a one-second pause (line 20), Jack first hesitates, and then instead of adding any information passes the initiative to ask questions back to the students by saying, "you can ask questions" (line 21). His response overlaps with Daniel's question, "any other information" (line 22), which passes the initiative back to Jack. After several turns of Jack and Daniel's efforts to push responsibility for requesting/supplying information to each other, Jack closes the interaction by saying "that's all that I have for now" (line 23).

(14) 13 Jack: [any questions?
14 Daniel: [okay, thanks
15 Jack: any other questions?
16 (6)
17 no?
18 Anna: no
19 Daniel: no, is it all?

20 (1)
21 Jack: Um- [you can ask questions
22 Daniel: [any other information?
23 Jack: that's all that I have for now

Example 15 is additional evidence of Group 2 holding park workers responsible for supplying information. After Gerri shares information about waterfalls, Daniel asks her, "Is that all?" (line 30). Gerri passes initiative back to the students (line 31), to which Daniel provides a closing statement (line 32).

(15) 28 Gerri: So that's wonderful!
29 (10)
30 Daniel: Is that all?
31 Gerri: that's it! Unless you have other ideas for the water
32 Daniel: okay, thank you!

Examples 12-15 demonstrate that Group 1 acted as autonomous learners by holding themselves responsible for obtaining information to complete the task (ex. 12, 13), whereas Group 2 did not do so and put this responsibility on the park workers (ex. 14, 15).

The results of the present study show that a 3D task with an environment exploration component mediated autonomy only in one of the two groups. This finding opens a discussion on why the two groups interpreted the learning context of the task and their learner roles differently. The following section provides several explanations of the results of this study.

DISCUSSION OF THE RESULTS

That individual learners or groups of learners interpret the task in their own ways is not uncommon. Studies on task-based learning report that learners' activity, or task-in-process, may differ from the task-as-workplan (e.g., Mori, 2002). Even when several groups of learners or several individual learners complete the same tasks, they may be engaged in different interactional activities (e.g., Coughlan & Duff, 1994; Foster, 1998; Roebuck, 2000). Ellis (2003) maintains that learners' activity is determined by their motives. Although exploring students' motives to act in certain ways was beyond the scope of the research project from which the above data was extracted, it is still possible to consider some of the reasons why the 3D task failed to mediate learner autonomy in Group 2—for example, by looking at each of the dimensions of autonomy as operationalized in this study in relation to the task instructions that students received.

Generating New Topics

Generating new topics was one of the ways for students to accomplish learner autonomy. Unlike Group 1, Group 2 did not generate any topics based on their observations. Although both groups were instructed to "explore the environment", they were not given specific instructions about whether they had to discuss their observations in their group. Lack of specific instruction about what exactly "explore the environment" involves could be what prevented Group 2 from generating and discussing topics.

Time could be another reason for Group 2 students not generating topics related to their observations. Since students had only 20 minutes to complete this task, talking to four park workers and exploring the environment may have seemed overwhelming, and in order to complete the task on time, students only talked to the park workers.

Eliciting Information and Controlling the Topics

Learners' ability to ask questions on specific topics and to control the topics was also considered as evidence of learner autonomy. In order to collect information about the island's resources, students were instructed to ask park workers questions. Such instructions leave room for interpretation of how to approach the task. Although Group 2 did not ask questions on specific topics, they still asked park workers general questions about how the landmarks could be used. Because students did not focus on specific topics, in order to keep interaction going and to provide learners with the information necessary for the task completion, park workers introduced topics themselves and scaffolded students' responses.

Student-Initiated Repair

Finally, learner autonomy was observed through learners' initiation of repair on incomprehensible input and on their own output. Group 2 did not initiate any repair leading to negotiation of meaning or modifying input and output. Foster (1998) highlights several reasons why students are reluctant to initiate repair on incomprehensible input: students may not initiate repair because it can slow down the task; or, learners are unwilling to be perceived as incompetent language users. Instead of initiating repair on a problematic item, students often pretend that they understand the message and wait for the next turn, hoping it will clarify what has not been understood. Lan et al. (2016) propose that students may not negotiate meaning because they treat task completion as a more important goal than the negotiation of meaning of lexical items.

Learner Autonomy and Task Outcome

Despite the fact that the task was designed to promote learner autonomy, the successful task outcome was measured not by students' autonomous actions in the environment exploration stage, but by their ability to present a survival plan. Thus, regardless of whether learner autonomy was achieved or not during that stage, students still could successfully achieve the task outcome.

Since learner autonomy plays an important role in language learning (Little, 2007; Littlewood, 1996), and 3D tasks with an environment exploration component have the potential to mediate learner autonomy, this raises a question of how 3D tasks could be designed to better mediate learner autonomy and provide learners with more effective learning experiences.

RECOMMENDATIONS

Several recommendations can be made to optimize the 3D task design so that the tasks with an environment exploration component could better mediate learner autonomy. Nunan (1997) argues that learner autonomy "is not an absolute concept" (p. 193), but can be developed with the help of learning materials designed to "encourage learners to develop autonomy" (p. 192). If the goal of an oral task is for students to develop fluency by engaging in autonomous learning, then learners can benefit from the following changes in the task design:

1. To promote learner autonomy, both reaching the task outcome (e.g., solving a problem) and students taking control of their learning as operationalized in the task (e.g., generating and controlling topics) should be considered as a successful task outcome.
2. For learners to benefit from the exploration stage, instructions should clearly communicate what exactly the task involves. Since 3D VWs can feature vast territories, instructions should specify which of the locations should be explored (e.g., the lake and the waterfalls); what needs to be observed at those locations and discussed in groups (e.g., whether the water is fresh and clean); and what else students would like to know that cannot be observed, e.g., whether there is fish in the lake. Such instructions will focus learners' attention on specific locations while providing them with the opportunity to brainstorm various topics and share their observations. The idea of sharing observations with group members is supported by Lan et al.'s (2016) research in that the tasks which require learners to pay attention to specific cues in the environment encourage them to incorporate their observations in their language production.
3. If learners are to interact with player avatars, both learners and the player avatars should be instructed to act in certain ways. For example, learners can ask only questions related to their observations, whereas player avatars can provide only requested information so that learners must communicate to complete the task.
4. To encourage students' vocabulary learning, students should be instructed to negotiate the meaning of unknown words. This will draw learners' attention to language input and prevent them from feeling intimidated by not knowing the vocabulary.

LIMITATIONS OF THE STUDY

The results of this study should be understood in the context that the data presented above is part of a larger project. Although the specific task was designed to promote learner autonomy, the goal of the project was different. Because the project did not aim to study learner autonomy, participants were not interviewed about the reasons for their approach to task completion. Other limitations are the small number of participants and that the study focused only on one task.

FUTURE RESEARCH DIRECTIONS

Although research on language learning in 3D VWs maintains that these immersive environments are facilitative to autonomous learning (Dalton, 2016; Deutschmann et al., 2009; Lan et al., 2016; Schwienhorst, 1998), this study shows that the 3D environment alone does not mediate autonomy in all learners. More research is needed to better explore why some learners are more responsive to mediation by these artifacts than the other learners, and how tasks could be designed to better facilitate autonomous learning. As shown in this study, the clarity of task instructions may also affect learner autonomy; examining the effect of task instructions on learners' interpretation of the task may help practitioners to develop teaching materials that foster autonomous learning.

The results of this study are based on the work of six participants completing only one task. Engaging more learners and using a variety of task types could shed more light on the interplay of the 3D tasks and learner autonomy.

Learner autonomy can take various shapes depending on the affordances available in a 3D environment. Collentine (2011), who examines learner autonomy in the context of text-based interaction, operationalizes autonomy as learners' choices of and decisions about which objects in the environment they interact with. She measures autonomy by how much text-based input learners decide to process and how often they re-read the messages. In the present study, where learners used a voice-based channel to interact with each other and the player avatars, autonomy was measured by learners' ability to generate and control topics, as well as to initiate repair. Since different affordances of the 3D environments provide learners with different learning experiences, it is worth exploring the ways in which autonomy can be accomplished and promoted in other 3D contexts.

CONCLUSION

In closing, the findings of the present study show that language-learning tasks with an environment exploration component have some potential to mediate autonomous learning in 3D worlds, but not all learners will be responsive to this type of mediation. Since learners may interpret a task in various ways, this chapter offers suggestions for how task design in 3D virtual worlds can be improved to better assist students in developing learner autonomy. This study focuses on teaching language in 3D VWs, but other disciplines can also benefit from this research; for example, 3D VWs can be used for teaching different subjects, such as history by having students explore excavation sites in 3D worlds. Students can benefit from the environment exploration component by generating new ideas to solve problems or make decisions, as well as by negotiating meaning of terms and concepts. Task-based learning in 3D VWs may contribute to the long-term educational goal of preparing students to become independent learners beyond the classroom context, as 3D worlds immerse learners in contexts and activities similar to those that they are likely to experience in real life.

REFERENCES

Benson, P. (2016). *Bibliography on autonomy in language learning.* Retrieved from https://dl.dropboxusercontent.com/u/61188845/Autonomy%20bibliography.pdf

Breen, M. (1989). The evaluation cycle for language learning tasks. In B. K. Johnson (Ed.), *The second language curriculum* (pp. 187–206). Cambridge, UK: Cambridge University Press. doi:10.1017/CBO9781139524520.014

Collentine, K. (2011). Learner autonomy in a task-based 3D world and production. *Language Learning & Technology, 15*(3), 50–67.

Cornille, F., Thorne, S. L., & Desmet, P. (2012). Digital games for language learning: From hype to insight? *ReCALL*, *23*(3), 243–356.

Cotterall, S. (1995). Readiness for autonomy: Investigating learner beliefs. *System*, *23*(2), 195–205. doi:10.1016/0346-251X(95)00008-8

Coughlan, P., & Duff, P. (1994). Same task, different activities: Analysis of SLA task from an activity theory perspective. In J. P. Lantolf & G. Appel (Eds.), *Vygotskian approaches to second language research* (pp. 173–193). Norwood, NJ: Ablex.

Dalton, G., & Devitt, A. (2016). Irish in a 3D world: Engaging primary school children. *Language Learning & Technology*, *20*(1), 21–33.

Darasawang, P., & Reinders, H. (2010). Encouraging autonomy with an online language support system. *CALL-EJ Online*, *11*(2), 1–9.

Deutschmann, M., Panichi, L., & Molka-Danielsen, J. (2009). Designing oral participation in Second Life: A comparative study of two language proficiency courses. *ReCALL*, *21*(2), 206–226. doi:10.1017/S0958344009000196

Ellis, R. (2003). *Task-based language learning and teaching*. Oxford, UK: Oxford University Press.

Foster, P. (1998). A classroom perspective on the negotiation of meaning. *Applied Linguistics*, *19*(1), 1–23. doi:10.1093/applin/19.1.1

Garcia, A. C. (2013). *An introduction to interaction: Understanding talk in formal and informal settings*. New York, NY: Bloomsbury Academic.

Gerhard, M., Moore, D., & Hobbs, D. (2004). Embodiment and copresence in collaborative interfaces. *Human-Computer Studies*, *61*(4), 453–480. doi:10.1016/j.ijhcs.2003.12.014

Heritage, J. (1984). *Garfinkel and Ethnomethodology*. Cambridge, UK: Polity Press.

Jefferson, G. (1984). Transcript notation. In J. M. Atkinson & J. Heritage (Eds.), *Structures of social action: Studies in conversation analysis* (pp. ix–xvi). Cambridge, UK: Cambridge University Press.

Kozlova, I. (2013). Online pedagogy: Development of the communicative skills in Russian online courses. *OLBI Working Papers, 5,* 57-70.

Kozlova, I., & Priven, D. (2015). ESL teacher training in 3D virtual worlds. *Language Learning & Technology*, *19*(1), 83–101.

Lan, Y. J., Kan, Y. H., Sung, Y. T., & Chung, K. E. (2016). Oral performance language tasks for CSL beginners in Second Life. *Language Learning & Technology*, *20*(3), 60–79.

Lantolf, J. P. (2000). Second language learning as a mediated process. *Language Teaching*, *33*(2), 79–96. doi:10.1017/S0261444800015329

Lantolf, J. P. (2013). Sociocultural Theory and the dialectics of L2 learner autonomy/agency. In P. Benson & L. Cooker (Eds.), *The applied linguistics individual: Sociocultural approaches to identity, agency and autonomy* (pp. 17–31). Bristol, CT: Equinos Publishing.

Lin, T., Wang, S., Grant, S., Chien, C., & Lan, Y. (2014). Task-based teaching approaches of Chinese as a foreign language in Second Life through teachers' perspectives. *Procedia Technology*, *13*, 16–22. doi:10.1016/j.protcy.2014.02.004

Little, D. (2007). Language learner autonomy: Some fundamental considerations revisited. *Innovation in Language Learning and Teaching*, *1*(1), 14–29. doi:10.2167/illt040.0

Littlewood, W. (1996). "Autonomy": An anatomy and a framework. *System*, *24*(4), 427–435. doi:10.1016/S0346-251X(96)00039-5

Mori, J. (2002). Task design, plan, and development of talk-in-interaction: An analysis of a small group activity in a Japanese language classroom. *Applied Linguistics*, *23*(3), 323–347. doi:10.1093/applin/23.3.323

Nunan, D. (1997). Designing and adapting materials to encourage learner autonomy. In P. Benson & P. Voller (Eds.), *Autonomy and independence in language learning* (pp. 192–203). London, UK: Longman.

Panichi, L., & Deutschmann, M. (2012). Language learning in virtual worlds: Research issues and methods. In M. Dooly & R. O'Dowd (Eds.), *Researching online foreign language interaction and exchange: Theories, methods and challenges* (pp. 205–231). Bern, Switzerland: Peter Lang.

Peterson, M. (2011). Towards a research agenda for the use of three-dimensional virtual worlds in language learning. *CALICO Journal*, *29*(1), 67–80. doi:10.11139/cj.29.1.67-80

Pica, T., Kanagy, R., & Falodun, J. (1993). Choosing and using communication tasks for second language instruction and research. In C. G. Crookes & S. M. Gass (Eds.), *Tasks and language learning: Integrating theory and practice* (pp. 9–34). Bristol, UK: Multilingual Matters.

Roebuck, R. (2000). Subjects speak out: How learners position themselves in psycholinguistic task. In J. P. Lantolf (Ed.), *Sociocultural theory and second language learning* (pp. 79–95). Oxford, UK: Oxford University Press.

Schroeder, R. (2002). Social interaction in virtual environments: Key issues, common themes, and a framework for research. In R. Schroeder (Ed.), *The social life of avatars: Presence and interaction in shared virtual environments* (pp. 1–18). London, UK: Springer-Verlag. doi:10.1007/978-1-4471-0277-9_1

Schwienhorst, K. (1998). The "third place": Virtual reality applications for second language learning. *ReCALL*, *10*(01), 118–126. doi:10.1017/S095834400000433X

Schwienhorst, K. (2003). Learner autonomy and tandem learning: Putting principles into practice in synchronous and asynchronous telecommunications environment. *Computer Assisted Language Learning*, *16*(5), 427–443. doi:10.1076/call.16.5.427.29484

Seedhouse, P. (2004). The interactional architecture of the language classroom: A Conversation Analysis perspective. *Language Learning Monograph Series*, *54*(S1).

Smith, K., & Craig, H. (2013). Enhancing the autonomous use of CALL: A new curriculum model in EFL. *CALICO Journal*, *30*(2), 252–278. doi:10.11139/cj.30.2.252-278 ten Have, P. (2007). *Doing conversation analysis: A practical guide* (2nd ed.). Thousand Oaks, CA: SAGE. doi:10.4135/9781849208895

Vanijdee, A. (2003). Thai distance English learners and learner autonomy. *Open Learning*, *18*(1), 75–84. doi:10.1080/02680510320000054130

Vygotsky, L. (1978). *Mind in society: The development of higher psychological processes*. Cambridge, MA: Harvard University Press.

KEY TERMS AND DEFINITIONS

Language Learner Autonomy: Learner responsibility for using language, choosing grammar and vocabulary, and making sure that they understand the input they receive.

Language-Learning Task: A goal-oriented learner-centered collaborative learning activity that involves using language in the classroom like it is used in the real-life context. While primary targeting learner ability to convey meanings, tasks may have a hidden focus on grammar that learners master when working on the task.

Mediation: A form of regulation of the learning processes. Within sociocultural theory, mediation of the learning processes occurs when learners interact with other members of the culture, with the objects created by the culture, and with themselves as they try to regulate their learning by imitating the models provided by more experienced interlocutors.

Negotiation of Meaning: Learner collaboration when trying to resolve issues during interaction that may lead to communication breakdowns or when the communication breakdown has already occurred.

APPENDIX

[yes Square brackets indicate the onset of overlapping utterances
(we have a question) Utterances in parentheses indicate transcriber's best guess
((runs to the lake)) Utterances in double parentheses indicate transcriber's comments
>>annoying<< Utterances in double "more than" and "less than" signs indicate that the they are pronounced quieter than the surrounding talk
xxx Signs of x's are used to indicate unintelligible utterances. Each "x" corresponds to one audible syllable
all water- dash indicates an interrupted utterance
(4) A four-second pause
(.) A pause shorter than one second
probably= =equal signs indicate latching utterances
=I saw them too
kokarca a foreign word

Chapter 4
Contextualizing Language Learning With Street View Panoramas

Ya-Chun Shih
National Dong Hwa University, Taiwan

ABSTRACT

The latest street view technology enables language learners to look around and navigate interactively from remote worldwide locations via the internet. In addition to the enhanced feeling of immersion, the realistic scenes in a street view panorama help to represent the real world and make language learning more engaging and meaningful. This chapter explores the potential for extending a virtual English as a foreign language classroom with online street view panoramas. The program aims to create an immersive environment within which students complete a task-based learning activity; the task design is based on Schank's (1996) goal-based scenarios. The results reveal that street view technologies hold great potential to enhance language learners' communicative competence. Future research is needed to look into learners' experience in this new learning environment and to examine the use of street view panoramas in other disciplines.

INTRODUCTION

Contextualizing learning reflects the belief that allowing language learners to use language appropriately in context is the best practice to engage language learners. It has been suggested that "appropriate language use is learned through context" (Opp-Beckman & Klinghammer, 2006a, p. 8). Language is best learned in an authentic context since learning is situated in the context, activities and culture (Lave, 1988). Additionally, Brown, Collins and Duguid (1989) argued that "situated cognition," a theory that suggests that knowledge construction, which is situated in context, is critical for learning. They also emphasized one important constituent aspect, "cognitive apprenticeship," whereby learners are stimulated and guided to acquire and employ cognitive tools and participate actively in authentic activities and situations bound to sociocultural and physical contexts. The role of situated cognition has been applied and emphasized

DOI: 10.4018/978-1-5225-3719-9.ch004

in the context of language and learning. For instance, Gee (2004) indicates researchers involved with situated cognition research generally hold the view that "language is tied to *people's experiences of situated action in the material and social world*" (p. 44). Accordingly, learning in context makes language learning and use more "situated" by linking language activities and instruction to authentic material and social contexts. This helps activate students' prior knowledge and experiences, and strengthens their ability to use language appropriately, according to the context.

Success in learning English as a foreign language (EFL) seems to be closely connected with authentic and practical use of English in real-life contexts. The lack of real-life contexts of using the target language leads to less situated and meaningful language learning in many EFL settings. Contexts provided by virtual environments create wide-ranging possibilities for both situated and meaningful language learning. Meaningful learning has five defining characteristics: *active, constructive, intentional, authentic*, and *cooperative* (Howland, Jonassen, & Marra, 2011; Jonassen, 1995). The contextual affordances of new technologies, e.g., avatar-based virtual worlds, give learners opportunities "to engage in goal-driven activity, authentic interactions, and collaborative problem-solving" ("Situated Cognition," 2015, "Perceiving and acting in avatar-based virtual worlds," para. 2). The context of virtual environments holds tremendous promise in terms of engaging learners in contextualized and meaningful language learning.

The incorporation of Google Street View (Google, 2007; Microsoft, 2009), which provides numerous vivid street-level panoramic views on a global scale into virtual environments, may be regarded as a response to the need for real-life contexts for meaningful language learning. Street View therefore supports the potential of educational technology to facilitate language learning and instruction in the context of situated recognition, and is particularly useful for providing language learners with authentic contexts and real-life situations within which language learning and use can take place. Furthermore, to maximize active, intentional and cooperative construction of knowledge and authenticity in language learning, we adopted the latest street view panorama technology with 3D avatars, which enables language learners to be immersed in a virtual environment comprised of realistic street views. Learners have the freedom to navigate this virtual environment by controlling their animated avatars. At the same time, they interact authentically and accomplish goal-oriented tasks collaboratively with other learners by employing text/voice chat. Both Street View technology, incorporating a large number of 360° street-level images, and panorama technology that allows users to view a given scene from arbitrary viewing angles, provide considerable potential for contextualizing meaningful language learning.

Despite the considerable potential, the incorporation of street view panorama technologies is only a preliminary step toward making language learning contextualized and meaningful. Researchers (e.g., Montoro & Hampel, 2011) also emphasize the paramount importance of task design. Therefore, we designed goal-based activities to engage learners in meaningful language learning. These activities encourage them to discover new ideas and solve problems, as well as interact and cooperate with their partners as they navigate the street view panoramas. This allows language learners to be exposed to and participate in situated real world landscapes representing the physical architecture, as well as the intangible atmosphere, of the target language and culture. The incorporation of street view panoramas, virtual environments, 3D avatars and goal-based tasks was intended to engage learners in the meaningful practice of language learning in contexts. While street view panorama technologies and goal-based learning tasks hold great potential to help achieve contextualized and meaningful language learning in theory, it is still unclear how this combination of technologies and pedagogical models would serve to involve students in English language use within the "real-world contexts" in practice. The main purpose of this chapter, therefore, is to demonstrate the systematic and curriculum implementation of the proposed system for contextualized and meaningful language learning in an EFL setting.

BACKGROUND

Contextualized language learning provides an overarching theme for this chapter. A range of concepts and ideas, namely, uses of authentic contexts and materials, virtual environments, and Google Maps/Earth/Street View, are closely related to contextualized language learning, a central element of all practices in this study.

Use of Authentic Contexts and Materials

Language learning in context as a pedagogical technique has been examined by previous researchers in the past 20 years. *Contextualization* has been explained as "meaningful language use for communicative purposes within a given situation or context. It helps students understand how language users construct language in a given context" (Opp-Beckman & Klinghammer, 2006b, p. 13). Shrum and Glisan (2004) refer to *contextualized language* as "language that is introduced and taught in context present[ing] real situations that encompass all aspects of a conversational exchange: the physical setting, the purpose of the exchange, the roles of the participants, the socially acceptable norms of interaction, in addition to the medium, topic, tone and register of the exchange" (p. 1). *Contextualized teaching and learning* is identified as a "concept of teaching and learning that helps teachers relate subject matter content to real world situations" (Berns & Erickson, 2001, p. 2). The *techniques* for contextualizing language learning or instruction in the classroom include the use of authentic materials and realia (Opp-Beckman & Klinghammer, 2006b, p. 18) through "working with real or simulated situations" and "paying attention to the physical setting of exchange" (p. 13). *Authentic materials*, also known as realia, can be described as anything "created with some real-life goal for, generally, native speakers" (Polio, 2014, p. 1). Authentic materials or realia lend virtual worlds "a level of authenticity with a real world place [which] may be required to give other students a sense of immersion" (Molka-Danielsen, Deutschmann & Panichi, 2009, p. 31).

The use of authentic contexts (e.g., street-view and authentic use of language) and authentic materials (e.g., advertisements and maps) serves as an approach to immersing language learners and contextualizing language learning. The combination of these two techniques (e.g., authentic use of language in context and use of authentic materials) has been suggested as a way of teaching target language in context using authentic materials, i.e., real-world objects ("Realia and Contextualization," n.d.), taken from a particular context to make language learning more meaningful.

Virtual Environments for Language Learning

Virtual environments pave the way for synthetic rendering and intuitive interaction and show growing potential for education, particularly in the context of language learning. Virtual environments (VEs) depict "a computer generated display that allows or compels the user (or users) to have a sense of being present in an environment other than the one they are actually in, and to interact with that environment"

(Schroeder, 1996, p. 25). Users can explore the environments by controlling their preferable 3D graphical representation, termed avatars, and also interact with other avatars. As a subset of VEs, multi-user virtual environments (MUVEs), e.g., Second Life and Active Worlds, have been proposed and implemented for language learning (Stockwell & Tanaka-Ellis, 2012, pp. 79-80). Research has been conducted to look into possible effects of exposure to MUVEs on language learning and related issues (e.g., Deutschmann & Steinvall, 2012; Lan, 2015; Peterson, 2010; Sve nsson, 2003; Toyoda & Harrison, 2002). One of the leading researchers in the field is Mats Deutschmann at Örebro University, Sweden, whose research has been focused on how VEs (e.g., MUVEs) can be used to engage language learners in contextualized and authentic learning contexts. Deutschmann and his colleagues employed Second Life to teach sociolinguistics aiming to promote greater gender awareness (Deutschmann & Steinvall, 2012), and he formulated a communicative model for designing language learning tasks within the framework of Access to Virtual and Action Learning live Online (Deutschmann & Panichi, 2013). Moreover, Molka-Danielsen, Deutschmann and Panichi's (2009) study on the Kamimo Islands project in Second Life examined the effect of "transient learning spaces" on supporting students' language learning in different phases of the learning process; several similar studies were conducted aiming to promote students' overall oral competence (Deutschmann et al., 2009) and linguistic behaviors, including the changes in floor space, turn-taking patterns, and supportive moves (Deutschmann & Panichi, 2009).

Other notable examples concerning virtual environments for language learning include the following. Wang, Calandra, Hibbard and Lefaiver (2012) incorporated Second Life into the teaching of English as a foreign language (EFL) and found that the virtual environment can effectively link universities and students across temporal, spatial, and cultural barriers. Similarly, Garrido-Inigo and Rodriguez-Moreno (2015) utilized the OpenSim platform as a tool for teaching French to tourism students at a university, including promotion of learners' reading, listening comprehension, and writing skills. Their development of the virtual environment in conjunction with appropriate instructional strategies led to a positive outcome in terms of the language acquisition process. In addition, Shih and Yang (2008) constructed a Virtual English Classroom, known as VEC3D, for online interactive language learning, particularly aimed at developing communicative competence. Along the same vein, Kim et al. (2009) designed a game-based simulation and tutoring system named BiLAT for practicing negotiation by relying on users' awareness of an Arab cultural context. Previous research has shown that virtual environments incorporating 3D avatars have the potential to engage learners in a variety of language learning settings, but the incorporation of street view into virtual environments is still in its infancy.

Educational Use of Google Maps, Google Earth and Google Street View

As stated on the Google Maps (n.d.), "The possibilities of using Google Maps, Earth and Street View are as endless as your imagination." A few studies have been conducted on the use of Google Maps and Google Earth in educational settings. Patterson (2007) used Google Earth to teach fundamental geographic and technological concepts, and indicated that Google Earth has great potential to help students to develop critical thinking, analytical, and inquiry skills. Chinnery (2008) coined the term "Google-Assisted Language Learning" and proposed the possibilities of using Google Maps and Google Earth both for language learning (e.g., using these technologies as discussion prompts) and for general pedagogical purposes. In contrast to Google Earth, which offers satellite imagery with a bird's-eye view, Google Street View (Google, 2007) is an online service that provides users with a street level view and 360° real-life imagery of popular worldwide locations. Similarly, Microsoft Bing Map Streetside (Microsoft, 2009) is another online service that offers a true-to-life view for users to explore, allowing them to familiarize themselves with local hotspots and destinations. Both the Google Street View and Microsoft Streetside systems offer users the option to zoom in and out to move closer to or further away from buildings or monuments, as if they are physically present at locations. The street-view panorama's inherent features of immersion and contextualization constitute opportunities for language learning. For instance, the language school known as Avatar Languages (2011) offers online lessons with Second Life, Skype and Google Docs, and the school's official website specifically points to the idea of promoting language learning using Google Street View: "Street View has the qualities of being both immersive and very useful…so it is easily incorporated into real-life activities that offer language learning opportunities" (para. 3-4).

Notwithstanding the immersive opportunities available through Google Street View, the platform on its own lacks the ability to give users the feeling of "being there" and to interact socially since it does not feature avatars (Victors, 2009), such as those found in Second Life (2003) and other 3D virtual environments. This makes it impossible to meet and interact with anyone in Google Street View. In contrast, Blue Mars (Avatar Reality, 2010) is a commercial platform with client-server architecture that offers a massively multiplayer online (MMO) virtual world consisting of an expanding set of independent user-operated cities with avatars. As an offshoot, Blue Mars Lite is a stand-alone client which integrates Google Street View into a virtual world to enable users to participate in various real-life settings. The availability of virtual 3D avatars provides the feeling of "being there" and enhances social interaction for users. Shih (2015) explored the possibilities of using Blue Mars Lite for language and culture learning. The results of the qualitative case study reveal that participants' culture learning of cultural knowledge and attitudes was promoted. However, since Blue Mars Lite is not specifically tailored for language learning in particular, it lacks the flexibility and adaptability required to support language learners. Thus, we need to create an innovative new system to allow more flexibility and provide additional possibilities for language learning.

SYSTEMATIC IMPLEMENTATION

The Virtual English Classroom 3D (VEC3D) is an online language learning system in which learners can interact with instructors and other learners through avatars in a virtual environment (Shih & Yang, 2008). VEC3D provides language learners with the interactive functions of text messages, voice chat, and real-time facial images. As an extension, we incorporated Google Street View with VEC3D to render the online world in the form of a global street view panorama wherein virtual objects are combined with real scenes. Google Maps with Street View provides 360° street-level imagery of popular locations worldwide, allowing virtual access to location-specific settings for language learning. Using virtual avatars in conjunction with real street views, language learners can explore real street-view scenes and interact with virtual objects or other avatars.

The implementation of the proposed language learning system with street view can be broken down into three steps. First, the Google Street View Image API provides functions to acquire static street view images through a standard HTTP request. A street view image can be specified by reference to several request parameters: the *size* parameter represents the output size of the acquired image in pixels; the *location* parameter contains either a text description string or a latitude/longitude value of the place of interest; the *heading* parameter indicates the horizontal viewing angle (i.e., the compass heading of the camera); the *pitch* parameter provides the vertical viewing angle (i.e., the up/down tilt of the camera relative to the horizon); and the *fov* parameter determines the horizontal field of view of the acquired image. With a smaller *fov*, images with a higher level of zoom can be acquired.

Second, the acquired images are stitched together according to their three-dimensional rotational angles corresponding to heading and pitch. An image mosaicking process can be applied to model a panorama in two ways. In one, a cylindrical panorama is constructed by projecting the acquired images onto the lateral surface of a cylinder. As shown in Figure 1(a), a cylindrical panorama provides a horizontal field of view of up to 360°. However, the vertical field of view is centered at the horizon with a practical limit of approximately 120°; hence, the ground and the sky cannot be shown. Alternatively, a spherical panorama is constructed by projecting the acquired images on the surface of a sphere. The field of view of a spherical panorama is three-dimensional (i.e., 360° horizontally and 180° vertically). The inherent problem with a spherical panorama is its geometric distortion, which can be corrected through a process of image warping.

Third, avatars are rendered and animated on a separate image layer, which differs from the image layer of the street views. Two image layers are then combined through an image blending process that involves aligning and placing the avatar layer in front of the street view layer (as shown in Figure. 1(b)). As part of the login process, users can select their representative avatars used for participating in the learning activities. Avatars can be dynamically rendered with four common actions (idle, walk, run, and wave) and one specific action (e.g., humans can jump, birdmen can fly, and mermaids can swim). Language learners can interact with each other through avatar actions, overhead text messages, and live voice chat. The rendering and animating functions of avatars imbue learners with the feeling that they somehow exist, albeit virtually, and enrich their immersive experience.

Finally, users are able to interact with street view images through a variety of controls. A *pan* control allows users to rotate the panorama images in three dimensions as if the avatar was spinning around (i.e., pivoting) at a location. A *zoom* control provides the ability to zoom in and out within the panorama images as if the avatar was moving backward and forward. A *link* control offers guide arrows on the screen for traveling to adjacent panorama images as if the avatar was walking or running to a neighboring spot. Because the photos in Google Street View are captured by a camera installed on a Google car, the routes along which users can move along the street are pre-set. The guide arrows show the directions in which users can move to neighboring spots where they can also spin around using the pan control. The combination of street view panoramas and VEC3D provides language learners with the ability to interact with each other using virtual avatars in a realistic street view panorama. The feeling of realism for language learners can be substantially enhanced when their animated avatars are surrounded by the street view panorama as the backdrop for the target language.

The wealth of availability of street view panoramas allows language learners to visit real-life sites around the world. A wide variety of 3D avatars with multiple user-controllable animation further enhances the feeling of realism. Used in conjunction with these technologies, the goal-based learning activities encourage language learners to freely explore realistic 3D places using the pan, zoom, and link controls. Multimodal communication between language learners is realized through real-time text chat, voice chat, and real-time facial images. As shown in Figure 2, the proposed system enriches the level of learner interactivity and helps to make language learning more immersive and meaningful.

Figure 1. Panorama construction and rendering of the Old Pack Horse restaurant in England by acquiring and stitching together Google Street View images. (a) 360° view of a cylindrical projection; (b) a perspective view in a spherical projection with two animated avatars

Figure 2. Different levels of interactivity (a) real-time communication through text/voice chat; (b) various avatars and real-time facial images; (c) various avatars with distinct animations (close-up views); (d)~(f) a scene with multiple perspectives achieved through pan control

THEORETICAL UNDERPINNINGS OF CONTEXTUALIZED CURRICULUM

Contextualized language learning requires the creation of contextualized tasks. A contextualized ESL (English as a Second Language) or ESOL (English for Speakers of Other Languages) curriculum is one that adopts "authentic materials, phrases and lexical items taken from a particular context" (Rymniak, 2011, p. 3-1), and "helps students learn language skills by teaching the skills using the authentic contexts in which students must use those skills in the real world" (Utech, 2008, p. 7). We selected and adapted authentic materials (e.g., advertisements and maps) for students to use as a way of exposing them to authentic contexts (i.e., Street View) in order to teach language skills, encourage communication, and motivate language learners. Within the framework of authentic materials and contexts provided by Street View panoramas, multiple language learners can freely explore, discuss, role-play, navigate, and interact with each other through their animated avatars and by using text/voice chat. The contextualized curriculum design process of this study is driven by three theoretical underpinnings: meaningful learning, the communicative approach, and Schank's goal-based scenarios (GBS) (1996).

Firstly, according to Jonassen (1995) and Howland et al. (2011), meaningful learning has five characteristics, namely, *active*, *constructive*, *intentional*, *authentic*, and *cooperative*. It is essential to consider these aspects when creating language learning activities for use within the framework of Street View panoramas to ensure that the former is pedagogically sound and will be beneficial to meaningful language learning. To address this concern, this study created activities designed to elicit learners' *active* participation, help learners *construct* their own knowledge, reinforce their learning *intentions*, and involve them in *authentic* contexts/materials and *cooperative* learning. In this study, teachers function more as guides and facilitators in the language learning process, rather than as imparters of knowledge or testers of learning, so as to empower language learners to engage in self-directed language learning. The goal is to let language learners solve problems by using a hands-on approach, making their own inferences and discoveries, and drawing their own conclusions.

Secondly, the communicative approach is also commonly known as communicative language teaching (CLT). The aim of CLT is to engage learners in language use and develop their communicative competence in authentic contexts, specifically in terms of the authentic use of language in real-life contexts for meaningful purposes (Savignon, 1997, 2001). Communicative competence refers to the ability to realize messages, understand the social contexts of language use, apply the grammatical rules, and use communication strategies to avoid communication breakdowns (Savignon, 1997). CLT has been described as "teaching practice that helps students develop their communicative competence in authentic context (which) is deemed an acceptable and beneficial form of instruction" ("Communicative Language Teaching," 2015, "Outline," para. 2), when such methods are employed to promote EFL learners' language use in authentic contexts (Littlewood, 2007) and communicative competence in real contexts (Larsen-Freeman, 2000). With the help of CLT teaching practice and task design, the proposed system allows real-life and learning-by-interacting simulations to engage students in both linguistic context (i.e., written/voice chat and real communication) and social or situational context (i.e., simulating real-life situations to necessitate real communication) as they interact with other people. With regard to its pedagogical implementation and curricular integration, instructors may incorporate the proposed system and tasks in their classrooms to simulate real-life situations and stimulate real conversations. By relying on these defining characteristics of the CLT approach, instructors can help learners develop their communicative competence. Additionally, the tasks in this study were designed according to CLT, particularly in terms of the types of activities assigned (e.g., describing a destination, requesting location information) and the use of instructional materials, which serve the role of enhancing communicative language use, and can be categorized into three types: text-based materials, task-based materials and realia (Ludescher, 2006). In this study, the *text-based materials* (e.g., mission descriptions, see Table 1) and *task-based materials* (e.g., map tasks, jigsaw type tasks, and conveying different information for different roles, see Table 1) were developed to support CLT. *Realia* that represent teaching with "authentic" and "from-life" materials consist of "language-based realia, such as signs, magazines, advertisements, and newspapers, or graphic and visual sources around which communicative activities can be built, such as maps, pictures, symbols, graphs, and charts" (Ludescher, 2006, Realia, para. 1). Both language-based realia (e.g., signs and advertisements in the Street View) and visuals (e.g., maps and Street View images) were used in this study to support task-based and goal-driven language learning employing a communicative approach.

Thirdly, the curriculum shares many features with Schank's (1996) goal-based scenarios (GBSs). GBSs constitute goal-driven learning-by-doing simulations in which learners meet goals by using target skills and related content. Such scenarios embody the principles of meaningful learning, and "stay in the tradition of situated learning approaches like cognitive apprenticeship" (Zumbach & Reimann, 1999, p. 3), in particular, when it comes to designing tasks and situating language learning in contexts to promote transfer to real-life situations. According to Schank and Cleary (1995), an instructional designer should go through six steps when creating a GBS (see Figure 3): Step 1: Identifying a set of target skills; Step 2: Developing missions which require the target skills; Step 3: Choosing a focus; Step 4: Creating a cover story which envelops the mission; Step 5: Planning the operations, and Step 6: Building learning environments to support the target skills.

Figure 3. Six sequential components of a GBS (Partly adapted from Schank & Cleary, 1995)

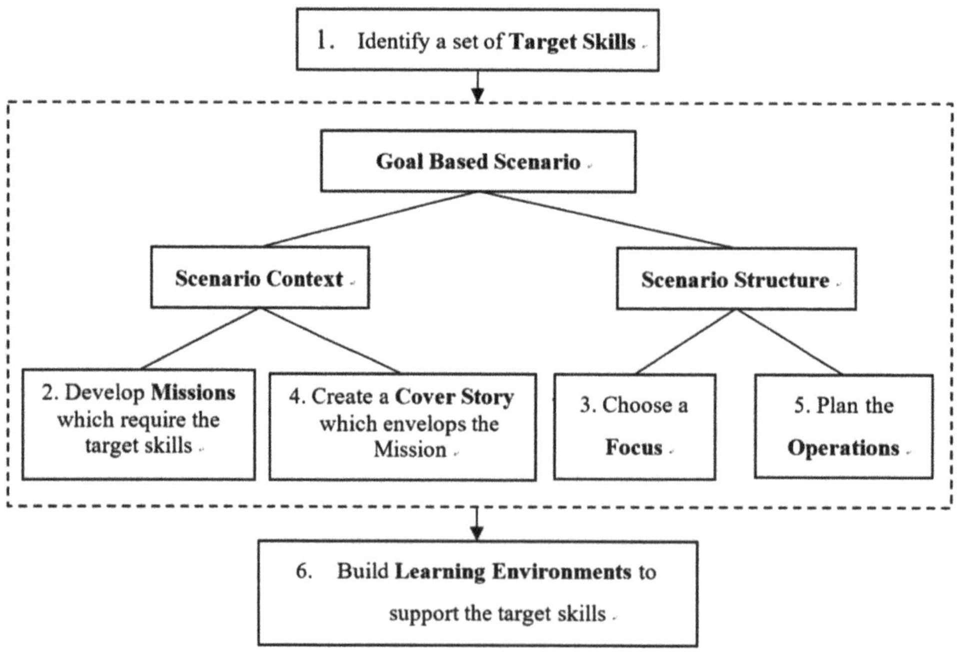

Task Design

Language learners, confronted with problems or questions, participate and role-play in simulated events in an authentic context provided by the Street View panorama to complete the goal-based tasks. We have designed a variety of language learning activities that add communicative and contextualized components to meaningful learning and goal-based tasks, such as a map task, virtual tour guide role play, a virtual field trip, home town introductions, and hotspot exploration, all of which allow for highly contextualized and communicative language use to occur in authentic contexts. Two of these tasks are described in Table 1. The students were grouped in pairs to accomplish tasks in a timely manner. Both the map view and the Street View were used for more authentic experiences.

The first mission of the GBS was entitled "Where am I in London Olympic Park?" It involved participants' role playing as leaders (Role A), choosing a favorite building in London Olympic Park (such as the Olympic Stadium, Aquatics Center, Orbit Tower, or Velodrome), searching for related information via the Internet, and locating themselves in the street view around or inside the building. Subsequently, leaders were asked to describe what they saw (e.g., the neighborhood, landscaping, spatial relationships, or architectural styles) using the target language, as wells as what was happening (e.g., a game, a show, or a parade taking place) in the zoomed-in street view as a means of giving hints to their partners that would allow them to guess the destination. Their partners (Role B) were also able to access online resources for their reference. Leaders answered their partner's questions for purposes of clarification (as shown in Figure 4).

Figure 4. Olympic Stadium in London

The second mission of the GBS was entitled “Getting Lost in New York City.” The cover story of this GBS was that the leader’s partner was lost in New York City. Only the leader (Role A) had a map containing locations of both group members. The leaders attempted to provide their partners (Role B) with directions through voice chat in the target language to help their partners to find the leaders (e.g., moving from the Empire State Building to Macy’s Department Store). Partners were able to report what they saw in the Street View and provide responses to the leader. Leaders had to guide their partners according to a map (e.g., “turn right at the next crossroads”) and include visual descriptions of what their partners would be seeing in the street views (e.g., “turn left after the big green building”). These activities expanded the act of giving directions beyond providing simple instructions into a plethora of more descriptive, immersive, contextualized, and interactive practices (as shown in Figure 5).

IMPLEMENTATION CONSIDERATIONS

Benefits and Challenges

We explored student and teacher perspectives regarding their experiences with the program. Their comments in discussions revealed their opinions concerning the classroom challenges and benefits associated with street view technology. For students, a common challenge was to familiarize themselves with the novel interface to manipulate street view panoramas. Additionally, although the proposed system is not

Figure 5. Times Square in New York City

Table 1. Detailed information about two goal-based scenarios

Mission	London Olympic Park	Getting Lost in New York City
Cover Story	Select your favorite building in London Olympic Park. Locate yourself in the street view around the building. Describe what you see using voice chat so your partner can try to guess where you are.	Your partner gets lost in NY city. Only you have a map with the information of you and your partner's locations. Give your partner directions through voice chat so your partner can come to you.
Roles	Leader (Role A): You have access to a Street View panorama around/inside your favorite building. Try to describe what you see (landscaping, spatial relationships, and architectural style) to your partner. Partner (Role B): You have access to online information about all the buildings in the park. Try to guess where your partner is. You can ask your partner questions for clarification.	Leader (Role A): You have access to a map with the information of you and your partner's locations. Give your partner directions so he/she can come to you. Partner (Role B): You have access to a Street View panorama. Try to follow your partner's directions to find him/her. You can report what you see in the street view so your partner knows your progress.
Target Skills	Participants' ability to describe/locate/name the building and question/answer with their partner in the target language will help their personal progress in communication skills.	Participants' ability to give/follow directions, provide/ understand feedback, and refine the solution with their partner in the target language will help their personal progress in communication skills.
Main Focus	Discovery: Participants discover new destinations in London.	Discovery: Participants discover new destinations in New York City.
Operation	Participants confront challenges or questions designed to elicit answers within a specific period of time. They search for online information, and receive detailed responses from their partners so they might adjust their plans, try new approaches, and accomplish tasks.	Participants confront challenges designed to elicit solutions within a specific period of time. They search for information via the Internet, using Google Maps to locate and map a destination, answer questions and gain detailed feedback from their partners so they might modify their proposal to provide new directions.
Goals	Participants need to: Role A: describe the scene of the target building and answer questions. Role B: understand the descriptions, pose questions, and find out answers.	Participants need to: Role A: discover solutions, give directions, understand feedback, and refine solutions. Role B: understand/follow directions, and provide feedback.
Overall Goals	• To practice effective interpersonal communication skills, enhance communication strategies, and improve oral communicative competence. • To understand the background information, terms, and expressions related to the events.	

computationally intensive on the client's side, smooth street view navigation requires a reasonably high Internet speed. Insufficient network bandwidth can increase the response time of user input and cause loss of interest. The following are example user comments regarding these challenges: "How do I go inside or get out at the entrance of a building?" "The shop sign is not clear enough. I cannot read the text." "The panorama download process freezes. Did I lose my Internet connection?" However, after overcoming the technical challenges, most participants successfully accomplished the assigned tasks in a timely manner. One of the participants commented, "After getting familiar with the system, I find it is easy to use." Moreover, participants can freely access the proposed system from remote locations. Thus, the technical challenges were not sufficiently substantial to diminish the enthusiasm that participants had for accomplishing the language learning activities. Their comments generally indicated that they enjoyed using the system to accomplish tasks and language learning: "I like my chosen avatar; the 3D model and its animations are detailed." "It is fun and I like it much better compared to the traditional language learning class." The program appears to provide a suitable context for task-based language learning for students.

From the participating teacher's perspective, instructors must be willing to innovate and incorporate new technology into their courses, develop the online curriculum, and familiarize themselves with the proposed system in advance. Although the instructor encountered the technical challenges posed by a system that is under continual development, the instructor's comments revealed the benefits of using street view panoramas to enhance language learning: "Teaching assistants' help is required to solve learners' technical problems in class." "It is important to encourage language learners engaging in the activities to describe and explain what they see." "We can use the street view panorama as a stimulus to get learners to use English." The instructor was generally satisfied with the program, and indicated that the benefits of the program outweigh the technical risks or challenges.

CONCLUSION AND FUTURE RESEARCH DIRECTIONS

For many EFL learners, the classroom is the only place to learn and use the target language. Enabled by recent 3D virtual reality technology, such as street view panoramas, learning the target language in authentic contexts and situations is possible now. This chapter presents a preliminary case study of the effect of contextualized language learning in virtual learning environments using Google Street View panoramas on language learner's communicative competence development. The instructional approach used in this study involves learners to interact in authentic contexts (e.g., London and New York), and use the target language and authentic materials (e.g., maps, landscape) in real-life environments in cooperation with peers. We use the latest street view panoramas and 3D animated avatar technology to facilitate optimal language learning. Online panoramas were constructed by acquiring and stitching street view images, and avatars were animated and superimposed on street view panoramas to make language learning more immersive and meaningful. We also designed contextualized language learning activities based on meaningful learning theory, the communicative approach, Schank's GBS (1996), and executed them in these contexts. Providing EFL learners with real contexts and real-life communicative tasks that elicit the use of authentic language and nurture cultural exploration offers students a chance to learn the target language via language activation "outside the classroom" (i.e., in the environment of Google Street View).

As identified in teacher and student comments, both student's and teacher's comfort levels with using street view panoramas play a large role in student's enjoyment, engagement, and learning outcomes in this learning environment. It is therefore imperative to develop and implement a well-thought-out technical support and technology integration plan to minimize the technical challenges and maximize the learning opportunities in the street view panoramas environment. Another area that needs further exploration relates to the research scope on communicative competence. As Berns (1984) indicated, "language study has to look at the use (function) of language in context, both its linguistic context (what is uttered before and after a given piece of discourse) and its social, or situational, context (who is speaking, what their social roles are, why they have come together to speak)" (p. 5). The field of communicative competence research has traditionally focused on the study of language use and discourse, which aims to reveal the dynamics of social interaction, in everyday sociocultural contexts (Duran, 1984). While it is important to continue the discourse analysis method with a focus on culturally oriented social interaction, it is necessary to expand the traditional research on communicate competence by considering emerging methods and areas that are relevant to the virtual environment, such as virtual ethnographic methods (Chrichton & Kinash, 2003), new communicative competencies necessary in virtual environments, and the dynamics of social interaction among learners in the virtual environment. We hope that our study on Google Street View panoramas technology in multi-user virtual environments helps advance research on communicative competence in all other disciplines.

ACKNOWLEDGMENT

This research was supported by the Ministry of Science and Technology R.O.C.

REFERENCES

Avatar Languages. (2011). *Google street view for language learning: A guide for teachers*. Retrieved February 3, 2017, from http://www.avatarlanguages.com/teaching/streetview.pdf

Avatar Reality. (2010). *Blue Mars*. Retrieved February 3, 2017, from http://www.bluemars.com/

Berns, M. S. (1984). Functional approaches to language and language teaching: Another look. In S. Savignon & M. S. Berns (Eds.), *Initiatives in communicative language teaching: A book of readings* (pp. 3–21). Reading, PA: Addison-Wesley.

Berns, R. G., & Erickson, P. M. (2001). Contextual teaching and learning: Preparing students for the new economy. *The Highlight Zone: Research @ Work, 5*, 2–9. (ERIC Document Reproduction Service No. ED452376)

Brown, J., Collins, A., & Duguid, P. (1989). Situated cognition and the culture of learning. *Educational Researcher, 18*(1), 32–42. doi:10.3102/0013189X018001032

Chinnery, G. (2008). You've got some GALL: Google-assisted language learning. *Language Learning & Technology, 12*(1), 3–11.

Chrichton, S., & Kinash, S. (2003). Virtual ethnography: Interactive interviewing online as method. *Canadian Journal of Learning and Technology, 29*(2), 101–115.

Communicative Language Teaching. (n.d.). In *Wikipedia*. Retrieved February 3, 2017, from https://en.wikipedia.org/wiki/Communicative_language_teaching

Deutschmann, M., & Steinvall. (2012). Identifying Identity: Using Second Life in the teaching of socio-linguistics for the raising of gender awareness. *The EuroCall Review, 20*(1), 49–53.

Deutschmann, M., & Panichi, L. (2009). Talking into empty space – Signaling involvement in a virtual language classroom in Second Life. *Language Awareness, 18*(3–4), 310–328. doi:10.1080/09658410903197306

Deutschmann, M., & Panichi, L. (2009). Talking into empty space? Signalling involvement in a virtual language classroom in Second Life. *Language Awareness, 18*(3-4), 310–328. doi:10.1080/09658410903197306

Deutschmann, M., & Panichi, L. (2013). Towards models for designing language learning in virtual worlds. *International Journal of Virtual and Personal Learning Environments*, *3*(4), 65-84.

Deutschmann, M., Panichi, L., & Molka-Danielsen, J. (2009). Designing oral participation in Second Life: A comparative study of two language proficiency courses. *ReCALL*, *21*(2), 206–226. doi:10.1017/S0958344009000196

Duran, R. P. (1984). Some implications of communicative competence research for integrative proficiency testing. In C. Rivera (Ed.), *Communicative competence approaches to language proficiency assessment: Research and application* (pp. 44–58). Clevedon, UK: Multilingual Matters.

Garrido-Inigo, P., & Rodriguez-Moreno, F. (2015). The reality of virtual worlds: Pros and cons of their application to foreign language teaching. *Interactive Learning Environments*, *23*(4), 453–470. doi:10.1080/10494820.2013.788034

Gee, J. P. (2004). *Situate language and learning: The critique of traditional schooling*. London: Routledge.

Google. (2007). *Street view in google earth*. Retrieved February 3, 2017, from http://support.google.com/earth/bin/answer.py?hl=en&answer=1067358

Google Maps. (n.d.). In *Google Maps Education Web site*. Retrieved February 3, 2017, from http://maps.google.com/help/maps/education/learn/

Howland, J., Jonassen, D., & Marra, R. (2011). *Meaningful learning with technology* (4th ed.). Allyn & Bacon.

Huang, Y., Chiu, P., Liu, T., & Chen, T. (2011). The design and implementation of a meaningful learning-based evaluation method for ubiquitous learning. *Computers & Education*, *57*(4), 2291–2302. doi:10.1016/j.compedu.2011.05.023

Jonassen, D. (1995). Supporting communities of learners with technology: A vision for integrating technology with learning in schools. *Educational Technology*, *35*, 60–63.

Kim, J., Hill, R., & Durlach, P. (2009). BiLAT: A game-based environment for practicing negotiation in a cultural context. *International Journal of Artificial Intelligence in Education*, *19*, 289–309.

Lan, Y. J. (2015). Contextual EFL learning in a 3D virtual environment. *Language Learning & Technology*, *19*(2), 16–32.

Larsen-Freeman, D. (2000). *Techniques and principles in language teaching*. Oxford, UK: Oxford University Press.

Lave, J. (1988). *Cognition in practice: Mind, mathematics, and culture in everyday life*. Cambridge, UK: Cambridge University Press. doi:10.1017/CBO9780511609268

Littlewood, W. (2007). Communicative and task-based language teaching in East Asian classrooms. *Language Teaching*, *40*(03), 243–249. doi:10.1017/S0261444807004363

Ludescher, F. (2006). *Communicative Language Teaching*. Retrieved February 3, 2017, from http://www2.vobs.at/ludescher/alternative%20methods/communicative_language_teaching.htm

Microsoft. (2009). *Bing StreetSide*. Retrieved February 3, 2017, from http://www.microsoft.com/maps/streetside.aspx

Molka-Danielsen, J., Deutschmann, M., & Panichi, L. (2009). Designing transient learning spaces in Second Life for language learning: A case study based on the Kamimo experience. *Designs for Learning, 2*(1), 22–33.

Montoro, C., & Hampel, R. (2011). Investigating language learning activity using a CALL task in the self-access centre. *Studies in Self-Access Learning Journal, 2*(3), 119–135.

Opp-Beckman, L., & Klinghammer, S. (2006a). *Shaping the way we teach English: Successful practices around the world.* Washington, DC: Office of English Programs, United States Department of State. Retrieved February 3, 2017, from http://ivantrainer.weebly.com/uploads/1/0/3/0/10309088/shaping_the_way_we_teachreading.pdf

Opp-Beckman, L., & Klinghammer, S. (2006b). *Shaping the way we teach English: Successful practices around the world.* Instructor's Manual. Washington, DC: Office of English Programs, United States Department of State. Retrieved February 3, 2017, from http://oelp.uoregon.edu/sites/oelp1.uoregon.edu/files/shaping_manual_aug2006.pdf

Patterson, T. (2007). Google Earth as a (Not Just) geography education tool. *The Journal of Geography, 106*(4), 145–152. doi:10.1080/00221340701678032

Peterson, M. (2010). Learner participation patterns and strategy use in Second Life: An exploratory case study. *ReCALL, 22*(3), 273–292. doi:10.1017/S0958344010000169

Polio, C. (2014). Using authentic materials in the beginning language classroom. *Clear News, 18*(1), 1–7.

Realia and Contextualization. (n.d.). *Gaining ground in teaching: Resources.* Retrieved February 3, 2017, from Michigan State University, Chinese Teacher Certification Program Web site: http://gaining.educ.msu.edu/resources/node/422

Rymniak, M. (2011). *Supporting skilled immigrants: A toolkit for ESL practitioners.* Global Talent Bridge, World Education Services. Retrieved February 3, 2017, from http://www.globaltalentbridge.org/toolkit/pdf/SupportingSkilledImmigrantsToolkit.pdf

Savignon, S. (1997). *Communicative competence: Theory and classroom practice.* New York, NY: McGraw-Hill.

Savignon, S. (2001). Communicative language teaching in the twenty-first century. In M. Celce-Murcia (Ed.), *Teaching English as a Second or Foreign Language.* Boston: Heinle & Heinle.

Schank, R. C. (1996). Goal-based scenarios: Case-based reasoning meet leaning by learning by doing. In D. Leake (Ed.), *Case-based reasoning: Experience, lessons & future directions.* AAAI Press/The MIT Press.

Schank, R. C., & Cleary, C. (1995). *Engines for education.* Hillsdale, NJ: Erlbaum Associates. Retrieved February 3, 2017, from http://www.engines4ed.org/hyperbook/nodes/NODE-233-pg.html

Schroeder, R. (1996). *Possible worlds: The social dynamic of virtual reality technologies*. Boulder, CO: Westview Press.

Second Life. (2003). Retrieved February 3, 2017, from http://secondlife.com

Shih, Y., & Yang, M. (2008). A collaborative virtual environment for situated language using VEC3D. *Journal of Educational Technology & Society*, *11*(1), 56–68.

Shih, Y., Yang, M., & Yang, F. (2013). Street-view panorama for cultural learning: implementation and curriculum design. *International Conference on Advanced Learning Technology*. doi:10.1109/ICALT.2013.107

Shih, Y. C. (2015). A virtual walk through London: Culture learning through a cultural immersion experience. *Computer Assisted Language Learning*, *28*(4), 1–22.

Shrum, J. L., & Glisan, E. W. (2004). *Teacher's handbook: Contextualized language instruction*. Boston: Heinle & Heinle.

Situation Cognition. (2015). In *Wikipedia*. Retrieved February 3, 2017, from https://en.wikipedia.org/wiki/Situated_cognition

Stockwell, G., & Tanaka-Ellis, N. (2012). Diversity in environments. In G. Stockwell (Ed.), *Computer-assisted language learning: Diversity in research and practice* (pp. 71–89). Cambridge, UK: Cambridge University Press. doi:10.1017/CBO9781139060981.005

Svensson, P. (2003). Virtual worlds as arenas for language learning. In U. Felix (Ed.), *Language learning online: Towards best practices* (pp. 123–143). Amsterdam, The Netherlands: Swets & Zeitlinger.

Toyoda, E., & Harrison, R. (2002). Categorization of text chat communication between learners and native speakers of Japanese. *Language Learning & Technology*, *6*(1), 82–99. Retrieved from http://llt.msu.edu/vol6num1/toyoda/default.html

Utech, J. L. (2008). *Contextualized curriculum for workplace education: An introductory guide*. Massachusetts Worker Education Roundtable. Retrieved February 3, 2017, from https://www.umass.edu/roundtable/projects/Integrated%20curr_guide%20p1.pdf

Vickers, H. (2009). *Google maps street view for language learning*. Retrieved February 3, 2017, from http://www.avatarlanguages.com/blog/google-street-view-languages/

Wang, C., Calandra, B., Hibbard, S., & Lefaiver, M. (2012). Learning effects of an experimental EFL program in Second Life. *Educational Technology Research and Development*, *60*(5), 943–961. doi:10.1007/s11423-012-9259-0

Zumbach, J., & Reimann, P. (1999). Assessment of a goal-based scenario approach: A hypermedia comparison. In P. Marquet, S. Mathey, A. Jaillet, & E. Nissen (Eds.), *Internet-based teaching and learning (IN-TELE) 98* (pp. 449-454). Frankfurt, Germany: Peter Lang. Retrieved February 3, 2017, from https://www.sbg.ac.at/mediaresearch/zumbach/download/1999_2006/book_chapters/zumbach_bookc_02.pdf

KEY TERMS AND DEFINITIONS

Authentic Context: Language is used, introduced, and learned in real situations. The term refers to the street-view and authentic use of language in this study.

Authentic Materials: The term refers to the resources of the target language which are used in real life instead of pedagogical purposes. The examples are newspapers, magazines, TV broadcasts, etc.

Contextualized Language Learning: Language learning occurs in a contextualized environment which combines opportunities for active participation in an authentic context.

Street View Panoramas: Google Maps with Street View provides 360° street-level imagery of global locations.

Virtual Environment: A computer generated display enables users to engage in a simulated world environment and interact with other users.

Chapter 5
The Affordances of 3D Virtual Learning Environments:
Designing for Learners' Interpersonal and Emotional Connections

Hisae Matsui
Princeton University, USA

Terence C. Ahern
West Virginia University, USA

ABSTRACT

The purpose of this chapter is to examine participants' perceived affordances of three-dimensional virtual learning environments (3D VLEs) in developing interpersonal emotional connections with their partners during the initial stage of the virtual exchange. To fulfill the purpose, two Japanese and two American students were paired and participated in sessions within two differently designed virtual environments using the same 3D virtual application. The results indicate that the participants tend to find avatars useful as a cue that helps in recalling previous conversations and in avoiding long silences. Additionally, the affordances of the 3D VLEs heightened the experience of co-presence. However, for non-native speakers, this experience also created increased anxiety. Finally, the results show the affordances affected the participants much more strongly during the first several sessions but were mitigated by other factors as the sessions continued.

INTRODUCTION

Globalization has transformed virtually all aspects of modern life, from the way we shop to the way we get our news. Not surprisingly, the waves of globalization have had an impact on foreign language education as well. Coupled with advances in information and communication technology, it is possible for students to have direct contact with different cultures through virtual technology. The Internet provides access to email, text cat, Skype, virtual environments, and other technologies that support prolonged

DOI: 10.4018/978-1-5225-3719-9.ch005

online intercultural exchanges between groups of students in various institutional settings who might otherwise not have the opportunity to interact (Belz & Thorne, 2006).

3D Virtual Learning Environments (3D VLEs) are relatively new tools in foreign language education, even though they are not a new phenomenon in and of themselves. These platforms have been attracting foreign language educators who are constantly looking for authentic opportunities for their students to interact with others in the target language (Panichi, Deutschmann, & Molka-Danielsen, 2010). Dalgarno and Lee (2010) noted that various unique characteristics of more advanced platforms of virtual environments could be adapted for educational purposes. Given the great variety of such tools that are available, an instructional designer needs a way to evaluate the relative advantages of competing candidates. The discrepancy between a learner's use of an instructional object and the anticipated instructional interaction is often attributed to a weak design and poor implementation of appropriate affordances (Kirschner, Strijbos, Kreijns, & Beers, 2004). When new technology is introduced into educational activities, it is crucial for both instructors and instructional designers to know not only all the possibilities for action that the piece of technology can offer, but also how it could be perceived or used by learners in the environment to utilize the piece of technology in instruction. However, due to the novelty of 3D VLEs, there has been little research done on the learner's perception of the available affordances. The purpose of this chapter, therefore, is to examine the learners' perceptions of the affordance of 3D virtual learning environments.

BACKGROUND

Affordance

The notion of affordances is derived from work in the field of visual perception carried out by Gibson (1979), who focused his work on direct perception, a form of perception that does not require mediation or internal processing by an actor. For Gibson, an affordance is directly perceivable information in an environment that is meaningful to an actor. In his theory, the existence of the affordance is independent of an actor's experiences and culture, whereas the ability to perceive the affordance may be dependent on these.

In contrast, Norman's view of affordance deals with designed objects. He describes an affordance as a design aspect that suggests how the object should be used (Bower, 2008). Norman (1988) noted that in current technologically driven society, many objects do not have accessibility at the core of their design, thereby restricting perceptions of their possibilities. Norman (1993) went on to distinguish between real and perceived affordances, claiming that the latter is more crucial to the design process since an affordance is of no utility to the potential user unless it is perceived. According to Norman, affordances provide strong pointers to the way things operate, and simple things should have their intended purpose strongly signaled in their design and should not require further explanation (Gall & Breeze, 2005). Norman also believed that while perception may be direct, our interpretation of things is based on our past knowledge and experience of our perception of those things; therefore, he places the emphasis on people's knowledge, memory and experience in the realization of affordances (Norman, 1988).

Although Gibson and Norman shared a basic concept of affordance, the distinction between Gibson's and Norman's definitions of affordance is important because it determines whether or not the term affordance encompasses usability or just utility (Kirschner et al., 2004). Gibson focused upon the fundamental characteristics of the object in relation to the user, which is a question of utility, while Norman placed more emphasis on how an object is perceived, which relates to usability and not just utility (Bower, 2008). Norman was interested much more in the perception of the user than in the invariant properties of the tool; therefore, he was interested in how the environment could be both symbolically and physically designed (Hammond, 2010). Considering that the learner's perception is formed by culture and context in foreign language education, this paper follows Noman's view of affordance, which attends to the user's perception.

A number of authors have used affordance in educational contexts. For example, Conole and Dyke (2004) believe that a better understanding of the nature and properties of technologies will lead to a more systematic application of the use of information and communication technology (ICT) for learning and teaching. Therefore, they emphasize the importance of analyzing how the affordances of ICT can be used to facilitate particular approaches to teaching and learning. Kennewell and his colleagues pointed out that many recent papers concerning the impact of ICT on teaching and learning refer to the affordances of ICT in order to account for the influence of environmental features on learning activity (Kennewell, Tanner, Jones, & Beauchamp, 2007). In the context of 3D VLEs, Dalgarno and Lee (2010) claimed that the technologies themselves do not directly cause learning to occur. Rather, they can afford certain learning tasks that themselves may result in learning or give rise to certain learning benefits. However, little is understood about the affordances of different technologies and how these properties might be exploited in particular learning and teaching contexts (Conole & Dyke 2004).

In the discussion of affordances in learning and teaching contexts, opportunities and constraints are often discussed as subsidiary ideas of affordance. Opportunities for actions are provided by features of the setting, usually in the form of tools which convey some indication of how they might be used (Kennewell et al., 2007). In conjunction with the idea of opportunities, the use of the related idea of constraints, which refers to a boundary, guide or structure for action, provides a more comprehensive characterization of the relationships between the environment and the people acting in and on that environment (Greeno et al., 1998). Even though constraints have no negative connotations, in some circumstances, constraints may be perceived as a barrier or an obstacle to action because perception of potential and structure for action will depend on the knowledge, skills and dispositions of the person acting, and will be relative to the setting and the goal (Hammond, 2010).

Learners can reach their learning goals using their knowledge, skills and dispositions and the opportunities of the features, which may provide potential for their actions towards their goals. At the same time, the constraints of the features may provide structure for their actions in a positive form or a negative form. Opportunities and constraints provide more comprehensive characterizations of the relationships between the environment and the people acting in and on that environment (Kennewell et al., 2007); hence, they are inherent in the makeup of affordance (Hammond, 2010).

Virtual Environments and Affordances

Virtual environments such as Second Life are not new. They can be traced back to the early days of MMOs (Massively Multiplayer Online games) and the online role-playing games known as MUDs (Multi-User Dungeons) (Ludlow & Wallace, 2007). Advances in computational power and network connectivity enabled MUDs to evolve into MOOs (MUDs, Object-Oriented), MUVEs (multi-user virtual environments), and MMORPGs (Massively-Multiplayer Online Role Playing Games) among others (Dieterle & Clarke, 2009).

Since "virtual worlds" have evolved through these many different forms, it is challenging to define what exactly virtual worlds are. Schroeder (1996) identified virtual reality technology as "a computer-generated display that allows or compels the user (or users) to have a sense of being present in an environment other than the one they are actually in, and to interact with that environment" (p. 25). Even though virtual environments are generally not created for educational purposes, these platforms have been attracting foreign language educators who are constantly looking for authentic opportunities for their students to interact with others in the target language (Panichi, Deutschmann, & Molka-Danielsen, 2010). Peterson (2012) found that the participants engaged in collaborative interaction including peer-scaffolding and they actively maintained a supportive atmosphere while completing tasks in Second Life. Dalgarno and Lee (2010) identified various unique characteristics of advanced platforms of virtual environments for educational purposes (see below), which are categorized under "aspects of their representational fidelity" and "aspects of the learner–computer interactivity they facilitate."

- **Aspects of Their Representational Fidelity:**
  - Realistic display of environment
  - Smooth display of view changes and object motion
  - Consistency of object behavior
  - User representation
  - Spatial audio
  - Kinesthetic and tactile force feedback
- **Aspects of the Learner–Computer Interactivity They Facilitate:**
  - Embodied actions, including view control, navigation and object manipulation
  - Embodied verbal and nonverbal communication
  - Control of environment attributes and behavior
  - Construction of objects and scripting of object behaviors

Among these characteristics of 3D VLEs, one of the obvious essential technological affordances in online intercultural exchanges would be "embodied verbal and nonverbal communication," because exchanging opinions is at the heart of online intercultural exchanges. However, it is unknown how other affordances are perceived by learners or what opportunities and constraints these features will give to learners in learning activities.

One aspect of representational fidelity that Dalgarno and Lee (2010) listed is "user representation," which involves the depiction of the user as an avatar through which he or she is able to develop and project an online identity (Dickey, 2003). This use of the user's image is considered to be an important element of the fidelity of representation online. The avatar helps create a sense of individuality that aides in co-presence, the sense of "being there together" with other geographically dispersed users in the remote environment, and enriches the social interactions occurring (Schroeder & Axelsson, 2006).

The term co-presence was originated by Goffman (1963) and was defined as a sense of being together in virtual environments where individuals become "accessible, available, and subject to one another" (p. 22). Since then, researchers have put forth various more specific definitions of the term. Even though there is no consensus definition of co-presence, there are mainly two groups of studies: studies that focus on people's perceptions of embodied agents and studies that focus on people's social responses to embodied agents (Bailenson et al., 2005).

While researchers in the former group take the view that co-presence occurs when a user not only perceives or feels that he or she is "present" within a virtual environment, but also perceives or feels that others are present there as well, researchers in the latter group view co-presence as a social, task-related, or physiological response to embodied agents (Bailenson et al., 2005).

In this research study, the participants knew they were communicating with real human beings through embodied agents (avatars) and whether or not the embodied agents were perceived and treated as if they were human was not the objective of the research; therefore, the term co-presence is used in terms of a user's perception or feeling that others are co-situated within an interpersonal environment (Swinth & Blascovich, 2002).

Socio-emotional processes are crucial for building effective structures and communities. Previous studies show that users can socially and psychologically feel connected to others by interacting through avatars and they can experience greater co-presence (Biocca et al., 2003; Schroeder, 2002). How this feature of 3D VLEs is perceived by learners is still unknown even though there are previous studies on general impressions of using 3D VLEs in instruction. Furthermore, there is no specific research that has been done to examine learners' perceptions on one of the main features of 3D VLEs such as co-presence.

The purpose of this study is to examine the relations between the visual design elements of a 3D VLE, which aims to promote co-presence, and interpersonal emotional connections between participants in the initial stage of online collaboration. The experiences of four participants were observed as they participated in conversational activities in two different virtual environments. Specifically, reflections after each session about overall impressions and verbal interactions during the activities were analyzed to investigate the possible significance of sharing environments virtually on the development of interpersonal emotional connections between participants in online intercultural exchanges.

RESEARCH METHODS

Four participants, two non-native speakers (NNS) of Japanese, Jennifer and Mary, from an American university and two native speakers (NS) of Japanese, Yoko and Keiko, from a Japanese university participated in this research. To avoid gender factors on emotional connections, all participants were arranged to be the same gender. Each participant was paired up with each participant from the other university and thus belonged to two different pairs. As shown in Table 1 below, four pairs were formed; two of these interacted in a café environment and the other two in an individual room environment. In this research, only four pairs were observed due to technical and institutional constraints that were outside the control of the researcher.

Table 1. Combinations of the participants

	Yoko (NS)	**Keiko (NS)**
Jennifer (NNS)	Pair 1: Individual room (Jennifer and Yoko)	Pair 2: Café (Jennifer and Keiko)
Mary (NNS)	Pair 3: Café (Mary and Yoko)	Pair 4: Individual room (Mary and Keiko)

Jennifer and Mary are female students from an American university and had both studied the first-year level of Japanese at the university. They were currently taking the second-year level of Japanese when they participated in this research. Jennifer is a 20-year-old female Chinese-heritage student who came to the United States when she was ten years old. Before they came to the United States, they had lived in Japan for two years. Therefore, even though she was taking second-year Japanese when she participated in the project, her proficiency level of Japanese language and cultural knowledge of Japan was higher than her peers in the class. Her level of speaking proficiency was assessed by a fully certified ACTFL tester of Japanese through an ACTFL Oral Proficiency Interview (OPI) and was rated as "Intermediate-High." Mary is a 20-year-old female student, coming to the United States from China when she was four-year-old. Unlike Jennifer, she has never been to Japan and has had limited contact with native Japanese speakers. Her level of speaking proficiency was was "Novice-High." Yoko and Keiko are female students from a Japanese university. They are both senior students in Intercultural Communication major. Yoko was 21-year-old and Keiko was 22-year-old at the time of the research.

The participants completed two surveys: one asking the participants' impressions of each section of the interaction and the other asking their impressions of the overall experience. The questionnaire for each session asked specifically if the participants thought they had more or less of an emotional connection with their partners than the last time and what made them feel that way in order to clarify the factors that participants perceive. The questionnaire for the overall experience was distributed only after the first set of sessions and the final set of sessions. It included questions asking participants to compare the two environments. Participants answered the questions in a narrative form in their native languages. The surveys were prepared online using a form tool provided by Google. A link to the online version of the questionnaire was sent to participants in Second Life and they were expected to answer the questionnaire after each session. The results from the surveys were anticipated to show transitions of perceived interpersonal emotional connection that participants would have from the first session to the last session.

Second Life was used for the virtual environment where sessions took place. The land within Second Life used for the sessions, which has an area of 4096 sq. mi. (64 x 64, 938 prims), was rented from New Media Consortium (NMC). The land had two settings: the café setting, which allowed participants to share a single environment, and the individual room setting, which provided separate environments for each participant (see Figure 1). The environment was closed to participants so that no other users could interrupt the sessions.

The sessions took place over a five-week period. During the period, each participant had five sessions in each pairing since the differentiation in design can often be observed with as few as five observations with each condition in single-subject research designs (Gast, 2010). In each session, participants had a twenty-minute-long conversation and answered the online survey questionnaire immediately thereafter, which took about five minutes. The topic of the conversation was open so as to elicit free and natural interaction.

Before the sessions started, the participants were given accounts in Second Life. Within the Second Life environment the participants were provided landmarks, which transport avatars to predetermined locations. Each participant chose their avatars from ten pre-made avatars. Because none of the participants had previous experience using Second Life, a one-hour training session was offered. The training included basic in-world operations, such as walking, sitting on a chair, teleporting, and talking, as well as how to log in and go to the assigned meeting place. The order of the sessions was random as long as the participants' schedules permitted, because random order is important in alternating treatments design

Figure 1. Café setting and individual room setting

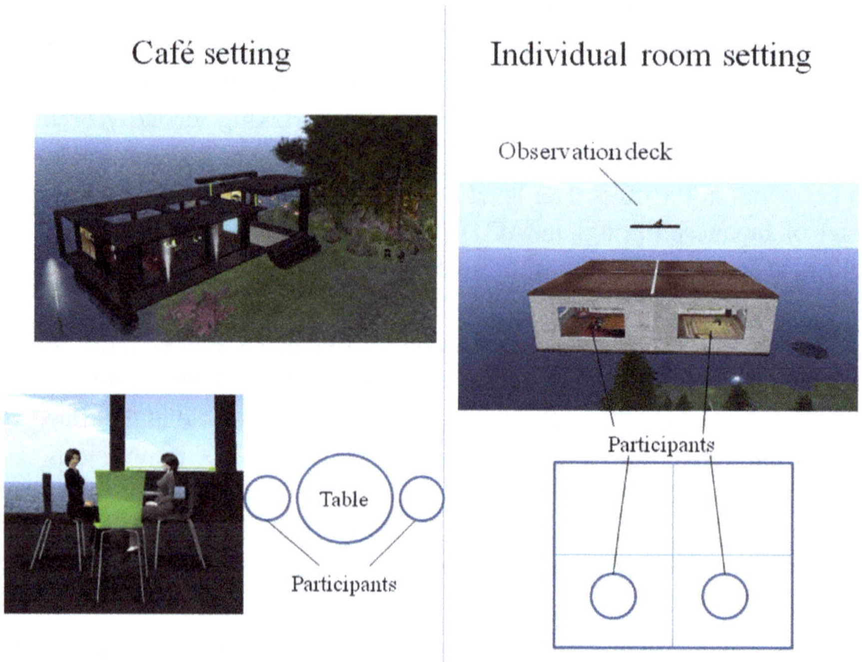

in order to increase the likelihood that the observed effects were the result of the treatment rather than some extraneous influence.

During the sessions, participants communicated using voice chat, which is an interactive communication application. In Second Life, one can choose whether or not voices are heard from either the avatar position or the camera position. In this study, all of the participants set it so that they would hear the sound from their avatar's positions. In the café setting, participants sat across from each other at a table so that they would able to see each other's avatars and were close enough to hear each other's voice. In the individual room setting, they could not see their interlocutor's avatar. However, they could still hear their interlocutor's voice because their rooms were located next to each other. In this setting, participants were free to do anything except for looking at their partner's avatar by controlling camera view.

All of the participants' interactions were recorded with Audacity, an audio software for recording and editing, to analyze the contents of the interactions. In both environments, the researcher logged in with the participants for recording and supporting purposes; however, her avatar was hidden under the water in the café environment and on the observation deck above the rooms in the individual room environment and thus out of sight of the participants. After each session, the questionnaire, which was explained under the "Instruments" section above, was distributed to ask the participants their impressions on the sessions for the analysis. Further details of the analysis will be explained in the following section.

RESULTS

In order to observe the change in participant's perception of the affordance of 3D VLEs, reflections from each participant were closely examined from the first session to the final session for each pair.

While participants' reflections were the main data used to investigate the change, the contents of the interactions and the times and lengths of silences were also used to search for the factors of the changes demonstrated throughout the sessions.

Pair 1: Jennifer and Keiko in the Café

In the first session, the pair introduced themselves and exchanged basic information. Jennifer described her interaction with Keiko as "an actual face-to-face conversation" in the café environment. However, she also pointed out that she had difficulty in conveying some of her ideas. Jennifer suggested that seeing the avatar of her partner gave her "a better sense of connection" than simply chatting with her partner in an individual room. Jennifer also mentioned that she felt that seeing another person's virtual character gave her "a stronger sense of personal interaction." She also said that her experience of meeting in the café had "more authenticity in terms of real-life interactions." Keiko felt that the café environment was a "very good place to interact with her partner," even though she wished the avatar would have had her partner's actual face. Examining their interactions, Keiko tended to ask more questions while responding minimally to her partner. After the first sessions in both environments, Keiko mentioned that the ability to see her partner's avatar affected her conscious awareness of her partner. She found it easier to talk to her partner when she could see her—even if it was only in the form of an avatar. After the second session at the cafe, Jennifer said she "felt more comfortable" sharing with Keiko about her "likes and typical holiday customs." On the other hand, Keiko's comments after the second session were generally negative. Keiko mentioned that even though she spoke in the same manner as the previous session, there were times when she felt an uncomfortable psychological distance from her partner. She was also not sure what they would talk about and how deep the topic would go.

During the fourth session, Jennifer asked Keiko what Japanese people do outside during the winter. Keiko used a term "*irumineeshon* (illumination)," referring to holiday lighting displays, when answering the question. They had an extended conversation about "*irumineeshon*" before Jennifer asked Keiko what "*irununeeshon*" was. It is not clear if Jennifer misunderstood what "*irumineeshon*" was or if she had simply been pretending to know. Overall, transitions between topics were very smooth and had no breaks between them. Jennifer's comments after the session were all positive. She stated that she felt that she connected with her partner better each time and noticed that the amount of "gaps" in their conversations also decreased every time. When considering the reason for this, she said that she thought that it was probably because they had started their conversation with topics that they both were familiar with and interested in. On the other hand, Keiko's comments were all negative. She realized once again how hard it is to deliver a message with only her voice. She also recognized the importance of accurate understanding of words and their meanings because there are many Japanese words which were adapted from English words, yet have different meanings from the original English meanings. It is clear that she was referring here to the misunderstanding caused by the term "*irumineeshon* (illumination)."

When it came to the fifth session, they talked about various topics. The topics seemed unrelated; however, they were loosely connected and the transitions were very smooth. Most of the time, Jennifer or Keiko voluntarily shifted the topic voluntarily by telling their own stories instead of asking their partner questions, which was common practice during the first set of sessions. Jennifer's comments for the final session were all positive. She looked back on the session and mentioned, "compared to earlier sessions, I definitely think that I have a more emotional connection with the other party." She also reviewed their relationship and mentioned that she and her partner "have moved from two strangers to close acquaintances" through the sessions and said that the café environment has "facilitated the process." Keiko's comments were also all positive. She compared the two environments and felt the ease of conveying the conversation depended on whether or not she could see her partner's avatar. She kept her tendency of asking more questions and giving minimal answers to her partner; however, the tone of the conversation was much more cheerful and the sequences of interaction through the conversation and topics suggested that these questions came from genuine curiosity in her partner rather than simply to fill the silences.

Pair 2: Mary and Yoko in the Café

The pair started off their first session with self-introductions. During the session, there was one communication breakdown. While Mary was trying to explain her family members, she could not express what she wanted to say. In spite of her partner's encouragement, Mary gave up on the explanation. After the first session in the cafe, Mary felt "quite closely connected" to her partner. However, she "struggled over when it would be appropriate to jump into the conversation" and noticed that oftentimes there were longer awkward pauses than she "would have expected in a face-to-face conversation."

Mary compared her first experiences in both environments and realized that she was "more engaged" in the conversation in the café but "more comfortable" in talking in the individual room. In the café environment, since she felt the conversation was more like talking to someone in person, she was "very invested in" continuing the conversation and expressing herself. She admitted that she even used gestures in front of the computer even though she knew her partner could not see her. She also realized that pauses and mistakes in the conversation made her feel they were more detrimental to the conversation in this environment than in the individual room environment. Mary even mentioned that she felt that while her partner in the café environment was much more willing to talk, she was more willing to talk in the individual room environment. These comments show how the environmental context affected her emotional state during each session.

Yoko reflected on her session and said that she was very nervous. Consequently, she was very careful in her selection of words as well as style of speech. Yoko did not know how much Japanese her partner would understand. In spite of her nervousness, she still thought that seeing her partner's avatar along with sharing an environment reduced the sense of insecurity that came from communicating with a stranger from a different county. Looking back on her first experience in both environments, Yoko indicated that once she became accustomed to Second Life, meeting someone in the café environment was just like meeting someone in person.

By the third session, Mary felt "a lot more comfortable" with her partner. As a result, she found that even though they talked "a bit more about more serious topics like religion and work," she felt "less awkward" than she did the previous time when they talked about "more silly, more personal topics." All of the comments from Yoko after the third session were also positive. Yoko felt that she could talk to her partner more comfortably as the topics shifted to more familiar everyday matters. As a result, Yoko started feeling that meeting her partner was similar to meeting her friends in everyday life.

There was a serious sound problem at the beginning of the fourth session. The length of the session ended up being cut to 10 minutes and 28 seconds, which was only half the length of the usual session. Despite the problems, Mary's comments were overall positive. Mary felt that they managed to have a "nice conversation" in what little time they had. She also felt "very comfortable" speaking with her partner, and she had the impression that they "responded well to each other's questions." Even when they had two very long pauses, Mary felt that they were "relatively non-awkward," and she felt like she and her partner "took turns redirecting the conversation from the pauses." Yoko also said she and her partner could talk comfortably and she started opening up a little more to her partner. Yoko also noticed that she started to feel relieved when she saw her partner's familiar avatar, just as she would upon seeing a familiar face in real life.

On the contrary, there were several very long silences during the final session. After a very long silence, which lasted for 29 seconds Mary broke the silence by asking a question with a wry laugh. It was clear that Mary had asked the question simply to end the silence. Mary looked back at the session and mentioned that she had to "constantly jump in to fill in the pauses," which were "pretty long and often." Although she managed to "steer the conversation into some new topics" that they haven't covered before," she strongly felt that both of them spoke in "really short and somewhat awkward sentences." Yoko mentioned that she was bracing herself because this was the final session. As a result, Yoko felt like she was not able to provide topics to talk about during the session as much as she wanted. In spite of the negative points, Yoko still thought it was easy for her to open up to her partner in the café environment partially because they met up before they went to the café and she was able to prepare herself for the conversation.

Pair 3: Jennifer and Yoko in the Individual Room

During the first session, Jennifer and Yoko mainly exchanged their basic information. After the session, Jennifer commented that "overall I did not feel nervous about speaking with a stranger in a language that I have only a rudimentary knowledge of." However, Jennifer noticed that talking in the individual room felt like "having a phone conversation with someone." She had difficulty in knowing when her partner had finished speaking; therefore, she sometimes interrupted her partner accidentally. Yoko mentioned that although she was relieved when she learned that her partner's language proficiency was relatively high, she felt "restless" and like she was talking to herself because sometimes her partner did not give "*aizuchi* (supportive responses)" to her utterances. Looking back on her first experience in both environments, Yoko often felt like she was talking to herself in the individual room because she could not find an "object" to talk to, and therefore struggled to keep her attention on her partner.

By the time they had their third session, Jennifer found that there were "more stalls in the conversation" during the session, which could be observed as silences, including a long silence, by the researchers. Yoko, on the other hand, reported that she felt more comfortable during this session than in the first or second session because she had gotten to know her partner better. Yoko mentioned that after experiencing both environments twice, she noticed the differences between the two environments more clearly. Not being able to see her partner's avatar frustrated her at times and made her feel uneasy in the individual room environment.

The fourth session started with a discussion of Thanksgiving and switched to driver's licenses. The rest of the session, which was approximately three-fourths of the session, was dominated by topics related to driver's licenses and lives with and without cars. After the session, Jennifer felt the session was "a little less connected between us" because "there were more breaks between our conversations than usual." Jennifer suspected that the topic they chose to guide their conversation was the cause of the breaks; however, she also admitted that she "did not feel quite comfortable to change the topic to something else" when the chance to do so arose in their conversation. This comment explains why three-fourths of the session was dominated by topics related to driver's licenses and lives with and without cars even though there were several breaks, which usually serve as triggers to change topics of the conversation. Yoko's comments were also negative. She felt more frustration because as she had become closer to her partner, she started having the urge to "meet" her. Even though she felt this closeness to her partner more than ever, she felt like she and her partner were often merely "temporizing," and she was having difficulty "bridging the psychological distance with her partner" – she likened it to "trying to seize clouds."

Their final session shows more distance between them. After checking if they could hear each other, there were long silences: an 8-second silence and a 5-second silence. Yoko broke the silence by asking a question. Instead of answering the question, Jennifer asked Yoko another question. After Yoko answered the question, there were two more long silences: one lasted for 10 seconds, and the other lasted for 9 seconds. There was no conversation based on information learned from the previous sessions. Jennifer's comments after the final session show the stale state of the relationship. She mentioned that she "did not feel any more or less emotional connection than previous sessions." Jennifer reflected on the previous session and found that she and her partner "did connect more" compared to the earlier sessions; however, she felt that the level of emotional connection "plateaued" once they reached a certain level. Yoko also mentioned that even though they had an animated conversation in the final session and had built a certain level of closeness with each other, she was not able to dispel an "unclearness" that she had had toward her partner throughout the sessions. She said she would prefer different means of communication or environments, such as Second Life in the café environment or Facebook, if there were another opportunity to interact with a person she did not know.

Pair 4: Mary and Keiko in the Individual Room

In their first session, they exchanged basic information such as academic year, hobbies, and plans after graduation. After the session, Mary reflected that she felt "slightly more comfortable in this session" than the session in the café environment. As a result, she felt that the conversation seemed to "flow more naturally" when she could not "see" her partner. Mary felt quite comfortable continuing the conversation and she also felt the few longer pauses "didn't feel particularly awkward or out of place." On the other hand, Keiko mentioned that she had experienced some difficulty because she could not see her partner's avatar.

Although there were two misunderstandings between them during the second session, Mary stated that she still felt quite comfortable continuing the conversation in this environment. Mary also mentioned that even the few longer pauses still "didn't feel particularly awkward or out of place." Contrary to her negative comments after the previous session, Keiko's comments turned out to be all positive. She found it was easier to talk to her partner this time around because she felt "less nervous" compared to the first session. She also felt she had "better mental preparation" this time around.

During the fourth session, there were two communication breakdowns. On the second breakdown, even though Keiko initially tried to explain the word that Mary did not understand, Keiko gave up on explaining after Mary said, "I don't understand." Then, Mary asked Keiko what her major was even though this question was asked in the first session. While Mary's comments after the fourth session turned out to be generally positive, Keiko's comments were negative and she noted the difficulty of expressing her opinions to her partner in this environment. This comment most likely came from the conversation breakdown she experienced as described above.

During the final session, Mary asked Keiko a question (what she was going to do after graduation) that she had already asked in the first session. There were a variety of topics discussed during this session, but some of them, such as post-graduation plans, had already been talked about in previous sessions.

After the last session, Mary's comments were generally positive. She felt "quite comfortable" with her partner during the session and she even thought this session was "the most comfortable" she felt with her partner among all the sessions. Despite the fact that she had a hard time hearing her partner at times and had to ask her partner to repeat, she felt "extremely comfortable" talking to her partner. On the other hand, Keiko's comments after the final session were all negative. She mentioned that she could not sweep away the sense of "discomfort," which she had been having since the first session. She also confessed that she tended to forget what she talked about with her partner in this environment because the sessions took place only once a week. There were no exchanges that were based on previously acquired knowledge.

Combined Results

As described above, each of the participants was affected by differences within each of the environments. The participants perceived the affordances for each environment differently. For example, co-presence, which the café environment afforded, added a level of comfort to the conversation for some of the participants while it caused nervousness for others.

Yoko and Keiko both expressed that they felt uneasy not being able to see their partner's avatar during the sessions. In the individual room, Yoko often felt like she was talking to herself or simply throwing her words at the wall and that made her feel unsure of their conversation. She also sometimes felt herself unable to focus her attention on her partner in the individual room because she could not find an "object" to talk to. Likewise, Keiko had a feeling that "something was wrong" in the environment when she was not able to see her partner's face. She also mentioned having a sense of anxiety over whether her partner was there or not when she could not see her partner's avatar. It should be concluded, from what has been said above, that they both found having visual representations of their partners added to their comfort with the conversations.

While Yoko and Keiko expressed their strong preferences for co-presence, Jennifer and Mary had more mixed impressions. Jennifer and Mary felt more of a sense of connection in the café environment than in the individual room environment but they felt a higher level of comfort in the individual room environment during the first session. Jennifer explained that the avatar gave her "a better sense of connection" and that she felt "a stronger sense of personal interaction" during the first session in the café environment. Mary also mentioned that she felt "quite closely connected" to her partner during the first session in the café environment. On the other hand, when it comes to the comfort level of interaction, both preferred the individual room. After their first experiences in both environments, Jennifer said she "did not feel nervous about speaking with a stranger" in the individual room and Mary also mentioned that she felt "slightly more comfortable" there. These comments show that they deepened their emotional connections with their partners, whereas they were more nervous in the café environment.

Despite the different impressions among participants, all the participants became relatively comfortable with having light conversations about recent events or their own cultures by the third session. The actual content of the conversations supports this observation. This phenomenon could be a result of adjusting to the restrictions of the media by adapting their language behavior to account for the absence of non-verbal cues usually used to build interpersonal impressions, as the social information processing perspective of mediated communication explains (Walther, 1992). After the third session, their emotional connections either became stronger or remained static. When there were no common interests or topics that they wanted to talk about, silences happened more frequently in later sessions.

Being able to see their partners' avatars in the environments also afforded the participants the ability to remember their partners and recall the content of their prior conversations. There were several instances in which the participants repeatedly asked the same questions during different sessions in the individual room environment with the same partner. On the other hand, there was no instance of this type of occurrence during the sessions within the café environment. Besides this, in the café environment, there were conversational sequences which were based on information that was given in previous sessions. This never happened in the individual room environment. Yoko constantly expressed her uncomfortableness in the individual room and suggested that the reason was a lack of visual cues. She explained that it was hard to remember what they talked about in the previous sessions without having visual cues. Keiko also pointed out a similar situation. She added that since they had sessions only once a week, it was very hard to remember what they had talked about in the individual room environment. Therefore, the visibility of the avatar seemed to help the participants remember what they talked about, which is necessary to understand a partner's views, perspectives and values through discussions.

Visibility of their partners' avatars also prevented the participants from having long silences. Each session had at least one instance of silence; however, longer silences, such as 19-second silences and 20-second silences, only happened in Jennifer and Yoko's sessions in the individual room environment. This pair's total number of silences also rose way above that of any other group. However, Mary and Keiko, the other pair in the individual room environment, did not have very long silences. One possible reason is Keiko's conversational patterns: she tended to give short answers and ask questions to her partners quickly. Although Mary did not experience longer silence in the individual room, she still noticed that the pauses in the conversation in the individual room "felt less awkward" since there seemed to be "less pressure to continue speaking for a long time." In addition, Jennifer thought that in the café environment, people will be "on their best behavior" because they feel like they are with the other party. This is also a possible motivation to avoid longer silences. Therefore, even though a speaker's personality and pair's compatibility may be a part of the reason, not being able to see the partner's avatars might also have contributed to the long silences.

DISCUSSION

In this study, participants had only one other person in their sessions with them; however, if there were three or more people in a group, participants might find avatars, as visual cues, more beneficial because they might be able to make connections between each group member's avatar and what he/she said during the sessions. Also, because co-presence worked as a prompter to avoid long silences, participants were, in a certain sense, forced to talk during the sessions. This may be especially beneficial for non-native speakers because some non-native speakers are hesitant to talk due to their fear of making mistakes. This effect, however, may give non-native speakers the impression that the interactions are less comfortable. In this research, non-native participants were in a second-year Japanese class and they were able to express basic facts and opinions; however, if they were novice speakers, the uncomfortableness might critically hinder their interactions.

The findings above make the following points clear:

- By using avatars as a visual cue, the participants were able to recall what they had talked about previously, thereby sustaining engagement.
- When faced with their partner's virtual presence, the participants tended to feel awkward if there was a long silence.
- Co-presence may also help both native speakers and non-native speakers to deepen their emotional connections, which is important, as Salmon (2000) said that "success comes with a strong foundation at stage two (online socialization)."
- For non-native speakers, however, the same co-presence may cause more anxiety about having interactions with their partners compared to the anxiety that they had in the environment with no co-presence. Whether the overall impressions turned out to be positive or negative may depend on a learner's personality and/or speaking proficiency.
- The differences in the environments may strongly affect, both negatively and positively, participants' emotional connections during the first several sessions; however, other factors, such as the topic of the conversation, increase their impact on emotional connections as the sessions go on.

Taking affordance framework into consideration, the findings listed above can be shown in the following diagram (Figure 2). The diagram, which was adapted from Hammond (2010)'s work, shows how affordance can be understood in the context of participants having interactions in 3D VLEs. The double-headed arrows in the diagram indicate that affordance points back to both agents and tools. One affordance, "environment shareable," gives participants an opportunity to see other avatars while simultaneously placing a constraint on realness: what they see is virtual reality, not a real environment or a real partner's face. This affordance subsequently affords participants the ability to see other avatars and to be together with their partners. The "other avatars visible" affordance helps learners to recall the content of their previous conversations while placing a constraint on having a long silence. The other sequential affordance, "able to be together," gives both native and non-native an opportunity for developing emotional connections; however, this affordance places a constraint on non-native speakers when it comes to expressing their opinions freely because of the social anxiety it can cause. As this diagram shows, affordance is a coming together of the perception and the property of software, which has a basis in physical properties.

Figure 2. Affordances of 3D VLEs

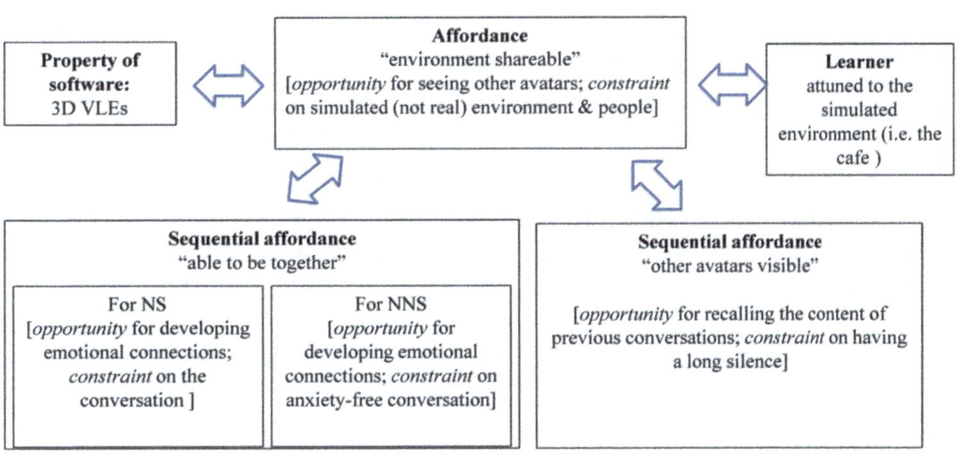

IMPLICATIONS

The results of the study suggest two important implications for the use of 3D MUVE to promote interpersonal and emotional connections. First, 3D MUVEs are an ideal environment to connect language learners who are geographically dispersed in real life. While the results show that native speakers are more comfortable with communicating in the 3D VLE using the visual design elements than non-native speakers, the study also reveals that non-native speakers can catch up and become comfortable by the third session. It is therefore important for instructors and instructional designers to plan ice-breaking and warm-up interaction sessions before moving students to the content-based and skill-focused learning activities.

Secondly, the results show that for learners with lower proficiency levels or learners who are afraid of making mistakes, the visual design elements of 3D VLEs may result in additional anxiety. One possible solution is to provide these students with less intimidating means of communication, such as e-mail and text chat, which might help to lower their anxiety levels, especially during the initial stage of the interaction process. On the other hand, some researchers question the benefits of a "less intimidating environment" (O'Dowd, 2006; Salaberry, 1996; Warschauer, 1997). In fact, all participants in this study stated that meeting in the café environment is similar to meeting someone in the real world. This suggests that the use of high fidelity visual elements in 3D VLEs can benefit language learners and better prepare them for the real-world interaction.

CONCLUSION

Due to its inherently social nature, 3D VLE is an optimal platform for online interaction, communication, and collaboration, and it holds great potential for language learners by engaging them in a real-life environment with authentic contexts, materials and social interaction. This study looks deeper into the visual features of 3D VLEs and examines how it affects language learners' perceptions of interpersonal and emotional connections with peers in this learning environment. Obviously, learners perceive the same technical feature and its affordance differently, depending upon their competency levels. In addition to competency levels, future research could look into learners' gender, personality and cultural background and examine how they affect learners' feeling of co-presence in 3D multi-user learning environments.

Learner's feeling of personal and emotional connection is an important aspect of any learning experience. Many studies have examined the effect of the affordances of 3D MUVEs on students' learning outcomes; the results of this study remind us that the affordances of a learning environment can affect a learner's emotional experience as well. Future research is needed to further explore the relationship between the affordances of 3D VLEs and learners' emotional experiences; for example, the effect of different types of affordances (e.g., visual, audio, text) on learners' feeling of co-presence. In addition, a categorization system that connects 3D VLE's technical affordances, emotional experience, and learning performance will help greatly in enhancing student learning experience and learning outcomes in this learning environment.

REFERENCES

Bailenson, J. N., Swinth, K., Hoyt, C., Persky, S., Dimov, A., & Blascovich, J. (2005). The independent and interactive effects of embodied-agent appearance and behavior on self-report, cognitive, and behavioral markers of copresence in immersive virtual environments. *Presence (Cambridge, Mass.)*, *14*(4), 379–393. doi:10.1162/105474605774785235

Belz, J. A., & Thorne, S. L. (2006). Introduction: Internet-mediated intercultural foreign language education and the intercultural speaker. In J. A. Belz & S. L. Thorne (Eds.), *Internet-mediated intercultural foreign language*. Boston, MA: Heinle & Heinle. doi:10.1079/9781845930639.0001

Biocca, F., Harms, C., & Burgoon, J. K. (2003). Toward a more robust theory and measure of social presence: Review and suggested criteria. *Presence (Cambridge, Mass.)*, *12*(5), 456–480. doi:10.1162/105474603322761270

Bower, M. (2008). Affordance analysis – matching learning tasks with learning Technologies. *Educational Media International*, *45*(1), 3–15. doi:10.1080/09523980701847115

Conole, G., & Dyke, M. (2004). What are the affordances of information and communication technologies? *ALT-J*, *12*(2), 113–124. doi:10.3402/rlt.v12i2.11246

Dalgarno, B., & Lee, M. J. W. (2010). What are the learning affordances of 3D virtual environments? *British Journal of Educational Technology*, *40*(6), 10–32. doi:10.1111/j.1467-8535.2009.01038.x

Dickey, M. D. (2003). Teaching in 3D: Pedagogical affordances and constraints of 3D virtual worlds for synchronous distance learning. *Distance Education*, *24*(1), 105–121. doi:10.1080/01587910303047

Dieterle, E., & Clarke, J. (2009). Multi-user virtual environments for teaching and learning. In M. Pagani (Ed.), *Encyclopedia of multimedia technology and networking* (2nd ed.; pp. 1033–1041). Hershey, PA: Information Science Reference. doi:10.4018/978-1-60566-014-1.ch139

Gall, M., & Breeze, N. (2005). Music composition lessons: The multimodal affordances of technology. *Educational Review*, *57*(4), 415–433. doi:10.1080/00131910500278314

Gibson, J. J. (1979). *The ecological approach to visual perception*. Boston, MA: Houghton Mifflin.

Goffman, E. (1963). *Behavior in public places*. New York, NY: The Free Press.

Greeno, J. (1998). The situativity of knowing, learning, and research. *The American Psychologist*, *53*(1), 5–26. doi:10.1037/0003-066X.53.1.5

Hammond, M. (2010). What is an affordance and can it help us understand the use of ICT in education? *Education and Information Technologies*, *15*(3), 205–217. doi:10.1007/s10639-009-9106-z

Hedberg, J. G., & Alexander, S. (1994). Virtual reality in education: Defining researchable issues. *Educational Media International*, *31*(4), 214–220. doi:10.1080/0952398940310402

Jarmon, L., Traphagan, T., Mayrath, M., & Trivedi, A. (2009). Virtual world teaching, experiential learning, and assessment: An interdisciplinary communication course in Second Life. *Computers & Education*, *53*(1), 169–182. doi:10.1016/j.compedu.2009.01.010

Kennewell, S., Tanner, H., Jones, S., & Beauchamp, G. (2007). Analyzing the use of interactive technology to implement interactive teaching. *Journal of Computer Assisted Learning*, *24*(1), 61–73. doi:10.1111/j.1365-2729.2007.00244.x

Kirschner, P., Strijbos, J., Kreijns, K., & Beers, P. J. (2004). Designing electronic collaborative learning environments. *Educational Technology Research and Development*, *52*(3), 47–66. doi:10.1007/BF02504675

Ludlow, P., & Wallace, M. (2007). *The Second Life Herald: The virtual tabloid that witnessed the dawn of the metaverse*. Cambridge, MA: MIT Press.

Norman, D. A. (1988). *The psychology of everyday things*. New York, NY: Basic Books.

Norman, D. A. (1993). *Things that make us smart: Defending human attributes in the age of the machine*. New York, NY: Basic Books.

O'Dowd, R. (2006). *Telecollaboration and the development of intercultural communicative competence*. Berlin, Germany: Langenscheidt.

Panichi, L., Deutschmann, M., & Molka-Danielsen, J. (2010). Virtual worlds for language learning and intercultural exchange: Is it for real? In S. Guth & F. Helm (Eds.), *Telecollaboration 2.0: Languages, literacies and intercultural learning in the 21st century* (pp. 165–195). New York, NY: Peter Lang.

Peterson, M. (2012). EFL learner collaborative interaction in Second Life. *ReCALL*, *24*(1), 20–39. doi:10.1017/S0958344011000279

Richards, S. B., Taylor, R., Ramasamy, R., & Richards, R. Y. (1999). *Single subject research: Applications in educational and clinical settings*. Belmont, CA: Wadsworth.

Salaberry, M. R. (1996). The theoretical foundation for the development of pedagogical tasks in computer mediated communication. *CALICO Journal*, *14*(1), 5–34.

Salmon, G. (2000). *E-moderating: The key to teaching and learning online*. New York, NY: Routledge. doi:10.4324/9780203465424

Schroeder, R. (1996). *Possible worlds: The social dynamic of virtual reality technologies*. Boulder, CO: Westview Press.

Schroeder, R. (2002). *Copresence and interaction in virtual environments: An overview of the range of issues*. Paper presented at the 5th Annual International Workshop on PRESENCE, Porto, Portugal.

Schroeder, R., & Axelsson, A. (Eds.). (2006). *Avatars at work and play: Collaboration and interaction in shared virtual environments*. London, UK: Springer-Verlag. doi:10.1007/1-4020-3898-4

Swinth, K., & Blascovich, J. (2002, October). *Perceiving and responding to others: Human-human and human-computer social interaction in collaborative virtual environments.* Paper presented at the 5th Annual International Workshop on PRESENCE, Porto, Portugal.

Tu, C. H., Yen, C., & Blocher, M. (2011). A study of the relationship between gender and online social presence. *International Journal of Online Pedagogy and Course Design, 1*(3), 33–49. doi:10.4018/ijopcd.2011070103

Walther, J. B. (1992). Interpersonal effects in computer-mediated interaction: A relational perspective. *Communication Research, 19*(1), 52–90. doi:10.1177/009365092019001003

KEY TERMS AND DEFINITIONS

3D Virtual Learning Environments (3D VLEs): A three-dimensional (3D) virtual environment that is used to create an immersive and interactive environment to facilitate learning.

Affordance: The perceived properties of the object. These fundamental properties primarily determine how the object could possibly be used.

Avatar: A graphical image that represents a person in the virtual world of the internet and computers.

Co-Presence: A user's perception or feeling that others are co-situated within an interpersonal environment.

Online Intercultural Exchange: A technology-enabled, sustained, people-to-people exchange that entails the engagement of groups of students in intercultural exchange, interaction, and collaboration with peers from partner classes in geographically distant locations.

Second Life: An online-based virtual world that is developed and owned by Linden Lab. Using their avatars, which can be customized, users can interact with places, objects, and other avatars.

Section 2
MUVE and Twenty-First Century Learning

Chapter 6

Integrating Virtual Spaces:
Connecting Affordances of 3D Virtual Learning Environments to Design for Twenty-First Century Learning

Peggy Hartwick
Carleton University, Canada

Nuket Savaskan Nowlan
Carleton University, Canada

ABSTRACT

This chapter explores perspectives from general learning theories in relation to affordances of 3D virtual learning environments (3DVLEs) in order to substantiate a theoretically informed pedagogical design process. Following this review, the authors describe 3DVLE space and task design used as part of an English for Academic Purpose (EAP) course at a Canadian university. The design process is then contextualized according to a Phillips, McNaught, and Kennedy's (2010, 2012) learning framework called Learning Environment, Learning Processes, and Learning Outcomes (LEPO). The authors share sample tasks and screen shots of the 3DVLE, as well as teacher and designer recommendations for future designs. In conclusion, the authors stress the importance of drawing on multiple learning theories to illuminate the affordances of the space. Further, they call for empirical research that makes use of telemetric data in the assessment of learner interaction in relation to achieving learning outcomes and predicting learner success.

INTRODUCTION

The 21st century student is evolving to include both digital natives and lifelong and global learners. Academic content is not limited to knowledge acquisition, now extending to include skills and competency development. Meanwhile, classrooms are no longer confined to four walls as a result of new online learning environments. Consequently, teaching is not simply the synchronous transmission of information; rather, it includes the facilitation of learning opportunities in multiple learning environments, some

DOI: 10.4018/978-1-5225-3719-9.ch006

unrestricted by time and place (Bransford, Brown, & Cocking, 2000; Haythornthwaite & Andrews, 2011; Illeris, 2003; Prensky, 2006). The delivery of post-secondary education has shifted to include a myriad of online spaces, such as multi-user 3-dimensional (3D) virtual learning environments (3DVLEs) in which users communicate in real-time in an Internet-hosted virtual environment. An understanding of how the affordances of 3DVLEs contribute to general learning may help educators develop more meaningful activities to be carried out in these learning spaces. Reflecting on the teaching and learning experiences in terms of how learners interact with in these online spaces has the potential to positively influence teaching practice and learning outcomes. Such knowledge could contribute to students' overall success in achieving 21st century learning outcomes, including mastery of subject content, and 21st century skills, including critical thinking, communication, and problem solving (Dede, 2010).

This chapter is motivated by the authors' experiences using 3DVLEs and will address the following two questions: (1) what are the pedagogical perspectives that inform instruction in 3DVLEs based on the affordances of the space? And, more specifically, (2) how might 3DVLEs be used to enhance 21st century skills in English for Academic Purpose (EAP) classrooms? To address these questions, the authors situate the key affordances of 3DVLEs outlined by Dalgarno and Lee (2010) in relation to general and specific learning theories. To accomplish this, they provide a broad review of traditional and contemporary learning theories in order to understand which theoretical approach (or combination of approaches) best supports learning in 3DVLEs based on the affordances of the space. To contextualize the learning process in relation to said affordances and activity design, the authors introduce a general learning framework proposed by Phillips, McNaught, and Kennedy (2010, 2012) called *Learning Environment, Learning Processes and Learning Outcomes* (LEPO). The authors then provide definitional context for a 3DVLE uniquely designed for an EAP course at a Canadian university (i.e., the *Learning Environment*). Next, they situate and describe a series of tasks (i.e., *Learning Processes*) specifically designed for and carried out in this context. The tasks could be replicated in most undergraduate university level courses, as the focus is on practicing research skills and facilitating the achievement of 21st century skills development through learning experiences (i.e., *Learning Outcomes*). The authors selected this framework as it blends characteristics from multiple learning theories. The framework also reflects the importance of environment and affordances of space reviewed in this chapter.

The chapter calls for ongoing research about 3DVLEs in order to substantiate teaching practice and space design in well-grounded theory. Specifically, it recommends empirical studies that measure levels of engagement in relation to achievement outcomes through the use of telemetrics that focus on frequency of interaction and communication in space. Overall, the chapter aims to contribute to a better understanding of how learning theories help to guide space and task design for 3DVLEs to best promote unique opportunities for learning through interaction and experience in and with the space in order to achieve 21st century learning outcomes.

BACKGROUND

A recurrent theme in academic literature on emerging pedagogies is a call for a modified or new learning theory to reflect learning in the many new online teaching spaces (Bransford et al., 2000; Dewey, 1938; Harasim, 2012; Haythornthwaite & Andrews, 2011; Illeris, 2003; Loke, 2015; Phillips et al., 2012; Savin-Baden, 2008; Savin-Baden, Gourlay, Tombs, Steils, Tombs, & Mawer, 2010). Historically well-known learning theories, while critical in accounting for how people learn generally, are problematic when applied to these new learning environments because many fail to account for how people learn with respect to the affordances of online space. To illustrate, behaviourists like B. F. Skinner argue that learning is a behaviour that can be changed by external stimuli, such as reward and punishment; cognitivists like Robert Gagné claim that learning is related to mental processes; and constructivists, like Vygotsky, understand learning in relation to personal, social interaction (Ally, 2008; Dede, 2007; Harasim, 2012). None of these adequately account for the affordances of online learning spaces, however, and so understanding and identifying relevant characteristics from existing theory and applying them to these ever-changing learning contexts proves challenging. Further, it is difficult to work within a strict dichotomy of learning theories, because learning depends a number of variables, such as technology, learner, expected outcomes, and defined space.

To capture these variables and to contextualize the learning processes described herein, the authors chose to employ the LEPO framework as a flexible and pragmatic approach. This framework helps clarify how learners learn in a range of environments and views learning as a social process in which the learner and teacher are active participants. Phillips et al.'s (2012) framework draws on characteristics from constructivist learning theories and other models of learning that emphasize interaction, student and teacher knowledge, experience, and reflection. For instance, the learning processes component of the framework draws on Bransford et al.'s (2000) four lenses of learning which include the learner's beliefs and knowledge experiences and, importantly, an understanding that learning activities create increased learner awareness through feedback. Under this framework, learning outcomes are based on demonstrated knowledge and skills acquired through the learning processes whereby the learner has engaged in the learning environments. The authors selected this framework because it helps capture their view of how people learn and it is broad enough to allow for a range of learning outcomes, including 21st century skills like problem solving and critical thinking. The following review identifies a range of relevant learning theories and helps substantiate the authors' decision to work within the LEPO framework.

General Learning Theories and Approaches

This section begins with a review of learning theories that have guided 20th century teaching practice—namely, behaviourism, cognitivism, constructivism, and socio-cultural theory—followed by a review of more contemporary 21st century approaches to learning. The purpose of this review is to relate theory to practice in 3DVLEs based on the key affordances of these unique online learning spaces. The authors explore key characteristics from traditional and contemporary theories to speculate whether, or if, the affordances of 3DVLEs facilitate achievement of learning outcomes. It is hoped that this section will illuminate the importance of drawing on diverse learning paradigms to inform 3DVLE space and task design.

Behaviourist, Cognitivist, and Constructivist Learning Theories

Behaviourist learning theory came to the forefront in education in the early 20th century and stems from the work of psychologists such as B. F. Skinner. Behaviourists believe that the correct instructional stimuli will elicit the desired learning outcomes, with an emphasis on practice and performance (Ally, 2008; Harasim, 2012). Behaviourism has a role in the understanding and design of learning spaces today, as certain basic learning outcomes depend on practice and repetition (Harasim, 2012). For instance, in current digital learning contexts, the act of accessing, manipulating, and adapting to online learning contexts to complete a task requires the learner to become adept at negotiating the space. This adeptness happens in time and with practice.

Moving away from behaviourist accounts, cognitivist learning theorists do not entirely reject the notion of stimulus and response, but rather seek to understand the intervening mental processes. Whereas behaviourists reject the unobservable components of thinking and learning, cognitivists view the mind as an information processor (Ally, 2008; Clark, 2001; Harasim, 2012) and understand learning and knowledge in terms of dynamic schematic representations of concepts that an individual shapes in their mind. Psychologist and instructional designer Robert Gagné specified a learning taxonomy based on anticipated outcomes (skills and strategies) and events of instruction. Though occasionally prescriptive and deliberate in practice, cognitivist learning theory and certainly Gagné's taxonomy contribute important theoretical elements for understanding online spaces. For instance, some of Gagné's *events of instruction*, such as providing feedback, can help explain the affordance of real-time voice and movement in terms of giving instruction, assistance, and feedback (Harasim, 2012).

Theories have moved on to consider learning more holistically and inseparable from the learner and social environment. Coinciding with the social movements of the 1970s, constructivist learning theorists view the learner as an active participant in their own learning process and the teacher as a facilitator of knowledge making. A prominent theorist of this school, Vygotsky, believes that knowledge is more than passive reception and memorization of information; he holds that learning occurs because of active engagement or experience in a social context. This approach departs significantly from behaviourist and cognitive views in which "...the lecture notes of the instructor get transferred to the notebooks of the students without passing through the brains of either" (Mazur, as cited in Harasim, 2012, p. 59).

Vygotsky (1986) stresses the social context in which the learning occurs and places great importance on interaction, communication, and experience. According to Vygotsky's concept *zone of proximal development* (ZPD), an individual's learning potential is reached with the assistance of a more capable peer through active problem solving and interaction (Ireson, 2008; Vygotsky, 1986). In keeping with the ZPD, it can be argued that, like a "more capable peer", the affordances of 3DVLEs provide the assistance needed for learning to occur, particularly as users collaborate in the online space with artifacts or objects (described by Vygotsky as *tools*). Indeed, both the virtual space and the objects within the space can be viewed as culturally created artifacts that shape the activity or task at hand.

Characteristics of constructivist and socio-cultural theory are evident in 21st century pedagogies. For instance, active learning and learning-by-doing (such as role-play), as well as scaffolded, experiential, and collaborative learning (Harasim, 2012) are all based on the premise that learning is an active process. Vygotsky's view continues to be influential today and underlies other approaches to learning. A notable adaptation is activity theory, which understands learning as a socially constructed process where learners interact in pursuit of a shared goal (Engeström, 2001; Ireson, 2008; Kaptelinin & Nardi, 2006). Importantly for 3DVLEs, activity theory extends beyond basic bi-directional interaction to consider the complex social context and the technologies in and with which subjects act. These multi-directional interactions are a key premise of the LEPO model.

Learning Into the 21st Century

While the abovementioned theories help account for how people learn more generally, Dede (2003) calls for a new model of education to better suit 21st century learners who are competent digitally and have high collaboration and critical thinking skills. Savin-Baden (2008) suggests that digital spaces have brought about new types of literacy, communication, and pedagogy. Loke (2015) advocates for a modified learning theory that better accounts for students' physical experiences, especially in 3DVLEs. According to Siemens (2005), contemporary learning theory needs to better reflect learners' needs and today's trends such as life-long learning, and broad competencies with technology and tools. Siemens proposes a connectivist theory that presupposes that the learner can make critical judgments in the knowledge making and acquisition process, and learning is about making connections between large amounts of information and decisions about what needs to be learned for tomorrow. Accordingly, connectivism is about knowing how to access new knowledge through technology and has relevance in that students need to be resourceful and take advantage of tools inside and outside of the 3DVLE to meet learning outcomes. For example, students working on a collaborative writing document in the environment can simultaneously access an online dictionary or website to gather more information about the topic.

A gap in connectivist theory with respect to 3DVLEs is that it places little emphasis on the role of the collective group and the activity and its mediating tools (a tenet of activity theory), such as language and space. Newer learning theories should continue to focus on aspects of socio-cultural theory, but also recognize the role of mediating tools. Scardamalia and Bereiter (2006) attempt this integration with respect to learning in relation to the Internet and technology. They comment on the range and diversity of learning approaches, including situated cognition and social constructivism. Scardamalia and Bereiter believe that learning occurs socially, and add the dimension that members are connected through and with technology. Essentially, learners are members of a community wherein understanding emerges through collective problem solving and is not confined to a classroom or individual—in other words, ours is a "… knowledge creating culture" (p. 97). Their beliefs are applicable to learning afforded by and in 3DVLEs.

In keeping with Siemens' (2005) and Scardamalia and Bereiter's (2006) push for new learning theories, Dede (2007) points out that models of education need to shift to keep up with a changing landscape of teaching and learning as emerging technologies are used in and as the classroom. His focus is preparing 21st century learners with skills such as critical thinking and problem solving. He challenges educators and institutions to transform education in terms of what we already know about learning and cognition and claims this transformation should include the delocalization of the classroom community as technologies help to distribute knowledge outside of the traditional classroom space. While he agrees that traditional pedagogies are still important, Dede believes that situated learning is the best theoretical approach to technology enabled collaboration: "Fortunately, emerging information communication technology that enable immersive, collaborative simulation now offer the capability to implement situated learning environments in classroom settings" (p. 23). The central notion of situated learning is that learning is an active process whereby cognition is shared and learning is achieved through collaboration and co-participation (Brown, Collins, & Duguid, 1989; Lave & Wenger, 1991; Rogoff, 1990). The assumption is that knowing how and knowing what are inseparable; further, it is through the collective act and use of authentic physical and social spaces that learning occurs, where "Learning and acting are interestingly indistinct, learning being a continuous, life-long process resulting from acting in situations" (Brown, Collins, & Duguid, 1989, p. 33).

Despite the importance placed on the needs of 21st century learners, skill development, and the incorporation of technology in education (Prensky, 2006), neither the connectivist nor the focus-on-skill approach adequately accounts for what is happening in terms of user interaction in and with the learning space. Gee (2007) claims, "Traditional views of learning stress the mind and not the body" (p. 71). He argues that traditional pedagogy continues to focus on the dissemination of content, concrete stages of development, and rigid curricula instead of emphasizing the strength of the space and the activity, such as collaborative problem solving. Gee (2004) and Gee and Hayes (2011) argue that traditional definitions of literacy and knowledge are overly rigid and do not account for technical and creative expertise, which are characteristics of 21st century learners. With respect to space, Gee and Hayes (2011) describe any virtual or physical learning space as an *affinity space* in which participants share the same interest and passion (affinity) for whatever activity they are embarking on together. As described, affinity spaces reflect many of the same theoretical constructs mentioned earlier, such as situated and experiential learning, guidance from a more capable peer, and shared or distributed knowledge (Gee, 2007; Gee & Hayes, 2011).

Savin-Baden (2008) likewise explores the notion of space in connection to learning. She explains how space affords opportunities for reflection, critique, and learning. She reflects on how digital spaces have provided novel opportunities for learning and knowledge building; these are characterized by the freedom to move and explore. Drawing on this and many of the characteristics from the above noted learning theories, this chapter's authors use Phillips et al.'s (2010) LEPO framework as a way of conceptualizing and understanding learning in 3DVLEs. This framework reflects the authors' shared understanding of the importance of space in affording learning opportunities by virtue of the learner's experiences interacting in and with these spaces. Importantly, this model describes learning as facilitated by an environment in which an activity is acted out and learning outcomes are subsequently demonstrated or achieved.

Under this broad framework the environment provides the context in which learners engage in learning processes and where learning outcomes are demonstrated. This model pertains to physical and digital learning environments, curriculum, and task design, and is underpinned by a view that learning is an interactive system. This framework is in line with the authors' views that learning is a social process in which the learner is engaged as an active participant. Learning is a process and outcomes are achieved because the activity and the affordances of the environment help the learner to achieve learning outcomes.-

Affordances of 3DVLEs

The term *affordance* in relation to learning was first coined by James Gibson and described as "... whatever it is about the environment that contributes to the kind of interaction that occurs" (as cited in Greeno, 1994, p. 338). Gibson (1979) defines an affordance as an *action opportunity* provided by the environment; while not always acted on, an affordance is the potential for action. Norman (2002), on the other hand, defines affordances in relation to an object and according to what is perceived or actual regarding the characteristics of the object or thing. From a design perspective, Norman claims an affordance pertains to what people see; he argues that if the user does not see or perceive the affordance, then it is not so. The notion of affordance is important in the context of 3DVLEs and in relation to the many characteristics revealed in learning theories wherein the learner (perceiver) interacts with the environment. For instance, opportunities for learning experiences, collaboration, and knowledge construction are presented in the environment and because of the affordances. According to the LEPO framework, the environment is an integral component of the learning process.

While much of the literature on 3DVLEs refers to the affordances and benefits of these spaces, Dalgarno and Lee (2010) argue that research pertaining to their educational uses and benefits is largely anecdotal. Their article conceptualizes the interactive nature of these environments in terms of affordances and explores the relationships between learning benefits and 3DVLEs' key characteristics. They propose a learning model for 3DVLEs that classifies affordances with respect to facilitating learning through task design. The model focuses particularly on the qualities of presence and immersion, which afford opportunities for user interaction and experience. Dalgarno and Lee claim that a so-called *fidelity of space* leads to users' sense of "being there" (presence), which subsequently increases user interaction. By theorizing the affordances of space this learning model helps distinguish 3DVLEs from other physical or online classroom spaces.

Affordance of Authentic Space

3DVLEs can be designed to replicate authentic geographical places like London and Madrid (Ibáñez, Garcia, Galan, Maroto, Morillo, & Kloos, 2011; Milton, Jonsen, Hirst, & Lindenburn, 2012), or authentic physical spaces like a classroom, archeological dig site, or nightclub (Arya, Hartwick, Graham, & Nowlan, 2012; Milton et al., 2012). The visual and spatial richness of 3DVLEs affords opportunities for experiential learning shaped by other users and by artifacts or 3D objects in the environment. In this way, 3DVLEs are mediums within which social interaction may occur. Further, learning opportunities can be mediated not just by the space, but through virtually rendered artifacts and non-player avatars, which are not controlled by a user, but rather purposefully designed for the activity (Dalgarno & Lee, 2010; Warburton, 2009). For example, in the 3DVLE the authors used in their EAP classrooms, non-player avatars are manipulated to the extent that they have pre-recorded dialogue that is not necessarily part of task instructions. The depth of space and range of artifacts, such as refrigerators in the houses, contribute to the fidelity and authenticity of space, affording learners experiences in both the visual and physical realm and facilitate social interaction and construction of knowledge through language. The representational authenticity of space in 3DVLEs is one of most significant and distinguishing characteristics of these learning spaces (Dalgarno & Lee, 2010). Not only is interaction with and because of the space meaningful, but the affordance of real-time, synchronous interaction are significant catalysts for learning. This fidelity leads to a true perception of immersion and "being there" for the user.

Affordance of Immersion

The rich fidelity of space gives users a sense of real-time presence or immersion. Dalgarno and Lee (2010) describe the sense of presence and co-presence as a consequence of the characteristics of the environment. The affordance of immersion includes the user's ability to personalize their own avatar according to traits like hair and skin colour, height, and weight, resulting in a 3D self. Contributing further to a sense of presence is the ability for avatar users to perform gestures, such as a hand-wave or shake, or bow, and even make facial expressions and head movement (Peterson, 2006). Further, the ability to create new avatar identities may differ from the user's "real-world" identity and provide them with new opportunities to interact socially while hiding behind an avatar persona (Wigham & Chanier, 2013). This is likely to contribute to increased self-efficacy and willingness to communicate, increased motivation, and increased risk-taking (Peterson, 2010; Peterson, 2011). Owing to the realistic and immersive qualities of the space, users feel that they are extensions of themselves as their avatar-self is genuinely engaged in completing the task. This extension of self helps users concentrate and focus on the task as opposed to focusing on themselves (Csikszentmihalyi, 2014). In this way, the affordance of immersion relates to the learning approaches highlighted earlier in terms of social interaction, experience, negotiation, and collaboration.

Implications

Understanding the many salient relationships between learning theories and the affordances or benefits of 3DVLEs is critical in terms of practical implications. For instance, if the benefits of 3DVLEs as defined learning spaces afford opportunities for synchronous interaction and mediation through tools and collaboration with others, then it is possible to contextualize these as learning spaces based on the learning principles from the previously mentioned theories, including negotiation of meaning and development of skills as a result of external social processes, influences, and interaction (Harasim, 2012; Kaptelinin & Nardi, 2006; Prensky, 2006; Vygotsky, 1986). These social processes are collaborative and interactive and hence promote learning as a result of the affordances of the space. Tasks Two through Five were designed so that users would make use of the space and tools within the space by clicking, moving, and gesturing to accomplish a task. Ideally, these experiences would lead to outcomes.

In sum, the conceptualization of the classroom has changed with the provision of online spaces and due to the learning affordances of these spaces, but how do these perspectives inform space and instructional design? The authors hold that these unique learning contexts may have the potential to facilitate learning for some learners in a blended context by creating alternative learning spaces. Similarly, the potential for distance language learning in these spaces is significant, as made evident by the number of studies involving virtual worlds and online language education (Kim, Lee, & Thomas, 2012). The next section provides a definitional framework of a unique 3DVLE used to carry out a series of tasks designed to achieve specified learning outcomes in an EAP classroom.

DESIGN PROCESS

With the addition of technology as an alternative space for teaching and learning, the practical implications of new online teaching and learning spaces are far-reaching and should consider the affordances, features, and benefits of each unique space in relation to established learning theories and understanding of how people learn. While 3DVLE platforms are easy to use, the shift from instruction in a physical or online space to a 3D space is challenging. A difficulty for educators is knowing how to create scenarios that will facilitate the achievement of specified learning outcomes in these new contexts. This section describes the design of a 3DVLE for a course and its associated activities that evolved from the authors' shared understanding of the affordances of space in relation to 21st century learning theories and is framed by LEPO, an integrative and flexible framework. The section first contextualizes the course and the rationale for using a 3DVLE, and then provides a definitional framework of the space (Learning Environment) and provides illustrative descriptions of specific spaces and sample tasks that were developed to help promote critical thinking, problems solving, collaboration, and effective communication (Learning Processes and Learning Outcomes), some of the 21st century skills identified by Dede (2010).

Course Context

The activities below were designed as part of an advanced level EAP course at a Canadian university. These courses are for students who have an English as a Second Language requirement as determined by a recognized English Language Proficiency test such as IELTS. Students achieving a mid-range score are placed in one of three levels of this program designed to refine academic English skills and language proficiency. Typically, students at the advanced level take up to three courses in their degree program at the same time; in this case, the EAP course outline states that the course is designed to "enhance academic language skills", while "developing critical thinking and problem solving skills."

While the course physically takes place on campus twice a week for three hours, a major component is a *Research Project*, worth 40% of the course grade, which includes 16 separate activities, four of which take place in a 3DVLE. Students access the 3DVLE from a lab on campus during regular class time. Throughout the term and as part of the *Research Project*, students are expected to demonstrate evidence of personal learning as they do preliminary research related to a commercial sustainable initiative and the overarching theme of "sustainable development" and based on their experiences interacting in a 3DVLE. Over the 12-week course, students are evaluated according to whether their chosen initiative meets its sustainable development goals according to suitable indicators derived from teacher-assigned sources. Of the eight learning outcomes for the *Research Project*, the outcomes most related to the students' experiences completing tasks in the 3DVLE include: describing in detail their major, program of study, and main topics from required courses; recognizing and interpreting career and educational preferences; evaluating the sustainability of their chosen sustainable initiative based on select indicators; and showing academic written and oral communication skills.

The rationale behind using a 3DVLE for these activities was to increase the potential for users to experience interactions made possible specifically due to the affordances of the environment and to observe how learners interact in and with these spaces. The authors believe that the 3DVLE experiences described below helped facilitate and enhance learning outcomes due to the affordances of the virtual space and the design of the tasks.

Definition of Whole Space (Learning Environment)

The following is a description of the 3DVLE and associated tasks. For context, 3DVLEs are Internet-hosted environments, which can be designed to graphically replicate real world places or scenarios and wherein users manipulate an avatar to purposefully communicate with other user avatars using voice over Internet protocol (VoIP). Users can also interact with physically represented artifacts like chairs and tables and use web-based tools, such as collaborative writing surfaces and text functions. The purpose of the interaction is determined by the assigned activity and desired learning outcomes (Hartwick, 2015).

The 3DVLE described herein originally replicated a university campus, including campus buildings and classrooms (Figure 1) and was a browser-based 3D platform by AvayaLive Engage. Over a four-year period, the space evolved to include new spaces, including an orientation maze. New space designs resulted from a recursive process involving a multidisciplinary team of 3D technical designers, educational designers, and subject matter experts. Importantly, the design team had support from managers, directors, and faculty deans. Each iteration of the space was determined by the design team and involved matching teaching objectives to space design and identifying how the space would help learners achieve outcomes that might not otherwise be possible in a physical classroom space. In line with the LEPO framework, this included developing the learning outcomes, authentic virtual world characteristics, options, and objects needed for successful activity implementation. Each activity-specific location is connected to the main university virtual campus.

Figure 1. Screenshot of university virtual campus

LEPO Framework: Learning Environments, Learning Processes, and Learning Outcomes

Phillips et al. (2012) credit the success of a well-designed learning environment to the relationship of activity design and learning design. For example, the design of an activity should prompt the learner to engage with the design of the environment. As noted above, the purpose of the *Research Project* is for students to do preliminary research related to the overarching theme of sustainable development. During regular class time, students develop language and academic skills through the same topic, such as by reading and learning about related sub-topics like sustainability indicators and the pillars of sustainable development. In addition to thematic content, students learn and practice academic skills, such as citing and referencing sources and reflective writing. The tasks described below are the result of the design team's more than four years of experience and modifications. The recursive process allowed team members to systematically account for the affordances of space and characteristics of how people learn, such as practice, collaboration, and interaction. Hence, tasks designed for this particular course and the 3DVLE were intended to help students achieve specified learning outcomes related to language, content, and skill and because of their experiences in class and in the 3DVLE. Tasks were intended to increase technical proficiency and elicit critical thinking and problem solving, which are to be demonstrated through actions and written language. This section describes five interrelated and sequential tasks, the latter four of which played out in the 3DVLE described above. The tasks designed and described in this chapter made use of five locations in the 3DVLE campus, namely *Orientation Maze*, *Career Island*, *Residences*, *Campus* and *Rainbow Stage*, and *Native Village* and *Market*. The tasks were designed to target students' content knowledge regarding an understanding of their majors and disciplines and thematic topic; language in terms of topic specific vocabulary; and self-awareness regarding their ability to make connections between experience and knowledge.

Activity One: Holland Code Assessment

Learning Environments

Although Activity One did not take place in the 3DVLE, it helped students develop an awareness of their interests, values, and possible major; it was also a necessary step to guide Activity Three by providing vocabulary related to personality traits and career preferences. Activity One was done in the physical classroom during class time and consisted of students taking a modified version of the Holland Code Assessment to identify personality traits, skills, and career preferences.

Learning Processes

Students ranked their top three personality traits (realistic, investigative, artistic, social, enterprising, and conventional) in relation to their choice in major and career preferences. The purpose of this activity was to assess language, content, and metacognitive skills based on use of specific vocabulary and ability to articulate traits, skills, and career preferences. This process promotes language use, while simultaneously having students predict, monitor and reflect on their learning trajectory. These processes are congruent with behaviourist, cognitive, constructivist, and 21st century learning theories.

Learning Outcomes

The students' metacognitive ability or self-awareness was reflected in their ability to make connections between the outcome of the Holland Code Assessment and their choice of major and experiences to date both in and out of class and in response to the following prompt: *Explain how the results of your Holland Code (category) related to your major. Use vocabulary from question 2 above. Your explanation should include your experiences to date.* As a result of this activity, students were able to articulate in writing their own personality traits as in, "I'm a curios person. Every time a question popped up in my head, I always right away looking for the answer." Further, they could reflect on choice of major in relation to Holland Code results as in, "The career possibilities described by the Holland code for the Investigate traits suits my current academic career and even my career plan. I'm currently in Biology major and I want to be a surgeon." Students also predicted future careers options, as in, "Also, I would like to work in a bank, so the computer skills that I am learning and the math course that I am study will help me in this career."

Activity Two: Spatial and Technical Orientation

Learning Environments

As previously mentioned, the *Orientation Maze* (Figure 2) was designed to give students a spatial and technical orientation to the environment before tackling other tasks. It was also used to determine which types of strategies students relied on to efficiently complete an activity (e.g., asking peers for help or going back and starting the maze again). The *Orientation Maze* is a virtual path that progressively guides students through the functions of the platform so they can be technically and spatially prepared to engage in upcoming tasks. Each of the seven maze sections is connected by a gate that students can

Figure 2. Screenshot of orientation maze

open only by performing an activity accurately, such as a movement or a gesture. The maze is designed to be followed without a facilitator. By the end of the maze, students will have successfully performed the most common features of the 3DVLE platform, thereby reducing technical and spatial barriers in future activities. Students can practice these skills until they feel confident enough to leave the maze and proceed to other tasks. Students can advance through the progressively more complex steps of the maze as they read directions and solve problems along the way.

Learning Processes

Understanding how to use the technology, reading to inform, and the ability to problem solve in authentic, new environments are considered important 21st century skills (Dede, 2010; P21 Partnership for 21st Century Learning, n.d.). In each of the seven maze sections, students are expected to perform a series of interactions by following posted written instructions and solving the challenge of opening the gate to advance to the next section of the maze. One such interaction has students attempt and practice various gestures to advance. This interaction is in line with behaviourist theories with regards to repetition and memory and importantly contributes to students' ultimate success in these environments with progressively more complex tasks. Further, each station of progression and instruction throughout the maze acts to scaffold the technical skill. Upon completion of the *Orientation Maze* and by way of the post orientation survey, the teacher helps students reflect on whether they made use of meta-cognitive skills and the available supports.

Learning Outcomes

Phillips et al. (2012) define learning outcomes as things that are demonstrable as a result of engagement. Upon successfully completing each section of the *Orientation Maze*, students were expected to demonstrate achievement of technical outcomes, reading comprehension, and problem solving by following a set of instructions. These instructions required that the student manipulate their avatar by using gestures (e.g., wave, nod), movement (e.g., left and right), changing their avatar appearance, and texting the teacher. By responding to the question below, students reflected on their personal learning strategies:

Which strategies did you use to complete Activity Two (circle as many that apply)?

1. I asked another avatar by using my headset and voice
2. I went back to the maze
3. I worked with another avatar
4. I followed/ watched a peer avatar
5. I did not use any strategy(ies)
6. Other
7. I gave up/ logged off

Activity Three: Explore Your Career

Learning Environments

Career Island represents a self-sustainable island in which learners explore various professional roles represented by non-player avatars positioned throughout the island in virtual rooms reflecting their role, such as a nurse in a small clinic (Figure 3) and a biologist in a research lab (Figure 4). The virtually rendered rooms further reflect the careers through animated artifacts, such as a patient in the clinic. This environment, while not authentic, may contribute to a sense of immersion and real-time presence. The non-player avatars, if clicked on, provide information about the type of person that might be suitable for the careers and present challenges typical to that field. For instance, in the research lab, the biologist has crumpled paper all over the floor and around the garbage bin, indicating the biologist is frustrated with

Figure 3. Screenshot of nurse's clinic on Career Island

her research. In the nurse's clinic, a patient appears to be having an allergic reaction. *Career Island*, as a learning environment, was designed to support the activity, while the activity purposefully made use of the artifacts and rooms in the environment. The objects and non-player avatars helped to scaffold the content-specific vocabulary and stimulate the learners' prior knowledge of these different career roles in order to facilitate the activity.

Learning Processes

For Activity Three, students chose two of eight possible careers based on the results of Activity One and their choice in major. Upon landing in *Career Island*, students looked for the area representing their career choice, e.g., *Town Centre Building* (engineer, Figure 5) or *Clinic* (nurse). Once they found the most relevant location, students were instructed to notice, observe, and interact with the space, including the non-player avatars who talked about the selected careers. In these spaces students are encouraged to observe the space and listen to non-player avatars talk about their profession. Upon leaving the space students completed a brief survey to challenge their observational skills and encourage them to think critically about both careers. The survey is provided within the virtual environment via web board where it can be answered within the virtual environment while their experience is still fresh. From both a constructivist and a connectivist perspective, these instructions assume that learners will actively collaborate and be resourceful by taking advantage of the objects and tools within and outside the environment in order to successfully complete the activity.

Learning Outcomes

Students ultimately had to explain how their experiences interacting in the career spaces related to what they had found out thus far about their own choice of major. The following is one student's response to her experience in the clinic:

Figure 4. Screenshot of biologist's lab on Career Island

The second career that I chose is nursing because I want to help people and know how to treat sick people, and give them the right medicine. According to Holland Code, the nursing area of study of social but I am not a social person but I like this career. According to 3D lesson, the nursing in the video talk about how to help people and you need to be attention to details.

This comment demonstrates her awareness of her personality traits as she justifies how nursing is a suitable career choice although she is not social. Additionally, students were asked to respond to two questions that targeted critical thinking. For example, students who selected the nurse career and who explored the clinic were asked to respond to the questions:

1. What do you think is wrong with the female patient in the clinic?
2. Have you ever cared for a sick animal?

Because of this interaction and drawing on personal, real-world experiences, one student responded as follows, "My friend used to have a dog before finally the dog died because of the inflammation of the pancreas and I used to help her."

Activity Four: Defining Sustainable Development

Learning Environments

In addition to *Career Island* and the *Orientation Maze*, the 3DVLE has two main functional areas, a downtown area with shops, a café, and three houses, and a virtual university campus. Each of the houses in the *Residences* section can be designed and textured to reflect the eating, consuming, and cultural habits of the hypothetical inhabitants. As such, walls, refrigerators, furniture and level of cleanliness can be textured to suit the learning task and outcomes. Figure 6 is a screenshot of a university student

Figure 5. Screenshot of engineer's work site

inspecting virtual refrigerator contents in a virtual house to get insight into residents' consumption habits. Activity Four was designed so that users would move and interact in these two main areas; learning became situated and outcomes were the result of the user's experiences interacting with and in the space. The *Campus* area and buildings are designed around a central courtyard and replicate, for the most part, a university in Ottawa, Canada. The area includes a library, virtual classrooms, and offices. To take advantage of the expansive space and users' perception of being outside, more recently an open-air classroom, called *Rainbow Stage* (Figure 7), was added. This space is ideal for group work as it includes six breakout stations complete with work surfaces and contained sounds.

Learning Processes

During class, students were given a worksheet on writing formal academic definitions. This included a list of definitions of sustainable development from which they were to identify specific details or characteristics that recurred across all definitions. The purpose of the worksheet was to scaffold the learner toward writing their own definition of the term. After completing the worksheet, students were tasked with exploring the *Residences* and making recommendations to a hypothetical family as to how they could be more environmentally sustainable in their home based on what they observed, such as recycling habits and refrigerator contents. This active exploration of the space, not an option in a physical classroom environment, was intended to promote collaboration, experiential learning, and learning-by-doing, which are especially characteristic of socio-cultural and 21st century pedagogies. Next, students were asked to individually explore the *Campus* and *Rainbow Stage*, and then in groups identify two sustainability initiatives from an economic and social perspective. As 3DVLEs allow for movement and exploration, ideally learners can connect these virtual experiences to learning; learning is therefore situated. This ability to move, explore, and create are related to Savin-Baden's (2008) notion of space and learning.

Learning Outcomes

Demonstrated outcomes for this activity included the use of formal and content specific language and proficiency in defining a term. Further, expected outcomes included problem solving and the ability to

Figure 6. Screenshot of virtual refrigerator contents

Figure 7. Screenshot of Rainbow Stage

think critically based on experiences in and within the space. One student's response clearly demonstrates the value of movement, exploration, and experience in the *Campus* space, "Firstly, we can use the new type energy. The sunlight is enough, so it is able to install some solar panel to collect solar energy." In this case, the student links their experience in the 3DVLE to sustainable initiatives from the class readings and course content. This experience would not have been possible in a traditional classroom space; this would have necessitated a tour of library or other campus building.

Activity Five: Applying Sustainable Development Indicators

Learning Environments

The 3D model of *Native Village* (Figure 8) was designed by the authors' university's multimedia students and includes an animated dance that allows users to experience an authentic part of Canada's First Nations culture. *Native Village* is a good entry point for stimulating discussion, the basis for task design, as it invokes opportunity for experiential learning. The *Market* (Figure 9) design is based on design-team members determining the need for any tasks related to food, shopping, and health. In connection with the theme of sustainable development it was expected that as students interact with the space, students may notice variation in products and costs, as well as ethical considerations such as fair trade items, thus prompting critical thinking and problem solving. These skills are compatible with previously identified 21st century skills.

Figure 8. Screenshot of native village

Figure 9. Screenshot of market

Learning Processes

In Activity Five, students were asked to explore the *Native Village* and *Market* in groups. As they explored the two areas, students were tasked with answering questions related to sustainable development using a collaborative writing surface. The affordance of real-time voice allowed for peer feedback, or what cognitive theorists might call an *event of instruction*; theoretically, the stance is that learning is a social process in that successful completion of the task may be due to interaction with a more knowledgeable peer. This assumption draws on socio-cultural, connectivist, and 21st century learning theories. More specifically, successful completion of the activity depended on students' collaboration, freedom to move and create, and a certain level of proficiency using a collaborative writing tool and moving and exploring in the 3DVLE. Writing prompts included reporting on the observed culture's social, environmental, and financial goals and practices based on a shared understanding of the topic and course readings.

Learning Outcomes

Demonstrated outcomes included evidence of topic-specific vocabulary and content knowledge in the shared written document. The ability to achieve outcomes successfully included demonstrating connections between experiences in and because of the space and due to collaborative thinking and problem solving. Ideally, students could account for their experiences by including references to the input of peers and the space. In response to the prompt, *Identify possible trade-offs, as defined in the reading, in terms of access to food in the Native Village compared to the Downtown market area*, one group responded collaboratively (as indicated by different coloured text-based responses):

Access to food is much more easy in Downtown because of the shops available. In the village they have to hunt to get the food, which is dangerous. Furthermore, people who live in downtown can try multi-cultural food and it is more convenient, but the people living in the village have access to specific food.

In this response, students demonstrate connections between their experiences exploring the space and have worked collaboratively in producing a relevant response. Also, there is evidence of attempts at using comparative language and examples, which are academic conventions expected at this level.

RECOMMENDATIONS

This section includes recommendations for designing a learning space and tasks in a 3DVLE based on the authors' collective experience and from the point of view of the teacher as designer. To date and as illustrated above, the authors have approached the task and space design for 3DVLE by systematically drawing on various learning theories, particularly as they pertain to the affordances of the environment and the promotion of learning experiences that may lead to the development of learning outcomes, such as critical thinking and collaboration. The authors have used Phillips et al.'s (2012) LEPO framework to demonstrate the potential of five tasks designed for a unique learning environment, processes, and expected outcomes.

The authors suggest making use of the affordance of real-time, multi-user, synchronous interaction through first-person voice, text, and movement in task design. This helps establish a sense of presence and facilitates opportunities for sharing and exchanging information, co-constructing meaning, and practicing newly acquired skills. These are characteristics of many learning theories addressed in the first section of this chapter and align with 21st century learning trends and constructivist perspectives.

To further support an authentic experience and promote engagement, entertaining design elements can be used throughout the 3DVLE, such as musical instruments in *Career Island*. The success of Tasks three, four, and five was due largely to the fidelity of space, which led to strong student engagement and interaction with other users and the space as students worked through problems and demonstrated critical thinking in order to respond to the task. The focus was on making sense of information through interaction, reflection, and learning about learning (Ally, 2008). These are possible because of the immersive and authentic affordances of the space.

According to Bransford et al. (2000), knowledge-centeredness refers to how the environment is organized so that it contributes to knowledge growth and skill. From this perspective, the authors recommend designing activities that consider a learner's prior knowledge, typically gathered by means of an introductory activity such as the *Orientation Maze* (Figure 10). The authors suggest that such preliminary activities be easily accomplishable in a reasonable amount of time so as not to discourage first time users. The authors further suggest that task design take advantage of such things as the authentic quality of 3DVLE spaces and their ability to promote content and skill development by means of tools and artifacts available in the space. For example, visual cues, including multiple collaboration surfaces and objects throughout the environment may help trigger memory and prior knowledge. The implication is that learners are free to explore, gather, select, and evaluate information anytime and from anywhere (Ally, 2008).

The authors recommend that a well-crafted 3DVLE educational space should provide tasks related to 3D-rendered, high-quality artifacts that learners can interact with – for example, custom designed non-player avatars with clickable voice options to create a truly immersive experience. Further, the design of a 3DVLE space for learning requires a strong understanding of the educational material and frequent collaboration between members of the design team. In this case, Career Island used non-player avatars to provide different career roles based on Holland Code vocations. The vocabulary used in non-player avatar recordings while explaining their career aligned with students' language level, the instructors' vision, and learning objectives of the activity. Importantly, 3DVLEs are living spaces that should continuously adapt to the design team's experience; thus, a good platform should support all abovementioned

Figure 10. Screenshot of an introductory activity in orientation maze

features, as well as be easy to modify and deploy on a server that students and instructors can access without difficulty.

The implications for learners in these 3D spaces extend to becoming more selective and critical of information, as well as more collaborative, yet at the same time more autonomous. Due to the complex nature of the space, the learner becomes more accountable and responsible for their own learning. However, considering that technology is a medium for instructional practice, it is ultimately what educators do with technology that matters: the designer is responsible for creating spaces that are motivating and engaging (Ally, 2008; Clark, 1994). Adding entertaining elements of surprise, such as musical instruments that can be played in the music room on Career Island (Figure 11), reminds student to be observant and investigative. As such, in addition to designing tasks that foster experience, interaction, and collaboration, the implications for design include ensuring a high-quality VoIP as a critical component of a successful 3DVLE. Further, based on the affordances of authentic space and immersion, a chosen 3DVLE platform should support avatar customization for students to personalize their own avatar, along with non-player avatar usability. Designers should be able to create spaces that are populated with non-playing avatars that are animated and include voice to create realistic opportunities for engagement.

Despite the complexity of design and opportunity for technical skill development, interaction, and collaboration, the authors noted in their course that their students worked through tasks at very different levels and speeds, and often students were observed working independently, even in tasks designed for collaboration. Students with stronger technical adeptness tended to move through the instructions very quickly and wander off task, while not necessarily benefitting from the spatial cues and experience. High flexibility and ease of user management capabilities should be considered when choosing a 3DVLE platform. Selected platforms should therefore support password-controlled authentication and group access control, volume, and interaction support.

Figure 11. Screenshot of music room on career island

FUTURE RESEARCH DIRECTIONS

It is an interesting and fulfilling time to be involved in 3DVLE research. This chapter has attempted to understand how the affordances of the space relate to characteristics of 20th and 21st century learning theories and how these can guide space and task design. Further research is needed in the area of curriculum and task design. The authors suggest the use of analytics in combination with observational data to clarify the role of space. Accordingly, research should appreciate and understand the role of the environment as a mediator in the learning process and use 3DVLE analytics to measure duration and frequency of interaction to understand the impact of space on performance. The authors are investigating the reliable use of learning analytics, defined as "the measurement, collection, analysis and reporting of data about learners and their contexts, for purposes of understanding and optimizing learning and the environments in which it occurs" (LAK '11, 2017). The use of learning analytics, or *telemetrics*, in 3DVLE contexts will help predict students' success and aid students in performing learning activities in the 3DVLE. This process will lead to more efficient assessment and provide timely feedback to students to increase the likelihood of successful learning outcomes. Knowledge obtained from telemetric data combined with student surveys, teacher observations, and task outcomes will help guide research, design, and practice in these unique online learning spaces.

Additionally, research in this area will contribute to decision-making in terms of supporting the development and use of these spaces as an extension of post-secondary institutions' physical classroom space. The potential for 3DVLEs in EAP and other learning contexts is exciting and a better understanding of these spaces will help target niche markets for post-secondary, online, and distance education. These spaces provide a rich and safe opportunity for learners to continue to develop technical skills, gain content knowledge, and practice meta-cognitive skills. Future research will help determine how and which tasks will help contribute to the achievement of learning outcomes and 21st century skills as an experience of interaction with the space.

CONCLUSION

Upon examination of the key affordances of 3DVLEs—namely, authenticity, immersion, and real-time interaction—it is evident that characteristics from a range of learning theories can be applied to a conceptualization of 3D classrooms. Concepts like *connected, experiential, collaborative, and interactive* are shared between the learning theories and approaches discussed above. Overall, a consideration of the role of space in learning, whether physical or virtual, is often overlooked and yet especially pertinent for understanding how people learn in 3DVLEs. As stressed throughout this chapter, understanding what is happening in and because of the space is critical to any theoretical approach to learning online and specifically in 3DVLEs.

Drawing on well-known learning theories and approaches is important as theories help to illuminate the path to proceed in our practice: "To move forward, to know where to invest our energies, we have need of theory" (Kaptelinin & Nardi, 2006, p. 23). And so, while the notion of online classrooms fits nicely within constructivist and socio-cultural learning theories in terms of their technological affordance of providing an environment or learning space where learners can collaborate, problem solve, and grow conceptually, these theories do not adequately capture the role of 3DVLE spaces in the active process of learning. Thus, a blended learning theory could help practitioners better understand how the affordances of the space contribute to qualities of active, collaborative learning. In other words, it should account for how learning takes place because of the affordances within a socially and culturally mediated system. It would be counter-productive to ignore earlier theories of learning in consideration of these spaces; moving forward, a blended model should consider the key affordances, learning outcomes, and the actual space and artifacts within the space.

ACKNOWLEDGMENT

The authors are grateful for the support of Dean John Osborne, Faculty of Arts and Social Sciences (Carleton University), Dr. Randall Gess, School of Linguistics and Language Studies (Carleton University), Dr. Ali Arya, School of Information Technology (Carleton University), and Dr. Janna Fox, School of Linguistics and Language Studies (Carleton University).

REFERENCES

P21 Partnership for 21st Century Learning. (n. d.). *Framework for 21st century learning*. Retrieved from http://www.p21.org/our-work/p21-framework

Ally, M. (2008). Foundations of educational theory for online learning. In T. Anderson (Ed.), *The theory and practice of online learning* (pp. 15–44). Edmonton, Canada: AU Press.

Arya, A., Hartwick, P., Graham, S., & Nowlan, N. (2012). Collaborating through space and time in educational virtual environments: 3 case studies. *The Journal of Interactive Technology & Pedagogy,* (2). Retrieved from http://jitp.commons.gc.cuny.edu/collaborating-through-space-and-time-in-educational-virtual-environments-3-case-studies/

Bransford, J. D., Brown, A. L., & Cocking, R. R. (2000). *How people learn: Brain, mind, experience, and school* (expanded ed.). Retrieved June 23, 2015, from http://www.nap.edu/openbook.php?record_id=9853

Brown, J. S., Collins, A., & Duguid, P. (1989). Situated cognition and the culture of learning. *Educational Researcher, 18*(1), 32–42. doi:10.3102/0013189X018001032

Clark, A. (2001). *Mindware: An introduction to the philosophy of cognitive science.* New York: Oxford University Press.

Clark, R. E. (1994). Media will never influence learning. *Educational Technology Research and Development, 42*(2), 21–29. doi:10.1007/BF02299088

Csikszentmihalyi, M. (2014). *Applications of flow in human development and education: The collected works of Mihaly Csikszentmihalyi.* Dordrecht, The Netherlands: Springer. doi:10.1007/978-94-017-9094-9

Dalgarno, B., & Lee, M. J. (2010). What are the learning affordances of 3D virtual environments? *British Journal of Educational Technology, 41*(1), 10–32. doi:10.1111/j.1467-8535.2009.01038.x

Dede, C. (2003). No cliché left behind: Why education policy is not like the movies. *Educational Technology, 43*(2), 5–10.

Dede, C. (2007). Reinventing the role of information and communications technologies in education. *Yearbook of the National Society for the Study of Education, 106*(2), 11–38. doi:10.1111/j.1744-7984.2007.00113.x

Dede, C. (2010). Comparing frameworks for 21st century skills. In J. Bellanca & R. Brandt (Eds.), 21st century skills: Rethinking how students learn (pp. 51-76). Bloomington, IN: Solution Tree Press.

Dewey, J. (1938). *Experience and education.* New York, NY: Touchstone.

Engeström, Y. (2001). Expansive learning at work: Toward an activity theoretical reconceptualization. *Journal of Education and Work, 14*(1), 133–156. doi:10.1080/13639080020028747

Gee, J. P. (2004). *Situated language and learning: A critique of traditional schooling.* New York, NY: Routledge.

Gee, J. P. (2007). *What video games have to teach us about learning and literacy.* New York: Palgrave MacMillan.

Gee, J. P., & Hayes, E. (2011). *Language and learning in the digital age.* New York: Routledge.

Gibson, J. J. (1979). *The ecological approach to visual perception.* Boston, MA: Houghton Mifflin.

Greeno, J. G. (1994). Gibson's affordances. *Psychological Review, 101*(2), 336–342. doi:10.1037/0033-295X.101.2.336 PMID:8022965

Harasim, L. M. (2012). *Learning theory and online technologies.* New York, NY: Routledge.

Hartwick, P., & Nowlan, N. (2012, March). *Learning as an avatar: Designing immersive spaces and facilitating 3D learning experiences.* Paper presented at INTED2012 6th International Technology, Education and Development Conference, Valencia, Spain.

Haythornthwaite, C. A., & Andrews, R. (2011). *E-learning theory and practice.* Thousand Oaks, CA: Sage. doi:10.4135/9781446288566

Ibáñez, M. B., Garcia, J. J., Galan, S., Maroto, D., Morillo, D., & Kloos, C. D. (2011). Design and implementation of a 3D multi-user virtual world for language learning. *Journal of Educational Technology & Society, 14*(4), 2–10.

Illeris, K. (2003). *Three dimensions of learning: Contemporary learning theory in the tension field between the cognitive, the emotional and the social.* Malabar, FL: Krieger.

Ireson, J. (2008). *Learners, learning and educational activity.* New York, NY: Routledge.

Kaptelinin, V., & Nardi, B. A. (2006). *Acting with technology: Activity theory and interaction design.* Cambridge, MA: MIT Press.

LAK '11. (2010). *LAK '11: 1st International Conference on Learning Analytics and Knowledge 2011.* Retrieved from https://tekri.athabascau.ca/analytics/

Lave, J., & Wenger, E. (1991). *Situated learning: Legitimate peripheral participation.* New York, NY: Cambridge University Press. doi:10.1017/CBO9780511815355

Loke, S. K. (2015). How do virtual world experiences bring about learning? A critical review of theories. *Australasian Journal of Educational Technology*, *31*(1), 112–122. doi:10.14742/ajet.2532

Milton, J., Jonsen, S., Hirst, S., & Lindenburn, S. (2012). Foreign language vocabulary development through activities in an online 3D environment. *Language Learning Journal*, *40*(1), 99–112. doi:10.1080/09571736.2012.658229

Norman, D. A. (2002). *The design of everyday things*. New York, NY: Basic Books.

Peterson, M. (2006). Learner interaction management in an avatar and chat-based virtual world. *Computer Assisted Language Learning*, *19*(1), 79–103. doi:10.1080/09588220600804087

Peterson, M. (2010). Massively multiplayer online role-playing games as arenas for second language learning. *Computer Assisted Language Learning*, *23*(5), 429–439. doi:10.1080/09588221.2010.520673

Peterson, M. (2011). Towards a research agenda for the use of three-dimensional virtual worlds in language learning. *CALICO Journal*, *29*(1), 67–80. doi:10.11139/cj.29.1.67-80

Piaget, J. (1959). *The language and thought of the child* (3rd ed.). London, UK: Routledge & Kegan Paul.

Prensky, M. (2006). *Don't bother me mom – I'm learning!* St. Paul, MN: Paragon House.

Prensky, M. (2007). *Digital game-based learning*. St. Paul, MN: Paragon House.

Rogoff, B. (1990). *Apprenticeship in thinking: Cognitive development in social context*. New York, NY: Oxford University Press.

Savin-Baden, M. (2008). *Learning spaces: Creating opportunities for knowledge creation in academic life*. New York, NY: McGraw Hill.

Savin-Baden, M., Gourlay, L., Mawer, M., Steils, N., Tombs, C., & Tombs, G. (2010). Situating pedagogies, positions and practices in immersive virtual worlds. *Educational Research*, *52*(2), 123–133. doi:10.1080/00131881.2010.482732

Scardamalia, M., & Bereiter, C. (2006). Knowledge building: Theory, pedagogy, and technology. In K. Sawyer (Ed.), *Cambridge handbook of the learning sciences* (pp. 97–118). New York, NY: Cambridge University Press.

Siemens, G. (2005). Connectivism: A learning theory for the digital age. *International Journal of Instructional Technology and Distance Learning*, *2*(1). Retrieved from http://er.dut.ac.za/handle/123456789/69

Vygotsky, L. S. (1986). *Thought and language*. Cambridge, MA: The MIT Press.

Warburton, S. (2009). Second Life in higher education: Assessing the potential for and the barriers to deploying virtual worlds in learning and teaching. *British Journal of Educational Technology*, *40*(3), 414–426. doi:10.1111/j.1467-8535.2009.00952.x

Wigham, C. R., & Chanier, T. (2013). Architecture students' appropriation of avatars. In M. N. Lamy & K. Zourou (Eds.), *Social networking for language education* (pp. 31–55). New York, NY: Palgrave Macmillan. doi:10.1057/9781137023384_3

KEY TERMS AND DEFINITIONS

Affordance: The quality or characteristic of the environment that contributes to increased opportunities for interaction or engagement, thereby contributing to learning.

Artifact: A 3D rendered object that exists in a digital environment designed to complement the space and/or task.

Avatar: A virtually rendered 3D self that can be personalized by the user according to the user's choice of certain traits, like clothing and hair color, height, and weight.

Learning Analytics: The measurement and collection of learner telemetric for optimizing 3DVLE task and space design.

Metacognition: A critical awareness of one's own thought process and understanding.

Non-Player Avatar: Virtually rendered avatar artifacts with which users can interact through clicking to prompt a voice or movement response.

Telemetric: 3DVLE user activity data that is captured remotely and logged for analysis.

Three-Dimensional Virtual Learning Environment (3DVLE): An internet-hosted space designed to replicate real places and objects and provide online users with the opportunity to interact with other users synchronously with voice, movement, or text.

Twenty-First Century Learning: The acquisition of content knowledge and skills, including critical thinking, problem solving, and collaboration.

Chapter 7
Creating Contexts for Collaborative Learning in a 3D Virtual World for Distance Education

Anders I. Mørch
University of Oslo, Norway

Valentina Caruso
Swiss Federal Institute for Vocational Education and Training, Switzerland

Melissa D. Hartley
West Virginia University, USA

Barbara L. Ludlow
West Virginia University, USA

ABSTRACT

The purpose of this chapter is to explore the contexts that teachers can create to promote collaborative learning in 3D virtual learning environments. The authors report on the findings of a case study using the 3D virtual world Second Life in a preservice teacher distance education program. Two types of contexts are identified: social interaction (social context) and instructor's scaffolding (pedagogical context). The anonymity represented by avatars in the 3D environment allowed learners to engage in social interaction and practice collaboration skills. Scaffolding involved several stages: scaffold the students' learning of the new technology, plan the course structure, implement the procedures during the lesson, and facilitate transitions between activities. The study also identifies the potential for a third context (emotional context), as the participants—both the instructor and the students—report a need to express emotions in many situations, but the environment does not seamlessly support this mode of communication.

DOI: 10.4018/978-1-5225-3719-9.ch007

INTRODUCTION

Second Life (SL) is a multiuser virtual environment (MUVE) configured as an online world in which individuals interact as avatars with people and objects in three-dimensional (3D) space. Avatars are visual representations of a user by an animated 3D figure controlled by the user through customization and movement. MUVEs offer educators new opportunities to design authentic learning experiences that would not be possible in a traditional classroom (Dieterle & Clarke, 2007). Educators have used SL for online instruction in colleges and universities in a variety of disciplines, from academic content to professional preparation (Wang & Burton, 2013). A specific building block in the SL environment used by developers and instructors for constructing buildings and disseminating content is the "box." This tool was also used by the students in the case we report from.

Previous research for using SL in different subject domains has found that collaborative activities in virtual learning environments can encourage empathic interaction between peers or team members working together (Miller & Wallis, 2011), and students often blur the distinction between themselves and their avatars when they immerse themselves in the 3D learning environment with the effect of making 3D virtual worlds as potential sites for embodied and extended cognition (Pasfield-Neofitou, Huang, & Grant, 2015). In a study of language teaching and learning in SL, examining the teacher's facilitating role, it was found that the teacher played important technical and social roles in the early phases of a learning activity to counterbalance the threshold of advanced technology and ensure the establishment of a collaborative learning environment (Wang, 2015).

However, to the best of our knowledge the previous research in 3D virtual worlds lacks best practices and examples of the specific teaching conditions that can promote collaborative learning. We address the discrepancy by exploring a case study in a preservice teacher distance education program at a southern university in United States where 34 students participated in the study, using SL as the learning environment. Faculty members have been teaching in SL for six and a half years, and it has been the educational platform for six online graduate courses at both master's and doctoral levels. It has also been incorporated into undergraduate, campus-based courses for role-play simulation. Since the use of SL was first piloted in 2011, over 1,000 students have used SL in their teacher preparation courses.

The use of a 3D virtual immersive environment, such as Second Life, offers students and faculty the illusion of being together in a classroom on campus, an experience quite different from that of engaging in asynchronous forums and information-sharing portals. Everyone interacts live in real time while viewing a visual representation (an avatar) of one another. The learning space is designed to look like a classroom, yet there are artifacts and tools in SL that cannot be found in any traditional classroom. Our working hypothesis, based on comments from previous course evaluations of the online teacher preparation program, is that it is possible to create a learning community in SL that is comparable to a campus-based classroom. However, it requires advance preparation of a skilled instructor and the use of the technology's unique features to create learning contexts appropriate for an online learning environment. For example, users in virtual worlds relate to one another based on presence, look, and feel, and they position themselves at a certain distance from each other while communicating, not unlike in the real world. When presenting new material during a lecture or when students ask for assistance, an instructor in a virtual world will glean information from students' movements, gestures, and verbal behavior. Moreover, developers and instructors need to be conscious of the decisions they make when either replicating or transcending conventions in face-to-face (f2f) communication for online environments.

Both strengths and limitations are associated with f2f communication, and these should be leveraged or avoided as appropriate (Hollan & Stornetta, 1992).

Therefore, we address the following research question in this chapter: "What contexts can the instructor create to promote collaborative learning in an online teacher preparation program in Second Life?" We explore two types of contexts judged important from a sociocultural perspective on learning and instruction: (1) Social context: Presence and awareness of others in the environment (e.g., the ability for an avatar to see other avatars and get a feel for their communicability), and (2) Pedagogical context: Techniques instructors use to scaffold learning activities (e.g., lecture, display board, note cards, adaptive feedback).

We consider these contexts enactive and dynamic rather than static and passive, and we refer to them as designed contexts, meaning they must be planned for and modifiable during a course (Mørch, Hartley, Ludlow, Caruso, & Thomassen, 2014). The rest of the chapter elaborates on these contexts and is organized as follows: First, we describe theoretical perspectives, followed by a survey of related work on using Second Life for teacher education and an overview of Second Life and the virtual campus adopted for our case study. We then describe the qualitative research method and present representative data extracts, and we analyze the findings. Finally, we discuss the research question, the implications for design, and suggestions for future work.

THEORETICAL PERSPECTIVES

Social Presence Theory and Model

Short, Williams, and Christie (1976) proposed the concept of social presence to describe the mediated sense of others' presence in remote communication, arguing this was a property of the medium itself. Applied to video conferencing, Berge's Instructor's Roles Model (Berge, 1995) posited four key roles for the instructor in distributed learning environments: pedagogical, social, managerial, and technical. One study of multiple online courses using Berge's model (Liu, Bonk, Magjuka, Lee, & Su, 2005) found that students rated instructors as effective in the pedagogical, managerial, and technical roles but did not emphasize enough the social role and in maintaining social presence. Berge (2008) has suggested that the four instructor roles were intensified when teaching in virtual worlds such as Second Life, which emphasize student exploration, interaction, and collaboration. A qualitative study of online instructors using virtual reality applications (Keskitalo, 2011) found that some were moving toward using more student-centered and problem-based pedagogy, but others were trying to replicate classroom conditions in the online environment rather than taking advantage of the new opportunities that the online environment offered in terms of exploration, interaction, and collaboration.

Focusing on the social role, Gunawardena (1995) applied the concept of social presence, suggesting that verbal and nonverbal behaviors to establish relationships with and among students were critical to successful online instruction. More recently, a large body of research has documented that social presence is an important predictor of student satisfaction with online courses. Jarmon (2008) suggested that users report heightened social presence in SL, which she termed an "embodied sense of social presence" (p. 1) and attributed to the ability to move avatars through space in real time. Dede (2009) has argued that the individually created SL avatars enhance the sense of social presence because they embody personal representations of each individual. Allmendringer (2010) suggested that the sense of social presence in virtual worlds might also be related to nonverbal signals made by avatars. Bulu (2012) suggested that social presence might be more important than immersion in predicting student satisfaction in virtual worlds. Furthermore, the relevance of the learning activity and flexibility in creating them might be more important than the accurate rendering of a real-world phenomenon, which could explain why some crudely rendered 3D worlds attract much interest if well designed (e.g., block-building games such as Minecraft).

Sociocultural Learning Theory: The Zone of Proximal Development

The sociocultural perspective on learning entails two levels: the first level is the social process between people supported by collaboration and instruction, and the second is an internal process of development through individual learning (Vygotsky, 1978). A key concept in Vygotsky's theory is the zone of proximal development (ZPD) that provides a bridge from individual learning to instruction. The ZPD refers to the potential for learning that is realized when new knowledge interacts with what a person already knows in a process that is mediated by artifacts, tools, and interaction (Wertsch, 2007) while being guided by instruction (e.g., feedback from teachers, parents, and more knowledgeable peers).

This implies that both verbal and nonverbal activity and physical things in the environment contribute to scaffold interaction. Thus, they should be considered during analysis of the collaborative learning process in f2f and distributed settings (Ludvigsen & Mørch, 2010; Säljö, 2010). Moreover, researchers studying collaborative learning in virtual worlds should be aware of both virtual and real influences that may affect learning in positive or negative directions. Educators preparing to teach in Second Life can anticipate and plan for these influences, supporting the positive and avoiding the negative (Mørch et al., 2014).

Scaffolding

Scaffolding is a concept and technique that can be traced back to Vygotsky's seminal research on the ZPD and variations of the technique according to different metaphors are in use today, including evolutionary growth and control (Vygotsky, 1978), cooperative problem solving (Wood, Bruner, & Ross, 1976), and cognitive apprenticeship (Collins, Brown, & Newman, 1989; Lave, 1988).

Wood, Bruner, and Ross (1976) coined the term "scaffolding" to explore the types of support provided by an adult for children who are learning how to carry out a task they could not perform alone. It builds on the knowledge children already have and adds new knowledge that adults and more knowledgeable peers bring to the situation to help the child learn. This suggests instructional feedback as a method for tutoring, keeping the students on track during problem solving. Two types of feedback are showing (direct intervention) and telling (verbal guidance), providing directions toward a solution, highlighting critical features, and giving examples of partial solutions along the way (Wood, Bruner, & Ross, 1976). Effective feedback is necessary not only to enrich students' learning experience (Hattie & Timperley, 2007; Price, Handley, Millar, & O'Donovan, 2010) but also to help students develop their self-regulated learning competence (Van den Boom, Paas, Van Merrienboer, & Van Gog, 2004).

The adult role in pedagogical practice is now often referred to as the skilled master, whereas the child or student is considered the learning apprentice through an educational process often termed "cognitive apprenticeship" (Collins, Brown, & Newman, 1989). Cognitive apprenticeship has roots in situated learning theory, and it is based on the idea that we learn most naturally when learning forms a relationship with the social situation in which it occurs (Lave, 1988). Furthermore, Dennen and Burner (2008) suggested that learning by cognitive apprenticeship has the great advantage of making visible the practices of skilled practitioners that may not be easily explained in a traditional lecture. In the context of SL, the environment and instructor assume a relevant role to support cognitive apprenticeship and effective feedback by providing the students with visible learning strategies (Hattie & Timperley, 2007) that create opportunities for collaborative learning.

ZPD, scaffolding, effective feedback, cognitive apprenticeship, and related concepts have stimulated educational technology developers over many years to build intelligent support systems and adaptive educational technology, including domain-specific critiquing systems (Fischer, Lemke, Mastaglio, & Morch, 1991; Mørch, Engeness, Cheng, Cheung, & Wong, 2017) and collaborative learning environments (Mørch, Dolonen, & Nævdal, 2006; Soller, Martinez, Jermann, & Muehlenbrock, 2005; Stahl, Koschmann, & Suthers, 2006).

In this study, instructional feedback involves a combination of technological tools, tasks, and instructor' scaffolding to support preservice teachers in practicing collaboration skills by making the learning process more visible through the virtual environment. Furthermore, the study aims at creating a new dimension of ZPD in the SL learning environment, drawing on the affordances and constraints of mediated interaction in virtual worlds. Finally, it explores to what extent an instructor can create social and pedagogical contexts and integrate them with an SL distance education course. We firmly believe that collaborative learning is not something that runs by pushing a button; it must be carefully planned and stimulated throughout the entire activity to be effective.

SECOND LIFE AND ROLE-PLAY IN TEACHER EDUCATION

Although the body of literature concerning SL practice in teacher education is limited (Muir, Allen, Rayner, & Cleland, 2013), researchers have suggested that 3D virtual worlds can be integrated throughout a teacher education program to provide preservice teachers with the experiences needed to apply teaching skills in real school settings. Based on these premises, Cheong, Yun, and Chollins (2009) used Second Life as an educational platform to guide 160 preservice teachers in practicing teaching skills collaboratively. The findings showed that SL seems particularly well suited as an experimental teaching method compared with traditional classroom-based methods.

Indeed, several studies have noted that this virtual environment provides a platform for collaborative learning activities by supporting social interaction, collaboration, and role-play (Muir et al., 2013; Vasileiou & Paraskeva, 2010). For example, in a mixed-methods study adopted for an education course (Gao, Noh, & Kohler, 2009), researchers compared role-playing in a face-to-face format and in SL, collecting quantitative and qualitative data on student perceptions and conducting an analysis of recorded transcripts of the exercises. Results showed no significant differences in the amount of communication in the two environments, but transcript analysis showed that students took more conversational turns in SL, but each turn was shorter than in the f2f environment. Furthermore, the students found the SL environment more interesting and less formal (Gao, Noh, & Kohler, 2009). In a pilot study of a distance education program (Caruso, Mørch, Thomassen, Hartley, & Ludlow, 2014), it was found that users of a 3D world feel less self-conscious and find it easier to familiarize themselves with social concepts, such as collaboration and knowledge sharing.

A distance education literature course was organized in SL to teach role-playing, and 15 primary and secondary school teachers participated (Vasileiou & Paraskeva, 2010). The 3D environment showed a positive influence on learner engagement and motivation, and it was found to be especially well suited for socialization and collaboration among the participants. It favored communication and collaboration, lowered the threshold for exposure, and made learning in groups more effective in a friendly atmosphere (Vasileiou & Paraskeva, 2010).

Role-playing instruction is a strategy broadly used in various educational settings in which participants assume different professional roles in a collaborative environment according to a given scenario. Given this premise, a well-designed role-playing game provides a platform for developing both social skills and professional knowledge, by which participants use the former to collectively reflect on their learning process (Dabbagh, 2005; Vasileiou & Paraskeva, 2010).

The aforementioned studies suggest that virtual role-play allows learners to become active participants, partly through increased motivation and encouragement of play and social interaction (Morse, Littleton, Macleod, & Ewins, 2009). Furthermore, role-playing in collaborative and distributed environments can be an effective way to develop and encourage empathic interaction not only between users but also between peers or team members working together (Miller & Wallis, 2011). However, outside of role-playing, these studies lack some of the key aspects involved in organizing educational courses in virtual worlds, as seen from a sociocultural perspective (e.g., instructor's scaffolding). This study aims to fill this gap and apply a broader range of sociocultural concepts in the analysis.

Second Life and the Virtual Campus

In SL, the college owns a private island (virtual land on which to build smaller worlds like a group of buildings, or a small town) and there are two virtual campuses on that island. Public transportation—via scripted teleporting—is available to take students between campuses. Each faculty member who teaches in SL has a main classroom for whole-group instruction, small-group buildings for collaborative group work, and office space for office hours. In the island's design, the small-group buildings were created to provide a place for students to work collaboratively without hearing their classmates' conversations. While there are other ways to meet this goal within SL, the faculty preferred this method when designing the campus. Therefore, all group buildings are 60 meters apart to create a sound barrier (Figure 1).

The main classrooms were designed for interactive lecture and individual activities. Therefore, there are display boards with presentation slides around the classroom, and the class walks from one display board to the next during the interactive lecture. Although it is possible to show a presentation without physically moving one's avatar from one display board to another, the faculty found that physically moving their avatars increased students' engagement during the interactive lecture.

All buildings are fully furnished, allowing the environment to feel like a professional classroom environment. The buildings have windows to prevent the feeling of claustrophobia when students and faculty are inside the buildings. In addition, every wall is set to "phantom," and there are no doors. In SL, when an object is set to phantom, one can walk through it. There are also no stairs on the island. Although an avatar can navigate stairs, doing so is cumbersome and unnecessary.

Figure 1. Bird eye's view of two buildings on the virtual campus in Second Life. The distance between buildings prevents noise interference and overhearing. Avatars can fly in and out of buildings.

The outside area of the campus is landscaped to create an inviting feeling for users. There are trees, flowers, bushes, and outside lounge seating (Figure 1). There is a tutorial skill practice area on one of the campuses, where students can view display boards of how to perform the skill (Figure 2) and practice the skills needed for class sessions. There is also a graduate student lounge where students can meet outside of class.

Figure 2. Pedagogical scaffolding in Second Life by display boards, used here for explaining how to use the box tool for sharing educational material

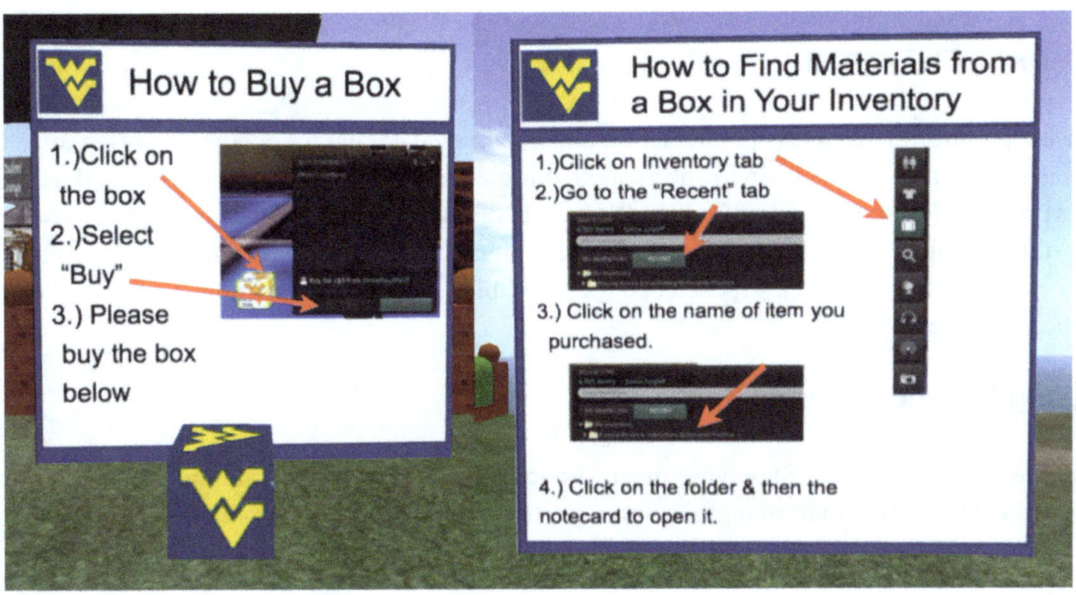

RESEARCH DESIGN AND DATA COLLECTION

A qualitative research method was the main approach to data collection, classification, selection and analysis, combining case study (Yin, 2003) and Internet ethnography (Hetland & Mørch, 2016). We examined the use of SL a graduate-level special-education preservice teacher preparation course, held at a Southern University in the United States. The course was arranged after working hours for full-time teachers and used SL as the primary educational platform. Thirty-four students took part in seven one-hour class sessions, each held online and divided into interactive lectures of theoretical concepts (15 minutes), individual activities (5 minutes), small-group activities in separate rooms (30 minutes), and role-play activities (10 minutes). All sessions were observed online and video-recorded with screen capture software. Afterward, we conducted interviews with students and the instructor (Caruso et al, 2014; Mørch et al., 2014). Interview guides are presented in the Appendices.

To collect and manage the data (spoken utterances, chat logs, and interviews) totaling 15 hours of raw video data, each session and interview were stored in a separate file and transcribed in their entirety using linguistic conventions according to interaction analysis (Jordan & Henderson, 1995). Interaction analysis was chosen because it is concerned with turn-taking in verbal communication (textual or oral), as well as how verbal communication interacts with body language–like intonation, gestures and movement, and nonverbal symbols used in chat (smileys and emotional abbreviations).

We categorized the interaction data into recurring themes, combining top-down (theory informed) and bottom-up (data-driven, open coding) classification processes. The initial categories were informed by our theoretical perspectives, which served as a lens for zooming in on the corpus. We initially grouped data into categories using an iterative, thematic coding technique inspired by Grounded Theory (Strauss & Corbin, 1998). Then we extended and adjusted the categories as we identified new instances of data (Caruso et al, 2014; Mørch et al., 2014). We present three of the categories below: (a) allowing for social interaction, (b) expressing emotions in SL, and (c) instructor's scaffolding. Illustrative examples of each of the three categories are reproduced below (Excerpts 1–10) and are critically examined in the subsequent section.

DATA PRESENTATION

We have reproduced 10 excerpts of interaction and interview data that we deemed representative of the three categories, and we use them to substantiate our claims. Each subsection is organized as follows: (a) short context description and/or finding, (b) excerpt of raw data, and (c) brief (common sense) explanation of the finding. The transcript notation we used includes the following symbols: (..) short pause, ((text)) comment by researcher, [..] excluded (non-audible) speech, and:: abruption of talk. The names of participants are fictitious.

Allowing for Social Interaction

The findings showed that the SL environment fostered a form of social interaction that is supportive of collaboration by catering to meaningful communication without expressing prejudices among its users.

Comparing Communication (Excerpt 1)

This excerpt is taken from a student's interview. She was asked what differences exist between communication in SL and communication in the real world.

I think it's easier to speak in SL because you don't see the other person looking at you, and [..] if I was in that room with other people, it would have taken me a little bit longer to get adjusted and acclimated to everyone's personalities. I think it's harder in real life because you can't just go to the chat wall and make a quick statement. You have to sit there and wait for people to stop talking. There are certain social norms you have to follow.

We can glean from the excerpt that the virtual learning environment in SL offered many opportunities for rich social interactions because the students felt more confident about taking part in learning activities due to freedom from the social norms required for face-to-face interactions. However, having an active role in SL learning activities also required oral skills combined with textual discourse (chat) abilities. Preservice teachers used both means of discourse. However, they seemed to prefer using chat to avoid the sound problems with the "speak" button and the noise associated with multiple people attempting to speak at the same time.

The learning environment on the college campus in SL was designed to promote social interaction. Small-group buildings were built to facilitate student interaction and group work. The buildings were 60 meters apart to eliminate interference in conversations during group activities. Students submitted personal pictures, and those pictures were used to decorate the walls within the group building to create a feeling of belonging.

Computer-Supported Collaboration (Excerpt 2)

Throughout the courses, students worked collaboratively in groups to complete activities during each session. Role-play activities were described on electronic notecards and stored in information-sharing containers (referred to as boxes), and students would purchase the materials for free (see Figure 2). Once students purchased the materials, they could access the materials from their inventory. These are idiosyncratic SL tools inherited from containers for packaging and purchasing goods in the SL marketplace (building units, furniture, clothing, etc.). Each student selected a role at the beginning of the semester and worked within that role throughout (time keeper, secretary, facilitator, leader, or organizer). In the anonymous student evaluations of the instruction at the end of each course, students were asked to rate, on a scale of one to five, whether collaborative problem solving and teamwork were encouraged via technologies. The scores ranged from 4.7 to 5.0, and the mean score across eight classes was 4.9. Students also commented about the collaborative learning within SL in the evaluations, stating, "This was an excellent learning experience and allowed us to actually collaborate and learn a lot more through an online class" and "The Second Life class was a great forum to promote collaboration with others." In the following excerpt, one of the groups had just finished planning the role-play scenario:

Janet: *We've got everything (...) in line now, which makes me feel a whole lot better.*
Heather: *I had no doubt that we could do it; we're superwomen.*
Stacy: *Go team! Ha-ha.*
Mandy: *We were just overachieving with trying to write a behavior plan.*
Heather: *I know, I think we were just... I tend to do that a lot, over-think things. But I'm glad that you guys met with her and realized it's not as much as we were making it out to be.*
Janet: *Ha-ha, we are super!*
Mandy: *I'm glad that we thought it was harder than it really was instead of (...) expecting it to be really easy and it turning out to be really difficult.*
Heather: *Yeah.*
Janet: *Exactly.*

Although some students encountered technical difficulties managing their own avatars, we found that the support of the virtual environment and the instructor were generally very good, enabling collaboration and increased motivation and engagement. The excerpt shows that even though some students had difficulties in the beginning and feared it would not work out (e.g., to engage in online role play), the opposite occurred for most of them, as the following line from Mandy illustrates: "I'm glad that we thought it was harder than it really was."

The Feeling of Belonging to a Group (Excerpt 3)

To see the value of working together as a team and to see each member of their group as a human being were two goals of the instructor. When working from a distance, using technology, individuals can easily forget that they are working with another person, and the distance may allow the individual a sense of anonymity not found in face-to-face interaction. While SL provides individuals with a visual representation of a human (avatar), it remains important that individuals form connections with one another on a human level to promote collaboration. The following excerpt, taken from the interview with the instructor, shows why SL was considered the more suitable distance educational platform in many respects, particularly in fostering social interactions among learners.

Second Life lends itself to social interaction as compared to Wimba ((a virtual classroom environment integrated with Blackboard)). So, for distance education, Second Life is my preferred educational platform for social interaction, because you actually get the physical presence of a person. In Wimba, unless you're using video conferencing you don't get that physical presence of a person. And so, the interaction is not as genuine. For example, at the end of this semester, when I was flying around to students, they'd finished working on one of the other groups role plays, and so they had a couple of minutes, and they were just talking, and I heard a student say to somebody in their group, Hey, what are you all takin' this summer? We should try to get in the same class. That would never happen in Wimba. Students just don't interact like that; they actually form relationships, and I think it's because of Second Life. I've even had students tell me, in previous semesters, that they felt they were in an undergraduate cohort again because they were actually making relationships, and they had friends, ((and that this class)) being held in Second Life, really helped them to feel like they were part of a group again, where they didn't feel disconnected from the online education. In Wimba, they didn't feel connected to other people.

The self-motivated communication shown in Excerpt 3 that led the students to form new relationships—not unlike the ways students socialize in residential college settings—is quite common in SL. Compared to other (asynchronous) platforms supporting online learning, SL seems particularly well suited for motivating distance education in terms of fostering social interactions. For example, it features a 3D graphical representation of the individual by means of avatars that are able to easily interact and communicate using audio or chat (Figure 3).

Expressing Emotions in Second Life

Nervousness Before a Role-Play (Excerpt 4)

The students had many opportunities to express their feelings while interacting in SL, and they revealed anxiety, excitement, joy, and frustration, which they mainly expressed during group work in the discussions areas. Before starting the excerpt below, one of the students (Andy) invited another (Rachel) to join him in the next role-play.

Rachel: *(Chat) You make me nervous . . . I'm an avoidance kind of person*
Andy: *(Chat) Lol, don't be nervous!!!!!!!*
Peter: *(Chat) I am, too!*
Rachel: *(Audio) You know, I haven't been in the defensive role. I don't mind it. I mean, you know, I'm saying (..) I'll try. I'll try. ((Laughing.))*

SL has a built-in gesture menu, though the students did not use this option as far as we could tell. This may have been due to a somewhat cumbersome invocation procedure. However, the students were intimately familiar with chatting and used chat in many situations to express feelings. In Excerpt 4, the

Figure 3. Participants and researchers are observing a role-play in the main lecture hall. Chat window to the left.

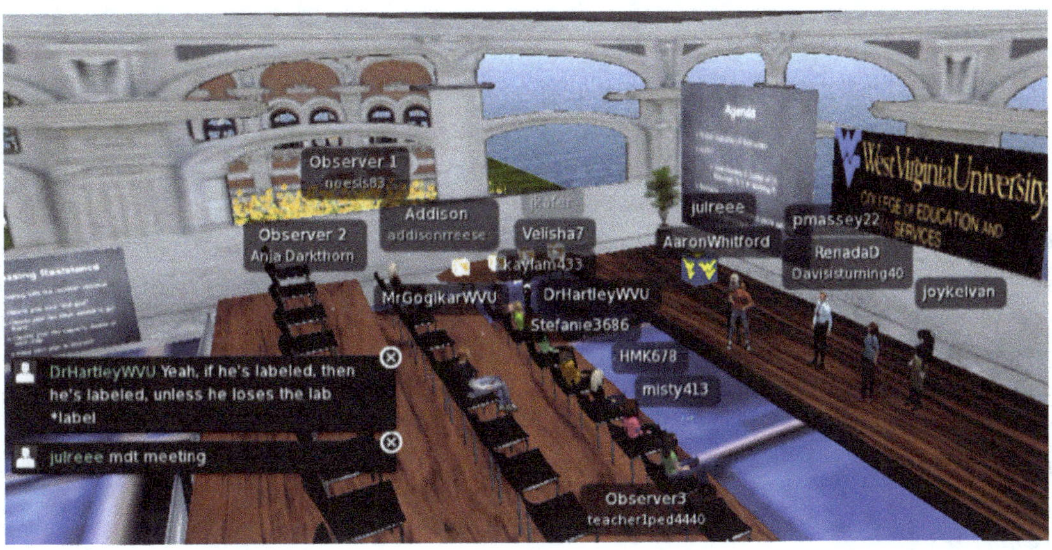

three chat lines were all exchanged within the same minute. Immediately preceding and following the chat exchange, Peter and Rachel attempted to formulate a question and answer it, respectively. Chat line communication was frequently intertwined with speech. The function of chat was to supplement the speech and to serve as a back channel, as shown in the excerpt. The students also used chat to respond to spoken questions from the instructor during lectures in the main hall. In that case, the students preferred to use chat to avoid audio problems; if several people pressed the "speak" button at the same time, sound problems would occur.

Wish There Were Better Emojis in SL (Excerpt 5)

The next excerpt depicts the instructor having just arrived in the students' group room, shown in Excerpt 4, to check the status of this group's work. As she landed in the room, she immediately started typing on her keyboard, an activity visible to the others and first noticed by Peter:

Peter: *(Audio) OK. Oops, she just came in too (..). Got that one on video.*
Instructor: *(Chat) No worries if you aren't finished!:)*
Instructor: *(Chat) I wish there were emojis in SL!*
Julia: *(Audio) Real quick, before everybody runs. The last question here was why she would have asked us to participate in this group activity, what her objective was, and why this is important to educators. And I'm pretty sure Andy and Rachel proved it in the last one; because we need effective communication with parents (..) as well as other educators.*
Peter: *(Chat) Exactly*

The instructor intended to tell the students that time was up, but she sensed the intensity of the situation (wrapping up joint work in a hurry), and she preferred to intervene unobtrusively, telling them without using words. To accomplish this, she started with a smiley face but realized this emoticon was too coarse grained for the situation ("I wish there were emojis in SL!"). Invoking the appropriate gesture from the gesture menu might take too much time, however; most SL users are not familiar with gesturing unless they use specific gestures frequently and program them into keyboard shortcuts.

Applying Gesture to Praise Students (Excerpt 6)

In this excerpt, the instructor explicitly invoked the "clap gesture" in SL, to praise a group of students who had just finished their role-play in front of the whole class (see Figure 3).

Instructor: *(Audio) Thank you, group, very much. Let me get my gestures ready here ((audio and avatar applause)). Yeey! Excellent job, group ((clapping hands)). And, um, I wanted to make sure, before we proceeded, would you all prefer that the last group go now, um, we may have to stay a couple of min:: - minutes after class in order to finish, or would you prefer to come next week? So yes is to go now; [..] if you would prefer next week (..), you can IM me (..) if you don't wanna say it in front of the group.*
Heather: *(Chat) Yes!*
Andy: *(Chat) Yes*
Julia: *(Chat) Yes*

Stacy: *(Chat) Now*
Peter: *(Chat) Go ahead*
Heather: *(Chat)Now*

The instructor is both clapping with the built-in gesture and physically clapping her hands, making the gesture both visible and audible to the students. This illustrates a deliberate effort at invoking gestures. It is different from the way gestures are invoked in most f2f situations, which is often automated and tacit for the speaker. However, many gestures are programmed into SL and invoked by keyboard commands, and when memorized, they can approximate second-hand nature (Figure 4). Excerpt 6 illustrates another typical situation of the lecture room; the instructor is the active speaker, with the students responding to questions by chat. This situation would be reversed in the small-group discussion areas, where the instructor would be the silent, listening partner, and the students would talk and chat, as shown in Excerpt 5.

The Instructor's Scaffolding

Scaffolding in SL in this case is quite elaborate. It demonstrates an active instructor who can manage the technology and students who put great effort into learning to use the technology.

Scaffold the Learning of SL (Excerpt 7)

It is recommended that instructors incorporate assignments into the course to scaffold SL learning. The subject-specific assignment given to the students was to apply the theoretical concepts taught in the class in a role-play in two stages, first to create the role play through collaborative group work with peers and then to act it (another group's) role play out. In complex learning environments like SL, incorporating

Figure 4. Role-play session in the main lecture hall. The person on the left raises his hand to ask question.

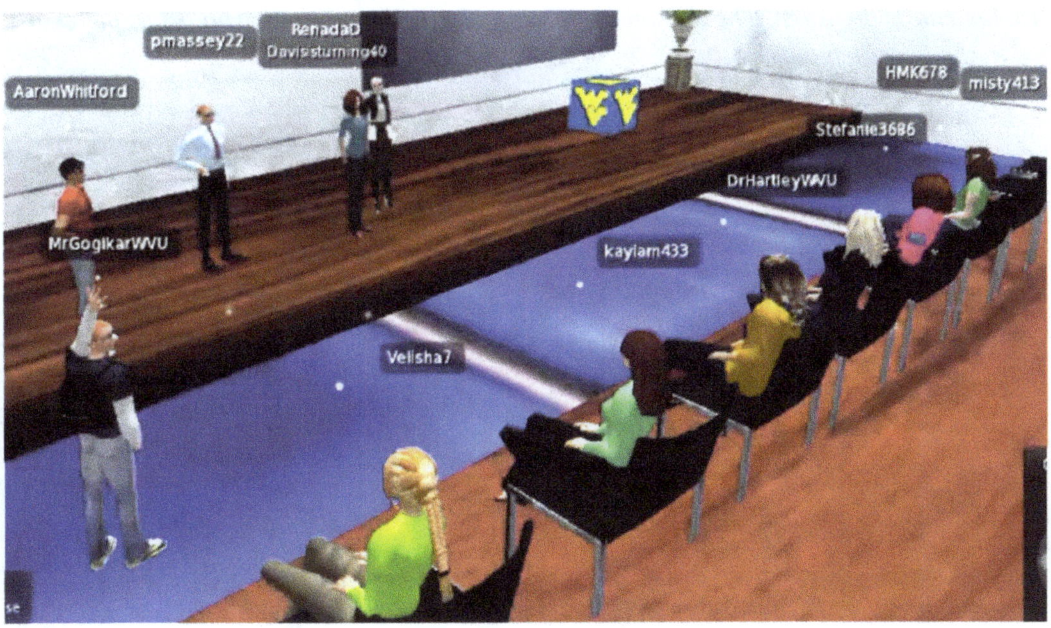

(technical) assignments ensures that students practice the skills necessary to participate in the class sessions. This is demonstrated in the following excerpt of an online interaction between two students and their instructor regarding a third student who is temporarily lost and needs help getting back to her group.

Laura: *That is why I do not fly; I walk or run. ((Laughs)) (..) OK, I think she's coming. (..)*
John: *((Instructor)), if one of our other people is flying around lost, tell them that (..) is there a way that we can get them to come here? ((Student)) seems to be a little lost.*
Instructor: *Oh yeah, I can—I can help. You said ((student)) is lost?*
John: *Yes, ((student)) A.*
Instructor: *OK, let me look on the mini-map. Oh, I found her; I'll bring her over. I'll be right back. ((Instructor flies away.))*

Some skills that should be demonstrated include the ability to do the following: fly, teleport, speak, landmark a location, send a friend request, buy materials from a box (see the box on the table in Figure 5), retrieve materials from their inventory, create a notecard, and share a notecard via a box.

The instructor we interviewed reported that the most efficient way for the preservice teachers to demonstrate these skills is by submitting screenshots or videos.

Structure (Excerpt 8)

Instructors should plan the class's structure. How will the class begin? How will the students demonstrate understanding? What are the expectations surrounding student participation? How will students participate? What activities will students be asked to do? While this list of questions is not exhaustive, these questions can begin to assist online instructors in thinking about how to prepare for teaching in

Figure 5. A group session in one of the discussion areas is using boxes for information sharing when the instructor enters the room. The person on the right is typing on the keyboard to the chat window displayed in the lower left corner.

SL. The following excerpt is from an interview with the instructor conducted by observer 3 (one of the researchers).

Observer3: *If you (..) were asked to teach this course (..) in a conventional face-to-face way, would you organize it in the same way or differently?*
Instructor: *That's a really good question, I taught this course to undergrad, face to face, and [..] I tried to incorporate role-play, because I really like role-play (..) I found that people aren't as apprehensive online ((as they are in f2f situations)).*

The excerpt shows that the instructor had previously taught the course to undergraduate students in a conventional (f2f) setting and incorporated role-play based on her teaching preferences and previous research; and when she compares this to online teaching she found role-playing to work even better; many of the students were less apprehensive when role-playing online. Role-playing became a stepping-stone to apply the theoretical concepts taught in the lectures (see Figure 3). Furthermore, the role-plays were created and played out by the students in collaborative activities (see Figures 4 and 5).

Procedures (Excerpt 9)

Instructors also need to determine the procedures needed in class and then explicitly teach those procedures to students. Examples of such procedures include where students will meet to begin class; how to complete, submit, and review a warm-up; how to complete individual and group activities; what artifacts support the activities; and how the class session will end. The following excerpt is from the instructor interview.

When I first started teaching in Second Life, before I went to the Sloan training I used to type everything into the chat text, but it would disappear, and so I'd have to type it again. Or, I'd IM every student individually by typing instructions, and it was very ineffective and very non-time efficient, because it would take me forever for getting that information to multiple people.

The instructor explains the rationale for using information sharing containers, boxes, as an efficient way of sharing information, rather than send individual messages by chat. The use of boxes was the most convenient way for her to communicate to several students (see Figure 5). However, the boxes are not always easy to manipulate, and the instructor provided scaffolds (see Figure 2). We observed a discrepancy in the perceived benefit of using this tool between the instructor and some of the students. This discrepancy became evident when some groups encountered difficulties in making the boxes available for the rest of the class to buy in order to share information with another group during role-play activity. The complexity of boxes and other educational resources can be attributed to two object types in SL: functional (manipulative) and decorative. Other functional objects are chairs and tables, whereas plants, pictures, and photos are examples of decorative objects. The instructor used both types when designing the interior of the group rooms.

Planned Transitions (Excerpt 10)

In addition to planning the structure and procedures, faculty members need to plan how students will transition between activities. The following excerpt is from the interview with the instructor in the same dialogue context as shown in Excerpt 8, preceding it by two and one-half minutes.

Observer3: *Could you say a little bit about that process, or, how do you perceive (..) going from theory to practice in this domain?*

Instructor: *Yeah, definitely, that was my goal [..] throughout the whole (..) course of the semester, for the live class sessions [..]. I tried to only do five to ten minutes of lecture, and then some sort of individual activity. In the past I've also done pair activities, and then five to ten more minutes of lecture. Then I'd have them do the group work, and my idea with the group work was that whatever topic we had been talking about that day, or whatever content I had been teaching them, I wanted them to practice those skills. And some skills I had them practice more than others.*

The excerpt shows the number of minutes assigned to different activities and the typical sequence of activities, going from theory to practice. It details iterations of key concepts and skills practice and the arrangement of this practice. In a class of 30–35 students, it is difficult for the instructor to know who has submitted an assignment that will be reviewed later because doing so requires determining who is still working. This could be done with a printed list, checking which students have submitted; however, it is more efficient to ask students to physically move to another location when they have finished. For example, once students finish the lecture (see Figure 3) and are ready to discuss it, they walk over to the discussion area (see Figure 5). When students physically relocate, the faculty can see how many students are still seated and working. The other students can see it too, so they know there is a little time remaining until they begin again.

GENERAL DISCUSSION

In this section, we summarize and discuss our findings by addressing the research question raised in the beginning of the chapter: "What contexts can the instructor create to promote collaborative learning in an online teacher preparation program in Second Life?" We answer the question by pointing to relevant data extracts and comparing them with the findings reported in related research in three areas: (a) social presence, (b) body language and gesturing, and (c) instructor's scaffolding.

The results of the data analysis indicate that the learning we observed in SL was directly influenced by students' social interactions and the instructor's scaffolding. They also indicate that a third type of context, emotional, was present in the interactions but under supported in the environment.

Social Presence

An overarching theme throughout our data is social presence. Short, Williams, and Christie (1976) first defined social presence as the degree of awareness of the other person in a communication. Even while unaware of the concept, the instructor was conscious of those relationships and engaged in multiple actions to create them.

There are several reasons social presence is high in SL. First, SL users are featured by a 3D-graphical representation referred to as avatars that are easily able to interact and communicate using speech or text chat. Second, the number of users aware of each other is critical to experiencing a sense of communal presence (Bulu, 2012). In our case, this was fulfilled, as the course had more than 30 participants (in addition to three observers) who were visible to the whole class during the lectures (see Figures 3–4) and co-located in small groups facing each other during round table discussions (see Figure 5). Third, the sense of anonymity represented by avatars in the 3D environment (Excerpts 1 and 3) allowed learners to engage more effectively in practicing collaboration skills of a certain complexity. According to Bulu (2012), students' interactions in an online world relate more to their relationships with the other students and with the instructor than to immersion or the extent to which they feel the environment is real and accurately rendered. This is supported by our findings regarding the ease by which avatars could meet, communicate, and form relationships in the online environment (Excerpt 3), using both direct (e.g., speech, text chat) and indirect (e.g., boxes, notecards, slides) means of communication, and in ways that were different from their interactions in the asynchronous learning environment of other classes.

Body Language and Gesturing

Previous research indicates that gesturing is important for communication and learning (Goldin-Meadow & Wagner, 2005). Arguably, the best approximation to gesturing in online environments (aside from video conferencing, which aims to replicate f2f communication) is provided by 3D virtual worlds. The participants in our study (both instructor and students) frequently felt a need to express emotions, but the environment did not provide a mode of gesture invocation that was as seamless as gesturing in ordinary communication. Gesturing had to be invoked explicitly by menu selection, a somewhat cumbersome procedure unless memorized as keyboard shortcuts.

The students relied instead on text chatting, which was used in synchronicity with speech on almost all occasions we observed (Excerpts 4 and 5). The students also used text chat and sometimes speech when responding to the instructor's questions in the main auditorium (Excerpt 6). When they met in the discussion areas, they would use all communication channels at their disposal, even commenting on each other's domestic background sounds (e.g., dog barking, baby crying, etc.). The instructor would typically use speech to communicate with the students in the main auditorium, and she used text chat to give feedback (e.g., praise) and ask questions (Excerpt 6). The instructor also used gestures, position, and movement (nonverbal behaviors, Excerpt 6) and combined verbal and nonverbal behaviors (Gunawardena, 1995) to interact. Hence, the instructor preferred SL to video conferencing or the asynchronous learning environment used in other courses at the college (Excerpt 3).

The Instructor's Scaffolding

The instructor's scaffolding activities (Excerpts 7–10) required thought, planning, and follow-up and were learned through hands-on experience in the Sloan training and while using SL as an educational platform over several years. In addition, they were field tested in multiple courses (Excerpt 9). The lessons learned are that in SL, the instructor must be more deliberate in designing the contexts that facilitate learning because f2f contexts cannot be taken for granted in virtual worlds (Mørch et al., 2014). On the other hand, when the students applied the theoretical concepts taught in role-play activities, they practiced collaboration skills, involving perspective-taking and cooperative problem solving, while being less apprehensive compared to a face-to-face course with role-plays (Excerpt 8). We also observed that an instructor's constructive feedback to the students in the lecture hall facilitated the group work and the transitioning between individual and collaborative learning activities. Other contributors to pedagogical scaffolding were well-designed virtual learning activities that allowed iterative skills practice in dedicated small-group rooms (Excerpt 10) and the instructor's continuous guidance and adaptive feedback while flying around the campus and visiting each of the working groups in a round-robin fashion (Excerpt 5).

Four types of scaffolding activities were essential for planning the course: (a) scaffold the students' learning of the new technology (Excerpt 7), (b) plan for the structure of the course (Excerpt 8), (c) implement the procedures in the virtual classroom (Excerpt 9), and (d) facilitate the transitions between activities (Excerpt 10) (Mørch et al., 2014). The instructor was trying to make the distance education experience more student-centered (Excerpts 8 and 10) and make use of technological artifacts (Excerpt 9), to extend and not merely replicate the traditional classroom, as indicated by Keskitalo (2011).

IMPLICATIONS FOR THE DESIGN OF ONLINE LEARNING CONTEXTS

Based on our findings, suggestions for new designs (technological features and pedagogical practices) include the following:

1. Use SL for experimentation (it is relatively low cost to design new contexts for collaborative learning and test out in small-scale experiments in semi-naturalistic settings).
2. Enact contexts other than those mentioned in the study (social, pedagogical, emotional) with implications for collaborative learning and the sociocultural perspective (cultural, institutional, etc.).
3. Render cultural and historical information in computer-based artifacts beyond mouse click actions and decorations of SL objects to also capture digital object modifications over time and cultural complexity beyond screen depth.
4. Increase support for scaffolding by computer-based feedback, using visualization and automated advice giving and leveraging adaptive feedback techniques and learning analytic methods and tools.
5. Increase support for gesturing in SL (e.g., allow users to define new gestures and invoke them by self-defined keyboard shortcuts).
6. Conduct work on Internet pedagogy by harnessing teaching principles for 3D virtual worlds.
7. Consider integrating SL with an asynchronous learning environment to supplement real-time interaction with time for independent problem solving and reflection (e.g., when working on assignments that allow multiple solution approaches, and individual preferences).
8. Follow up with research designs employing quantitative methods to identify causal effects of specific relationships of contexts to motivation, collaboration, and learning.
9. Follow up with new case studies, using virtual worlds other than SL (e.g., Minecraft), and identify best practices for creating contexts for collaborative learning in 3D virtual worlds.

CONCLUSION

The findings from this study indicate that carefully designed contexts for collaborative learning can increase the support of a 3D virtual world such as SL and that skilled instructors can accomplish the design work as part of course preparation and execution. This type of synchronous online learning environment provides a semi-naturalistic setting for practicing collaborative skills and role-playing, mediated by a new class of artifacts—end-user modifiable 3D objects (Caruso, Hartley, & Mørch, 2015; Mørch, Caruso, & Hartley, 2017).

Although SL cannot replace real classroom practice and does not intend to do so, the results we report suggest that SL had a major impact as an alternative to residential college education for this teacher preparation program, facilitating access to student teachers who live far away from the college campus.

SL also provides an arena for those who feel self-conscious in f2f situations (e.g., when role-playing or answering a question from the instructor in front of the class). SL engaged all the participants who could master the technology, which involved a learning curve for some of the students. The instructor provided technical assistance to students who needed it. The initial learning curve disappeared quickly upon successive use of the learning environment.

However, some limitations should be noted; the learning activities depended on the active participation of both instructor and students. This implies instructor and students will benefit from adopting a constructivist learning philosophy of active learning through the use of tools (Mørch, Caruso, & Hartley, 2017). However, planning and direct instruction are important for steering students in the right direction; without some scaffolding, they will be lost. The success of role-play as a learning method also depends on the students' serious treatment of the assignment and on the instructor's planning of the learning activities according to educational goals. In one of the interviews, a student said, "There are other classes I think Second Life wouldn't work very well, but with a specific style of course where we were learning how to collaborate with people, I thought Second Life was absolutely a wonderful tool!"

Despite the potential of 3D virtual worlds in education, research interest in this field is still in an embryonic stage. Thus, 3D virtual worlds need to be integrated throughout teacher education programs to provide preservice teachers with the necessary experience in online role-playing to apply professional skills in real school settings. In this area, there is plenty of opportunity for more research.

The findings of this study were limited to a single case study (one institution), and it was conducted with a convenience sampling method (the instructor responded to a request for participation sent by the researchers to the Second Life Educators mailing list (SLED). A third limitation was the insufficient number of interviews with the students. This can be attributed to the fact that students were asked to take part in an interview after the end of the course during a time frame that coincided with end-of-semester holidays and busy workdays (the participants were working as teachers in school settings).

REFERENCES

Allmendringer, K. (2010). Social presence in synchronous learning environments: The role of nonverbal signals displayed by avatars. *Educational Psychology Review*, *22*(1), 41–56. doi:10.1007/s10648-010-9117-8

Berge, Z. L. (1995). Facilitating computer conferencing: Recommendations from the field. *Educational Technology*, *35*(1), 22–30.

Berge, Z. L. (2008). Changing instructor's roles in virtual worlds. *The Quarterly Review of Distance Education*, *9*(4), 407–414.

Bulu, S. T. (2012). Place presence, social presence, co-presence and satisfaction. *Virtual Worlds. Computers & Education*, *58*(1), 154–161. doi:10.1016/j.compedu.2011.08.024

Caruso, V., Hartley, M. D., & Mørch, A. I. (2015). End-user development in Second Life: Meta-design, tailoring, and appropriation. In P. Diaz, V. Pipek, & C. Ardito (Eds.), *Proceedings 5th international symposium end-user development 2015* (pp. 92–108). Berlin: Springer. doi:10.1007/978-3-319-18425-8_7

Caruso, V., Mørch, A. I., Thomassen, I., Hartley, M., & Ludlow, B. (2014). Practicing collaboration skills through role-play activities in a 3D virtual world. In R. Huang, Kinshuk, & N.-S. Chen (Eds.), The new development of technology enhanced learning (pp. 165–184). Berlin: Springer.

Cheong, D. U., Yun, S., & Chollins, C. (2009). Is Second Life effective for pre-service teachers' teaching practice? In I. Gibson, R. Weber, K. McFerrin, R. Carlsen, & D. A. Willis (Eds.), *Proceedings of society for information technology & teacher education international conference 2009* (pp. 1418–1421). Chesapeake, VA: AACE.

Collins, A., Brown, J. S., & Newman, S. E. (1989). Cognitive apprenticeship: Teaching the crafts of reading, writing, and mathematics. In L. B. Resnick (Ed.), *Knowing, learning, and instruction: Essays in honor of Robert Glaser* (pp. 453–494). Hillsdale, NJ: Lawrence Erlbaum.

Dabbagh, N. (2005). Pedagogical models for E-Learning: A theory-based design framework. *International Journal of Technology in Teaching and Learning*, *1*(1), 25–44.

Dede, C. (2009). Immersive interfaces for engagement and learning. *Science*, *233*(5910), 66–69. doi:10.1126/science.1167311 PMID:19119219

Dennen, V. P., & Burner, K. J. (2008). The cognitive apprenticeship model in educational practice. *Educational Communication and Technology*, *3*, 425–439.

Dieterle, E., & Clarke, J. (2007). Multi-user virtual environments for teaching and learning. In M. Pagani (Ed.), *Encyclopedia of multimedia technology and networking* (pp. 1033–1041). Hershey, PA: Idea Group.

Fischer, G., Lemke, A. C., Mastaglio, T., & Morch, A. I. (1991). The role of critiquing in cooperative problem solving. *ACM Transactions on Information Systems*, *9*(2), 123–151. doi:10.1145/123078.128727

Gao, F., Noh, J. J., & Koehler, M. J. (2009). Comparing role-playing activities in Second Life and face-to-face environments. *Journal of Interactive Learning Research*, *20*(4), 422–443.

Goldin-Meadow, S., & Wagner, S. M. (2005). How our hands help us learn. *Trends in Cognitive Sciences*, *9*(5), 234–241. doi:10.1016/j.tics.2005.03.006 PMID:15866150

Gunawardena, C. N. (1995). Social presence theory and implications for interaction and collaborative learning in computer conferences. *International Journal of Educational Telecommunications*, *1*(2–3), 147–166.

Hattie, J., & Timperley, H. (2007). The power of feedback. *Review of Educational Research*, *77*(1), 81–112.

Hetland, P., & Mørch, A. I. (2016). Ethnography for investigating the Internet. *Seminar.net: Media. Technology and Lifelong Learning*, *12*(1), 1–14.

Hollan, J., & Stornetta, S. (1992). Beyond being there. In *Proceedings CHI'92* (pp. 119–125). New York, NY: ACM Press. doi:10.1145/142750.142769

Jarmon, J. (2008). Pedagogy and learning in the virtual world of Second Life. In P. Rogers, G. Berg, J. Boettcher, C. Howard, L. Justice, & K. Schenk (Eds.), *Encyclopedia of distance and online learning* (pp. 1–11). Hershey, PA: Idea Group.

Jordan, B., & Henderson, A. (1995). Interaction analysis: Foundation and practice. *Journal of the Learning Sciences*, *4*(1), 39–103. doi:10.1207/s15327809jls0401_2

Keskitalo, T. (2011). Teacher's conceptions and approaches to teaching in virtual reality and simulation-based learning environments. *Teachers and Teaching*, *17*(1), 131–147. doi:10.1080/13540602.2011.538503

Lave, J. (1988). *Cognition in practice: Mind, mathematics and culture in everyday life*. Cambridge, UK: Cambridge University Press. doi:10.1017/CBO9780511609268

Liu, X., Bonk, C. J., Magjuka, R. J., Lee, S. H., & Su, B. (2005). Exploring four dimensions of online instructor roles: A program level case study. *Journal of Asynchronous Learning Networks*, *9*(4), 29–48.

Ludvigsen, S., & Mørch, A. (2010). Computer-supported collaborative learning: Basic concepts, multiple perspectives, and emerging trends. In B. McGaw, P. Peterson, & E. Baker (Eds.), *The international encyclopedia of education* (Vol. 5, pp. 290–296). Oxford, UK: Elsevier. doi:10.1016/B978-0-08-044894-7.00493-0

Miller, F., & Wallis, J. (2011). Social Interaction and the role of empathy in information and knowledge management: A literature review. *Journal of Education for Library and Information Science*, *52*(2), 122–132.

Mørch, A. I., Caruso, V., & Hartley, M. D. (2017). End-user development and learning in Second Life: The evolving artifacts framework with application. In F. Paterno & V. Wulf (Eds.), *New perspectives in end-user development*. Berlin: Springer. doi:10.1007/978-3-319-60291-2_13

Mørch, A. I., Dolonen, A. I., & Nævdal, J. E. (2006). An evolutionary approach to prototyping pedagogical agents: From simulation to integrated system. *Journal of Network and Computer Applications*, *29*(2–3), 177–199.

Mørch, A. I., Engeness, I., Cheng, V. C., Cheung, W. K., & Wong, K. C. (2017). Essay Critic: Writing to learn with a knowledge-based design critiquing system. *Journal of Educational Technology & Society*, *20*(2), 216–226.

Mørch, A. I., Hartley, M. D., Ludlow, B. L., Caruso, V., & Thomassen, I. (2014). The teacher as designer: Preparations for teaching in a Second Life distance education course. In *Proceedings of 2014 IEEE International Conference on Advanced Learning Technologies (ICALT 2014)* (pp. 691–693). Los Alamitos, CA: IEEE Computer Society. doi:10.1109/ICALT.2014.201

Morse, S., Littleton, F., Macleod, M., & Ewins, R. (2009). The theatre of performance appraisal: Role-play in Second Life. In C. Wankel & J. Kingsley (Eds.), *Higher education in virtual worlds: Teaching and learning in Second Life* (pp. 181–201). Bingley, UK: Emerald Group.

Muir, T., Allen, J. M., Rayner, C. S., & Cleland, B. (2013). Preparing pre-service teachers for classroom practice in a virtual world: A pilot study using Second Life. *Journal of Interactive Media in Education*, *2013*(1), 3. doi:10.5334/2013-03

Pasfield-Neofitou, S., Huang, H., & Grant, S. (2015). Lost in Second Life: Virtual embodiment and language learning via multimodal communication. *Educational Technology Research and Development*, *63*(5), 709–726. doi:10.1007/s11423-015-9384-7

Price, M., Handley, K., Millar, J., & O'Donovan, B. (2010). Feedback: All that effort, but what is the effect? *Assessment & Evaluation in Higher Education*, *35*(3), 277–289. doi:10.1080/02602930903541007

Säljö, R. (2010). Digital tools and challenges to institutional traditions of learning: Technologies, social memory and the performative nature of learning. *Journal of Computer Assisted Learning*, *26*(1), 53–64. doi:10.1111/j.1365-2729.2009.00341.x

Short, J. A., Williams, E., & Christie, B. (1976). *The social psychology of telecommunications*. London, UK: Wiley.

Soller, A., Martinez, A., Jermann, P., & Muehlenbrock, M. (2005). From mirroring to guiding: A review of state of the art technology for supporting collaborative learning. *International Journal of Artificial Intelligence in Education*, *15*, 261–290.

Stahl, G., Koschmann, T., & Suthers, D. (2006). Computer-supported collaborative learning. In R. K. Sawyer (Ed.), *The Cambridge handbook of the learning sciences* (pp. 409–425). Cambridge, UK: Cambridge University Press.

Strauss, A., & Corbin, J. (1998). *Basics of qualitative research: Techniques and procedures for developing grounded theory*. Thousand Oaks, CA: Sage.

Van den Boom, G., Paas, F., Van Merrienboer, J. J., & Van Gog, T. (2004). Reflection prompts and tutor feedback in a web-based learning environment: Effects on students' self-regulated learning competence. *Computers in Human Behavior*, *20*(4), 551–567. doi:10.1016/j.chb.2003.10.001

Vasileiou, V., & Paraskeva, F. (2010). Teaching role-playing instruction in Second Life: An exploratory study. *Journal of Information. Information Technology and Organizations*, *5*, 25–50.

Vygotsky, L. (1978). *Mind in society: The development of higher psychological processes*. Cambridge, MA: Harvard University Press.

Wang, A. (2015). Facilitating participation: Teacher roles in a multiuser virtual learning environment. *Language Learning & Technology*, *19*(2), 156–176.

Wang, F., & Burton, J. K. (2013). Second Life in education: A review of publications from its launch to 2011. *British Journal of Educational Technology*, *44*(3), 357–371. doi:10.1111/j.1467-8535.2012.01334.x

Wertsch, J. V. (2007). Mediation. In H. Daniels, M. Cole, & J. V. Wertsch (Eds.), *The Cambridge companion to Vygotsky* (pp. 178–192). New York, NY: Cambridge University Press. doi:10.1017/CCOL0521831040.008

Wood, D., Bruner, J. S., & Ross, G. (1976). The role of tutoring in problem solving. *Journal of Child Psychology and Psychiatry, and Allied Disciplines*, *17*(2), 89–100. doi:10.1111/j.1469-7610.1976.tb00381.x PMID:932126

Yin, R. K. (2003). *Case study research: Design and methods*. London: Sage.

KEY TERMS AND DEFINITIONS

3D Virtual World: A web-based simulated world where three-dimensional graphical representations of individuals (i.e., avatars) can interact with each other by using text-based or voice-based tools. Avatars can move around in 3D space and explore buildings and other objects by simple commands, and users get a feel for the presence of others and distances to virtual objects.

Collaborative Learning: An educational approach that involves groups of learners working together to solve a problem, simulate a scientific inquiry, share knowledge, or create a product, such as a role-play script, presentation of a topic or concept map.

Design Context: Representations in virtual environments that model and extend environmental attributes of face-to-face interaction, such as movement, body language, emotion, social presence, objects, power, and instruction. Design contexts are persistent, dynamic, and updated incrementally by the computer or by users during sessions in virtual environments.

Preservice Teacher: A college or university student who is enrolled in a teacher education program with the goal of obtaining professional licensure prior to service as a teacher in elementary or secondary schools.

Role Play: A technique for teaching communication and problem-solving skills in groups when participants take on specific roles associated with different viewpoints (e.g., a profession, a culture, a workplace). The participants are involved in "as-if" or simulated actions, where the aim is to construct an approximation of aspects of a real-life situation that is impractical, expensive, or risky to carry out in the real world.

Second Life (SL): A 3D virtual world developed by Linden Labs and launched in 2003. The users download a client program, 3D viewer, which is free of charge. The SL world is composed of islands with buildings and owning an island requires payment. A 3D design environment based on simple geometric shapes (e.g., cubic shaped boxes) is integrated with the SL environment and allows residents to build virtual objects such as buildings and furniture.

Sociocultural Perspective: One of the branches in psychology (also called cultural psychology) used to understand how the society (social practices and culture) influences the way people interact in groups and, specifically, the social conditions that shape learning as it occurs in people as part of authentic (non-laboratory) learning activities mediated by culture-specific tools.

Special Education: Individualized programs and services delivered to students with disabilities or other special learning needs delivered by specially trained teachers in elementary or secondary schools.

Virtual Ethnography: An application of ethnographic methods for internet research, implying that social interactions carried out in an online world are subject to similar methods to those used when studying distant cultures. An example of a common data collection technique is to use screen capture software for video recording computer screen activity, as seen from a distant observer's screen in the real world who are co-located with informants in the virtual world.

APPENDIX 1

Interview Guide for Instructor

1. Description of the course
    a. How many times have you held this course in SL?
    b. Did you teach in F2F before in SL?
    c. What were the decisions for this course to be held in SL?
    d. Is the course held entirely in SL?
2. Scaffolding techniques
    a. What are the scaffolding techniques used? (technological and pedagogical)
    b. How did you create the scaffolds in the SL environment? And which ones work the best?
    c. In which way were the artifacts you made available in SL useful for collaborative and role playing activities?
    d. What was your role in supporting the collaborative activities in SL?
3. Social interaction and communication
    a. In which way does SL make social interaction easy or difficult?
    b. How can SL support communication within the groups?
    c. What advantages and disadvantages do you see, by comparing virtual world communication to its real world counterpart?
4. Collaborative interaction and learning
    a. Do you think that SL is a good environment for enabling students' collaborative interaction?
    b. Which features make the collaborative activities in SL better or worse than their real world equivalents?
    c. Could you please describe some activities that differ the most between SL and RL learning?
    d. Could you please describe some activities that differ the least between SL and RL learning?
    e. What attitude do students display toward using SL for collaborative activities?
    f. In what ways are students assessed in the course (individually and/or collaboratively)?
5. Artifacts
    a. How did the artifacts that you created (campus buildings, presentation slides and so on) facilitate role-playing activities and collaboration among the groups?
6. Role-play
    a. Why did you choose to teach theoretical concepts through role-play scenarios?
    b. How did you organize role-playing activities?
    c. Where did you get the ideas for the scenarios?
    d. Is Second Life especially well-suited for this?
    e. What advantages and disadvantages do you see, by comparing the role-playing activities to their real world equivalents?
    f. Do the sequence of the activities organized in Second Life by you, follow the same sequence of the events when organized for face-to-face seminars (if not, why?)
    g. (If not, to the previous question) What aspects of Second Life allow you to do things in new ways? (i.e. what are the unique features of SL that are useful, and why are they so?)

7. Flexibility
   a. (Self-organized learning): We observed that sometimes the students were working on their own in the work group buildings to apply the concepts and to create role playing games. You were not always present, but it counted as hours of your teaching, I suppose. Does this mean that Second Life can help make teaching and learning more flexible?
   b. (Flexibility of teaching): a) Can you teach the course while you are on travel or located in some other location than your university or home location? b) Are you at home or in your office when you teach your course in Second Life?
   c. (Flexibility of learning): Can the students who are physically co-located at the same place as you attend your lecture in a seminar room (where you are located), or is it required that all students always follow the course in SL from their own location?

APPENDIX 2

Interview Guide for Students

1. Introduction
   a. Presentation
   b. The interview will be recorded
2. Student information
   a. Avatar's name
   b. Age
   c. Gender
   d. Full time or part time student
   e. Group which you participated in and name of hall/building
3. Description of the course
   a. Course's name
   b. What is the course about?
   c. How is the course organized?
   d. Is the course held entirely in SL, if not what off-line sessions are there?
   e. What tools other than Second Life do you use in the course?
   f. What is the "percentage" you use Second Life among all the tools in the course?
   g. What are the three most important things you gain from participation in the course?
4. Description of activities in Second Life
   a. Describe your group's activities in SL
   b. Describe your individual activities in SL
   c. How easy was it to access the material provided by the teacher?
   d. Did you at any time feel that you did not have access to the information you needed?
   e. Did the use of SL for this course motivate you in any specific ways? (Please, elaborate briefly. If not, why?)

5. Teaching and learning activities
    a. Did the SL teaching methods give you the same amount of information, as you would get in classical lectures?
    b. Describe the activities that are most beneficial to your learning? What were the effective skills that were demonstrated in your group?
    c. Were there other skills that would have also been more appropriate to use? (If so, what were they?)
    d. Would you like to use Second Life for learning activities in the future?
6. Second Life environment
    a. Have you used SL for other courses than this one? If yes, which ones?
    b. How long did it take you to feel comfortable with the environment?
    c. Have you experienced any technical difficulties with Second Life?
    d. According to you, what are the main differences between learning in Second Life vs. learning in real life?
    e. Describe the activities that differ the most between Second Life and real life learning.
    f. Describe the activities that differ the least between Second Life and real life learning.
7. Social interaction and communication
    a. Which methods did you use to communicate with other avatars?
    b. Did you find any difficulties to interact and socialize within the group?
    c. Do you think SL makes social interaction easy or difficult?
    d. Which differences can you identify between communication in SL and communication in real world? (both strengths and weaknesses)
    e. Do you also use SL at your own time? If "Yes", what activities you are engaged with?
8. Collaborative activities
    a. How was your collaborative activity organized (e.g. by teacher, self-organized)?
    b. How were 'roles' assigned or did group members have equal status?
    c. Do you feel that you learned more as part of a group than you would have working alone? (elaborate)
    d. Compared to their real world equivalents, in which ways did SL support your collaborative activities?
    e. Compared to their real world equivalents, in which ways did SL hinder your collaborative activities?
    f. there anything you would have done differently if you were the teacher?
9. Role play
    a. What was your role as group member?
    b. How did the role-play allow you to apply the concepts taught in the course?
    c. What advantages and disadvantages do you see in virtual role-play compared to its real world counterpart?
    d. What were the objectives of the role-play?
    e. What outcomes did your group produce?

10. Artifacts
    a. What artifacts were involved in collaborative activities?
    b. Are the SL buildings similar to the real ones in the campus?
    c. What artifacts allowed you to practice the skills needed for the class?
    d. How were the boxes and the notecards created? (individually or collaboratively)
    e. How did these artifacts facilitate role-playing activities and collaboration among the groups?
    f. How were the artifacts created in SL (boxes, presentation slides, etc.) related to their real world counterpart (text book, articles, etc.)
11. Teacher's role
    a. What was the teacher's role in supporting your learning activities in SL?

Chapter 8
Team-Based Learning and Team-Based Playing:
How *World of Warcraft* and Similar Games Can Make Better Learners

Abi Johnson
The College of Saint Rose, USA

ABSTRACT

Certain aspects of the popular online game World of Warcraft embody the tenets of Larry Michaelsen's team-based learning instructional method. However, team-based learning can fail when implemented incorrectly. This chapter aims to provide a theoretical basis for using World of Warcraft as an example of successful teamwork in order to better inform student understanding of collaborative, team-based learning, and introduce incoming college freshmen to the type of active, participatory learning that is critical to higher education. Through literature review and study of World of Warcraft itself, the author has established a framework for a future research avenue in unifying MUVEs and team-based learning. The author believes that using World of Warcraft as an introductory activity in a team-based learning style course can accelerate new team bonding, and can establish learning practices (such as individual accountability and preparedness for class) to benefit the entire college experience and subsequent professional career.

INTRODUCTION

Team-based learning, developed by Larry Michaelsen in 1979, is an instructional method designed with three purposes: to help facilitate learning in large classes, to allow students to take responsibility for their own learning, and to change the instructor's focus from delivering content to demonstrating for students why their subjects are significant (Michaelsen, Knight, & Fink, 2004a). Team-based learning provides students opportunities to learn collaboratively and to teach each other, in order to facilitate deeper learning. It works on four tenets: (1) each group must be properly formed and managed, (2) students must be accountable for their work in and out of the group, (3) assignments must promote both

DOI: 10.4018/978-1-5225-3719-9.ch008

learning and group development, and (4) students must receive frequent and timely feedback on their work (Michaelsen, 2004b).

Bad group experiences cause students and instructors to shy away from further attempts. Hard-working students dislike when they are forced to treat other students as obstacles to be overcome, or when the entire group gets the same grade for one students' hard work. Shy or socially anxious students may dislike being forced to meet outside of class to complete a group project. Problems and uncomfortable experiences like these will cause students to dislike group learning, and can cause students to give instructors low student evaluation scores. It is therefore necessary, especially for first-year students, to introduce team-based learning properly and correctly.

The video game *World of Warcraft,* developed by Blizzard Entertainment and released in 2004, is classified as a massively multiplayer online role-playing game (MMORPG). It can also be classified as a multi-user virtual environment (MUVE), a living online space in which players interact with each other in the virtual environment in real time (Qian, 2015). Although it is possible to play *World of Warcraft* alone, a great deal of content is designed for small player groups (up to five players), including specific zones of the game world called dungeons. These small player groups function best when adhering to the tenets of team-based learning: the groups must be formed carefully and managed well, each player must be accountable to themselves and to the group, the activities in the game must encourage team development as well as promote learning about the game itself, and players must receive frequent and timely feedback on what they are doing correctly or incorrectly.

Students enter the higher education environment unprepared for the style of learning employed there, as a result of being taught this "skill and drill" method of reciting information rather than critically engaging with it. As a result, they are often unprepared for the rigors and demands of higher education and its associated learning style. Team-based learning, when successfully and correctly implemented, can help to smooth this transition, and introduces the intrinsic skills students need to succeed in this environment. It is therefore possible to eradicate the ineffectual "skill and drill" K-12 learning style when students enter the college environment by employing *World of Warcraft* as a working example of how team-based learning can help them succeed. This chapter will outline a theoretical application of *World of Warcraft* as an introductory module or assignment for a course taught using the team-based learning method. It will address potential problems of the approach, as well as provide introductory information on team-based learning itself.

BACKGROUND

Jane McGonigal (2011), a proponent of using video game concepts to improve various nongaming processes ("gamifying"), calls games "hard work that we choose for ourselves" (p. 28) and breaks games down into four concepts: rules, a goal, a feedback system, and voluntary participation. These four concepts could also be used to describe a classroom, especially a classroom where team-based learning is utilized. Unlike the K-12 educational space, higher education is "hard work [students] choose for themselves" (McGonigal, 2011, p. 28). Higher education is a great expense, and the landscape of the "average college student" is rapidly changing (Freedman, 2013). A bachelor's degree is no longer a guarantee of an entry-level position. Students need to possess a different set of skills in today's job market: skills such as problem-solving and the ability to interact effectively (Fink, 2004). James Paul Gee (2014) argues that some of these skills (such as teamwork and critical thinking) are best learned actively, and that video games are an example of such active learning (Gee, 2014). The link between games and learning is so profound that books on game design, such as Raph Koster's (2005) *Theory of Fun for Game Design,* place emphasis on designing video games based around the way human beings learn, in order to create games that players enjoy.

Traditional games, like soccer or solitaire, establish a set of rules at the outset and require someone (a coach or another player) to demonstrate to neophytes how to play. Early video games worked in a similar manner: they used thick manuals or in-game tutorials to teach newcomers the rules and methods of play. As video games evolved as a medium, however, it became clearer to designers and players that video games were uniquely situated to instead teach players how to play through the act of playing. This is the potential that excites Gee, Koster, and others. Video games encourage their players to learn and continue learning because it is by learning that they are able to "beat" the game: "motivation is built into the game itself" (Lee, Eustace, Fellows, Bytheway, & Irving, 2005, p. 449). Games can teach students how to learn without being explicitly walked through a process: how to use contextual, systemic, and environmental clues to determine how to proceed in a situation.

Charles, Charles, McNeill, Bustard, and Black (2011) contend that the importance of a university education does not all lie in content knowledge or domain-specific skills. The importance of a university education lies in "understanding the processes and systems" (Charles et al., 2011, p. 638) that will allow students to continue learning throughout their lives. If instructors set up good learning habits, both implicit and explicit, students will have a solid foundation in what true learning looks like, and will go on to greater success, in the academy and outside of it (Charles et al., 2011). Team-based learning functions on a system of modules and a cycle of learning that is conducive to immersive learning while also establishing this foundation in appropriate, university-level learning.

McGonigal (2011) defines games through four concepts: rules, a goal, a feedback system, and voluntary participation. The higher education classroom operates on these same four concepts. Classrooms have rules, a goal, a feedback system, and voluntary participation on the part of the student. Rules are outlined clearly, both by the institution and the syllabus. The goal of the course is similarly clearly stated in the syllabus and should be reflected in each activity and reading the students participate in. The feedback system takes the form of grading and of instructor comments during class discussions. Voluntary participation is equally essential to success in the university environment, but it cannot be tied only to the idea of attending class and participating in discussions. Voluntary participation can be segmented into at least three sections: adequately preparing for class, attending class (and participating in classwork), and completing homework. Higher education is an extraordinary expense, and, unlike a K-12 education, is not mandatory. Therefore, participation, to whatever extent, in the higher education system is wholly voluntary. Voluntary participation of a level that is appropriate for success in higher education needs to be taught, and instructors need to make their expectations clear; but first, instructors need to capture their students' attention. Gamifying learning can be a tool by which instructors can both capture attention and supplement textbook learning in order to keep that attention, bridging the gap for less self-motivated learners.

However, because the idea of gamifying learning is rather broad and vague, attempts to capture student attention by using this method can fail. Jamin Warren (2017), founder of the media company Killscreen, finds that what is referred to as gamifying can instead simply be "limited to points and leaderboards, rather than encouraging systems thinking" (Warren, 2017, n.p.). Much of adult life is a series of systems:

bureaucratic systems such as filing taxes or procuring insurance, professional systems like networking, the workplace itself, and professional development, or even systems like navigating public transit. This is the potential that excites proponents of gamifying learning: when students learn to think in terms of systems and to improve those systems by closely examining their rules, they are better prepared for life as adult citizens. If instructors can facilitate students' voluntary participation through gamifying learning, students can prepare themselves for adult life by learning to metacognate, and by understanding the value of active learning.

Higher education, then, needs to prepare students for the modern professional environment at its least effective, and teach its students how to examine systems in order to continue to learn at its most effective. Standardized testing and Common Core curriculums in the K-12 arena cause students to become bogged down in a learning model Gee calls "skill-and-drill" (Gee, 2014, p. 159), and it therefore becomes important for incoming college freshmen to relearn how to learn in the college environment (Charles et al., 2011). The university and the academy beyond it are large systems, and a university education that will prove valuable beyond the classroom is an education that teaches students systems thinking. It is not enough for a college graduate to understand the domain skills and content of their discipline; they must also understand the way to work together with others, the way to solve problems (sometimes without guidance), and the way to think critically (Fink, 2004). Video games, like *World of Warcraft*, can promote appropriate learning skills in college students, demonstrate active learning, as well as facilitate systems thinking and critical thinking.

What, then, of working collaboratively? Di Blas and Paolini (2014) call for collaborative learning as the remedy for the K-12 ailments; de Freitas (2007) finds that use of computer games benefits collaborative learning, and Gee (2014) cites several learning principles, embodied in video games, which deal directly with Michaelsen's team-based learning ideas. By working in teams, students are always operating from the advantage of the "sum of their parts:" team learning allows the group as a whole to accomplish more than even the best student in the group working alone (Fink, 2004). In this paper, "collaborative" learning is defined as learning that is more open-ended and student-led; learning related to higher-level concepts often found in the university classroom. "Cooperative" learning, then, is learning related to more foundational concepts which rely on there being a "correct" answer to the questions posed to students, and in which the instructor is the ultimate authority (Rockwood, 1995). Team-based learning falls under the "collaborative" side: in team-based learning, the instructor takes a step back to allow the learning teams to arrive at conclusions themselves, fostering higher-order thinking and discussion.

The *World of Warcraft* assignment is designed as an introductory activity to help students understand the first phase of team-based learning (the readiness assurance process), to foster a positive team dynamic, and to actively teach students the benefits of correctly implemented team learning. An entire team-based learning module, which extends beyond the readiness assurance process, is intended to take place over two to three weeks of class time (Michaelsen, 2004b). The *World of Warcraft* assignment, as outlined in this chapter, is not intended to take up so much time in a semester.

Team-based learning teaches more than simply course content; it teaches students how to learn successfully and they understand that in order to succeed in higher education, they must be accountable for themselves and arrive in class prepared and ready to learn. Through application of the three phases of team learning (Michaelsen, 2004a), students understand the process by which they are expected to learn in a team-based learning course, and better understand the way to learn in a higher education environment and beyond. In combining a strict teaching methodology with a rules-based, systemic game, Galarneau's (2005) conundrum is solved: the game is tied to a specific pedagogical approach, fostering a positive attitude towards an often-maligned learning style. *World of Warcraft* is a fun game contained in a short, concise team-building exercise, resting on the strong foundation of team-based learning, a profound pedagogical method.

The author conducted a literature review concerning collaborative learning and virtual worlds, consisting of various studies and other writing on these topics. Although the studies varied in specific aims, the connecting thread seemed to be the intense need for debriefing, metacognition, and reflection when employing gamified learning. Therefore, a deeper discussion of this problem exists below, in the section titled "Making Clear Connections to What is Learned."

LEARNING TO LEARN VIA *WORLD OF WARCRAFT'S* DUNGEON SYSTEM

Many types of exercises and class assignments can help foster cohesive teams while simultaneously providing a deep understanding of course content. The *World of Warcraft* exercise meets the criteria Michaelsen (2004b) outlined for a successful assignment. Namely, it encourages using concepts (albeit outside of class concepts) to solve problems, supports give-and-take discussions, prompts cross-team comparisons, and allows for prompt and detailed feedback (Michaelsen, 2004b). The *World of Warcraft* assignment is designed to provide a hands-on activity demonstrating the specific behaviors associated with team-based learning and, by extension, learner-centered learning. Therefore, the assignment is designed to instruct good learning habits and develop a successful learning process, rather than teach specific skills or course content, like math or writing (Rahim, 2013). *World of Warcraft* is a tool being used in this case to teach team-based learning. After the *World of Warcraft* assignment ends, the instructor has fostered a positive environment in which to continue to use team-based learning as a method to teach subject knowledge.

James Paul Gee (2014) believes that students learn to solve problems and learn actively through playing games; lessons that high school "skill-and-drill" teaching cannot truly teach. Video games encourage their players to become problem solvers, persistent people "who [do] not see mistakes as errors but as opportunities for reflection and learning" (Gee, 2014, p. 80). By combining these two ideas, instructors can overcome negative concepts of group work or poorly implemented team-based learning, and set their students up to "learn how to learn" in the higher education environment.

World of Warcraft, and its dungeon system specifically, can function as a working example of team-based learning and the readiness assurance process. Players "prepare" by completing individual quests alone, using input from the game itself or in conjunction with other resources, such as YouTube videos or *World of Warcraft*-specific Web sites. As expansions, classes, races, or other content are added to (or removed from) the game, players continue this research constantly throughout their time playing. Every class undergoes certain changes throughout *World of Warcraft*'s lifespan, and players must be prepared to accommodate those changes through the way that they play.

A "dungeon" in *World of Warcraft* is a specific multi-room zone which is designed for groups composed of a maximum of five players. Players must work collaboratively to defeat the enemies and monsters inside of the dungeon, and ultimately to defeat the "Boss" of the dungeon: a very strong final enemy which cannot be defeated without strategy and planning (Blizzard Entertainment, 2017a). Players assume roles within their group, and, with good communication, good planning, and a good team dynamic, it is possible to defeat the boss and complete the dungeon. Successfully completing dungeons requires a high level of cohesion and relies upon a well-functioning group. Michaelsen defines team-based learning within four tenets. Below, these tenets are broken down and connected to successful team function in *World of Warcraft*'s dungeons.

Tenet 1: Learning Groups Are Permanent, Small, and Correctly Formed

Group formation is as critical in *World of Warcraft* as it is in the team-based learning classroom. The ideal team-based learning group, according to Michaelsen (2004b), is permanent, consists of 5-7 members with even skill levels and abilities, and does not contain subgroups (i.e. spouses, roommates, or members of the same sports team). Although standard player groups are not formed by an outside party and often contain subgroups such as spouses or friends, they are composed of up to 5 members and they are composed of members with even skill level and ability. They are not always permanent, although they have potential to be: players can create or join a "guild," and, in doing so, gain access to several in-game perks as well as a consistent pool of known players to play with.

Tenet 2: Group Members Are Accountable for Individual and Group Participation

Accountability in *World of Warcraft* is very straightforward. Players are automatically accountable for their own research; they cannot access the Dungeon Finder feature until level 15, meaning they will need to play for a considerable amount of time and become very accustomed to the way their character should be played before attempting a dungeon with others. The first 10 levels are a sort of tutorial, introducing the player to the quest system, the history of their chosen race and class, and the controls of the game. Players who intend to attain a certain level of mastery within *World of Warcraft* may be further encouraged by others in their group ("guild") to seek outside resources, such as forums or wiki-style websites, to improve their playing and increase their chances of success within the game. Interviews conducted by Voulgari and Komis (2010) explain that players of MMORPGs find it extremely unlikely that a player would achieve proficiency without these additional, out-of-game resources.

Once in a dungeon group, each player chooses a role, based on the race, class, and abilities they have chosen for their character. Many different combinations of roles are possible, but the standard formation includes a "tank" player, a "healer" player, and some damage-dealing players, sometimes referred to as damage per second or "DPS" players (Blizzard Entertainment, 2017a.). Each player's role has its own set of necessary skills and responsibilities, without which the team cannot succeed. Tanks are responsible for drawing enemy fire by attacking first. Healers are responsible for healing and otherwise supporting the tank and DPS players as they take damage. DPS players are responsible for actually dealing damage to enemy creatures within the dungeon (Blizzard Entertainment, 2017a). If each player does not commit to their role, the group as a whole suffers. Players who rush ahead and break formation run a large risk of being killed by the waves of enemies inside the dungeon, leaving the rest of the team undefended. Players who are not intimately familiar with their role, and their team members' roles, can cause the entire team to fail.

Tenet 3: Group Activities Must Promote Both Learning and Group Development

The dungeons themselves are designed by the developers at Blizzard Entertainment to be fun, challenging, and to require groups to work well together. In order for groups to become true learning teams, they must work together for 20-25 hours (Michaelsen, 2004b), the rough equivalent of 40 lower-level dungeons (taking 30 minutes each). Playing together teaches group members more about the game or system itself, while concurrently teaching players to understand appropriate and inappropriate feedback. Members will "develop a genuine appreciation of each other's contribution to the group success" (Michaelsen, 2004b, pp. 34), and see the value in working together towards a common goal. Working in a group for an extended period of time in this manner introduces the concept of "discriminatory" feedback (Michaelsen, 2004b, p. 33); the difference between constructive and destructive ways to communicate with team members. One of Oliver and Carr's (2009) study participants noted the difference in feedback style between a group matched by *World of Warcraft*'s algorithm and a "family-like guild" (Oliver & Carr, 2009, p. 452) in which players will continue to interact in the future. The algorithm-matched group was unlikely to provide feedback on mistakes at all, since players were unlikely to ever communicate again. A guild in which there is a consistent pool of friendly players to choose from, who discuss both in- and out-of-game topics, is more likely to better understand appropriate feedback and respond accordingly. Since there is an expectation that players will not only interact again, but likely attempt another dungeon together, the feedback system needs to be supportive and encourage the entire team to improve, while simultaneously fostering a good group environment.

Tenet 4: Group Members Must Receive Frequent and Immediate Feedback on Their Performance

Players in any video game, but particularly in *World of Warcraft*, receive frequent and immediate feedback as they play: being killed by the monsters inside a dungeon teaches players what not to do, and the input from the game (i.e., the speed at which enemy health bars decrease) instantaneously alerts a player to the effectiveness of the current strategy. This type of instant feedback lets players identify how and where they went wrong while the experience is still fresh in their mind (Fink, 2004). The death mechanic in *World of Warcraft* asks a player to navigate from the graveyard to their corpse, which is sometimes an awkward or frustrating journey. If the player died from a steep fall, for example, the corpse will be located at the bottom of a ravine. Once body and spirit are reunited, the player must escape from whatever caused his/her death, with reduced health. In the case of a dungeon, the player will need to make this journey to his/her corpse, and then rejoin his/her group in the dungeon (although it is possible that another player can resurrect the dead player). If the player died in an area that was too difficult for his/her level, or if he/she was killed by a strong boss enemy, he/she may repeat this death process several times before managing to move a safe distance from the danger. The alternative to this process is to be resurrected by a non-player character called the Spirit Healer. If the player chooses to be resurrected, all of his/her armor (including unworn armor in his/her inventory) takes 25% damage, and the player is affected by "Resurrection Sickness" for 10 minutes, decreasing all of his/her attributes and the amount of damage he/she can deal by 75%. If the player dies many times in a row, his/her armor becomes less effective and he/she must pay in-game currency to repair it. Dying in *World of Warcraft* is frustrating for the player and his/her teammates, and therefore the feedback is clear: work as a team, follow the guidelines laid out in the game, and only take on challenges that are appropriate.

The Readiness Assurance Process

The "backbone" (Michaelsen, 2004b, p. 43) of team-based learning is its readiness assurance process. This is the element of team-based learning that most resembles the way *World of Warcraft* players approach the game, and approach serious play. The readiness assurance process works within a system of modules, and includes the readiness assurance tests. Outside of class, before the module begins, students are expected to prepare by doing the reading or otherwise studying basic concepts. In class, students take an individual readiness assurance test, then take the same test collaboratively in their groups. The instructor grades the individual tests while the students take the group tests, so the students receive immediate feedback on both their individual and group performance. After the feedback, there is an optional appeals phase, at which point students are allowed to refer to their assigned reading material and appeal any questions they missed. Finally, the instructor provides oral feedback, in order to clarify any misunderstandings or confusion on the part of the students (Michaelsen, 2004b). The diagram in Figure 1 presents the portions of the *World of Warcraft* assignment that correspond to out-of-class and in-class activities, and also links each section of the assignment with the readiness assurance process present in team-based learning. Note that in standard classroom use of team-based learning, an optional appeals process exists between steps 2 and 3 as indicated in Figure 1. The appeals process is not present in the figure.

Figure 1. A diagram explaining the out-of-class and in-class processes associated with the Readiness Assurance Process. Image is based on ideas present in Team-Based Learning: a Transformative Use of Small Groups in College Classes, by L.K. Michaelsen, 2004, Sterling, VA: Stylus.

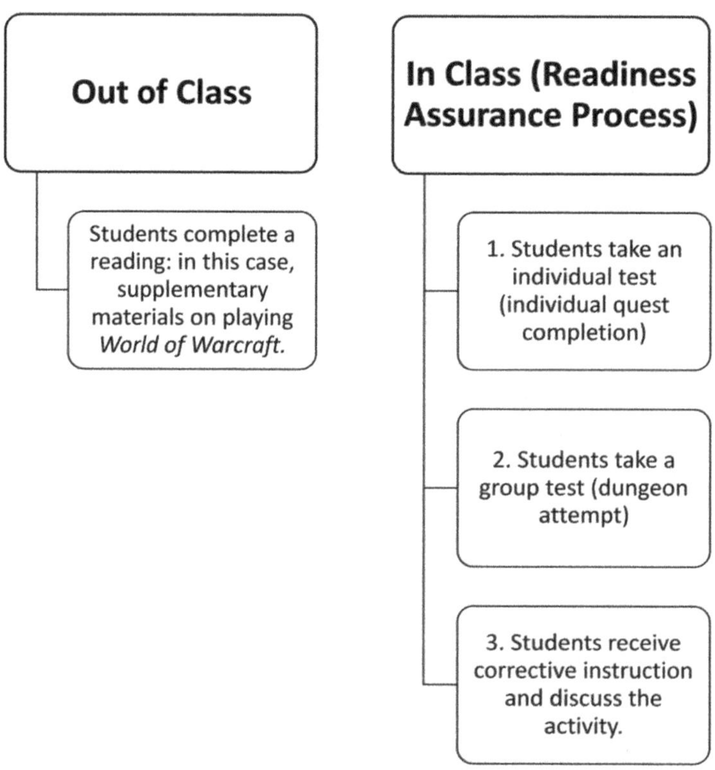

In *World of Warcraft,* players are "tested" on their individual skills constantly; each enemy they encounter and quest they perform requires them to use their skills and understanding of the game to complete a task. MUVEs like *World of Warcraft* ask their players to always be thinking, problem solving, and adapting. The quest system in *World of Warcraft* asks players to strategize and plan methodically before proceeding. Players receive a group of quests in a settlement or other "quest hub," and the actual locations of the task to be performed are spread out from that area. Each player has his/her own preferred strategy for establishing an order to completing these quests, in order to be most efficient. Items from one quest might aid or abet another, and it is important to consider these effects before accepting certain quests.

Players who attempt a dungeon together are more strenuously tested as an entire group. They must plan and strategize for the waves of various lesser enemies in the earlier zones of the dungeon, each with their own specific weaknesses and strengths. Once the players have cleared these nuisance creatures, they must deal with "mini bosses:" slightly stronger single enemies. The last room in the dungeon will contain the "boss," the strongest enemy the dungeon has to offer. Each dungeon has its own set of obstacles and problems to overcome, and the group must work well together and must prove that they have done their research on this particular dungeon in order to complete it successfully. If the players succeed at completing the quest or the dungeon, they are rewarded with experience points and in-game items and currency; positive feedback. If they fail and are killed, the negative feedback is similarly instantaneous and clear.

As in team-based learning, after *World of Warcraft* groups have played together for an extended period of time, they become familiar with each other and are more able to understand how best to mitigate personnel problems. If a player who is responsible for dealing damage to enemies runs ahead without the rest of his/her group and is killed by a monster, he/she could attempt to blame the healer for not following him/her closely, but his/her teammates will know where the true fault lies. Addressing issues like these in a constructive, helpful manner is as critical in player groups as it is in learning groups. Teams need to function with the understanding that every member of the team is there to support the others, and that members who do not support each other or who jeopardize the rest of the team by behaving recklessly or slacking off will not be tolerated, and will not succeed.

Unlike in classroom team-based learning, learners are sometimes encouraged to appeal, no true appeals phase occurs in *World of Warcraft*. Players are not encouraged to appeal to Blizzard Entertainment on the way a dungeon should be played, but they are free to make suggestions, requests, or voice concerns on the various official *World of Warcraft* forums.

THE *WORLD OF WARCRAFT* TEAM-BASED LEARNING ASSIGNMENT

Team-based learning is an intensive teaching and learning method. It is important to demonstrate to students that in this class they will be expected to come prepared to learn every day. Requiring work before the first day of the course discourages a relaxed student attitude about the first day of the course, and about the course in general (Michaelsen, 2004a). Some instructors like to use the syllabus itself as the first "assignment" in the readiness assurance process. By using *World of Warcraft* or a similar MUVE instead, the effectiveness of team-based learning can be actively demonstrated to students instead of explained. Students will almost immediately understand why their instructor has chosen to teach using team-based learning, and they will be quickly shown how the rest of the class will be conducted and what the instructor expects from them. They will be free from having to make small talk with new group members, potentially in an online discussion forum or other sterile environment, and will instead have a shared goal to discuss: learning the mechanics of *World of Warcraft* and succeeding in their dungeon attempt. Further, any students who have taken a course in which team-based learning was poorly implemented, or in which casual group work was called team-based learning, will need some convincing to accept that truly immersive team-based learning can be successful rather than a distraction. By utilizing a game-based reintroduction to team-based learning, students will quickly see the difference between a group paper or presentation and what is expected in a team-based learning course.

The following is an outline, based in literature review and the connection between successful learning teams and successful playing teams, of how the *World of Warcraft* assignment could be set up and implemented in a semester-long class with a meeting time of approximately one hour and 15 minutes. The assignment can theoretically be modified for shorter class times (40-50 minutes), and would be even more successful and practical in courses with extended class times (2 hours or more). The assignment is designed to promote learning of the team-based learning teaching method (to set a precedent for the rest of the course), and to accelerate early team development in newly-formed teams. The assignment is not designed to teach specific course content or a domain-specific skill. Nor, as it is presented here, is it intended to be used throughout the entire duration of a course. The *World of Warcraft* assignment, as described in this chapter, is intended as a single activity designed to teach team-based learning itself. It could, of course, be modified and adapted to a specific discipline or field, such as game design, communications, or education studies. Figure 2 presents a flow chart of the general phases of the *World of Warcraft* assignment, which is described in greater detail in the following sections.

Before the First Day

This is the time for the instructor to find a group-forming approach that suits him/her. It is possible to form the groups randomly, perhaps using a tool embedded in the instructor's learning management system, or to use a tool, such as a discussion board, to collect information about his/her students and group them through that information. However, collecting information and forming teams based around that information before the class starts may prove difficult (Michaelsen, 2004b). The instructor sends students the syllabus, the names of the other students in their group, and some introductory materials on *World of Warcraft*. He/she explains that the first day of class will be devoted to playing this game, in order to build team camaraderie and to demonstrate the use of team-based learning. The instructor encourages questions via email or the learning management system on the syllabus itself, since he/she will not be going over it in class on the first day. The instructor tells the students that he/she expects them to log in to the game, read the introductory materials, and create their character before the first day of class.

Figure 2. A flow chart demonstrating the general phases of the World of Warcraft assignment

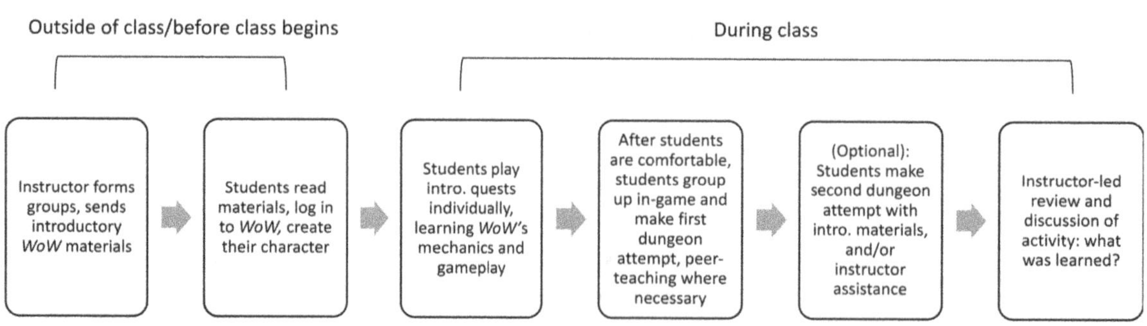

On the First Day

The first day of class will vary slightly, based on the length of time for which the class meets. Shorter class times, around 40-50 minutes, might require modifications of the exercise. Further relevant details are provided in the following, in the section on online courses and other modifications.

On the first day, the instructor sets his/her students up with computers. He/she gives them a period of class time in which to play the introductory quests, and a period of time in which to attempt a dungeon in their groups. The dungeon and the team readiness assessment test are alike in that they allow for peer teaching; if some students in a group are more familiar with video games as a whole or MMORPGs/ *World of Warcraft* specifically, they can help others in their team acclimatize to playing. Trying the dungeon together unites new group members in a common goal and encourages close teamwork. The action of attempting the dungeon mimics the individual readiness assessment test scoring; players who struggle with mechanics or gameplay will struggle in front of their teammates, who can propose solutions or helpful advice. If a player could not successfully complete the individual quests, other players who were more successful can lend advice or suggestions during the dungeon, since doing so is beneficial to the entire team.

Grading the *World of Warcraft* assignment could consist of a pass/fail system: Did the team successfully defeat the boss and "complete" the dungeon? It could also consist of a graded system based on team effectiveness, although this requires closer observation on the part of the instructor. If a team did not successfully defeat the boss, but worked well together, there is room for a higher grade. It is also possible to grade based on how many zones of the dungeon the team successfully managed to complete. Michaelsen (2004b) suggests public comparison between the group scores: the instructor should consider posting the scores on the board or having an open discussion about how far each group progressed in the dungeon. The grades on the *World of Warcraft* assignment can be kept as extra credit or allowed to be "dropped" later, since this exercise is intended as introductory practice.

Close instructor observation is suggested during this exercise, so that students who are struggling with working together or in mastering the mechanics of *World of Warcraft* receive necessary assistance. However, it is encouraged that instructors do not intervene, unless the team is truly falling apart. Indeed, part of the importance of the entire exercise is to allow students to peer teach and succeed by supporting each other.

The author suggests reserving the last 15 minutes of class for discussion of the activity, or this discussion could take place as homework on an online discussion board. Students need to understand very clearly the reason they played an MMORPG in class in order to relate the skills they may not have realized they learned with the skills they are expected to transfer to the classroom (Oliver & Carr, 2009; Voulgari & Komis, 2010). Debriefing hones students' skills of reflection and metacognition for future situations. The activity's two purposes (group cohesion and understanding of the logic behind team-based learning) should be addressed as frequently as possible before, during, and after the activity.

After the First Day

If the last 15 minutes of class were not used to discuss the activity, the instructor asks that students turn in a brief reflection of the exercise. Do they feel comfortable with the readiness assurance process? Do they understand the significance of each tenet of team-based learning? The instructor ensures that students understand the parallels between the activity they have just performed and the way the course will be managed: so long as students come to class prepared, work cohesively in their teams, and are responsible to (and, to an extent, for) each other, they will succeed in the class. Unevenly weighted group effort (one player attempting to be the "superstar" or another person attempting to slack off) will not work as it may have in previous group experiences. Every individual must participate and contribute equally.

Online Courses and Other Modifications

For an online course, the process before the first day remains the same, with the exception of asking the students to make a time to play together within the first week of the course opening. After the course opens, the instructor sets up the discussion board and the rest of the modules. Instructors may need to look into setting up a Discord server or other voice chat system to facilitate communication between team members. *World of Warcraft* does have its own native voice chat system, but it requires players to be "friends" within the Battle.net interface, which some students may be uncomfortable with.

It is, of course, possible to continue the *World of Warcraft* exercise as more than simply an introductory activity. Courses in subjects like game design, gamification, or educational technology can expand the team-based learning/*World of Warcraft* metaphor. Courses in fields like gender studies have potential to use the MUVE as an exploration of identities, intersectionality, or to examine play itself. At institutions where a trimester system or other type of shorter term is in use, or perhaps in eight-week courses, this exercise could be implemented as a full-term demonstration of how and why team-based learning is so successful. It could even be used outside of class, in future faculty-based learning groups.

For shorter class meeting times (40-50 minutes), it is possible to extend the *World of Warcraft* activity from a one or two class endeavor to a full week. It is also possible to require students to complete most of the individual "leveling" of their character outside of class, so as to preserve class time for the dungeon activity, although this does impede the team-based learning metaphor slightly.

ISSUES AND RECOMMENDATIONS

This chapter provides a theoretical application of *World of Warcraft* as an individual, preparatory assignment in a course taught using the team-based learning method. The following are potential problems or obstacles the author considered in implementing this exercise, and potential solutions or suggestions the author proposes to combat these problems.

Peer Assessment

Michaelsen (2004b) is a proponent of peer assessment as a tool to balance group grading and to allow students to grow. If an instructor simply uses peer assessment as a method to determine which students regularly contributed to group work in order to discern which students deserve which grades, and the assessments are never shown to students, anonymous peer assessment is absolutely appropriate and effective. Using peer assessment merely as a means to a grade leaves the matter of peer feedback open; instructors need to encourage appropriate and timely peer-to-peer feedback during the activity itself (and during continuing group work). Again, peer-to-peer feedback, whether in person or anonymously, needs to be of a level of quality and general respect.

L. Dee Fink (2004), however, suggests employing peer assessment "only if students are given proper training and the teacher monitors the process sufficiently" (Fink, 2004, p. 18). When team-based learning is successful, the result is not only a close understanding of course concepts, but a tight-knit team of 5-7 individuals who have become intimately familiar with one another's patterns of speech, opinions, and level of participation. The author is therefore skeptical that, in successful learning teams, peer assessment can ever truly be "anonymous." The premise of anonymity can engender potential for overly harsh, critical assessment that is not conducive to the learning environment and can even prove destructive to team morale (Michaelsen, 2004b). Team-based learning relies upon team members providing constructive, honest feedback, not using peer assessment as a tool for passive aggression, hostility, or lazily giving everyone the same grade.

Oliver and Carr's (2009) study participants note that the style of feedback present in a "family-like guild" (Oliver & Carr, 2009, p. 452) is different from the style of feedback when players are strangers. This is the type of peer assessment that is important in the *World of Warcraft* assignment specifically: feedback tailored to and appropriate for a group of people who work very closely together and intend to do so for the remainder of the semester. By using anonymous peer assessment only as a tool to influence individual grades, the instructor can keep the student-to-student feedback appropriate and helpful, and reduce potential hostility. In the *World of Warcraft* assignment itself, peer feedback is significant. In a course taught using team-based learning, peer assessment is significant.

Expenses Related to the *World of Warcraft* Assignment

World of Warcraft accounts are free until a player reaches level 20, which would be sufficient for the individual's character creation and questing portions of the assignment. However, free accounts have limited functionality, including the inability to form a group of players, and therefore to attempt a dungeon (Blizzard Entertainment, 2017b). *World of Warcraft* ordinarily operates on a subscription basis. Players are charged approximately US$15 a month in order to have full access to the game. Each expansion (additional worlds, campaigns, and content) costs around US$40. Expansions are not required; the base game alone is all that would be required to successfully implement the *World of Warcraft* assignment in a course. Purchasing the base *World of Warcraft* game (with no expansions) gives the player a one-month allotment of "game time," and costs US$20.

The author finds that the time requirement involved in progressing to level 15 is essential to understanding how to play *World of Warcraft* successfully, but it is understandable, especially in a shorter class period, that an instructor would not want to devote so much time to one introductory activity. In this vein, it is possible, through a paid *World of Warcraft* account, to pay an additional fee to "boost" a character to level 100. The difficulty with attempting to expedite the process of reaching a level able to participate in dungeons lies in the fact that *World of Warcraft* scales its difficulty: a level 15 dungeon is exponentially simpler than a level 100 dungeon, and understanding the various toolbars and skills of a level 15 character is much simpler than understanding those of a level 100 character. A Hunter class character at level 4, for example, has six potential abilities and spells out of 12 available toolbar slots. A Shaman class character at level 100 utilizes a total of 24 toolbar slots, having gained a second toolbar and a great deal of additional abilities. It is not recommended for the instructor to create a pool of characters for student use. Blizzard Entertainment does not approve of multiple users sharing *World of Warcraft* characters, and this would require an unrealistic amount of pre-class preparation on the instructor's part.

Not all students will come to campus with laptop computers. Some may rely entirely upon campus computer labs and other facilities. *World of Warcraft* will run successfully on most computers, but broadband Internet access is required to play. Students who need to use public computers, such as those in campus computer labs or libraries, may have difficulty completing any parts of the assignment that are expected to be conducted out of class. In order to ensure fairness to students who did not choose to bring computers to campus, the assignment could be adapted to take place entirely in-class, in a computer lab environment. This would take up more class time, of course, but it is possible to restructure the assignment to adjust for this. If the teacher's institution allows instructors to reserve labs for certain periods of time, he/she could also speak with his/her lab administrators about installing *World of Warcraft* on specific machines, and giving access to students without computers during a certain reserved time period. Students who experience slow connections may also report frustration. Rahim (2013) solved this dilemma by granting a longer period of time for the virtual meetings themselves. Classes with shorter meeting times could extend the *World of Warcraft* activity to two class days.

Using a MMORPG or other MUVE in this manner is, as di Blas and Paolini (2014) note, a "special event breaking the school's routine and requiring a significant effort" (di Blas & Paolini, 2014, p. 66). The author recognizes that both team-based learning and the use of an MMORPG, even as an introductory exercise, can require significant front-end effort on the part of the instructor, but believes that the end result is worth this work, especially when used in introductory courses designed for incoming freshmen.

If the US$20 fee should prove problematic, an alternative to requiring students to pay for *World of Warcraft* and its subscription would be to choose an MMORPG that is free to play, such as *Guild Wars 2* or *Aion Online*. The only true requirements for an MMORPG appropriate to this assignment would be the presence of group-based quest and dungeon-type content. Be aware that different games refer to these activities differently ("quests" might be "missions," for example). If an instructor is set on using *World of Warcraft* specifically, the author suggests approaching a Blizzard Entertainment representative directly regarding other options.

Assigning Groups

Assigning regular team-based learning groups is recommended to be done on the first day of class, in person (Michaelsen, 2004b). However, because groups for the *World of Warcraft* assignment require an additional characteristic (mixed level of video game skill), assigning these groups may prove more challenging. Although efforts to mitigate these challenges can be implemented (using an online discussion board to collect information about students or assigning the groups in class on the first day), it is always possible that students will form subgroups of their own accord during the semester, or that an instructor will not "catch" all potential problems at the outset. Requiring students to participate in an online discussion board before the class meets for the first time might prove difficult as well, especially if students who have been assigned a group drop the course or new students add it.

Regardless of the method used to place students in groups, it is important that students do not choose their own groups. Students are likely to choose their friends or other students they have some type of relationship with, which creates a subgroup within the learning team. These subgroups may then band together and neglect other members of the team, and create a bad learning environment for those outside of the subgroups. If this tenet of team-based learning fails, it is likely to take others with it: if students don't feel included in the group as a whole, they are not likely to be accountable to each other (Tenet 2). Through semester-long team development, and assignments specifically chosen to foster team-building (such as the *World of Warcraft* assignment itself), students will "transform," as Michaelsen's (2004) title suggests, from a group of students into a cohesive learning team.

It is the instructor's responsibility to adapt the entire *World of Warcraft* assignment in ways they find appropriate to their own course. If one person has a group-assigning system they find to work well, there is no reason not to use it for this assignment. After all, the main focus of this assignment is the demonstration of active learning through team-based learning, not creating a professional *World of Warcraft* team, and the teams will need to continue to work well together on course material after the MUVE assignment is over.

Student Familiarity With Video Games

Student familiarity with video games may differ greatly. Some students may take well to the *World of Warcraft* exercise, and find they have no trouble learning to play with the in-game materials and the materials the instructor provides. Other students may find learning to play the game more burdensome, potentially even to the point that they feel the assignment is impossible. If some students cannot manage to work past the individual questing phase, the success of the dungeon attempt is threatened. Without a full, working 5-person team, the dungeon attempt is very likely to fail. However, students unfamiliar with video games need not despair: Rahim (2013) found that use of forums devoted to the MUVE, additional reading, and student knowledge-sharing were sufficient to overcome this challenge.

If the instructor is considering the *World of Warcraft* assignment and is unsure of his/her students' comfort level with video games, it is prudent to first determine that the students will be able to manage successfully. This assignment, and team-based learning in general, requires a good deal of course restructuring. The goal is to prove how well team-based learning works, not discourage further attempts! It is critical that the groups have at least one team member who is familiar with video games in general, and ideally MMOs/MUVE-style games in particular, to help mitigate this problem. The instructor should assure students during the exercise that this is only an introductory activity, and that their success in the entire course is not weighted on their success in *World of Warcraft*, and that the "grade" they receive for this assignment is not a grade that will be held against them in the course as a whole.

Making Clear Connections to What Is Learned

The main concern raised throughout the related works in the literature review centered on the connection between the activity in the virtual world and the learning skill the virtual world was intended to teach. This section addresses the concerns raised or answered by specific authors.

Voulgari and Komis (2010) noted through their interviews that students did not seem to acknowledge that they had been exposed to specific cooperative or learning skills by playing cooperative games. However, "a wide range of different skills practiced emerged in the answers…even of those who reported that they learn[ed] nothing" (Voulgari & Komis, 2010, pp. 182). This lack of awareness of the intrinsic skills taught by structured, cooperative gameplay can be combated with a high level of instructor input and discussion after the *World of Warcraft* assignment: Pivec and Pivec (2011) stress the importance of post-activity reflection in order for players to truly learn from the games they play. Instructors should therefore carefully "draw out" the connections during class discussions of the activity, perhaps through careful question phrasing. "What did playing *World of Warcraft* as a team teach you about good group work?" could invite more useful answers than "What did you learn from the *World of Warcraft* assignment?" Alternatively, di Blas and Paolini's (2014) participants did acknowledge that they had learned successful group work, and 85% of Rahim's (2013) students reported on a survey that they learned skills through *Second Life* that enabled them to achieve the objectives of the wider learning activity.

Oliver and Carr (2009) express concern that it can be difficult to link video games not expressly created for education to educational goals and objectives. However, they addressed this issue by specifically choosing study participants who regularly interacted both inside and outside of *World of Warcraft*. They believed that players who interact with each other both inside and outside of an MMORPG were more likely to draw the conclusion between what they do in-game and what they do outside of it; when students group up in a *World of Warcraft* party and then complete classwork in the same group, the correlation between skills used to complete a task within the game and skills used to learn outside of it becomes clearer. De Freitas (2006) corroborates this: previous research did not allow enough pre- or post-exercise reflection or supporting activities to correlate game activities and real-world learning, and therefore stated learning outcomes were not reached. By integrating the game (and discussion thereof) more carefully into the curriculum, it is possible to teach these learning process skills successfully. De Freitas and Oliver (2006), in establishing a framework for assessing games learning, place heavy emphasis on linking the in-game and out-of-game learning through reflection, briefing, and debriefing.

De Freitas (2006) additionally found that using games in collaborative learning settings helped reinforce learning outcomes or higher-level concepts, and notes an "implicit link between discovery learning and working in teams" (de Freitas, 2006, p. 353), which are the exact goals of the *World of Warcraft* assignment.

FUTURE RESEARCH DIRECTIONS

Although the author briefly communicated with a Blizzard Entertainment employee (J. Kartje, personal communication, March 16-April 4, 2017) via email, it would be interesting to continue that avenue of conversation and investigate other ways to implement *World of Warcraft* in the classroom. Recently, other "commercial off-the-shelf" video games (video games that exist solely for entertainment) have begun to branch out into the educational sphere. In November 2016, the popular open-world game Minecraft released a special "Education Edition" (Mojang, 2017), which was designed to be used by educators in the classroom. Another MUVE, *Second Life*, has been used in the educational field successfully (Carr, Oliver, & Burn 2008), and the game itself features classroom environments and other types of learning spaces. If the trend continues, it could prove lucrative for Blizzard Entertainment and useful for university instructors to work together to develop a similar solution for *World of Warcraft* and other similar MUVEs.

There is a great deal of writing regarding video games of all types/genres and collaborative learning, but there is very little on linking any MMORPG or MUVE with team-based learning specifically. Therefore, the most logical future research would be to move the *World of Warcraft* assignment from the theoretical space to the practical space, and teach team-based learning through *World of Warcraft* in a classroom. The ideal next step is to work with college faculty and Blizzard Entertainment representatives to implement the assignment in a Communications or Education course, and in doing so to collect empirical data on the efficacy and success of the assignment, as well as areas of the assignment that could be strengthened or improved. Further, it is of course possible to conduct this activity using a different MUVE or MMO, so long as the game chosen features group play options and a dungeon-like mechanic.

CONCLUSION

When students learn that they will be expected to participate in teams, the idea can seem like a nightmare version of the bad group projects they have been involved with in the past. Team-based learning only serves students and instructors when it is implemented exactly and correctly, every time. It is a specific system that works well when students understand all that it requires and involves, and student "buy-in" may be limited or otherwise hampered by biases and bad previous experiences. It is therefore necessary, especially when attempting to use team-based learning at an institution where it is not widely used or not widely used well, to overcome these biases and to show students, not tell them, why learning teams are so valuable.

Video games teach human beings to learn, through use of their systems, rules, and inherent problem solving. The concept of "gamifying" any process, including learning, is essentially tying learning to an existing system that works well; in this case, video games. Tying team-based learning to a system like a MUVE, with its own set of structured rules, roles, and systems forces both instructors and students to learn its tenets and to use the system correctly, which allows instructors to return to their course content with students who are ready, willing, and able to learn in teams. It allows students to learn how to learn, sets them up for a good university experience, and teaches them crucial critical thinking, problem solving, and teamwork skills: skills that are becoming increasingly valuable in the contemporary working environment.

Both gamifying learning and team-based learning are potentially excellent teaching methods which are often utilized incorrectly and therefore fail. Just as instructors cannot create a Jeopardy!- style review game or use points and leaderboards throughout a semester and call their class gamified, so they cannot use casual groups and claim to be teaching in the team-based learning style. Using *World of Warcraft* to teach team-based learning harnesses the inherent ways that collaborative video games ask their players to learn (both individually and as a group) and the best practices of team-based learning, and makes both methods simple to demonstrate to students. The volume of Michaelsen's work creates a literal "rulebook" to follow when implementing team-based learning, so it is easy for an instructor to understand the method's value. Imparting this value to students through a team-building exercise both aligns neatly with Michaelsen's intentions for the method and with Gee and others' theories on active learning, exemplifying both in one short activity.

REFERENCES

Blizzard Entertainment. (2017a). *New player's guide: Part four.* Retrieved from https://worldofwarcraft.com/en-us/game/new-players-guide/part-four

Blizzard Entertainment. (2017b). *World of Warcraft Starter Edition Limitations.* Retrieved from https://us.battle.net/support/en/article/World-of-Warcraft-Starter-Edition-Limitations

Carr, D., Oliver, M., & Burn, A. (2008, May). *Learning from online worlds: Teaching in Second Life.* Retrieved from https://learningfromsocialworlds.wordpress.com/

Charles, D., Charles, T., McNeill, M., Bustard, D., & Black, M. (2011). Game-based feedback for educational multi-user virtual environments. *British Journal of Educational Technology*, *42*(4), 638–654. doi:10.1111/j.1467-8535.2010.01068.x

Curry, K. (2010). Warcraft and civic education: MMORPGs as participatory cultures and how teachers can use them to improve civic education. *Social Studies*, *101*(6), 250–253. doi:10.1080/00377990903493879

De Freitas, S., & Oliver, M. (2006). How can exploratory learning with games and simulations within the curriculum be most effectively evaluated? *Computers & Education*, *46*(3), 249–264. doi:10.1016/j.compedu.2005.11.007

De Freitas, S. I. (2006). Using games and simulations for supporting learning. *Learning, Media and Technology*, *31*(4), 343–358. doi:10.1080/17439880601021967

Di Blas, N., & Paolini, P. (2014). Multi-user virtual environments fostering collaboration in formal education. *Journal of Educational Technology & Society*, *17*(1), 54–69.

Dirksen, J. (2012). *Design for how people learn*. Berkeley, CA: New Riders.

Fink, L. D. (2004). Beyond small groups: Harnessing the extraordinary power of learning teams. In L. K. Michaelsen, A. B. Knight, & L. D. Fink (Eds.), *Team-based learning: A transformative use of small groups in college teaching* (pp. 3–26). Sterling, VA: Stylus.

Freedman, J. (2013). The typical college student is not a 'typical' college student (and other fun college demographics data). *Forbes*. Retrieved from https://www.forbes.com/sites/joshfreedman/2013/09/20/the-typical-college-student-is-not-a-typical-college-student-and-other-fun-college-demographics-data/#6f370f107c5a

Galarneau, L. (2005). Authentic learning experiences through play: Games, simulations and the construction of knowledge. *Proceedings of DiGRA 2005 Conference: Changing Views - Worlds in Play*. Retrieved from http://www.digra.org/digital-library/publications/authentic-learning-experiences-through-play-games-simulations-and-the-construction-of-knowledge/

Gee, J. P. (2014). *What video games have to teach us about learning and literacy*. New York, NY: Palgrave Macmillian.

Koster, R. (2005). *Theory of fun for game design*. Scottsdale, AZ: Paraglyph Press.

Lee, M. J. W., Eustace, K., Fellows, G., Bytheway, A., & Irving, L. (2005). Rochester Castle MMORPG: Instructional gaming and collaborative learning at a Western Australian school. *Australasian Journal of Educational Technology*, *21*(4), 446–469. doi:10.14742/ajet.1314

McGonigal, J. (2011). *Reality is broken: Why games make us better and how they can change the world*. New York, NY: Penguin.

Michaelsen, L. K. (2004b). Getting started with team-based learning. In L. K. Michaelsen, A. B. Knight, & L. D. Fink (Eds.), *Team-based learning: A transformative use of small groups in college teaching* (pp. 27–53). Sterling, VA: Stylus.

Michaelsen, L. K. (2004c). Preface. In L. K. Michaelsen, A. B. Knight, & L. D. Fink (Eds.), *Team-based learning: A transformative use of small groups in college teaching* (pp. vii–xi). Sterling, VA: Stylus.

Michaelsen, L. K., Knight, A. B., & Fink, L. D. (Eds.). (2004a). *Team-based learning: A transformative use of small groups in college teaching*. Sterling, VA: Stylus.

Mojang. (2017). *Frequently asked questions.* Retrieved from https://education.minecraft.net/support/faq/

Oliver, M., & Carr, D. (2009). Learning in virtual worlds: Using communities of practice to explain how people learn from play. *British Journal of Educational Technology*, *40*(3), 444–457. doi:10.1111/j.1467-8535.2009.00948.x

Pivec, P., & Pivec, M. (2011). Digital games: Changing education, one raid at a time. *International Journal of Game-Based Learning*, *1*(1), 1–18. doi:10.4018/ijgbl.2011010101

Qian, Y. (2015). 3D multi-user virtual environments in science education. In T. Heafner, R. Hartshorne, & T. Petty (Eds.), Exploring the effectiveness of online education in K-12 environments pp. 308-330. Hershey, PA: IGI Global. doi:10.4018/978-1-4666-6383-1.ch015

Rahim, N. F. A. (2013). Collaboration and knowledge sharing using 3D virtual world on Second Life. *Education for Information*, *30*(1-2), 1–40. doi:10.3233/EFI-130928

Rockwood, H. S. (1995). Cooperative and collaborative learning. *The National Teaching & Learning Forum, 4*(6), 8-9. doi: 10.1002/ntlf.10024

Voulgari, I., & Komis, V. (2010). 'Elven Elder LVL59 LFP/RB. Please PM Me:' immersion, collaborative tasks and problem-solving in massively multiplayer online games. *Learning, Media and Technology*, *2*(35), 171–202. doi:10.1080/17439884.2010.494429

Warren, J. (2017, February 13). *Games as a means and an end.* Retrieved from https://shiftcommission.work/games-as-means-and-an-end-8fb79b51b6e6

KEY TERMS AND DEFINITIONS

Dungeon: A special zone in a MMORPG. Unlike the rest of the game world, dungeons are only inhabited by one player or group of players at a time. The dungeon features several rooms, specific enemies stronger than other enemies of their level, and a very strong enemy called a boss. Successfully completing dungeons gives players better rewards than completing standard quests: unique equipment, more gold, etc.

Gamifying: The process of using the traits of games to improve a system that is unrelated to games. Gamifying should emphasize systems thinking and exploration/manipulation of rules.

MMORPG: Massively Multiplayer Online Roleplaying Game. A type of video game designed to be played by thousands of players at once, online. Players inhabit the same virtual space, perform the same tasks, and at times work together in the virtual world.

Module: A section of a course consisting of a preparation period (including the readiness assurance process), an application period (including homework, simple group assignments, and complex group assignments), and an assessment period (including review and a culminating team project or exam).

Quest: A specific task to be completed in *World of Warcraft* or other roleplaying games. Many types of quests exist, from collection quests (pick up 10 objects from a field with enemies) to quests asking the player to defeat a certain number of a certain type of enemy.

Readiness Assurance Process: The cycle between individual tests, team tests, appeals, and corrective instruction and feedback from the instructor.

Readiness Assurance Test: A short multiple-choice test consisting of approximately 20 questions on the content of the readings. The test is taken twice: once as individuals and once as a team.

Team-Based Learning: A teaching method, developed by Larry Michaelsen, divides the students into small teams of 5-7 individuals and the course content into modules. It has very specific principles and tenets and differs greatly from standard group work.

Chapter 9
Factors Affecting Primary School Students' Learning Experiences When Using MUVEs:
Development and Validation of a Scale

Emmanuel Fokides
University of the Aegean, Greece

Pinelopi Atsikpasi
University of the Aegean, Greece

ABSTRACT

3D multi-user virtual environments (MUVEs) are considered a technological advancement that, in the coming years, will have a significant impact on how students learn. On the other hand, the factors that shape the learning experience in such applications are not well studied. This chapter is an attempt to fill that gap. It reports the development and validation of a scale to measure the factors that come into play when primary school students use MUVEs in formal educational settings. Perceived learning effectiveness, perceived ease of use, presence, motivation, perceived application realism, interactions, enjoyment, as well as collaboration were used to develop a questionnaire that initially included 34 items. A total of 352 sixth-grade primary school students used a MUVE in formal educational settings and the aforementioned questionnaire was administered to them. The exploratory and confirmatory factor analysis revealed the existence of 7 factors and 24 items that were retained in the final version of the scale. The factor structure of the questionnaire is also discussed.

DOI: 10.4018/978-1-5225-3719-9.ch009

INTRODUCTION

Information and communication technologies have significantly increased the level of independence students have when learning. They have also multiplied and diversified the ways in which students can learn and interact with the learning material. One technology that attracts the interest of educators and researchers is virtual reality (VR). VR is an "umbrella" term and various sub-genres do exist, one of which is 3D multi-user virtual environments (MUVEs). In recent years, there is a growing use of MUVEs in diverse educational settings (e.g., formal and informal learning) and in almost all learning domains (Merchant, Goetz, Cifuentes, Keeney-Kennicutt, & Davis, 2014). This calls for the use of instruments and methods assessing not only the learning outcomes they yield, but also assessing the interactions between a number of key factors that affect students' learning experience when using them. By knowing how certain subjective constructs and MUVEs' features interplay with each other, we can have an in-depth understanding of how MUVEs affect the learning outcomes. This, in turn, will allow us to develop strategies to maximize the impact of the positive elements and, at the same time, to minimize the impact of the negative ones, thus increasing the odds of achieving better results in terms of knowledge acquisition.

There are certain steps in this process, the first one being the development and validation of scales to measure the factors that come into play when students use MUVEs for educational purposes. The study presents the development of a scale to measure exactly this. A number of factors, namely perceived learning effectiveness, perceived ease of use, presence, motivation, perceived application's realism, interactions, enjoyment, as well as collaboration, were included in the scale. The reasoning for selecting these factors, the research methodology, and the results of the exploratory and confirmatory factor analysis of the scale are discussed in the coming sections.

BACKGROUND

VR applications are 3D simulations of real or imaginary environments that "fool" the human senses; users have the feeling of being in a real environment (Hew & Cheung, 2010). Depending on the hardware and software used, VR can vary from fully immersive (that uses sophisticated equipment, such as head-mounted displays and haptic devices for the provision of somatosensory feedback), to simple "low-tech" desktop applications (that use just mid-range computers) (Levin, 2011). Furthermore, in MUVEs, multiple users can simultaneously use the same simulation; thus, they can interact not only with the virtual objects but also with each other. Principles drawn from constructivism provide the theoretical framework for the educational uses of MUVEs (Dickey, 2005). According to this theory, learning is an active process and knowledge is constructed on the basis of what learners already understand and as they make connections between new and old information (Ertmer & Newby, 2013). Social interaction, peer feedback, collaboration between users, visual and audio stimuli are but a few of their features that have an educational interest (Zheng & Newgarden, 2011). These, lead to, probably, the most significant benefits for education, that of incentives for learning and active learning (O'Neil, Wainess, & Baker, 2005).

There are numerous studies, in all levels of education, demonstrating the educational benefits when using VR/MUVEs. For example, in science education, the non-textually mediated presentation of the content, allows students to understand complex concepts (Squire, Barnett, Grant, & Higginbotham, 2004). Moreover, by encompassing both small and large scales, by allowing side-by-side comparisons, and by presenting the content in multiple perspectives in time as well as in space, issues related to scientific misconceptions can be addressed (Barnett, Yamagata-Lynch, Keating, Barab, & Hay, 2005).

While most of studies related to the educational uses of MUVEs report, more or less, satisfactory learning outcomes, there is too much speculation on why these results were achieved, with the focus being on the teaching methods that were used and, in general, on the educational settings (Merchant et al., 2014). Fewer studies have examined which factors, other than the above, are involved and how they interact with each other. More importantly, the inclusion of psychological factors is not common. As Yaman, Nerdel, and Bayhuber (2008) noted, the learner's psychological perspective has hardly been studied in computer simulation-based learning. On the other hand, studies that examined such factors, provide useful insights. For example, Merchant, Keeney-Kennicutt, and Goetz (2015) examined the acceptance of MUVEs when teaching chemistry to undergraduate students. deNoyelles, Hornik, and Johnson (2014) correlated certain aspects of self-efficacy in MUVEs with course learning, having as a target group university students, but this time financial accounting was the learning subject. On another instance, presence was the factor of interest and the target group was, once again, university students (Hassell, Goyal, Limayem, & Boughzala, 2012). Jia, Bhatti, and Nahavandi (2014) found that self-efficacy and perceived system efficacy have an impact on the effectiveness of virtual training systems. Pre-service teachers' satisfaction in MUVEs, in correlation with the learning outcomes, was examined by Vrellis, Avouris, and Mikropoulos (2016). Merchant, Goetz, Keeney-Kennicutt, Kwok, Cifuentes and Davis (2012) used the learners' characteristics (self-efficacy and presence) and usability, in order to develop a model that tried to explain the observed learning outcomes in desktop VR. Finally, on a more systematic inclusion of factors, Lee, Wong, and Fung (2010) also developed a model to explain the learning outcomes in VR. Their model used a number of VR's features together with presence, motivation, cognitive beliefs, control, and reflective thinking, while the target group was, this time, secondary school students and the learning subject was the frog's anatomy.

The abovementioned studies had little in common. Besides having different factors as key determinants of the learning outcomes or of the learning experience, they examined different types of VR/MUVEs, and the learning subjects were also diverse. Thus, it can be argued that:

- While there are many studies examining the relationship between VR and the learning outcomes, they are either focused on the educational settings or on specific VR's features (e.g., presence). Fewer studies encompassed three or more factors that come into play in an educational VR/MUVE. Thus, more research is needed toward a more comprehensive inclusion of factors.
- Taking into account the specific characteristics of MUVEs (e.g., in-world collaboration), there is a good chance that the results of studies that examined non-multiuser VR applications are not applicable to MUVEs.
- The emphasis appears to be on young adults, while younger ages, for example, primary school students, are still understudied.
- The small the sample sizes and the specialized learning subjects do not allow the generalization of the results.

On the basis of the above, the purpose of the study was to develop a scale that will allow the examination of a wide range of factors involved in the learning experience when using MUVEs. Because of the lack of studies in younger ages, it was decided that the target group would be primary school students aged around 12 (sixth-grade).

THEORETICAL AND EMPIRICAL BASIS OF THE INSTRUMENT

In order to develop a scale for measuring the factors that affect, and ultimately shape, the learning experience in MUVEs, one has to determine which factors to include. Salzman, Dede, Loftin, and Chen (1999), were among the first to propose a model of how immersive VR's affordances work with other factors in shaping the learning process and the learning outcomes. They theorized that: (a) VR's features (e.g., multisensory cues and 3D immersion) are likely to influence learning (learning process and outcomes), (b) the concept being learned is likely to moderate how VR's capabilities influence the learning process, (c) the learner's characteristics (e.g., spatial ability, gender, computer experience) should play a role in shaping the learning process and may also interact with VR's features in influencing learning, and (d) it is likely that VR's affordances, as well as individual characteristics, affect both the interaction experience (e.g., usability) and the learning experience (e.g., presence, motivation), which, in turn, influence learning (Figure 1).

Although the model identified by Salzman and her colleagues provided useful insights on what factors can be considered for inclusion on the scale, one has to keep in mind that it was proposed for immersive VR systems and also collaboration, a key MUVEs' feature, is absent. Therefore, other technology-mediated models relevant to VR and MUVEs as well as to ICT tools, in general, were considered. It was found that these models not only use a variety of factors but even if they have common factors, these are not viewed in the same way. For example, in some cases, technology factors are illustrated in terms of technology features while in others they are illustrated in terms of quality and accessibility. However, the literature review revealed eight factors that are commonly used for explaining the learning processes and outcomes when individuals, regardless of their age, use MUVEs and other ICT tools. These factors can be roughly grouped into three major categories:

Figure 1. Salzman et al.'s theoretical model

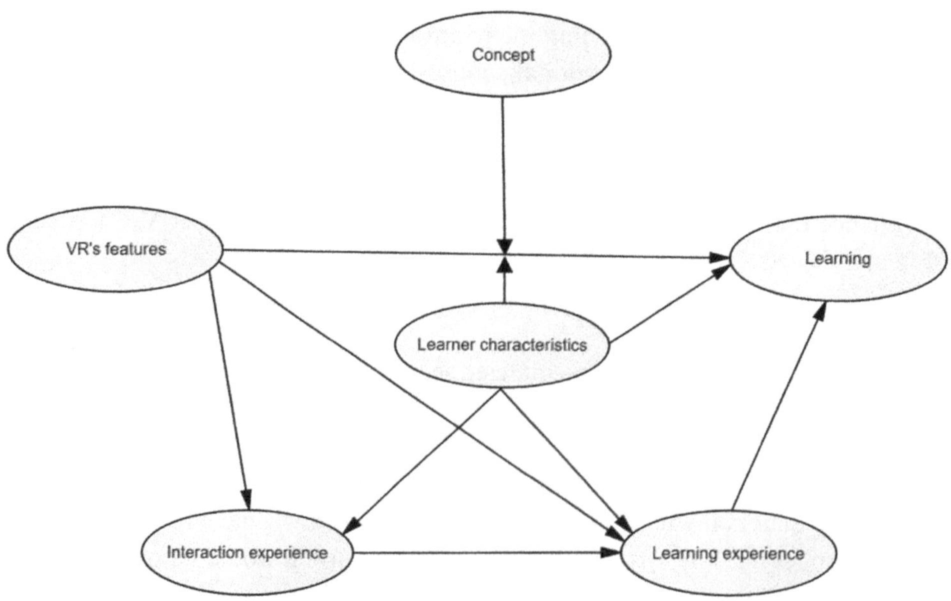

MUVEs' Features, Affordances, and Constraints

- **Perceived Realism:** From a technical perspective, the simulation's realism varies depending on how detailed the virtual objects are and, in general, how close to reality their behavior is. On the other hand, it is a subjective feature, because individuals perceive it differently and also plays an important role in one's experience when using MUVEs or VR applications in general (Dalgarno & Lee, 2010; Lee et al., 2010).
- **Interaction:** In addition to realism, increased interactions with the objects included in the simulation, also add to the user's experience (Dalgarno & Lee, 2010, Lee et al., 2010).
- **Perceived Ease of Use:** Perceived ease of use has been found to play a major role in one's experience when using diverse ICT tools (Davis, Bagozzi, & Warshaw, 1989). As a construct, it is included in a large number of studies that utilize the Technology Acceptance model (Davis et al., 1989) which tries to interpret people's intentions to use technological tools and, by extension, the learning outcomes resulting from their use. It is also included in models regarding VR (Lee et al., 2010; Sun, Tsai, Finger, Chen, & Yeh, 2008).
- **Collaboration:** As it was already mentioned, MUVEs allow social interactions, peer feedback, and collaboration between users, that are all considered as important elements in the learning processes that take place in MUVEs (Zheng & Newgarden, 2011).

State of Mind

- **Enjoyment:** The fun and, in general, the pleasure which one feels in a MUVE, can be defined as the degree to which a user considers that its use is an enjoyable experience (Ducoffe, 1996). Studies have shown that the positive feelings, such as fun and enjoyment, contribute to knowledge acquisition (Harrington, 2012).
- **Presence:** Presence is defined as the sense one has in a VR application that he/she is present there and not in the real world (Rizzo, Wiederhold, & Buckwalter, 1998). Studies indicated that as a factor is affecting the learning outcomes (Bulu, 2012; Lee et al., 2010). One might argue that presence should be included as a factor in a MUVE only if sophisticated equipment, such as head-mounted displays, are used. Actually, presence has generated a lot of debate that dates back at the first VR applications. There are researchers who supported that it solely depends on the equipment used (e.g., North & North, 2016; Schuemie, Van Der Straaten, Krijin, & Van Der Mast, 2001). Others supported the idea that it heavily depends on the individual's personality (e.g., Nunez, 2004), arguing that even reading a book can generate the feeling of presence. Studies have indicated that presence is indeed a factor in desktop VR applications and that it significantly influences the learning outcomes (e.g., Lee et al., 2010). Since the matter is not resolved, it was decided to include presence as a construct in the present study, even if it was planned not to use equipment that enhances presence in a MUVE.

Learning Enabling Features

- Perceived usefulness is also a construct in the Technology Acceptance Model and refers to the extent to which a person believes that using an ICT tool would enhance his/her productivity and performance and affects the course of the learning process (Hong & Tam, 2006). Perceived usefulness is also considered as a construct in other studies regarding VR's impact on learning (e.g., Lee et al., 2010; Sharda et al., 2004; Sun et al., 2008). In this study, perceived usefulness was considered as perceived learning effectiveness, the extent to which a person believes that a MUVE is a learning enabler, a facilitator of the learning process, compared to other teaching methods.
- Incentives for learning/motivation. Modern cognitive theories do not consider incentives for learning as a static attribute but as inherently volatile and sensitive to the way the content is presented (Linnenbrink & Pintrich, 2002). Researchers believe that the 3D presentation of the MUVE, interaction with its objects and the increased control on what the user selects to view, can influence motivation and, as a result, the learning outcomes (McLellan, 2004).

Having selected the factors, the next step was to develop the scale itself. For that matter, a number of questionnaires were considered that satisfied the following inclusion or exclusion criteria: (a) to have been tested and validated in studies concerning VR or MUVEs, (b) in multiple item factors (factors that were examined using multiple questions) the questions that had high loadings were selected, while (c) questions with intermediate or low loadings were excluded, and (d) questions coming from single variable factors (factors that were examined using only one question) were considered for inclusion only if their loadings were exceptionally high.

Specifically, five questions regarding perceived learning effectiveness were adapted from the corresponding questions in the Computer Attitude Scale (Selwyn, 1997) measuring perceived usefulness. This scale is used and validated in a large number of studies examining intentions to use diverse technologies (including MUVEs) in an educational context (e.g., Teo & Lee, 2010; Teo & Noyes, 2011). The five questions measuring perceived ease of use were also the ones used in the above-mentioned scale. For measuring presence, five questions from Novak's, Hoffman's and Yung's (2000) presence questionnaire were used. The Intrinsic Motivation Inventory is a multidimensional measurement for assessing participants' subjective experience of enjoyment related to a given activity (McAuley, Duncan, & Tammen, 1989; Tamborini, Bowman, Eden, Grizzard, & Organ, 2010). Four items from this scale were used for assessing the enjoyment when using a MUVE. Witmer's and Singer's (1998) questionnaire for assessing presence, provided a total of seven questions for measuring perceived realism and interaction. For measuring motivation, four questions were adapted from two relevant questionnaires (Martens, Bastiaens, & Kisrcher, 2007; McAuley et al., 1989). Finally, four questions for measuring collaboration were improvised, since no questionnaires that satisfied the inclusion criteria were found.

The pool of questions was translated into Greek by three groups. Each group consisted of one psychologist and one computer science professional with experience in MUVEs, both experts having proficiency in the English language. The resulting three different versions were back-translated into English and then viewed by another group of five experts. A unified version was obtained through a consensus meeting held with these experts aiming to assess the semantic adaptation and, thus, the initial version of the MUVEs learning factors scale (MLFS) was formulated, having a total of 34 questions.

METHOD

To confirm the factorial structure of MLFS and for validating it, a pilot project was designed and implemented. For that matter, it was decided to use a MUVE that was developed and used in previous research projects. Space exploration and the related facts and concepts are the themes of this MUVE, which was developed using OpenSimulator (http://opensimulator.org/). There are two levels in the MUVE. On the ground level, the technology behind space exploration is presented. A wealth of highly detailed 3D models is included; from the first rockets to the space shuttle, space suits, rocket engines, a rocket launch pad, moon vehicles, the Mars Rover, to name but a few (Figure 2). Scripts allow interactions to take place; the user can launch the Apollo 11, ignite rocket engines, disassemble a multistage rocket and see its stages, put rockets side by side and compare them, teleport from one place to another. Videos and slide presentations are also included, providing more detailed information on all objects. The second level is placed high in the sky and presents man-made satellites. Gravity is set to zero so that users can float in space. As in the first level, the users can interact with objects (e.g., put satellites side by side and compare them or disassemble them and get information on each of their main parts).

As already mentioned, the study's target group was sixth-grade primary school students (12-year-olds). A total of 385 students participated in the study, coming from 18 primary schools in Athens, Greece. It has to be noted that these schools were selected out of a larger number of schools that responded af-

Figure 2. Screenshots from the application

firmatively to the email invitation that was sent to them. Prior to the beginning of the project, students' parents were briefed about the project, its methodology, and objectives. Their written consent for their children's participation was obtained. Written consent was also obtained from the schools' headmasters. The sixth-grade teachers of the participating schools were also briefed and they were explicitly asked not to intervene in terms of trying to teach students anything related to the MUVE or to try to assist them in any way other than providing technical assistance when needed.

Students used the MUVE for a total of eight hours (four two-hour sessions). They were free to explore the environment, talk to each other, and to collaborate in-world. Since the study's objective was to record the students' learning experience in a MUVE, no in-classroom teaching intervention took place. Immediately following the end of the fourth session, MLFS was administered to students. The scale was presented as a list of the 34 items, alternately displayed so that no two items from the same construct appear adjacently, alongside a 5-point Likert scale (worded "Strongly Agree", "Agree", "Neutral", "Disagree" and "Strongly Disagree"). Students were advised that the scale was a survey, not a test and that there were no correct or incorrect answers. They were asked to indicate whether they agree or disagree with each statement and to answer as honestly as possible. Scores were obtained by allocating numerical values to responses: "Strongly Agree" is scored 5, "Agree" is scored 4; "Neutral" is scored 3; "Disagree" is scored 2 and "Strongly Disagree" is scored 1.

The project lasted for about four months, from early February to early June 2016 (it was not implemented simultaneously in all schools).

RESULTS ANALYSIS

Prior to conducting any statistical analysis, all questionnaires were checked for missing data and unengaged responses (cases with no variance in their responses). The number of valid questionnaires left after the initial screening was 352. Since the MLFS was based on translated and adapted versions of questions from multiple sources and a number of questions had to be improvised, an Exploratory Factor Analysis (EFA) had to be conducted in order to establish the underlying dimensions between the variables and the latent constructs. The initial sample was randomly split into sub-samples with 250 cases each, multiple times and, for each, EFA was conducted. The sub-samples' sizes satisfied Cattell's (1978) rule for a sample to variable ratio of 3-6:1 and an absolute minimum of 250 observations. For assessing the underlying structure of the 34 items in the initial version of MLFS, principal axis factor analysis (PAF) with oblique rotation was used. That is because, PAF accounts for the covariation among variables (Kline, 2005) and oblique rotation is considered to produce more accurate results for research involving human behaviors (Costello & Osborne, 2005).

In all cases, the EFA suggested 7 independent and distinct underlying constructs (one less than it was hypothesized). Also, in all cases, some items (4 to 7) had to be dropped, either because they loaded very low on their respective factor or because they were highly correlated with more than one factor. In the coming paragraph, the most strict solution is reported.

The data were well suited for factorial analysis, since the Kaiser-Meyer-Olkin (KMO) Measure of Sampling Adequacy index was .89, the Bartlett's Test of Sphericity was significant ($p < .001$), and the extraction communalities were well above the .5 level (Hair, Black, Babin, Anderson, & Tatham, 2006; Tabachnick & Fidell, 2007) (Table 1). Seven factors were extracted using both the Kaiser's (1960) criterion (eigenvalue > 1) and the more recommended scree test (Costello & Osborne, 2005) (Table 1, Figure

Table 1. Principal axis factor analysis of the retained items

Item	Factor Loadings							Communalities
	Enj	PEU	PLE	Pre	Real	Mot	Col	
Enj2	.93							.87
Enj4	.87							.77
Enj1	.76							.63
Enj3	.76							.59
PEU4		.85						.66
PEU2		.79						.67
PEU1		.77						.63
PEU3		.74						.67
PLE2			.86					.74
PLE1			.82					.69
PLE3			.73					.63
PLE4			.73					.62
Pre2				.92				.80
Pre3				.79				.61
Pre4				.74				.57
Pre1				.74				.64
Real2					.86			.70
Real1					.76			.57
Real4					.73			.59
Real3					.71			.56
Mot1						.85		.69
Mot3						.79		.75
Mot2						.77		.69
Mot4						.70		.68
Col2							.87	.70
Col3							.84	.74
Col1							.74	.63
Eigenvalues	9.20	3.66	1.88	1.79	1.53	1.29	1.02	
% variance explained (Total 67.05)	32.90	12.33	5.80	5.33	4.50	3.57	2.62	
Cronbach's α Total = .91	.90	.88	.89	.87	.85	.90	.86	

Notes. Extraction Method: PAF. Rotation Method: Oblique. Values < .30 are omitted for clearance of presentation. Enj: Enjoyment, PEU: perceived ease of use, PLE: perceived learning effectiveness, Pre: presence, Real: realism, Mot: motivation, Col: collaboration

3). These constructs were named as follows: enjoyment (Enj), perceived ease of use (PEU), perceived learning effectiveness (PLE), presence (Pre), realism (Real), motivation (Mot), and collaboration (Col). Interaction was merged with realism, as it will be further elaborated in the coming section. Seven items had to be dropped, all the retained items loaded high on their respective factors (> .6) and each factor averaged above the .7 level, as recommended by Hair et al. (2006). There were no significant cross-loadings between the retained items and there were no correlations between the factors greater than .7. The total variance explained by the 7 components was 67.05%. The reliability scores of all constructs using Cronbach's alpha was between .85 and .90 and the overall score was .91 (Table 1), suggesting that the internal consistency of the constructs and of the overall scale was satisfactory (deVellis's, 2003).

The final version of the MLFS with the 27 retained items and construct representations is shown in the Appendix.

The resulting factor structure was inputted into AMOS 24 to perform Confirmatory Factor Analysis (CFA). This time, the whole sample was used. Table 2 and Figure 4 show the results of the CFA. The standardized estimates ranged from .73 to .95 and were regarded as very good (Hair, Black, Babin, & Anderson, 2010). All of the R^2 values were above .50, suggesting that items explained more than half the amount of variance of the latent variable that they belong. All the fit indices appeared to be good, with the exception of χ^2 (Table 3). It has to be noted that χ^2 is too sensitive when the sample size exceeds 200 cases. If so, there is a great tendency for it to indicate significant differences (Hair et al., 2006). Therefore, this anomaly was assumed to be applicable in the present study ($N = 352$).

For assessing convergent validity, the average variance extracted (AVE) was measured and it was also checked whether the measurement items were loaded with significant *t*-values on their theoretical constructs. The AVE in all cases was above the .50 level as suggested by Hair et al. (2010). In addition, all the reflective indicators were significant at the .001 level (Table 2). The presence of discriminant validity was evaluated by comparing the square root of the AVE for any given factor with the correlations between that factor and all other factors. Since the variance shared between a factor and any other factor was less than the variance that the construct shares with its measures, as Fornell, Tellis, and Zinkhan (1982) suggested, it was concluded that the discriminant validity was satisfactory in all cases (Table 4).

Figure 3. Scree plot of the eigenvalues

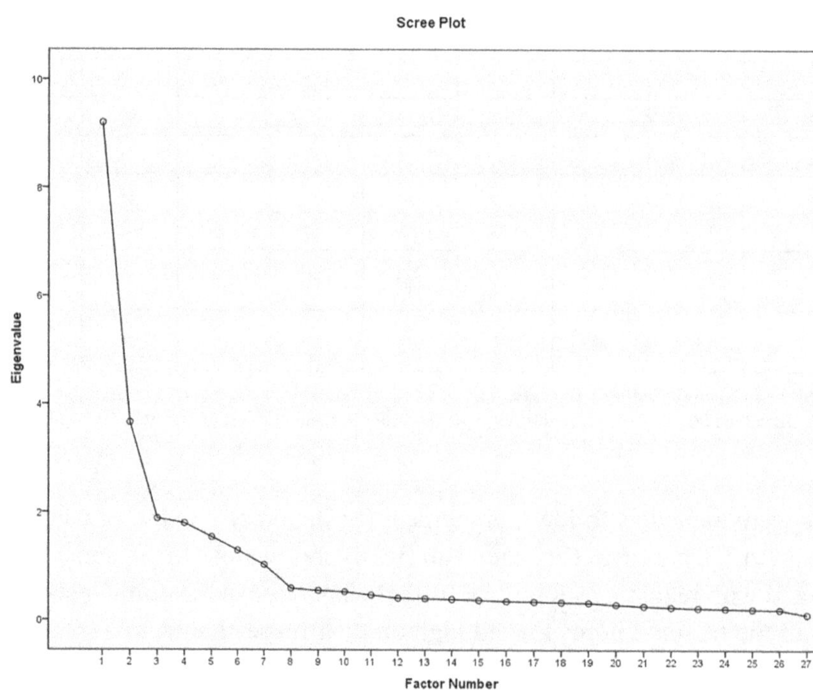

Table 2. Results for the measurement model

Item	SE	*t*-value	R^2	AVE
Enj2	.95	-	.90	.70
Enj4	.90	27.78	.81	
Enj1	.76	18.99	.57	
Enj3	.73	17.97	.54	
PEU4	.84	-	.61	.64
PEU2	.81	15.59	.67	
PEU1	.86	16.07	.64	
PEU3	.83	15.92	.66	
PLE2	.87	-	.74	.67
PLE1	.79	16.76	.69	
PLE3	.75	18.84	.62	
PLE4	.79	16.83	.63	
Pre2	.78	-	.76	.64
Pre3	.80	16.98	.62	
Pre4	.82	15.90	.56	
Pre1	.81	17.17	.63	
Real2	.83	-	.68	.60
Real1	.73	14.25	.53	
Real4	.78	15.27	.60	
Real3	.75	14.75	.57	
Mot1	.83	-	.65	.69
Mot3	.79	17.86	.73	
Mot2	.86	19.44	.70	
Mot4	.79	18.67	.69	
Col2	.81	-	.66	.68
Col3	.87	16.57	.75	
Col1	.79	15.55	.62	

Notes. - This value was fixed at 1.00 for model identification purposes. SE: standardized estimate. AVE: average variance extracted.

Finally, scores from items on each subscale were summed to provide individual scores on each construct. The 27 individual scores were also collectively summed to provide a total score representing the individuals' overall learning experience in MUVEs (ranging from 0 to 135) (Table 5). As a normative guide to interpretation, the scores obtained with a sample of 352 sixth-grade primary school students gave cut-off scores: at the 25th percentile of 80; at the 50th percentile of 88; and at the 75th percentile of 97 (with an overall range of scores from 47 to 122). Thus, a score below the 25th percentile (80) can be interpreted as a relatively negative experience, whereas a score above the 75th percentile (97) can be interpreted as a relatively positive learning experience when using a MUVE (Table 5).

Figure 4. Results of the CFA

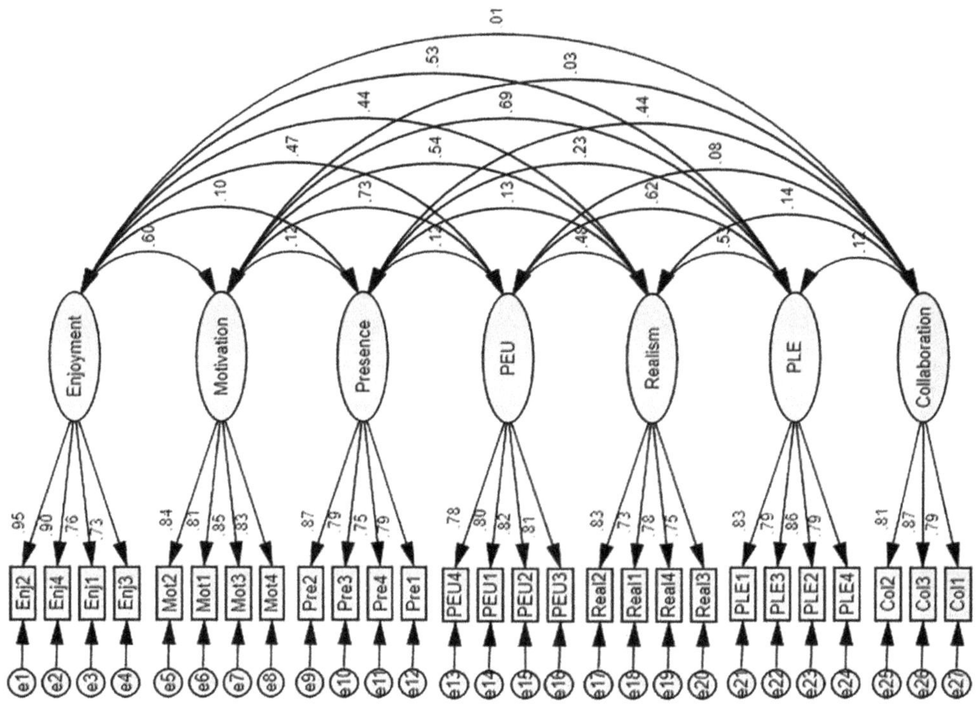

Table 3. Fit indices of the research model

	Result	Recommendation	Reference
χ^2	χ^2 (303, N = 352) = 547.95, $p < .001$	ns at $p < .05$	Schumacker & Lomax, 2010
χ^2/df	1.81	1 - 3	Kline, 2005
SRMR	.035	< .05	Klem, 2000; McDonald & Ho, 2002
TLI	.953	≥ .95	Hu & Bentler, 1999
NFI	.914	≥ .90	Bentler & Bonett, 1980
RMSEA	.048	<.05	McDonald & Ho, 2002
CFI	.96	≥ .95	Hu & Bentler, 1999

Note. ns: not significant

SOLUTIONS AND RECOMMENDATIONS

Out of the initial 34 items and the inclusion of 8 factors in the original scale, 27 items were retained belonging to 7 factors in the final version. It has to be emphasized that the wording was kept as simple as possible since the questionnaire is addressed to young students. This necessity together with the fact that almost all questions were originally in English (with the exception of the questions measuring perceived collaboration, that were improvised), might have indeed the question "Real2: When interacting with the virtual objects, these interactions seemed like real," although it was supposed to measure interaction, it

Table 4. Convergent and discriminant validity

Factor	CR	AVE	Enj	Mot	Pre	PEU	Real	PLE	Col
Enj	.90	.70	(.84)						
Mot	.90	.69	.60	(.83)					
Pre	.88	.64	.10	.12	(.80)				
PEU	.88	.64	.47	.73	.12	(.80)			
Real	.86	.60	.44	.55	.13	.48	(.77)		
PLE	.89	.67	.53	.69	.23	.62	.53	(.82)	
Col	.86	.68	.005	.03	.44	.08	.14	.12	(.82)

Notes. CR: Critical ratio. AVE: Average Variance Extracted. Diagonal in parentheses: square root of AVE extracted from observed variables. Off-diagonal: correlations between constructs

Table 5. Factors' totals and percentiles

Factor	*min*	*max*	*M*	*SD*	Percentiles		
					25	50	75
Presence (20)	5	19	12.32	3.04	10	12	14
Collaboration (15)	3	14	6.20	2.47	4	6	8
PLE (20)	8	20	15.68	2.90	14	16	18
PEU (20)	8	20	14.77	2.83	13	15	17
Motivation (20)	4	20	13.59	3.26	11	14	16
Realism (20)	5	19	12.41	2.61	10	13	14
Enjoyment (20)	5	20	13.83	3.05	12	14	16
Total (135)	47	122	88.80	12.89	80	88	97

Note. Maximum score for each factor is reported in parenthesis

proved to be the question with the second strongest loading in perceived realism. The other two questions that were also supposed to measure interaction also loaded to realism, but their loadings were rather small (< .50) and it was decided to drop them. As a result, interaction is not represented as a construct in the final scale. Though other studies examined these two factors separately (e.g., Dalgarno & Lee, 2010; Lee et al., 2010), the findings of the present study suggest that it can be merged with realism. A plausible explanation is that since no specialized equipment was used, that allowed increased interactions, these were viewed as part of the application's realistic representation of the virtual environment.

In general, Hair et al.'s (2006) recommendation for high items' loading (> .60) and high factors' average (> .7) was strictly followed, leading to the exclusion of 7 items in total. Even so, in the final scale, there are no factors having less than 3 items as suggested by Raubenheimer (2004). Actually, only one factor (collaboration) is measured using 3 items, while all the other factors are measured with 4. Yet, the total variance explained by the 27 items was 67.05%, which is more than satisfactory (Hair et al., 2010). Therefore, it can be argued that MLFS is a quite balanced scale since no factor is overrepresented. Moreover, MLFS's reliability and internal consistency, as a whole and per construct, was well above the .70 threshold (85 to .91) which is considered "acceptable" in most social science research situations (deVellis's, 2003). The same holds true for its convergent and discriminant validity since no problems were noted during the CFA. Thus, it can be concluded that MLFS seems to be a quite robust scale and short, in terms of how many items it has, and, thus, it can be administered in 5 to 10 minutes.

Collaboration had the lowest mean score ($M = 6.20$, $max = 15$), well below the mid-point. Apparently, collaboration did not work well when students used the MUVE and expressed their dissatisfaction to the relevant questions. This finding has to be further studied since other scholars indicated that it is an important factor in shaping the learning outcomes in a MUVE (Zheng & Newgarden, 2011). The short duration of the project in each school (8 hours) is a plausible explanation. Almost certainly, more time was needed so as students to get aquatinted with the software, master its use, and start collaborating efficiently.

Presence and the application's realism had the second and third lowest mean scores respectively. Since no specialized equipment was used, that could have enhanced the sense of presence, this finding was expected. While the results confirm that it is a factor in a MUVE, as others had noted (e.g., Lee et al., 2010), the relatively low mean score suggests that its role might not be that important compared to other factors. The same applies for perceived realism. It was confirmed that it is a factor, as previous literature suggested (Dalgarno & Lee, 2010; Lee et al., 2010), but of a lesser importance. MUVEs require well-equipped computers (in terms of hardware) in order to run smoothly. Alas, about the half of the participating schools had mid- to low-range computers. Accordingly, the settings regarding the quality of the simulation were set to low, and this had a negative impact on students' perception of the application's realism.

The mean scores of incentives for learning and enjoyment were well above the mid-point. The presence of enjoyment as a factor in the scale confirmed Harrington's (2012) views that fun and enjoyment contribute to the overall learning experience when using MUVEs. The same applies for motivation. It seems that students are motivated to learn when using VR/MUVEs applications as others had previously noted (e.g., McLellan, 2004).

Finally, the factors with the highest mean scores were perceived ease of use and perceived learning effectiveness. Given that students are "digital natives" (Prensky, 2001), it was expected that they would not face significant problems when using the application and this was reflected in their answers to the relevant questions. As for perceived learning effectiveness, it has to be reminded that it was a modified version of perceived usefulness. It seems that students formed the view that MUVEs are useful (as facilitators of their learning), confirming previous research on the importance of usefulness in one's experience when using MUVEs (e.g., Lee et al., 2010; Sharda et al., 2004).

Research has demonstrated that VR and MUVEs applications can produce satisfactory results when they are used for educational purposes. While this holds true, there is no common consensus on why individuals learn in these environments. Though studies scrutinizing the impact of certain factors on the learning outcomes do exist, each analyzed either one or a different set of factors and each used different instruments for validating these factors. On the other hand, in this study, by reviewing the relevant literature, seven subjective factors were located and a scale for measuring them was developed and tested. The scale's considerable internal consistency, stability, and validity are indicators that, indeed, these factors are involved in one's learning experience when using MUVEs. Thus, the study's contribution to research is that it proposes an instrument for measuring multiple factors at the same time. Even more, the scale is flexible; it can be used in a variety of VR/MUVEs application, by excluding certain factors, without altering the validity of the instrument. That is because the questionnaire's items load quite strongly on their respective factors and with minimal cross-correlations. For example, the scale can be easily used in a single-user VR application, by excluding the items measuring collaboration, since in this type of applications collaboration among users cannot take place.

There are limitations to this study that have to be taken into consideration. Despite being meticulous in methodology, one can never be certain about the accuracy -or honesty- of the participants' answers. The data were collected from primary school students in Greece and the sample size, although adequate for statistical analysis, could have been larger. Therefore, the study's results cannot easily be generalized to other samples. Time restrictions, imposed by the schools, did not allow the project to last for more than 8 hours (at each school). If students had more time at their disposal, their views might have been different. Finally, all of the questionnaire's items measured subjective factors (e.g., perceived realism, perceived ease of use, enjoyment, etc.). Thus, perceived learning effectiveness, which, in essence, is the perception of how much one thinks that he/she had learned when using MUVEs, does not verify/ guarantee that he/she has actually learned something. Consequently, the scale, without the inclusion of items measuring knowledge acquisition, cannot be used for measuring the objective learning outcomes.

FUTURE RESEARCH DIRECTIONS

Further validations are required for establishing the scale's validity and applicability. Perceived realism and perceived interactions require an in-depth examination, since, in this study, these two factors were merged. Additional factors can be considered that contribute in shaping the learning experience in MUVEs. Also, future studies can examine whether the scale can be used in different levels of education, in different types of VR applications, as well as in other types of emerging technologies (e.g., augmented reality) and, thus, increase its usefulness to the researchers. The full potential of the scale can be realized if, in future studies, the subjective factors that it measures are compared with data that measure the actual learning outcomes (e.g., through knowledge acquisition tests). By doing so, it would be possible to make multiple comparisons, examine how the factors interact with each other and with the learning outcomes, and draw useful conclusions. For example, it would be possible examine if and how subjective factors influence the learning outcomes or if (and to what extent) perceived learning differs from actual learning.

CONCLUSION

Within the theoretical framework laid out by Salzman and her colleagues, a scale has been developed for measuring a number of factors involved in the learning experience of students (aged around 12) when they use MUVEs. The scale consists of seven factor analytically distinct subscales with high internal consistency, stability, and validity. Those teaching in primary schools can use the scale to devise suitable strategies for curricular integration. The scale can also be used as a post-course outcome measure of the effectiveness of MUVEs. Researchers can use the scale as a comparative measure of the learning experience when using MUVEs in primary education, as well as revealing the extent of inequalities between students according to gender, race, and efficacy in using computers. In conclusion, the study contributes to the growing body of research on the educational impact of MUVEs and it is hoped that the scale will be of use to educators and researchers.

REFERENCES

Barnett, M., Yamagata-Lynch, L., Keating, T., Barab, S. A., & Hay, K. E. (2005). Using virtual reality computer models to support student understanding of astronomical concepts. *Journal of Computers in Mathematics and Science Teaching*, *24*(4), 333–356.

Bentler, P. M., & Bonett, D. G. (1980). Significance tests and goodness of fit in the analysis of covariance structures. *Psychological Bulletin*, *88*(3), 588–606. doi:10.1037/0033-2909.88.3.588

Bulu, S. T. (2012). Place presence, social presence, co-presence, and satisfaction in virtual worlds. *Computers & Education*, *58*(1), 154–161. doi:10.1016/j.compedu.2011.08.024

Cattell, R. B. (1978). *The scientific use of factor analysis*. New York: Plenum; doi:10.1007/978-1-4684-2262-7

Costello, A. B., & Osborne, J. W. (2005). Best practices in exploratory factor analysis: Four recommendations for getting the most from your analysis. *Practical Assessment, Research & Evaluation*, *10*(7), 1–9.

Dalgarno, B., & Lee, M. J. (2010). What are the learning affordances of 3-D virtual environments? *British Journal of Educational Technology, 41*(1), 10-32. doi: 10.1111/j.1467-8535.2009.01038.x

Davis, F. D., Bagozzi, R. P., & Warshaw, P. R. (1989). User acceptance of computer technology: A comparison of two theoretical models. *Management Science*, *35*(8), 982–1003. doi:10.1287/mnsc.35.8.982

deNoyelles, A., Hornik, S., & Johnson, R. D. (2014). Exploring the dimensions of self-efficacy in virtual world learning: Environment, task, and content. *Journal of Online Learning and Teaching / MERLOT*, *10*(2), 255.

deVellis, R. F. (2003). *Scale development: Theory and applications* (2nd ed.). Newbury Park, CA: SAGE.

Dickey, M. D. (2005). Brave new (interactive) worlds: A review of the design affordances and constraints of two 3D virtual worlds as interactive learning environments. *Interactive Learning Environments*, *13*(1-2), 121–137. doi:10.1080/10494820500173714

Ducoffe, R. H. (1996). Advertising value and advertising on the web. *Journal of Advertising Research*, *36*(5), 21–35.

Ertmer, P. A., & Newby, T. J. (2013). Behaviorism, cognitivism, constructivism: Comparing critical features from an instructional design perspective. *Performance Improvement Quarterly*, *26*(2), 43–71. doi:10.1002/piq.21143

Fornell, C., Tellis, G. J., & Zinkhan, G. M. (1982). Validity assessment: A structural equations approach using partial least squares. In *An assessment of marketing thought & practice* (pp. 405–409). Chicago: American Marketing Association.

Hair, J. F., Black, W. C., Babin, B. J., & Anderson, R. E. (2010). *Multivariate data analysis: International version* (7th ed.). Pearson.

Hair, J. F., Black, W. C., Babin, B. J., Anderson, R. E., & Tatham, R. L. (2006). *Multivariate data analysis* (Vol. 6). Upper Saddle River, NJ: Pearson Prentice Hall.

Harrington, M. C. (2012). The virtual trillium trail and the empirical effects of freedom and fidelity on discovery-based learning. *Virtual Reality (Waltham Cross)*, *16*(2), 105–120. doi:10.1007/s10055-011-0189-7

Hassell, M. D., Goyal, S., Limayem, M., & Boughzala, I. (2012). Effects of presence, copresence, and flow on learning outcomes in 3D learning spaces. *Administrative Issues Journal: Education, Practice, and Research*, *2*(1), 62–73. doi:10.5929/2011.2.1.4

Hew, K. F., & Cheung, W. S. (2010). Use of three-dimensional (3-D) immersive virtual worlds in K-12 and higher education settings: A review of the research. *British Journal of Educational Technology*, *41*(1), 33–55. doi:10.1111/j.1467-8535.2008.00900.x

Hong, S. J., & Tam, K. Y. (2006). Understanding the adoption of multipurpose information appliances: The case of mobile data services. *Information Systems Research*, *17*(2), 162–179. doi:10.1287/isre.1060.0088

Hu, L., & Bentler, P. M. (1999). Cutoff criteria for fit indexes in covariance structure analysis: Conventional criteria versus new alternatives. *Structural Equation Modeling*, *6*, 1-55. doi:/10.1080/10705519909540118

Jia, D., Bhatti, A., & Nahavandi, S. (2014). The impact of self-efficacy and perceived system efficacy on effectiveness of virtual training systems. *Behaviour & Information Technology*, *33*(1), 16–35. doi: 10.1080/0144929X.2012.681067

Kaiser, H. F. (1960). The application of electronic computers to factor analysis. *Educational and Psychological Measurement*, *20*(1), 141–151. doi:10.1177/001316446002000116

Klem, L. (2000). Structural equation modeling. In L. Grimm & P. Yarnold (Eds.), *Reading and understanding multivariate statistics* (Vol. 2). Washington, DC: American Psychological Association.

Kline, R. B. (2005). *Principles and practice of structural equation modeling* (2nd ed.). New York: Guilford Press.

Lee, E. A. L., Wong, K. W., & Fung, C. C. (2010). How does desktop virtual reality enhance learning outcomes? A structural equation modeling approach. *Computers & Education*, *55*(4), 1424–1442. doi:10.1016/j.compedu.2010.06.006

Levin, M. F. (2011). Can virtual reality offer enriched environments for rehabilitation? *Expert Review of Neurotherapeutics*, *11*(2), 153–155. doi:10.1586/ern.10.201 PMID:21306202

Linnenbrink, E. A., & Pintrich, P. R. (2002). Motivation as an enabler for academic success. *School Psychology Review*, *31*(3), 313–327.

Martens, R., Bastiaens, T., & Kirschner, P. A. (2007). New learning design in distance education: The impact on student perception and motivation. *Distance Education*, *28*(1), 81–93. doi:10.1080/01587910701305327

McAuley, E., Duncan, T., & Tammen, V. V. (1989). Psychometric properties of the intrinsic motivation inventory in a competitive sport setting: A confirmatory factor analysis. *Research Quarterly for Exercise and Sport*, *60*(1), 48–58. doi:10.1080/02701367.1989.10607413 PMID:2489825

McDonald, R. P., & Ho, M. R. (2002). Principles and practice in reporting structural equation analyses. *Psychological Methods*, *7*(1), 64–82. doi:10.1037/1082-989X.7.1.64 PMID:11928891

McLellan, H. (2004). Virtual realites. In D. H. Jonassen (Ed.), *Handbook of research on educational communications and technology*. Mahwah, NJ: Erlbaum Associates.

Merchant, Z., Goetz, E. T., Cifuentes, L., Keeney-Kennicutt, W., & Davis, T. J. (2014). Effectiveness of virtual reality-based instruction on students' learning outcomes in K-12 and higher education: A meta-analysis. *Computers & Education, 70*, 29–40. doi:10.1016/j.compedu.2013.07.033

Merchant, Z., Goetz, E. T., Keeney-Kennicutt, W., Kwok, O. M., Cifuentes, L., & Davis, T. J. (2012). The learner characteristics, features of desktop 3D virtual reality environments, and college chemistry instruction: A structural equation modeling analysis. *Computers & Education, 59*(2), 551–568. doi:10.1016/j.compedu.2012.02.004

Merchant, Z., Keeney-Kennicutt, W., & Goetz, E. (2015). Predicting undergraduate students' acceptance of second life for teaching chemistry. *Journal of Online Learning and Teaching / MERLOT, 11*(2).

North, M. M., & North, S. M. (2016). A comparative study of sense of presence of traditional virtual reality and immersive environments. *AJIS. Australasian Journal of Information Systems, 20*. doi:10.3127/ajis.v20i0.1168

Novak, T. P., Hoffman, D. L., & Yung, Y.-F. (2000). Measuring the customer experience in online environments: A structural modeling approach. *Marketing Science, 19*(1), 22–42. doi:10.1287/mksc.19.1.22.15184

Nunez, D. (2004, November). How is presence in non-immersive, non-realistic virtual environments possible? In *Proceedings of the 3rd International Conference on Computer Graphics, Virtual Reality, Visualisation and Interaction in Africa* (pp. 83-86). ACM. doi:10.1145/1029949.1029964

O'Neil, H. F., Wainess, R., & Baker, E. L. (2005). Classification of learning outcomes: Evidence from the computer games literature. *Curriculum Journal, 16*(4), 455–474. doi:10.1080/09585170500384529

Prensky, M. (2001). Digital natives, digital immigrants part 1. *On the Horizon, 9*(5), 1–6. doi:10.1108/10748120110424816

Raubenheimer, J. (2004). An item selection procedure to maximise scale reliability and validity. *SA Journal of Industrial Psychology, 30*(4), 59–64. doi:10.4102/sajip.v30i4.168

Rizzo, A. A., Wiederhold, M. D., & Buckwalter, J. G. (1998). Basic issues in the use of virtual environments for mental health applications. In G. Riva, B. K. Widerhold, & E. Molinari (Eds.), *Virtual environments in clinical psychology and Neuroscience* (pp. 22–42). Amsterdam: IOS Press.

Salzman, M. C., Dede, C., Loftin, R. B., & Chen, J. (1999). A model for understanding how virtual reality aids complex conceptual learning. *Presence (Cambridge, Mass.), 8*(3), 293–316. doi:10.1162/105474699566242

Schuemie, M. J., Van Der Straaten, P., Krijin, M., & Van Der Mast, C. A. P. G. (2001). Research on presence in virtual reality: A survey. *Cyberpsychology & Behavior, 4*(2), 183–210. doi:10.1089/109493101300117884 PMID:11710246

Schumacker, R. E., & Lomax, R. G. (2010). *A beginner' guide to structural equation modeling* (3rd ed.). New York: Routledge.

Selwyn, N. (1997). Students' attitudes toward computers: Validation of a computer attitude scale for 16-19 education. *Computers & Education*, *28*(1), 35–41. doi:10.1016/S0360-1315(96)00035-8

Sharda, R., Romano, N. C. Jr, Lucca, J. A., Weiser, M., Scheets, G., Chung, J. M., & Sleezer, C. M. (2004). Foundation for the study of computer-supported collaborative learning requiring immersive presence. *Journal of Management Information Systems*, *20*(4), 31–63. doi:10.1080/07421222.2004.11045780

Squire, K., Barnett, M., Grant, J. M., & Higginbotham, T. (2004, June). Electromagnetism supercharged!: Learning physics with digital simulation games. In *Proceedings of the 6th International Conference on Learning Sciences* (pp. 513-520). International Society of the Learning Sciences.

Sun, P.-C., Tsai, R. J., Finger, G., Chen, Y.-Y., & Yeh, D. (2008). What drives a successful e-Learning? An empirical investigation of the critical factors influencing learner satisfaction. *Computers & Education*, *50*(4), 1183–1202. doi:10.1016/j.compedu.2006.11.007

Tabachnick, B. G., & Fidell, L. S. (2007). *Using multivariate statistics*. Boston, MA: Pearson Education.

Tamborini, R., Bowman, N. D., Eden, A., Grizzard, M., & Organ, A. (2010). Defining media enjoyment as the satisfaction of intrinsic needs. *Journal of Communication*, *60*(4), 758–777. doi:10.1111/j.1460-2466.2010.01513.x

Teo, T., & Lee, C. B. (2010). Explaining the intention to use technology among student teachers: An application of the Theory of Planned behaviour (TPB). *Campus-Wide Information Systems*, *27*(2), 60–67. doi:10.1108/10650741011033035

Teo, T., & Noyes, J. (2011). An assessment of the influence of attitude and perceived enjoyment on the intention to use technology among pre-service teachers: A structural equation modelling approach. *Computers & Education*, *57*(2), 1645–1653. doi:10.1016/j.compedu.2011.03.002

Vrellis, I., Avouris, N., & Mikropoulos, T. A. (2016). Learning outcome, presence and satisfaction from a science activity in Second Life. *Australasian Journal of Educational Technology*, *32*(1), 59–77. doi:10.14742/ajet.2164

Witmer, B. G., & Singer, M. J. (1998). Measuring presence in virtual environments: A presence questionnaire. *Presence (Cambridge, Mass.)*, *7*(3), 225–240. doi:10.1162/105474698565686

Yaman, M., Nerdel, C., & Bayrhuber, H. (2008). The effects of instructional support and learner interests when learning using computer simulations. *Computers & Education*, *51*(4), 1784–1794. doi:10.1016/j.compedu.2008.05.009

Zheng, D., & Newgarden, K. (2011). Rethinking language learning: Virtual worlds as a catalyst for change. *International Journal of Learning and Media*, *3*(2), 13–36. doi:10.1162/ijlm_a_00067

KEY TERMS AND DEFINITIONS

Multiuser Virtual Environments (MUVEs): 3D virtual environments where multiple users can simultaneously use the same simulation.

Perceived Ease of Use: The subjective view that an application or an ICT tool can be handled/used with no problems.

Perceived Realism: The view one has regarding how close to reality a VR application is.

Perceived Usefulness: The extent to which a person believes that using an ICT tool would enhance his/her productivity and performance.

Presence: The sense one has in a virtual reality application that he/she is present there and not in the real world.

Scale: Concept, device, or procedure used in arranging, measuring, or quantifying events, objects, or phenomena.

Virtual Reality: A technology that allows a user to interact with a computer-simulated environment, whether this environment is a simulation of the real world or an imaginary world.

APPENDIX

Table 6. The MLFS scale

Factor	Item	
Perceived learning effectiveness	PEL1	I feel that MUVEs can ease the way I learn
	PEL2	MUVEs are a much easier way to learn compared to the usual teaching
	PEL3	Why use a MUVE? There are easier ways to learn what I want to learn*
	PEL4	MUVEs can make learning more interesting
Perceived ease of use	PEU1	Learning to use the MUVE was easy for me
	PEU2	I found the MUVE easy to use
	PEU3	Whenever I used the MUVE I needed help because it was not easy for me to use it*
	PEU4	It was easy for me to become skillful at using the MUVE
Presence	Pr1	I forgot about my immediate surroundings when I used the MUVE
	Pr2	When I used the MUVE I often forgot where I am
	Pr3	When I used the MUVE, the virtual world was more real than the real world
	Pr4	When I used the MUVE, I felt that my body was in the room, but my mind was inside the world created by the MUVE
Enjoyment	En1	My experience in the MUVE was quite enjoyable
	En2	I would describe my experience in the MUVE as very interesting
	En3	The experience in the MUVE was fun
	En4	I enjoyed experiencing the virtual world in the MUVE very much

continued on following page

Table 6. Continued

Factor	Item	
Motivation	Mo1	When using the MUVE, I had the impulse to learn more about space exploration**
	Mo2	I tried to explore all the MUVE because everything was so interesting
	Mo3	I wasn't interested in learning using this type of computer program*
	Mo4	This type of computer program did not hold my attention*
Collaboration	Co1	I was displeased because it was impossible to collaborate with others in a MUVE; everyone had a mind of his own*
	Co2	It was interesting that in the MUVE I was doing things together with my fellow students
	Co3	With my fellow students, we were able to jointly decide where to go and what to do in the MUVE
Realism	Real1	The visual display quality of the MUVE distracted me from doing other things
	Real2	When interacting with the virtual objects, these interactions seemed like real
	Real3	There were times when the virtual objects became more real and present for me compared to the real ones
	Real4	The virtual objects seemed like the real objects to me

Notes. * = Item for which scoring was reversed; ** = Replace with the learning subject of the MUVE

Section 3

MUVE:

Exploring the Future

Chapter 10
Multi-User Mixed Reality Environments for Distance Learning

Anasol Peña-Rios
University of Essex, UK

Victor Callaghan
University of Essex, UK

Michael Gardner
University of Essex, UK

ABSTRACT

Technological innovation is changing every aspect of our lives and extending into education, where it is introducing profound changes to both the traditional classroom and online learning environments. This chapter explores the future of MUVEs, focusing particularly on immersive mixed reality learning environments and the challenges involved in the shift to multidimensional environments in education. It reviews the earlier developments in MUVEs and identifies a barrier to their deployment in science and engineering education: their inability to support physical collaborative laboratory work. The chapter then explains how advances in mixed-reality research may offer a solution to this problem through a case study of a cutting-edge example of such an approach, the BReal Lab, together with a summary of evaluation results gained from a trial involving students in 5 different countries. Finally, the chapter concludes by reflecting on the issues raised and speculates on possible future directions that work on mixed-reality MUVEs might take.

INTRODUCTION

The use of online technology has opened opportunities for students to learn, without being constrained to a particular time or space. On-demand content allows learners to have 24/7 access to materials and resources, collaborating synchronously (e.g., chat, video conferences) and asynchronously (e.g., forums,

DOI: 10.4018/978-1-5225-3719-9.ch010

wikis) with their peers, introducing social interaction which has been shown to be a key element on the learning process (Dillenbourg, Järvelä, & Fischer, 2009; Nicholson, 2008; Smith & Macgregor, 1992). Multi-user virtual environments (MUVEs) provide a 3D virtual canvas for users to populate with 3D representations of the real world, or simplifying visualisations of complex abstractions, enabling multiple simultaneous participants to access virtual contexts, interact with digital artefacts, communicate with other participants and experience situations that reflect real world dynamics (Dede et al., 2005). Traditionally MUVEs have been regarded as standalone entities separated from the real world, where users can create virtual worlds which could follow realistic physical laws and rules (e.g., gravity), or, where advantageous, differ from reality (e.g., flying, non-human avatars, etc.). They bring a sense of community and belonging which provides conditions for free and open dialogue, critical debate, negotiation and agreement, which are the foundations of education (Garrison & Kanuka, 2004). Moreover, they provide opportunities for distant participants to engage and participate in collaborative learning scenarios. Through immersion of the simulation and engagement with authentic tasks, the learners are supported in understanding the principles and concepts together with acquiring the reasoning and procedural skills needed to test their ideas (Dieterle & Clarke, 2006).

This chapter addresses innovative learning spaces created by combining MUVEs and mixed reality technologies with a particular focus on multi-user immersive reality environments, identifying relevant technologies and highlighting current trends for future advances in technology and educational applications. In doing so, the first section of this chapter introduces concepts relating to multidimensional spaces and proposes the use of mixed reality in a distributed learning environment, establishing potential benefits of using such environments over current alternatives for hands-on activities. The second section describes some of the technologies and underlying pedagogies involved in different implementations of mixed reality learning environments. In the third section, this chapter identifies the challenges faced in the shift to multi-user mixed reality learning environments. The fourth section illustrates the ideas being advocated through the presentation of an exemplar system, BReal Lab, a proof-of-concept of a multi-user, mixed reality, learning laboratory prototype, tested across three continents with culturally diverse learners. This section includes a summary of the findings from these tests. Finally, the chapter concludes by reflecting on the discussion and considering future research directions for multidimensional spaces in education.

BACKGROUND

E-Learning is perhaps the best-known form of distance learning, involving students accessing online education materials through network enabled computers, in much the same way as we might browse regular libraries and books. It is generally understood as encompassing all forms of electronically supported learning and teaching (Rosenberg, 2000). Thus, the traditional learning paradigm has shifted to a blended learning scenario, with the possibility of combining traditional classroom methods with computer-mediated activities. Garrison and Kanuka (2004) defined a continuum of e-learning with face-to-face (F2F) enhanced classrooms in one end and complete online experiences on the other, where Blended Learning is situated on any point that mixes these two approaches. Blended Learning can be understood as the thoughtful integration of F2F instructional learning experiences with computer-mediated learning experiences. The use of the term "learning experiences" is important because immersive technologies, such as virtual, augmented or mixed reality, have opened up limitless design possibilities which can be applied to many contexts. Therefore, the use of Blended Learning represents a fundamental reconceptualization and reorganisation of the teaching and learning dynamic (Garrison & Kanuka, 2004), introducing more complexity into the design of learning experiences.

Virtual learning environments (VLE), build on these ideas by providing rich teaching templates and teaching content, helping to improve the learners' ability for analysing problems and exploring new concepts (Pan, Cheok, Yang, Zhu, & Shi, 2006). Based on their interfaces, they can be classified into the three following major categories (Dede, 2004; Moore, 1995):

- Text-based or "World to the desktop" interfaces such as Learning Management Systems (LMS), Massive Open Online Courses (MOOCs), forums, video recorded conferences, etc. which provide instant access to distant experts and archives, enabling collaborations, mentoring relationships, and virtual communities-of-practice.
- Desktop or "*Alice-in-Wonderland*" multi-user virtual environments (MUVE) interfaces, based on three-dimensional models, in which participants' represented as avatars interact with computer-based agents and digital artefacts in virtual contexts. In education, they are commonly known as three-dimensional Virtual Learning Environments (3D VLEs) (e.g., serious games, virtual worlds in education, etc.).
- Interfaces for ubiquitous computing or "*Immersive experiences*", based on mixed and virtual reality, linking virtual resources back to the physical world. These interfaces are characterised by the role of "smart objects" and "intelligent contexts" in learning and doing. This area is highly topical with the current profusion of the internet-of-things, augmented reality mobile applications, smart-glasses (e.g., Microsoft HoloLens) and immersive virtual reality devices (e.g., Oculus Rift).

In particular, interfaces for ubiquitous computing allow the creation of multidimensional spaces. A multidimensional space can be defined as a hybrid environment where physical and virtual worlds couple together to create the seamless illusion of continuity.

Weiser (1999) in his essay "*The computer for the 21st century,*" described virtual reality as perhaps the "most diametrically opposed" concept to his vision of ubiquitous computing, in which technology integrates seamlessly into the physical world so as to become indistinguishable from it (i.e., somewhat invisible); whereas, in contrast, virtual reality "*attempts to make a world inside the computer [...] focusing on simulating the world rather than on invisibly enhancing the world that already exists*" (p. 1). The term, "*virtual reality*" was first used in 1986 by Jaron Lanier, the founder of VPL Corporation (Mann, 2002; Steuer, 1992; Yoh, 2001), and it is usually referred as "*the sense of artificial reality*". Thus, Virtual Reality (VR) refers to a highly-interactive computer-generated environment which creates a synthetic experience for the user, allowing a person to have a sense of being present in an environment other than the one the person is actually in, by substituting the primary sensory input with data received produced by a computer (Heim, 1998; Ijsselsteijn, 2006; Kim, 2005; Schroeder, 1996). Weiser's VR concerns reflect two limitations, a) the separation that virtual reality imposes to reality; and b) humans' capability to be present and fully engaged in one reality at a time. Lifton (2007) defined this as the *vacancy problem*, "*a noticeable and profound absence of a person from one world, either physical or virtual, while they are participating in the other*" (p. 41).

Mixed Reality (MR) tries to solve the vacancy challenge by combining physical and virtual elements in a shared environment. Milgram and Kishino (1994) proposed a continuum to represent the different degrees of separation between virtuality and reality, defining anything amid the ends as mixed reality (Figure 1). MR is a spectrum that connects wholly physical to wholly virtual environments, illustrating the possible arrangements for the co-existence of physical and computer-generated elements in real-time.

Within the Reality-Virtuality Continuum's scope, Augmented Reality (AR) is probably the most popular combination. AR describes an environment where the physical world is enhanced by adding computer-generated objects to make them appear as if they co-exist in the same dimension (Pastoor & Conomis, 2005). Therefore, AR supplements reality rather than completely replacing it. In contrast, Augmented Virtuality (AV) describes an environment primarily virtual, which is enhanced by adding physical objects and physical world's data. This is generally done by adding raw video data onto markers within a virtual environment (Pastoor & Conomis, 2005; Tamura, Yamamoto, & Katayama, 2001).

Nowadays, and with the increasing popularity of the Internet-of-Things (IoT), MR has new possibilities for mixing virtual elements with smart (physical) objects in real-time. The Internet-of-Things is based on standard and interoperable communication protocols where physical "things" have identities, physical attributes, and virtual personalities; joining the virtual world of *information* with the physical world of *things*, and creating a dynamic global network infrastructure with self-configuring capabilities (Gershenfield, Krikorian, & Cohen, 2004; Sundmaeker, Guillemin, & Friess, 2010; Uckelmann, Harrison, & Michahelles, 2011). Smart objects are autonomous physical/digital objects augmented with sensing, processing, and network capabilities which can interpret their local situation and status, and can communicate with other smart objects and interact with human users (Kortuem, Kawsar, Fitton, & Sundramoorthy, 2010).

One example of these possibilities is the so-called Ubiquitous Virtual Reality, a paradigm that combines VR with ubiquitous computing, extending VR capabilities into a physical space, not confining it within a simulated space (Jang, Kim, & Woo, 2005; Lee, Oh, Shin, & Woo, 2008; Oh & Woo, 2013). In learning, this paradigm creates a correlation between virtual and physical spaces to adjust them to the purposes of the learning experience, creating what is also known as "mirror worlds". A different possibility is to include mappings not only between spaces but also between physical and virtual objects that exist within those spaces. Dual Reality (DR) (also known as *Cross-Reality*) is the underpinning concept behind this. It can be defined as "*an environment resulting from the interplay between the physical world and the virtual world. While both worlds are complete unto themselves, they are also enriched by their ability to mutually reflect, influence, and merge into one another*" (Lifton & Paradiso, 2009, p. 1). DR might seem a modification of AV or AR, or even a mix between them, however, AV consists of a virtual environment complemented with physical elements; in comparison to AR, which is mainly based

Figure 1. Mixed reality continuum (Milgram & Kishino, 1994)

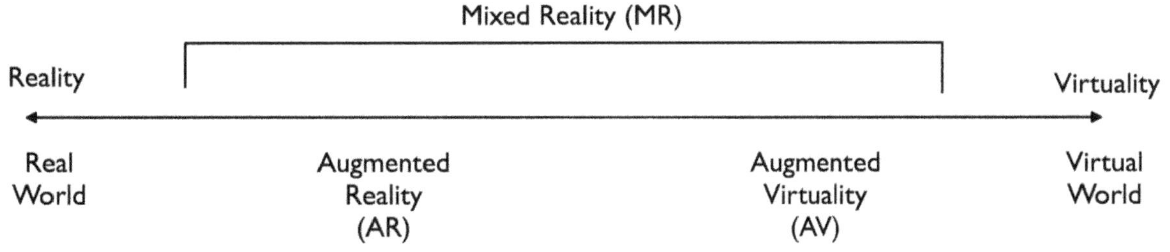

on a physical environment enhanced with virtual elements. In contrast, a DR environment is complete by itself, but elements inside the virtual environment are directly linked with its physical counterparts, interchanging a flux of data in real-time, which allows them to react simultaneously, creating *digital twins*. Figure 2 shows this data flux within Milgram's Reality-Virtuality Continuum.

The diverse use of technology towards the creation of multi-dimensional learning environments reflect the changes in the learning paradigms, suggesting a relationship between blended learning with mixed reality technologies. Figure 3 illustrates this relationship within an adapted version of Garrison's continuum of e-Learning and Milgram's Reality-Virtually continuum, including traditional F2F education, located at the "Reality" extreme of the continuum, and online learning at the "Virtuality" end.

Figure 2. Dual reality within Milgram's Taxonomy (Pena-Rios, 2016)

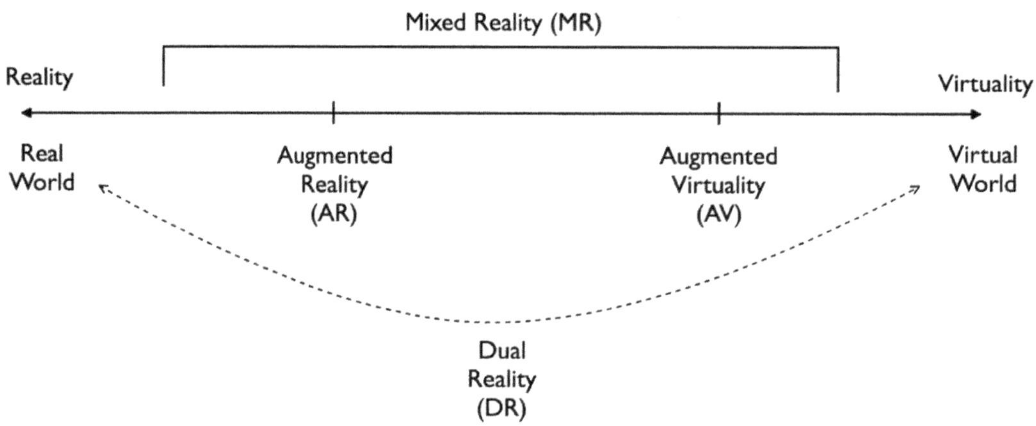

Figure 3. Milgram's Reality-Virtually continuum vs Garrison's continue of e- learning (adapted) (Pena-Rios, 2016)

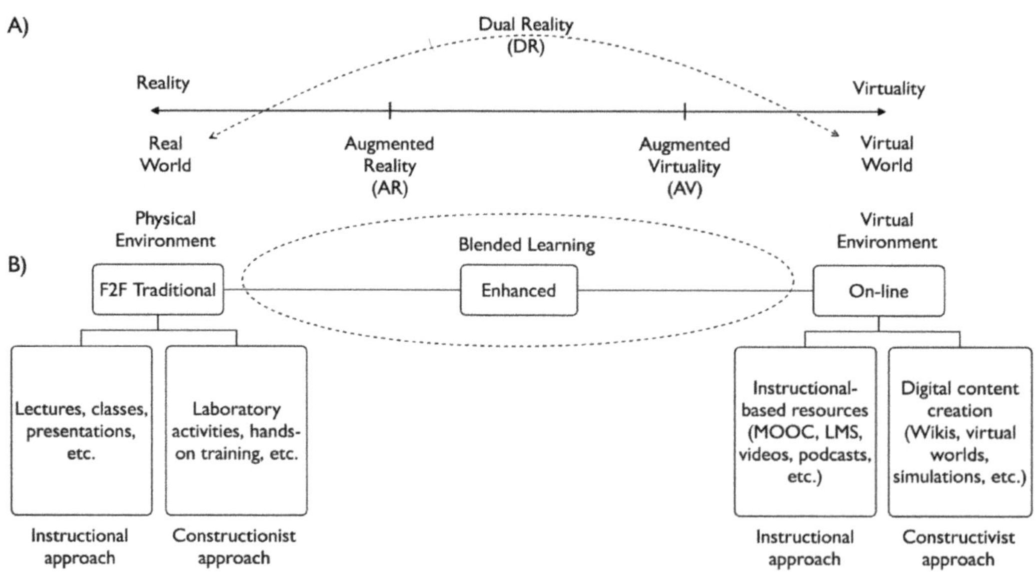

Multi-User Mixed Reality Learning Environments

Mixed Reality Learning Environments (MRLE) combine physical and virtual resources to enhance the learning process. This includes a broad range of applications in which some elements of the physical world (e.g., physical space, physical objects, students) can be blended with digital objects (Kirkley & Kirkley, 2004). Teachers and learners have started to embrace the use of digital tools in education, and they expect to increase their use due to the novelty that immersive headsets provide (e.g., Oculus Rift, HTC Vive, Microsoft Hololens) combined with the pervasiveness of mobile devices. Schrader (2008) described the use of technology in education based on the role it takes on a learning activity. He defined four types of interaction:

- **About Technology:** When the end goal is to learn how it works or how to use a particular technology (e.g., programming languages).
- **From Technology:** When technology is the teacher and/or provides the content (e.g., online courses).
- **With Technology:** When technology frees cognitive space for attention to higher-level skills (e.g., calculator).
- **Within Technology:** When technology is the context, creating a mechanism of interaction between content and experience (e.g., MUVEs).

Immersive Learning (IL) happens when creating experiences that focus on learning within the technology (Gardner & Elliott, 2014). This can be from technology embedded in the physical space (i.e. intelligent classrooms) to virtual learning spaces (i.e. MUVEs). IL could be defined as the combination of Blended Learning with diverse immersive technology that can support self-directed and collaborative group-based learning activities. An Immersive Learning Environment (ILE) can be defined as a technology-based educational setting which provides rich and complex content-based learning (usually computer-generated), deeply involving learner's senses and therefore, giving a profound sense of immersion; with the result of enhancing the user experience. This type of environment usually includes sensory stimulus feedback (visual, haptic, auditory) and occasionally, the possibility of combining virtual and physical spaces, or the integration of mobile capabilities to engage and motivate differentiated learner groups. Smart classrooms, MUVEs and MRLEs are some implementations of immersive learning environments.

Immersion can be used in different contexts and degrees, however, the most commonly used is spatial immersion, which occurs when an individual has the impression that a simulated world looks and feels "real" and he or she is really "there" (also known as Presence) (Dede, 1995; Ijsselsteijn, 2006). This feeling of "being there" is the key element that allows constructivist approaches, such as problem-based learning, challenge-based learning, and competency-based learning, to be used in Immersive Learning to create richer and more hands-on, real-world experiences for students. When immersive learning experiences are designed for collaboration, they can take advantage of learners' immersive feeling of "being there with others" (co-presence), allowing them to participate and interact in a more natural way, even when the participants are not in the same geographical place, enhancing the learning experience. Therefore, it is important to identify and match a learning environment with the needs of the learners and the learning goal.

The use of VR, AR and other immersive technologies combined with ubiquitous computing, mobile and wearable devices allow participants' use of virtual interactive resources as they move through the physical world, fostering an increasing number of educational applications, and creating new learning experiences combining both ends of the physical - digital spectrum. The use of immersive VR headsets that allow learners to immerse in 360-degree animations and models, along with AR glasses that enable interaction with the learning environment, complemented with gesture and voice recognition capabilities, enable numerous innovative scenarios. For example, HoloMuse is an AR application for Microsoft's HoloLens, which allows users to actively engage and learn about archaeological artefacts from a museum collection without taking away from the experience of viewing an original artefact within the context of an exhibit. It enables users to pick up, rotate, scale, and alter a holographic image of an original archaeological artefact using in-air gestures. Users can also curate their own exhibit or customize an existing one by selecting artefacts from a virtual gallery and placing them within the physical world so that they are viewable only using the device (Pollalis, Fahnbulleh, Tynes, & Shaer, 2017). Similarly, the Augmented Reality Collaborative Application (ARCA) (Alzahrani et al., 2015) uses AR to insert holographic-like images of remote students into a shared local environment to enable communication between students that are physically present (local students) with students that are digitally present (remote students) in a way that is analogous to real world meetings with the aim of providing all participants with a sense of place, in terms of location, vision and sound (Figure 7b). Visual integration was achieved using markers with tablets, smart phones and/or immersive glasses to insert the imagery, bringing new opportunities for supporting learning and teaching within educational classrooms and laboratories.

AR has good potential for creating MRLEs, however, several alternatives exist. For example, Shanghai Jiao Tong University in China, has created a multi-user mixed reality environment based on two approaches: a) live classroom broadcasting, delivered in real-time (e.g., audio, lecture video, presentation video) to remote multi-modal receivers (e.g. 'standard natural classrooms', home computer, IPTV, mobile phone) via Internet; and b) web-based learning, providing lectures and material on demand (Zhang, Callaghan, Shen, & Davies, 2011). Other approaches, such as University of Essex' MiRTLE (Figure 4a) (Callaghan et al., 2008; Gardner & O'Driscoll, 2011), or University of Hawaii's Holodeck (Figure 4b) (Schmidt, Kevan, Mckimmy, & Fabel, 2013), seek to reunite students in a physical classroom with those in different geographical locations, with the goal of fostering a sense of community amongst remote and physically-present students (Horan, Gardner, & Scott, 2009). Using a MUVE connected to a live video streaming of the physical classroom, remote students could share lectures with students located in physical classrooms, participating in class discussions through chat/voice tools in the virtual world. These examples follow a fairly traditional instructional approach which combines a physical space (where students meet in-person) with a virtual one (where students meet as avatars facilitated through live video streaming into the virtual world).

Tolentino et al. (2009) presented the Situated Multimedia Arts Learning Laboratory (SMALLab), a semi-immersive learning environment that incorporated gesture recognition within a 15x15-foot-space utilising projections on to an interactive floor surface (Figure 5a). Their approach is based on the concept of embodied learning, where the interface is, to certain extent, responsive to students' movements, capturing their gestures and tracking their position. A similar project, the MEteor simulation game (Lindgren & Moshell, 2011) comprised a 30x10-foot interactive environment utilising both wall and floor projection displays which allowed students to predict an asteroid's movement using their bodies (Figure 5b).

Figure 4. Examples of mixed reality environments in instructional approaches. (a) MiRTLE (Gardner & O'Driscoll, 2011). (b) Holodeck (Schmidt et al., 2013)

Figure 5. Examples of mixed reality environments in embodied learning. (a) SMALLab (Birchfield & Johnson-Glenberg, 2010). (b) MEteor simulation game (Lindgren & Moshell, 2011)

Ibáñez, Delgado Kloos, Leony, Garcia Rueda, and Maroto (2011) presented an application for "second language" learning, where students could make a phone call by touching a 3D mobile phone to a teacher's smartphone (Figure 6a). Using geotagged information sent by the physical smartphone, students could "walk" with the teacher via a virtual representation of the street. The project created mirrored connections between 3D objects inside the MUVE with physical objects. Similarly, the PhyMEL project (Physical, Mental and Emotional Learning) (Fernández Panadero, De la Cruz Barquero, Delgado Kloos, & Moran Nuñez, 2014) uses a wheelchair simulator to train and promote awareness of the challenges faced by people with disabilities and people they relate to (medical staff, people with other disabilities, architects and general public). Interaction between virtual and physical worlds is achieved by controlling the wheelchair simulator (Figure 6b). These projects follow experiential learning approaches, which can be understood as "processes whereby knowledge is created through the transformation of experience" (Kolb, 1984, p. 41).

Alrashidi, Alzahrani, Gardner, and Callaghan (2016) presented the IoT-Lens project (Figure 7a), which uses AR for revealing and learning about hidden technologies, such as visualising computational processes or messages. In their particular case (although it's not an essential feature of the method) they chose to

Figure 6. Examples of mixed reality environments in experiential learning. (a) Second Language Learning Activity (Ibañez Espiga et al., 2011). (b) PhyMEL (Fernández Panadero et al., 2014)

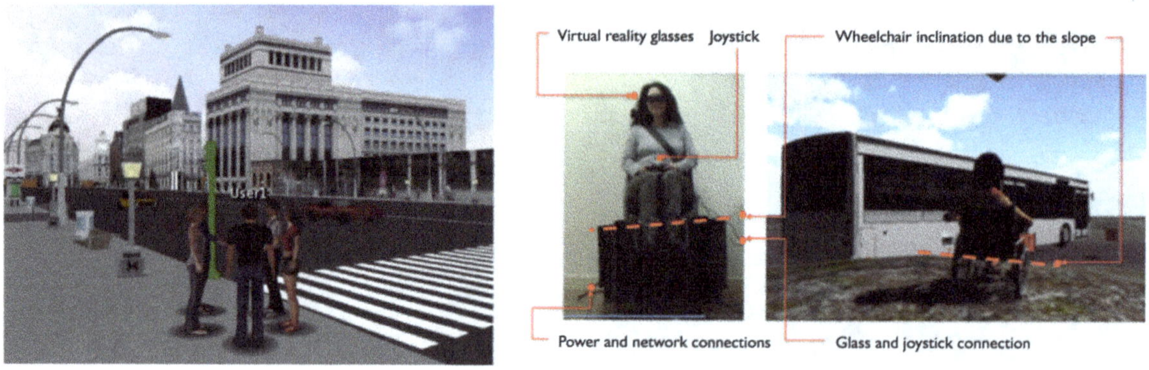

Figure 7. Examples of mixed reality environments in constructivism approaches. (a) IoT-Lens (Alrashidi et al., 2016). (b) ARCA (Alzahrani et al., 2015)

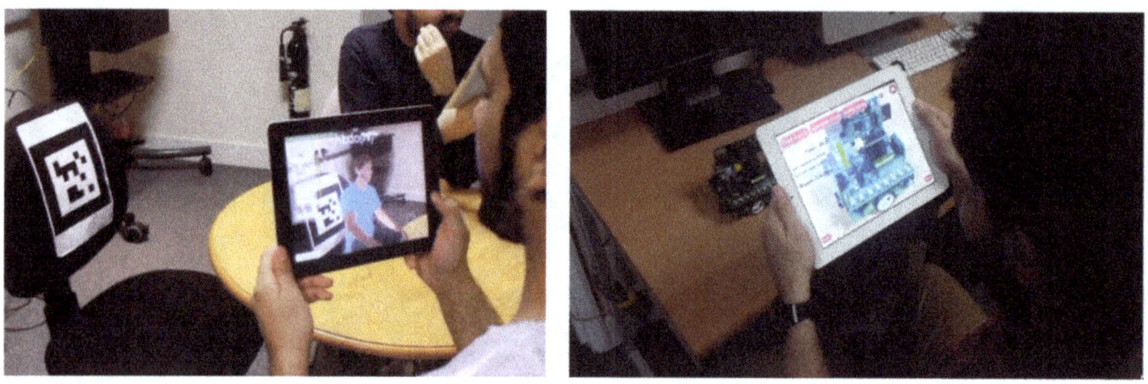

use pluggable electronic boards to create different mash-ups (e.g., desktop robots). Messages between boards were "sniffed" to reveal the learning process, monitoring and guiding the student. This project uses a constructivist approach in which the learner actively constructs or builds ideas and internalises concepts, rules, and general principles which may consequently be applied in a practical real-world.

These projects illustrate some of the possible combinations arising from mixing virtual and physical environments. Other variations can be found in projects such as MiRTLE and Holodeck which encoded live students as avatars projecting than on the rear wall of a physical classroom in a way that allowed teachers in a traditional classroom to see and interact with remotely located students. In other examples, SMALLab and MEteor showed connection between users' actions and virtual elements; the language learning mixed reality implementation presented by Ibañez Espiga et al. (2011), PhyMEL and the IoT-Lens projects exemplified bi-directional mappings between objects: virtual phone to physical phone (second language learning app), the wheelchair simulation (PhyMEL) and the desktop robots (IoT-Lens). These examples indicate that instructional and embodied learning approaches create mappings in a more abstract way, connecting environments and participants, whereas experiential and constructivist approaches focus more on mappings between objects. Figure 8 illustrates some of these mappings.

Figure 8. Possible mappings between environments (Lifton, 2007)

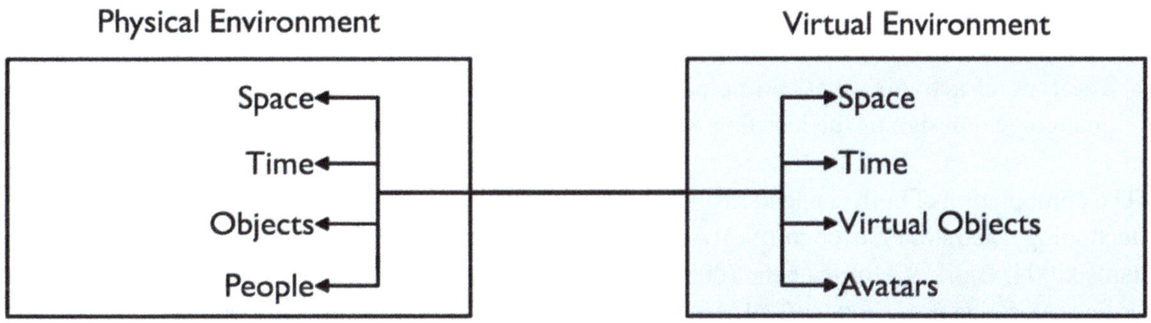

CHALLENGES IN THE SHIFT TO MULTI-USER MIXED REALITY LEARNING ENVIRONMENTS

Current trends in educational technology research aim to create a multidimensional space, where virtual and physical elements are combined; allowing students to use the best of both paradigms. The change from desktop-based interfaces to mixed reality interfaces is being driven by the psychologically immersive characteristic innate nature of virtual and augmented reality experiences, which induce a strong sense of "*presence*" which, for learning, is advantageous. This sense of presence is variable and depends on the situation that the learner is confronted with. Achieving self-presence (sense that my avatar is me), social presence (sense that others are with me) and spatial presence (sense that I am in the environment) is challenging for any mixed reality learning environment. For example, in such a space, a student could work in a regular physical environment, enjoying enhanced social integration, while utilising the possibilities that virtual learning environments and immersive technology provides. Delgado Kloos et al. (2014) classified this shift to multi-dimensional learning environments in three categories:

- A physical-digital dimension, where students and teachers share a common environment; physical, virtual or mixed.
- A local-global dimension, where students can be in the same physical location or distributed around the world.
- A formal-informal dimension, which allows learning to be managed along a range of possibilities from formal (with defined outcomes, e.g., lectures, laboratory sessions) or informal (where outcomes are undefined, e.g., makerspace and museum activities).

Consequently, designing and implementing effective multi-dimensional learning environments represents a big challenge to educators, considering the mix of pedagogical approaches with technological innovations. A diversity of resources could be available for the creation of innovative learning environments to enhance the learning process; however, this process cannot be completed without establishing learning goals based on correct designs to ensure that the activities are properly structured with clear learning objectives, regardless of the pedagogical methods utilised. To achieve this, it is important to consider two main elements (Figure 9):

1. Infrastructure of the learning environment, which can help to create the sense of presence; and is related to how to use technological innovation to implement a valuable learning environment which supports the pre-designed learning activities; and
2. The type of activities that can be performed within the learning environment, and involves the pedagogical design of the learning activity towards achieving the desired learning outcomes.

The combination of both can lead to different degrees of immersion; achieving spatial immersion via the technology; and strategic (cognitive) (Adams, 2004; Bjork & Holopainen, 2005), narrative (emotional) (Adams, 2004; Bjork & Holopainen, 2005) and actional immersion (Dede, 1995) through the learning activities. As a side note, Fowler (2015) warns about the use of term immersion in pedagogy, as it risks being confused with the meanings being used in technology and psychology. Pedagogical immersion can identify and empathise with the concept-to-be-learnt, which is critical to understanding it. Thus, the ability to make the "concept-to-be-learnt" more concrete is a key component to task immersion.

One of the main challenges for Mixed Reality Learning Environments concerns to finding ways to appropriately measure learning outcomes. As pointed out by Gardner and Elliott (2014), learning within the technology creates a pedagogical shift that requires teachers to think about measuring outcomes in non-traditional ways. Thus, it is necessary to evaluate students' learning gains and propose adequate (and, perhaps, new) mechanisms for assessment; rethinking how to measure and demonstrate subject mastery and acquisition of soft skills such as creativity and collaboration. Therefore, the design of the learning environment takes particular relevance in relation to the expected outcomes. Stiles (2000) identified some of the issues when designing technology-based learning solutions:

- Failure to engage the learner.
- Mistaking "interactivity" for engagement.
- Focussing on content rather than outcomes.

Figure 9. Mixed reality learning environments framework (Pena-Rios, 2016)

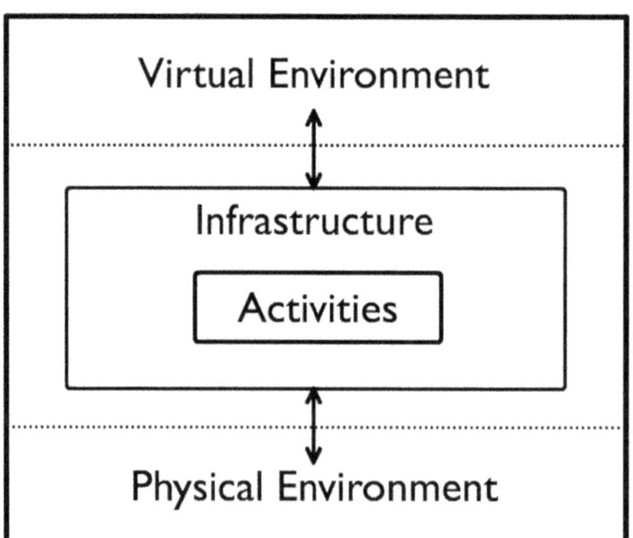

- Mirroring traditional didactic (educational) approaches on the technology.
- Failure to recognise the social nature of learning, generating a genuine sense of isolation, which leads to less effective learning.

In particular, the challenge of recognising the social nature of learning is something that needs to be seriously considered when creating solutions for people in geographically dispersed locations. Currently, most of the approaches focus on emulating the classroom, which introduces the challenge of how to maintain the social collaboration between peers (fellow learners). This is important because collaboration is a key aspect of learning since it can promote creativity, critical thinking and dialogue to assist with deeper levels of knowledge generation; promoting initiative and, when conducted internationally, addressing issues of culture (Vallance, 2009). Dede (2004) points the need to create learning environments based on "*mediated immersion*" and "*distributed-learning communities*", with "*knowledge distributed across a community and a context, as well as within an individual, able to provide a balance among experiential learning, guided mentoring and collective reflection*" (p. 1). He adds that MUVEs and real-world settings augmented with virtual information can provide the capability to create "*problem-solving communities in which participants can gain knowledge and skills through interacting with other participants who have varied levels of skills, enabling legitimate peripheral participation driven by intrinsic sociocultural forces*" (Dede, 2004, p. 13). Mixed reality learning environments aim to build up the invisible bridge between contents and users by situating the learner in highly-interactive environments where they can interrelate with the environment as well as with peers, concentrating on their assigned tasks without the necessity of being conscious of the user interface, as illustrated with the examples in the previous section.

A DISTRIBUTED MIXED REALITY FRAMEWORK FOR DISTANCE LEARNERS

As discussed previously, the effectiveness of the learning environment depends largely on the correct design of the learning activity. To date, the lack of support for hands-on collaborative immersive experiences has proven to be a serious shortcoming for distance learners, particularly in the domain of science and engineering where hands-on activities are of fundamental importance (Clough, 2002; Gomes & Bogosyan, 2009; Ma & Nickerson, 2006; Magin & Reizes, 1990; Nersessian, 1989), and a significant challenge to online education researchers. Hands-on activities allow learners to correlate concepts with authentic tasks; and when performed in meaningful realistic settings, they help in developing problem-solving skills.

Current approaches to hands-on activities for distance learners are commonly limited to: a) watching online videos of experiments, b) remote off-site experiments that can be triggered using software interfaces, and c) three-dimensional (3D) simulations. Whilst physical and virtual laboratories try to achieve similar objectives, such as exploring the nature of science, developing team work abilities, cultivating interest in science, promoting conceptual understanding, and developing inquiry skills (Bonde et al., 2014), they have different affordances (de Jong, Linn, & Zacharia, 2013) which has consequences for learning. In contrast to virtual laboratories, physical laboratories provide students with the possibility of working directly with physical equipment, which emphasize design and problem-solving skills, dealing with unanticipated events, such as measurement errors (de Jong et al., 2013). Additionally, they offer the possibility to engage in teamwork and collaboration with peers and colleagues. On the other hand, virtual experiments offer cost-effective alternatives to physical laboratories giving students the opportunity to use experimental systems that are beyond their reach. Additionally, they can simplify learning by highlighting specific information and removing confusing details (Trundle & Bell, 2010), such as irregularities in the equipment or unanticipated consequences; or modifying model characteristics, such as the time scale, making the interpretation of certain phenomena easier (de Jong et al., 2013). While the lower cost and increased convenience has some superficial appeal, it also presents educational disadvantages, including: a) the lack of interaction with real equipment, thus the activity is commonly performed with idealized data and restricted options (Ma & Nickerson, 2006); b) limited learning scenarios, thus changing the learning goals sometimes requires a restructuring of the whole implementation (Ma & Nickerson, 2006); c) a difficulty in carrying out collaborative work with other learners which leads to reduced user engagement (Nedic, Machotka, & Nafalski, 2003).

Although many comparison studies report no differences between physical and virtual laboratories (de Jong et al., 2013; Klahr, Triona, & Williams, 2007; Triona & Klahr, 2003; Wiesner & Lan, 2004); due to its nature, simulated and remote labs are more focused in supporting the acquisition of conceptual knowledge whereas physical laboratories have advantages in allowing students acquire some practical skills such as problem-solving thinking and teamwork (de Jong et al., 2013; Ma & Nickerson, 2006).

The use of immersive technologies in laboratory activities has the potential to overcome some of the reported issues of engineering fidelity, psychological fidelity and collaboration. In this regard, MRLEs can provide support for collaborative hands-on activities which are common in university science and engineering laboratories. A possible scenario for distance learners which would allow them collaborative hands-on activities, could be a mixed reality laboratory which blends physical laboratory apparatus with virtual representations by using computer networks as the glue to join together both soft and hard components that students use collaboratively to construct working computer systems. Our original vision was drawn from a somewhat futuristic scenario for an "education pod" that incorporated advanced mixed reality with AI (Callaghan 2010). Our work built on that vision, differs from others in that it is neither remote control nor simulation, but, rather, building composite systems comprising components that reside in distributed locations (with the students that built them). This is an extension of the commonly used approach to building computers by plugging components together where the connecting bus becomes the Internet, rather than a local backplane. In this model, processes (software) and processors (hardware) are the core components connected by the system. In that sense, it fit the Internet-of-Things model perfectly. Figure 10 illustrates this possibility for connecting multiple separated components, linking them to a common system by interconnecting and synchronising their elements, creating the illusion of one common extended system. This notion of sharing extends up the model into the user space. Synchronisation between physical objects and virtual objects creates mirrored objects (also known as *digital twins*) that exist in both worlds simultaneously. While all hardware objects have software twins, software objects do not necessarily need twins (twinning is primarily a mechanism to synchronise virtual and physical versions of the same component). Real-time synchronisation that allows an object's existence in both worlds is defined as a dual reality (or cross-reality) state. The three components of the proposed environment are:

1. The *physical world*, where the user and the physical objects are situated;
2. The *virtual world*, where the physical-world data will be reflected using 3D virtual objects, allowing multiple users/environments to be interconnected;

Figure 10. Distributed mixed reality environment interactions (Pena-Rios, 2016)

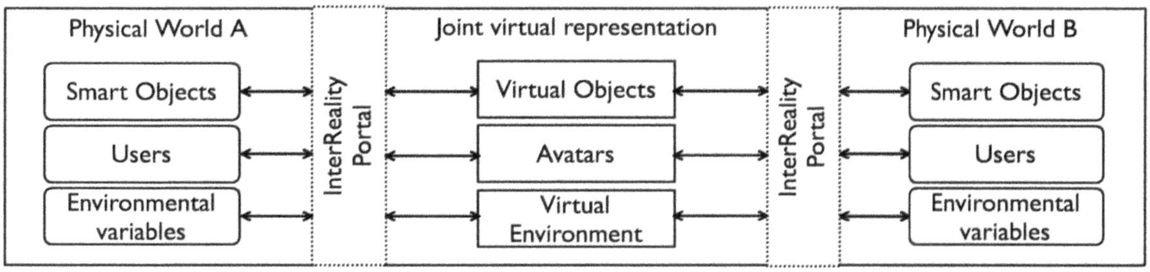

3. The *inter-reality portal*, a human-computer interface (HCI) which receives and processes in real-time data generated by the physical environment, so it can be mirrored by its virtual counterpart. The fundamental task of the inter-reality portal is to detect changes in one environment and translate them into appropriate actions within the other environment.

Based on the conceptual model in Figure 10, the authors proposed a framework for interconnecting multiple distant learning environments, allowing bidirectional communication between environments, smart objects and users using a synchronising mechanism to mix distributed physical and virtual devices (Pena-Rios, Callaghan, Gardner, & Alhaddad, 2014). By way of an illustration of the different combinations that can be used to create a *digital twin*, we can imagine that two users (A and B) are collaborating in the creation of a clock alarm. User A has the speakers which play the alarm sound and user B has the "snooze" button and the LCD that shows the time. All the objects have a mirrored virtual representation within the virtual world; therefore, all of them are *digital twins*. However, when combined, they create a mixed reality clock alarm that reproduces the sound in space A and can be stopped with the button in space B. The final mashup can be seen in the virtual world and users can interact with it from there. For example, user A which only has the speakers could press the virtual "snooze" button with the same effect as if he/she had pressed the physical one. In addition to the communication between pieces (i.e., speakers, LCD, a button), a program needs to be included in the final mashup to add the desired functionality (e.g., stop the sound when pressing the "snooze" button). This program is considered as an additional virtual component (with no physical representation) which allows the combination of available functions for each *digital twin* (i.e. speakers sound, detection of a button press). Thus, in addition to the combination between mirrored physical/virtual elements, the mashup can include a combination of soft and hard components that allows it to achieve a desired behaviour.

Figure 11 shows the conceptual model of a complete inter-reality system composed of an inter-reality portal and one *digital twin*. The diagram illustrates a one-to-one relationship between one physical object and one virtual object in a local mixed reality space (*digital twin*); however, when connecting a second inter-reality system in a remote mixed reality space, it is necessary to synchronise multiple *digital twins*, and thus managing multiple dual reality states. The goal of this interconnected learning environment is to enable hands-on activities for distance learners based in a collaborative group-based learning session.

Within the framework, the Context-awareness agent (CAag) periodically requests information from the physical object to identify any change on the object. When a change is detected the information is sent to the Mixed reality agent (MRag) which translates this as an action in the virtual object. When this process is replicated on a second inter-reality system, the Dual reality agent (DRag) coordinates the

Figure 11. Distributed mixed reality framework (Pena-Rios, 2016)

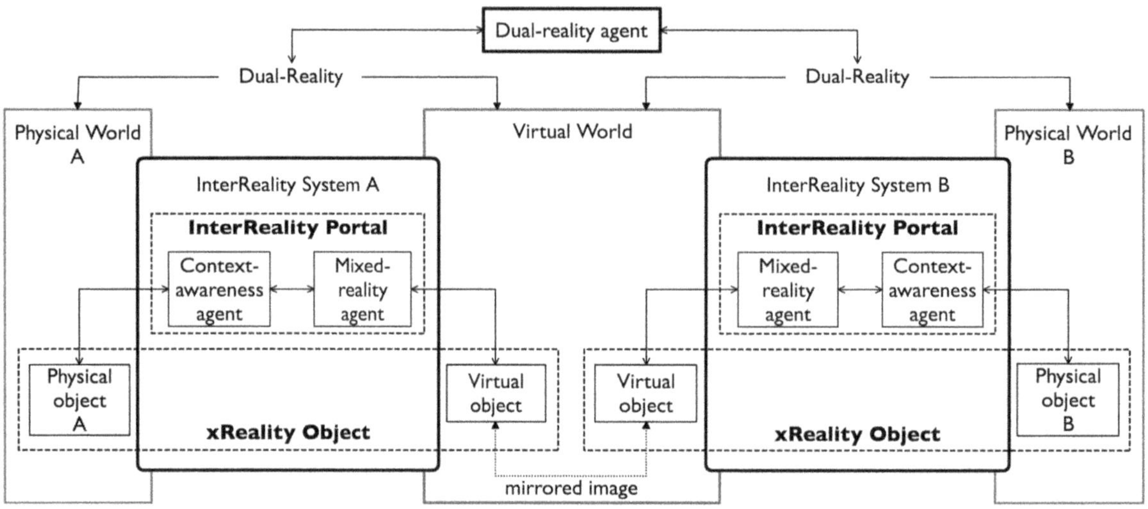

synchronisation between multiple environments following these predefined rules (Pena-Rios, Callaghan, Gardner, & Alhaddad, 2012):

1. A change in a virtual object of a given inter-reality system results in identical changes to all mirrored virtual objects in any subscribing inter-reality portal.
2. A change in a physical object of a given inter-reality system results in changes to the virtual representation of the physical device in all subscribing inter-reality portals; and in changes to the physical objects linked to those virtual representations.

Therefore, a change in a physical object "A" is reflected first in its linked virtual representation within the local inter-reality system; and then sent via the Dual reality agent to any remote inter-reality system connected at that time. The remote inter-reality system first reflects the change in the virtual representation, and then changes the status in the physical object "B". When this mechanism is replicated using multiple *digital twins* in each physical space, it is possible to mirror distant physical spaces and thus joining multiple distant environments based on a distributed mixed reality architecture.

The proposed framework allows different mashups between local *digital twins* and distant *digital twins*. Scenario S1 in Figure 12 shows a single xReality object owned by one user in a local environment. This represents the ideal single dual reality relationship that has been described in previous sections, which is formed by the synchronisation between one physical object (situated in the local environment) and one virtual object (described as a one-to-one relationship). When an additional user joins, he/she can interact with the remote physical object via the shared virtual representation (scenario S2); or via a local physical object linked to the same virtual representation (scenario S3), creating a many-to-one relationship (many physical objects connected to one virtual representation). The relationship between physical and virtual objects described in scenario S3 represents an extended mixed reality environment, in which an element is reflected in the virtual environment and linked using its virtual entity to another object in a remote space, showing a continuous shared element within spaces (physical-virtual-physical) with multiple dual reality states.

Figure 12. Interactions between digital twins (Pena-Rios, Callaghan, Gardner, & Alhaddad, 2015)

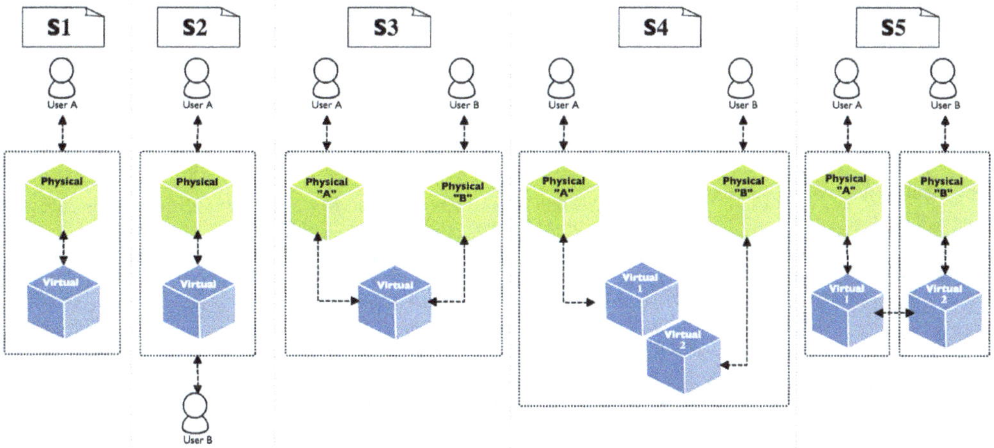

Single dual-reality state (ideal)	Single dual-reality state (shared)	Multiple dual-reality states (ideal)	Multiple dual-reality states (complementary)	Multiple dual-reality states (duplicated)
one-to-one (1:1)	one-to-one (1:1)	many-to-one (n:1)	many-to-many (n:n)	one-to-one (1:1)

The scenarios described so far use only one physical object in the local environment or one in both, the local and the remote space; however, when adding more physical objects to each environment it is possible to create mashups between multiple *digital twins*. Scenario S4 describes a collaborative session where users combine *digital twins* that physically exist in the owner's local environment, but can be shared and combined using its virtual representation in the virtual world, creating a complete new object in the virtual. As an analogy, this can be seen as a puzzle where each of the participants has one or more pieces that allow the completion of the final object inside the virtual world. Finally, scenario S5 shows the possibility of having two or more *digital twins* that do not complement to each other, but instead, both exist as separate entities inside the common virtual space.

In addition to the challenges previously described, the proposed distributed mixed reality framework presents the challenge of bridging the model of distributed *digital twins* to a pedagogical model of constructionist hands-on activities to produce a solution for distributed mixed reality laboratories. To solve this, we adopted deconstructionism as a key concept to unify a constructionist pedagogy, with a set of mirrored physical/virtual objects and their supporting soft components (e.g., programs, software processes, threads, apps), which can be constructed and deconstructed in different mashups to support hands-on activities. This is effective because a constructionist pedagogy regards learning is a consequence of the correlation between performing active tasks that construct meaningful tangible objects in the physical world and relating them to personal experiences and ideas. Table 1 summarises the affordances of the proposed distributed mixed reality framework. The aim of such framework is to support collaborative hands-on activities within distance learners based on a MRLE formed by multiple interconnected multidimensional spaces.

Table 1. Distributed mixed reality framework affordances (Pena-Rios, Callaghan, Gardner, & Alhaddad, 2014)

Affordances	Description
Simulation of physical objects	Enable the use of virtual objects.
Emulation using a mixture of physical and virtual mirrored objects (*digital twins*)	Instantiation of diverse scenarios of single and multiple dual reality states.
Creation of physical-virtual mashups using a deconstructionist model	Creation of mashups using services available in static and nomadic smart objects.
Collaborative sessions between 2 or more users	Support the use and sharing of *digital twins* within an environment, regardless its physical location.

Case Study: The Blended Reality Lab (BReal Lab)

The Blended Reality Lab (BReal Lab) (Pena-Rios, Callaghan, Gardner, & Alhaddad, 2014) (Figure 13) was built as a proof-of-concept implementation of the Distributed Mixed Reality Framework described earlier. It uses a mix of mirrored physical and virtual objects as a means of creating a platform to allow geographically dispersed team members to work together on collaborative hands-on activities.

As such, it comprises the mechanisms needed to allow users to interact with physical and virtual worlds. It is formed by:

Figure 13. The Blended Reality Lab (BReal Lab)

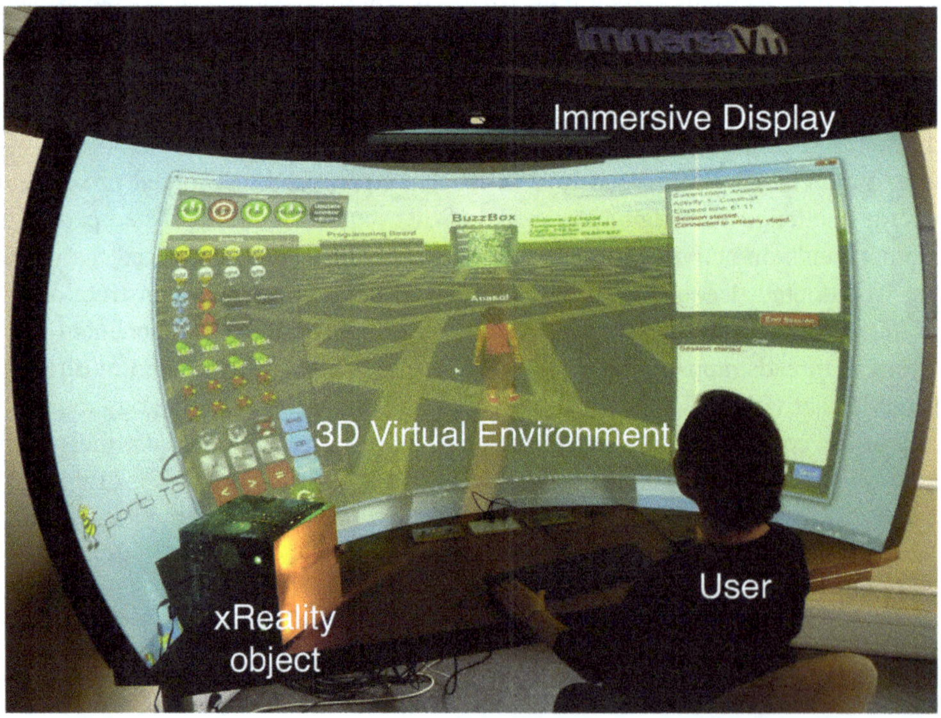

1. The *InterReality Portal*, a visual interface that allows the connection between physical and virtual worlds, creating the blended reality space that hosts the learning activities (Pena-Rios, Callaghan, Gardner, & Alhaddad, 2014). The interface is formed by components in both the physical and the virtual world aiming to achieve enough psychological immersion to maintain engagement with the tasks.
2. *Cross-Reality (xReality) objects***,** which are networked smart objects able to maintain a virtual representation of themselves in real time (Pena-Rios et al., 2014); and can be considered as the implementation of the *digital twins* concept.

To facilitate experimental evaluation, a collaborative learning activity in which students could create simple IF-THEN-ELSE behavioural rules to control a xReality object was designed. Based on this, a hypothetical scenario was established as follows:

- First, by giving the participants an environment that consisted of a simulated (virtual) (and for some, emulated (mixed reality)) domestic room (a bedroom) (Figure 14) and asking the question: *"If you lived in an intelligent house, how would you program your house to wake you up in the mornings?"*.
- Second, by providing them with a special end-user programming tool, designed to follow the principles of programming via analogy (i.e., using graphical icons or physical representations), whereby participants could create these behavioural rules via a "Programming Board" inside the InterReality Portal (Figure 16).

The objective of the learning activity was to illustrate concepts of ambient intelligence (AmI) using a co-creative approach to encourage students to create as many behavioural rules as possible based on the hypothetical situation using basic programming logic principles. Ambient intelligence (AmI) is defined as a discipline that incorporates artificial intelligence to everyday environments making them sensitive and responsive to the presence of people (Cook et al., 2009). The learning activity was inspired by earlier pioneering work on the embedded-internet (the forerunner of the Internet-of-Things) (Chin & Callaghan, 2003) and internet-of-things appliances (Scott & Chin, 2013). Figure 14 describes the learning activity in the context of IMS Learning Design Specification.

Physical implementation of the xReality objects was done using a Raspberry Pi (RPi) and Fortito's BuzzBoard Educational Toolkit range, a set of diverse pluggable network-aware hardware boards which can be interconnected allowing rapid prototyping of Internet-of-Things (IoT) applications by pugging together combinations of modules (Callaghan, 2012; Wang, Callaghan, Lear, & Colley, 2011). In particular, two assemblies of BuzzBoard components were utilised, a wheeled desktop robot (the BuzzBot) and a desktop smart-room (the BuzzBox). Fortito's BuzzBox, is a desktop-size emulation of a smart-room formed by six 25x25cm (10×10 inches) panels with embedded actuators (a variable speed ventilator fan, a controllable heater, 4 dimmable 'warm white' LED lights, 8 push buttons, 8 tricolour LED's) and two pluggable interchangeable sensors (temperature and light). Audio functionality was added using RPi's embedded audio hardware and a pair of speakers. Additionally, a virtual proximity sensor was available in the 3D interface. This virtual sensor measured the distance between the avatar and the virtual box, and it was available for every participant regardless if they had the physical object. Virtual components were implemented using a bespoke MUVE that acted as the link between a) physical and virtual worlds, and b) local and remote environments. It was developed using Unity3D, a cross-platform game engine for

Figure 14. Description of the learning activity (IMS Unit of Learning)

Mixed-reality Learning Activity

LEARNING OBJECTIVES

a) Understand the concept of Ambient Intelligence.
b) Create functional rules for a smart house.
c) Teamwork in distance learning.

CONDITIONS

- Access to Internet.
- Access to a PC with the client software installed.
- Watch the introductory video.

1:1

1:1

ACTIVITIES

1) Familiarize with the mixed-reality environment.
2) Understand the activity and the hypothetical situation.
3) Agree with other team members on the rules to be programmed.
4) Create rules in collaboration with other team members.
5) Execute the rules.

creating interactive 3D content. It contained a virtual representation of all the elements of the physical learning environment; namely, representations of the user (personified in an avatar), virtual counterparts of xReality objects and a virtual representation of the environment itself (Figure 15).

Functionality of the xReality object was depicted as a list of available services for the BuzzBoards, using their different actuators and sensor capabilities (e.g., lights on and off, fan on and off, alarm sound on and off, etc.) on the left menu of the GUI main screen (Figure 15). By combining different modularised components in a xReality object, several functionalities (services) become available on the menu. These services represent atomic functions which can be combined into a nuclear function (program) to allow bi-directional communication between both worlds. When two BuzzBoxes were used together, the InterReality Portal detected both and linked them to the same virtual representation of the BuzzBox, creating a physical-virtual-physical connection between the two objects. Thus, when an actuator was triggered (e.g., a light), the action was replicated: first, in the BuzzBox in environment A; then, in the virtual BuzzBox shared for all the participants in the session; and finally in the environment B. In the case of the sensors, if a participant had a sensor plugged to the BuzzBox, it was shared across environments. However, if another participant had the same sensor connected, then the InterReality portal uses the one belonging to the participant who had joined the session first. Additionally, as mentioned before, the tool includes a series of conditional instructions (IF, THEN, ELSE), logical operators (AND, OR), and mathematical operators (GREATER THAN, LESS THAN, EQUAL THAN) which can be added to create a program. As an example, Figure 16 illustrates an IF-THEN-ELSE behavioural rule written in the "*Programming Board*", which was designed on the principles of programming via analogy (i.e. using graphical icons or physical representations).

Figure 15. xReality Objects Implementation Examples. Desktop robot (top) and domestic room (bottom)

Figure 16. BReal lab programming tool

Graphical rule construction

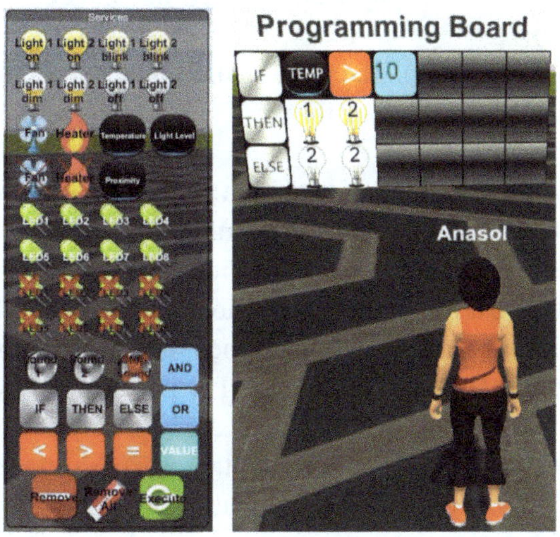

Rule interpretation

```
IF TEMPERATURE is greater THAN 10
THEN turn LIGHT_1 AND LIGHT_2 on
ELSE turn LIGHT_1 AND LIGHT_2 off
```

In a similar fashion to the relationship between services (atomic functions) and programs (nuclear functions), the physical modules (i.e., the sets of autonomous networked resources) represent atomic functions on the physical world, as they can be (re)constructed into different combinations creating new physical mashups (nuclear functions). It is the combination of differing hardware and software components (programs) that creates a complete functional xReality object.

Evaluation Findings

The BReal Lab was tested with 52 undergraduate and postgraduate students from eight different universities in six countries, namely China, Malaysia, Mexico, UAE, USA and UK between March and May 2015 (Pena-Rios, 2016), ranging from 19 to 55 years old, with a mean value of 30 years old in both genders (mode = 28) (Figure 17a). In terms of cultural background, participants identified themselves as nationals of 14 different countries, where 69.23% had a good level of English understanding, ranging from native to professional working proficiency, and 30.77% had limited or elementary proficiency. The level of studies that participants were doing at the time of the experiment varied, with 23.08% pursuing a PhD, 50.0% studying for a postgraduate degree and 26.92% doing an undergraduate course (Figure 17b). Their courses ranged from Computer Science (61.54%), and related subjects such as Electronic and Electrical Engineering (3.85%) and Computer Engineering (3.85%) to Learning Design and Technology (21.15%) and a broader range of topics (9.61%) (e.g., Economics, Linguistics, Politics, Graphic Design). Each session lasted 30 minutes and the activity was designed to have each student seated in front of one computer connected to the InterReality Portal MUVE. Thus, each one of the students needed to work with their own equipment. As not all the students were in possession of the physical bits of the xReality object implementation (i.e., Raspberry Pi and BuzzBoards), they worked with three types of sensors/actuators:

1. *Virtual Sensors/Actuators* which does not exist in the physical world but can be used to form the rules (e.g. virtual proximity sensor, when an avatar moves close to a virtual representation of the xReality object);
2. *Remote Shared Sensors/Actuators* are tangible sensors physically located in a remote environment, but can be used to form the rules (e.g. a temperature sensor physically located in China can be shared and used for all the members of the session);
3. *Local Sensors/Actuators* are those physical sensors available in the local environment and shared with other participants. Their values were updated in real-time for all the participants in the session.

The motivation underpinning the BReal Lab was to offer a collaborative platform where multiple remote students could interact with objects and each other in a similar way to traditional team-work spaces. To analyse this, we used two sources: a) 4-point Likert questionnaires answered by users after the trials, and b) data taken from the proof-of-concept BReal Lab demonstrator log. Results from the collaboration and user studies, suggested a high degree of participants' engagement and satisfaction, indicating a positive acceptance of the mixed reality extended synchronised space. Participants reported preference towards the use of physical/virtual mirrored objects (xReality) over simulated (virtual) objects in hands-on activities, which suggested that the *digital twin* concept underlying the proposed models delivered a good experience. For example, 83.33% indicated that having a physical component made a difference for them when performing the activity; and 75% reported that they concentrated their attention more in the physical component of the xReality object (i.e., BuzzBox or BuzzBot) rather than on the

Figure 17. Participants' demographics (Pena-Rios, 2016). (a) Age distribution. (b) English level and Country of Origin.

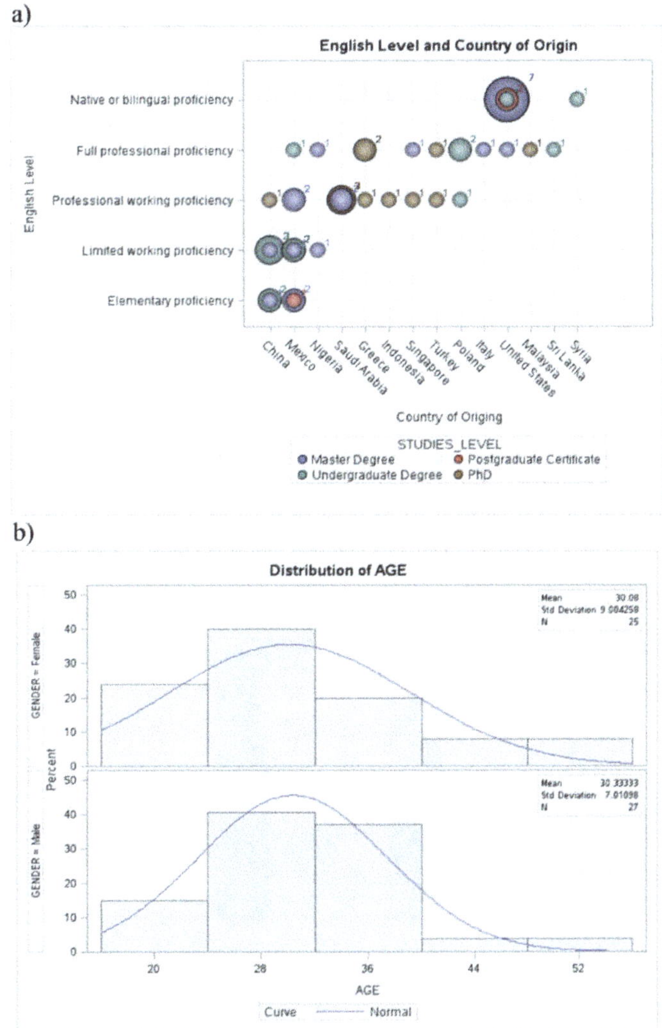

virtual component. Moreover, 80.77% of the participants and instructors stated they would use similar technology in their courses if it were available (median = 1, "Very likely"); recognising the added-value physical/virtual mirrored objects brought to hands-on learning activities for online learning (Pena-Rios, Callaghan, Gardner, & Alhaddad, 2015).

Regarding collaboration, 78.26% (median = 1, "Very good") responded that their experience of collaborating with students in other locations was good (Figure 18a), however, collaboration in general was challenging, as the tools for interaction were limited to: a) a chat window in the user interface, b) avatar representation of participants, c) the "programming board", and d) the xReality object (Buzz-Box). Additionally, a number of factors influenced the results of this evaluation, for example, sessions were organised from a minimum of two students up to a maximum of twenty-one students, working in geographically separated locations, and who did not know each other on beforehand. This created a mix of participants with different sociocultural backgrounds, and with different personal preferences, which were reflected in their feedback; which included GUI design issues related to the responsiveness and location to the chat window; the social anxiety that comes from collaborative activities for introverted students; and a general preference of spoken over written communication. In this regard, results from the chat analysis revealed the high use of emoticons to transmit emotions over the use of written positive feedback (Emoticons 5.85% versus "Expressing Positive Feedback" 1.01%). Emoticons are symbols representing facial expressions, used to express non-verbal cues in written communication (Walther and D'Addario, 2001). These results supported user's feedback stating that the use of written text for communication was not enough for the interaction needed. An interesting aspect to notice is that the dynamics between participants never included negative feedback. Available data is not enough to determine why there was an absence of negative feedback, as this could have been related to the controlled conditions of the experiment, where participants knew the feedback was being recorded.

Figure 18. Analysis of Collaboration (Pena-Rios, 2016). (a) Collaboration analysis. (b) Level of interaction

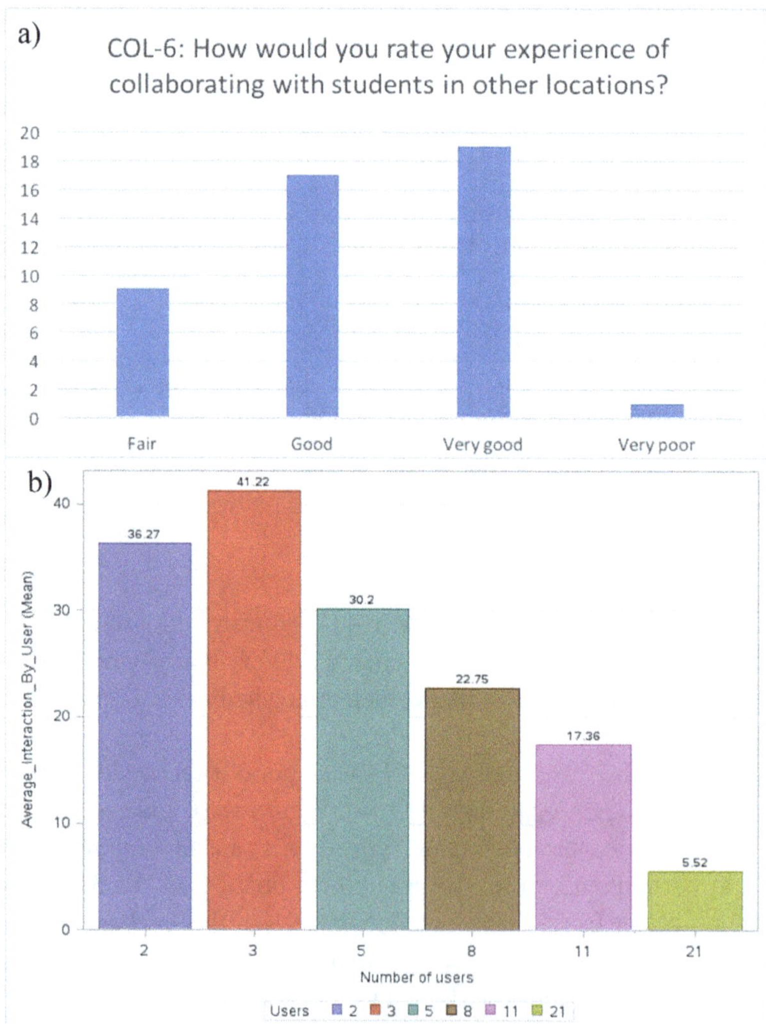

Nonetheless, participants' views about the BReal Lab demonstrator's capacity to allow remote participants working together was considered useful by 69.57% of participants, and the possibility of working with other students located in different parts of the world was regarded as attractive by users, and it was mentioned as one of the reasons for using the proposed technology. Moreover, team dynamics, in larger multicultural groups without an established leader (a role that is usually embodied in teachers and instructors), were revealed in some users participating as spectators only, with more confident participants leading the decisions over the activity. To calculate the amount of participation, the number of interactions were analysed, based on the number of participants that collaborated in a session. Results from the number of interactions made by each participant showed that the highest level of interaction occurred in sessions with 3 participants (Figure 18b), suggesting that BReal Lab sessions with up to 3 participants would lead to more equitable participation and involvement of the users, supporting literature findings suggesting that the smaller the group, the more likely each member participates, regardless if it is a face-to-face or online group (Hare, 1981; Chidambaram & Tung, 2005; Piezon and Donaldson, 2005). This was a reminder that communication and collaboration in distance environments can be more difficult than face-to-face interaction, as social aspects inherent to human behaviour are constantly present, regardless the technology used, thus, it is necessary to design user interfaces that respect these natural characteristics.

FUTURE RESEARCH DIRECTIONS

Our ongoing research is directed to the challenge of measuring individual and group learning outcomes. This involves many challenges, such as observing users' behaviour dynamically and collecting evidence of learning; particularly those related to soft skills, such as communication and negotiation, which are difficult to automatically detect and assess even in standard classroom-based situations. Moreover, the ability to identify individual learners' contributions to a group activity in real-time represents a big challenge, particularly if several learners are contributing at the same time.

To do so, we are working towards a novel computational framework that is able to correlate observations of students in physical settings with those in virtual worlds. The work is focusing on methods that identify and classify learning evidence relating to group working rather than mapping all these elements to specific learning outcomes. More specifically, we have devised a model we refer to as "The Observation Lens" (Felemban et al., 2016) (Figure 19) which proposes different levels of granularity for observing students and recording evidence of collaborative learning, that varies according to the level of observation. At its lowest level, "Events Detection", it simulates an instructor who is watching a collaborative activity from a general viewpoint without looking deeply into the content of what is happening. At the next level up, "The Learning Interactions level", it seeks to capture social and environmental interactions. Above this, "The Students' Success" level, captures actions taken by teachers observing students' success, such as counting the number of correct answers (correct answers reinforce events, or the opposite for delays on incorrect answers). The fourth and final level is "The Performance Outcomes", which relates to the skills and knowledge the students have acquired from the learning activities.

Figure 19. Observation Lens model (Felemban et al., 2016)

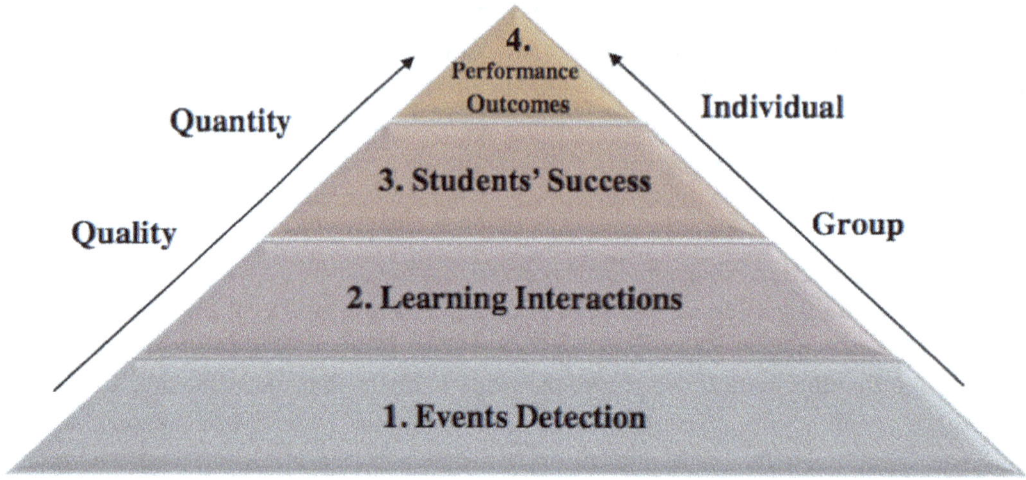

To achieve this, the BReal Lab has been extended to use an agent-based approach to record and label learning evidence from the mixed reality activities, thereby simulating the observations normally made by a teacher. To achieve this, we use software agents to track learners progress, collecting actions such as clicks, together with the use of natural agents (students) to perform peer evaluations on each other to assess the quality of the learning performance. This is part of an ongoing research that is somewhat outside the focus of this chapter, but more detail is provided in other publications by Felemban et al. (2016).

CONCLUSION

This chapter has provided an overview of applications of MUVEs in education. In particular, it has explained that while advances in technology have resulted in a significant increase in learners taking online courses, there remain significant technological impediments to the wider uptake of such approaches in STEM education, principally the lack of support for hands on collaborative engineering lab work. The chapter has explained how MRLEs offer a solution to this problem and the authors presented examples of different Multi-User Mixed Reality Learning Environments and supporting pedagogies, with the goal of illustrating the possibilities that these environments represent. Additionally, this chapter described a distributed mixed reality framework and its implementation, called the BReal Lab, which enabled dispersed online learners to collaborate online in computer engineering lab activities. We also reported on a case study involving an evaluation of over 50 students in six countries. The study showed that this approach provided a workable solution to the problem of providing computer engineering students with hands on laboratory activities, recording acceptable levels of student progress and satisfaction. While our expectation was that students would always prefer to learn in a traditional physical environment, it was pleasing to find that mixed reality settings increased the student's engagement and motivation. In addition to improving student engagement, a key benefit of the collaborative activities was the opportunity to expose students to people from different socio-cultural backgrounds, working together in group activities, based on the perspective that learning is an active (and inherently social) process. Current pedagogical trends are focusing on the creation of richer and more hands-on, real-world learning experiences; yet, institutions, researchers and practitioners continue to be challenged regarding how to generate and use these in spaces alongside traditional approaches. The challenges for multi-user mixed reality learning environments can be summarised as being a) the design and creation of functional learning environments, redesigning learning spaces to resemble real-life situations to foster skills such as collaboration and innovation in active learning situations; b) adaptation of pedagogical methods, rethinking the roles of educators and c) measuring outcomes in non-traditional ways, in situations where learners, instead of being mere participants and consumers of knowledge, they learn by experiencing, doing, and creating, demonstrating newly acquired skills in more concrete and creative ways.

Finally, while much research remains to be done before MRLEs can be deployed commercially; we hope that this chapter will be a catalyst for encouraging more research into what we believe is an area with good potential to improve online education.

ACKNOWLEDGMENT

We are grateful to Samah Felemban for the description of the Observation Lens.

REFERENCES

Adams, E. (2004). *Postmodernism and the three types of immersion*. Retrieved from https://www.gamasutra.com/view/feature/130531/the_designers_notebook_.php

Alrashidi, M., Alzahrani, A., Gardner, M., & Callaghan, V. (2016). A pedagogical virtual machine for assembling mobile robot using augmented reality. In *Proceedings of the 7th Augmented Human International Conference 2016*. Geneva, Switzerland: ACM. doi:10.1145/2875194.2875229

Alzahrani, A., Gardner, M., Callaghan, V., & Alrashidi, M. (2015). Towards measuring learning effectiveness considering presence, engagement and immersion in a mixed and augmented reality learning environment. *Immersive Learning Research Network Conference (iLRN 2015)*, 252–264. doi:10.3233/978-1-61499-530-2-252

Birchfield, D., & Johnson-Glenberg, M. (2010). A next gen interface for embodied learning. *International Journal of Gaming and Computer-Mediated Simulations*, *2*(1), 49–58. doi:10.4018/jgcms.2010010105

Bjork, S., & Holopainen, J. (2005). *Patterns in game design*. Charles River Media.

Bonde, M. T., Makransky, G., Wandall, J., Larsen, M. V., Morsing, M., Jarmer, H., & Sommer, M. O. A. (2014). Improving biotech education through gamified laboratory simulations. *Nature Biotechnology*, *32*(7), 694–708. doi:10.1038/nbt.2955 PMID:25004234

Callaghan, V. (2010). *Tales from a Pod*. Paper presented at Creative Science 2010 (CS'10), Kuala Lumpur, Malaysia.

Callaghan, V. (2012). *Buzz-Boarding; practical support for teaching computing based on the internet-of-things*. Retrieved from http://orbit.dtu.dk/files/105633882/Improving_biotech_education.pdf

Callaghan, V., Gardner, M., Horan, B., Scott, J., Shen, L., & Wang, M. (2008). A mixed reality teaching and learning environment. *Hybrid Learning and Education*, 54–65. doi: 10.1007/978-3-540-85170-7_5

Chalabi, M. (2014). *Distance learning: Who's doing it now?* Retrieved from http://www.theguardian.com/education/datablog/2014/jan/30/distance-learning-higher-education-moocs

Chidambaram, L., & Tung, L. L. (2005). Is out of sight, out of mind? An empirical study of social loafing in technology-supported groups. *Information Systems Research, 16*(2), 149–168. doi:10.1287/isre.1050.0051

Chin, J., & Callaghan, V. (2003). *Embedded-internet devices: A means of realizing the pervasive computing vision.* Paper presented at IADIS International Conference, Algarve, Portugal.

Clough, M. P. (2002). Using the laboratory to enhance student learning. *Learning Science and the Science of Learning*, 85–94.

Cook, D. J., Augusto, J. C., & Jakkula, V. R. (2009). Ambient intelligence: Technologies, applications, and opportunities. *Pervasive and Mobile Computing*, *5*(4), 277–298. doi:10.1016/j.pmcj.2009.04.001

Dede, C. (1995). The evolution of constructivist learning environments: Immersion in distributed, virtual worlds. *Educational Technology*, *35*(5), 46–52.

Dede, C. (2004). Planning for 'neomillennial' learning styles: Implications for investments in technology and faculty. *Educating the Net Generation*, 226–247.

Dede, C., Clarke, J., Ketelhut, D. J., Nelson, B., & Bowman, C. (2005). *Students' motivation and learning of science in a multi-user virtual environment*. Paper presented at American Educational Research Association Conference, Montreal, Canada.

Delgado Kloos, C., Ibañez Espiga, M. B., Fernández Panadero, C., Muñoz Merino, P. J., Estévez Ayres, I., Crespo García, R. M., & Pérez Sanagustín, M. (2014). A multidimensional analysis of trends in educational technology. *Proceedings of the IEEE Frontier in Education Conference (FIE'14)*, 395–398. doi:10.1109/FIE.2014.7044053

Dieterle, E., & Clarke, J. (2006). Multi-user virtual environments for teaching and learning. Encyclopedia of Multimedia Technology and Networking, 1033–1041.

Dillenbourg, P., Järvelä, S., & Fischer, F. (2009). The evolution of research on computer-supported collaborative learning. In N. Balacheff, S. Ludvigsen, T. de Jong, A. Lazonder, & S. Barnes (Eds.), *Technology-enhanced learning: Principles and products* (pp. 3–19). Heidelberg, Germany: Springer. doi:10.1007/978-1-4020-9827-7_1

Felemban, S., Gardner, M., & Callaghan, V. (2016). *Virtual observation lenses for assessing online collaborative learning environment.* Paper presented at the Second Immersive Learning Research Network Conference (iLRN 2016), Santa Barbara, CA.

Fernández Panadero, C., De la Cruz Barquero, V., Delgado Kloos, C., & Moran Nuñez, D. (2014). PhyMEL-WS: Physically experiencing the virtual world. Insights into mixed reality and flow state on board a wheelchair simulator. *Journal of Universal Computer Science*, *20*(12), 1629–1648.

Fowler, C. (2015). Virtual reality and learning: Where is the pedagogy? *British Journal of Educational Technology*, *46*(2), 412–422. doi:10.1111/bjet.12135

Gardner, M., & Elliott, J. B. (2014). The immersive education laboratory: Understanding affordances, structuring experiences, and creating constructivist, collaborative processes, in mixed reality smart environments. *Transactions on Future Intelligent Educational Environments*, *1*(1), 1–13.

Gardner, M., & O'Driscoll, M. L. (2011). MiRTLE (Mixed reality teaching and learning environment): From prototype to production and implementation. In D. Hernandez-Leo, C. Delgado-Kloos, & J. I. Asencio-Pérez (Eds.), *Proceedings of the Across Physical and Virtual Spaces (AcrossSpaces) Workshop in conjunction with ECT-TEL 2011* (pp. 21–28). Palermo, Italy: Academic Press.

Garrison, D. R., & Kanuka, H. (2004). Blended learning: Uncovering its transformative potential in higher education. *The Internet and Higher Education*, *7*(2), 95–105. doi:10.1016/j.iheduc.2004.02.001

Gartner. (2015). *Gartner says 6.4 billion connected "things."* Retrieved from http://www.gartner.com/newsroom/id/3165317

Gershenfield, N., Krikorian, R., & Cohen, D. (2004). The internet of things. *Scientific American*, *291*(4), 76–81. doi:10.1038/scientificamerican1004-76 PMID:15487673

Gomes, L., & Bogosyan, S. (2009). Current trends in remote laboratories. *IEEE Transactions on Industrial Electronics*, *56*(12), 4744–4756. doi:10.1109/TIE.2009.2033293

Hanson, K., & Shelton, B. E. (2008). Design and development of virtual reality: Analysis of challenges faced by educators. *Journal of Educational Technology & Society*, *11*(1), 118–131.

Hare, A. P. (1981). Group size. *The American Behavioral Scientist*, *24*(5), 695–708. doi:10.1177/000276428102400507

Heim, M. (1998). *Virtual realism*. Oxford, UK: Oxford University Press.

Horan, B., Gardner, M., & Scott, J. (2009). *MiRTLE: A mixed reality teaching & learning environment*. Retrieved from https://www.researchgate.net/publication/234773595_MiRTLE_a_mixed_reality_teaching_learning_environment

Ibañez Espiga, M. B., Delgado Kloos, C., Leony, D., Garcia Rueda, J. J., & Maroto, D. (2011). Learning a foreign language in a mixed reality environment. *IEEE Internet Computing*, *15*(6), 44–47. doi:10.1109/MIC.2011.78

Ijsselsteijn, W. A. (2006). History of telepresence. *3D videocommunication: Algorithms, concepts and real-time systems in human centred communication*, 5–21. doi:10.1002/0470022736.ch1

Jang, S., Kim, S., & Woo, W. (2005). When VR meets ubicomp. *Virtual Reality (Waltham Cross)*, 1–2.

Jong, T., Linn, M. C., & Zacharia, Z. C. (2013). Physical and virtual laboratories in science and engineering education. *Science*, *340*(6130), 305–308. doi:10.1126/science.1230579 PMID:23599479

Kim, G. J. (2005). *Designing virtual reality systems: The structured approach*. Heidelberg, Germany: Springer.

Kirkley, S. E., & Kirkley, J. R. (2004). Creating next generation blended learning environments using mixed reality, video games and simulations. *TechTrends*, *49*(3), 42–53. doi:10.1007/BF02763646

Klahr, D., Triona, L. M., & Williams, C. (2007). Hands on what? The relative effectiveness of physical versus virtual materials in an engineering design project by middle school children. *Journal of Research in Science Teaching*, *44*(1), 183–203. doi:10.1002/tea.20152

Kolb, D. A. (1984). *Experiential learning: Experience as the source of learning and development*. Englewood Cliffs, NJ: Prentice Hall.

Kortuem, G., Kawsar, F., Fitton, D., & Sundramoorthy, V. (2010). Smart objects as building blocks for the Internet of things. *IEEE Internet Computing*, *14*(1), 44–51. doi:10.1109/MIC.2009.143

Lee, Y., Oh, S., Shin, C., & Woo, W. (2008). *Recent trends in ubiquitous virtual reality*. Paper presented at 2008 International Symposium on Ubiquitous Virtual Reality, Hainan Island, China. doi:10.1109/ISUVR.2008.27

Lifton, J. H. (2007). *Dual reality: An emerging medium*. Retrieved from https://dspace.mit.edu/handle/1721.1/41707

Lifton, J. H., & Paradiso, J. (2009). *Dual reality: Merging the real and virtual*. Paper presented at First International Conference on Facets of Virtual Environments (FaVE'09), Berlin, Germany.

Lindgren, R., & Moshell, J. M. (2011). Supporting children's learning with body-based metaphors in a mixed reality environment. In *Proceedings of the 10th International Conference on Interaction Design and Children* (pp. 177–180). ACM. doi:10.1145/1999030.1999055

Ma, J., & Nickerson, J. V. (2006). Hands-on, simulated, and remote laboratories. *ACM Computing Surveys*, *38*(3), 1–24. doi:10.1145/1132960.1132961

Magin, D. J., & Reizes, J. A. (1990). Computer simulation of laboratory experiments: An unrealized potential. *Computers & Education*, *14*(3), 263–270. doi:10.1016/0360-1315(90)90009-V

Mann, S. (2002). Mediated reality with implementations for everyday life. *Presence (Cambridge, Mass.)*, *11*(2), 158–175. doi:10.1162/1054746021470603

Milgram, P., & Kishino, F. (1994). A taxonomy of mixed reality visual displays. *IEICE Transactions on Information and Systems*, *E77–D*(12), 1321–1329.

Moore, P. (1995). Learning and teaching in virtual worlds: Implications of virtual reality for education. *Australian Journal of Educational Technology*, *11*(2), 91–102.

Nedic, Z., Machotka, J., & Nafalski, A. (2003). *Remote laboratories versus virtual and real laboratories*. Paper presented at the 33rd Annual Frontiers in Education, Westminster, CO. doi:10.1109/FIE.2003.1263343

Nersessian, N. J. (1989). Conceptual change in science and in science education. *Synthese*, *80*(1), 163–183. doi:10.1007/BF00869953

Nicholson, P. (2008). A history of e-learning: Echoes of the pioneers. In B. Fernandez Manjon (Ed.), *Computers and education: E-Learning, from Theory to practice* (pp. 1–11). Springer.

Oh, Y., & Woo, W. (2013). Ubiquitous virtual reality environments. In S. Price, C. Jewitt, & B. Brown (Eds.), *The SAGE handbook of digital technology research* (pp. 374–386). Thousand Oaks, CA: SAGE. doi:10.4135/9781446282229.n25

Pan, Z., Cheok, A. D., Yang, H., Zhu, J., & Shi, J. (2006). Virtual reality and mixed reality for virtual learning environments. *Computers & Graphics*, *30*(1), 20–28. doi:10.1016/j.cag.2005.10.004

Pastoor, S., & Conomis, C. (2005). Mixed reality displays. In O. Schreer, P. Kauff, & T. Sikora (Eds.), 3D videocommunication: Algorithms, concepts and real-time systems in human centred communication (pp. 261-280). Hoboken, NJ: John Wiley & Sons. doi:10.1002/0470022736.ch14

Pena-Rios, A. (2016). *Exploring mixed reality in distributed collaborative learning environments* (Doctoral dissertation). University of Essex, UK.

Pena-Rios, A., Callaghan, V., Gardner, M., & Alhaddad, M. J. (2012). Remote mixed reality collaborative laboratory activities: Learning activities within the InterReality portal. *Proceedings of the 2012 IEEE/WIC/ACM International Conference on Web Intelligence and Intelligent Agent Technology Workshops (WI-IAT'12)*, 362–366. doi:10.1109/WI-IAT.2012.43

Pena-Rios, A., Callaghan, V., Gardner, M., & Alhaddad, M. J. (2014). Using mixed reality to develop smart environments. In *10th International Conference on Intelligent Environments* (pp. 182–189). Shanghai, China: IEEE Computer Society.

Pena-Rios, A., Callaghan, V., Gardner, M., & Alhaddad, M. J. (2015). *Experiments with collaborative blended-reality laboratory technology for distance learners.* Paper presented at the 1st Immersive Learning Research Network Conference 2015 (iLRN 2015), Prague, Czech Republic.

Piezon, S. L., & Donaldson, R. L. (2005). Online groups and social loafing: Understanding student-group interactions. *Online Journal of Distance Learning Administration*, *8*(4). Retrieved from http://www.westga.edu/~distance/ojdla/winter84/piezon84.htm

Pollalis, C., Fahnbulleh, W., Tynes, J., & Shaer, O. (2017). HoloMuse: Enhancing engagement with archaeological artifacts through gesture-based interaction with holograms. In *Proceedings of the Tenth International Conference on Tangible, Embedded, and Embodied Interaction* (pp. 565–570). New York, NY: ACM. doi:10.1145/3024969.3025094

Rosenberg, M. (2000). *E-Learning: Strategies for delivering knowledge in the digital age*. Columbus, OH: Mcgraw-hill.

Schmidt, M., Kevan, J., Mckimmy, P., & Fabel, S. (2013). *The best way to predict the future is to create it: Introducing the Holodeck@UH mixed reality teaching and learning environment.* Paper presented at the 36th Annual Convention of the Association for Educational Communications and Technology, Anaheim, CA.

Schroeder, R. (1996). *Possible worlds: The social dynamic of virtual reality technology*. Boulder, CO: Westview Press.

Scott, G., & Chin, J. (2013). A DIY approach to pervasive computing for the internet of things: A smart alarm clock. *Proceedings of the 5th Computer Science and Electronic Engineering Conference (CEEC'13)*, 57–60. doi:10.1109/CEEC.2013.6659445

Smith, L., & Macgregor, J. T. (1992). *What is collaborative learning? Collaborative learning: A sourcebook for higher education.* Washington, DC: Office of Educational Research and Improvement.

Steuer, J. (1992). Defining virtual reality: Dimensions determining telepresence. *Journal of Communication*, *42*(4), 73–93. doi:10.1111/j.1460-2466.1992.tb00812.x

Stiles, M. J. (2000). *Effective learning and the virtual learning environment.* Paper presented at European Universities Information Systems Congress (EUNIS 2000).

Sundmaeker, H., Guillemin, P., Friess, P., & Woelfflé, S. (2010). Vision and challenges for realising the Internet of Things. *Cluster of European Research Projects on the Internet of Things. European Commision*, *3*(3), 34–36. doi:10.2759/26127

Tamura, H., Yamamoto, H., & Katayama, A. (2001). Mixed reality: Future dreams seen at the border between real and virtual worlds. *IEEE Computer Graphics and Applications*, *21*(6), 64–70. doi:10.1109/38.963462

The Immersive Learning Research Network. (2015). *Immersion (definition).* Retrieved from http://wiki.immersivelrn.org/ariel/wiki

The Open University. (2015). *Facts & figures - About the OU.* Retrieved from http://www.open.ac.uk/about/main/sites/www.open.ac.uk.about.main/files/files/fact_figures_1415_uk.pdf

Tolentino, L., Birchfield, D., Megowan-Romanowicz, C., Johnson-Glenberg, M. C., Kelliher, A., & Martinez, C. (2009). Teaching and learning in the mixed reality science classroom. *Journal of Science Education and Technology*, *18*(6), 501–517. doi:10.1007/s10956-009-9166-2

Triona, L. M., & Klahr, D. (2003). Point and click or grab and heft: Comparing the influence of physical and virtual instructional materials on elementary school students' ability to design experiments. *Cognition and Instruction*, *21*(2), 149–173. doi:10.1207/S1532690XCI2102_02

Trundle, K. C., & Bell, R. L. (2010). The use of a computer simulation to promote conceptual change: A quasi-experimental study. *Computers & Education*, *54*(4), 1078–1088. doi:10.1016/j.compedu.2009.10.012

Uckelmann, D., Harrison, M., & Michahelles, F. (2011). An architectural approach towards the future Internet of Things. In D. Uckelmann, M. Harrison, & F. Michahelles (Eds.), *Architecting the internet of things* (pp. 1–25). Springer Berlin; doi:10.1007/978-3-642-19157-2_1

Vallance, M. (2009). Experiential learning, virtual collaboration and robots. Riding the Hype Cycle: The Resurgence of Virtual Worlds, 1–18.

Walther, J. B., & D'Addario, K. P. (2001). The impacts of emoticons on message interpretation in computer-mediated communication. *Social Science Computer Review*, *19*(3), 324–347. doi:10.1177/089443930101900307

Wang, M., Callaghan, V., Lear, M., & Colley, M. (2011). *Teaching next generation computing skills: The challenge of embedded computing.* Paper presented at iCampus 2011, Nottingham, UK.

Weiser, M. (1999). The computer for the 21st century. *SIGMOBILE: Mobile Computing and Communications Review*, *3*(3), 3–11.

Wiesner, T. F., & Lan, W. (2004). Comparison of student learning in physical and simulated unit operations experiments. *Journal of Engineering Education*, *93*(3), 195–204. doi:10.1002/j.2168-9830.2004.tb00806.x

Yoh, M. S. (2001). *The reality of virtual reality*. Paper presented at the Seventh International Conference on Virtual Systems and Multimedia, Berkeley, CA.

Zhang, T., Callaghan, V., Shen, R., & Davies, M. (2011). *Virtual classrooms: Making the invisible, visible*. Paper presented at iCampus 2011, Nottingham, UK.

KEY TERMS AND DEFINITIONS

Blended Learning: Thoughtful integration of face-to-face (F2F) learning with computer-mediated learning experiences.

Blended Reality: User's interaction in real time between two environments (physical-local and virtual-distant) extending them to work as if they were one, simultaneously blending traces of one into another.

Cross-Reality Objects: A physical object linked to its virtual representation, sharing information in real-time. Also known as *digital twin*.

Digital Twin: Same as cross-reality object.

Dual Reality/Cross-Reality (xReality): Interaction between physical and virtual elements within an environment where each object (physical or virtual) is complete by itself (exists without the other), but it is enriched by bi-directional communication reflecting information in real time.

Immersive Learning: The combination of blended learning with diverse immersive technology (e.g., augmented reality, virtual reality, etc.) that can support self-directed and collaborative group-based learning activities. It happens when creating experiences that focus on learning within the technology based on a strong sense of presence.

Mirror Worlds: A representation of the physical world that attempts to map it in a digital format accurately.

Mixed-Reality Environment: A collection of interrelated elements existing in a physical space and a virtual environment achieving users' perception of integration between both worlds.

Mixed-Reality Learning Environment: Learning environments that combine physical and virtual resources to enhance the learning process.

Multidimensional Space: A hybrid environment where physical and virtual worlds couple together to create the seamless illusion of continuity.

Virtual Object: 3D representation of an object without any links to a physical object.

Chapter 11
The Learners' Isle:
A Multi-User Virtual Environment to Foster Learner Agency and Motivation

Menucha Birenbaum
Tel Aviv University, Israel

Elhanan Gazit
Tel Aviv University, Israel

ABSTRACT

The multi-user virtual environment (MUVE) described in this chapter is aimed to promote learner agency and motivation by engaging students in authentic and challenging learning experiences aligned with educational goals to foster twenty-first century competencies. Principles of assessment for learning (AfL) and gamification will be integrated to design a MUVE governed by students. The students will engage in learning, assessment, and instruction-related activities. They will also initiate, manage, and monitor the activities. The relationship between The Learners' Isle virtual environment and the physical classroom environment will be complementary and reciprocal. The teacher (a digital immigrant) and the students (the digital natives) will be partners in the teaching-learning process. The design principles of The Learners' Isle, a scenario to illustrate blended learning, and its conceptualization through an activity theory framework will be presented. In addition, this chapter will discuss the educational context characteristics conducive to successful implementation of the MUVE.

INTRODUCTION

Much has been written since the mid-80's about the incongruence between goals of education in the knowledge age and prevalent traditional practices of instruction, learning, and assessment. Such practices are consistent with the teaching-focused paradigm (Kember, 1997) according to which the teacher imparts discrete chunks of knowledge and uses summative assessment to measure the extent to which the students recall them. Such practices were congruent with the goals of education in the industrial age that aimed at preparing workers for the production line. But they are not suitable for achieving the

DOI: 10.4018/978-1-5225-3719-9.ch011

current goals of education, which are adapted to the rapid renewal of knowledge and its complexity. Successful functioning in the knowledge society requires nurturing the 21st century skills (Binkley et al., 2012; Organisation for Economic Co-operation and Development, 2003) for preparing students to become lifelong learners. Hence the shift in paradigm from teaching-focused to learning-focused (Barr & Tagg, 1995). According to the latter, the teacher assumes the role of a guide or a manager of a knowledge-construction site (Biggs, 1999), the students are active participants in their learning, and the assessment becomes an integral part of the teaching-learning process and informs decisions made during its navigation (Birenbaum, 1996; Black & Wiliam, 1998).

Although the 21st century skills have been defined operatively along with suitable instruction and assessment practices, their implementation is challenging (Voogt, Erstad, Dede, & Mishra, 2013). One obstacle lies in students' low motivation and inadequate skills to engage in deep learning and become agentic learners (Ferguson, Phillips, Rowley, & Friedlander, 2015; Yazzie-Mintz, 2006). The current chapter describes a MUVE that aims to tackle the obstacle. It combines principles of assessment for learning (AfL)–a pedagogical approach consistent with the learning-centered paradigm–with principles of gamification–a gameful approach to learning–in order to foster learner agency and motivation to enact it.

The chapter comprises three parts. The first presents a brief account of the main constructs, which highlights the potential of AfL and gamification to promote learner agency and motivation. The second part introduces the guiding principles of the proposed MUVE and describes its features. Next, it presents a hypothetical scenario of blended learning between the MUVE and the classroom and its conceptualization through an activity theory framework. The last part includes suggestions for implementing the MUVE and concluding remarks.

Learner Agency

Agency is a multi-faceted, situated and relational phenomenon (Rajala, Martin, & Kumpulainen, 2016). It refers to one's capacity and propensity to take purposeful initiative (Ferguson et al., 2015). To be agentic is "to intentionally make things happen by one's actions" (Bandura, 2001, p. 2).

As a psychological construct, agency embodies belief systems, self-regulation, and a variety of structures or functions through which personal influence is actualized (Bandura, 2001). It is thus closely related to autonomy and to power relations in human activity (Rajala et al., 2016). Self-efficacy—the faith in one's ability to succeed in achieving one's goals—is a key element of agency (Bandura, 1997). Other factors associated with learner agency include conception of intelligence as a growing entity (Dweck, 2006), consciousness, mastery orientation, and future orientation (Ferguson et al., 2015).

Although agency refers to both, the capacity and the willingness to take action, classroom observations show that a student may be agentic in a different way in the activity that develops in two groups or learning sites as evident from their interest and engagement with the work (Siry, Wilmes, & Haus, 2016). Moreover, agentic students under certain circumstances may choose not to enact their agency. The current chapter therefore differentiates between the capacity to take action and the willingness or motivation to exercise it.

From a sociological perspective, agency is the "socioculturally mediated capacity to act" (Ahearn, 2001, p. 112). Such capacity is constructed in social interactions using mediating structures (Sewel, 1992). Structures are constituted by cultural rules (or schemas) and resources that mutually imply and sustain each other over time (Giddens, 1979; Sewell, 1992). Schemas are generalizable procedures applied in a variety of interactions (Sewell, 1992). In classroom contexts, they may refer to types of curriculum, forms of instruction and learning, etc. Resources are of two kinds–human and nonhuman (Giddens, 1979). In classroom contexts, the former may refer to teaching and learning capabilities, related emotions, conceptions, self-beliefs etc., and the latter, to instructional materials and learning tools. Structures and agency maintain a dialectic relationship that is fluid, dynamic and recursive. Structures empower social actions and agentic acts sustain the reproduction of structures making possible their transformation (Sewell, 1992). In classroom, the dialectical interplay of agency and structure implies that instructional structures mediate the learner's agency and in turn, the learner's ability to enact agency mediates the structures (Siry et al., 2016). In these reciprocal relations tension and contradictions can occur, which may lead to classroom transformation (Siry et al., 2016).

Justifications to promote learner agency have recently advanced. Renshaw (2016) argued that agency is an aspect of human functioning. Therefore, the focus should be on its quality (what is a worthwhile agency) rather than its quantity (the extent of being agentic). Asserting that the worth of agency is related to culture, Renshaw (2016), using dimensions suggested by Biesta (2007), provided justification for agency promotion by looking at the grounds on which learner agency was regarded as worthwhile. The three dimensions were: (1) qualification (knowledge and skills); (2) subjectification (characteristics of the self); and (3) socialization (daily habits and beliefs consistent with membership in society). While the first dimension justified agency on epistemological grounds (i.e., producing knowledge outcomes for all students), the second gave precedence to disposition empowerment over knowledge of specific facts. The third justified a type of learner agency related to norms and expectations of a given society.

Policy makers ascribe great importance to the development of learner agency (Istanxe & Kools, 2013) and researchers explore instructional patterns that support it. Recent studies focused on agency attributes as exhibited in conventional instruction contexts (e.g., Ferguson et al., 2015; Rajala et al., 2016). They send a message regarding the urgent need to address the role of learner agency in teaching, high-stakes assessments, and research.

Assessment for Learning (AfL)

AfL is a formative approach to improving teaching and learning. It helps making learning visible (Hattie, 2012) to teachers and students while learning is happening so that appropriate modifications can be made to advance learning (Wiliam, 2011). AfL researchers and practitioners who engage in teacher training and professional development believe that AfL is effective in fostering learner agency (Earl, 2006; James et al., 2007; Willis & Cowie, 2014).

AfL, as defined by the Assessment Reform Group, is "the process of seeking and interpreting evidence for use by learners and their teachers to decide where the learners are in their learning, where they need to go, and how best to get there" (ARG, 2002, p. 2). A more recent definition stated that "AfL is part of everyday practice by students, teachers, and peers that seeks, reflects upon, and responds to information from dialogue, demonstration, and observation in ways that enhance ongoing learning" (Fairtest, 2009, p. 2).

These definitions implied the following about AfL: (1) the goal of the assessment is to advance learning; (2) its social nature rests on dialogue between the assessor (teacher or peers) and learner; (3) it has a dynamic nature and continuous enactment; (4) it utilizes a variety of tools and strategies to make learning explicit (visible); and (5) inferences are derived through an interpretive and integrative manner. For learners, the definitions pointed to their active-reflective role in the assessment. They participate in formulating objectives, developing rubrics, and performing self- and peer assessment. Therefore, AfL offers the learners an opportunity to exercise self-regulation, co-regulation, and socially shared regulation (Hadwin & Oshige, 2011; Pintrich, 1995).

From a socio-cognitive perspective, AfL is consistent with conceptions of the educational process as a socio-cultural dialogue and of learning as a collaborative construction of knowledge (Brown, Collins, & Duguid, 1989; Lave & Wenger, 1991). It is responsive to the interplay between individual and collective knowledge construction whereby they constantly feed each other. According to Willis and Cowie (2014), "AfL can [...] be conceptualized as more than a series of techniques or strategies; as part of a dialectical and cultural process of increasing understanding and control of the learning process by the learner—that is, exercising agency" (p. 25). However, this conceptualization may not be reflected in educational practice because the potential of AfL is unrealized in various education systems (Klenowski, 2009). Some scholars attribute this to teachers who enact AfL according to the letter rather than embrace its spirit (Marshall & Drummond, 2006). Others attribute it to students' lack of motivation to engage in learning (Salmela-Aro, Muotka, Alho Hakkarainen, & Lonka, 2016) and invest efforts in performing school-type tasks they consider irrelevant and disconnected from their real-life experiences (Prensky, 2003). Yet, they eagerly invest efforts in learning to improve their skills in other contexts, including extreme sports and digital games (Brown, 2011). Hence, there is a need to develop innovative pedagogies and learning environments suitable for digital natives (Prensky, 2001). This chapter will propose an AfL-based MUVE that integrates gamification principles.

Gamification

There is a growing interest to integrate gamification into the formal teaching system. This stems from the need to create experiences that encourage students' commitment to and engagement in the learning process, and to increase their motivation to pursue meaningful learning.

Gamification is defined as "the use of game design elements in non-game contexts" (Deterding, Dixon, Khaled, & Nacke, 2011, p.1). The gameful mindset is founded on the belief that we were born to play. Koster (2013) argues that increasing motivation and interest in games stemmed from the tasks and challenges that are built into the rules of the game. Faced with increasing challenges during the game, players advance and win by exhibiting comprehension and control. These struggles are both entertaining and educational.

In other words, gamification for learning consists of using a new way of thinking, a gameful minset, which uses game design dynamics and mechanics elements, such as levels, challenges, system's roles for player engagement, rewards, real-time action-feedback loops etc., in order to promote learners' agency, perseverance, problem solving, creativity, and collaboration skills.

- **Enhancing Learner Internal Motivation and Agency in a Virtual Learning Environment (VLE):** According to Gee (2004), digital games are complex semiotic systems. Uncertainty prevails in these environments. Unlike the requirements for success in real world games (e.g., basketball or football), successful gamers must decipher the rules and underlying mechanics of the game space. This is similar to Neo's learning process in *The Matrix* film (Gazit, 2017).

Gameful design principles create an engaging VLE and increase the learner's motivation and agency. For the sake of simplicity, the following principles are discussed:

1. **Autonomy:** This is a powerful driving force to boost internal learning motivation according to the self-determination theory (Ryan & Deci, 2000). Gamers' self-efficacy and motivation are enhanced by free choice and avatar customization, and by their ability to modify game space features and the gameplay journey (Gazit, 2009, 2017). Compared to classroom learning, the degree of autonomy granted to gamers within a video game is much higher. Like gamers in video games, the VLE should afford a high level of autonomy for the learner.
2. **Mastery and Competence:** These two forces also boost internal learning motivation according to the self-determination theory (Ryan & Deci, 2000). Unlike formal teaching, video games serve as internal motivation engines as they boost mastery and competence through challenges and levels designed to mirror a gamer's real-time skills (Gazit, 2009, 2017). To promote the learner's agency and internal motivation, the VLE should be gamified and include a semi-automated Hero's Journey engine for both teachers and students. This VLE engine will create an adjustable virtual learning space, which includes real-time challenges and levels suited to the learner's real-time knowledge and skills.
3. **Ownership, Transparency, and Reflection:** Kline, Dyer-Witheford, and de Peuter (2003) argued that the appeal of video games comes from the cybernetic loop between the player and the game as the gamer uses the joystick to outperform the program. Gamers structure their individual game experience through technological empowerment, consumer sovereignty, and cultural creativity. Hence, the VLE space should be designed around "the learner as the owner of his creation" aspect. The space, much like video games, should support the learner's ownership of the learning process and outcomes. Video games empower gamers by allowing them to control the narrative and meaning (Rushkoff, 1999). According to Rushkoff (1999), video game play is immersion in a world from a participant's point of view. This world reflects the values and actions of both the player and the community members (Rushkoff, 1999). Therefore, the VLE space should provide real-time feedback for the learner's actions and performance. Transparency and reflective learning should enable the leaner to acquire knowledge. The VLE space design should also include real-time assessment tools to reflect the learner's progress.
4. **Relatedness:** This is a powerful driving force to boost internal learning motivation according to the self-determination theory (Ryan & Deci, 2000). Contrary to myth, most gamers are not isolated from society. Instead, they play collaboratively in groups and guilds, which increase their relatedness and social skills. Such characteristics elevate the internal motivation of gamers and enhance their agentic capacity (Gazit, 2017). The VLE space should be a social engine, which includes collaborative tasks and challenges (solving a riddle, hacking a code to escape, etc.). In the space design, the learner should successfully complete the tasks through collaboration and teambuilding skills.

Dispositions and Competencies

Table 1 presents dispositions and competencies of students in classrooms where AfL has been successfully enacted (Birenbaum, 2014, 2016), marked as AfL lens. The gamification lens category is based on ethnographic studies of players in online digital games (Gazit, 2009; Lavee & Gazit, 2012; McGonigal, 2011).

Table 1. Dispositions and competencies of learners in classrooms with AfL and players in digital games

AfL Lens	Gamification Lens
Attribute value to learning Feel responsible for learning	Enjoy learning and improving skills
Curious Eager to know Inquisitive	Curious
Enjoy challenging learning tasks	Always see the challenge
Set learning objectives Monitor performance to achieve goals	Goal-oriented
Exhibit self-regulation	Possess leadership/management skills
Exhibit self-efficacy for learning	Optimistic in ability to succeed Optimistic in abilities of their group
Motivated to learn	Motivated to succeed
Critical thinkers Reflective	Systemic thinkers
Creative	Creatively solve problems Easily switch between roles/characters
Value formative assessment Crave feedback Provide constructive feedback	Eager and accustomed to feedback
Comfortable with mistakes Learn from mistakes	Consider failure integral to learning
Exhibit initiative Resourceful	Take risks Step out of comfort zone
Diligent Hardworking	Persistent when faced with obstacles Learn by observation and replays Learn under uncertainty Adaptable
Enjoy working in teams	Work in teams Empathetic

As shown in Table 1, similar attributes are visible through AfL and gamification lenses. These include attributes related to self-regulation, self-efficacy, and motivation, which are main components of agency. The conceptualization of AfL, gamification, and agency is based on the socio-cognitive theory (Bandura, 1986) and the self-determination theory (Ryan & Deci, 2000). These are both rooted in the perception of humans as proactive beings (with cognitive and metacognitive abilities) who are capable of self-regulation and reflection, rather than as creatures that react, are activated by environmental forces or driven by internal impulses. According to these theories, the combination of autonomy, socialization, and self-efficacy enhance intrinsic motivation. Therefore, it is not surprising to see similar attributes through AfL and gamification lenses.

Gamification to Upgrade AfL

Despite the shared theoretical foundation between AfL and gamification, there is a difference between how students learn in school vs. how they learn in games or real world activities. As game players in video games, students are enthusiastically learning in either a group or individual setting. Learning takes place by mindfully utilizing feedback. When engaged in extreme sports, learners receive feedback, analyze their mistakes, learn strategies by observing a model (or champion), test the strategies, and compare their performance to the model. In general, they are characterized by embracing change and eagerly learning to improve performance (Brown, 2011).

By contrast, in school, even when feedback is available, many students do not aim to improve their performance (Crisp, 2007). In conventional classrooms, learners feel like submissive subjects to obscure teaching and assessment dictates. They do not feel that their learning aligns with real world experiences. The current G (Gameful) generation (Gazit, 2017), is exposed to school teaching methods based on epistemological beliefs and perceptions that were appropriate for achieving the educational goals of the past. Therefore, it is not surprising that many teachers fail to engage students in lessons and learning tasks since they perceive these tasks as a burdensome necessity. Consequently, the motivated students orient themselves toward performance goals rather than learning goals, especially when it lines up with policies adhering to external test-based accountability (Berliner, 2011). Moreover, it is difficult to update teaching and assessment methods to competently utilize digital technologies. Teachers are reluctant to apply such technologies, which students then view as the preservation of archaic instruction. As the generation gap grows between teachers (digital immigrants) and students (digital natives), students will view the schooling experience as unattractive and irrelevant (Prensky, 2001).

Gamification is therefore proposed for upgrading AfL-based teaching, learning, and assessment experiences in school. Specifically, a gameful learning MUVE, titled "The Learners' Isle", is proposed. This environment, along with the classroom's physical learning environment, will offer a bi-level blended learning space.

THE LEARNERS' ISLE

This section will describe the characteristics of the Learners' Isle and the activities that can take place there. It will conclude with a scenario illustrating blended learning between the two learning environments–the physical and the virtual–and its conceptualization through an activity theory framework.

Characteristics of the Learners' Isle

To foster learner agency and motivation, teaching can no longer be a planned process executed solely by the teacher while the students are submissive subjects. Students should understand its language, recognize its tools, and be partners in planning, executing, and monitoring the process in collaboration with the teacher.

The goals of the Learners' Isle can be addressed according to the three dimensions advanced by Renshaw (2016) to justify fostering learner agency:

1. **Qualification:** The goal is to evoke deep learning through student participation in the instruction and assessment processes that would be adapted to the media utilization of digital natives.
2. **Subjectification:** The goal is to empower students to become self-efficacious in their ability to self- and co-regulate their learning, and to socially share regulation of collaborative learning.
3. **Socialization:** The goal is to socialize students to norms and skills required for proper functioning in the 21st century.

The Learners' Isle offers students a virtual, multi-purpose activity space. To encourage students to engage in the instruction, learning, and assessment processes, they are held accountable for the space's design and management.

The Isle, which is always accessible, contains learning and teaching resources, virtual facilities, and tools for school work and challenging leisure activities. Students design, build, and shape the space according to their preferences (as in a Minecraft environment), and operate and maintain it. Learners' Isle guidelines and activity targets are formulated by the collaborative efforts of students and teachers.

The Isle can be utilized for knowledge management by documenting the collective knowledge constructed during classroom discussion (i.e., knowledge maps, lesson summaries, exemplary performances, etc.). Students can also manage inventories of strategies, tools, applications for instruction and assessment, standards, and rubrics. Furthermore, they can assemble a library of relevant resources, construct models and illustrations for instructional purposes, develop learning games, offer peer assessment, conduct synchronous and asynchronous discussions, perform experiments, present exhibitions, and host conferences to present learning outcomes.

The activity in the Isle offers students the opportunity to develop expertise, assist and guide peers, work in teams, solve authentic problems, and cope with challenges. The activity is expected to promote deep learning, self-regulation, co-regulation, and socially-shared regulation. It is expected to increase motivation for excellence, empower transparent students (those who shy away from class participation), foster self- and collective-efficacy (Pajares, 1996), and create a sense of cohesion. Students' personal identities may expand due to gained experiences from roles like those in the current workplace. These workplace experiences require competencies unrealized by students in their regular school work. Therefore, the Learners' Isle activity has the potential to foster learner agency and motivation.

Activities in the Learners' Isle

Students design and construct activity sites in accordance with the purpose of the Isle, including buildings (activity centers), infrastructure, and landscape. The construction process is led by enthusiastic students who have worked with digital construction software (like Minecraft). Once the Isle is created, the activity centers are put into action.

- **Information and Resource Centers:** Student visit these centers for advice, training, and shared information. The teams who run the centers are responsible for tasks including: locating, collecting, organizing, and cataloging information resources and learning tools; disseminating information and tools; providing consultation services to peers and teachers; and initiating educational activities and events within the classroom, school, and community (exhibitions and conferences).

- **Learning Activity Centers:** Students use these centers to work on assignments and/or develop instructional materials with specialized software.
- **Leisure Activity Centers:** Students come here to play, exercise, debate, and learn about extracurricular topics.
- **The Isle Administration Hub:** The hub consists of the cyber, development, and communication centers. Students who run the hub manage the virtual environment, and the internal and external communication.
- **Knowledge Dissemination Center:** This center includes conference halls, museum, and galleries to display, present, and discuss learning outcomes.

The heads of the centers are elected by their classmates based on their qualifications and their election campaign's vision for the center. Then, team members are selected based on the posts' qualifications. Officials in the Isle are represented by avatars.

Each center's performance is assessed based on the activity log produced by the automated system. Center teams are motivated to excel; team members feel responsible for the success of the team. The activity in the Learners' Isle follows procedures, regulations, norms, and ethics rules in accordance with those in effect at the school.

Conceptualization of the Blended-Learning Activity

Blended learning consisting of activities in both spaces—the physical (classroom) and the virtual (Learners' Isle)—can be conceptualized using an activity theory framework (Engeström, 2001)—a suitable framework for studying human activity as a complex socially-situated phenomenon. It emphasizes the role of mediation through cultural tools for achieving the object of the activity. Two activity systems will be described, compared, and examined with regard to tensions, interrelations, and learning as a result of engagement in activities.

Figure 1 presents the structure of a balanced activity system (Engeström, 2001) from the perspective of the learner (subject). The system consists of one large triangle formed by four triangles. The two middle triangles form a rhombus with four vertices: (1) subject (learner); (2) object (of study); (3) mediating tools for learning; and (4) community (classmates). The vertices of the two triangles on the sides of the rhombus (rules and division of labor) are the contextual conditions in which the activity is conducted. The vertices of all triangles are connected by two-way arrows representing reciprocal influences. They converge on the center, which is marked by an ellipse representing the teacher. The mid-perpendicular of the two central triangles (connecting tools and community) is referred to as axis of mediation. This is made up of three sources of assistance for the learner to cope with the challenges of the object: (1) tools; (2) teacher; and (3) community.

The structure in Figure 1 fits the physical and virtual activity systems. Yet, the systems differ in three ways: (1) the teacher's role and dominance; (2) the division of labor between teacher and students, and among students; and (3) the rules under which the activity is conducted. To illustrate the differences, a hypothetical scenario illustrates activities in each system during a study unit titled "Introduction to Descriptive Statistics, for Middle School."

Figure 1. Structure of the activity system (based on Engeström, 2001)

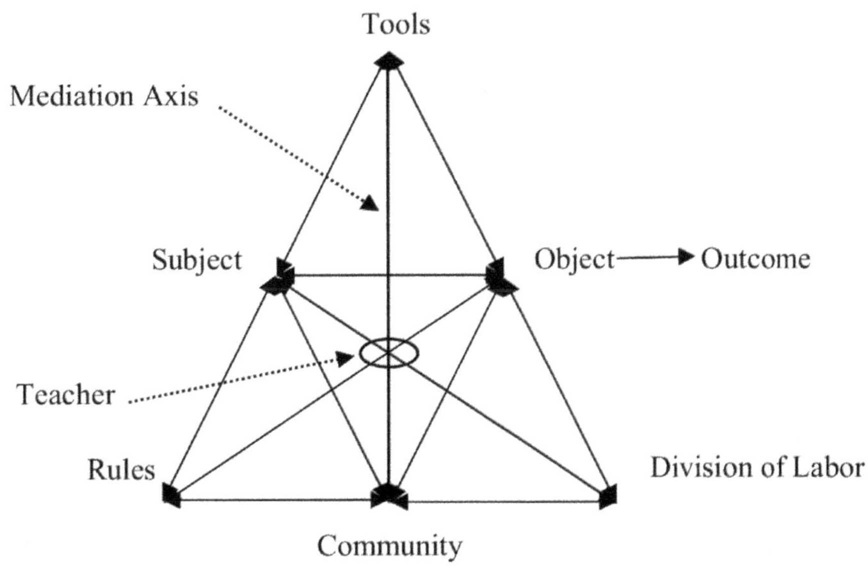

The lesson exposing students to the unit takes place in the classroom. The teacher, who holds an AfL mindset (Birenbaum, 2014, 2016), asks questions to elicit students' prior knowledge about statistics and its applications in daily life. The classroom discourse follows AfL cycles (Ruiz-Primo, 2011). The communication pattern in the discourse is multi-directional. Relevant information is recorded on the interactive white board. The teacher assigns tasks to student groups. Tasks include examples of data represented in graphs (e.g., salary broken by education level and gender, household electricity consumption broken by season and region, national math test scores broken by gender and sector, etc.). Two groups receive the same graph. Groups interpret the graph and compare interpretations with the counterpart group. The groups discuss their interpretations and attempt to identify the source of disagreements. The teacher observes the groups, making notes of possible difficulties. In the plenary, a group member presents and interprets the graph. The class discusses the interpretation and draws conclusions based on the data. During the discussion, key terms are mentioned and defined, including frequency distribution, values of central tendency (mean, mode, and median), etc. The lesson concludes with a visual summary or concept map presenting the network of concepts. A traffic-light feedback is used by the teacher to prepare subsequent lessons. With this method, students provide individual feedback on green, yellow, or red sticky notes to state that they understood, partially understood, or misunderstood the lesson. Those lessons will also reflect an AfL approach. They are intended to explicate the statistical concepts mentioned at the introductory lesson.

From an activity theory perspective, the activity in the classroom lesson can be described as follows:

1. The learner (subject) works to achieve the object (mastery of the learning unit) through mediation of tools, teacher, and peers (the mediation axis in Figure 1).
2. The teacher offers scaffolding to individual students, groups, and the class based on diagnostic information gathered from dialogues, task performance, and students' feedback notes.
3. Classmates assess their peers' performance according to rubrics, which the teacher developed in cooperation with the students.

4. The division of labor is characterized by the dominance of the teacher in managing and organizing the lesson, leading the discussion, assigning tasks, and offering instructional aids. The teacher may use instructional materials developed by students.
5. Participants agree upon and follow rules that regulate classroom discussion and group work.
6. Management tactics and tools—think-discuss (with neighbor)-share (with class), traffic-light cards, personal erasable boards, etc.—allow students time to think before responding to a question. It also provides the teacher with a snapshot of the whole class understanding.
7. Students work collaboratively according to a clear division of roles.
8. Legitimizing of errors, a prevalent norm in the classroom, is fostered through learning experiences. For example, tests are returned to students without scores. The students are expected to correct the test's highlighted errors after discussing the cause of the errors with their peers. Other learning experiences include discussions on wrong solutions and asking students to develop test items to elicit misconceptions. Such experiences make learning visible, and raise students' awareness about learning from errors.

The described activity system takes place in a physical space (classroom). A complementary activity system takes place in the virtual space. The Learners' Isle allows students to independently explore a topic or work on the teacher's group assignments. For example, one group assignment asks learners to generate an empirical (research) question that would interest the group. This task requires data collection on three variables. Data can be collected through an online survey (e.g., a question about reading preferences of boys and girls of different age groups) or an experiment (e.g., a question about the time that it takes two types of seeds to sprout under different light conditions). Students are asked to organize the data in tables and graphs, interpret the information, and draw conclusions to answer the research question. Data collection tools include online questionnaires, observations, and experiments. The statistical lab provides software for data organization, analysis, and presentation of the findings. A rubric, developed in cooperation with the students, is attached to the task instructions. The task is divided into performance stages. Upon completion of each stage, the group submits a progress report. Feedback is received from the teacher and peers before advancing to the next stage. Finally, each group prepares a creative poster summary to be presented in the virtual exhibition hall.

From an activity theory perspective, the activity system that takes place in the Learners' Isle can be described as follows:

1. The subject (a group of students performing the task [the object]) collaborate on utilizing the affordances along the mediation axis.
2. The teacher's role changes compared to the classroom role. The teacher now functions as a supervisor of a construction site.
3. Teacher dominance decreases compared to the students.
4. The teacher tracks activities on the Isle. If necessary, the teacher will intervene through the center's heads. However, students can always access the teacher for consultation.
5. The division of labor within the group is determined by its members.
6. Each student or group can turn to specialized centers as needed. For instance, students can use the information center to retrieve relevant information for formulating their empirical question. Training in use of an application for conducting online surveys is offered by the resource center. The graphic center provides consultation on poster design.

7. The rules on activity management are determined by the students and approved by the teacher. These are documented in the regulation book.
8. Groups have a forum for synchronous and asynchronous discussions. This is open to all participants in the Isle. There are also forums in leisure activity centers. All forums are smartphone accessible.
9. The activity of each center is recorded, including feedback regarding services.
10. The center's team gains points on the nature of their activities (e.g., providing consultation, retrieving and managing information, initiating activities, etc.).

Tasks and challenges in the Learners' Isle are designed according to the gameful design principles previously outlined. Students can suggest tasks and challenges, and enter them into the system for review and approval by the teacher and peers. Team members receive immediate feedback on performance through the computerized reward system. Likewise, the team receives feedback and rewards for its collective performance.

The Learners' Isle computerized reward system consists of rules and regulations governing the automated scoring and reward structure. It also manages and displays qualitative formative assessment, including feedback from the teacher and peers. The assessment rules and regulations result from discussions between the students and the teacher. These are agreed upon by all participants. Scoring reports are available and transparent to participants. Once a semester, the team publishes an evaluation regarding the center's activities. Based on the system's data, this reflects on the center's performance (i.e., reaching objectives) and suggests performance improvements for the upcoming semester.

As in video games, the learners receive more than medals or points, including new tools, authorizations for new centers or center upgrades, and nominations for more advanced and challenging roles. The team in charge of developing the gaming space monitors the effectiveness of the reward system and updates it as needed.

Figure 1 shows a balanced activity system. However, since it is a complex and dynamic system with mutual influences between its components, reality may prove tensions and contradictions between the components. They can result from the uncertainty inherent in adopting new AfL methods, new roles and identities of the students and the teacher, pressure to meet accountability requirements of the education system, and parental expectations for success in high-stake tests. Such tensions and contradictions may become a catalyst for change since it is a challenge to reach a resolution to restore system equilibrium, thus increasing the potential for improvement (Cowan & Butler, 2013).

As illustrated in the presented scenario, the two activity systems are coordinated and interrelated. They feed each other constantly leading to coevolution and creation of a "third space" (Gutierrez, Rymes, & Larson, 1995) where expansive learning evolves (Engeström, 2001).

Students' personal learning from participation in the two activity systems is recorded in a digital portfolio. This includes artifacts created and tasks performed by the student (individually or collaboratively) during the course of learning, feedback notes from the teacher and peers, awards, self-assessment and reflective notes on the effects of systems participation on learning.

IMPLEMENTING THE LEARNERS' ISLE

This section will address contextual conditions conducive to successful implementation of the Learners' Isle as illustrated in the hypothetical scenario. It will also review preparatory measures for implementation. The implementation suggestions are based on professional literature regarding the introduction of innovative ICT-based pedagogies in schools (Harris, 2002; Law, Pelgrum & Plomp, 2008) and the cultivation of school-based professional learning communities (McLaughlin & Talbert, 2006) and an assessment culture (Birenbaum, 2014, 2016).

Contextual Conditions

A classroom that would appreciate activities provided by the Learners' Isle is characterized by a climate of growth, relationships of trust, and mutual respect between the teacher and students. The classroom has norms of mutual support, transparency, openness, and legitimacy of errors. Students feel confident to try, dare, initiate, set challenges, and believe in their abilities. The classroom is experienced in teamwork, peer teaching, and self- and peer-assessment.

The classroom teacher is caring, thinks outside the box, and views themselves as an educator rather than an agent who imparts knowledge. The teacher cultivates values, empowers students, enhances self-efficacy, and fosters critical thinking, creativity, and social competencies. Professionally, the teacher feels supported by critical friends (Costa & Kallick, 1993) in a cohesive school-based professional learning community (McLaughlin & Talbert, 2006). Team members are motivated to improve the learning skills of students and nurture their agency. They proudly believe in their collective capacity to meet challenges. They exhibit constructivist conceptions of instruction, learning, and assessment, and attach value to cultivating students' interest in their educational discipline. The team thinks outside the box, is enthusiastic and open to new experiences, exhibits an inquisitive disposition, and practices professional accountability and internal regulation (O'Day, 2002). Team members feel supported by a school management that sets a high priority on fostering agency among staff and students (Elmore, 2004).

Schools with these properties of organizational culture (Birenbaum, 2016) are conducive to the successful implementation of the Learners' Isle and to mindful integration of the virtual and physical activity systems.

Preparation for the Implementation

Once the Learners' Isle becomes operational, the following preparatory actions are suggested for classrooms where conditions are conducive to the implementation of the MUVE:

1. Discuss with students the difference between learning at school and learning in non-school contexts (e.g., when performing extreme sports or playing video games, etc.). Try to understand what makes the learning exciting, challenging, and engaging.
2. Introduce the concept and potential of the Learners' Isle. Examine the possibilities offered by the MUVE.
3. As students gain interest, jointly decide on the goals they would like to achieve. Discuss the Isle activities and the following questions:
    a. What are the short- and long-term objectives?
    b. Which centers should be on the Isle?
    c. What is the nature of the activity?
    d. What are the expected outcomes of the activity?
    e. What would be the criteria for quality control?

   f. What would be the limits of autonomy granted to the students?
   g. What would be the norms, procedures, and rules that govern the activities in the Isle?
   h. What kind of support does the teacher provide?
   i. How are the activities assessed?
4. Student questions should also be addressed. The questions above would be discussed by the teaching staff to examine options, consider possible tensions and contradictions, and suggest design alternatives.
5. Supported by critical friends, the teacher would lead student discussions regarding the purpose, goals, and achievement strategies for the Isle.
6. Once a consensus and shared vision are reached, the teacher would support the students in planning and constructing the Isle.
7. Elections would take place.
8. Once the Isle is ready for use, the teacher would orchestrate the blended learning between the two activity systems.

CONCLUDING REMARKS

The chapter described a MUVE aimed to foster learner agency and motivation to enact it. In view of the rapid developments in learning technology nowadays, it becomes important to address challenges related to fostering learner agency. The following questions posed in the chapter address such challenges:

1. What is learner agency and why is it important to foster it?
2. What are the barriers to fostering learner agency in schools?
3. What is the potential of AfL to foster learner agency?
4. How can gamification upgrade AfL?
5. What are the main features of a MUVE aimed to foster learner agency?
6. How can the activity in the Learners' Isle foster learning agency?
7. What characterizes blended learning between the two systems that leads to expansive learning?
8. What characterizes a conducive context for successful implementation of the Learner Isle?

The answers to those questions offer a working framework for designing affordances to cultivate agentic lifelong learners capable of applying 21st century skills. Several design-related aspects discussed in the chapter are still tentative. They will be put to the real test as the MUVE becomes operational and implemented in schools. This will open intriguing research and development opportunities.

REFERENCES

Ahearn, L. M. (2001). Language and agency. *Annual Review of Anthropology*, *30*(1), 109–137. doi:10.1146/annurev.anthro.30.1.109

Assessment Reform Group (ARG). (2002). *Assessment for learning: 10 principles* [Leaflet/poster]. Cambridge, UK: University of Cambridge. Retrieved December 21, 2012, from https://assessmentreformgroup.files.wordpress.com/2012/01/10principles_english.pdf

Bandura, A. (1986). *Social foundations of thought and action: A social cognitive theory*. Englewood Cliffs, NJ: Prentice Hall.

Bandura, A. (1997). *Self-efficacy: The exercise of control*. New York, NY: Worth Publishers.

Bandura, A. (2001). Social cognitive theory: An agentic perspective. *Annual Review of Psychology*, *52*(1), 1–26. doi:10.1146/annurev.psych.52.1.1 PMID:11148297

Barr, R. B., & Tagg, J. (1995, November). From teaching to learning: A new paradigm for undergraduate education. *Change*, 13–25.

Berliner, C. D. (2011). Rational responses to high stakes testing: The case of curriculum narrowing and the harm that follows. *Cambridge Journal of Education*, *41*(3), 287–302. doi:10.1080/0305764X.2011.607151

Biesta, G. (2007). Why "what works" won't work: Evidence-based practice and the democratic deficit in educational research. *Educational Theory*, *57*(1), 1–22. doi:10.1111/j.1741-5446.2006.00241.x

Biggs, J. B. (1999). *Teaching for quality learning at university: What the student does*. London, UK: Society for Research into Higher Education.

Binkley, M., Erstad, O., Herman, J., Raizen, S., Ripley, M., Miller-Ricci, M., & Rumble, M. (2012). Defining twenty-first century skills. In P. Griffin, B. McGaw, & E. Care (Eds.), *Assessment and teaching of 21st century skills* (pp. 17–66). Dordrecht, The Netherlands: Springer Netherlands. doi:10.1007/978-94-007-2324-5_2

Birenbaum, M. (1996). Assessment 2000: Towards a pluralistic approach to assessment. In M. Birenbaum & F. J. R. C. Dochy (Eds.), *Alternatives in assessment of achievements, learning processes and prior knowledge* (pp. 4–29). Boston, MA: Kluwer. doi:10.1007/978-94-011-0657-3_1

Birenbaum, M. (2014). Conceptualizing assessment culture in school. In C. Wyatt-Smith, V. Klenowski, & P. Colbert (Eds.), *Designing assessment for quality learning* (pp. 285–302). Dordrecht, The Netherlands: Springer. doi:10.1007/978-94-007-5902-2_18

Birenbaum, M. (2016). Assessment culture versus testing culture: The impact on assessment for learning. In D. Laveault & L. Allal (Eds.), *Assessment for learning: Meeting the challenge of implementation* (pp. 275–292). New York, NY: Springer International. doi:10.1007/978-3-319-39211-0_16

Black, P., & Wiliam, D. (1998). Assessment and classroom learning. *Assessment in Education: Principles, Policy & Practice*, *5*(1), 7–74. doi:10.1080/0969595980050102

Brown, J. S. (2011, August). *Innovation expert John Seely Brown on new ways of learning in a rapidly-changing world*. Retrieved from https://www.youtube.com/watch?v=bGdpbba1i9c

Brown, J. S., Collins, A., & Duguid, P. (1989). Situated cognition and the culture of learning. *Educational Researcher*, *18*(1), 32–42. doi:10.3102/0013189X018001032

Costa, A. L., & Kallick, B. (1993). Through the lens of critical friend. *Educational Leadership*, *51*(2), 49–51.

Cowan, P., & Butler, R. (2013, October). Using activity theory to problematize the role of the teacher during mobile learning. *SAGE Open*, 1–13.

Crisp, B. R. (2007). Is it worth the effort? How feedback influences students' subsequent submission of assessable work. *Assessment & Evaluation in Higher Education*, *32*(5), 571–581. doi:10.1080/02602930601116912

Deterding, S., Dixon, D., Khaled, R., & Nacke, L. (2011). From game design elements to gamefulness: Defining "gamification." In *Proceedings of the 15th International Academic MindTrek Conference: Envisioning Future Media Environments* (pp. 9-15). New York, NY: ACM. doi:10.1145/2181037.2181040

Dweck, C. S. (2006). *Mindsets: The new psychology of success*. New York, NY: Random House.

Earl, L. M. (2006). *Rethinking classroom assessment with purpose in mind: Assessment for learning, assessment as learning, assessment of learning*. Government of Manitoba.

Elmore, R. F. (2004). *School reform from the inside out: Policy, practice, and performance*. Cambridge, MA: Harvard Education Press.

Engeström, Y. (2001). Expansive learning at work: Toward an activity theoretical reconceptualization. *Journal of Education and Work*, *14*(1), 133–156. doi:10.1080/13639080020028747

Fairtest. (2009, March). *Position Paper on Assessment for Learning*. Paper presented at the Third International Conference on Assessment for Learning, Dunedin, New Zealand. Retrieved December 21, 2012, from www.fairtest.org/position-paper-assessment-learning

Ferguson, R. F., Phillips, S. F., Rowley, J. F. S., & Friedlander, J. W. (2015). *The influence of teaching beyond standardized test scores: Engagement, mindsets, and agency*. Research Report: The Achievement Gap Initiative at Harvard University. Retrieved from http://www.agi.harvard.edu/publications.php

Gazit, E. (2009). A window on digital games interactions in home settings. In R. E. Ferdig (Ed.), *Handbook of research on effective electronic gaming in education* (Vol. 1, pp. 127–145). Hershey, PA: IGI Global. doi:10.4018/978-1-59904-808-6.ch008

Gazit, E. (2017). *The gameful heroes' future: How gaming and virtual reality technologies are reshaping our learning world*. Manuscript in preparation.

Gee, J. P. (2004). *What video games have to teach us about learning and literacy*. Basingstoke, UK: Palgrave Macmillan.

Giddens, A. (1979). *Central problems in social theory: Action, structure and contradiction in social analysis*. Berkeley, CA: University of California Press. doi:10.1007/978-1-349-16161-4

Gutierrez, K., Rymes, B., & Larson, J. (1995). Script, counterscript, and underlife in the classroom: James Brown versus "Brown v. Board of Education." *Harvard Educational Review*, *65*(3), 445–471. doi:10.17763/haer.65.3.r16146n25h4mh384

Hadwin, A. F., & Oshige, M. (2011). Self-regulation, coregulation, and socially shared regulation: Exploring perspectives of social in self-regulated learning theory. *Teachers College Record, 113*(2), 240–264.

Harris, S. (2002). Innovative pedagogical practices using ICT in schools in England. *Journal of Computer Assisted Learning, 18*(4), 449–458. doi:10.1046/j.0266-4909.2002.00256.x

Hattie, J. (2012). *Visible learning for teachers: Maximizing impact on learning*. New York, NY: Routledge.

James, M., McCormick, R., Black, P., Carmichael, P., Drummond, M.-J., Fox, A., … Wiliam, D. (2007). Improving learning how to learn: Classrooms, schools and networks. London, UK: Routledge.

Kember, D. (1997). A reconceptualisation of the research into university academics' conceptions of teaching. *Learning and Instruction, 7*(3), 255–276. doi:10.1016/S0959-4752(96)00028-X

Klenowski, V. (2009). Assessment for learning revisited: An Asia-Pacific perspective. *Assessment in Education: Principles, Policy & Practice, 16*(3), 263–268. doi:10.1080/09695940903319646

Kline, S., Dyer-Witheford, N., & de Peuter, G. (2003). *Digital play: The interaction of technology, culture, and marketing*. Montreal, Canada: McGill-Queen's University Press.

Koster, R. (2013). *A theory of fun for game design*. Sebastopol, CA: O'Reilly Media.

Lave, J., & Wenger, E. (1991). *Situated learning: Legitimate peripheral participation*. New York, NY: Cambridge University Press. doi:10.1017/CBO9780511815355

Lavee, Z., & Gazit, E. (2012). World of Warcraft (WOW) guild conflict management insights for organizations leadership building. In Y. Yair, & E. Shmueli (Eds.), *Proceedings of the 10th Annual Conference of MEITAL-The Israeli Inter-University Center for E-Learning (IUCEL)* (pp. 66-73). Rehovot, Israel: Weizmann Institute of Science.

Law, N., Pelgrum, W. J., & Plomp, T. (2008). *Pedagogy and ICT use in schools around the world: Findings from the IEA SITES 2006 study*. Springer.

Marshall, B., & Drummond, M. J. (2006). How teachers engage with assessment for learning: Lessons from the classroom. *Research Papers in Education, 21*(2), 133–149. doi:10.1080/02671520600615638

McGonigal, J. (2011). *Reality is broken: Why games make us better and how they can change the world*. London, UK: Penguin.

McLaughlin, M. W., & Talbert, J. E. (2006). *Building School-based Teacher Learning Communities: Professional Strategies to Improve Student Achievement*. New York, NY: Teachers College.

O'Day, J. A. (2002). Complexity, accountability, and school improvement. *Harvard Educational Review, 72*(3), 293–327. doi:10.17763/haer.72.3.021q742t8182h238

Organisation for Economic Co-operation and Development (OECD). (2003). *Key competencies for a successful life and well-functioning society. The definition and selection of key competencies: Executive summary (Summary of report by S. D. Rychen & L. H. Salganik)*. Kirkland, WA: Hogrefe and Huber.

Pajares, F. (1996). Self-efficacy beliefs in academic settings. *Review of Educational Research, 66*(4), 543–578. doi:10.3102/00346543066004543

Pintrich, R. R. (1995). *Understanding self-regulated learning*. San Francisco, CA: Jossey-Bass.

Prensky, M. (2001). Digital natives, digital immigrants. *New Horizons (Baltimore, Md.)*, *9*(5), 10–16.

Prensky, M. (2003). Digital game-based learning. *Theoretical and Practical Computer Applications in Entertainment*, *1*(1). doi:10.1145/950566.950596

Rajala, A., Martin, J., & Kumpulainen, K. (2016). Agency and learning: Researching agency in educational interactions. *Learning Culture and Social Interaction*, *10*, 1–3. doi:10.1016/j.lcsi.2016.07.001

Renshaw, P. (2016). On the notion of worthwhile agency in reformist pedagogies. *Learning. Culture and Social Interaction*, *10*, 60–63. doi:10.1016/j.lcsi.2016.07.002

Ruiz-Primo, M. A. (2011). Informal formative assessment: The role of instructional dialogues in assessing students' learning. *Studies in Educational Evaluation*, *37*(1), 15–24. doi:10.1016/j.stueduc.2011.04.003

Rushkoff, D. (1999). *Playing the future: What we can learn from digital kids*. New York, NY: New River Trade.

Ryan, R. M., & Deci, E. L. (2000). Intrinsic and extrinsic motivations: Classic definitions and new directions. *Contemporary Educational Psychology*, *25*(1), 54–67. doi:10.1006/ceps.1999.1020 PMID:10620381

Salmela-Aro, K., Muotka, J., Alho, K., Hakkarainen, K., & Lonka, K. (2016). School burnout and engagement profiles among digital natives in Finland: A person-oriented approach. *European Journal of Developmental Psychology*, *13*(6), 704–718. doi:10.1080/17405629.2015.1107542

Sewell, W. H. Jr. (1992). A theory of structure: Duality, agency, and transformation. *American Journal of Sociology*, *98*(1), 1–29. doi:10.1086/229967

Siry, C., Wilmes, S., & Haus, J. M. (2016). Examining children's agency within participatory structures in primary science investigations. *Learning Culture and Social Interaction*, *10*, 4-16.

Voogt, J., Erstad, O., Dede, C., & Mishra, P. (2013). Challenges to learning and schooling in the digital networked world of the 21st century. *Journal of Computer Assisted Learning*, *29*(5), 403–413. doi:10.1111/jcal.12029

Wiliam, D. (2011). What is assessment for learning? *Studies in Educational Evaluation*, *37*(1), 3–14. doi:10.1016/j.stueduc.2011.03.001 PMID:22114905

Willis, J., & Cowie, B. (2014). Assessment as a generative dance: Connecting teaching, learning and curriculum. In C. Wyatt-Smith, V. Klenowski, & P. Colbert (Eds.), *Designing assessment for quality learning. The enabling power of assessment* (Vol. 1, pp. 23–37). New York, NY: Springer. doi:10.1007/978-94-007-5902-2_2

Yazzie-Mintz, E. (2006). *Voices of students on engagement: A report on the 2006 high school survey of student engagement*. Center for Evaluation & Education Policy, Indiana University. Retrieved from http://files.eric.ed.gov/fulltext/ED495758.pdf

KEY TERMS AND DEFINITIONS

Activity Theory: A conceptual and methodological framework for studying human activity as a complex socially situated phenomenon. It emphasizes the role of mediation through cultural tools for achieving the object of the activity.

Assessment for Learning (AfL): Formative assessment that makes learning visible to teachers and students while learning is happening so that appropriate modifications can be made to advance learning.

Blended Learning: An instructional practice that mindfully integrates in-person and online learning experiences.

Expansive Learning: Constructing new knowledge through active reflective participation in activity systems maintaining reciprocal relations to expand the object of activity.

Gameful Learning Design: A mindset framework of working principles that is used to enhance learner agency and motivation.

Gamification: The implementation of game design elements in non-game contexts in order to boost engagement and to solve problems.

Learner Agency: Students' capacity to initiate and carry out activities that will advance their learning.

Chapter 12
The Added Value of the Hybrid Virtual Learning Approach:
Using Virtual Environments in the Real Classroom

Athanasios Christopoulos
University of Bedfordshire, UK

Marc Conrad
University of Bedfordshire, UK

Mitul Shukla
University of Bedfordshire, UK

ABSTRACT

This chapter maps the types of interactions that relate to the use of virtual worlds in hybrid virtual learning scenarios. Students were asked to state their opinions regarding their experiences and were also observed along the way. The results highlight that the learning activities and students' attitudes and experiences greatly affect learner engagement. It is vital, though, that instructional designers plan the learning activities thoughtfully and provide learners with enough time and support. Offering content with examples of the expectations of the teaching team can be invaluably helpful. Furthermore, a game-like content can be considered a great source of motivation. Moreover, the vividness of the virtual world makes the learning process more stimulating and less tedious. Additionally, avatars enable users to interact with the content and increase the opportunities for interactions with others. Nevertheless, learners' simultaneous co-presence in the physical classroom is a more immediate and preferred option, since it offers increased opportunities for collaboration.

DOI: 10.4018/978-1-5225-3719-9.ch012

INTRODUCTION

The term virtual environment was coined around the 1950s, when a machine named 'Sensorama,' able to provide the illusion of reality using stereoscopic 3-Dimensional (3D) images, was introduced to the public (Ellis, 1994). Ever since, the continuous evolution of Computer Science has greatly impacted on this field. The potential of these 3D artificial environments was very promising, as they seemed to offer a relatively cheap way to simulate various tasks. In these environments, users interacted simultaneously and in real time both with the content and with others, without the need to be physically co-located. All the above attracted the educators' interest, and a new term 'Virtual Learning' was coined (Bredl et al., 2012; Childs, 2010; de Freitas et al., 2010).

Educational institutions initially introduced the use of virtual environments in their Distance Learning courses as an innovative, interactive, and engaging way of delivering their course material. The academic staff in the University of Bedfordshire (host of the project) followed accordingly, using the virtual environment platform 'Second Life', as a supplementary tool to their traditional teaching methods (Conrad, 2011; Conrad et al., 2010; Conrad et al., 2009). The first experience and feedback received from students were highly encouraging, aiding towards the grounding of such virtual environments, as well as the ongoing active research in the field.

Numerous and various terms have been coined for Hybrid Virtual Learning (HVL). In this study, HVL is defined as the simultaneous co-presence of both the teaching team and the students, both in the physical classroom and in the virtual world. A large portion of the existing literature concludes that developing high levels of immersion is the key to success if better learning results are to be achieved. However, it is really intriguing that, in this study, high levels of immersion were not present, due to the students' continuous interaction when altering between the two environments (physical and virtual). Based on this anecdotal observation, we sought for information on the impact that immersion has on Hybrid Virtual Learning models. Interestingly enough, the review of the literature suggested that most researchers focus primarily on the intrinsic elements that affect learner engagement, while they partially, if not completely, disregard the existence of the physical environment. Consequently, after identifying this research gap, a hypothesis was formed that a synergy between learner engagement and interactions might exist. As we actually had access both to the person who interacts (real identity) and to their avatar (virtual identity), it was decided to systematically evaluate the impact of interactions in both environments, as a combination and not as individual components.

This chapter will offer an overview of the history of and developments in the use of virtual environments by different providers over the past years, along with a discussion on the experiments and findings. In the conclusions section, an evaluation will be provided regarding the different kinds of interactions and their impact on learner engagement.

INTERACTION AND ENGAGEMENT

Activities that include 3D content creation and exploration as well as student collaboration have been extensively studied (Carter, 2012; Hockey et al., 2010). Schrader (2008) has identified four different combinations that link technology and learning, which are, namely, 'learning about technology', 'learning from technology', 'learning with technology', and 'learning in technology'. Users are represented by avatars (artificial figures), interacting that way with both the content and others. Some examples of that interaction are: object creation and manipulation, terrain editing and navigating around the world, chatting, and the use of gestures (Allison et al., 2012; Bredl et al., 2012; Dalgarno and Lee, 2010; Herbet et al., 2012; Hockey et al., 2010).

Vygotsky's Social Constructivist Learning Theory (1978) is still considered a cornerstone with great practical applications in learning within virtual worlds, even if recent research (Padróset al., 2012; Veletsianos, 2009) may have slightly differentiated from it. According to Vygotsky (1978), students construct their cognitive structures through interactions, while engagement through any kind of activity motivates them to learn. Jones (2013) underlines that virtual worlds enable learners to develop, alter, and enhance their content in accordance to their needs, allowing them to construct their cognitive schemas and engage with the phenomena they study. Indeed, interacting within virtual worlds can be very beneficial for learners (Christopoulos, 2013; Dalgarno & Lee, 2010), as learning becomes more student-centered and self-directed (Zhao et al., 2010), whilst the educator gets the role of the designer, instructor, and supporter of the activities (Anasol et al., 2012; Schrader, 2008).

Even though the importance of interactions upon learning activities has been extensively discussed (Camilleri et al., 2013; Childs, 2010; Christopoulos, 2013; de Freitas et al., 2009), very few attempts have been made to develop frameworks for the evaluation of their impact on these activities (Bronack et al., 2006; de Freitas & Oliver, 2006).

In addition, most of the existing taxonomies focus on the interactivity of virtual worlds per se, and not on the interactions that can—or need to—be developed. Camilleri et al. (2013) studied in detail the in-world interactions aiming to explain how students learn in-world, but disregarded the perspective of learning in the physical classroom (e-Learning experiment). Childs (2010), who investigated the skills students acquire when they start using virtual worlds, formed a taxonomy which classified interactions into four categories:

1. **Interacting With the World:** Motion, maneuvering, way-finding, camera positions, mouselook.
2. **Interacting With Others:** Local/private chat, using the minimap to find people and move towards them.
3. **Interacting With the Avatar:** Changing the avatar's appearance, animating avatars.
4. **Finding and Searching:** Creating landmarks and teleporting to new locations.

Nevertheless, this taxonomy did not include the content development process, or the programming skills that students need to acquire in order to shape the world. Steuer (1992) concluded that the factors affecting the virtual worlds' interactivity are speed and range, whilst Chafer and Childs (2008) reported that manipulability, reciprocation, and responsiveness also affect it.

All the aforementioned studies can be truly helpful for educators who need an approach to measure the interactivity of their virtual environments. However, what needs to be pointed out is that all of them—partially or even completely—disregard the interactions that take place in the physical classroom.

Levesque and Lelièvre (2011), who examined interactions as a combination in a Hybrid Virtual Learning scenario, reported that a complex network of interactions was observed being developed between the two environments. Special mention was also made regarding the way interactions occurred both among students, and between the students and the world. As a concluding remark, they suggest that further research should be conducted, since there are more parameters that have to be identified and considered in terms of interactions. De Freitas et al. (2010) also underline the need for further investigation in the potential and the affordances of hybrid spaces. Elliott et al. (2012) point out a lack of a detailed taxonomy of all the interactions related to the use of virtual worlds in an educational context.

Based on the aforementioned recommendations for a further investigation of interactivity and engagement, a series of different experiments was conducted for the purposes of this study. The main aim was to identify whether or not interactions affect learner engagement in Hybrid Virtual Learning scenarios, and, if so, taxonomise them based on their impact. We also wish to provide a framework and a substantial guide to educators and instructional designers who want to develop such engaging and interactive learning activities, by developing a better understanding of the affordances to design more expedient activities.

INSTITUTIONAL CONTEXT

In 2007 the University of Bedfordshire utilised Second Life in various teaching and research projects. These projects were integrated into the Project Management course, designed for the final year undergraduate and postgraduate students. Students were asked to apply the PRINCE2® Project Management methodology to build an educational showcase. The general setup of this latter assignment, and in particular the difficulty in dealing with large student numbers, has been discussed in Conrad et al. (2009). The added value of using Second Life in enhancing the acquisition of Project Management skills is presented in Conrad (2011) within the context of situated learning (Herrington & Oliver, 2000).

However, issues with the Linden Lab—as the service provider of Second Life—regarding the termination of the educational discount (Harrison, 2010), made it imperative to explore alternative solutions. It was, therefore, decided to seek alternative options without compromising the delivery of the classes. Two providers were trialed, namely, Dreamland Metaverse, a company that offers regions within the OSgrid infrastructure, and ReactionGrid Inc.,with their own dedicated grid infrastructure. Both worlds are based on the OpenSimulator technology, which aims to be compatible with Second Life clients, and provides in-world a 'look and feel' similar to Second Life. Since 2013, the OpenSimulator technology has been used to develop an institutionally hosted virtual world, resourced from the university and supported by the in-house technical support team. A brief presentation of the units' structure is provided below.

Unit A: Event Oriented Programming (Undergraduate)

This is a four-week course where the Linden Scripting Language (LSL) is introduced to underpin the understanding of Event Driven Programming (Ferg, 2006). Weekly lectures consist of the theoretical concepts plus material adapted from the Second Life LSL wiki. In the practical sessions students write scripts with simple functionality. These are deployed in-world and tested by the students' avatars. Typical examples include objects that change color or produce messages when touched. The implementation of object-to-object interaction explores the various uses of communication channels.

Unit B and C: Project Management (Undergraduate and Postgraduate)

These are, respectively, a twenty-four-week (undergraduate level) unit, and a twelve-week (postgraduate level) one on Project Management. Students are required to build an educational showcase as part of a

PRINCE2® managed project. The average amount of time that students are expected to spend in-world ranges between six to eight weeks (Undergraduate), or four to eight weeks (Postgraduate). For details about the general setup of the assignment, reference can be made to Conrad et al. (2009).

RESEARCH METHODS

After reviewing the literature, we concluded that the topic of interactivity and engagement was an interesting area to further examine, especially since it had not been widely investigated. Thus, in order to contextualize the focus of this study, the following hypothesis was developed:

The use of Hybrid Virtual Learning models results in higher levels of engagement with the learning material, thanks to the wide network of interactions that is being developed between the environments. And the following research questions were generated:

How do interactions affect learner engagement when Hybrid Virtual Learning models are used? Also, how do learners' personal choices and preconceptions, regarding the use of virtual worlds in education, enhance or constrain the educators' plans to develop engaging and interactive learning experiences?

The study used a mixed-methods research design that allows for the triangulation of the primary data, leads to a deeper insight of the phenomena, and, hence, enhances the validity and diversity of the results. Students' actions and behaviors were monitored through observations, whilst their thoughts and tendencies were recorded through surveys. The survey's statements were developed and analyzed under the principles of the Likert Scale methodology, as described in Kothari (2014). The data collected from the observations and the open-ended questions of the a posteriori survey were analyzed using the Grounded Theory coding process, as described by Strauss & Corbin (1998).

EXPERIMENTS' SETUP

To contextualise the study and also examine the impact that the instructional designers' decisions have on learners' interactions and engagement, a combination of three different experiments (abbreviated as E1, E2 and E3) was proposed and tested using the aforementioned teaching units (Unit A, B, and C). All these units are under the Computer Science 'umbrella;' however, the knowledge acquisition and the learning outcomes are slightly different. Therefore, in order to distinguish each one (Unit A, B, and C) in relation to each experiment, three different identifiers were used. The Event Driven Programming unit is abbreviated as 'a,' whilst the Undergraduate Project Management unit as 'b,' and the Postgraduate Project Management unit as 'c.' The combination of the experiments' number (1, 2, and 3) with each unit code (a, b, and c) resulted in having 3 sub-experiments (e.g., E1a, E2a… EXy) every year.

Students who participated in E1a, E2a, and E3a, were expected to acquire strong and solid knowledge related to the structure and functionality of the event-driven programming embedded in Graphical User Interface (individual assignment). In the rest sub-experiments, the emphasis of the learning outcome was more on the scenario management (group project), and less on the knowledge acquisition related to the 3D development, or the programming language per se.

Each one of these experiments was tested against different student cohorts, so as to broaden the opportunities to collect diverse data, and provide strong conclusions. Participation in the study (in both the surveys and the observations) was voluntary, and all the enrolled students were invited to participate. In other words, no filtering in terms of setting up 'standards' or specific criteria, such as age, gender, nationality, were made. Likewise, no particular selection, such as prior experience in similar platforms or generic interest in using or not virtual worlds/games, was made either.

Experiment 1

The content developed by former university students was used to contextualize E1 (Table 1). In particular, the most outstanding projects were selected and used as example showcases for the newcomers, aiming to identify how such content can increase the opportunities for interaction both with the content and with other students (Figure 1).

At this point it should be mentioned that only one island was available by this time, and, thus, high levels of server instability were observed, due to the server load. As a result, the frequent sim crashes affected the overall process and engagement in a negative way.

Experiment 2

Educators who have used virtual worlds stress the importance of providing students with enough time to familiarise themselves with the world and its tools. However, the strict university time frames make that hard or even impossible (Christopoulos, 2013). Considering that this is a time-consuming process, it is questionable whether or not instructional designers can facilitate, or even speed up this process. To examine this matter, an orientation area was developed that included theoretical information and practical exercises and focused on: the avatars' editing appearance process, the communication channels, and the use and development of gestures or animations. The aforementioned material was present in a 'school- like' building next to a sandbox area, which contained mostly technical information related to object creation and manipulation. In this area, students could freely experiment without 'messing up' their workspaces. The orientation building was surrounded by a park and a meeting point, where students could meet up or rest, away from their workspaces (Figure 2). The aim of this experiment was to examine whether or not this process can help students acquire all the knowledge and skills required to cope with the world, by increasing the incentives for interaction, and, therefore, engagement (Table 2).

The content developed by former students became unavailable, in order to focus explicitly on one parameter. In addition, further technical work on the server side was conducted, to improve the world's stability.

Table 1. Overview of the first experiment

Participant Group	E1a	E1b	E1c
Participants' academic level	Undergraduate	Undergraduate	Postgraduate
Period	November 2013—January 2014	January —March 2014	April —June 2014
Duration (weeks/hours)	4 weeks / 12 hours	8 weeks / 16 hours	8 weeks / 16 hours

Figure 1. Snapshot of a mix & match students' work in progress and completed (example) showcases

Table 2. Overview of the second experiment

Participant Group	E2a	E2b	E2c
Participants' academic level	Undergraduate	Undergraduate	Postgraduate
Period	November 2014—January 2015	January —March 2015	April —June 2015
Duration (weeks/hours)	4 weeks/12 hours	6 weeks/ 12 hours	6 weeks/ 12 hours

Experiment 3

For this experiment, the following content was available to students: an amusement park, a small lake, a café, a maze, and an avatar-racing game (Figure 3).

The employment of the leisure games aimed at evoking strong childhood memories, and further enhancing the already playful nature of the virtual world. Interacting with the games would increase the opportunities for interaction, not only with the content of the virtual world, but also with other students (collaboration, exploration). Thus, the aim of this content was to investigate whether or not it can have an impact on interactions, and, hence, learner engagement, especially with those students who had negative preconceptions regarding using the virtual world at first hand. On top of that, the educational games aimed at aiding the educational process (knowledge revision, rewards for their assignments). In

Figure 2. Snapshot of the orientation building, the sandbox, and the meeting park

Table 3. Overview of the third experiment

Participant Group	E3a	E3b	E3c
Participants' academic level	Undergraduate	Undergraduate	Postgraduate
Period	November 2015—January 2016	January —March 2016	May —June 2016
Duration (weeks/hours)	4 weeks/ 12 hours	6 weeks / 12 hours	4 weeks / 8 hours

both cases, as this content was fairly massive, students could also be benefited by getting some ideas for their own projects (Table 3).

As with the previous experiments, the content from E1 or E2 became unavailable. Additional technical work was conducted and the available island was expanded from one to three, so as to further increase the stability of the world

DISCUSSION OF THE FINDINGS

For convenience reasons, the primary data of this study have been outsourced in the form of Appendices, and can be accessed from http://perisic.com/marc-conrad/students/AddedValue.pdf. The following sections will provide a synopsis of the data collected through the observations (Appendix 1) and surveys (Appendices 2-3). Some student behaviors and actions were observed more frequently than others which were rarely or never observed. Students' choices to act in certain ways can draw a clear and consistent picture regarding their attitude towards the use of a virtual world in the context of their academic studies.

The sample of the a priori survey (334) consisted of both undergraduate and postgraduate university students with a relatively short prior experience in such environments. The sample of the a posteriori

Figure 3. Snapshots of the leisure areas and the educational games

survey (472) reported that the student-to-world interactions played a more important role in their engagement, as opposed to the student-to-student ones (Appendices 2-3).

Preconceptions and Attitude Towards Virtual Worlds

After the first year of this study, due to the negative rumors about the virtual world spread by former students, we deemed necessary to administer one more questionnaire. The a priori questionnaire was distributed to students prior to their first contact with the virtual world, questioning their thoughts and preconceptions as to the use of this technology for educational practices. Furthermore, as sub-experiments b and c ran in the context of a group project, not all the students were required to actively engage with the world. Thus, a small difference in the total number of students who filled in the a priori and the a posteriori questionnaire can be seen. In addition, students who had participated in the Event Driven Programming classes (unit a), also attended the (compulsory) Project Management classes (unit b). This justifies the considerably high numbers of students with minor prior experience (up to a month) in the use of virtual worlds like Second Life and/or OpenSim.

Most participants with experience reported that it was quite positive (87), though a considerable number of them maintained a neutral position (53). Only few expressed a negative one (7). In any case, for more than half of the sample, this would be the first time that such a platform was being used. Interestingly, the vast majority had heard positive (133) or very positive (31) comments about this technology, and only a few had heard negative (19) ones. Despite their positive stance and preconceptions, participants seemed mindful regarding the contribution of a virtual world in an educational project, as most of them responded negatively (113) or maintained a neutral stance (101). Cross-examining these findings, two questions are raised:

- **Value of Using a Virtual World:** Why did students find the use of a virtual world in an educational context of little or no value, despite the fact that their stance and preconceptions were generally positive?
- **Experience in Using a Virtual World:** Why would students still want to engage in activities in the virtual world, despite the fact that they thought this was not a worthwhile experience?

These questions identify an area where further investigation has to be conducted to shed light on the way that students perceive virtual worlds when it comes to higher education—as opposed to leisure and socialization purposes.

Virtual World but 'Real' Emotions

Students experienced various feelings ranging from happiness and enjoyment to confusion, displeasure, and disappointment. Each one of these emotions affected their interactions and engagement with the virtual world very diversely. Furthermore, the levels of engagement students had with the virtual world differed completely from the levels of engagement they had with their task.

Students' personal preferences and preconceptions, prior experiences, and adaptability to new technologies, directly affected the way they perceived and adapted to the world. Thus, some students were more comfortable with using it, whilst others found difficulty even to navigate within it. In any case, only a few students were observed to intensely dislike this technology.

The main incidents that generated negative feelings or dissatisfaction were the server latencies/crashes, and the difficulty students had to manipulate virtual objects or non-functional scripts. The former affected engagement in two opposite ways, as some students opted to spend more time expanding their knowledge and improving their work, whilst others gave up. On the other hand, the intermediate breaks in order to edit their avatars' appearance, explore the world, and 'play' with others, positively influenced their emotions and experience. Students' decision to work in groups or individually also affected their engagement. With only few exceptions, students who decided to work alone, or completely isolated from others, were less engaged with the virtual world, and were often observed struggling to deal with its tools. On the other hand, those who decided to work in groups were observed helping and influencing each other, and, consequently, the teaching team would interfere only when deemed absolutely necessary.

The design and development process of 3D objects, using the in-world tools, attracted students' attention and resulted in higher levels of engagement. On the other hand, the use of third-party software resulted in having an almost complete lack of engagement with the virtual world, as students were focused exclusively on achieving good results. Furthermore, higher levels of engagement were observed after reaching half way through the completion of their assignment. This can be justified in two ways: either because students were more familiar and comfortable with the world and its tools, or because of the need to complete and submit their assignment. In any case, students were also observed being completely detached from the virtual world from time to time, as they were performing tasks related to other needs of their assignment, browsing the web, or discussing matters unrelated to the university.

The 'Trending' Topics

Content development and scripting were often the highlights of students' talks. However, the 'hard-to-use' (quoting students' comments) in-world building and scripting tools triggered discussions about the use of a third party software, too. The negative comments heard were mainly referring to the technology per se (graphics, scripting language, latency/server crashes). On the other hand, students were observed being content with their achievements, or surprised when getting unexpected results.

Students' emotional experience and comments were positive and enthusiastic, especially during exploration. Nevertheless, some students' willingness to 'secure'—prevent others from entering—their workspaces, caused disappointment to others. Furthermore, those who struggled with the in-world tools claimed that this technology is used exclusively in such environments, and, thus, no 'true' knowledge is gained. On top of that, they reported that their experience was disadvantageous and doubtful, since it had nothing to offer them as a learning tool. However, students were willing to share with each other their knowledge and thoughts (peer-tutoring) when requests for feedback and suggestions were made (peer-learning). That eliminated the negative preconceptions and thoughts, as seen from the positive concluding remarks.

Students' verbal interaction with the teaching team covered topics related to the marking scheme, informal feedback, suggestions for development and demonstrations related to the in-world tools. Especially during the early stages, requests for objects removal were made to the server administrator, as students' workflow was being negatively affected. Hence, the following question is raised: why did students not opt to contact their fellow students in order to solve their issues, but, instead, addressed the issue to the teaching team?

Students were also observed discussing matters outside the scope of their project, though related to the virtual world. Some of the topics discussed were: access of the world from portable devices (tablets), use of hardware to improve the Virtual Reality experience (headsets), inclusion of this virtual world technology in other university units. It is noteworthy that a small portion of students was often detached from the classroom discussing matters irrelevant to the project or the virtual world.

Several students complained because of the limited number of scripts they were allowed to use per team in the Project Management units. In fact, one of them proposed to setup his own virtual world so as to have 'unlimited' number of scripts, which was welcomed by several students who also expressed their willingness to work undistracted. These proposals were, of course, rejected by the teaching team. However, they are a significant indication of the different way a portion of students perceived the in-world interactions, who worked in-world only to fulfill the requirements of their assignment—hence the 'ease' of the extra scripts—and get good grades.

Alternative Communication Channels

Most students, with only few exceptions, used the chat tool infrequently and only when deemed absolutely necessary. This is because either they were physically co-located, or, when this was not possible, they would opt to use 'social media platforms' or 'VoIP tools' (quoting students' comments). In fact, the lack of embedded VoIP system was pointed out as a drawback of this technology. Considering how frequently the chat tool was used, several were the times when internet slang language was observed. On top of that, students who were motivated by and being used to virtual games, were even observed using command lines that do not exist in this world. The above instances indicate that students did have experience with similar online tools, yet they were reluctant to use the chat tool because they did not prefer it.

In-world communication was more intense during the first practical sessions, as students were observed greeting each other, commenting on others' avatars or artifacts. On-the-spot help requests were also observed, though. When the subject was too complicated, students would opt to move closer (physically) to their fellow students and hold a face-to-face conversation. Usually the matters being discussed were related to their project or the world, and the language used was English. However, some students used their mother tongue, hindering this way the researcher's understanding of the conversation topic. Furthermore, even when communication was in English, if the discussed matters were unrelated to the university, distance was discreetly maintained.

Though rarely, students' emotions or feelings were also imprinted in-world. This was not only observed but further confirmed from the server's chat logs. During exploration, phrases revealing excitement, happiness or admiration could be seen. On the other hand, students who were struggling with the in-world tools expressed their dissatisfaction in the global chat. Furthermore, students with inappropriate behavior received several 'warning' messages, delivering senders' irritation or frustration. Lastly, the server freezes or crashes caused intense disappointment to students, often discussed in the global chat.

Those who discovered the gestures' library were observed testing them at least once, and even motivated others to do so. Students who role-played or used their avatars as part of their assignment's needs, were even observed developing their own gestures combinations. Some of them also used poseballs (scripted objects) to animate their avatars. However, nearly all students avoided the often or unnecessary use of the non-verbal communication channels. In addition, some of them even removed the default animated typing move, as they considered it to be 'too annoying' (quoting students' words). Even though various emoticons were observed both in the public chat and in private messages expressing students' feelings and emotions, the frequency was not as often as it is accustomed in the social media.

Transition From 'Real' to 'Virtual' Identity

The default avatar appearance was considered 'ugly' and 'basic' (quoting students' comments), leading most students to alter it almost immediately after entering the world for the first time. This action was taking place more intensely during the first sessions, though some students were working on it up until the completion of their projects. Some of the avatar-related interactions students experienced include: exchange of ideas, provision of feedback, or even control of the others' avatars. Using mostly the in-world tools, students modified the avatars' appearance (body shape, skin/hair color and clothing) to resemble either their 'real' identity, or role-play (opposite gender, imaginary creatures, and robots). Nevertheless, some students made slight or no modifications at all.

Due to the lack of knowledge, various questions or requests were raised, especially at the early stages. Students who removed their avatars' clothing or stretched their shape to the limit, sought help to restore appearance to default. In fact, they even admitted feeling ashamed when taunted by their fellow students. Moreover, they expressed their wish for an option to buy and sell outfits using virtual currency. Others sought ways and options to have a 'health pool' for their avatars. All the above give a clear indication that students developed the sense of in-world presence, and considered themselves part of the world.

Indirect and unintended references to avatars were made mainly during the first sessions, and more intensely from those who edited their avatars' appearance. Nevertheless, as students were using the first person to communicate with others in most occasions, we cannot safely claim whether or not they had identified themselves with their avatars. References to avatars using the second person were more direct and easier to detect, though rare. Even more infrequent were the references observed addressing avatars in the third person or even as an object. In most occasions, these references were expressing admiration and joy. Comments with a 'sexual' content were also observed, referring to those students who role-played, or those with 'attractive' avatars. In rare cases, expressions revealing anger or frustration could be heard, addressed to students with inappropriate avatars' appearance or behavior. In the role-play spectrum, well-known quotes originating from movies or books were heard, while at the same time students were imitating the corresponding actions in the physical classroom. Lastly, students who had no changes in their avatars' appearance worriedly commented on their fellow students' willingness to put effort on this process, as they considered it a waste of time or unnecessary.

'Behind' the Avatar

Avatars affect users' virtual embodiment, which renders them one of the most important features that virtual worlds have to offer (Childs, 2010). Editing the avatars' appearance was among the first types of interaction students—especially those with prior experience—had. However, the more engaged students were becoming with the world, the keener they were to make more complex and detailed modifications on their avatars. From the teaching team's perspective, there were no restrictions, as long as the modifications were in an acceptable and appropriate way. Most of the students decided to replicate their real identity, as they considered the virtual world to be an extension of the physical classroom. Roleplaying is also an option that virtual worlds offer. Thus, students—especially those coming from the Games and Animation course—made some intense and detailed modifications on their avatars, such as dwarfs, super heroes, or fiction characters. Finally, it is noteworthy that a few students modified their avatars for the needs of their assignment.

The in-world references to avatars were limited or almost non-existent. Nevertheless, the inappropriate behavior of some students led others to make requests—or even warn them—to stop disturbing them. Even though avatars were named after students' real identity and chat logs were being maintained, not all of them were minding their language or behavior. Thus, some important considerations are posed: Is students' unusual behavior or misbehavior due to their personality, or to the 'freedom' the virtual world offers in the wider context of 'immersion' or 'engagement?' Would students have become more 'engaged' with the world if they had had the option to choose a nickname instead of their real identity? As these were out of the scope of our study, researchers are suggested to further examine them in the future.

'Real' Task in a Virtual World

Interactions played an important role in student engagement, though not all of them were equally intense. Having pre-existing content was deemed to be extremely helpful for the student cohorts who participated in E1, whilst those from E2 and E3 very often mentioned the lack of example showcases. Students expressed the difficulty and disappointment to deal with the virtual world and its tools, at least initially. Nevertheless, it should be mentioned that only few students showed interest in visiting and going through the orientation area, as observed during E2. In addition, the leisure games and areas attracted the attention and interest of most students, whereas the educational ones left almost all of them completely uninterested.

The types of interactions that students had with the world can be classified into four categories:

- **Content Exploration** *(i)*
- **Use of the Building and Scripting Tools** *(ii)*
- **Avatar Appearance Modification** *(iii)*
- **Communication with Others** *(iv)*

As avatars *(iii)* and communication *(iv)* have already been discussed, the following two sub-categories will elaborate on the first two categories.

Content Exploration (i)

The opportunities for exploration, especially during the first practical sessions, were limited (excluding E1). Over time, students were observed visiting others' workspaces to get ideas for their own projects or to provide feedback. Nevertheless, students who blocked access to their workspaces—in an attempt to prevent others from copying their ideas—cannot be disregarded. This reduced the opportunities for interactions, hindering the enhancement of in-world interactivity (content/students), which was a primary aim when designing students' workspaces.

The impact of the orientation area was rather disappointing, at least initially. Students who explored this area and invested time in familiarizing themselves with the world and its tools, found it easier to work and collaborate with others in the long run. However, the majority showed lack of interest to go through this process and disregarded, almost completely, its existence. As a result, they were observed struggling and often making questions which could have been answered if they had chosen to be properly oriented. Over time, students were observed visiting the orientation area, after being advised to do so by other students.

The impact of the leisure and educational content was diverse. Students were observed visiting the leisure areas often enough. However, they were not always observed playing with the games. On the other hand, only a few were observed visiting or even using the maze, whilst none of them used the racing-knowledge game. This becomes more interesting after considering that particular emphasis was given (by the teaching team) to the fact that students could revise their knowledge on a weekly basis and also get unique rewards for their projects. At this point several questions are raised: Why did the educational games not attract students' attention as much as the leisure ones? Is the virtual world already a 'game-like' environment leaving no space for the traditional learning approaches? Or, did students perceive the virtual world merely as a workspace to fulfill the requirements of their assignment and score high marks, instead of a 'leisure box'? In any case, students got inspired by this content and developed (mini) games as part of their own assignment.

Building and Scripting Tools (ii)

During the first practical sessions, with only few exceptions, students spent their time performing actions irrelevant to their projects, yet related to the virtual world. The quick adaptability that some students had, and their willingness to help those who were struggling, speeded up this process making it more enjoyable and less stressful. In any case, most of the students usually became fully familiar with the mechanisms of the world about halfway through the assignment. It is noteworthy, though, that only a few students were keen to explore the full potential of the programming language. This can be attributed to their fear in causing technical issues to the server, to their unfamiliarity with this language, or even to the fast-paced nature of these assignments. On the other hand, much attention was placed on the designing process of 3D objects. In short, students would spend most of their time designing their own 3D objects, and, consequently, using or slightly editing premade scripts that can be found on the web. It is worth mentioning that only a few students used the more advanced tools of the world (e. g. poseballs, animations). Lastly, students' willingness to share their code or objects resulted in having overloaded workspaces, something which negatively affected the stability of the physical server.

The Attributes That Affect Engagement

The interactions students can have both with the virtual objects and with others make the use of a virtual world a worthwhile investment. Participants stated, in the a posteriori survey, that the in-world interactions made the practical session and the learning material more attractive, compared to studying in the traditional sense. As the learning material was becoming more appealing, greater levels of engagement were reported. This is also indicated by the fact that students enjoyed the sessions, as noted in the corresponding statements. The elements that contributed the most to achieving the above are the vividness of the environment, the freedom given to students to observe their creations 'alive,' and the ludic nature of the virtual world. What also facilitated the learning process and helped students experience the knowledge are the real-time awareness of the results of their work, and the immediate feedback they could get from others. The continuous alteration of the students' focus between the real and the virtual world does not seem to have affected the sense of in-world presence. In fact, this justifies the reasons why interactions with others (in-world) were less intense. Indeed, when students were physically co-located, their communication needs were covered in-class. However, in cases where this was not feasible, they would—at least initially—opt to use the in-world communication tools to cover them.

Student-to-world interactions seem to have a substantially great impact on learner engagement in four aspects:

- **Content:** Interactions with the content, as an exclusive feature of virtual worlds, have some unique impacts and benefits on learning. An increased level of willingness and enthusiasm to participate in practical sessions was reported. However, students noted that their interactions with their fellow students had similar—yet slightly more limited—impact on their perception and attitude regarding the world.
- **Object creation:** The 3D design and scripting were the core parts of these assignments. The reflection of their responses provides a clear indication that this kind of activities can significantly increase student engagement with the learning material.
- **3D:** The 3D element turned coding into a stimulating activity, since students were able to design and observe 3D objects performing actions. Participants also stated that interacting with the content of the world helped them experience the learning material and have real-time awareness of the results of their work, since these were visualised in 3D representations.
- **Creations:** Overall, students enjoyed more using their own creations. Exploring others' artefacts helped them get ideas for their own work, but not all of them would opt to use them. Thus, it can be said that the more the content was, the greater the levels of enjoyment were, too.

Student-to-student interactions did not seem to have influenced student engagement as extensively as the student-to-world ones. Nevertheless, their impact on some points was highlighted, and are presented below:

- **Assignment:** In one case it was recorded that student-to-student interactions had a more positive impact—compared to the student-to-world one—as they made the practical session and the assignment more interesting.
- **Collaboration:** Students became more open and positive to collaborations, since the use of this medium encouraged them to cooperate in order to acquire the necessary skills to work on their assignment.
- **Peer-Learning/Tutoring:** Cross-examining the responses given in the statements regarding the 'learning from' and 'teaching' others, participants claimed that they felt more involved in the teaching/learning process. However, this is more intense when it comes to 'teaching others' and less when 'being taught' from others.
- **Enjoyment:** The unexpected results and mistakes—especially those deriving from the programming language—made students laugh, which made the process much more enjoyable.
- **Breaks from Work:** The opportunity to have small breaks and perform actions irrelevant to their project was something that was also acknowledged and highlighted as important.

Engagement or Necessity?

Students would usually go online at the starting time of the practical session and leave right after its scheduled completion. In some cases, they were observed leaving the virtual world before the completion of the session. Only rarely would they come online delayed. Those who showed interest in this educational approach would stay in-world more than expected, or come online even prior to the session's starting time. In cases where the assignment was part of a group work, those responsible for the development of the virtual showcase would usually enter the world at the starting point of the session. However, even in those cases, they were not always interacting with the virtual world, as their work was getting interrupted to help their team members on other matters. As a side note, it should be mentioned that most students would remain online past the working hours of the practical sessions. Even though their actions were not observed during these hours, the results of their work could be seen during the weekly observations, as the server logs also confirm.

FUTURE RESEARCH DIRECTIONS

As students and researchers were part of the same university, biases or preconceptions might have affected participants' attitude and behavior, when they were being observed, or when they would answer the surveys. Even though all the necessary measures were taken to differentiate the role of the researcher from that of the educator (cross-examination of the primary data and significant population to generate reliable generalizations), it is highly suggested that the proposed experiments be repeated using different student cohorts, as well as by researchers that will ideally be external to the university environment.

Furthermore, educators, greatly affected by the 'immersion craze' which originated from the entertainment industry, dedicated much time and effort to develop the so-called 'immersive virtual worlds' or 'immersive learning activities'. Indeed, immersion can have a positive impact on users' engagement in virtual games or distance learning scenarios; not to say that it is possibly the key to success. Nevertheless, is the same theory applying in Hybrid Virtual Learning models? Is immersion a necessity to engage students with the virtual world and the learning activities? In our study we attempted to draw a new research direction and provide researchers and instructional designers with alternative focus points. Thus, what is also recommended for further examination is to identify the factors that make such setups successful in other educational fields (outside the spectrum of Computer Science). In addition, the vast evolution of the Virtual Reality technology provides opportunities for new design principles, which should be explored after taking into account the aspect of interactivity in both environments (physical and virtual). Moreover, in our experiments we examined the most common educational scenarios (i.e. use of pre-existing content, orientation process, educational/leisure games) individually, as suggested in the literature. It is, therefore, advised that the aforementioned scenarios be examined as a combination, and even within different setups employed, such as the use of Artificial Intelligence agents. Lastly, in the previous sections, during the presentation of our findings, various questions arose. Nevertheless, as they were not in the context or scope of this study, they could not be examined, and, thus, are proposed for further examination.

CONCLUSION

The importance of examining interactions both in the virtual world and in the physical classroom, in conjunction with one another and not in isolation, has been confirmed in this study. In fact, this is the essence of employing Hybrid Virtual Learning models: maximizing the benefits of each educational practice. Indeed, both types of interactions play a crucial role in learner engagement, as they contribute to enhancing the benefits deriving from using the virtual world alone. Unlike virtual games, where the sense of in-world presence, the so-called 'immersion, is a key factor, when it comes to educational practices immersion does not seem to have much relevance or effect (if any). Furthermore, the in-world student-to-student interactions seem to have a slightly lesser impact on learner engagement, compared to the student-to-world ones. Nevertheless, their impact on engagement and learning truly exists and should not be disregarded.

The role of educators or instructional designers is that of a 'game changer' in the teaching and learning process. Learners' personal preferences, choices, or preconceptions, might come in contrast with the instructional design. However, it is of vital importance that educators provide learners with clear information and instructions regarding the relevant content, and even encourage them to use it, as it has been designed and developed in their favor. Undoubtedly, not every learner will be attracted by the same design approach. Nevertheless, the higher the levels of interactivity are, the higher the chances to attract students' attention and engagement with the process will be. Therefore, instructional designers should pay special attention when designing and developing educational content, since the main reason for doing so is to motivate students to develop and expand their knowledge through it.

Providing students with pre-existing content or example showcases should be an integral part of the content of the virtual world, as well. The existence of such content has many advantages, as it allows students to have a comparison measurement against their aims and goals, and also provides them with ideas for development and experimentation. It also turns the virtual world into a more 'real' or 'alive' environment, which is conducive to the feeling of being part of a wider community.

Students really need to have some form of guidance related to the world and its tools, especially at the early stage, be it through the use of an orientation area or any other similar method. However, the freedom that virtual worlds offer, and the human instinct to explore the unknown, make it hard to patronize procedures. Thus, chances are that students will rather attempt to explore the world and its tools by themselves, instead of going through a specific process. Nevertheless, having an information 'fountain' available at any given point comes handy.

Lastly, both leisure and educational games have potentially higher chances of attracting learners' attention, and can, therefore, engage them with the virtual world. Some may be inspired, while others may perceive them purely as a way to break their routine and entertain themselves. Either way, the existence of these games can help students familiarize themselves with the in-world tools, or even make them perceive the learning process in a more enjoyable way. Nevertheless, the impact of this content on the learning process may be considered minimal or even non-existent.

REFERENCES

Allison, C., Campbell, A., Davies, C. J., Dow, L., Kennedy, S., & McCaffery, J. P. (2012). Growing the use of Virtual Worlds in education: an OpenSim perspective. In *Proceedings of the 2nd European Immersive Education Summit: EiED 2012* (pp. 1–13). Paris, France: Universidad Carlos III de Madrid.

Anasol, P. R., Callaghan, V., Gardner, M., & Alhaddad, M. J. (2012). End-user programming and deconstrutionalism for co-creative laboratory activities in a collaborative mixed-reality environment. In Gardner, M., Garnier, F., & Kloos, C. D. (Eds.), *Proceedings of the 2nd European Immersive Education Summit: EiED 2012* (pp. 1-13). Paris, France: Universidad Carlos III de Madrid.

Bredl, K., Groß, A., Hünniger, J., & Fleischer, J. (2012). The avatar as a knowledge worker? how immersive 3d virtual environments may foster knowledge acquisition. *The Electronic Journal of Knowledge Management, 1*(10), 15–25. Retrieved from, http://www.ejkm.com/issue/download.html?idArticle=316

Bronack, S., Rield, R., & Tashner, J. (2006). Learning in the Zone: A social constructivist framework for distance education in a 3-dimensional virtual world. *Proceedings of Interactive Learning Environments, 14*(3), 219–232. doi:10.1080/10494820600909157

Camilleri, V., de Freitas, S., Montebello, M., & McDonagh-Smith, P. (2013). A case study inside virtual worlds: Use of analytics for immersive spaces. In *Proceedings of the 3rd International Conference on Learning Analytics and Knowledge* (pp. 230–234). Leuven, Belgium: ACM. doi:10.1145/2460296.2460341

Carter, B. (2012). Virtual harlem: An innovative past, an evolving present and an exciting future. In *Proceedings of the 2nd European Immersive Education Summit: EiED 2012* (pp. 1–13). Paris, France: Universidad Carlos III de Madrid.

Chafer, J., & Childs, M. (2008). The impact of the characteristics of a virtual environment on performance: Concepts, constraints and complications. In *Proceedings of the Researching Learning in Virtual Environments* (pp. 94-105). Milton Keynes, UK: Open University Press.

Childs, M. (2010). *Learners' experience of presence in virtual* worlds (Unpublished doctoral dissertation). University of Warwick, Coventry, UK.

Christopoulos, A. (2013). *Higher education in virtual worlds: The use of Second Life and Opensim for educational practices* (Unpublished Master thesis). University of Bedfordshire, Luton, UK.

Cohen, L., Manion, L., & Morrison, K. (2011). *Research Methods in Education* (7th ed.). London, UK: Routledge Taylor & Francis.

Conrad, M. (2011). Teaching Project Management in Second Life. In G. Vincenti & J. Braman (Eds.), *Proceedings of Multi-User Virtual Environments for the Classroom: Practical Approaches to Teaching in Virtual Worlds*. Hershey, PA: Idea Group. doi:10.4018/978-1-60960-545-2.ch019

Conrad, M., Neale, J., & Charles, A. (2010). This is my body: The use and effects of the avatar in the virtual world. *International Journal for Infonomics*, *3*(4), 1–9. doi:10.20533/iji.1742.4712.2010.0039

Conrad, M., Pike, D., Sant, P., & Nwafor, C. (2009). Teaching large student cohorts in Second Life. In *Proceedings of the 1st International Conference on Computer Supported Education*. Lisboa, Portugal: SciTePress.

de Freitas, S., & Oliver, M. (2006). How can exploratory learning with games and simulations within the curriculum be most effectively evaluated? *Computers & Education - Virtual Learning*, *46*(3), 249-264.

de Freitas, S., Rebolledo-Mendez, G., Liarokapis, F., Magoulas, G., & Poulovassilis, A. (2009). Developing an evaluation methodology for immersive learning experiences in a Virtual World. In *Proceedings of the Conference in Games and Virtual Worlds for Serious Applications* (pp. 43–50). Coventry, UK: IEEE Computer Society. doi:10.1109/VS-GAMES.2009.41

de Freitas, S., Rebolledo-Mendez, G., Liarokapis, F., Magoulas, G., & Poulovassilis, A. (2010). Learning as immersive experiences: Using the four-dimensional framework for designing and evaluating immersive learning experiences in a virtual world. *British Journal of Educational Technology*, *41*(1), 69–85. doi:10.1111/j.1467-8535.2009.01024.x

Elliott, J. B., Gardner, M., & Alrashidi, M. (2012). Towards a framework for the design of mixed reality immersive education spaces. In *Proceedings of the 2nd European Immersive Education Summit: EiED 2012* (pp. 1–13). Paris, France: Universidad Carlos III de Madrid.

Ellis, S. R. (1994). What are virtual environments? *IEEE Computer Graphics and Applications*, *14*(1), 17–22. doi:10.1109/38.250914 PMID:7757252

Ferg, S. (2006). *Event-Driven Programming: Introduction, Tutorial, History*. Retrieved from http://eventdrivenpgm.sourceforge.net

Garnier, F., & Kloos, C. D. (Eds.). (2012). *Proceedings of the 2nd European Immersive Education Summit: EiED 2012*. Paris, France: Universidad Carlos III de Madrid.

Harrison, D. (2010). Linden Lab to end Second Life educational discounts. *The Journal: Transforming Education Through Technology*. Retrieved from, https://thejournal.com/articles/2010/11/03/linden-lab-to-end-second-life-educational-discounts.aspx

Herbet, A., Thompson, F., & Garnier, F. (2012). Immaterial art stock: Preserve, document and disseminate the pioneering works of art created inside online immersive platforms. In M. Gardner, F. Garnier, & C. D. Kloos (Eds.), *Proceedings of the 2nd European Immersive Education Summit* (pp. 101–113). Paris, France: Universidad Carlos III de Madrid.

Herrington, J., & Oliver, R. (2000). An instructional design framework for authentic learning environments. *Educational Technology Research and Development*, *48*(3), 23–48. doi:10.1007/BF02319856

Hockey, A., Esmail, F., Jimenez-Bescos, C., & Freer, P. (2010). Built environment education in the era of virtual learning. *Proceedings of the W089 - Special Track 18th CIB World Building Congress*, 200–217.

Jones, D. (2013). An alternative (to) reality. Understanding learning in virtual worlds. In M. Childs & A. Peachey (Eds.), *Human-computer interaction series* (pp. 1–20). London, UK: Springer.

Kothari, C. R. (2004). *Research methodology: Methods & Techniques* (2nd ed.). Delhi, India: New Age International Publisher.

Levesque, J., & Lelièvre, E. (2011). Creation and communication in virtual worlds: Experimentations with OpenSim. In S. Richir, & A. Shirai (Eds.) *Proceedings of the Virtual Reality International Conference* (pp. 22–24). Laval, France: ACM.

Moyles, J. (2002). Observation as a research tool. In M. Coleman & A. J. Briggs (Eds.), *Research Methods in Education with SPSS*. London, UK: Sage.

Padrós, A., Romero, M., & Usart, M. (2012). Measuring the knowledge convergence process in the collaborative game metavals. *Procedia Computer Science*, *15*, 193–202. doi:10.1016/j.procs.2012.10.071

Schrader, P. G. (2008). Learning in technology: Reconceptualising immersive environments. *Journal of Association for the Advancement of Computing in Education*, *4*(16), 457–475.

Shaughnessy, J. J., Zechmeister, E. B., & Zechmeister, J. S. (2003). *Research methods in psychology* (6th ed.). New York, NY: McGraw-Hill.

Steuer, J. (1992). Defining virtual reality: Dimensions determining telepresence. *Journal of Communication*, *42*(2), 73–93. doi:10.1111/j.1460-2466.1992.tb00812.x

Strauss, A., & Corbin, J. (1998). *Basics for Qualitative Research: Techniques and Procedures for Developing Grounded Theory* (2nd ed.). Thousand Oaks, CA: SAGE.

Veletsianos, G. (2009). The impact and implications of virtual character expressiveness on learning and agent-learner interactions. *Journal of Computer Assisted Learning*, *25*(4), 345–357. doi:10.1111/j.1365-2729.2009.00317.x

Vygotsky, L. S. (1978). *Mind Society: The Development of Higher Mental Processes*. Cambridge, MA: Harvard University Press.

Wilkinson, J. (2000). Direct Observation. In G. M. Breakwell, S. Hammond, & C. Fife-Shaw (Eds.), *Research Methods in Psychology* (2nd ed.). London, UK: Sage.

Zhao, H., Sun, B., Wu, H., & Hu, X. (2010). Study on building a 3D interactive virtual learning environment based on OpenSim platform. *Proceeding of the International Conference on Audio, Language and Image Processing*, 1407–1411. doi:10.1109/ICALIP.2010.5684986

KEY TERMS AND DEFINITIONS

Exploratory Learning: Students are encouraged to explore the world's content and construct the necessary knowledge.

Game-Based Learning: Students build their knowledge by playing. It turns the traditional learning into a more entertaining and joyful process, making it more interesting and attractive.

Hybrid Virtual Learning: Virtual worlds are used in conjunction with the traditional classroom learning.

OpenSimulator: The open source alternative of the Second Life™ virtual world owned by Linden Lab.

Virtual World: A three-dimensional computer-generated environment designed and shared by individuals in real time.

Chapter 13
Create-and-Learn:
Education "in" a Synthetic Learning Environment

Michael Vallance
Future University Hakodate, Japan

ABSTRACT

The aim of this chapter is to argue how create-and-learn pedagogy can be used to direct and drive the development of virtual reality applications in academic settings. The chapter discusses the development of a synthetic learning environment that provides a context for new learning and twenty-first century education. A case study of an interdisciplinary project by university undergraduates in Japan designing, modeling, and programming a rudimentary virtual nuclear power plant provides the scenario for reflecting on the learning experiences. The chapter attempts to answer the question: How can education-appropriate virtual reality technology support students in their learning endeavors? The participation "in" technology, described in this chapter, advances the development of particular skill sets, applies knowledge to innovative situations, empowers positive attitudes to active learning, and promotes ethical considerations of the impact of technological implementations.

INTRODUCTION

The developments of technology and the ubiquity of digital media in recent years has accelerated the dynamic paradigm shift in education from 'sit-and-listen' didactic tuition to a 'create-and-learn' discursive pedagogy. To illustrate and make sense of this, the chapter will discuss the design and development of a Synthetic Learning Environment that provides a context for new learning and 21st century education, and subsequently present a case for interdisciplinary education informed by the development of a virtual environment.

The implementation is enacted by a 'try-and-explore' approach to support a 'create-and-learn' pedagogy. This is supported in Japan. For instance, the Japanese government is concerned about the skill sets of its declining workforce in adapting to the new world of work, despite continuing high Math and Science rankings in the global PISA assessments (OECD, 2016). Accordingly, to implement its 'Overhaul

DOI: 10.4018/978-1-5225-3719-9.ch013

of Organization and Overall Operations of National University Corporations' the Japanese Ministry of Education, Culture, Sports, Science and Technology (*Monbu-kagaku-shō*) is requiring all universities to reform their Diploma Policy to meet the needs of a changing demographic. This National University Reform Plan (2015) requires universities to consider knowledge, skills, attitudes, values, and ethics, which have been categorized into four broad classifications: Ways of Thinking; Ways of Working; Ways of Living in the World; Tools for Working.

Being located in Japan, the project outlined in this chapter is accordingly contextualized by the Fukushima Dai'ichi nuclear plant accident of March 11, 2011. The disaster revealed much about Japan's lack of preparedness for nuclear accidents (Lochbaum *et al,* 2014). Despite the brave efforts of its labor force leading up to, and in the aftermath of, the reactor explosions, it became apparent that coordination and communication were disorganized. Moreover, the citizens of Fukushima needed to be better informed and equipped to make sense of the official and social information in order to have a better understanding of the causes of the accident along with its long-term effects. An accessible virtual environment was consequently considered a safe technology space to engage students and the general population (i.e., non-experts) in learning about the Fukushima Dai'ichi nuclear plant situation. It was therefore decided to develop a virtual environment for effective, experiential learning of elementary nuclear power concepts conceptualized by a nuclear accident scenario, and subsequently test users' understanding.

The chapter reports the work-in-progress and is organized as follows. First, an interpretation of learning as a social constructivist effort is provided. Then the notion that technology is now so pervasive that arguments for and against technology use have become irrelevant is presented. Mixed reality environments are then illustrated, in particular a Synthetic Learning Environment. The research project and its implementation are then summarized as a Case Study contextualized by the Fukushima nuclear accident of 2011. A surprising diversion from the project's original goal is then discussed, with implications for future research in Synthetic Learning Environments.

CONSIDERING LEARNING

Active Learning

The process of learning is the acquisition of new skills or new forms of knowledge and understanding (Selwyn, 2017). Bloom (1956) described learning in terms of three overlapping domains involving the manual and physical skills of 'doing' (the psychomotor domain), emotions, attitudes as 'feeling' (the affective domain), and capability and knowledge as 'thinking' (the metacognitive domain). Bloom and colleagues subsequently proposed a taxonomy of knowledge consisting of factual knowledge (relating to a specific discipline), procedural knowledge (techniques and procedures), declarative knowledge (relationship between concepts) and meta-cognitive knowledge (knowledge of one's cognitive demands, limitations and strategies). Anderson *et al.* (2001) updated the taxonomy by mapping the cognitive processes of creating, evaluating, analyzing, applying, understanding and remembering onto the four knowledge dimensions of metacognitive, procedural, conceptual, and factual knowledge. The rationale is that where the two dimensions intersect, a learning objective can be identified. For example, the learning objective that may be associated with 'metacognition' and 'evaluate' could be 'reflect'. The object of the verb (what is being reflected on) is determined by the particular learning domain, problem or context. Anderson *et al.* (*ibid*) recognized though that a learning objective ('what' is to be learnt) is not the same as a learning activity ('how' it is learnt). They reasoned, like Bloom (1956) before them, that teaching situations require clear objectives of the learning expected of the students. Consequently, the taxonomy has become a tried-and-tested heuristic for teachers, course designers and policy makers in developing learning objectives (see Table 1).

Learning objectives are implemented through tasks, whether the task be making notes from a lecture, conducting an experiment in a laboratory, participating in an online discussion, or being actively engaged in out-of-class fieldwork. In any task design it is important to consider its difficulty for the intended learners. Task designers such as school teachers and higher education practitioners need to provide tasks commensurate with the expected successful outcomes that will be developed by the learners. In task design the instructor, as designer, must be aware of the kinds of cognitive load associated with learning. Mayer (2014) outlines three kinds of cognitive load: extraneous where cognitive processes do not support the learning objectives (e.g., distracting features); essential where cognitive processing is aimed at mentally representing the content (e.g., selecting relevant information and organizing it); generative where cognitive processing is making sense of the content (e.g., reorganizing the information and integrating it with prior knowledge). The design and implementation of tasks that account for cognitive load subsequently require an informed pedagogy that promotes active learning (Dewey, 1938; Papert, 1993; Piaget, 1972).

Active learning processes of accommodation (accepting new experiences) and assimilation (making sense of new experiences based upon what is known) form the foundation of a social constructivist pedagogy (Piaget, 1972). Knowledge is not merely a commodity to be transmitted, encoded and retained, but is personal experience to be actively constructed (Papert & Harel, 1993; Vygotsky, 1986). This supposition is supported by Kolb (1984) who states learning is a ''process whereby knowledge is created through the transformation of experience" (p. 41). Vallance and Towndrow (2016) and others (*cf.* Lave & Wenger, 1991) have reasoned that a practical implementation for such active and experiential learning is for students to consider, analyze, solve and make personal meaning from engaging problems. They argue that interdisciplinary problem-solving, in particular, presents opportunities for reciprocation between declarative and procedural knowledge in which personal input and collaborative efforts support cognitive connection that can lead to understanding of concepts and theories in multiple contexts (referred to as 'situated cognition').

Table 1. Anderson et al.'s (2001) updated Bloom's taxonomy

Subject	Cognitive Process	Knowledge Dimension (or Type of Content)
The learner will …	remember (recall, recognize)	Factual knowledge of discrete, isolated, content elements.
	understand (classify, interpret, summarize)	Conceptual knowledge of more complex, organized forms.
	apply (execute, implement)	Procedural knowledge of how to do something.
	analyze (attribute, differentiate, organize)	Metacognitive knowledge (have a general awareness of and about one's own cognition).
	evaluate (check, critique)	
	create (generate, plan, produce)	

Learning 'in' Technology

The integration of technology in teaching and learning has received a great deal of attention. Pedagogical approaches using technology have varied widely due to disparate beliefs about the role of technology (IT or ICT) and the impact of technological advancements (Cuban, 2002; Honey & Kanter, 2013; Ito, 2009; Sandholtz & Dwyer, 1997). However, Vallance and Towndrow (2016) proposed that the notion of IT integration is neither relevant, useful or accurate anymore. For instance, there was a time when we learnt 'from' IT; especially computers that housed pre-programmed expert knowledge and information (Kulik & Kulik, 1991). Later, this relationship developed into one where individuals working alone or in groups learnt 'with' IT. The central idea here was that IT provided us with tools to get certain jobs done more efficiently and effectively (Jonassen *et al.,* 1998). Today, 3D virtual world contexts and social media show that IT has become its own legitimate context for learning and being (de Freitas *et al.,* 2010). In other words, we can now teach and learn 'in' technology and this modality will come to dominate how IT assimilates within our lives, and become a central pillar in what it means to know, learn and grow. Vallance and Towndrow (2016) suggest, "… IT is not just a part of our lives, toolwise, but now forms an important constituent of who we are as people."

This premise is supported by Shrader (2008). He states that learning 'about' technology is learning about tools such as its operation and functions, whether that tool be a computer or a motorcycle. He goes on to state that learning 'from' technology implies that the technology itself is the instructor, and is supported by content delivery. Images of Artificial Intelligence (AI) may come to mind, but in reality the closest we have come is so-called Intelligent Tutoring Systems and Computer Assisted Instruction. In addition, learning 'with' technology may be exemplified by the simple calculator to support mathematical calculations. Use of spreadsheets, databases and concept mapping tools are also examples of learners learning 'with' technology. The argument here is that the technology frees up space for deeper cognitive engagement. Schrader acknowledges this and develops an argument for an additional perspective: learning 'in' technology. He reasons that due to technology being so pervasive nowadays, it has become part of us (e.g., social media), and it may be considered a natural extension of the way we view the world and, therefore, ourselves (*cf.* Turkle, 2011).

Assessment of Learning

Traditionally, paper-based assessments are primarily used for capturing the education experience and newly acquired knowledge. However, a 3D virtual space such as a Synthetic Learning Environment is open-ended with many pathways to success, hence formative evaluations such as post-hoc questionnaires and interviews may be used to get more detailed information from users about their experiences with the system. Also, summative evaluations can be used to compare various techniques in a single experiment. Additionally, a task-based usability evaluation can be structured whereby users are given specific tasks to perform and evaluators may keep track of errors made by the user (*cf.* Bowman, 2004). Nevertheless, assessment in virtual spaces is challenging.

First, there are the physical issues. For example, when donning a Head Mounted Display (HMD) to view a virtual space, the physical world is blocked from the user's view. This means that the evaluator must ensure that the user does not bump into objects or walls, or that the cables stay untangled. Another example involves a common method in traditional evaluation called a 'think-aloud' protocol. This refers to a situation in which the user talks aloud about what he is thinking/doing in the interface. However, many virtual applications use speech input, which would render this evaluation method unsuitable.

In addition, issues related to the evaluator must be considered. For instance, an evaluator can break the user's sense of presence by talking to the user, touching the user, or making changes to the environment during an evaluation. If 'presence' is considered important to the task, the evaluator has to avoid contact with the user during the immersive experience. Moreover, to be quite candid, there are currently a lack of evaluators who can truly be considered experts in virtual space assessment.

Finally, it is problematic to generalize the results of an experiment or evaluation because usually the evaluation is done with a particular type of hardware or a single type of environment. Transfer is therefore difficult to determine as virtual technologies encompass a wide variety of different devices, software systems and environments.

Due to this lack of uniformity, pedagogical approaches need to accommodate physical constraints, virtual space explorations, and students' experiences. Standardized testing as a form of assessment is therefore inappropriate. Alternatively, formative assessment via diagnostics alongside personal learning plans could be used. Students can track themselves, subsequently leading to better metacognition and meta-learning awareness.

To conclude this section, assessment in virtual spaces is challenging and no solution is readily apparent. Education should not impose unrealistic assessment criteria but allow students to learn from one another 'in' the virtual technologies.

Synthetic Learning

The next wave of technology that will have a dramatic impact on our daily lives and education is virtual reality (VR), augmented reality (AR) and mixed reality (MR). These environments will further deepen a person's immersion 'in' technology so that a learner, for instance, will truly be in a sensory-based realm when communicating virtually or engaged in some form of physical activity; whether in a multi-player game or a high-stakes training simulation. Dalgarno and Lee (2010) argue that the advances in representational fidelity and users' interactions are the characteristics that will drive the adoption of 3D virtual environments, particularly in education. They state that the functional properties of spatial knowledge representation, engagement, experiential learning, contextual learning and collaborative learning will further virtual reality, augmented reality and mixed reality adoption.

Consequently, there needs to be a shift in the education - research paradigm as researchers look at ways to evaluate learners in these virtual spaces. Schrader (2008) states, "… teachers and researchers might continue to examine gains in knowledge ('about' or 'from') or human-computer interactions ('with') as possible units of analysis" (p. 467). He goes on to state: "However, because the environment affords a profound degree of interaction otherwise unaccounted for using these levels of analysis, researchers must evaluate performance and learning in other ways" (*ibid*). He recommends that the educator should not deliver instruction 'in' the virtual world. Rather, educators need to create and provide the circumstances by which students engage in learning 'in and out of' a virtual space. See Figure 1, for example, which illustrates students portraying their virtual artifact in the real world. Consequently, the pedagogical implications of learning 'in' technology need to be researched. The next section explains learning 'in' a 3D virtual technology, termed a Synthetic Learning Environment.

Figure 1. Viewing a robot model as an example of augmented reality

Synthetic Learning Environments (SLE) is a term described by Canon-Bowers and Bowers (2008) as, "a learning environment characterized in terms of a particular technology, subject matter, learner characteristics, and pedagogical principles; a synthetic experience, as opposed to real-world interaction with an actual device or process, is created for the learner through a simulation, game, or other technology" (p.318). The synthetic experience becomes a platform for learning, "by augmenting, replacing, creating or managing an actual learner's experience with the world" (*ibid*). They rationalize that well-designed Synthetic Learning Environments provide meaningful contexts for learning to occur through significant experiences, and support the notion that 'expertise' is subsequently developed through experience. It is well known that experts connect new information to existing knowledge. By gaining experiences in a Synthetic Learning Environment a student is able to organize isolated definitions and superficial understandings of terms and concepts into meaningful, connected, and well-organized set of schema that can be transferred to other contexts. This notion is supported by Dalgarno *et al.* (2002) who state: "By exploring and manipulating a 3D virtual environment the learner will develop a spatial model of the concepts represented and that, for certain types of concepts, this spatial model is central to thorough conceptual understanding" (p. 152).

On the other hand, what Synthetic Learning Environments can bring to education is difficult to realize at present because the purpose of a university education is still being determined. For instance, the university may be considered as an imaginary institution: it lives through the imaginaries of its staff and students, and the society in which it is located. Often these imaginaries play against one another: employability against lifelong-learning; play against serious; holistic against specialized. However, virtual environments are designed experiences for a particular user to support active and interactive learning, and they are about building knowledge through meaningful actions in a simulated and stimulating context. Cautiously, deFreitas and Neumann (2009) suggest that the appeal, immersivity and immediacy of virtual worlds can support experiential learning but education requires a re-consideration of how, what, when, and where we learn. To have educational value, Synthetic Learning Environments need well-ordered problem solving contexts, meaningful goals, possibility spaces, feedback and information, empowerment, and reward (Hale & Stanney, 2014).

IMPLEMENTATION OF A SYNTHETIC LEARNING ENVIRONMENT

There is a lot of literature promoting the benefits of games and recent 3D iterations in education from mainstream media (Rhodes, 2016) to corporations (McGonigal, 2012) to academia (Aldrich, 2004). Mayer's (2014) extensive research though offers some caution: "Many strong claims are made for the educational value of computer games, but there is little strong empirical evidence to back up those claims" (p.16). Mayer (*ibid*) seeks: "Better evidence-based theories of how people learn from games" (p.164). Even the term 'gamification' has been ridiculed as he states that there is simply "… no support for the gamification principle" (*ibid*., p.122). Historically, many technology integrations have found that it is not the technology medium that causes learning but the instructional method, and for effective instruction one requires to be a good learning task designer (*cf.* Sandholtz *et al.,* 1997). Moreover, Cuban (2002) concluded his 'oversold and underused' argument by stating that few have pursued the deep and comprehensive changes in the existing system of schooling required to realize the fundamental changes espoused by the promoters of new technologies. The end point, he concluded, is that the effort and expenditure involved in promoting the use of IT in education have been wasted or misguided, or both. The implementation of the project was therefore undertaken heedful of the historical words of experienced practitioners.

Research Aim

The research project aims to determine the impact of a Synthetic Learning Environment beyond the rhetoric of potentiality to realistic, authentic, practical real-world implementations in higher education and high schools in Japan and, later, UK. The rationale is that participation 'in' technology will support students' development of particular skill sets, apply knowledge to innovative situations, empower positive attitudes to active learning, and promote ethical considerations of the impact of technological implementations.

Case Study: Virtual Fukushima Dai'ichi Nuclear Power Plant

As outlined above, the Japanese government is concerned about the skill sets of its declining workforce in adapting to the new world of work. The Higher Education Bureau of *Monbu-kagaku-shō* state: "... cultivating true competencies to learn which enables students to live through the coming era will be impossible if we simply continue education in current styles." It has been argued that trans-boundary, cross-cultural participation can facilitate development of 21st century skills, apply knowledge to innovative situations, empower positive attitudes to active learning, influence emotional values associated with care and understanding, and promote ethical considerations of the impact of technological implementations (Vallance *et al.,* 2015).

The ongoing case study presented in this chapter presupposes that a Synthetic Learning Environment project provides participants with not only a real-life experience with innovative technologies, but also cross-cultural working with Japanese and non-Japanese students; as desired by Japan's Education Bureau. It is reasoned that the active, experiential and interdisciplinary learning can be implemented if learners consider, analyze, solve and make personal meaning from engaging problems 'in' a Synthetic Learning Environment.

Participants

Four participants were engaged in developing the Synthetic Learning Environment of the Fukushima Dai'ichi nuclear power plant with maneuverable robots. One participant was an external professional Unity application developer while the other three were undergraduate students in the researcher's university lab. The developer set the project in motion by creating two main Scenes in the Unity Project. A modeled robot was added along with code to enable its control. Actions such as exploding radioactive bins and a tsunami flood were later added. The three students (all male, aged 19 -20) had no prior Unity programming or 3D modeling experience. They had never before worked on a project together, had diverse interest, limited understanding of the Fukushima accident beyond general media reports, and had never used a Head Mounted Display such as the Oculus Rift. However, they were motivated by the possibility of creating a tangible Synthetic Learning Environment that would be utilized locally (in Japan) and internationally (in a UK school). The students met with the researcher once-a-week throughout two semesters (30 weeks total) but had access to the lab and its resources (hardware and software) 24/7. Language of communication among students was, of course, Japanese but all could communicate adequately in English with the researcher and external colleagues. The Synthetic Learning Environment was developed in English and Japanese.

Synthetic Learning Environment Design

Direct instruction is a predictable pedagogy. A Synthetic Learning Environment though is complex and diverse, with challenging multi-modal and multi-sensory experiences, involving a multitude of narratives in demanding cognitive and physical activities. In developing the Synthetic Learning Environment, students' technical competency needed to be integrated with an expressive capacity through design and aesthetic appreciation. An interdisciplinary pedagogy, reminiscent of the Bauhaus training of artists to integrate material production techniques (i.e., technical knowledge) and mastery of expressive forms (i.e., aesthetic knowledge) into a single holistic approach (Lerner, 2005) was therefore utilized.

It has already been mentioned that the Fukushima Dai'ichi nuclear power plant disaster of March 2011 revealed much about Japan's lack of preparedness for nuclear accidents, and was therefore used as the context for the Synthetic Learning Environment (see above). In developing this Synthetic Learning Environment, the student developers adopted the Successive Approximation Model (SAM) to design, construct and implement their 3D virtual creations. SAM is a development model that uses a continuous iterative process to design, make and play. This was deemed more effective than using the traditional Instructional Design standard ADDIE model (Analysis, Design, Development, Implementation and Evaluation). The ADDIE model was considered limiting as each stage would have had to be corrected before moving onto the next stage. The SAM model allows for more diverse, creative, innovative and unusual possibilities during the creative process as opposed to an evaluation at the 'end' of a process.

To engage the student developers in the active design and construction of their learning environments both in the 3D virtual space and the real world lab, a virtual Fukushima space was subsequently designed for training and familiarity with virtual maneuvers, interactions and 'emotion-mind' conflict that often results in motion sickness when using a Head Mounted Display. Users maneuver a virtual robot with a first-person viewpoint (fpv) using the built-in controller to pick up radioactive bins. A radiation meter in the bottom right corner indicates radioactivity levels that provide a clue as to the nearness of the radioactive bins. A birds-eye view is offered via a virtual drone that can be maneuvered over the Fukushima space seeking out the location of the radioactive bins (see Figure 2). If the robot crashes, then the radioactive bins explode. In addition, after a 6-minute interval a tsunami alarm is activated and the area will flood (see Figure 3).

The virtual structures are 3D models built by the students who had no prior experience of modeling or familiarity with modeling software (i.e., Blender). The animations with Unity were programmed by the students, again with limited experience (see Figure 4). Unity uses C# programming language and students are familiar and do program using similar languages C+ and Java.

Donning the Oculus Rift Head Mounted Display (see Figure 7), users must maneuver a virtual robot to locate and pick up radioactive bins. Users must also gather information among debris and inside buildings. A control room (see Figure 5) with monitors of the Fukushima plant (see Figure 6), together with display panels throughout the space, provide additional information regarding the causes of the accident. There is also a cross-section of Reactor no. 2 plus complete cooling towers; see the drone's camera view in Figure 2. All these structures provide a realistic scenario for users to learn about the basics of nuclear power and explore disaster situations.

Figure 2. The virtual Fukushima space

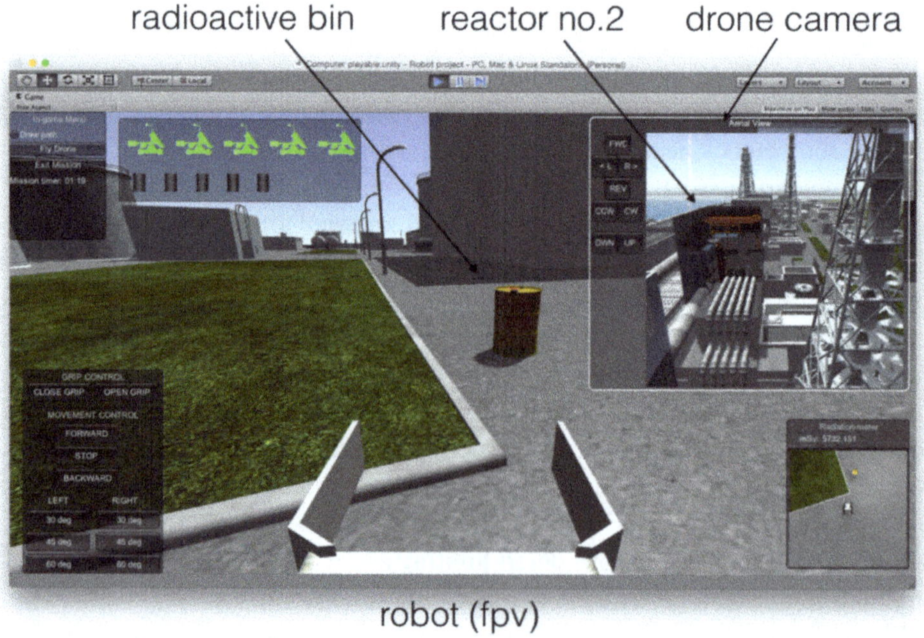

Figure 3. A flooded Fukushima space

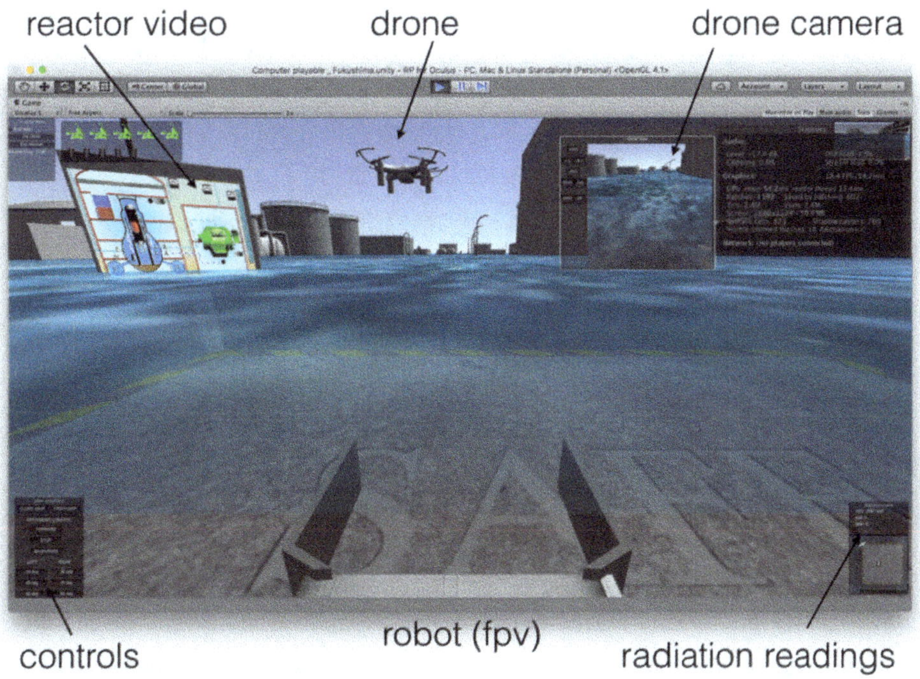

Figure 4. Programming water flow in a pipe as an animation in Unity

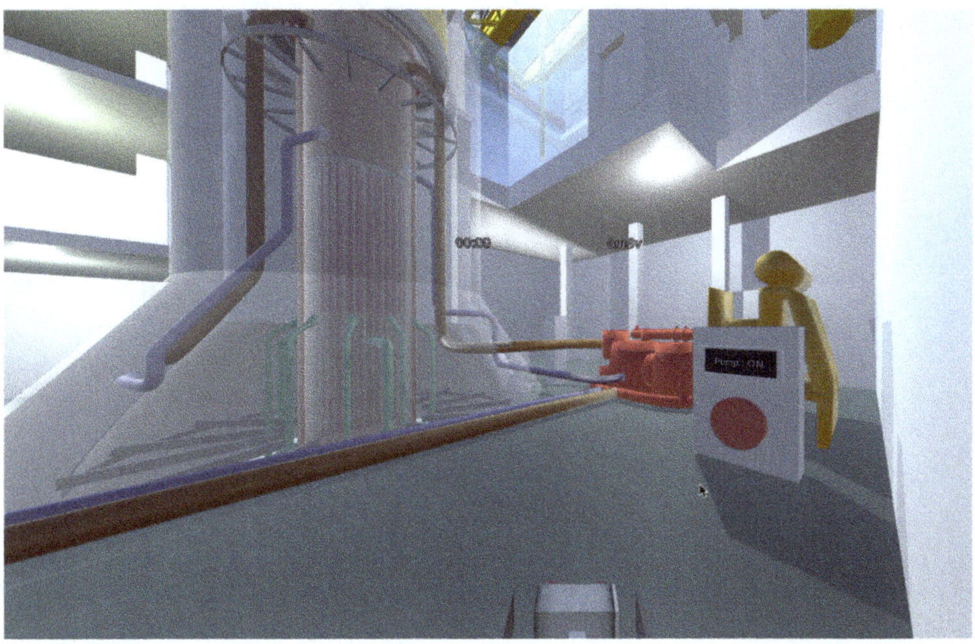

Figure 5. Control room

Figure 6. Monitors viewing Fukushima space from Control room

Figure 7. Using the Oculus Rift Head Mounted Display

OBSERVATIONS

Create-and-Learn Experiences

In addition to designing, programming and building 3D structures, the students had to locate accurate information about the Fukushima accident. It became apparent though that many reports in the media were not as straightforward as they initially appeared. Depending on the media outlet, news reports could be biased, sometimes contradictory, and even lacking in important detail. For instance, the Japanese government was slow to release specific details of the disaster and its severity (Onishi & Fackler, 2011) and implemented a 20 km exclusion zone, while the USA government advised Americans to leave the area within 80 km of the plant. The student developers therefore had to study the timeline of events that led to the Fukushima disaster and the aftermath of the reactor explosions on March 12th and 15th in greater detail than initially anticipated. They learned how to source for credible information regarding the technical complexities of the nuclear power plant and the challenges ahead for workers and the environment (Guizzo, 2011). They watched video recordings of local anti-nuclear protestors in Japan, and listened to the arguments against nuclear power put forward by two Japanese ex-Prime Ministers, Abe and Koizumi; who both visited Hakodate (the location of this university project). The students compared, analyzed and discussed the information in their endeavor to create a veritable Synthetic Learning Environment for their juniors at university and Secondary/ High schools. These discussions led to a number of interesting developments. The students:

- **Modified the Basic Robot:** The students found that exposure to radiation damages robots and its electronics (Guizzo, 2011) and so built that metric into the project. Consequently, as the virtual robot is maneuvered, its performance declines over time.
- **Adjusted the Cameras:** The camera view from the robot to the user declines over time due to the radiation exposure and its screen image degrades unless the robot is returned to a safe area in the virtual environment.
- **Added a Virtual Drone:** Recent use of drones to survey buildings and debris is incorporated into the environment. The drone camera is viewable directly in the Fukushima space and also in the Control Room (see Figures 2 and 5).
- Constructed 3D models by replicating its material, dimensions, scale and aesthetics.
- Programmed the maneuvering of robots with different wheel and track combinations and subsequent friction values and their effect on robot movements.
- Calculated water flow velocity in the pipes in order to keep the reactor cool.
- Designed water pipe layout with bends and valves to and from emergency pumps.
- Included different types of radiation (alpha, beta and gamma) prominent in the disaster space inside the reactor space and outside of the buildings.
- Calculated the different radiation exposure values and their subsequent effect on the environment. Even the metric used for radiation causes confusion with regular citizens.
- Incorporated their own game-play experiences to develop tasks that would allow promote active participation and immersion of the users. This is a good example of transfer of learning.
- Stated clearly the learning task objectives as the students did not want the users so to perceive the Synthetic Learning Environment as a game, but as a participatory learning experience.
- Considered ways of evaluating users' accomplishments and subsequent procedural and declarative knowledge (knowing 'how' and knowing 'what' respectively) as they retrieved the radioactive bins and collected information for post-task evaluations. This was the most challenging aspect: how to assess users 'in' a virtual environment (see the Assessment of Learning section above).

The developments were also not simply the domain of the students. Due to the reduction in funding allocation, it was not possible to seek the advice of a nuclear expert so the researcher participated in a refresher course entitled The Science of Nuclear Energy hosted by UK's Open University. The project became an exciting researcher – student team effort.

To sum up, educators considering the use of virtual environments must give deliberate consideration to the purpose of the designed space, its intended learning outcomes, the cognitive load associated with the activities, the instructional strategies, the motivation of the users, the affordances offered by the space and activities and, if relevant, the user assessment criteria. Virtual environments need to be engaging, intuitive and satisfying. As Koenig *et al.* (2013) state: "The simple presence of educational content in a simulation does not guarantee its efficacy" (p. 49).

Education 'in' a Synthetic Learning Environment

The project illustrated in this chapter began as an ambitious endeavor involving a professional programmer, corporate support and government funding. The research bid was successful but, due to national budget cuts, the funding was much reduced. By recruiting inexperienced undergraduate students, and utilizing existing hardware where possible, the goals of the research remained intact. However, during the course of the project it became apparent that the development of the 'product' to be 'tested' was taking place right in front of us every day. The inexperienced students as designers, programmers and testers were deeply engaged in the 'try-and-explore' paradigm leading to a 'create-and-learn' situation. In other words, a development of situational awareness where the students organized information around goals and determined meaningful information from sometimes quite abstract representations. As the researcher supported students as designers, modelers, programmers and testers, an apprenticeship, experiential model of learning through trying, exploring and creating evolved (see Figure 8).

The goal of the research remained: to develop a virtual environment for effective, experiential learning of elementary nuclear power concepts conceptualized by a nuclear accident scenario, and subsequently test users' understanding. However, the students' development of the Synthetic Learning Environment began to represent the desired education paradigm shift from instructor-driven, traditional didactic pedagogies to more collaborative, self-determined active learning. The students began to learn from each other "through a dynamic form of reciprocal apprenticeship, exploring creative solutions to problems, negotiating worldviews, and socially constructing skills and knowledge" (Marone, 2016). As evidenced by the project development, students started to think like designers, think like programmers, and think in a shared construction space. They were creating a Synthetic Learning Environment through shared modelling, designing and programming (see Figure 9) and, as a result, were developing new skills and insights (*cf.* Illich, 1971), particularly observed in their create-and-learn experiences (see above). In effect, students were learning 'in' technology.

The students were also able to transfer their own learning to unique situations. They began to transfer knowledge, generalize concepts experienced in developing the virtual Fukushima, its components and its activities. Through their transboundary interactions the students developed communication and social skills, digital literacy, and recognition of multi-modal literacies. These are the traits often considered of experts.

Figure 8. Experiential learning diagram

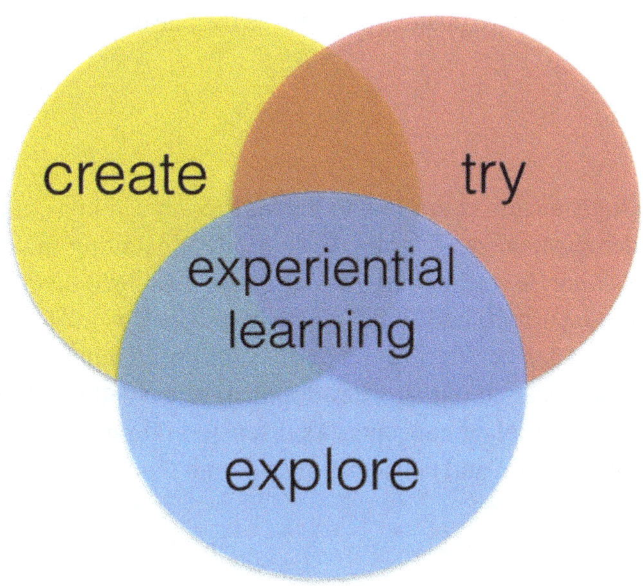

Figure 9. Creating a synthetic learning environment

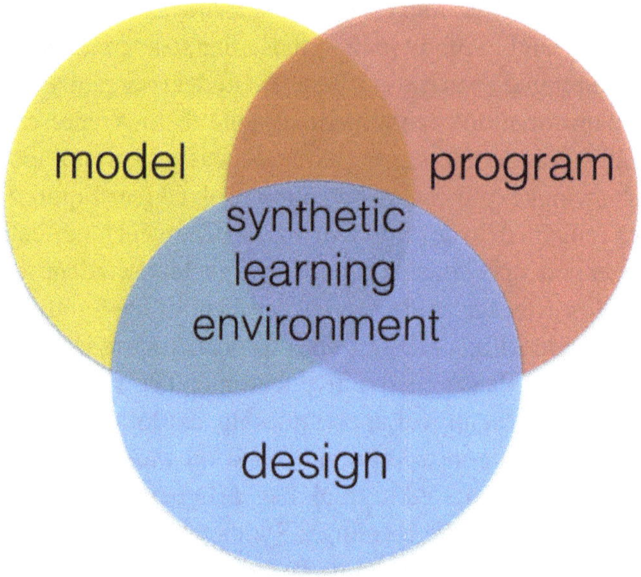

Referring to Anderson *et al's* neo-Bloomian taxonomy (see Table 1), it has been observed throughout this project that the students have been engaged in a multitude of cognitive processes: recalling prior knowledge in their programming; classifying radiation issues to be incorporated into the environment; applying a number of skills in the designs and implementations; analyzing problems and forming constructive solutions; evaluating each other's contributions in constructing a collaborative space; and creating 3D object designs, animations and learning tasks.

In conclusion, the project has revealed how an interdisciplinary approach enabled students to gain knowledge through collaborative effort. Joichi Ito, Director of the MIT Media Lab, suggests the way ahead in education is to support such endeavors where learning processes and peer collaborations are valued above end products such as certificates and exam scores; he calls it 'antidisciplinary' (Ito, 2014).

LIMITATIONS

The number of participating students is too low to generalize any findings, although it is posited that this chapter sufficiently demonstrates an ongoing Case Study illustrating the development of a virtual environment to support learning 'in' technology. It is also acknowledged that the observations from this project cannot be scaled up to current, traditional classroom scenarios in Higher Education or schools. However, the findings in this chapter can be applied to small group, interdisciplinary project-learning scenarios. Finally, the research started out as a development of a Synthetic Learning Environment for users to learn basic nuclear power plant concepts. As discussed though, active learning was occurring within the student development team and consequently became the focus for the Case Study described in this chapter.

FUTURE WORK

Virtual simulations allow remotely located students to enter as avatars to communicate and collaborate with other students. This has previously been possible using Second Life, OpenSim and JIBE. Remote collaborations are currently being explored in this project using the Oculus Rift HMD with emerging applications such as AltspaceVR, Engage and vTime. There are also physical environments known as a CAVE (Cave Automatic Virtual Environment) that blend the physical space with a virtual environment.

It is additionally anticipated that such user-accessible simulations with citizens controlling a virtual robot will also create an awareness and understanding of disaster recovery, and not simply rely upon retrospective information from unprepared experts. Consequently, as well as capturing data for analysis of cognitive processes, an additional affordance is to familiarize participants with the complexities of nuclear power; given that there is much confusion about the situation at present in Japan.

To conclude, the experiences involved in designing the Synthetic Learning Environment in this ongoing project have revealed, through researcher observation and student reflection, how a 3D virtual simulation for real world collaboration engenders a transformative pedagogy for learning 'in' technology.

CONCLUSION

Learning is an extremely complex process that occurs within the learner, is unobserved, occurs at random and in chaotic ways, is a response to a personal need and, often, occurs to resolve some ambiguity. It is associated with making new linkages in the brain involving ideas, emotions, and experiences that lead to new understandings about oneself or the world. The Case Study in this chapter has illustrated how developing a Synthetic Learning Environment with collaborative effort can result in valued learning outcomes. No empirically-based claims have been made but the ongoing project has shown how such development can be leveraged to support Japan's desire to update its Education system with a more 'active learning' pedagogy. Without highlighting a Case Study such as this, Japan's education practices and policies will simply 'bolt on' existing didactic pedagogies and assessments to new physical environments.

The subsequent maturation of immersive technologies has profound implications for Higher Education. Research into the efficacy of 3D virtual collaborations for effective learning must be persevered in order to determine their educational value and promote new, transformative learning. Therefore, engaging students to develop, experience and learn 'in' Synthetic Learning Environments will better inform and prepare Higher Education Institutes for future changes in education, learning, curricula and pedagogy.

ACKNOWLEDGMENT

The research is being supported by JAIST *kakenhi* [grant number 15K01080]. Many thanks to Gabriel Campitelli (gabriel.campitelli@gmail.com) for the initial developments of the Unity project, and students Yuto Kurashige, Tomohiro Sasaki and Takurou Magaki in the iVERG lab at Future University Hakodate, Japan.

REFERENCES

Aldrich, C. (2004). *Simulations and the future of learning*. San Francisco, CA: Pfeiffer.

Anderson, L. W., Krathwohl, D. R., Airasian, P. W., Cruicshank, K. A., Mayer, R. E., Pintrich, P. R., & Wittrock, M. C. et al. (2001). *A taxonomy for learning, teaching and assessing: A revision of Bloom's taxonomy of educational objectives*. New York, NY: Longman.

Bloom, B. S. (Ed.). (1956). *Taxonomy of Educational Objectives, the classification of educational goals. Handbook 1: Cognitive Domain*. New York, NY: McKay.

Bowman, D., Kruijff, E., LaViola, J. J., & Poupyrev, I. P. (2004). *3D User interfaces: Theory and practice*. Boston, MA: Addison-Wesley.

Canon-Bowers, J. A., & Bowers, C. A. (2008). Synthetic learning environments. In J. M. Spector, D. M. Merrill, J. van Merrienboer, & M. P. Drsicoll (Eds.), *Handbook of research on educational communications and technology* (pp. 317–327). New York, NY: Routledge.

Cuban, L. (2002). *Oversold & underused: Computers in the classroom*. Cambridge, MA: Harvard University Press.

Dalgarno, B., & Lee, M. (2010). What are the learning affordances of 3-D virtual environments? *British Journal of Educational Technology*, *41*(1), 10–32. doi:10.1111/j.1467-8535.2009.01038.x

deFreitas, S., & Neumann, T. (2009). The use of 'exploratory learning' for supporting immersive learning in virtual environments. *Computers & Education*, *52*(2), 343–352. doi:10.1016/j.compedu.2008.09.010

de Freitas, S., Rebolledo-Mendez, G., Liarokapis, F., Magoulas, G., & Poulovassilis, A. (2010). Learning as immersive experiences: Using the four-dimensional framework for designing and evaluating immersive learning experiences in a virtual world. *British Journal of Educational Technology*, *41*(1), 69–85. doi:10.1111/j.1467-8535.2009.01024.x

Dewey, J. (1938). *Experience and education*. New York, NY: Touchstone.

Guizzo, E. (2011). Fukushima Robot Operator Writes Tell-All Blog. *IEEE Spectrum*, *23*. Retrieved from http://spectrum.ieee.org/automaton/robotics/industrial-robots/fukushima-robot-operator-diaries

Hale, K. S., & Stanney, K. M. (Eds.). (2014). *Handbook of virtual environments: Design, implementation, and applications*. Boca Raton, FL: CRC Press. doi:10.1201/b17360

Honey, M., & Kanter, D. E. (2013). *Design make play: Growing the next generation of STEM innovators*. London, UK: Routledge.

Illich, I. (1971). *Deschooling society*. London, UK: Marion Boyars.

Ito, J. (2014, October 2). Antidisciplinary [Weblog post]. MIT Media Lab Blog. Retrieved February 9, 2017, from https://joi.ito.com/weblog/2014/10/02/antidisciplinar.html

Ito, M. (2009). *Engineering play. A cultural history of children's software*. Cambridge, MA: MIT Press.

Jonassen, D. H., Peck, K. L., & Wilson, B. G. (1998). *Learning WITH technology: A constructivist perspective*. Columbus, OH: Prentice-Hall.

Koenig, A., Iseli, M., Wainess, R., & Lee, J. J. (2013). Assessment methodology for computer-based instructional simulations. *Military Medicine*, *178*(10S), 47–54. doi:10.7205/MILMED-D-13-00217 PMID:24084305

Kolb, D. A. (1984). *Experiential learning: Experience as the source of learning and development.* Englewood Cliffs, NJ: Prentice-Hall.

Kulik, C. L. C., & Kulik, J. A. (1991). Effectiveness of computer-based instruction: An updated analysis. *Computers in Human Behavior*, *7*(1–2), 75–94. doi:10.1016/0747-5632(91)90030-5

Lave, J., & Wenger, E. (1991). *Situated learning: Legitimate peripheral participation*. Cambridge, UK: Cambridge University Press. doi:10.1017/CBO9780511815355

Lerner, F. (2005). Foundations for design: Continuing the Bauhaus Vorkurs vision. *Studies in Art Education*, 211–226.

Lochbaum, D., Lyman, E., & Stranahan, S. Q. (2014). *Fukushima. The story of a nuclear disaster*. New York, NY: The New Press.

Marone, V. (2016). Playful constructivism: Making sense of digital games for learning and creativity through play, design, and participation. *Journal of Virtual Worlds Research*, *9*(3), 1–18.

Mayer, R. E. (2014). *Computer games for learning. An evidence-based approach.* Cambridge, MA: MIT Press.

McGonigal, J. (2012). *Reality is broken: Why games make us better and how they can change the world.* London, UK: Vintage Books.

National University Reform Plan. (2015). Retrieved December 13, 2016, from http://www.mext.go.jp/en/news/topics/detail/1372655.htm

OECD. (2016). *Programme for International Student Assessment (PISA).* Retrieved December 13, 2016, from https://www.oecd.org/pisa/

Onishi, N., & Fackler, M. (2011). *Japan Held Nuclear Data, Leaving Evacuees in Peril.* Retrieved February 9, 2017, from http://www.nytimes.com/2011/08/09/world/asia/09japan.html?_r=1

Papert, S. (1993). *Mindstorms: Children, computers, and powerful ideas.* New York, NY: Basic Books.

Papert, S., & Harel, I. (1993). *Constructionism.* New York, NY: Ablex.

Piaget, J. (1972). Intellectual evolution from adolescence to adult. *Human Development*, *15*(1), 1–12. doi:10.1159/000271225

Rhodes, M. (2016). Forget the School Bus - The Most Magical Field Trip Is in VR. *Wired.* Retrieved February 9, 2017 from https://www.wired.com/2016/06/went-vr-field-trip-tomorrow-heres-saw/

Sandholtz, J. M., Ringstaff, C., & Dwyer, D. C. (1997). *Teaching with technology: Creating student-centered classrooms*. New York, NY: Teachers College Press.

Schrader, P. G. (2008). Learning in technology: Reconceptualizing immersive environments. *AACE Journal*, *16*(4), 457–475.

Selwyn, N. (2017). *Education and technology: Key issues and debates* (2nd ed.). London, UK: Bloomsbury Academic.

Turkle, S. (2011). *Alone together: Why we expect more from technology and less from each other*. New York, NY: Basic books.

Vallance, M., Martin, S., & Naamani, C. (2015). A situation that we had never imagined: Post-Fukushima virtual collaborations for determining robot task metrics. *International Journal of Learning Technology*, *10*(1), 30–49. doi:10.1504/IJLT.2015.069453

Vallance, M., & Towndrow, P. A. (2016). Pedagogic transformation, student-directed design and computational thinking. *Pedagogies*, *11*(3), 218–234. doi:10.1080/1554480X.2016.1182437

Vygotsky, L. (1986). *Thought and language*. Cambridge, MA: MIT Press.

KEY TERMS AND DEFINITIONS

Antidisciplinary: An endeavor that is not a sum of disciplines but something entirely new. It is something that defies the traditional academic disciplines with predictable studies and determined frameworks and methods.

Bloom's Taxonomy: A classification of learning objectives.

Cognitive Processes: The performance of some specific cognitive activity that affects mental contents; the process of thinking.

Fukushima Dai'ichi Nuclear Power Plant: An inoperable nuclear power plant located in northern Japan which suffered major damage due to an earthquake and tsunami on March 11, 2011.

Oculus Rift: A virtual reality head mounted display with external touch controllers.

Synthetic Learning Environment: A learning environment characterized in terms of a particular technology, subject matter, learner characteristics, and pedagogical principles; a synthetic experience, as opposed to real-world interaction with an actual device or process, created for the learner through a simulation, game, or other technology.

Unity: A software platform used for developing games and virtual reality content.

Compilation of References

Adams, E. (2004). *Postmodernism and the three types of immersion*. Retrieved from https://www.gamasutra.com/view/feature/130531/the_designers_notebook_.php

Ahearn, L. M. (2001). Language and agency. *Annual Review of Anthropology*, *30*(1), 109–137. doi:10.1146/annurev.anthro.30.1.109

Aldrich, C. (2004). *Simulations and the future of learning*. San Francisco, CA: Pfeiffer.

Allison, C., Campbell, A., Davies, C. J., Dow, L., Kennedy, S., & McCaffery, J. P. (2012). Growing the use of Virtual Worlds in education: an OpenSim perspective. In *Proceedings of the 2nd European Immersive Education Summit: EiED 2012* (pp. 1–13). Paris, France: Universidad Carlos III de Madrid.

Allmendringer, K. (2010). Social presence in synchronous learning environments: The role of nonverbal signals displayed by avatars. *Educational Psychology Review*, *22*(1), 41–56. doi:10.1007/s10648-010-9117-8

Ally, M. (2008). Foundations of educational theory for online learning. In T. Anderson (Ed.), *The theory and practice of online learning* (pp. 15–44). Edmonton, Canada: AU Press.

Alrashidi, M., Alzahrani, A., Gardner, M., & Callaghan, V. (2016). A pedagogical virtual machine for assembling mobile robot using augmented reality. In *Proceedings of the 7th Augmented Human International Conference 2016*. Geneva, Switzerland: ACM. doi:10.1145/2875194.2875229

Alzahrani, A., Gardner, M., Callaghan, V., & Alrashidi, M. (2015). Towards measuring learning effectiveness considering presence, engagement and immersion in a mixed and augmented reality learning environment. *Immersive Learning Research Network Conference (iLRN 2015)*, 252–264. doi:10.3233/978-1-61499-530-2-252

Anasol, P. R., Callaghan, V., Gardner, M., & Alhaddad, M. J. (2012). End-user programming and deconstrutionalism for co-creative laboratory activities in a collaborative mixed-reality environment. In Gardner, M., Garnier, F., & Kloos, C. D. (Eds.), *Proceedings of the 2nd European Immersive Education Summit: EiED 2012* (pp. 1-13). Paris, France: Universidad Carlos III de Madrid.

Anderson, L. W., Krathwohl, D. R., Airasian, P. W., Cruicshank, K. A., Mayer, R. E., Pintrich, P. R., & Wittrock, M. C. et al. (2001). *A taxonomy for learning, teaching and assessing: A revision of Bloom's taxonomy of educational objectives*. New York, NY: Longman.

Arya, A., Hartwick, P., Graham, S., & Nowlan, N. (2012). Collaborating through space and time in educational virtual environments: 3 case studies. *The Journal of Interactive Technology & Pedagogy*, (2). Retrieved from http://jitp.commons.gc.cuny.edu/collaborating-through-space-and-time-in-educational-virtual-environments-3-case-studies/

Assessment Reform Group (ARG). (2002). *Assessment for learning: 10 principles* [Leaflet/poster]. Cambridge, UK: University of Cambridge. Retrieved December 21, 2012, from https://assessmentreformgroup.files.wordpress.com/2012/01/10principles_english.pdf

Avatar Languages. (2011). *Google street view for language learning: A guide for teachers*. Retrieved February 3, 2017, from http://www.avatarlanguages.com/teaching/streetview.pdf

Avatar Reality. (2010). *Blue Mars*. Retrieved February 3, 2017, from http://www.bluemars.com/

Bailenson, J. N., Swinth, K., Hoyt, C., Persky, S., Dimov, A., & Blascovich, J. (2005). The independent and interactive effects of embodied-agent appearance and behavior on self-report, cognitive, and behavioral markers of copresence in immersive virtual environments. *Presence (Cambridge, Mass.)*, *14*(4), 379–393. doi:10.1162/105474605774785235

Bandura, A. (1986). *Social foundations of thought and action: A social cognitive theory*. Englewood Cliffs, NJ: Prentice Hall.

Bandura, A. (1997). *Self-efficacy: The exercise of control*. New York, NY: Worth Publishers.

Bandura, A. (2001). Social cognitive theory: An agentic perspective. *Annual Review of Psychology*, *52*(1), 1–26. doi:10.1146/annurev.psych.52.1.1 PMID:11148297

Barab, S. A. (2003). An introduction to the special issue: Designing for virtual communities in the service of learning. *The Information Society*, *19*(3), 197–201. doi:10.1080/01972240309467

Barab, S. A., Thomas, M., Dodge, T., Carteaux, R., & Tuzun, H. (2005). Making learning fun: Quest Atlantis, a game without guns. *Educational Technology Research and Development*, *5*(1), 86–108. doi:10.1007/BF02504859

Barab, S., Dodge, T., Tuzun, H., Job-Sluder, K., Jackson, R. C., & Gilbertson, J. (2007). The Quest Atlantis Project: A socially-responsive play space for learning. In B. E. Shelton & D. A. Wiley (Eds.), *The educational design of computer games* (pp. 159–186). Rotterdam, The Netherlands: Sense Publishers.

Barnett, M., Yamagata-Lynch, L., Keating, T., Barab, S. A., & Hay, K. E. (2005). Using virtual reality computer models to support student understanding of astronomical concepts. *Journal of Computers in Mathematics and Science Teaching*, *24*(4), 333–356.

Barr, R. B., & Tagg, J. (1995, November). From teaching to learning: A new paradigm for undergraduate education. *Change*, 13–25.

Belz, J. A., & Thorne, S. L. (2006). Introduction: Internet-mediated intercultural foreign language education and the intercultural speaker. In J. A. Belz & S. L. Thorne (Eds.), *Internet-mediated intercultural foreign language*. Boston, MA: Heinle & Heinle. doi:10.1079/9781845930639.0001

Benson, P. (2016). *Bibliography on autonomy in language learning*. Retrieved from https://dl.dropboxusercontent.com/u/61188845/Autonomy%20bibliography.pdf

Bentler, P. M., & Bonett, D. G. (1980). Significance tests and goodness of fit in the analysis of covariance structures. *Psychological Bulletin*, *88*(3), 588–606. doi:10.1037/0033-2909.88.3.588

Berge, Z. L. (1995). Facilitating computer conferencing: Recommendations from the field. *Educational Technology*, *35*(1), 22–30.

Berge, Z. L. (2008). Changing instructor's roles in virtual worlds. *The Quarterly Review of Distance Education*, *9*(4), 407–414.

Berliner, C. D. (2011). Rational responses to high stakes testing: The case of curriculum narrowing and the harm that follows. *Cambridge Journal of Education*, *41*(3), 287–302. doi:10.1080/0305764X.2011.607151

Berns, R. G., & Erickson, P. M. (2001). Contextual teaching and learning: Preparing students for the new economy. *The Highlight Zone: Research @ Work*, *5*, 2–9. (ERIC Document Reproduction Service No. ED452376)

Berns, M. S. (1984). Functional approaches to language and language teaching: Another look. In S. Savignon & M. S. Berns (Eds.), *Initiatives in communicative language teaching: A book of readings* (pp. 3–21). Reading, PA: Addison-Wesley.

Biesta, G. (2007). Why "what works" won't work: Evidence-based practice and the democratic deficit in educational research. *Educational Theory*, *57*(1), 1–22. doi:10.1111/j.1741-5446.2006.00241.x

Biggs, J. B. (1999). *Teaching for quality learning at university: What the student does.* London, UK: Society for Research into Higher Education.

Binkley, M., Erstad, O., Herman, J., Raizen, S., Ripley, M., Miller-Ricci, M., & Rumble, M. (2012). Defining twenty-first century skills. In P. Griffin, B. McGaw, & E. Care (Eds.), *Assessment and teaching of 21st century skills* (pp. 17–66). Dordrecht, The Netherlands: Springer Netherlands. doi:10.1007/978-94-007-2324-5_2

Biocca, F., Harms, C., & Burgoon, J. K. (2003). Toward a more robust theory and measure of social presence: Review and suggested criteria. *Presence (Cambridge, Mass.)*, *12*(5), 456–480. doi:10.1162/105474603322761270

Birchfield, D., & Johnson-Glenberg, M. (2010). A next gen interface for embodied learning. *International Journal of Gaming and Computer-Mediated Simulations*, *2*(1), 49–58. doi:10.4018/jgcms.2010010105

Birenbaum, M. (1996). Assessment 2000: Towards a pluralistic approach to assessment. In M. Birenbaum & F. J. R. C. Dochy (Eds.), *Alternatives in assessment of achievements, learning processes and prior knowledge* (pp. 4–29). Boston, MA: Kluwer. doi:10.1007/978-94-011-0657-3_1

Birenbaum, M. (2014). Conceptualizing assessment culture in school. In C. Wyatt-Smith, V. Klenowski, & P. Colbert (Eds.), *Designing assessment for quality learning* (pp. 285–302). Dordrecht, The Netherlands: Springer. doi:10.1007/978-94-007-5902-2_18

Birenbaum, M. (2016). Assessment culture versus testing culture: The impact on assessment for learning. In D. Laveault & L. Allal (Eds.), *Assessment for learning: Meeting the challenge of implementation* (pp. 275–292). New York, NY: Springer International. doi:10.1007/978-3-319-39211-0_16

Bjork, S., & Holopainen, J. (2005). *Patterns in game design.* Charles River Media.

Black, P., & Wiliam, D. (1998). Assessment and classroom learning. *Assessment in Education: Principles, Policy & Practice*, *5*(1), 7–74. doi:10.1080/0969595980050102

Blizzard Entertainment. (2017a). *New player's guide: Part four.* Retrieved from https://worldofwarcraft.com/en-us/game/new-players-guide/part-four

Blizzard Entertainment. (2017b). *World of Warcraft Starter Edition Limitations.* Retrieved from https://us.battle.net/support/en/article/World-of-Warcraft-Starter-Edition-Limitations

Bloom, B. S. (Ed.). (1956). *Taxonomy of Educational Objectives, the classification of educational goals. Handbook 1: Cognitive Domain.* New York, NY: McKay.

Blumenfeld, P. C., Soloway, E., Marx, R. W., Krajcik, J. S., Guzdial, M., & Palincsar, A. (1991). Motivating project-based learning: Sustaining the doing, supporting the learning. *Educational Psychologist*, *26*(3-4), 369–398. doi:10.1080/00461520.1991.9653139

Bonde, M. T., Makransky, G., Wandall, J., Larsen, M. V., Morsing, M., Jarmer, H., & Sommer, M. O. A. (2014). Improving biotech education through gamified laboratory simulations. *Nature Biotechnology*, *32*(7), 694–708. doi:10.1038/nbt.2955 PMID:25004234

Bower, M. (2008). Affordance analysis – matching learning tasks with learning Technologies. *Educational Media International*, *45*(1), 3–15. doi:10.1080/09523980701847115

Bowman, D., Kruijff, E., LaViola, J. J., & Poupyrev, I. P. (2004). *3D User interfaces: Theory and practice*. Boston, MA: Addison-Wesley.

Boyle, E. A., Hainey, T., Connolly, T. M., Gray, G., Earp, J., Ott, M., & Pereira, J. et al. (2016). An update to the systematic literature review of empirical evidence of the impacts and outcomes of computer games and serious games. *Computers & Education*, *94*, 178–192. doi:10.1016/j.compedu.2015.11.003

Bransford, J. D., Brown, A. L., & Cocking, R. R. (2000). *How people learn: Brain, mind, experience, and school* (expanded ed.). Retrieved June 23, 2015, from http://www.nap.edu/openbook.php?record_id=9853

Bransford, J. D., & Schwartz, D. L. (1999). Rethinking transfer: A simple proposal with multiple implications. *Review of Research in Education*, *24*(1), 61–100. doi:10.3102/0091732X024001061

Bredl, K., Groß, A., Hünniger, J., & Fleischer, J. (2012). The avatar as a knowledge worker? how immersive 3d virtual environments may foster knowledge acquisition. *The Electronic Journal of Knowledge Management, 1*(10), 15–25. Retrieved from, http://www.ejkm.com/issue/download.html?idArticle=316

Breen, M. (1989). The evaluation cycle for language learning tasks. In B. K. Johnson (Ed.), *The second language curriculum* (pp. 187–206). Cambridge, UK: Cambridge University Press. doi:10.1017/CBO9781139524520.014

Bressler, D. M., & Bodzin, A. M. (2016). Investigating flow experience and scientific practices during a mobile serious educational game. *Journal of Science Education and Technology*, *25*(5), 795–805. doi:10.1007/s10956-016-9639-z

Bronack, S., Rield, R., & Tashner, J. (2006). Learning in the Zone: A social constructivist framework for distance education in a 3-dimensional virtual world. *Proceedings of Interactive Learning Environments*, *14*(3), 219–232. doi:10.1080/10494820600909157

Brown, J. S. (2011, August). *Innovation expert John Seely Brown on new ways of learning in a rapidly-changing world.* Retrieved from https://www.youtube.com/watch?v=bGdpbba1i9c

Brown, J. S., Collins, A., & Duguid, P. (1989). Situated cognition and the culture of learning. *Educational Researcher*, *18*(1), 32–42. doi:10.3102/0013189X018001032

Bulu, S. T. (2012). Place presence, social presence, co-presence and satisfaction. *Virtual Worlds. Computers & Education*, *58*(1), 154–161. doi:10.1016/j.compedu.2011.08.024

Callaghan, V. (2010). *Tales from a Pod.* Paper presented at Creative Science 2010 (CS'10), Kuala Lumpur, Malaysia.

Callaghan, V. (2012). *Buzz-Boarding; practical support for teaching computing based on the internet-of-things*. Retrieved from http://orbit.dtu.dk/files/105633882/Improving_biotech_education.pdf

Callaghan, V., Gardner, M., Horan, B., Scott, J., Shen, L., & Wang, M. (2008). A mixed reality teaching and learning environment. *Hybrid Learning and Education*, 54–65. doi: 10.1007/978-3-540-85170-7_5

Camilleri, V., de Freitas, S., Montebello, M., & McDonagh-Smith, P. (2013). A case study inside virtual worlds: Use of analytics for immersive spaces. In *Proceedings of the 3rd International Conference on Learning Analytics and Knowledge* (pp. 230–234). Leuven, Belgium: ACM. doi:10.1145/2460296.2460341

Canon-Bowers, J. A., & Bowers, C. A. (2008). Synthetic learning environments. In J. M. Spector, D. M. Merrill, J. van Merrienboer, & M. P. Drsicoll (Eds.), *Handbook of research on educational communications and technology* (pp. 317–327). New York, NY: Routledge.

Cardellini, L. (2006). Fostering creative problem solving in chemistry through group work. *Chemistry Education Research and Practice*, *7*(2), 131–140. doi:10.1039/B5RP90019K

Carr, D., Oliver, M., & Burn, A. (2008, May). *Learning from online worlds: Teaching in Second Life*. Retrieved from https://learningfromsocialworlds.wordpress.com/

Carter, B. (2012). Virtual harlem: An innovative past, an evolving present and an exciting future. In *Proceedings of the 2nd European Immersive Education Summit: EiED 2012* (pp. 1–13). Paris, France: Universidad Carlos III de Madrid.

Caruso, V., Mørch, A. I., Thomassen, I., Hartley, M., & Ludlow, B. (2014). Practicing collaboration skills through role-play activities in a 3D virtual world. In R. Huang, Kinshuk, & N.-S. Chen (Eds.), The new development of technology enhanced learning (pp. 165–184). Berlin: Springer.

Caruso, V., Hartley, M. D., & Mørch, A. I. (2015). End-user development in Second Life: Meta-design, tailoring, and appropriation. In P. Diaz, V. Pipek, & C. Ardito (Eds.), *Proceedings 5th international symposium end-user development 2015* (pp. 92–108). Berlin: Springer. doi:10.1007/978-3-319-18425-8_7

Cattell, R. B. (1978). *The scientific use of factor analysis*. New York: Plenum; doi:10.1007/978-1-4684-2262-7

Chafer, J., & Childs, M. (2008). The impact of the characteristics of a virtual environment on performance: Concepts, constraints and complications. In *Proceedings of the Researching Learning in Virtual Environments* (pp. 94-105). Milton Keynes, UK: Open University Press.

Chaiklin, S., & Lave, J. (Eds.). (1993). *Understanding practice: Perspectives on activity and context*. Cambridge, UK: Cambridge University Press. doi:10.1017/CBO9780511625510

Chalabi, M. (2014). *Distance learning: Who's doing it now?* Retrieved from http://www.theguardian.com/education/datablog/2014/jan/30/distance-learning-higher-education-moocs

Charles, D., Charles, T., McNeill, M., Bustard, D., & Black, M. (2011). Game-based feedback for educational multi-user virtual environments. *British Journal of Educational Technology*, *42*(4), 638–654. doi:10.1111/j.1467-8535.2010.01068.x

Chen, J. A., Metcalf, S. J., & Tutwiler, M. S. (2014). Motivation and beliefs about the nature of scientific knowledge within an immersive virtual ecosystems environment. *Journal of Contemporary Educational Psychology*, *39*(2), 112–123. doi:10.1016/j.cedpsych.2014.02.004

Cheong, D. U., Yun, S., & Chollins, C. (2009). Is Second Life effective for pre-service teachers' teaching practice? In I. Gibson, R. Weber, K. McFerrin, R. Carlsen, & D. A. Willis (Eds.), *Proceedings of society for information technology & teacher education international conference 2009* (pp. 1418–1421). Chesapeake, VA: AACE.

Chidambaram, L., & Tung, L. L. (2005). Is out of sight, out of mind? An empirical study of social loafing in technology-supported groups. *Information Systems Research*, *16*(2), 149–168. doi:10.1287/isre.1050.0051

Childs, M. (2010). *Learners' experience of presence in virtual* worlds (Unpublished doctoral dissertation). University of Warwick, Coventry, UK.

Chin, J., & Callaghan, V. (2003). *Embedded-internet devices: A means of realizing the pervasive computing vision.* Paper presented at IADIS International Conference, Algarve, Portugal.

Chinnery, G. (2008). You've got some GALL: Google-assisted language learning. *Language Learning & Technology, 12*(1), 3–11.

Chrichton, S., & Kinash, S. (2003). Virtual ethnography: Interactive interviewing online as method. *Canadian Journal of Learning and Technology, 29*(2), 101–115.

Christopoulos, A. (2013). *Higher education in virtual worlds: The use of Second Life and Opensim for educational practices* (Unpublished Master thesis). University of Bedfordshire, Luton, UK.

Clark, A. (2001). *Mindware: An introduction to the philosophy of cognitive science*. New York: Oxford University Press.

Clark, D., Tanner-Smith, E., Killingworth, S., & Bellamy, S. (2013). *Digital games for learning: A systematic review and meta-analysis*. Menlo Park, CA: SRI International.

Clarke, J., Dede, C., Ketelhut, D. J., & Nelson, B. (2006). A Design-based research strategy to promote scalability for educational innovations. *Educational Technology, 46*(3), 27–36.

Clark, R. E. (1994). Media will never influence learning. *Educational Technology Research and Development, 42*(2), 21–29. doi:10.1007/BF02299088

Clough, M. P. (2002). Using the laboratory to enhance student learning. *Learning Science and the Science of Learning*, 85–94.

Cohen, L., Manion, L., & Morrison, K. (2011). *Research Methods in Education* (7th ed.). London, UK: Routledge Taylor & Francis.

Collentine, K. (2011). Learner autonomy in a task-based 3D world and production. *Language Learning & Technology, 15*(3), 50–67.

Collins, A., Brown, J. S., & Newman, S. E. (1989). Cognitive apprenticeship: Teaching the crafts of reading, writing, and mathematics. In L. B. Resnick (Ed.), *Knowing, learning, and instruction: Essays in honor of Robert Glaser* (pp. 453–494). Hillsdale, NJ: Lawrence Erlbaum.

Communicative Language Teaching. (n.d.). In *Wikipedia*. Retrieved February 3, 2017, from https://en.wikipedia.org/wiki/Communicative_language_teaching

Conole, G., & Dyke, M. (2004). What are the affordances of information and communication technologies? *ALT-J, 12*(2), 113–124. doi:10.3402/rlt.v12i2.11246

Conrad, M. (2011). Teaching Project Management in Second Life. In G. Vincenti & J. Braman (Eds.), *Proceedings of Multi-User Virtual Environments for the Classroom: Practical Approaches to Teaching in Virtual Worlds*. Hershey, PA: Idea Group. doi:10.4018/978-1-60960-545-2.ch019

Conrad, M., Neale, J., & Charles, A. (2010). This is my body: The use and effects of the avatar in the virtual world. *International Journal for Infonomics, 3*(4), 1–9. doi:10.20533/iji.1742.4712.2010.0039

Conrad, M., Pike, D., Sant, P., & Nwafor, C. (2009). Teaching large student cohorts in Second Life. In *Proceedings of the 1st International Conference on Computer Supported Education*. Lisboa, Portugal: SciTePress.

Cook, D., Bialoskursky, Y., Fulton, B., Fitch, M., & Gonzales, J. (2017, January 27). *Game design patterns for building friendships*. Retrieved from http://www.lostgarden.com/2017/01/game-design-patterns-for-building.html

Cook, D. J., Augusto, J. C., & Jakkula, V. R. (2009). Ambient intelligence: Technologies, applications, and opportunities. *Pervasive and Mobile Computing, 5*(4), 277–298. doi:10.1016/j.pmcj.2009.04.001

Cornille, F., Thorne, S. L., & Desmet, P. (2012). Digital games for language learning: From hype to insight? *ReCALL, 23*(3), 243–356.

Costa, A. L., & Kallick, B. (1993). Through the lens of critical friend. *Educational Leadership, 51*(2), 49–51.

Costello, A. B., & Osborne, J. W. (2005). Best practices in exploratory factor analysis: Four recommendations for getting the most from your analysis. *Practical Assessment, Research & Evaluation, 10*(7), 1–9.

Cotterall, S. (1995). Readiness for autonomy: Investigating learner beliefs. *System, 23*(2), 195–205. doi:10.1016/0346-251X(95)00008-8

Coughlan, P., & Duff, P. (1994). Same task, different activities: Analysis of SLA task from an activity theory perspective. In J. P. Lantolf & G. Appel (Eds.), *Vygotskian approaches to second language research* (pp. 173–193). Norwood, NJ: Ablex.

Cowan, P., & Butler, R. (2013, October). Using activity theory to problematize the role of the teacher during mobile learning. *SAGE Open*, 1–13.

Crawford, B. (2000). Embracing the essence of inquiry: New roles for science teachers. *Journal of Research in Science Teaching, 37*(9), 916–937. doi:10.1002/1098-2736(200011)37:9<916::AID-TEA4>3.0.CO;2-2

Crisp, B. R. (2007). Is it worth the effort? How feedback influences students' subsequent submission of assessable work. *Assessment & Evaluation in Higher Education, 32*(5), 571–581. doi:10.1080/02602930601116912

Csikszentmihalyi, M. (2014). *Applications of flow in human development and education: The collected works of Mihaly Csikszentmihalyi*. Dordrecht, The Netherlands: Springer. doi:10.1007/978-94-017-9094-9

Cuban, L. (2002). *Oversold & underused: Computers in the classroom.* Cambridge, MA: Harvard University Press.

Curry, K. (2010). Warcraft and civic education: MMORPGs as participatory cultures and how teachers can use them to improve civic education. *Social Studies, 101*(6), 250–253. doi:10.1080/00377990903493879

Dabbagh, N. (2005). Pedagogical models for E-Learning: A theory-based design framework. *International Journal of Technology in Teaching and Learning, 1*(1), 25–44.

Dalgarno, B., & Lee, M. J. (2010). What are the learning affordances of 3-D virtual environments? *British Journal of Educational Technology, 41*(1), 10–32. doi:10.1111/j.1467-8535.2009.01038.x

Dalgarno, B., Lee, M. J. W., Carlson, L., Gregory, S., & Tynan, B. (2011). An Australian and New Zealand scoping study on the use of 3D immersive virtual worlds in higher education. *Australasian Journal of Educational Technology, 27*(1), 1–15. doi:10.14742/ajet.978

Dalton, G., & Devitt, A. (2016). Irish in a 3D world: Engaging primary school children. *Language Learning & Technology, 20*(1), 21–33.

Darasawang, P., & Reinders, H. (2010). Encouraging autonomy with an online language support system. *CALL-EJ Online, 11*(2), 1–9.

Davis, F. D., Bagozzi, R. P., & Warshaw, P. R. (1989). User acceptance of computer technology: A comparison of two theoretical models. *Management Science, 35*(8), 982–1003. doi:10.1287/mnsc.35.8.982

Dawley, L. (2009). Social network knowledge construction: Emerging virtual world pedagogy. *On the Horizon, 17*(2), 109–121. doi:10.1108/10748120910965494 de Freitas, S., & Oliver, M. (2006). How can exploratory learning with games and simulations within the curriculum be most effectively evaluated? *Computers & Education - Virtual Learning, 46*(3), 249-264.

De Freitas, S. I. (2006). Using games and simulations for supporting learning. *Learning, Media and Technology, 31*(4), 343–358. doi:10.1080/17439880601021967

de Freitas, S., & Neumann, T. (2009). The use of 'exploratory learning' for supporting immersive learning in virtual environments. *Computers & Education, 52*(2), 343–352. doi:10.1016/j.compedu.2008.09.010

De Freitas, S., & Oliver, M. (2006). How can exploratory learning with games and simulations within the curriculum be most effectively evaluated? *Computers & Education, 46*(3), 249–264. doi:10.1016/j.compedu.2005.11.007

de Freitas, S., Rebolledo-Mendez, G., Liarokapis, F., Magoulas, G., & Poulovassilis, A. (2009). Developing an evaluation methodology for immersive learning experiences in a Virtual World. In *Proceedings of the Conference in Games and Virtual Worlds for Serious Applications* (pp. 43–50). Coventry, UK: IEEE Computer Society. doi:10.1109/VS-GAMES.2009.41

de Freitas, S., Rebolledo-Mendez, G., Liarokapis, F., Magoulas, G., & Poulovassilis, A. (2010). Learning as immersive experiences: Using the four-dimensional framework for designing and evaluating immersive learning experiences in a virtual world. *British Journal of Educational Technology, 41*(1), 69–85. doi:10.1111/j.1467-8535.2009.01024.x

Dede, C. (2004). Planning for 'neomillennial' learning styles: Implications for investments in technology and faculty. *Educating the Net Generation*, 226–247.

Dede, C. (2009b). Learning context: Gaming, simulations, and science learning in the classroom. In *National Research Council Workshop on Gaming and Simulations.* Retrieved from http://www7.nationalacademies. org/bose/Gaming_Sims_Commissioned_Papers.html

Dede, C. (2010). Comparing frameworks for 21st century skills. In J. Bellanca & R. Brandt (Eds.), 21st century skills: Rethinking how students learn (pp. 51-76). Bloomington, IN: Solution Tree Press.

Dede, C., Clarke, J., Ketelhut, D. J., Nelson, B., & Bowman, C. (2005). *Students' motivation and learning of science in a multi-user virtual environment.* Paper presented at American Educational Research Association Conference, Montreal, Canada.

Dede, C. (1995). The evolution of constructivist learning environments: Immersion in distributed, virtual worlds. *Educational Technology, 35*(5), 46–52.

Dede, C. (2003). No cliché left behind: Why education policy is not like the movies. *Educational Technology, 43*(2), 5–10.

Dede, C. (2007). Reinventing the role of information and communications technologies in education. *Yearbook of the National Society for the Study of Education, 106*(2), 11–38. doi:10.1111/j.1744-7984.2007.00113.x

Dede, C. (2009a). Immersive interfaces for engagement and learning. *Science, 323*(5910), 66–69. doi:10.1126/science.1167311 PMID:19119219

Delgado Kloos, C., Ibañez Espiga, M. B., Fernández Panadero, C., Muñoz Merino, P. J., Estévez Ayres, I., Crespo García, R. M., & Pérez Sanagustín, M. (2014). A multidimensional analysis of trends in educational technology. *Proceedings of the IEEE Frontier in Education Conference (FIE'14)*, 395–398. doi:10.1109/FIE.2014.7044053

Dennen, V. P., & Burner, K. J. (2008). The cognitive apprenticeship model in educational practice. *Educational Communication and Technology, 3*, 425–439.

deNoyelles, A., Hornik, S., & Johnson, R. D. (2014). Exploring the dimensions of self-efficacy in virtual world learning: Environment, task, and content. *Journal of Online Learning and Teaching / MERLOT, 10*(2), 255.

Deterding, S., Dixon, D., Khaled, R., & Nacke, L. (2011). From game design elements to gamefulness: Defining "gamification." In *Proceedings of the 15th International Academic MindTrek Conference: Envisioning Future Media Environments* (pp. 9-15). New York, NY: ACM. doi:10.1145/2181037.2181040

Deutschmann, M., & Steinvall. (2012). Identifying Identity: Using Second Life in the teaching of sociolinguistics for the raising of gender awareness. *The EuroCall Review, 20*(1), 49–53.

Deutschmann, M., & Panichi, L. (2009). Talking into empty space – Signaling involvement in a virtual language classroom in Second Life. *Language Awareness, 18*(3–4), 310–328. doi:10.1080/09658410903197306

Deutschmann, M., & Panichi, L. (2013). Towards models for designing language learning in virtual worlds. *International Journal of Virtual and Personal Learning Environments, 3*(4), 65-84.

Deutschmann, M., Panichi, L., & Molka-Danielsen, J. (2009). Designing oral participation in Second Life: A comparative study of two language proficiency courses. *ReCALL, 21*(2), 206–226. doi:10.1017/S0958344009000196

deVellis, R. F. (2003). *Scale development: Theory and applications* (2nd ed.). Newbury Park, CA: SAGE.

Dewey, J. (1938). *Experience and education.* New York, NY: Touchstone.

Di Blas, N., & Paolini, P. (2014). Multi-user virtual environments fostering collaboration in formal education. *Journal of Educational Technology & Society, 17*(1), 54–69.

Dickey, M. D. (2003). Teaching in 3D: Pedagogical affordances and constraints of 3D virtual worlds for synchronous distance learning. *Distance Education, 24*(1), 105–121. doi:10.1080/01587910303047

Dickey, M. D. (2005). Brave new (interactive) worlds: A review of the design affordances and constraints of two 3D virtual worlds as interactive learning environments. *Interactive Learning Environments, 13*(1-2), 121–137. doi:10.1080/10494820500173714

Dickey, M. D. (2005). Engaging by design: How engagement strategies in popular computer and video games can inform instructional design. *Educational Technology Research and Development, 53*(2), 67–83. doi:10.1007/BF02504866

Dickey, M. D. (2011). The pragmatics of virtual worlds for K-12 educators: Investigating the affordances and constraints of ActiveWorlds and SecondLife with K-12 in-service teachers. *Educational Technology Research and Development, 59*(1), 1–20. doi:10.1007/s11423-010-9163-4

Dieterle, E., & Clarke, J. (2006). Multi-user virtual environments for teaching and learning. Encyclopedia of Multimedia Technology and Networking, 1033–1041.

Dieterle, E. (2009). Neomillennial learning styles and River City. *Children, Youth and Environments, 19*(1), 245–278.

Dieterle, E., & Clarke, J. (2009). Multi-user virtual environments for teaching and learning. In M. Pagani (Ed.), *Encyclopedia of multimedia technology and networking* (2nd ed.; pp. 1033–1041). Hershey, PA: Information Science Reference. doi:10.4018/978-1-60566-014-1.ch139

Dillenbourg, P. (1999). What do you mean by collaborative learning? In P. Dillenbourg (Ed.), *Collaborative-learning: Cognitive and computational approaches* (pp. 1–19). Oxford, UK: Elsevier.

Dillenbourg, P., Järvelä, S., & Fischer, F. (2009). The evolution of research on computer-supported collaborative learning. In N. Balacheff, S. Ludvigsen, T. de Jong, A. Lazonder, & S. Barnes (Eds.), *Technology-enhanced learning: Principles and products* (pp. 3–19). Heidelberg, Germany: Springer. doi:10.1007/978-1-4020-9827-7_1

Dirksen, J. (2012). *Design for how people learn.* Berkeley, CA: New Riders.

Divjak, B., & Tomić, D. (2011). The impact of Game-based learning on the achievement of learning goals and motivation for learning mathematics-literature review. *Journal of Information and Organizational Sciences*, *35*(1), 15–30.

Ducoffe, R. H. (1996). Advertising value and advertising on the web. *Journal of Advertising Research*, *36*(5), 21–35.

Duffy, T. M., & Cunningham, D. J. (1996). Constructivism: Implications for the design and delivery of instruction. In D. H. Jonassen (Ed.), *Handbook of research for educational communications and technology* (pp. 170–198). New York, NY: Macmillan.

Duran, R. P. (1984). Some implications of communicative competence research for integrative proficiency testing. In C. Rivera (Ed.), *Communicative competence approaches to language proficiency assessment: Research and application* (pp. 44–58). Clevedon, UK: Multilingual Matters.

Duschl, R. A., Schweingruber, H. A., & Shouse, A. W. (2007). *Taking science to school. Learning and teaching science in grades K-8*. Washington, DC: National Academies Press.

Dweck, C. S. (2006). *Mindsets: The new psychology of success*. New York, NY: Random House.

Earl, L. M. (2006). *Rethinking classroom assessment with purpose in mind: Assessment for learning, assessment as learning, assessment of learning*. Government of Manitoba.

ECO. (n.d.). *Build a civilization in a simulated ecosystem*. Retrieved May 4, 2017, from https://www.strangeloopgames.com/eco/

Elliott, J. B., Gardner, M., & Alrashidi, M. (2012). Towards a framework for the design of mixed reality immersive education spaces. In *Proceedings of the 2nd European Immersive Education Summit: EiED 2012* (pp. 1–13). Paris, France: Universidad Carlos III de Madrid.

Ellis, R. (2003). *Task-based language learning and teaching*. Oxford, UK: Oxford University Press.

Ellis, S. R. (1994). What are virtual environments? *IEEE Computer Graphics and Applications*, *14*(1), 17–22. doi:10.1109/38.250914 PMID:7757252

Elmore, R. F. (2004). *School reform from the inside out: Policy, practice, and performance*. Cambridge, MA: Harvard Education Press.

Engeström, Y. (2001). Expansive learning at work: Toward an activity theoretical reconceptualization. *Journal of Education and Work*, *14*(1), 133–156. doi:10.1080/13639080020028747

Ertmer, P. A., & Newby, T. J. (2013). Behaviorism, cognitivism, constructivism: Comparing critical features from an instructional design perspective. *Performance Improvement Quarterly*, *26*(2), 43–71. doi:10.1002/piq.21143

Fairtest. (2009, March). *Position Paper on Assessment for Learning*. Paper presented at the Third International Conference on Assessment for Learning, Dunedin, New Zealand. Retrieved December 21, 2012, from www.fairtest.org/position-paper-assessment-learning

Felemban, S., Gardner, M., & Callaghan, V. (2016). *Virtual observation lenses for assessing online collaborative learning environment*. Paper presented at the Second Immersive Learning Research Network Conference (iLRN 2016), Santa Barbara, CA.

Ferg, S. (2006). *Event-Driven Programming: Introduction, Tutorial, History*. Retrieved from http://eventdrivenpgm.sourceforge.net

Ferguson, R. F., Phillips, S. F., Rowley, J. F. S., & Friedlander, J. W. (2015). *The influence of teaching beyond standardized test scores: Engagement, mindsets, and agency.* Research Report: The Achievement Gap Initiative at Harvard University. Retrieved from http://www.agi.harvard.edu/publications.php

Fernández Panadero, C., De la Cruz Barquero, V., Delgado Kloos, C., & Moran Nuñez, D. (2014). PhyMEL-WS: Physically experiencing the virtual world. Insights into mixed reality and flow state on board a wheelchair simulator. *Journal of Universal Computer Science, 20*(12), 1629–1648.

Fink, L. D. (2004). Beyond small groups: Harnessing the extraordinary power of learning teams. In L. K. Michaelsen, A. B. Knight, & L. D. Fink (Eds.), *Team-based learning: A transformative use of small groups in college teaching* (pp. 3–26). Sterling, VA: Stylus.

Fischer, G., Lemke, A. C., Mastaglio, T., & Morch, A. I. (1991). The role of critiquing in cooperative problem solving. *ACM Transactions on Information Systems, 9*(2), 123–151. doi:10.1145/123078.128727

Fishman, B., Dede, C., & Means, B. (2015). Teaching and technology: New tools for new times. In D. Gitomer & C. Bell (Eds.), *Handbook of research on teaching* (5th ed.). Washington, DC: American Educational Research Association.

Fornell, C., Tellis, G. J., & Zinkhan, G. M. (1982). Validity assessment: A structural equations approach using partial least squares. In *An assessment of marketing thought & practice* (pp. 405–409). Chicago: American Marketing Association.

Foster, A. (2008). Games and motivation to learn science: Personal identity, applicability, relevance and meaningfulness. *Journal of Interactive Learning Research, 19*(4), 597–614.

Foster, P. (1998). A classroom perspective on the negotiation of meaning. *Applied Linguistics, 19*(1), 1–23. doi:10.1093/applin/19.1.1

Fowler, C. (2015). Virtual reality and learning: Where is the pedagogy? *British Journal of Educational Technology, 46*(2), 412–422. doi:10.1111/bjet.12135

Freedman, J. (2013). The typical college student is not a 'typical' college student (and other fun college demographics data). *Forbes*. Retrieved from https://www.forbes.com/sites/joshfreedman/2013/09/20/the-typical-college-student-is-not-a-typical-college-student-and-other-fun-college-demographics-data/#6f370f107c5a

Furtak, E. M. (2006). The problem with answers: An exploration of guided scientific inquiry teaching. *Science Education, 90*(3), 453–467. doi:10.1002/sce.20130

Galarneau, L. (2005). Authentic learning experiences through play: Games, simulations and the construction of knowledge. *Proceedings of DiGRA 2005 Conference: Changing Views - Worlds in Play*. Retrieved from http://www.digra.org/digital-library/publications/authentic-learning-experiences-through-play-games-simulations-and-the-construction-of-knowledge/

Gall, M., & Breeze, N. (2005). Music composition lessons: The multimodal affordances of technology. *Educational Review, 57*(4), 415–433. doi:10.1080/00131910500278314

Gao, F., Noh, J. J., & Koehler, M. J. (2009). Comparing role-playing activities in Second Life and face-to-face environments. *Journal of Interactive Learning Research, 20*(4), 422–443.

Garcia, A. C. (2013). *An introduction to interaction: Understanding talk in formal and informal settings*. New York, NY: Bloomsbury Academic.

Gardner, M., & O'Driscoll, M. L. (2011). MiRTLE (Mixed reality teaching and learning environment): From prototype to production and implementation. In D. Hernandez-Leo, C. Delgado-Kloos, & J. I. Asencio-Pérez (Eds.), *Proceedings of the Across Physical and Virtual Spaces (AcrossSpaces) Workshop in conjunction with ECT-TEL 2011* (pp. 21–28). Palermo, Italy: Academic Press.

Gardner, M., & Elliott, J. B. (2014). The immersive education laboratory: Understanding affordances, structuring experiences, and creating constructivist, collaborative processes, in mixed reality smart environments. *Transactions on Future Intelligent Educational Environments*, *1*(1), 1–13.

Garnier, F., & Kloos, C. D. (Eds.). (2012). *Proceedings of the 2nd European Immersive Education Summit: EiED 2012*. Paris, France: Universidad Carlos III de Madrid.

Garrido-Inigo, P., & Rodriguez-Moreno, F. (2015). The reality of virtual worlds: Pros and cons of their application to foreign language teaching. *Interactive Learning Environments*, *23*(4), 453–470. doi:10.1080/10494820.2013.788034

Garrison, D. R., & Kanuka, H. (2004). Blended learning: Uncovering its transformative potential in higher education. *The Internet and Higher Education*, *7*(2), 95–105. doi:10.1016/j.iheduc.2004.02.001

Gartner. (2015). *Gartner says 6.4 billion connected "things."* Retrieved from http://www.gartner.com/newsroom/id/3165317

Gaydos, M. (2015). Seriously considering design in educational games. *Educational Researcher*, *44*(9), 478–483. doi:10.3102/0013189X15621307

Gazit, E. (2017). *The gameful heroes' future: How gaming and virtual reality technologies are reshaping our learning world.* Manuscript in preparation.

Gazit, E. (2009). A window on digital games interactions in home settings. In R. E. Ferdig (Ed.), *Handbook of research on effective electronic gaming in education* (Vol. 1, pp. 127–145). Hershey, PA: IGI Global. doi:10.4018/978-1-59904-808-6.ch008

Gee, J. P. (2008). Learning and games. *The Ecology of Games: Connecting Youth, Games, and Learning, 3*, 21-40.

Gee, J. P. (2003). What video games have to teach us about learning and literacy. *Computers in Entertainment*, *1*(1), 20–20. doi:10.1145/950566.950595

Gee, J. P. (2004). *Situate language and learning: The critique of traditional schooling*. London: Routledge.

Gee, J. P. (2004). *Situated language and learning: A critique of traditional schooling*. New York, NY: Routledge.

Gee, J. P. (2007). *What video games have to teach us about learning and literacy*. New York: Palgrave MacMillan.

Gee, J. P. (2009). Deep learning properties of good digital games. In U. Ritterfeld, M. Cody, & P. Vorderer (Eds.), *Serious games: Mechanisms and effects* (pp. 67–82). Abingdon, UK: Routledge.

Gee, J. P., & Hayes, E. (2011). *Language and learning in the digital age*. New York: Routledge.

Gerhard, M., Moore, D., & Hobbs, D. (2004). Embodiment and copresence in collaborative interfaces. *Human-Computer Studies*, *61*(4), 453–480. doi:10.1016/j.ijhcs.2003.12.014

Gershenfield, N., Krikorian, R., & Cohen, D. (2004). The internet of things. *Scientific American*, *291*(4), 76–81. doi:10.1038/scientificamerican1004-76 PMID:15487673

Gibson, J. J. (1979). *The ecological approach to visual perception*. Boston, MA: Houghton Mifflin.

Giddens, A. (1979). *Central problems in social theory: Action, structure and contradiction in social analysis*. Berkeley, CA: University of California Press. doi:10.1007/978-1-349-16161-4

Goffman, E. (1963). *Behavior in public places*. New York, NY: The Free Press.

Goldin-Meadow, S., & Wagner, S. M. (2005). How our hands help us learn. *Trends in Cognitive Sciences*, *9*(5), 234–241. doi:10.1016/j.tics.2005.03.006 PMID:15866150

Gomes, L., & Bogosyan, S. (2009). Current trends in remote laboratories. *IEEE Transactions on Industrial Electronics*, *56*(12), 4744–4756. doi:10.1109/TIE.2009.2033293

Google Maps. (n.d.). In *Google Maps Education Web site*. Retrieved February 3, 2017, from http://maps.google.com/help/maps/education/learn/

Google. (2007). *Street view in google earth*. Retrieved February 3, 2017, from http://support.google.com/earth/bin/answer.py?hl=en&answer=1067358

Greeno, J. (1998). The situativity of knowing, learning, and research. *The American Psychologist*, *53*(1), 5–26. doi:10.1037/0003-066X.53.1.5

Greeno, J. G. (1994). Gibson's affordances. *Psychological Review*, *101*(2), 336–342. doi:10.1037/0033-295X.101.2.336 PMID:8022965

Grotzer, T. A., Kamarainen, A., Tutwiler, M. S., Metcalf, S., & Dede, C. (2013). Learning to reason about ecosystems dynamics over time: The challenges of an event-based causal focus. *Bioscience*, *63*(4), 288–296. doi:10.1525/bio.2013.63.4.9

Guizzo, E. (2011). Fukushima Robot Operator Writes Tell-All Blog. *IEEE Spectrum*, *23*. Retrieved from http://spectrum.ieee.org/automaton/robotics/industrial-robots/fukushima-robot-operator-diaries

Gunawardena, C. N. (1995). Social presence theory and implications for interaction and collaborative learning in computer conferences. *International Journal of Educational Telecommunications*, *1*(2–3), 147–166.

Gutierrez, K., Rymes, B., & Larson, J. (1995). Script, counterscript, and underlife in the classroom: James Brown versus "Brown v. Board of Education." *Harvard Educational Review*, *65*(3), 445–471. doi:10.17763/haer.65.3.r16146n25h4mh384

Hadwin, A. F., & Oshige, M. (2011). Self-regulation, coregulation, and socially shared regulation: Exploring perspectives of social in self-regulated learning theory. *Teachers College Record*, *113*(2), 240–264.

Hair, J. F., Black, W. C., Babin, B. J., & Anderson, R. E. (2010). *Multivariate data analysis: International version* (7th ed.). Pearson.

Hair, J. F., Black, W. C., Babin, B. J., Anderson, R. E., & Tatham, R. L. (2006). *Multivariate data analysis* (Vol. 6). Upper Saddle River, NJ: Pearson Prentice Hall.

Hale, K. S., & Stanney, K. M. (Eds.). (2014). *Handbook of virtual environments: Design, implementation, and applications*. Boca Raton, FL: CRC Press. doi:10.1201/b17360

Hammond, M. (2010). What is an affordance and can it help us understand the use of ICT in education? *Education and Information Technologies*, *15*(3), 205–217. doi:10.1007/s10639-009-9106-z

Hanson, K., & Shelton, B. E. (2008). Design and development of virtual reality: Analysis of challenges faced by educators. *Journal of Educational Technology & Society*, *11*(1), 118–131.

Harasim, L. M. (2012). *Learning theory and online technologies*. New York, NY: Routledge.

Hare, A. P. (1981). Group size. *The American Behavioral Scientist*, *24*(5), 695–708. doi:10.1177/000276428102400507

Harrington, M. C. (2012). The virtual trillium trail and the empirical effects of freedom and fidelity on discovery-based learning. *Virtual Reality (Waltham Cross)*, *16*(2), 105–120. doi:10.1007/s10055-011-0189-7

Harrison, D. (2010). Linden Lab to end Second Life educational discounts. *The Journal: Transforming Education Through Technology*. Retrieved from, https://thejournal.com/articles/2010/11/03/linden-lab-to-end-second-life-educational-discounts.aspx

Harris, S. (2002). Innovative pedagogical practices using ICT in schools in England. *Journal of Computer Assisted Learning*, *18*(4), 449–458. doi:10.1046/j.0266-4909.2002.00256.x

Hartwick, P., & Nowlan, N. (2012, March). *Learning as an avatar: Designing immersive spaces and facilitating 3D learning experiences*. Paper presented at INTED2012 6th International Technology, Education and Development Conference, Valencia, Spain.

Hassell, M. D., Goyal, S., Limayem, M., & Boughzala, I. (2012). Effects of presence, copresence, and flow on learning outcomes in 3D learning spaces. *Administrative Issues Journal: Education, Practice, and Research*, *2*(1), 62–73. doi:10.5929/2011.2.1.4

Hattie, J. (2012). *Visible learning for teachers: Maximizing impact on learning*. New York, NY: Routledge.

Hattie, J., & Timperley, H. (2007). The power of feedback. *Review of Educational Research*, *77*(1), 81–112.

Haythornthwaite, C. A., & Andrews, R. (2011). *E-learning theory and practice*. Thousand Oaks, CA: Sage. doi:10.4135/9781446288566

Hedberg, J. G., & Alexander, S. (1994). Virtual reality in education: Defining researchable issues. *Educational Media International*, *31*(4), 214–220. doi:10.1080/0952398940310402

Heim, M. (1998). *Virtual realism*. Oxford, UK: Oxford University Press.

Herbet, A., Thompson, F., & Garnier, F. (2012). Immaterial art stock: Preserve, document and disseminate the pioneering works of art created inside online immersive platforms. In M. Gardner, F. Garnier, & C. D. Kloos (Eds.), *Proceedings of the 2nd European Immersive Education Summit* (pp. 101–113). Paris, France: Universidad Carlos III de Madrid.

Heritage, J. (1984). *Garfinkel and Ethnomethodology*. Cambridge, UK: Polity Press.

Herrington, J., & Oliver, R. (2000). An instructional design framework for authentic learning environments. *Educational Technology Research and Development*, *48*(3), 23–48. doi:10.1007/BF02319856

Hetland, P., & Mørch, A. I. (2016). Ethnography for investigating the Internet. *Seminar.net: Media. Technology and Lifelong Learning*, *12*(1), 1–14.

Hew, K. F., & Cheung, W. S. (2010). Use of three-dimensional (3-D) immersive virtual worlds in K-12 and higher education settings: A review of the research. *British Journal of Educational Technology*, *41*(1), 33–55. doi:10.1111/j.1467-8535.2008.00900.x

Hmelo-Silver, C. E., Duncan, R. G., & Chinn, C. A. (2007). Scaffolding and achievement in problem-based and inquiry learning: A response to Kirschner, Sweller, and Clark (2006). *Educational Psychologist*, *42*(2), 99–107. doi:10.1080/00461520701263368

Hockey, A., Esmail, F., Jimenez-Bescos, C., & Freer, P. (2010). Built environment education in the era of virtual learning. *Proceedings of the W089 - Special Track 18th CIB World Building Congress*, 200–217.

Hollan, J., & Stornetta, S. (1992). Beyond being there. In *Proceedings CHI'92* (pp. 119–125). New York, NY: ACM Press. doi:10.1145/142750.142769

Honey, M., & Kanter, D. E. (2013). *Design make play: Growing the next generation of STEM innovators*. London, UK: Routledge.

Hong, S. J., & Tam, K. Y. (2006). Understanding the adoption of multipurpose information appliances: The case of mobile data services. *Information Systems Research*, *17*(2), 162–179. doi:10.1287/isre.1060.0088

Horan, B., Gardner, M., & Scott, J. (2009). *MiRTLE: A mixed reality teaching & learning environment*. Retrieved from https://www.researchgate.net/publication/234773595_MiRTLE_a_mixed_reality_teaching_learning_environment

Howe, C. (2014). Optimizing small group discourse in classrooms: Effective practices and theoretical constraints. *International Journal of Educational Research*, *63*, 107–115. doi:10.1016/j.ijer.2013.03.011

Howland, J., Jonassen, D., & Marra, R. (2011). *Meaningful learning with technology* (4th ed.). Allyn & Bacon.

Hu, L., & Bentler, P. M. (1999). Cutoff criteria for fit indexes in covariance structure analysis: Conventional criteria versus new alternatives. *Structural Equation Modeling*, *6*, 1-55. doi: /10.1080/10705519909540118

Huang, Y., Chiu, P., Liu, T., & Chen, T. (2011). The design and implementation of a meaningful learning-based evaluation method for ubiquitous learning. *Computers & Education*, *57*(4), 2291–2302. doi:10.1016/j.compedu.2011.05.023

Ibañez Espiga, M. B., Delgado Kloos, C., Leony, D., Garcia Rueda, J. J., & Maroto, D. (2011). Learning a foreign language in a mixed reality environment. *IEEE Internet Computing*, *15*(6), 44–47. doi:10.1109/MIC.2011.78

Ibáñez, M. B., Garcia, J. J., Galan, S., Maroto, D., Morillo, D., & Kloos, C. D. (2011). Design and implementation of a 3D multi-user virtual world for language learning. *Journal of Educational Technology & Society*, *14*(4), 2–10.

Ijsselsteijn, W. A. (2006). History of telepresence. *3D videocommunication: Algorithms, concepts and real-time systems in human centred communication*, 5–21. doi:10.1002/0470022736.ch1

Illeris, K. (2003). *Three dimensions of learning: Contemporary learning theory in the tension field between the cognitive, the emotional and the social*. Malabar, FL: Krieger.

Illich, I. (1971). *Deschooling society*. London, UK: Marion Boyars.

Ireson, J. (2008). *Learners, learning and educational activity*. New York, NY: Routledge.

Ito, J. (2014, October 2). Antidisciplinary [Weblog post]. MIT Media Lab Blog. Retrieved February 9, 2017, from https://joi.ito.com/weblog/2014/10/02/antidisciplinar.html

Ito, M. (2009). *Engineering play. A cultural history of children's software*. Cambridge, MA: MIT Press.

James, M., McCormick, R., Black, P., Carmichael, P., Drummond, M.-J., Fox, A., … Wiliam, D. (2007). Improving learning how to learn: Classrooms, schools and networks. London, UK: Routledge.

Jang, S., Kim, S., & Woo, W. (2005). When VR meets ubicomp. *Virtual Reality (Waltham Cross)*, 1–2.

Jarmon, J. (2008). Pedagogy and learning in the virtual world of Second Life. In P. Rogers, G. Berg, J. Boettcher, C. Howard, L. Justice, & K. Schenk (Eds.), *Encyclopedia of distance and online learning* (pp. 1–11). Hershey, PA: Idea Group.

Jarmon, L., Traphagan, T., Mayrath, M., & Trivedi, A. (2009). Virtual world teaching, experiential learning, and assessment: An interdisciplinary communication course in Second Life. *Computers & Education*, *53*(1), 169–182. doi:10.1016/j.compedu.2009.01.010

Jefferson, G. (1984). Transcript notation. In J. M. Atkinson & J. Heritage (Eds.), *Structures of social action: Studies in conversation analysis* (pp. ix–xvi). Cambridge, UK: Cambridge University Press.

Jia, D., Bhatti, A., & Nahavandi, S. (2014). The impact of self-efficacy and perceived system efficacy on effectiveness of virtual training systems. *Behaviour & Information Technology*, *33*(1), 16–35. doi:10.1080/0144929X.2012.681067

Johnson, D. W., & Johnson, R. T. (1996). *Cooperation and the use of technology. In Handbook of research for educational communications and technology* (pp. 1017–1044). Abingdon, UK: Routledge.

Johnson, D. W., & Johnson, R. T. (1996). Cooperation and the use of technology. In D. Jonassen (Ed.), *Handbook of research for educational communications and technology*. New York, NY: Macmillan.

Johnson, D. W., & Johnson, R. T. (2005). New developments in social interdependence theory. *Genetic, Social, and General Psychology Monographs*, *131*(4), 285–358. doi:10.3200/MONO.131.4.285-358 PMID:17191373

Johnson, D. W., Johnson, R. T., & Stanne, M. B. (2000). *Cooperative learning methods: A meta-analysis. University of Minnesota*. Minneapolis, MN: Cooperative Learning Center.

Jonassen, D. (1999). Designing constructivist learning environments. In C. M. Reigeluth (Ed.), Instructional-design theories and models: A new paradigm of instructional theory pp. 215-239. Hillsdale, NJ: Lawrence Erlbaum Associates.

Jonassen, D. (1995). Supporting communities of learners with technology: A vision for integrating technology with learning in schools. *Educational Technology*, *35*, 60–63.

Jonassen, D. H., Peck, K. L., & Wilson, B. G. (1998). *Learning WITH technology: A constructivist perspective*. Columbus, OH: Prentice-Hall.

Jones, D. (2013). An alternative (to) reality. Understanding learning in virtual worlds. In M. Childs & A. Peachey (Eds.), *Human-computer interaction series* (pp. 1–20). London, UK: Springer.

Jong, T., Linn, M. C., & Zacharia, Z. C. (2013). Physical and virtual laboratories in science and engineering education. *Science*, *340*(6130), 305–308. doi:10.1126/science.1230579 PMID:23599479

Jordan, B., & Henderson, A. (1995). Interaction analysis: Foundation and practice. *Journal of the Learning Sciences*, *4*(1), 39–103. doi:10.1207/s15327809jls0401_2

Kafai, Y. B. (2010). The world of Whyville: An introduction to Tween Virtual Life. *Games and Culture*, *5*(1), 3–22. doi:10.1177/1555412009351264

Kaiser, H. F. (1960). The application of electronic computers to factor analysis. *Educational and Psychological Measurement*, *20*(1), 141–151. doi:10.1177/001316446002000116

Kamarainen, A. M., Metcalf, S., Grotzer, T., & Dede, C. (2012). *EcoMUVE: Shifts in affective beliefs and values about science through learning experiences in immersive virtual environments*. Paper presented at American Educational Research Association (AERA) Conference, Vancouver, Canada.

Kamarainen, A., Metcalf, S., Grotzer, T., & Dede, C. J. (2015). Exploring ecosystems from the inside: How immersion in a multi-user virtual environment supports epistemologically grounded practices in ecosystem science instruction. *Journal of Science Education and Technology*, *24*(2), 148–167. doi:10.1007/s10956-014-9531-7

Kaptelinin, V., & Nardi, B. A. (2006). *Acting with technology: Activity theory and interaction design*. Cambridge, MA: MIT Press.

Kember, D. (1997). A reconceptualisation of the research into university academics' conceptions of teaching. *Learning and Instruction*, *7*(3), 255–276. doi:10.1016/S0959-4752(96)00028-X

Kennewell, S., Tanner, H., Jones, S., & Beauchamp, G. (2007). Analyzing the use of interactive technology to implement interactive teaching. *Journal of Computer Assisted Learning*, *24*(1), 61–73. doi:10.1111/j.1365-2729.2007.00244.x

Keskitalo, T. (2011). Teacher's conceptions and approaches to teaching in virtual reality and simulation-based learning environments. *Teachers and Teaching*, *17*(1), 131–147. doi:10.1080/13540602.2011.538503

Ketelhut, D. J., Nelson, B. C., Clarke, J., & Dede, C. (2010). A multi-user virtual environment for building and assessing higher order inquiry skills in science. *British Journal of Educational Technology*, *41*(1), 56–68. doi:10.1111/j.1467-8535.2009.01036.x

Kiang, D. (2014). *Minecraft 101: The underwater dome project.* Retrieved from https://www.iste.org/explore/articleDetail?articleid=155

Kim, G. J. (2005). *Designing virtual reality systems: The structured approach.* Heidelberg, Germany: Springer.

Kim, J., Hill, R., & Durlach, P. (2009). BiLAT: A game-based environment for practicing negotiation in a cultural context. *International Journal of Artificial Intelligence in Education*, *19*, 289–309.

King, A., Marietta, G., & Gehlbach, H. (2014). The role of role-taking: Social perspective taking and interpersonal relationships in virtual simulations. In D. B. Zandvliet (Ed.), *Interpersonal relationships in education: From theory to practice* (pp. 95–110). Rotterdam, The Netherlands: Sense Publishers. doi:10.1007/978-94-6209-701-8_7

Kirkley, S. E., & Kirkley, J. R. (2004). Creating next generation blended learning environments using mixed reality, video games and simulations. *TechTrends*, *49*(3), 42–53. doi:10.1007/BF02763646

Kirschner, P., Strijbos, J., Kreijns, K., & Beers, P. J. (2004). Designing electronic collaborative learning environments. *Educational Technology Research and Development*, *52*(3), 47–66. doi:10.1007/BF02504675

Klahr, D., Triona, L. M., & Williams, C. (2007). Hands on what? The relative effectiveness of physical versus virtual materials in an engineering design project by middle school children. *Journal of Research in Science Teaching*, *44*(1), 183–203. doi:10.1002/tea.20152

Klem, L. (2000). Structural equation modeling. In L. Grimm & P. Yarnold (Eds.), *Reading and understanding multivariate statistics* (Vol. 2). Washington, DC: American Psychological Association.

Klenowski, V. (2009). Assessment for learning revisited: An Asia-Pacific perspective. *Assessment in Education: Principles, Policy & Practice*, *16*(3), 263–268. doi:10.1080/09695940903319646

Kline, R. B. (2005). *Principles and practice of structural equation modeling* (2nd ed.). New York: Guilford Press.

Kline, S., Dyer-Witheford, N., & de Peuter, G. (2003). *Digital play: The interaction of technology, culture, and marketing.* Montreal, Canada: McGill-Queen's University Press.

Koenig, A., Iseli, M., Wainess, R., & Lee, J. J. (2013). Assessment methodology for computer-based instructional simulations. *Military Medicine*, *178*(10S), 47–54. doi:10.7205/MILMED-D-13-00217 PMID:24084305

Kolb, D. A. (1984). *Experiential learning: Experience as the source of learning and development.* Englewood Cliffs, NJ: Prentice Hall.

Kortuem, G., Kawsar, F., Fitton, D., & Sundramoorthy, V. (2010). Smart objects as building blocks for the Internet of things. *IEEE Internet Computing*, *14*(1), 44–51. doi:10.1109/MIC.2009.143

Koster, R. (2005). *Theory of fun for game design.* Scottsdale, AZ: Paraglyph Press.

Koster, R. (2013). *A theory of fun for game design.* Sebastopol, CA: O'Reilly Media.

Kothari, C. R. (2004). *Research methodology: Methods & Techniques* (2nd ed.). Delhi, India: New Age International Publisher.

Kozlova, I. (2013). Online pedagogy: Development of the communicative skills in Russian online courses. *OLBI Working Papers, 5,* 57-70.

Kozlova, I., & Priven, D. (2015). ESL teacher training in 3D virtual worlds. *Language Learning & Technology, 19*(1), 83–101.

Kulik, C. L. C., & Kulik, J. A. (1991). Effectiveness of computer-based instruction: An updated analysis. *Computers in Human Behavior, 7*(1–2), 75–94. doi:10.1016/0747-5632(91)90030-5

LAK '11. (2010). *LAK '11: 1st International Conference on Learning Analytics and Knowledge 2011*. Retrieved from https://tekri.athabascau.ca/analytics/

Lantolf, J. P. (2000). Second language learning as a mediated process. *Language Teaching, 33*(2), 79–96. doi:10.1017/S0261444800015329

Lantolf, J. P. (2013). Sociocultural Theory and the dialectics of L2 learner autonomy/agency. In P. Benson & L. Cooker (Eds.), *The applied linguistics individual: Sociocultural approaches to identity, agency and autonomy* (pp. 17–31). Bristol, CT: Equinos Publishing.

Lan, Y. J. (2015). Contextual EFL learning in a 3D virtual environment. *Language Learning & Technology, 19*(2), 16–32.

Lan, Y. J., Kan, Y. H., Sung, Y. T., & Chung, K. E. (2016). Oral performance language tasks for CSL beginners in Second Life. *Language Learning & Technology, 20*(3), 60–79.

Larsen-Freeman, D. (2000). *Techniques and principles in language teaching*. Oxford, UK: Oxford University Press.

Laurel, B. (1993). *Computers as theatre*. New York, NY: Addison-Wesley.

Lavee, Z., & Gazit, E. (2012). World of Warcraft (WOW) guild conflict management insights for organizations leadership building. In Y. Yair, & E. Shmueli (Eds.), *Proceedings of the 10th Annual Conference of MEITAL-The Israeli Inter-University Center for E-Learning (IUCEL)* (pp. 66-73). Rehovot, Israel: Weizmann Institute of Science.

Lave, J. (1988). *Cognition in practice: Mind, mathematics, and culture in everyday life*. Cambridge, UK: Cambridge University Press. doi:10.1017/CBO9780511609268

Lave, J., & Wenger, E. (1991). *Situated learning: Legitimate peripheral participation*. New York, NY: Cambridge University Press. doi:10.1017/CBO9780511815355

Law, N., Pelgrum, W. J., & Plomp, T. (2008). *Pedagogy and ICT use in schools around the world: Findings from the IEA SITES 2006 study*. Springer.

Lee, Y., Oh, S., Shin, C., & Woo, W. (2008). *Recent trends in ubiquitous virtual reality*. Paper presented at 2008 International Symposium on Ubiquitous Virtual Reality, Hainan Island, China. doi:10.1109/ISUVR.2008.27

Lee, E. A. L., Wong, K. W., & Fung, C. C. (2010). How does desktop virtual reality enhance learning outcomes? A structural equation modeling approach. *Computers & Education, 55*(4), 1424–1442. doi:10.1016/j.compedu.2010.06.006

Lee, M. J. W., Eustace, K., Fellows, G., Bytheway, A., & Irving, L. (2005). Rochester Castle MMORPG: Instructional gaming and collaborative learning at a Western Australian school. *Australasian Journal of Educational Technology, 21*(4), 446–469. doi:10.14742/ajet.1314

Lerner, F. (2005). Foundations for design: Continuing the Bauhaus Vorkurs vision. *Studies in Art Education*, 211–226.

Levesque, J., & Lelièvre, E. (2011). Creation and communication in virtual worlds: Experimentations with OpenSim. In S. Richir, & A. Shirai (Eds.) *Proceedings of the Virtual Reality International Conference* (pp. 22–24). Laval, France: ACM.

Levin, M. F. (2011). Can virtual reality offer enriched environments for rehabilitation? *Expert Review of Neurotherapeutics, 11*(2), 153–155. doi:10.1586/ern.10.201 PMID:21306202

Lifton, J. H. (2007). *Dual reality: An emerging medium.* Retrieved from https://dspace.mit.edu/handle/1721.1/41707

Lifton, J. H., & Paradiso, J. (2009). *Dual reality: Merging the real and virtual.* Paper presented at First International Conference on Facets of Virtual Environments (FaVE'09), Berlin, Germany.

Li, M. C., & Tsai, C. C. (2013). Game-based learning in science education: A review of relevant research. *Journal of Science Education and Technology, 22*(6), 877–898. doi:10.1007/s10956-013-9436-x

Lindgren, R., & Moshell, J. M. (2011). Supporting children's learning with body-based metaphors in a mixed reality environment. In *Proceedings of the 10th International Conference on Interaction Design and Children* (pp. 177–180). ACM. doi:10.1145/1999030.1999055

Linnenbrink, E. A., & Pintrich, P. R. (2002). Motivation as an enabler for academic success. *School Psychology Review, 31*(3), 313–327.

Lin, T., Wang, S., Grant, S., Chien, C., & Lan, Y. (2014). Task-based teaching approaches of Chinese as a foreign language in Second Life through teachers' perspectives. *Procedia Technology, 13*, 16–22. doi:10.1016/j.protcy.2014.02.004

Little, D. (2007). Language learner autonomy: Some fundamental considerations revisited. *Innovation in Language Learning and Teaching, 1*(1), 14–29. doi:10.2167/illt040.0

Littlewood, W. (1996). "Autonomy": An anatomy and a framework. *System, 24*(4), 427–435. doi:10.1016/S0346-251X(96)00039-5

Littlewood, W. (2007). Communicative and task-based language teaching in East Asian classrooms. *Language Teaching, 40*(03), 243–249. doi:10.1017/S0261444807004363

Liu, X., Bonk, C. J., Magjuka, R. J., Lee, S. H., & Su, B. (2005). Exploring four dimensions of online instructor roles: A program level case study. *Journal of Asynchronous Learning Networks, 9*(4), 29–48.

Lochbaum, D., Lyman, E., & Stranahan, S. Q. (2014). *Fukushima. The story of a nuclear disaster.* New York, NY: The New Press.

Loke, S. K. (2015). How do virtual world experiences bring about learning? A critical review of theories. *Australasian Journal of Educational Technology, 31*(1), 112–122. doi:10.14742/ajet.2532

Ludescher, F. (2006). *Communicative Language Teaching.* Retrieved February 3, 2017, from http://www2.vobs.at/ludescher/alternative%20methods/communicative_language_teaching.htm

Ludlow, P., & Wallace, M. (2007). *The Second Life Herald: The virtual tabloid that witnessed the dawn of the metaverse.* Cambridge, MA: MIT Press.

Ludvigsen, S., & Mørch, A. (2010). Computer-supported collaborative learning: Basic concepts, multiple perspectives, and emerging trends. In B. McGaw, P. Peterson, & E. Baker (Eds.), *The international encyclopedia of education* (Vol. 5, pp. 290–296). Oxford, UK: Elsevier. doi:10.1016/B978-0-08-044894-7.00493-0

Magin, D. J., & Reizes, J. A. (1990). Computer simulation of laboratory experiments: An unrealized potential. *Computers & Education, 14*(3), 263–270. doi:10.1016/0360-1315(90)90009-V

Ma, J., & Nickerson, J. V. (2006). Hands-on, simulated, and remote laboratories. *ACM Computing Surveys, 38*(3), 1–24. doi:10.1145/1132960.1132961

Mann, S. (2002). Mediated reality with implementations for everyday life. *Presence (Cambridge, Mass.), 11*(2), 158–175. doi:10.1162/1054746021470603

Marone, V. (2016). Playful constructivism: Making sense of digital games for learning and creativity through play, design, and participation. *Journal of Virtual Worlds Research, 9*(3), 1–18.

Marshall, B., & Drummond, M. J. (2006). How teachers engage with assessment for learning: Lessons from the classroom. *Research Papers in Education, 21*(2), 133–149. doi:10.1080/02671520600615638

Martens, R., Bastiaens, T., & Kirschner, P. A. (2007). New learning design in distance education: The impact on student perception and motivation. *Distance Education, 28*(1), 81–93. doi:10.1080/01587910701305327

Mayer, R. E. (2014). *Computer games for learning. An evidence-based approach.* Cambridge, MA: MIT Press.

McAuley, E., Duncan, T., & Tammen, V. V. (1989). Psychometric properties of the intrinsic motivation inventory in a competitive sport setting: A confirmatory factor analysis. *Research Quarterly for Exercise and Sport, 60*(1), 48–58. doi:10.1080/02701367.1989.10607413 PMID:2489825

McDonald, R. P., & Ho, M. R. (2002). Principles and practice in reporting structural equation analyses. *Psychological Methods, 7*(1), 64–82. doi:10.1037/1082-989X.7.1.64 PMID:11928891

McGonigal, J. (2008). Why I love bees: A case study in collective intelligence gaming. In K. Salen (Ed.), *The ecology of games: Connecting youth, games, and learning* (pp. 199–227). Cambridge, MA: MIT Press.

McGonigal, J. (2011). *Reality is broken: Why games make us better and how they can change the world.* New York, NY: Penguin.

McLaughlin, M. W., & Talbert, J. E. (2006). *Building School-based Teacher Learning Communities: Professional Strategies to Improve Student Achievement.* New York, NY: Teachers College.

McLellan, H. (2004). Virtual realites. In D. H. Jonassen (Ed.), *Handbook of research on educational communications and technology.* Mahwah, NJ: Erlbaum Associates.

Merchant, Z., Goetz, E. T., Cifuentes, L., Keeney-Kennicutt, W., & Davis, T. J. (2014). Effectiveness of virtual reality-based instruction on students' learning outcomes in K-12 and higher education: A meta-analysis. *Computers & Education, 70*, 29–40. doi:10.1016/j.compedu.2013.07.033

Merchant, Z., Goetz, E. T., Keeney-Kennicutt, W., Kwok, O. M., Cifuentes, L., & Davis, T. J. (2012). The learner characteristics, features of desktop 3D virtual reality environments, and college chemistry instruction: A structural equation modeling analysis. *Computers & Education, 59*(2), 551–568. doi:10.1016/j.compedu.2012.02.004

Merchant, Z., Keeney-Kennicutt, W., & Goetz, E. (2015). Predicting undergraduate students' acceptance of second life for teaching chemistry. *Journal of Online Learning and Teaching / MERLOT, 11*(2).

Metcalf, S. J., Kamarainen, A., Grotzer, T. A., & Dede, C. (2013a). *Collaborative learning in virtual environments: Role-based exploration of causality in ecosystems over time and scale.* Paper presented at Conference on Computer Supported Collaborative Learning (CSCL), Madison, WI.

Metcalf, S. J., Tutwiler, M. S., Kamarainen, A. M., Grotzer, T. A., & Dede, C. (2013b). *Multi-user virtual environments to promote middle school ecosystem science learning and attitudes about science.* Paper presented at American Educational Research Association (AERA) Conference, San Francisco, CA.

Metcalf, S. J., Chen, J. A., Kamarainen, A. M., Frumin, K. M., Vickrey, T. L., Grotzer, T. A., & Dede, C. (2014). Shifts in student motivation during usage of a multi-user virtual environment for ecosystem science. *International Journal of Virtual and Personal Learning Environments, 5*(4), 1–15. doi:10.4018/IJVPLE.2014100101

Metcalf, S. J., Kamarainen, A. M., Cooke, C. B., Turkay, S., Grotzer, T., & Dede, C. (2016). Teacher perceptions of the practicality and effectiveness of immersive ecological simulations. In K. Terry & A. Cheney (Eds.), *Utilizing virtual and personal learning environments for optimal learning* (pp. 22–45). Hershey, PA: Information Science Reference. doi:10.4018/978-1-4666-8847-6.ch002

Michaelsen, L. K. (2004b). Getting started with team-based learning. In L. K. Michaelsen, A. B. Knight, & L. D. Fink (Eds.), *Team-based learning: A transformative use of small groups in college teaching* (pp. 27–53). Sterling, VA: Stylus.

Michaelsen, L. K. (2004c). Preface. In L. K. Michaelsen, A. B. Knight, & L. D. Fink (Eds.), *Team-based learning: A transformative use of small groups in college teaching* (pp. vii–xi). Sterling, VA: Stylus.

Michaelsen, L. K., Knight, A. B., & Fink, L. D. (Eds.). (2004a). *Team-based learning: A transformative use of small groups in college teaching*. Sterling, VA: Stylus.

Microsoft. (2009). *Bing StreetSide*. Retrieved February 3, 2017, from http://www.microsoft.com/maps/streetside.aspx

Mikropoulos, T. A., & Natsis, A. (2011). Educational virtual environments: A ten-year review of empirical research (1999–2009). *Computers & Education, 56*(3), 769–780. doi:10.1016/j.compedu.2010.10.020

Milgram, P., & Kishino, F. (1994). A taxonomy of mixed reality visual displays. *IEICE Transactions on Information and Systems, E77–D*(12), 1321–1329.

Miller, F., & Wallis, J. (2011). Social Interaction and the role of empathy in information and knowledge management: A literature review. *Journal of Education for Library and Information Science, 52*(2), 122–132.

Milton, J., Jonsen, S., Hirst, S., & Lindenburn, S. (2012). Foreign language vocabulary development through activities in an online 3D environment. *Language Learning Journal, 40*(1), 99–112. doi:10.1080/09571736.2012.658229

Mojang. (2017). *Frequently asked questions.* Retrieved from https://education.minecraft.net/support/faq/

Molka-Danielsen, J., Deutschmann, M., & Panichi, L. (2009). Designing transient learning spaces in Second Life for language learning: A case study based on the Kamimo experience. *Designs for Learning, 2*(1), 22–33.

Montoro, C., & Hampel, R. (2011). Investigating language learning activity using a CALL task in the self-access centre. *Studies in Self-Access Learning Journal, 2*(3), 119–135.

Moore, P. (1995). Learning and teaching in virtual worlds: Implications of virtual reality for education. *Australian Journal of Educational Technology, 11*(2), 91–102.

Mørch, A. I., Caruso, V., & Hartley, M. D. (2017). End-user development and learning in Second Life: The evolving artifacts framework with application. In F. Paterno & V. Wulf (Eds.), *New perspectives in end-user development*. Berlin: Springer. doi:10.1007/978-3-319-60291-2_13

Mørch, A. I., Dolonen, A. I., & Nævdal, J. E. (2006). An evolutionary approach to prototyping pedagogical agents: From simulation to integrated system. *Journal of Network and Computer Applications, 29*(2–3), 177–199.

Mørch, A. I., Engeness, I., Cheng, V. C., Cheung, W. K., & Wong, K. C. (2017). Essay Critic: Writing to learn with a knowledge-based design critiquing system. *Journal of Educational Technology & Society, 20*(2), 216–226.

Mørch, A. I., Hartley, M. D., Ludlow, B. L., Caruso, V., & Thomassen, I. (2014). The teacher as designer: Preparations for teaching in a Second Life distance education course. In *Proceedings of 2014 IEEE International Conference on Advanced Learning Technologies (ICALT 2014)* (pp. 691–693). Los Alamitos, CA: IEEE Computer Society. doi:10.1109/ICALT.2014.201

Mori, J. (2002). Task design, plan, and development of talk-in-interaction: An analysis of a small group activity in a Japanese language classroom. *Applied Linguistics*, *23*(3), 323–347. doi:10.1093/applin/23.3.323

Morse, S., Littleton, F., Macleod, M., & Ewins, R. (2009). The theatre of performance appraisal: Role-play in Second Life. In C. Wankel & J. Kingsley (Eds.), *Higher education in virtual worlds: Teaching and learning in Second Life* (pp. 181–201). Bingley, UK: Emerald Group.

Moyles, J. (2002). Observation as a research tool. In M. Coleman & A. J. Briggs (Eds.), *Research Methods in Education with SPSS*. London, UK: Sage.

Muir, T., Allen, J. M., Rayner, C. S., & Cleland, B. (2013). Preparing pre-service teachers for classroom practice in a virtual world: A pilot study using Second Life. *Journal of Interactive Media in Education*, *2013*(1), 3. doi:10.5334/2013-03

Murray, J. H. (1998). *Hamlet on the holodeck: The future of narrative in cyberspace*. Cambridge, MA: MIT Press.

National Research Council. (2005). *How students learn: History, mathematics, and science in the classroom*. Washington, DC: The National Academies Press. doi:10.17226/10126

National Research Council. (2011). *Learning science through computer games and simulations*. Washington, DC: The National Academies Press. doi:10.17226/13078

National Research Council. (2012). *A framework for K-12 science education: Practices, crosscutting concepts, and core ideas*. Washington, DC: The National Academies Press. doi:10.17226/13165

National University Reform Plan. (2015). Retrieved December 13, 2016, from http://www.mext.go.jp/en/news/topics/detail/1372655.htm

Nedic, Z., Machotka, J., & Nafalski, A. (2003). *Remote laboratories versus virtual and real laboratories*. Paper presented at the 33rd Annual Frontiers in Education, Westminster, CO. doi:10.1109/FIE.2003.1263343

Nelson, B., & Ketelhut, D. J. (2007). Scientific inquiry in educational multi-user virtual environments. *Educational Psychology Review*, *19*(3), 265–283. doi:10.1007/s10648-007-9048-1

Nersessian, N. J. (1989). Conceptual change in science and in science education. *Synthese*, *80*(1), 163–183. doi:10.1007/BF00869953

NGSS Lead States. (2013). *Next generation science standards: For states, by states*. Washington, DC: The National Academies Press.

Nicholson, P. (2008). A history of e-learning: Echoes of the pioneers. In B. Fernandez Manjon (Ed.), *Computers and education: E-Learning, from Theory to practice* (pp. 1–11). Springer.

Norman, D. A. (1988). *The psychology of everyday things*. New York, NY: Basic Books.

Norman, D. A. (1993). *Things that make us smart: Defending human attributes in the age of the machine*. New York, NY: Basic Books.

Norman, D. A. (2002). *The design of everyday things*. New York, NY: Basic Books.

North, M. M., & North, S. M. (2016). A comparative study of sense of presence of traditional virtual reality and immersive environments. *AJIS. Australasian Journal of Information Systems*, *20*. doi:10.3127/ajis.v20i0.1168

Novak, T. P., Hoffman, D. L., & Yung, Y.-F. (2000). Measuring the customer experience in online environments: A structural modeling approach. *Marketing Science*, *19*(1), 22–42. doi:10.1287/mksc.19.1.22.15184

Nunan, D. (1997). Designing and adapting materials to encourage learner autonomy. In P. Benson & P. Voller (Eds.), *Autonomy and independence in language learning* (pp. 192–203). London, UK: Longman.

Nunez, D. (2004, November). How is presence in non-immersive, non-realistic virtual environments possible? In *Proceedings of the 3rd International Conference on Computer Graphics, Virtual Reality, Visualisation and Interaction in Africa* (pp. 83-86). ACM. doi:10.1145/1029949.1029964

O'Day, J. A. (2002). Complexity, accountability, and school improvement. *Harvard Educational Review*, *72*(3), 293–327. doi:10.17763/haer.72.3.021q742t8182h238

O'Dowd, R. (2006). *Telecollaboration and the development of intercultural communicative competence.* Berlin, Germany: Langenscheidt.

O'Neil, H. F., Wainess, R., & Baker, E. L. (2005). Classification of learning outcomes: Evidence from the computer games literature. *Curriculum Journal*, *16*(4), 455–474. doi:10.1080/09585170500384529

OECD. (2016). *Programme for International Student Assessment (PISA).* Retrieved December 13, 2016, from https://www.oecd.org/pisa/

Oh, Y., & Woo, W. (2013). Ubiquitous virtual reality environments. In S. Price, C. Jewitt, & B. Brown (Eds.), *The SAGE handbook of digital technology research* (pp. 374–386). Thousand Oaks, CA: SAGE. doi:10.4135/9781446282229.n25

Oliver, M., & Carr, D. (2009). Learning in virtual worlds: Using communities of practice to explain how people learn from play. *British Journal of Educational Technology*, *40*(3), 444–457. doi:10.1111/j.1467-8535.2009.00948.x

Onishi, N., & Fackler, M. (2011). *Japan Held Nuclear Data, Leaving Evacuees in Peril.* Retrieved February 9, 2017, from http://www.nytimes.com/2011/08/09/world/asia/09japan.html?_r=1

Opp-Beckman, L., & Klinghammer, S. (2006a). *Shaping the way we teach English: Successful practices around the world.* Washington, DC: Office of English Programs, United States Department of State. Retrieved February 3, 2017, from http://ivantrainer.weebly.com/uploads/1/0/3/0/10309088/shaping_the_way_we_teachreading.pdf

Opp-Beckman, L., & Klinghammer, S. (2006b). *Shaping the way we teach English: Successful practices around the world.* Instructor's Manual. Washington, DC: Office of English Programs, United States Department of State. Retrieved February 3, 2017, from http://oelp.uoregon.edu/sites/oelp1.uoregon.edu/files/shaping_manual_aug2006.pdf

Organisation for Economic Co-operation and Development (OECD). (2003). *Key competencies for a successful life and well-functioning society. The definition and selection of key competencies: Executive summary (Summary of report by S. D. Rychen & L. H. Salganik).* Kirkland, WA: Hogrefe and Huber.

P21 Partnership for 21st Century Learning. (n. d.). *Framework for 21st century learning.* Retrieved from http://www.p21.org/our-work/p21-framework

Padrós, A., Romero, M., & Usart, M. (2012). Measuring the knowledge convergence process in the collaborative game metavals. *Procedia Computer Science*, *15*, 193–202. doi:10.1016/j.procs.2012.10.071

Pajares, F. (1996). Self-efficacy beliefs in academic settings. *Review of Educational Research*, *66*(4), 543–578. doi:10.3102/00346543066004543

Panichi, L., & Deutschmann, M. (2012). Language learning in virtual worlds: Research issues and methods. In M. Dooly & R. O'Dowd (Eds.), *Researching online foreign language interaction and exchange: Theories, methods and challenges* (pp. 205–231). Bern, Switzerland: Peter Lang.

Panichi, L., Deutschmann, M., & Molka-Danielsen, J. (2010). Virtual worlds for language learning and intercultural exchange: Is it for real? In S. Guth & F. Helm (Eds.), *Telecollaboration 2.0: Languages, literacies and intercultural learning in the 21st century* (pp. 165–195). New York, NY: Peter Lang.

Pan, Z., Cheok, A. D., Yang, H., Zhu, J., & Shi, J. (2006). Virtual reality and mixed reality for virtual learning environments. *Computers & Graphics*, *30*(1), 20–28. doi:10.1016/j.cag.2005.10.004

Papert, S. (1993). *Mindstorms: Children, computers, and powerful ideas*. New York, NY: Basic Books.

Papert, S., & Harel, I. (1993). *Constructionism*. New York, NY: Ablex.

Paraskeva, F., Mysirlaki, S., & Papagianni, A. (2010). Multiplayer online games as educational tools: Facing new challenges in learning. *Computers & Education*, *54*(2), 498–505. doi:10.1016/j.compedu.2009.09.001

Pasfield-Neofitou, S., Huang, H., & Grant, S. (2015). Lost in Second Life: Virtual embodiment and language learning via multimodal communication. *Educational Technology Research and Development*, *63*(5), 709–726. doi:10.1007/s11423-015-9384-7

Pastoor, S., & Conomis, C. (2005). Mixed reality displays. In O. Schreer, P. Kauff, & T. Sikora (Eds.), 3D videocommunication: Algorithms, concepts and real-time systems in human centred communication (pp. 261-280). Hoboken, NJ: John Wiley & Sons. doi:10.1002/0470022736.ch14

Patterson, T. (2007). Google Earth as a (Not Just) geography education tool. *The Journal of Geography*, *106*(4), 145–152. doi:10.1080/00221340701678032

Pena-Rios, A. (2016). *Exploring mixed reality in distributed collaborative learning environments* (Doctoral dissertation). University of Essex, UK.

Pena-Rios, A., Callaghan, V., Gardner, M., & Alhaddad, M. J. (2015). *Experiments with collaborative blended-reality laboratory technology for distance learners.* Paper presented at the 1st Immersive Learning Research Network Conference 2015 (iLRN 2015), Prague, Czech Republic.

Pena-Rios, A., Callaghan, V., Gardner, M., & Alhaddad, M. J. (2012). Remote mixed reality collaborative laboratory activities: Learning activities within the InterReality portal. *Proceedings of the 2012 IEEE/WIC/ACM International Conference on Web Intelligence and Intelligent Agent Technology Workshops (WI-IAT'12)*, 362–366. doi:10.1109/WI-IAT.2012.43

Pena-Rios, A., Callaghan, V., Gardner, M., & Alhaddad, M. J. (2014). Using mixed reality to develop smart environments. In *10th International Conference on Intelligent Environments* (pp. 182–189). Shanghai, China: IEEE Computer Society.

Peterson, M. (2006). Learner interaction management in an avatar and chat-based virtual world. *Computer Assisted Language Learning*, *19*(1), 79–103. doi:10.1080/09588220600804087

Peterson, M. (2010). Learner participation patterns and strategy use in Second Life: An exploratory case study. *ReCALL*, *22*(3), 273–292. doi:10.1017/S0958344010000169

Peterson, M. (2010). Massively multiplayer online role-playing games as arenas for second language learning. *Computer Assisted Language Learning*, *23*(5), 429–439. doi:10.1080/09588221.2010.520673

Peterson, M. (2011). Towards a research agenda for the use of three-dimensional virtual worlds in language learning. *CALICO Journal*, *29*(1), 67–80. doi:10.11139/cj.29.1.67-80

Peterson, M. (2012). EFL learner collaborative interaction in Second Life. *ReCALL*, *24*(1), 20–39. doi:10.1017/S0958344011000279

Piaget, J. (1959). *The language and thought of the child* (3rd ed.). London, UK: Routledge & Kegan Paul.

Piaget, J. (1972). Intellectual evolution from adolescence to adult. *Human Development*, *15*(1), 1–12. doi:10.1159/000271225

Pica, T., Kanagy, R., & Falodun, J. (1993). Choosing and using communication tasks for second language instruction and research. In C. G. Crookes & S. M. Gass (Eds.), *Tasks and language learning: Integrating theory and practice* (pp. 9–34). Bristol, UK: Multilingual Matters.

Piezon, S. L., & Donaldson, R. L. (2005). Online groups and social loafing: Understanding student-group interactions. *Online Journal of Distance Learning Administration*, *8*(4). Retrieved from http://www.westga.edu/~distance/ojdla/winter84/piezon84.htm

Pintrich, R. R. (1995). *Understanding self-regulated learning*. San Francisco, CA: Jossey-Bass.

Pivec, P., & Pivec, M. (2011). Digital games: Changing education, one raid at a time. *International Journal of Game-Based Learning*, *1*(1), 1–18. doi:10.4018/ijgbl.2011010101

Plass, J. L., Homer, B. D., & Kinzer, C. K. (2015). Foundations of game-based learning. *Educational Psychologist*, *50*(4), 258–283. doi:10.1080/00461520.2015.1122533

Podolefsky, N. S., Rehn, D., & Perkins, K. K. (2013). Affordances of play for student agency and student-centered pedagogy. In AIP Conference Proceedings: Vol. 1513. *No. 1* (pp. 306–309). AIP. doi:10.1063/1.4789713

Polio, C. (2014). Using authentic materials in the beginning language classroom. *Clear News*, *18*(1), 1–7.

Pollalis, C., Fahnbulleh, W., Tynes, J., & Shaer, O. (2017). HoloMuse: Enhancing engagement with archaeological artifacts through gesture-based interaction with holograms. In *Proceedings of the Tenth International Conference on Tangible, Embedded, and Embodied Interaction* (pp. 565–570). New York, NY: ACM. doi:10.1145/3024969.3025094

Prensky, M. (2001). Digital natives, digital immigrants part 1. *On the Horizon*, *9*(5), 1–6. doi:10.1108/10748120110424816

Prensky, M. (2001). Digital natives, digital immigrants. *New Horizons (Baltimore, Md.)*, *9*(5), 10–16.

Prensky, M. (2003). Digital game-based learning. *Theoretical and Practical Computer Applications in Entertainment*, *1*(1). doi:10.1145/950566.950596

Prensky, M. (2006). *Don't bother me mom – I'm learning!* St. Paul, MN: Paragon House.

Prensky, M. (2007). *Digital game-based learning*. St. Paul, MN: Paragon House.

Price, M., Handley, K., Millar, J., & O'Donovan, B. (2010). Feedback: All that effort, but what is the effect? *Assessment & Evaluation in Higher Education*, *35*(3), 277–289. doi:10.1080/02602930903541007

Qian, Y. (2015). 3D multi-user virtual environments in science education. In T. Heafner, R. Hartshorne, & T. Petty (Eds.), Exploring the effectiveness of online education in K-12 environments pp. 308-330. Hershey, PA: IGI Global. doi:10.4018/978-1-4666-6383-1.ch015

Quintana, C., Reiser, B. J., Davis, E. A., Krajcik, J., Fretz, E., Duncan, R. G., & Soloway, E. et al. (2004). A scaffolding design framework for software to support science inquiry. *Journal of the Learning Sciences*, *13*(3), 337–386. doi:10.1207/s15327809jls1303_4

Rahim, N. F. A. (2013). Collaboration and knowledge sharing using 3D virtual world on Second Life. *Education for Information*, *30*(1-2), 1–40. doi:10.3233/EFI-130928

Rajala, A., Martin, J., & Kumpulainen, K. (2016). Agency and learning: Researching agency in educational interactions. *Learning Culture and Social Interaction*, *10*, 1–3. doi:10.1016/j.lcsi.2016.07.001

Raubenheimer, J. (2004). An item selection procedure to maximise scale reliability and validity. *SA Journal of Industrial Psychology*, *30*(4), 59–64. doi:10.4102/sajip.v30i4.168

Realia and Contextualization. (n.d.). *Gaining ground in teaching: Resources*. Retrieved February 3, 2017, from Michigan State University, Chinese Teacher Certification Program Web site: http://gaining.educ.msu.edu/resources/node/422

Renshaw, P. (2016). On the notion of worthwhile agency in reformist pedagogies. *Learning. Culture and Social Interaction*, *10*, 60–63. doi:10.1016/j.lcsi.2016.07.002

Rhodes, M. (2016). Forget the School Bus - The Most Magical Field Trip Is in VR. *Wired*. Retrieved February 9, 2017 from https://www.wired.com/2016/06/went-vr-field-trip-tomorrow-heres-saw/

Richards, S. B., Taylor, R., Ramasamy, R., & Richards, R. Y. (1999). *Single subject research: Applications in educational and clinical settings*. Belmont, CA: Wadsworth.

Rizzo, A. A., Wiederhold, M. D., & Buckwalter, J. G. (1998). Basic issues in the use of virtual environments for mental health applications. In G. Riva, B. K. Widerhold, & E. Molinari (Eds.), *Virtual environments in clinical psychology and Neuroscience* (pp. 22–42). Amsterdam: IOS Press.

Rockwood, H. S. (1995). Cooperative and collaborative learning. *The National Teaching & Learning Forum*, *4*(6), 8-9. doi: 10.1002/ntlf.10024

Roebuck, R. (2000). Subjects speak out: How learners position themselves in psycholinguistic task. In J. P. Lantolf (Ed.), *Sociocultural theory and second language learning* (pp. 79–95). Oxford, UK: Oxford University Press.

Rogoff, B. (1990). *Apprenticeship in thinking: Cognitive development in social context*. New York, NY: Oxford University Press.

Roschelle, J. (1992). Learning by collaborating: Convergent conceptual change. *Journal of the Learning Sciences*, *2*(3), 235–276. doi:10.1207/s15327809jls0203_1

Roseman, J. E., & Koppal, M. (2008). Using national standards to improve K-8 science curriculum materials. *The Elementary School Journal*, *109*(2), 104–122. doi:10.1086/590521

Rosenberg, M. (2000). *E-Learning: Strategies for delivering knowledge in the digital age*. Columbus, OH: Mcgraw-hill.

Ruiz-Primo, M. A. (2011). Informal formative assessment: The role of instructional dialogues in assessing students' learning. *Studies in Educational Evaluation*, *37*(1), 15–24. doi:10.1016/j.stueduc.2011.04.003

Rushkoff, D. (1999). *Playing the future: What we can learn from digital kids*. New York, NY: New River Trade.

Rutten, N., Van Joolingen, W. R., & Van der Veen, J. T. (2012). The learning effects of computer simulations in science education. *Computers & Education*, *58*(1), 136–153. doi:10.1016/j.compedu.2011.07.017

Ryan, R. M., & Deci, E. L. (2000). Intrinsic and extrinsic motivations: Classic definitions and new directions. *Contemporary Educational Psychology*, *25*(1), 54–67. doi:10.1006/ceps.1999.1020 PMID:10620381

Ryan, R. M., & Deci, E. L. (2000). Self-determination theory and the facilitation of intrinsic motivation, social development, and well-being. *The American Psychologist*, *55*(1), 68–78. doi:10.1037/0003-066X.55.1.68 PMID:11392867

Rymniak, M. (2011). *Supporting skilled immigrants: A toolkit for ESL practitioners*. Global Talent Bridge, World Education Services. Retrieved February 3, 2017, from http://www.globaltalentbridge.org/toolkit/pdf/SupportingSkilledImmigrantsToolkit.pdf

Salaberry, M. R. (1996). The theoretical foundation for the development of pedagogical tasks in computer mediated communication. *CALICO Journal, 14*(1), 5–34.

Säljö, R. (2010). Digital tools and challenges to institutional traditions of learning: Technologies, social memory and the performative nature of learning. *Journal of Computer Assisted Learning, 26*(1), 53–64. doi:10.1111/j.1365-2729.2009.00341.x

Salmela-Aro, K., Muotka, J., Alho, K., Hakkarainen, K., & Lonka, K. (2016). School burnout and engagement profiles among digital natives in Finland: A person-oriented approach. *European Journal of Developmental Psychology, 13*(6), 704–718. doi:10.1080/17405629.2015.1107542

Salmon, G. (2000). *E-moderating: The key to teaching and learning online*. New York, NY: Routledge. doi:10.4324/9780203465424

Salzman, M. C., Dede, C., Loftin, R. B., & Chen, J. (1999). A model for understanding how virtual reality aids complex conceptual learning. *Presence (Cambridge, Mass.), 8*(3), 293–316. doi:10.1162/105474699566242

Sandholtz, J. M., Ringstaff, C., & Dwyer, D. C. (1997). *Teaching with technology: Creating student-centered classrooms*. New York, NY: Teachers College Press.

Savery, J. R., & Duffy, T. M. (1995). Problem based learning: An instructional model and its constructivist framework. *Educational Technology, 35*(5), 31–38.

Savignon, S. (1997). *Communicative competence: Theory and classroom practice*. New York, NY: McGraw-Hill.

Savignon, S. (2001). Communicative language teaching in the twenty-first century. In M. Celce-Murcia (Ed.), *Teaching English as a Second or Foreign Language*. Boston: Heinle & Heinle.

Savin-Baden, M. (2008). *Learning spaces: Creating opportunities for knowledge creation in academic life*. New York, NY: McGraw Hill.

Savin-Baden, M., Gourlay, L., Mawer, M., Steils, N., Tombs, C., & Tombs, G. (2010). Situating pedagogies, positions and practices in immersive virtual worlds. *Educational Research, 52*(2), 123–133. doi:10.1080/00131881.2010.482732

Scardamalia, M., & Bereiter, C. (2006). Knowledge building: Theory, pedagogy, and technology. In K. Sawyer (Ed.), *Cambridge handbook of the learning sciences* (pp. 97–118). New York, NY: Cambridge University Press.

Schaller, D. T., Goldman, K. H., Spickelmier, G., Allison-Bunnell, S., & Koepfler, J. (2009). *Learning in the wild: What Wolfquest taught developers and game players*. Retrieved from http://www.archimuse.com/mw2009/papers/schaller/schaller.html

Schank, R. C., & Cleary, C. (1995). *Engines for education*. Hillsdale, NJ: Erlbaum Associates. Retrieved February 3, 2017, from http://www.engines4ed.org/hyperbook/nodes/NODE-233-pg.html

Schank, R. C. (1996). Goal-based scenarios: Case-based reasoning meet leaning by learning by doing. In D. Leake (Ed.), *Case-based reasoning: Experience, lessons & future directions*. AAAI Press/The MIT Press.

Schmidt, M., Kevan, J., Mckimmy, P., & Fabel, S. (2013). *The best way to predict the future is to create it: Introducing the Holodeck@UH mixed reality teaching and learning environment*. Paper presented at the 36th Annual Convention of the Association for Educational Communications and Technology, Anaheim, CA.

Schrader, P. G. (2008). Learning in technology: Reconceptualising immersive environments. *Journal of Association for the Advancement of Computing in Education, 4*(16), 457–475.

Schrader, P. G. (2008). Learning in technology: Reconceptualizing immersive environments. *AACE Journal, 16*(4), 457–475.

Schroeder, R. (2002). *Copresence and interaction in virtual environments: An overview of the range of issues*. Paper presented at the 5th Annual International Workshop on PRESENCE, Porto, Portugal.

Schroeder, R. (1996). *Possible worlds: The social dynamic of virtual reality technologies*. Boulder, CO: Westview Press.

Schroeder, R. (1996). *Possible worlds: The social dynamic of virtual reality technology*. Boulder, CO: Westview Press.

Schroeder, R. (2002). Social interaction in virtual environments: Key issues, common themes, and a framework for research. In R. Schroeder (Ed.), *The social life of avatars: Presence and interaction in shared virtual environments* (pp. 1–18). London, UK: Springer-Verlag. doi:10.1007/978-1-4471-0277-9_1

Schroeder, R., & Axelsson, A. (Eds.). (2006). *Avatars at work and play: Collaboration and interaction in shared virtual environments*. London, UK: Springer-Verlag. doi:10.1007/1-4020-3898-4

Schuemie, M. J., Van Der Straaten, P., Krijin, M., & Van Der Mast, C. A. P. G. (2001). Research on presence in virtual reality: A survey. *Cyberpsychology & Behavior*, *4*(2), 183–210. doi:10.1089/109493101300117884 PMID:11710246

Schumacker, R. E., & Lomax, R. G. (2010). *A beginner' guide to structural equation modeling* (3rd ed.). New York: Routledge.

Schwienhorst, K. (1998). The "third place": Virtual reality applications for second language learning. *ReCALL, 10*(01), 118–126. doi:10.1017/S095834400000433X

Schwienhorst, K. (2003). Learner autonomy and tandem learning: Putting principles into practice in synchronous and asynchronous telecommunications environment. *Computer Assisted Language Learning*, *16*(5), 427–443. doi:10.1076/call.16.5.427.29484

Scott, G., & Chin, J. (2013). A DIY approach to pervasive computing for the internet of things: A smart alarm clock. *Proceedings of the 5th Computer Science and Electronic Engineering Conference (CEEC'13)*, 57–60. doi:10.1109/CEEC.2013.6659445

Second Life. (2003). Retrieved February 3, 2017, from http://secondlife.com

Seedhouse, P. (2004). The interactional architecture of the language classroom: A Conversation Analysis perspective. *Language Learning Monograph Series, 54*(S1).

Selwyn, N. (1997). Students' attitudes toward computers: Validation of a computer attitude scale for 16-19 education. *Computers & Education*, *28*(1), 35–41. doi:10.1016/S0360-1315(96)00035-8

Selwyn, N. (2017). *Education and technology: Key issues and debates* (2nd ed.). London, UK: Bloomsbury Academic.

Sewell, W. H. Jr. (1992). A theory of structure: Duality, agency, and transformation. *American Journal of Sociology*, *98*(1), 1–29. doi:10.1086/229967

Sharda, R., Romano, N. C. Jr, Lucca, J. A., Weiser, M., Scheets, G., Chung, J. M., & Sleezer, C. M. (2004). Foundation for the study of computer-supported collaborative learning requiring immersive presence. *Journal of Management Information Systems*, *20*(4), 31–63. doi:10.1080/07421222.2004.11045780

Shaughnessy, J. J., Zechmeister, E. B., & Zechmeister, J. S. (2003). *Research methods in psychology* (6th ed.). New York, NY: McGraw-Hill.

Shih, Y. C. (2015). A virtual walk through London: Culture learning through a cultural immersion experience. *Computer Assisted Language Learning*, *28*(4), 1–22.

Shih, Y., & Yang, M. (2008). A collaborative virtual environment for situated language using VEC3D. *Journal of Educational Technology & Society, 11*(1), 56–68.

Shih, Y., Yang, M., & Yang, F. (2013). Street-view panorama for cultural learning: implementation and curriculum design. *International Conference on Advanced Learning Technology*. doi:10.1109/ICALT.2013.107

Short, J. A., Williams, E., & Christie, B. (1976). *The social psychology of telecommunications*. London, UK: Wiley.

Shrum, J. L., & Glisan, E. W. (2004). *Teacher's handbook: Contextualized language instruction*. Boston: Heinle & Heinle.

Siemens, G. (2005). Connectivism: A learning theory for the digital age. *International Journal of Instructional Technology and Distance Learning, 2*(1). Retrieved from http://er.dut.ac.za/handle/123456789/69

Siry, C., Wilmes, S., & Haus, J. M. (2016). Examining children's agency within participatory structures in primary science investigations. *Learning Culture and Social Interaction, 10*, 4-16.

Situation Cognition. (2015). In *Wikipedia*. Retrieved February 3, 2017, from https://en.wikipedia.org/wiki/Situated_cognition

Slater, M. (2009). Place illusion and plausibility can lead to realistic behaviour in immersive virtual environments. *Philosophical Transactions of the Royal Society of London. Series B, Biological Sciences, 364*(1535), 3549–3557. doi:10.1098/rstb.2009.0138 PMID:19884149

Smith, B., & MacGregor, J. (1992). What is collaborative learning? In A. Goodsell, M. Mahler, V. Tinto, B. L. Smith, & J. MacGreger (Eds.), *Collaborative learning: A sourcebook for higher education* (pp. 9–22). University Park, PA: National Center on Postsecondary Teaching, Learning and Assessment.

Smith, K., & Craig, H. (2013). Enhancing the autonomous use of CALL: A new curriculum model in EFL. *CALICO Journal, 30*(2), 252–278. doi:10.11139/cj.30.2.252-278

Smith, L., & Macgregor, J. T. (1992). *What is collaborative learning? Collaborative learning: A sourcebook for higher education*. Washington, DC: Office of Educational Research and Improvement.

Soller, A., Martinez, A., Jermann, P., & Muehlenbrock, M. (2005). From mirroring to guiding: A review of state of the art technology for supporting collaborative learning. *International Journal of Artificial Intelligence in Education, 15*, 261–290.

Squire, K., Barnett, M., Grant, J. M., & Higginbotham, T. (2004, June). Electromagnetism supercharged!: Learning physics with digital simulation games. In *Proceedings of the 6th International Conference on Learning Sciences* (pp. 513-520). International Society of the Learning Sciences.

Squire, K. (2011). *Video games and learning: Teaching and participatory culture in the digital age*. New York, NY: Teachers College Press.

Stahl, G., Koschmann, T., & Suthers, D. (2006). Computer-supported collaborative learning. In R. K. Sawyer (Ed.), *The Cambridge handbook of the learning sciences* (pp. 409–425). Cambridge, UK: Cambridge University Press.

Stake, J. E., & Nickens, S. D. (2005). Adolescent girls' and boys' science peer relationships and perceptions of the possible self as scientist. *Sex Roles, 52*(1), 1–11. doi:10.1007/s11199-005-1189-4

Starkey, P. L. (2013). *The effects of digital games on middle school students' mathematical achievement* (Doctoral dissertation). Lehigh University, Bethlehem, PA.

Steffens, K., Bannan, B., Dalgarno, B., Bartolomé, A. R., Esteve-González, V., & Cela-Ranilla, J. M. (2015). Recent developments in technology- enhanced learning: A critical assessment. *RUSC. Universities and Knowledge Society Journal*, *12*(2), 1–14.

Steinkuehler, C. A., & Williams, D. (2006). Where everybody knows your (screen) name: Online games as "third places". *Journal of Computer-Mediated Communication*, *11*(4), 885–909. doi:10.1111/j.1083-6101.2006.00300.x

Steinkuehler, C., & Duncan, S. (2008). Scientific habits of mind in virtual worlds. *Journal of Science Education and Technology*, *17*(6), 530–543. doi:10.1007/s10956-008-9120-8

Steinkuehler, C., & Squire, K. (2014). Videogames and learning. In R. K. Sawyer (Ed.), *The Cambridge handbook of the learning sciences* (pp. 377–396). Cambridge, UK: Cambridge University Press. doi:10.1017/CBO9781139519526.023

Steuer, J. (1992). Defining virtual reality: Dimensions determining telepresence. *Journal of Communication*, *42*(4), 73–93. doi:10.1111/j.1460-2466.1992.tb00812.x

Stevens, R., Satwicz, T., & McCarthy, L. (2008). In-game, in-room, in-world: Reconnecting video game play to the rest of kids' lives. *The Ecology of Games: Connecting Youth, Games, and Learning*, *9*, 41-66.

Stiles, M. J. (2000). *Effective learning and the virtual learning environment*. Paper presented at European Universities Information Systems Congress (EUNIS 2000).

Stockwell, G., & Tanaka-Ellis, N. (2012). Diversity in environments. In G. Stockwell (Ed.), *Computer-assisted language learning: Diversity in research and practice* (pp. 71–89). Cambridge, UK: Cambridge University Press. doi:10.1017/CBO9781139060981.005

Strauss, A., & Corbin, J. (1998). *Basics for Qualitative Research: Techniques and Procedures for Developing Grounded Theory* (2nd ed.). Thousand Oaks, CA: SAGE.

Strauss, A., & Corbin, J. (1998). *Basics of qualitative research: Techniques and procedures for developing grounded theory*. Thousand Oaks, CA: Sage.

Sundmaeker, H., Guillemin, P., Friess, P., & Woelfflé, S. (2010). Vision and challenges for realising the Internet of Things. *Cluster of European Research Projects on the Internet of Things. European Commision*, *3*(3), 34–36. doi:10.2759/26127

Sun, P.-C., Tsai, R. J., Finger, G., Chen, Y.-Y., & Yeh, D. (2008). What drives a successful e-Learning? An empirical investigation of the critical factors influencing learner satisfaction. *Computers & Education*, *50*(4), 1183–1202. doi:10.1016/j.compedu.2006.11.007

Svensson, P. (2003). Virtual worlds as arenas for language learning. In U. Felix (Ed.), *Language learning online: Towards best practices* (pp. 123–143). Amsterdam, The Netherlands: Swets & Zeitlinger.

Swinth, K., & Blascovich, J. (2002, October). *Perceiving and responding to others: Human-human and human-computer social interaction in collaborative virtual environments*. Paper presented at the 5th Annual International Workshop on PRESENCE, Porto, Portugal.

Tabachnick, B. G., & Fidell, L. S. (2007). *Using multivariate statistics*. Boston, MA: Pearson Education.

Tabak, I., & Reiser, B. J. (1997). *Complementary roles of software-based scaffolding and teacher-student interactions in inquiry learning*. Paper presented at The 2nd International Conference on Computer Support for Collaborative Learning, Toronto, Canada. doi:10.3115/1599773.1599809

Tamborini, R., Bowman, N. D., Eden, A., Grizzard, M., & Organ, A. (2010). Defining media enjoyment as the satisfaction of intrinsic needs. *Journal of Communication*, *60*(4), 758–777. doi:10.1111/j.1460-2466.2010.01513.x

Tamura, H., Yamamoto, H., & Katayama, A. (2001). Mixed reality: Future dreams seen at the border between real and virtual worlds. *IEEE Computer Graphics and Applications*, *21*(6), 64–70. doi:10.1109/38.963462

ten Have, P. (2007). *Doing conversation analysis: A practical guide* (2nd ed.). Thousand Oaks, CA: SAGE. doi:10.4135/9781849208895

Teo, T., & Lee, C. B. (2010). Explaining the intention to use technology among student teachers: An application of the Theory of Planned behaviour (TPB). *Campus-Wide Information Systems*, *27*(2), 60–67. doi:10.1108/10650741011033035

Teo, T., & Noyes, J. (2011). An assessment of the influence of attitude and perceived enjoyment on the intention to use technology among pre-service teachers: A structural equation modelling approach. *Computers & Education*, *57*(2), 1645–1653. doi:10.1016/j.compedu.2011.03.002

The Immersive Learning Research Network. (2015). *Immersion (definition)*. Retrieved from http://wiki.immersivelrn.org/ariel/wiki

The Open University. (2015). *Facts & figures - About the OU*. Retrieved from http://www.open.ac.uk/about/main/sites/www.open.ac.uk.about.main/files/files/fact_figures_1415_uk.pdf

Tolentino, L., Birchfield, D., Megowan-Romanowicz, C., Johnson-Glenberg, M. C., Kelliher, A., & Martinez, C. (2009). Teaching and learning in the mixed reality science classroom. *Journal of Science Education and Technology*, *18*(6), 501–517. doi:10.1007/s10956-009-9166-2

Toyoda, E., & Harrison, R. (2002). Categorization of text chat communication between learners and native speakers of Japanese. *Language Learning & Technology*, *6*(1), 82–99. Retrieved from http://llt.msu.edu/vol6num1/toyoda/default.html

Trindade, J., Fiolhais, C., & Almeida, L. (2002). Science learning in virtual environments: A descriptive study. *British Journal of Educational Technology*, *33*(4), 471–488. doi:10.1111/1467-8535.00283

Triona, L. M., & Klahr, D. (2003). Point and click or grab and heft: Comparing the influence of physical and virtual instructional materials on elementary school students' ability to design experiments. *Cognition and Instruction*, *21*(2), 149–173. doi:10.1207/S1532690XCI2102_02

Trundle, K. C., & Bell, R. L. (2010). The use of a computer simulation to promote conceptual change: A quasi-experimental study. *Computers & Education*, *54*(4), 1078–1088. doi:10.1016/j.compedu.2009.10.012

Tu, C. H., Yen, C., & Blocher, M. (2011). A study of the relationship between gender and online social presence. *International Journal of Online Pedagogy and Course Design*, *1*(3), 33–49. doi:10.4018/ijopcd.2011070103

Turkle, S. (2011). *Alone together: Why we expect more from technology and less from each other*. New York, NY: Basic books.

Uckelmann, D., Harrison, M., & Michahelles, F. (2011). An architectural approach towards the future Internet of Things. In D. Uckelmann, M. Harrison, & F. Michahelles (Eds.), *Architecting the internet of things* (pp. 1–25). Springer Berlin; doi:10.1007/978-3-642-19157-2_1

Utech, J. L. (2008). *Contextualized curriculum for workplace education: An introductory guide*. Massachusetts Worker Education Roundtable. Retrieved February 3, 2017, from https://www.umass.edu/roundtable/projects/Integrated%20curr_guide%20p1.pdf

Vallance, M. (2009). Experiential learning, virtual collaboration and robots. Riding the Hype Cycle: The Resurgence of Virtual Worlds, 1–18.

Vallance, M., Martin, S., & Naamani, C. (2015). A situation that we had never imagined: Post-Fukushima virtual collaborations for determining robot task metrics. *International Journal of Learning Technology*, *10*(1), 30–49. doi:10.1504/IJLT.2015.069453

Vallance, M., & Towndrow, P. A. (2016). Pedagogic transformation, student-directed design and computational thinking. *Pedagogies*, *11*(3), 218–234. doi:10.1080/1554480X.2016.1182437

Van den Boom, G., Paas, F., Van Merrienboer, J. J., & Van Gog, T. (2004). Reflection prompts and tutor feedback in a web-based learning environment: Effects on students' self-regulated learning competence. *Computers in Human Behavior*, *20*(4), 551–567. doi:10.1016/j.chb.2003.10.001

Vanijdee, A. (2003). Thai distance English learners and learner autonomy. *Open Learning*, *18*(1), 75–84. doi:10.1080/02680510320000054130

Vasileiou, V., & Paraskeva, F. (2010). Teaching role-playing instruction in Second Life: An exploratory study. *Journal of Information. Information Technology and Organizations*, *5*, 25–50.

Veletsianos, G. (2009). The impact and implications of virtual character expressiveness on learning and agent-learner interactions. *Journal of Computer Assisted Learning*, *25*(4), 345–357. doi:10.1111/j.1365-2729.2009.00317.x

Vickers, H. (2009). *Google maps street view for language learning*. Retrieved February 3, 2017, from http://www.avatarlanguages.com/blog/google-street-view-languages/

Voogt, J., Erstad, O., Dede, C., & Mishra, P. (2013). Challenges to learning and schooling in the digital networked world of the 21st century. *Journal of Computer Assisted Learning*, *29*(5), 403–413. doi:10.1111/jcal.12029

Voulgari, I., & Komis, V. (2010). 'Elven Elder LVL59 LFP/RB. Please PM Me:' immersion, collaborative tasks and problem-solving in massively multiplayer online games. *Learning, Media and Technology*, *2*(35), 171–202. doi:10.1080/17439884.2010.494429

Vrellis, I., Avouris, N., & Mikropoulos, T. A. (2016). Learning outcome, presence and satisfaction from a science activity in Second Life. *Australasian Journal of Educational Technology*, *32*(1), 59–77. doi:10.14742/ajet.2164

Vygotsky, L. (1978). *Mind in society: The development of higher psychological processes*. Cambridge, MA: Harvard University Press.

Vygotsky, L. S. (1978). *Mind Society: The Development of Higher Mental Processes*. Cambridge, MA: Harvard University Press.

Vygotsky, L. S. (1986). *Thought and language*. Cambridge, MA: The MIT Press.

Walther, J. B. (1992). Interpersonal effects in computer-mediated interaction: A relational perspective. *Communication Research*, *19*(1), 52–90. doi:10.1177/009365092019001003

Walther, J. B., & D'Addario, K. P. (2001). The impacts of emoticons on message interpretation in computer-mediated communication. *Social Science Computer Review*, *19*(3), 324–347. doi:10.1177/089443930101900307

Wang, M., Callaghan, V., Lear, M., & Colley, M. (2011). *Teaching next generation computing skills: The challenge of embedded computing*. Paper presented at iCampus 2011, Nottingham, UK.

Wang, A. (2015). Facilitating participation: Teacher roles in a multiuser virtual learning environment. *Language Learning & Technology*, *19*(2), 156–176.

Wang, C., Calandra, B., Hibbard, S., & Lefaiver, M. (2012). Learning effects of an experimental EFL program in Second Life. *Educational Technology Research and Development*, *60*(5), 943–961. doi:10.1007/s11423-012-9259-0

Wang, F., & Burton, J. K. (2013). Second Life in education: A review of publications from its launch to 2011. *British Journal of Educational Technology*, *44*(3), 357–371. doi:10.1111/j.1467-8535.2012.01334.x

Warburton, S. (2009). Second Life in higher education: Assessing the potential for and the barriers to deploying virtual worlds in learning and teaching. *British Journal of Educational Technology*, *40*(3), 414–426. doi:10.1111/j.1467-8535.2009.00952.x

Warren, J. (2017, February 13). *Games as a means and an end.* Retrieved from https://shiftcommission.work/games-as-means-and-an-end-8fb79b51b6e6

Warren, S. J., Stein, R. A., Dondlinger, M. A., & Barab, S. A. (2009). A look inside a MUVE design process: Blending instructional design and game principles to target writing skills. *Journal of Educational Computing Research*, *40*(3), 295–321. doi:10.2190/EC.40.3.c

Webb, N. M., Farivar, S. H., & Mastergeorge, A. M. (2002). Productive helping in cooperative groups. *Theory into Practice*, *41*(1), 13–20. doi:10.1207/s15430421tip4101_3

Weiser, M. (1999). The computer for the 21st century. *SIGMOBILE: Mobile Computing and Communications Review*, *3*(3), 3–11.

Wertsch, J. V. (2007). Mediation. In H. Daniels, M. Cole, & J. V. Wertsch (Eds.), *The Cambridge companion to Vygotsky* (pp. 178–192). New York, NY: Cambridge University Press. doi:10.1017/CCOL0521831040.008

Wiesner, T. F., & Lan, W. (2004). Comparison of student learning in physical and simulated unit operations experiments. *Journal of Engineering Education*, *93*(3), 195–204. doi:10.1002/j.2168-9830.2004.tb00806.x

Wigham, C. R., & Chanier, T. (2013). Architecture students' appropriation of avatars. In M. N. Lamy & K. Zourou (Eds.), *Social networking for language education* (pp. 31–55). New York, NY: Palgrave Macmillan. doi:10.1057/9781137023384_3

Wiliam, D. (2011). What is assessment for learning? *Studies in Educational Evaluation*, *37*(1), 3–14. doi:10.1016/j.stueduc.2011.03.001 PMID:22114905

Wilkinson, J. (2000). Direct Observation. In G. M. Breakwell, S. Hammond, & C. Fife-Shaw (Eds.), *Research Methods in Psychology* (2nd ed.). London, UK: Sage.

Williams, M., Linn, M. C., Ammon, P., & Gearhart, M. (2004). Learning to teach inquiry science in a technology-based environment: A case study. *Journal of Science Education and Technology*, *13*(2), 189–206. doi:10.1023/B:JOST.0000031258.17257.48

Willis, J., & Cowie, B. (2014). Assessment as a generative dance: Connecting teaching, learning and curriculum. In C. Wyatt-Smith, V. Klenowski, & P. Colbert (Eds.), *Designing assessment for quality learning. The enabling power of assessment* (Vol. 1, pp. 23–37). New York, NY: Springer. doi:10.1007/978-94-007-5902-2_2

Winn, W. (2003). Learning in artificial environments: Embodiment, embeddedness and dynamic adaptation. *Technology, Instruction. Cognition and Learning*, *1*(1), 87–114.

Witmer, B. G., & Singer, M. J. (1998). Measuring presence in virtual environments: A presence questionnaire. *Presence (Cambridge, Mass.)*, *7*(3), 225–240. doi:10.1162/105474698565686

Wood, D., Bruner, J. S., & Ross, G. (1976). The role of tutoring in problem solving. *Journal of Child Psychology and Psychiatry, and Allied Disciplines*, *17*(2), 89–100. doi:10.1111/j.1469-7610.1976.tb00381.x PMID:932126

Yaman, M., Nerdel, C., & Bayrhuber, H. (2008). The effects of instructional support and learner interests when learning using computer simulations. *Computers & Education*, *51*(4), 1784–1794. doi:10.1016/j.compedu.2008.05.009

Yazzie-Mintz, E. (2006). *Voices of students on engagement: A report on the 2006 high school survey of student engagement.* Center for Evaluation & Education Policy, Indiana University. Retrieved from http://files.eric.ed.gov/fulltext/ED495758.pdf

Yin, R. K. (2003). *Case study research: Design and methods*. London: Sage.

Yoh, M. S. (2001). *The reality of virtual reality.* Paper presented at the Seventh International Conference on Virtual Systems and Multimedia, Berkeley, CA.

Zhang, T., Callaghan, V., Shen, R., & Davies, M. (2011). *Virtual classrooms: Making the invisible, visible.* Paper presented at iCampus 2011, Nottingham, UK.

Zhao, H., Sun, B., Wu, H., & Hu, X. (2010). Study on building a 3D interactive virtual learning environment based on OpenSim platform. *Proceeding of the International Conference on Audio, Language and Image Processing*, 1407–1411. doi:10.1109/ICALIP.2010.5684986

Zheng, D., & Newgarden, K. (2011). Rethinking language learning: Virtual worlds as a catalyst for change. *International Journal of Learning and Media*, *3*(2), 13–36. doi:10.1162/ijlm_a_00067

Zimmerman, C. (2011). Developing scientific thinking in the context of video games: Where to next? In F. C. Blumberg (Ed.), *Learning by playing: Video gaming in education* (pp. 54–68). Oxford, UK: Oxford University Press.

Zumbach, J., & Reimann, P. (1999). Assessment of a goal-based scenario approach: A hypermedia comparison. In P. Marquet, S. Mathey, A. Jaillet, & E. Nissen (Eds.), *Internet-based teaching and learning (IN-TELE) 98* (pp. 449-454). Frankfurt, Germany: Peter Lang. Retrieved February 3, 2017, from https://www.sbg.ac.at/mediaresearch/zumbach/download/1999_2006/book_chapters/zumbach_bookc_02.pdf

About the Contributors

Yufeng Qian, Ed.D., is a doctoral faculty in the Graduate School of Education at Northeastern University. She teaches research methods courses and serves as the doctoral research chair in the Doctor of Education program. Prior to joining Northeastern, she worked at Dartmouth College for the online professional education programs. Previously, she was Associate Professor of Education at St. Thomas University, teaching in the Doctor of Education and Master of Science in Education programs. Dr. Qian's research interests include the design, development and assessment of technology-enhanced learning environments, emerging learning technologies, and the design of authentic learning tasks and modeling, coaching, and scaffolding strategies for active and deep learning. She is the author of numerous journal articles and book chapters on emerging learning technologies and innovative learning environments. In addition, she provides editorial review for SAGE and IGI Global. Qian holds a Doctor of Education in Educational Technology from Lehigh University, and a Master of Education in TESOL from State University of New York at Buffalo. She was the recipient of 2017 CPS Award for Teaching Excellence at Northeastern University.

* * *

Terence C. Ahern is an Associate Professor in Instructional Design and Technology in the College of Education and Human Resources at West Virginia University. He received his Ph.D. in Instructional Systems Design from the Pennsylvania State University. Ahern's research interests are in the use of instructional technology in the classroom. He has published extensively in the areas of distance education, social network media and games. Currently, he is using his expertise in instructional design and programming to create game-based learning environments for the middle school classroom.

Pinelopi Atsikpasi holds a Master's Degree in Educational Science from the Department of Primary Education, University of the Aegean, Greece. Her research interests include educational uses of Virtual and Augmented Reality, and the use of tablets to enhance teaching and learning.

Menucha Birenbaum is a Professor Emeritus of educational assessment at Tel Aviv University, Israel. She earned her Ph.D. in educational psychology (quantitative and evaluative research methodologies) at the University of Illinois at Urbana-Champaign, USA, and her MA in education (research methodologies, measurement, and evaluation) at Tel Aviv University. Menucha's current research focuses on formal and informal assessment for learning (AfL) and school related contextual factors that facilitate or hinder the successful implementation of AfL, on learning environments that foster learner agency, and on large-scale diagnostic assessment.

Victor Callaghan is a Professor of Computer Science at the University of Essex (UK). He holds a B.Eng and PhD in Electronics and Computing from Sheffield University. Presently, he is based at Essex University where he is an Emeritus Professor of Computer Science and co-director of the Immersive Education group at Essex. He is the current president of the Association for the Advancement of Intelligent Environments and the director of the Creative Science Foundation (www.creative-science.org) which promotes STEM education and careers. At Essex, he established and directed mobile robotics and the Intelligent Environments before co-founding the Immersive Education group at Essex University. He has authored over 300 papers in international journals, conferences and has been principal investigator on numerous research projects attracting over 6 million pounds in funding. He founded the international annual IEEE sponsored conference, Intelligent Environments (www.intenv.org - being program chair for the first 8 years) which is now managed by the Association for the Advancement of Intelligent Environments and includes the journal for Ambient Intelligence and Smart Environments. He was a founding member of the Technology, Innovation, Entrepreneurship and Education conference and past program chair of Active Media Technology, Pervasive Computing & Applications and Ubiquitous Intelligence & Computing conferences He is co-editor of the Transactions of Future Intelligent Educational Environments and Science and Fiction, plus a member of the editorial teams of Pervasive Computing & Communications, Ambient and Intelligence and Smart Environments journals and editor of countless books.

Valentina Caruso is a Junior Researcher at the Swiss Federal Institute for Vocational and Educational Training (SFIVET) in Lugano, and a PhD Student at the University of Fribourg, Switzerland. Her current research interests include the use of educational technologies in dual vocational systems, end-user development and collaborative learning in 3D virtual worlds.

Athanasios Christopoulos obtained his BSc (Hons) in 2011 and MSc by Research in Computer Science in 2013 from the University of Bedfordshire, UK. Subsequently, he joined, once again, the Institute for Research in Applicable Computing of the same University, as a Ph.D. candidate whilst, he was appointed as Research Demonstrator in the Department of Computer Science & Technology. His current research focuses on Virtual Reality and in particular on the effects of interactions on learner engagement.

Marc Conrad works for the Faculty of Creative Arts, Technology and Science at the University of Bedfordshire as a Principal Lecturer in Computer Science. Being educated as a mathematician, where he received his PhD, his research interests are now in areas as diverse as Virtual Worlds, Algebraic Number Theory, Software Engineering, Project Management, Trust, Security and Art. Together with his colleague Tim French he developed a lightweight mathematical model of trust propagation that identifies how much experience matters to establish trust. Marc Conrad is also the inventor of a framework to evaluate virtual worlds. His personal web site is http://perisic.com/marc-conrad.

Chris Dede is the Timothy E. Wirth Professor in Learning Technologies at Harvard's Graduate School of Education (HGSE). His fields of scholarship include emerging technologies, policy, and leadership. From 2001-2004, he was Chair of the HGSE department of Teaching and Learning. In 2007, he was honored by Harvard University as an outstanding teacher, and in 2011 he was named a Fellow of the American Educational Research Association. From 2014-2015, he was a Visiting Expert at NSF, Directorate of Education and Human Resources. Chris has served as a member of the National Academy of Sciences Committee on Foundations of Educational and Psychological Assessment, a member of the U.S. Department of Education's Expert Panel on Technology, and a member of the 2010 National Educational Technology Plan Technical Working Group. In 2013, he co-convened a NSF workshop on new technology-based models of postsecondary learning; and in 2015 he led two NSF workshops on data-intensive research in the sciences, engineering, and education. His edited books include: Scaling Up Success: Lessons Learned from Technology-based Educational Improvement, Digital Teaching Platforms: Customizing Classroom Learning for Each Student, and Teacher Learning in the Digital Age: Online Professional Development in STEM Education.

Emmanuel Fokides is a lecturer in the Department of Primary School Education, University of the Aegean, Greece. His research and teaching focus on the educational uses of Virtual Reality, Augmented Reality, Digital Storytelling, and Serious Games. Since 1994, he has been involved in a number of research projects on distance and lifelong learning and the educational uses of Virtual and Augmented Reality. His work is published in several academic journals, conference proceedings, and scholarly books.

Michael Gardner has a B.Sc (Hons) in Computer Science (1984) and a Ph.D in Computer Science (1991) from Loughborough University in the UK. Previously he worked for 15 years as a Research Scientist at the British Telecommunications (Adastral Park) research labs at Martlesham Heath in the UK. He then helped setup and became the Deputy Director of Chimera, the Institute for Social and Technical Research at the University of Essex. Currently he is a Senior Lecturer in the School of Computer Science and Electronic Engineering at the University of Essex, and serves as the Director of the Immersive Education Laboratory. He has published over 100 papers in academic journals, conference proceedings, and scholarly books. His research interests are focused on understanding the affordances of immersive education technologies and developing systems to support co-creative collaboration in mixed-reality environments. He is on the board of the newly created Immersive Learning Research Network (iLRN), which aims to develop and support a community of educators, scholars, and practitioners dedicated toward research in and on digitally-enhanced immersive learning environments.

Elhanan Gazit has an M.A (Hons) in Science Education and a Ph.D. in the Learning Sciences, both from Tel-Aviv University, Israel. His research interests are focused on digital games studies, gameful design and immersive 3D learning environments. He is a lecturer at Tel-Aviv University, teaching the use of gamification for enterprise, brands, and educational systems. He lectures on the intersection of gaming, eSports, media and culture. Elhanan advises leading Fortune 500 companies and startups on using his gameful design framework for creating engaging experiences for boosting results to success. He delivers gamification lectures and workshops for enterprise and startups on branding, marketing, management training, learning, and eSports. Additionally, he mentors B.Sc Computer Science students on virtual and augmented reality games development at Afeka Tel-Aviv Academic College of Engineering. He serves as a business mentor for startups of the Inno-Negev Technology Accelerator at the Center for Entrepreneurship & Hi-Tech Management, Ben-Gurion University of the Negev, Israel. Currently, he writes his book: The Gameful Heroes' Future (in preparation). His other scholarly activities include heading the Israeli Chapter of the Digital Games Research Association (DiGRA).

Tina Grotzer is a cognitive scientist whose research identifies ways in which understandings about the nature of causality impact our ability to understand complexity in our world. Her work has important implications for how we deal with global and ecological issues and is concerned with the environmental injustices that result from our inability to reason well about complexity. She is a member of the faculty at the Harvard Graduate School of Education and at the Center for Health and the Global Environment. She received a Career Award from NSF in 2009 and a Presidential Career Award for Scientists and Engineers in 2011. She is the author of Learning Causality in a Complex World: Understandings of Consequence (2012) as well as numerous articles, book chapters, and resources for teachers.

Melissa D. Hartley is a teaching associate professor at West Virginia University in the Department of Special Education. Her primary research interests include using virtual reality simulations to improve preservice and inservice teachers' skills in using evidenced-based instructional practices.

Peggy Hartwick is an instructor and PhD candidate in the School of Applied Linguistics and Language Studies at Carleton University, Canada. As the recipient of Brightspace's Innovation Award in Teaching and Learning in 2015, Peggy thoughtfully combines technology and pedagogy. She is passionate about the success of her students and promotes learning engagement through creative teaching design.

Abi Johnson graduated from the University at Albany with a Bachelor's degree in Women's, Gender and Sexuality Studies, and a Master's degree in the same. Her research focus is in women, identity, and video games, as well as using video games in higher education. She is the developer of the Twine game transmissions, which was a portion of her thesis, "Playing like a Girl." She is an Instructional Technology Specialist at The College of Saint Rose.

Amy Kamarainen is a senior research manager at the Harvard Graduate School of Education where she manages research related to both the EcoXPT and EcoMOD projects. Amy is an ecosystem scientist who holds a B.S. in Zoology from Michigan State University and a Ph.D. from the University of Wisconsin – Madison. Her Ph.D. work focused on studying the movement and fate of pollutants in aquatic ecosystems using environmental sensors, historical data, and models. She applies her understanding of ecosystems science and research to the design and evaluation of technologies that support science learning inside and outside of the classroom.

Iryna Kozlova is a lecturer in the TESOL Program, Graduate School of Education, University of Pennsylvania. She earned her Ph.D. from Georgia State University and taught Applied Linguistics, and English and Russian as additional languages at the universities and colleges in the United States, Canada, and Ukraine. Iryna's research focuses on the use of second/foreign language spoken discourse in the classroom setting and in casual conversation, task-based learning, and the application of technology for language teaching and teacher training. For innovative approaches to teaching, Iryna received a Teaching Achievement Award (2014) at Carleton University and an Honorable Mention in the International E-Learning category of the International e-Learning Association Awards (2013) for the team project "Language Teaching and Learning in 3D Virtual Learning Environment".

Barbara L. Ludlow, Ed.D., is Professor and Chair in the Department of Special Education at West Virginia University, where she has been a member of the faculty for over 35 years. She earned an Ed.D. from West Virginia University, an M.Ed. from the University of Delaware, an M.A. from Cornell University, and a B.A. from St, John's University. Previously she was a special education teacher in public school systems in Wilmington, Delaware and Buckhannon, West Virginia. She has authored numerous articles on teacher education in special education and is a leading authority on rural special education and on technology-based delivery of personnel preparation programs. She has authored three professional reference books on distance education, online instruction, and virtual reality. Dr. Ludlow has served as the executive editor of two major professional journals and currently serves on editorial boards of multiple major journals in the disciplines of special education and disability services.

Hisae Matsui is a lecturer in the Department of East Asian Studies at Princeton University. She received her Ed.D. in Technology Education and M.A. in TESOL/Linguistics from West Virginia University. Her scholarly interests are focused on various forms of technology integration in foreign language pedagogy. Her research areas include tele-collaboration between native and non-native speakers, affordances of technological tools in educational context, and personalized instruction in the foreign language classroom.

Shari Metcalf is Project Director for the EcoLearn Group at the Harvard Graduate School of Education and has held this position since 2008. Projects under her direction include EcoMUVE, EcoMOBILE, EcoXPT, and EcoMOD. Her research focuses on educational technology projects in STEM education, including research on computer-based data collection and analysis tools for middle school science students. Her PhD research involved the design and development of Model-It, a software tool for students building models of dynamic systems. Her professional interest centers on the design of modeling, simulation, and immersive environments to support inquiry-based STEM learning.

Anders Mørch is professor in Department of Education, University of Oslo, Norway. He received his PhD in Informatics from the University of Oslo and an M.S. in Computer Science from the University of Colorado, Boulder. He developed educational software at NYNEX Science and Technology Center, New York. His general research interest is to understand how tools and artifacts help people learn, and more specifically, collaborative learning in virtual worlds, interfaces supporting learning (critiquing systems, pedagogical agents, learning analytics), end-user development, and design-based models of human learning and development (evolving artifacts framework). Contact him at http://www.uv.uio.no/iped/english/people/aca/andersm/index.html.

Anasol Peña-Rios is a postdoctoral researcher within the School of Computer Science and Electronic Engineering at the University of Essex (UK), and a research fellow at British Telecom Research Labs in Adastral Park (UK). She holds a Ph.D. in Computer Science and a M.Sc. in Advanced Web Engineering, both from the University of Essex in UK. Previously, she completed a B.Eng. in Information Technology at the Instituto Politécnico Nacional in Mexico. Her research focus on the use of immersive intelligent environments for decision-making support, knowledge management, co-creative collaboration and learning. She serves as board member of the Immersive Learning Research Network, and Associate Editor for MERLOT (Multimedia Educational Resources for Learning and Online Teaching) Computer Science Task Force. She has published multiple peer-reviewed papers, and actively works as co-organiser of different conferences, workshops, and reviewer in international journals.

Louisa Rosenheck is a designer and researcher of educational technologies in the MIT Education Arcade. She manages the design, content, and development of educational games and simulations, and oversees the research on how games can be effectively used in both formal and informal educational settings. In addition, she supports other designers and organizations in creating innovative educational technology and curriculum. Through capacity building partnerships on local and international educational technology programs, she aims to increase the deep learning in games and tools being produced for education.

Joe Sanchez is a Professor at Queens College, City University of New York, in the Graduate School of Library and Information Studies. He applies a critical lens to investigate virtual and augmented reality, instructional technologies, and social informatics.

Nuket Savaskan Nowlan is currently pursuing a PhD in the School of Information Technology at Carleton University, Canada. She has a Master of Engineering in Technology Information Management from Carleton University, Canada, and a B.Sc. in Electrical Engineering from Boğaziçi University, Turkey. Her research is focused on 3D virtual environments, understanding their role in education, and assessing the design of learning space.

Ya-Chun Shih received her M.A. and Ph.D. degrees in Curriculum and Instruction (Bilingual Education emphasis) from Pennsylvania State University. She is currently Associate Professor in the Department of English at National Dong Hwa University, Taiwan. Dr. Shih's current research focuses on integrating virtual reality technologies into language learning. She has investigated the effect of virtual reality assisted language learning on students' achievement of English as a foreign language. She has also explored issues related to the use of 3D collaborative virtual environments within a social and cultural context. Under Dr. Shih's leadership, the VEC3D (3D Virtual English Classroom), an interdisciplinary research team of instructional designers and computer science experts, designed and developed a variety of innovative language learning platforms. Dr. Shih and her research team are expanding beyond the traditional language learning environments and pedagogy by incorporating emerging technologies into daily lessons and communicative activities.

Mitul Shukla has worked at the University of Bedfordshire since 2004. His research interest is primarily around social media technologies and how people communicate with one another using these mediating technologies. He is particularly interested in the affective impact and complex communication capability in using mediating technologies. Previously he worked as a lead on the JISC funded Building Capacities programme at the University of Bedfordshire. The project investigated how research staff at the University of Bedfordshire were supported as well as the processes involved in being a post-graduate research student. Shukla has also been involved in other JISC funded umbrella projects assisting other universities with their research. In 2007 Mitul worked on a £1 million Arts Council project developing digital technology use within the Arts sector.

Eric Torres is a PhD student in Education at Harvard University. His research interests include topics in epistemology, adult learning, curricular design, and related questions.

Michael Vallance conducts research in the Department of Media Architecture at Future University Hakodate, Japan. He has been involved in educational technology design, implementation and research for over twenty years, working closely with higher education institutes, schools and media companies in UK, Singapore, Malaysia and Japan. His 3D virtual world design and tele-robotics research has been funded by the UK Prime Minister's Initiative (PMI2) and the Japan Advanced Institute of Science and Technology (JAIST). In 2012 he was awarded second prize in the Distributed Learning category by the United States Department of Defense for his research in virtual collaboration. His website is at http://www.mvallance.net.

Index

Q

R

S

T

U

V

www.ingramcontent.com/pod-product-compliance
Lightning Source LLC
LaVergne TN
LVHW060303011026
849161LV00011B/2765
9781522537199